Major Problems in American
Foreign Relations

MAJOR PROBLEMS IN AMERICAN HISTORY SERIES

GENERAL EDITOR
THOMAS G. PATERSON

Major Problems in American Foreign Relations
Volume I: To 1920

DOCUMENTS AND ESSAYS

SEVENTH EDITION

EDITED BY

DENNIS MERRILL

UNIVERSITY OF MISSOURI–KANSAS CITY

THOMAS G. PATERSON

UNIVERSITY OF CONNECTICUT

WADSWORTH
CENGAGE Learning

Australia • Brazil • Japan • Korea • Mexico • Singapore • Spain • United Kingdom • United States

Major Problems in American Foreign Relations Volume I: To 1920, Seventh Edition
Dennis Merrill, Thomas G. Paterson

Senior Publisher: Suzanne Jeans

Acquisitions Editor: Jeffrey Greene

Development Editor: Terri Wise

Editorial Assistant: Megan Chrisman

Senior Marketing Manager: Katherine Bates

Marketing Coordinator: Lorreen Pelletier

Marketing Communications Manager: Christine Dobberpuhl

Associate Content Project Manager: Anne Finley

Senior Art Director: Cate Rickard Barr

Print Buyer: Linda Hsu

Senior Rights Acquisition Account Manager, Text: Katie Huha

Text Researcher: Mary Dalton-Hoffman

Production Service: Pre-Press PMG

Senior Photo Editor: Jennifer Meyer Dare

Photo Researcher: Stacey Dong

Cover Designer: Gary Ragaglia, Metro Design

Cover Image: "China, Canton Factories," Post, 1780, oil painting on glass, unknown Chinese artist, M3156. © Peabody Essex Museum.

Compositor: Pre-Press PMG

For product information and technology assistance, contact us at **Cengage Learning Customer & Sales Support, 1-800-354-9706**

For permission to use material from this text or product, submit all requests online at **www.cengage.com/permissions**. Further permissions questions can be emailed to **permissionrequest@cengage.com**.

Library of Congress Control Number: 2009926347

ISBN-13: 978-0-495-80016-3

ISBN-10: 0-495-80016-3

Wadsworth
20 Channel Center Street
Boston, MA 02210
USA

Cengage Learning products are represented in Canada by Nelson Education, Ltd.

For your course and learning solutions, visit **www.cengage.com**.

Purchase any of our products at your local college store or at our preferred online store **www.ichapters.com**.

Printed in the United States of America
1 2 3 4 5 6 7 13 12 11 10 09

For Theresa Hannon and
Rebecca Putnam

Contents

C H A P T E R   7
Westward Expansion and Indian Removal
Page 173

D O C U M E N T S

E S S A Y S

C H A P T E R   8
Manifest Destiny, Texas, and the War with Mexico
Page 206

D O C U M E N T S

C H A P T E R   9
Expansion to the Pacific and Asia
Page 233

CHAPTER 10
The Diplomacy of the Civil War
Page 265

CHAPTER 11
Becoming a World Power in the Late Nineteenth Century
Page 295

CHAPTER 14
Theodore Roosevelt, the Big Stick, and U.S. Hegemony in the Caribbean
Page 395

CHAPTER 15
Woodrow Wilson, the First World War, and the League Fight
Page 427

E S S A Y S

F U R T H E R   R E A D I N G

Maps

Preface

Soon after al Qaeda's devastating attacks on U.S. soil on September 11, 2001, President George W. Bush declared a global war on terror. Washington officials mobilized the nation's vast security apparatus and bolstered the U.S. presence world-wide through wars, military interventions, covert operations, electronic surveillance of telephone and Internet conversations, detention and torture of suspected terrorists, economic sanctions, foreign military aid, and diplomatic pressure. Added to the accelerating pace of economic and cultural globalization, the anti-terrorism campaign has stimulated an expansive dialogue at home and abroad about America's role in world affairs. Newspaper headlines, television reports, and the Internet's blogosphere bombard Americans every day with news from around the globe. We have learned that other societies and peoples often emulate U.S. values, but they also lament the erosion of their own cultural traditions in an interconnected world and identify the United States as the culprit. Among the world's poor, resentment runs strong against the inequalities inherent in the U.S.-led global economy. Everyone, everywhere, is endangered by global environmental degradation, climate change, and the depletion of natural resources. At home, a sizable portion of Americans' tax dollars pays for the nation's overseas presence. And it seems that everything from gas at the pump, to the clothes we buy, to the security of our bank accounts carries a rising global price tag. Foreign relations worry the families of hundreds of thousands of U.S. military personnel stationed abroad, many of them in harm's way. Despite the dizzying rate of change, many of these concerns are not new. The American people have in fact long participated in world affairs—and so has their government; this book seeks to explain why, how, and where.

This volume explores America's many intersections with the world from the American Revolution through the era of World War I. It shows how Americans from various walks of life participate in the world community. It examines why and how American leaders devised policies to protect, manage, and extend U.S. interests abroad. The documents and essays in *Major Problems in American Foreign Relations* reveal that searching debate—among Americans and foreign peoples, and among scholars who study the past—has surrounded most issues. Indeed, Americans have spiritedly debated one another about their place in the world, their wars, their territorial expansion, their overseas commitments, their trade policies, and the status of their principles and power. With comparable vigor they have debated the people of other nations about the spread of U.S. interests, culture, and ideologies. This book captures the reasoning and the passion that informed these debates by probing the factors that influenced decisionmakers, the processes by which decisions are made, and the impact of those decisions on the United States and other nations.

We use the phrase *American Foreign Relations* in the title because the subject matter encompasses the myriad ways in which peoples, cultures, economies, national governments, nongovernmental organizations, regional associations, and international institutions interact. The term "foreign policy" seems inadequate to account for this wide array of activities and actors because it focuses largely on governmental decision-making and on policy itself. "Diplomacy" falls short because it refers primarily to negotiations or communications among states and organizations. "International history" seems so broad a term that it loses meaning, while at the same time it underplays a legitimate emphasis on *American* foreign relations. The phrase "foreign relations" comes closest to the emphases in this volume because it explains the totality of interactions—economic, cultural, political, military, environmental, and more—among peoples, organizations, states, and systems.

For this seventh edition, we have integrated into our chapters some of the very best recent scholarship, adding selections that are based on new archival findings or that raise provocative questions and points of discussion. Since the publication of our last edition, scholars in the disciplines of history and international relations have produced an array of excellent new studies on America's early foreign relations which seek to position the nation's post 9/11 attitudes and behaviors within a historical context. Some of the new literature spotlights cultural relations and the ways in which culturally constructed attitudes about class, gender, race, and national identity have shaped American's perceptions of the world and subsequently its overseas relationships. In this volume, almost one half of the essays are new, including selections by Michael L. Krenn, Walter L. Hixson, Robert Kagan, John Lamberton Harper, Joseph J. Ellis, John E. Lewis Jr., Piero Gleijeses, Stuart Banner, McCabe Keliher, Michael H. Hunt, Kristin L. Hoganson, Paul A. Kramer, Robert W. Tucker, and Erez Manela. Many new documents have also been added to help illustrate themes by these scholars. As before, we have included in both essays and documents foreign voices and statements by people of color so as to illuminate the wide array of participants in foreign relations and to suggest the ways in which America has influenced other peoples and nations.

Like other volumes in this series, *Major Problems in American Foreign Relations* approaches its subject in two ways: first, through primary sources; and second, through the interpretations of scholars. We invite readers to contend with a diversity of viewpoints and approaches on critical issues. Documents introduce each chapter's problem, identify key questions, reveal the flavor of the times, and convey the intensity of the debate. Through encounters with documents, students can immerse themselves in the historical moment, shape their own perspectives, and test the explanations of the essayists. The essays demonstrate that different scholars read documents differently, come to quite different conclusions, or choose to focus on different aspects of an issue. Students' interaction with the documents and essays build an appreciation for the complexity of historical problems, a fascination about historical inquiry, and a recognition that events and personalities once buried in the past carry contemporary meaning for students as both scholars and citizens. Introductions and headnotes in each chapter start this empowering and rewarding process.

Instructors and students who want to continue their study of foreign relations history are invited to join the Society for Historians of American Foreign Relations

(SHAFR). This organization publishes a superb journal, *Diplomatic History*, and an informative newsletter, *Passport*; offers book, article, and lecture prizes and dissertation research grants; sponsors summer institutes led by leading professors; and holds an annual conference where scholars, including graduate students, present their new research results and interpretations. Dues are reasonable. The organization has published a bibliographical work entitled *American Foreign Relations Since 1600: A Guide to the Literature* (2003), edited by Robert L. Beisner and Kurt W. Hanson, which is available for purchase and updated regularly online. This indispensable guide includes citations of journal articles, books, memoirs, document collections, and other sources, organized by topic and period. For information on SHAFR, contact the SHAFR Business Office, Ohio State University, Department of History, 106 Dulles Hall, 230 West 17th Avenue, Columbus, OH 43210; or email shafr@osu.edu. *Diplomatic History* maintains a Web site at www.cohums.ohio-state.edu/history/projects/diplh. For online discussion of topics in the history of U.S. foreign relations, consult the electronic journal *H-DIPLO* Web page at http://h-net2.msu.edu/~diplo.

We are very pleased to acknowledge the many generous people who have helped us with both documents and essays, advised us about content, and caught errors. Detailed, constructive written reviews were provided by: Max Friedman, American University; W. Bruce Leslie, SUNY College at Brockport; and Anne Paulet, Humboldt State University. We also appreciate the assistance of J. Garry Clifford and Mary Wolfskill. Robert Shaffer delivered a helpful review of the sixth edition of *Major Problems in American Foreign Relations* in *Passport*. The Wadsworth/Cengage staff deserves special thanks. Imaginative, thorough, and understanding, Wadsworth/Cengage editors shaped this book for the better. We especially thank development editor Terri Wise and permissions editors Mary Dalton-Hoffman and Katie Huha.

We are also grateful to friends, colleagues, and students who contributed in various ways to the first six editions: Stanley J. Adamiak, Lloyd E. Ambrosius, Carol Anderson, Harold Barto, Miriam Biurci, Richard Dean Burns, Richard H. Collin, John W. Coogan, Bruce Cummings, Joe Decker, Bruce dePyssler, John Dobson, Gregory E. Dowd, Michael Ebner, Francis Gay, Mark Gilderhus, Mary A. Giunta, James Goode, Gerald Gordon, Laura Grant, Kenneth J. Hagan, Peter L. Hahn, Paul W. Harris, Gordon E. Harvey, John Herron, James Hindman, Elizabeth Cobbs Hoffman, Jane Hunter, Michael Hunt, Holly Izard, Donald Johnson, Robert B. Kane, Lawrence Kaplan, Ellen Kerley, Warren Kimball, Carla Klausner, Karen Kupperman, Melvyn Leffler, Reba Libby, Douglas Little, Jean Manter, Frederick Marks, James Matray, Elizabeth McKillen, John Merrill, Jean-Donald Miller, Carl Murdoch, Brian Murphy, Sharon Murphy, Charles Neu, Patrick Peebles, Stephen Pelz, Alan Perry, Carol Petillo, Eileen Rice, Andrew Rotter, Reneé Schloss, Kenneth E. Shewmaker, Katherine S. W. Siegal, James F. Siekmeier, Martha Lund Smalley, Mark Stoler, Harry Stout, William Steuck, John Sylvester, Paul Varg, Jean L. Woy, Marvin Zahniser, and Thomas Zoumaras.

We welcome comments, suggestions, and criticisms from students and instructors so that we can continue to improve this book.

D.M
T.G.P

Explaining American Foreign Relations

Why did the United States expand into a world power from the colonial era to the early twentieth century? How did Americans conduct themselves on the world stage as they pursued the path to power? The explanations abound. Some scholars stress the role of ideology: democratic idealism, Christian mission, the American slogan of Manifest Destiny, individualism, and marketplace principles. Others highlight self-interest rather than ideals: the quest for capitalist investment and trading opportunities, the drive for security and strategic advantage, and the pursuit of prestige and national honor. Still others accent the American political environment: a workable federal union and an elastic constitution, the two-party system, the influence of public opinion, and government support for expansion (removal of Indians, land grants, and a strong military). Some historians of U.S. foreign relations emphasize how culture has shaped America's interactions with the world. Culture differs from ideology in that it is less self-conscious and less rigid. By culture, we mean an evolving constellation of values, beliefs, myths, language, symbols, and assumptions about what it is to be an American, and what it is to be "foreign." These perceptions grow out of popular constructions of class, race, gender, sexuality, age, and national identity that are always being reconsidered and negotiated by different groups within society and refashioned in light of international experiences. Of course, U.S. foreign relations have also been influenced by geographic and physical realities: geography, location in the Western Hemisphere, ocean barriers, the presence of weak neighbors, population growth, and abundant natural resources.

Most problems in American foreign relations have many causes. Yet historians disagree on the weight that should be attached to each. Different approaches yield different conclusions about the nature of America's international behavior. Some scholars perceive the United States as a champion of global democracy, an exceptional or unique nation because of its devotion to liberty and humanitarianism. Others maintain that the United States has been exceptional in its resolve to remain isolated from the rest of the world, an isolationism that has only occasionally been breached for purposes of self-defense. Some scholars question America's uniqueness, portraying the United States as an emerging great power whose founders practiced "realpolitik" and held their own with Europe's most accomplished diplomats. More critical scholarship depicts the United States as an aggressive empire builder that has subjugated others economically, militarily, politically, and culturally. Finally, diplomatic style and technique also come under scrutiny. Some see the United States as internationalist in its willingness to broker alliances and multilateral undertakings. Others maintain that American leaders jealousy guard their independence and more often than not opt to act unilaterally.

This chapter provides a sampling of different approaches to the study of American foreign relations and raises basic questions that run throughout this entire book. What have been the enduring fundamental characteristics and wellsprings of the American people and nation in a changing world? What can a historical perspective teach us about America and the world?

✸ E S S A Y S

In the opening essay, Bradford Perkins of the University of Michigan confronts the question of uniqueness. To explain U.S. foreign relations, he emphasizes a peculiarly American character shaped by republican values and the credo of individualism and reinforced by America's wealth in land and resources. Looking through their distinctive prism, Americans have seen themselves at odds with the rest of the world and have made decisions based on their assumption of uniqueness. In the second essay, the late William Appleman Williams, who taught history at the University of Wisconsin and Oregon State University, argues that "tragedy" has marked U.S. foreign relations because the American people, driven by an "Open Door" economic expansionism that has meant coercing others, have violated their own ideals. In the third essay, Norman A. Graebner, professor emeritus at the University of Virginia, argues that the nation's early diplomats were not guided by idealism. Rather, in a display of realism, the founders pragmatically advanced U.S. interests by manipulating Europe's balance of power.

In the fourth essay, Andrew Rotter of Colgate University explores how popular notions of masculinity and femininity shaped nineteenth-century America's embrace of republican expansionism and industrial-era imperialism. Prevailing ideas of gender, according to Rotter, likewise influenced how Americans viewed other societies and peoples, especially those over whom the United States exerted control. In the fifth essay, Michael L. Krenn of Appalachian State University in North Carolina explains the enduring power of racial thinking in U.S. foreign relations. Adaptable and resilient, racism facilitated territorial conquest in the nineteenth century, the pursuit of overseas markets at the turn of the twentieth century, and America's subsequent rise to global power. In the last essay, Walter L. Hixson of the University of Akron critically assesses how culture and myth-making have nourished and reinforced structures of authority at home and spawned a militant U.S. foreign policy. According to Hixson, Americans have imagined a national identity that trumpets their exceptional place in history as agents of modern enlightenment; manly, Anglo-Saxon expansionism; and Christian uplift. This deeply rooted "myth of America" has underpinned popular consent for hegemonic wars and marginalized dissenters as unpatriotic.

The Unique American Prism

BRADFORD PERKINS

Americans considered themselves a model society, one destined to transform the world. As John Quincy Adams's father wrote in 1765, expressing what was already a widespread view, "I always consider the settlement of America with reverence

Bradford Perkins, *The Creation of a Republican Empire, 1776–1865*, vol. 1 of *The Cambridge History of American Foreign Relations*. Copyright © 1993. Reprinted with the permission of Cambridge University Press.

and wonder, as the opening of a grand scheme and design of Providence for the illumination and emancipation of the slavish part of mankind all over the earth." The success of the Revolution and the establishment of republican government increased such feelings, and most Americans believed, although historians still debate the degree of accuracy in their claims, that the French and Latin American revolutions, as well as the European revolts of 1848, confirmed the argument. Thus it was possible for Herman Melville to write, in his novel, *White Jacket*, published in 1850, "we bear the ark of the liberties of the world. . . . And let us always remember that with ourselves, almost for the first time in the history of earth, national selfishness is unbounded philanthropy; for we cannot do good to America, but we give alms to the world." From one end of John Quincy Adams's life to the other, Americans endlessly demanded that they be respected as a model for the world.

Before the Civil War, this thought usually was harmless arrogance; only occasionally, in happy contrast to later times, did a price have to be paid. Many other nations have phases of arrogance in their history, some of them nearly as long as the American. This . . . form of "expansion" is . . . a function of the inherent egocentrism of any nation's diplomacy. The American form differed; the central meaning did not.

The form sprang, of course, from American cultural values. In all nations, those who make decisions are influenced not merely by the information at their disposal but by the values they bring to the consideration of that information. When the United States was born, and for many years thereafter, foreign policy decisions in most countries were made by and subject to the scrutiny of a relative few, at most of a legislature. George Canning, after he became foreign secretary of Great Britain in 1822, is considered the first European diplomatist who sought broader support from the political public as a whole. In the United States, things were quite different from the outset. Revolutionary leaders and, later on, government officials had to seek national concurrence in their policies; the policies had to coincide with or be justified in terms of national values. In sum, from the beginning, "the cultural setting [was] less a backdrop than a vital cog in the workings of foreign affairs."

The core beliefs lasted so long—to our own time—and became so embedded in the American outlook that they seem unremarkable today. However, although drawn in part from the thinking of others, particularly in seventeenth-century England, they were radical departures from the dominant values of Europe at the time of the Revolution and for many years continued to be far more pervasive than in other countries. Moreover, they gained strength from the apparently confirming events of the years from independence to the Civil War. Indeed, it is impossible to understand American foreign policy without recognizing the profound, persistent impact of an ideology that emerged during the colonial and early national periods.

The most important belief was a commitment to republicanism, a striking departure from an otherwise nearly universal commitment to monarchy. Although Europeans might debate the proper extent of royal power, at least until the French Revolution (and in most countries the debate would continue for many more years), the stability provided by monarchical institutions was generally considered essential to political order.

Largely as a consequence of lessons they rightly or wrongly drew from the pre-Revolutionary controversy, but also because their colonial experiments in local republicanism had been generally successful, the Americans rejected this concept. "By the eighteenth century," [the historian] Edmund S. Morgan notes, "the sovereignty of the people was taken for granted." Of course, he adds, in practice, even in the most egalitarian colonies, elites dominated, but this was seldom discussed: "Popular sovereignty . . . became the prevailing fiction in a society whose government was traditionally the province of a relatively small elite."

For a generation or more after independence, Americans worried about the fate of their experiment in popular government. Jeremiahs at one end of the political spectrum or the other frequently bewailed the failures of republicanism as currently practiced. Some feared that republicanism would be destroyed by demagoguery; others saw the looming shape of aristocratic control or Caesarism. Still, no true American suggested that the concept itself be abandoned, only that distortions be corrected. Americans agreed that republicanism—and the United States as its preeminent practitioner—represented the hope of the present and the future.

Closely allied with republicanism, ever more so as the nation progressed, was the concept of individualism, both political and economic. The predominance of individualism was the central theme—sometimes the object of praise, often of criticism—of the great commentary, *Democracy in America,* published by Alexis de Tocqueville in 1835. Unlike French republicans after 1789, the Americans seldom talked of a "national will" transcending the views of individuals. Although government intervened in economic matters much more than is suggested by polemicists expressing reverence for the policies of the Founding Fathers, and although, too, cooperative economic efforts became increasingly important, individual free enterprise was the model form, as befitted the nation of farms and farmers that America was at its birth. As Thomas Jefferson wrote in 1815, uniting the themes of republicanism and individualism, America was a "model of government, securing to man his rights and the fruits of his labor, by an organization constantly subject to his own will."

The virtually universal endorsement of republicanism and individualism by no means translated into unanimity regarding foreign affairs. Indeed, disputatious, sometimes violent disagreements over policy began well before the celebrated clash between Hamiltonian and Jeffersonian views in the 1790s and continued beyond the Civil War. However, differences over policy should not obscure the common body of beliefs shared by virtually every American, beliefs that deeply influenced both sides in all the debates and both gave impetus to and placed limits upon the rival policies put forward.

Their credo—one could call it their ideology, were not the latter word so laden with negative implications; one could call it their ideals, were not that word so laden with favorable ones—meant that Americans and, to a very large extent, their presumably more sophisticated leaders instinctively distrusted monarchical, statist regimes. . . .

Every nation views others in the world through a prism shaped by its own experience. Even today, American statesmen, and those who record their actions, often overlook this simple, almost self-evident point. As [the historian] Reginald Stuart observes, "Americans have historically found it difficult to step outside of themselves when judging others. And they have rarely realized how much their own values unconsciously smudged the lenses through which they viewed the world." The belief system, the product of experience, conditions the way in which Americans have viewed world developments and consequently how they have responded to them.

Every nation, of course, has its own prism—the Russian view of world events, for example, is warped by memories of the series of invasions from Charles XII of Sweden early in the eighteenth century through Hitler in the twentieth—but each is, like the American, unique. America's commercial policies cannot be explained if one ignores the nation's devotion to individualism; closed systems and statist controls were by definition condemned, and "open doors" were preferable. America's drive for territory, in large part the product of greed, derived essential strength from the prism of cultural values, which allowed Americans to see themselves as bringing progress and improvement to Louisiana or Florida or Oregon or Mexico.

Similarly, the reaction of Americans to revolutions abroad was essentially a projection of their vision of their own. They had, they firmly believed, risen against tyranny, avoided sanguinary excesses and social turmoil, created a republic—such was God's path for the world. Thus they welcomed antimonarchical risings but, in a frequently repeated "cycle of hope and disappointment," recoiled when revolutions went beyond the purely political sphere to repression, Bonapartism, and deep social change. The Terror divided Americans previously nearly unanimously in favor of the French Revolution. The "Springtime of Revolutions" in 1848, antimonarchical and nationalist explosions in half a dozen European countries triggered by a Paris rising, roused applause, but the radical violence that developed in France soon alienated many Americans. Between these dates, in 1830, still another French revolution, a move in the direction of liberalism but not even a republican one, earned praise from President [Andrew] Jackson because of "the heroic moderation which . . . disarmed revolution of its terrors." The contrast is instructive.

In reacting as they did, Americans too often failed to remember two special circumstances that had made their kind of revolution possible. Alexis de Tocqueville, perhaps the most perceptive foreign analyst of American society, drew attention to them 150 years ago. "Nothing," he wrote, "is more fertile in marvels than the art of being free, but nothing is harder than freedom's apprenticeship." Virtually self-governing throughout most of their history as colonies, they came to freedom with patterns of behavior and thought that made republicanism both logical and easy; they did not have to exorcise political privileges of rank or transform the economic order to create conditions in which republicanism could thrive. Others were not so lucky, and when they went past what Americans considered the proper boundaries of revolution, they lost American sympathies.

Because national egotism was strong, the inability of others to create individualist republicanism was explained in terms of their inferiority to Americans. Thus Jefferson wrote of the people in Europe in 1787, "A thousand years would not place them on that high ground on which our common people are now setting out." When revolution broke out while he was American minister in Paris, Jefferson at first considered limited monarchy rather than republicanism the appropriate solution for France, because the French were so ill-prepared for self-government. Years later, when the Latin Americans rose against Spanish rule, virtually every American welcomed the revolt but many, including Jefferson, rightly doubted that true republicanism would follow. "They have not the first elements of good or free government," John Quincy Adams asserted. "Arbitrary power, military and ecclesiastical, was stamped upon their education, upon their habits, and upon all their institutions."

These two apparently dissimilar reactions are in fact reflections of the same facet of the prism. Republicanism in the American style was the higher form of government. Those who compromised it might be inherently inferior as a result of their history, but in any event they sinned. Throughout their history, Americans have regarded foreign nations in this way.

A sentence in *Democracy in America* also encapsulates the second distortion provided by the prism. In a characteristic tone, Tocqueville wrote, "Their fathers gave them a love of equality and liberty, but it was God who, by handing a limitless continent over to them, gave them the means of long remaining equal and free." The Americans were blessed with abundant land and resources. There was of course poverty, perhaps most notably in the cities that burgeoned before the Civil War. There was slavery: One out of six Americans was a slave when the first census was taken in 1790, one out of eight—four million in all—when the Civil War began. For the great preponderance of Americans, however, conditions were much better than in other nations; in particular, the proportion of landowners was higher than elsewhere. Above all, although there were of course periodic slumps, a high rate of economic growth prevailed.

[Economic growth] eased the path to republicanism, contributed to national stability, and strengthened the devotion to individualism. "We supposed that our revelation was 'democracy revolutionizing the world,'" a historian has written, "but in reality it was 'abundance revolutionizing the world.'" In other nations, or at least many of them, political change evoked class conflict and rivalry over economic shares, creating what from the American point of view was unrepublican turmoil. Such tensions existed in the United States, but comparatively speaking they were muted. Americans simply could not understand "the contrast between [for example] the three or four Frances that tore at each other's throats and the one America that hustled its way into the future."

The prism concept suggests one other line of thought. For years it has been fashionable among scholars to distinguish between ideals and self-interest as motives of foreign policy, to see them as polar opposites. In fact, mingling is the norm; conflict between national interest and national culture is the exception. And for this the prism is largely responsible. As Max Weber wrote many years ago, "Interests (material and moral), not ideas, dominate directly the actions of men. Yet the 'images of the world' created by these ideas have very often served as switches determining the tracks on which the dynamism of interests kept action going." In sum, material interests, culture, and the prism combine in a complex interplay that creates foreign policy.

There is no clearer illustration of the compatibility of the three factors than the devotion to isolationism. The Americans sought commerce with all the world, but they refused to become involved in the politics of other continents and, in particular, to align themselves with any other power. Sometimes compromised in practice, notably in the alliance with France, which was essential to the success of the Revolution, political isolation was an unvarying desire and increasingly became fixed dogma, even though the word itself was not used to describe policy until the twentieth century. Such a policy was obviously prudent: A state with all interests save the commercial confined to its own periphery was made stronger in that area by the width of the Atlantic Ocean. A power weak by world standards could only suffer from involvement in the wars of greater ones, and an uninvolved power could hope, at a time when the rights of neutrals were taken more seriously than later, to profit greatly from wartime trade.

At the same time, involvement in the sordid politics of Europe could be and was regarded by the Americans as contaminating, a descent to the level of court intrigues and amoral national selfishness contrary to the principles of republicanism. Involvement would force compromises of principle, expose simple but honest American diplomats to the wiles of cynically tricky Europeans, and, perhaps above all, dim the "beacon of liberty," the light to the world held forth by the United States. These beliefs in turn created the prism through which Americans viewed developments across the seas, an angle of vision that conditioned interpretations of actual developments and confirmed the mind-set that had created the prism in the first place.

The Open Door Policy: Economic Expansion and the Remaking of Societies

WILLIAM APPLEMAN WILLIAMS

In the realm of ideas and ideals, American policy is guided by three conceptions. One is the warm, generous, humanitarian impulse to help other people solve their problems. A second is the principle of self-determination applied at the international level, which asserts the right of every society to establish its own goals or objectives, and to realize them internally through the means it decides are appropriate. These two ideas can be reconciled; indeed, they complement each other to an extensive degree. But the third idea entertained by many Americans is one which insists that other people cannot *really* solve their problems and improve their lives unless they go about it in the same way as the United States.

This feeling is not peculiar to Americans, for all other peoples reveal some degree of the same attitude toward the rest of the world. But the full scope and intensity of the American version is clearly revealed in the blunt remark of former Secretary of State Dean G. Acheson. He phrased it this way in explaining and defending the American program of foreign aid as it was being evolved shortly after the end of World War II: "We are willing to help people who believe the way we do, to continue to live the way they want to live."

This insistence that other people ought to copy America contradicts the humanitarian urge to help them and the idea that they have the right to make such key decisions for themselves. In some cases, the American way of doing things simply does not work for the other people. In another instance it may be satisfactory, but the other society may prefer to do it in a different way that produces equally good results—perhaps even better ones. But even if the American way were the *only* effective approach, the act of forcing it upon the other society—and economic and political pressure are forms of force—violates the idea of self-determination. It also angers the other society and makes it even less apt to accept the American suggestion on its own merits. Hence it is neither very effective nor very idealistic to try to help other people by insisting from the outset that they follow closely the lead and the example of the United States on all central and vital matters.

The same kind of difficulty arises in connection with the economic side of American foreign policy. The United States needs raw materials and other goods and services from foreign countries, just as it needs to sell some of its own goods and services to them. It might be able literally to isolate itself and survive, but that is not the issue. Not even the isolationists of the late 1920's and early 1930's advocated that kind of foreign policy. The vital question concerns instead the way in which America gets what it needs and exports what it wants to sell.

Most Americans consider that trade supplies the answer to this problem. But trade is defined as the exchange of goods and services between producers dealing with each other in as open a market as it is possible to create, and doing this without one of them being so beholden to the other that he cannot bargain in a meaningful and effective way. Trade is not defined by the transfer of goods and services under conditions established and controlled largely by one of the parties.

Here is a primary source of America's troubles in its economic relations with the rest of the world. For in expanding its own economic system throughout much of the world, America has made it very difficult for other nations to retain any economic independence. This is particularly true in connection with raw materials. Saudi Arabia, for example, is not an independent oil producer. Its oil fields are an integrated and controlled part of the American oil industry. But a very similar, if often less dramatic, kind of relationship also develops in manufacturing industries. This is the case in countries where established economic systems are outmoded or lethargic, as well as in the new, poor nations that are just beginning to industrialize. American corporations exercise very extensive authority, and even commanding power, in the political economy of such nations.

Unfortunately, there is an even more troublesome factor in the economic aspect of American foreign policy. That is the firm conviction, even dogmatic belief, that America's *domestic* well-being depends upon such sustained, ever-increasing overseas economic expansion. Here is a convergence of economic practice with intellectual analysis and emotional involvement that creates a very powerful and dangerous propensity to define the essentials of American welfare in terms of activities outside the United States.

It is dangerous for two reasons. First, it leads to an indifference toward, or a neglect of, internal developments which are nevertheless of primary importance. And second, this strong tendency to externalize the sources or causes of good things leads naturally enough to an even greater inclination to explain the lack of the good life by blaming it on foreign individuals, groups, and nations. This kind of externalizing evil serves not only to antagonize the outsiders, but further intensifies the American determination to make them over in the proper manner or simply push them out of the way.

The over-all result of these considerations is that America's humanitarian urge to assist other peoples is undercut—even subverted—by the way it goes about helping them. Other societies come to feel that American policy causes them to lose their economic, political, and even psychological independence. . . .

In summation, the true nature and full significance of the Open Door Policy can only be grasped when its four essential features are fully understood.

First: it was neither a military strategy nor a traditional balance-of-power policy. *It was conceived and designed to win the victories without the wars.* In a truly perceptive and even noble sense, the makers of the Open Door Policy understood that war represented the failure of policy. Hence it is irrelevant to criticize the Open Door Policy for not emphasizing, or not producing, extensive military readiness.

Second: it was derived from the proposition that America's overwhelming economic power would cast the economy and the politics of the poorer, weaker, underdeveloped countries in a pro-American mold. . . .

Third (and clearly related to the second point): the policy was neither legalistic nor moralistic in the sense that those criticisms are usually offered. It was extremely hard-headed and practical. In some respects, at any rate, it was the most impressive intellectual achievement in the area of public policy since the generation of the Founding Fathers.

Fourth: unless and until it, and its underlying *Weltanschauung,* were modified to deal with its own consequences, the policy was certain to produce foreign policy crises that would become increasingly severe.

Once these factors are understood, it becomes useful to explore the way that ideological and moralistic elements became integrated with the fundamentally secular and economic nature of the Open Door Policy. The addition of those ingredients served to create a kind of expansionism that aimed at the marketplace of the mind and the polls as well as of the pocketbook.

Taken up by President Theodore Roosevelt and his successors, the philosophy and practice of secular empire that was embodied in the Open Door Notes [of 1899–1900] became the central feature of American foreign policy in the twentieth century. American economic power gushed into some underdeveloped areas within a decade and into many others within a generation. It also seeped, then trickled, and finally flooded into the more developed nations and their colonies until, by 1939, America's economic expansion encompassed the globe. And by that time the regions where America's position was not extensively developed were precisely the areas in which the United States manifested a determination to retain and expand its exploratory operations—or to enter in force for the first time.

Throughout these same years, the rise of a new crusading spirit in American diplomacy contributed an outward thrust of its own and reinforced the secular expansion. This righteous enthusiasm was both secular, emphasizing political and social ideology, and religious, stressing the virtues (and necessities) of Protestant Christianity. In essence, this twentieth-century Manifest Destiny was identical with the earlier phenomenon of the same name.

Americans assumed a posture of moral and ideological superiority at an early date. Despite the persistence of the Puritan tradition, however, this assertiveness took predominantly secular forms. Supernatural authority was invoked to explain and account for the steady enlargement of the United States, but the justifications for expansion were generally based on standards derived from this world. The phrase "Manifest Destiny," for example, symbolized the assertion that God was on America's side rather than the more modest claim that the country had joined the legions of the Lord. As that logic implied, the argument was that America was the "most progressive" society whose citizens made "proper use of the soil." For these and similar reasons, it was added, the laws of "political gravitation" would bring many minor peoples into the American system.

Though it had appeared as early as the eve of the American Revolution, the assertion that the expansion of the United States "extended the area of freedom" gained general currency after the War of 1812. President Andrew Jackson seems to have coined the phrase, with his wildcatting intellectual supporters making many variations. One of the more persuasive and popular, which won many converts during and after the war with Mexico, stressed America's responsibility to extend its authority over "semi-barbarous people." By thus taking up the duty of "regeneration and civilization," America could perform the noble work of teaching inferiors to appreciate the blessings they already enjoyed but were inclined to overlook. In turn, this would prepare them for the better days to follow under America's benevolent leadership.

Near the end of the century, American missionaries and domestic religious leaders began to impart a more theological tone to this crusading fervor. This resulted in part from the effort by the clergy to marry traditional Christianity with the new doctrine of evolution and in that way adjust their theology to the latest revelations, and also to sustain their influence in the age of science. Josiah Strong was an innovator of that kind. As a Congregationalist minister in whom the frontier experience and outlook exercised an important influence, Strong concluded that the theory of evolution only substantiated the doctrine of predestination. America had been handpicked by the Lord to lead the Anglo-Saxons in transforming the world. "It would seem," he explained with reference to the American Indians and other benighted peoples, "as if these inferior tribes were only precursors of a superior race, voices in the wilderness crying: Prepare ye the way of the Lord."

Ever since New England ministers had accepted the challenge of saving the heathens of Hawaii, a crusade that began in the eighteenth century, American missionaries had been noticeably concerned about Asia—and in particular China. As the Reverend Hudson Taylor explained in 1894, there was "a great Niagara of souls passing into the dark in China." Though they never lost faith, a growing number of missionaries did get discouraged enough to question whether hell-fire sermons on the dangers of damnation were an approach sufficient unto the need. Some thought fondly of the sword of righteousness, and toyed with the idea of a "Society for the Diffusion of Cannon Balls." That kind of crusade was never organized, but the missionaries did begin in the 1890's to demand formal support and protection from the American Government.

This request, while never acted upon with the same vigor as those from business groups, did receive sympathetic and favorable consideration. For one thing, the religious stake in China was significant: America had over 500 missionaries in that country, and their schools claimed a total student body of nearly 17,000 Chinese. Many churches had also supported intervention in Cuba. But the most important factor was the way that the missionary movement began to evolve an approach that offered direct support to secular expansion.

Missionaries had always tended to operate on an assumption quite similar to the frontier thesis. "Missionaries are an absolute necessity," explained the Reverend Henry Van Dyke of Princeton in 1896, "not only for the conversion of the heathen, but also, and much more, for the preservation of the Church. Christianity is a religion that will not keep." Religious leaders began to link the missionary movement with economic expansion in what the Reverend Francis E. Clark of the Christian Endeavor organization called "the widening of our empire." The Board of Foreign Missions also welcomed such expansion as "an ally."

Then, beginning in the mid-1890's, the missionaries began to change their basic strategy in a way that greatly encouraged such liaison with secular expansionists. Shifting from an emphasis on the horrors of hell to a concern with practical reform as the lever of conversion, they increasingly stressed the need to remake the underdeveloped societies. Naturally enough, they were to be reformed in the image of the United States. Such changes would lead to regeneration identified with Christianity and witnesses for the Lord would accordingly increase.

Not only did this program mesh with the idea of American secular influence (how else were the reforms to be initiated?), but it was very similar to the argument that American expansion was justified because it created more progressive societies. Missionaries came to sound more and more like political leaders who were themselves submerging their domestic ideological differences at the water's edge in a general agreement on expansion as a reform movement.

The domestic reformer [Robert] La Follette offers an excellent example of this convergence of economic and ideological expansion that took place across political lines. He approved taking the Philippines because it would enable America "to conquer [its] rightful share of that great market now opening [in China] for the world's commerce." Expansion was also justified because the United States had a "bounden *duty* to establish and *maintain* stable government" in the islands. Pointing out that from the beginning "the policy of this government has been to expand," La Follette justified it on the grounds that "it has *made men free.*" Thus, he concluded, "we can legally and morally reserve unto ourselves perpetual commercial advantages of priceless value to our foreign trade for all time to come" by taking the Philippines.

Theodore Roosevelt's outlook reveals an even more significant aspect of this progressive integration of secular and ideological expansionism. His concern for economic expansion was complemented by an urge to extend Anglo-Saxon ideas, practices, and virtues throughout the world. Just as his Square Deal program centered on the idea of responsible leaders using the national government to regulate and moderate industrial society at home, so did his international outlook revolve around the idea of American supremacy being used to define and promote the interests of "collective civilization."

Thus it was necessary, he warned in his Presidential Message of December 1901, to exercise restraint in dealing with the large corporations. "Business concerns which have the largest means at their disposal . . . take the lead in the strife for commercial supremacy among the nations of the world. America has only just begun to assume the commanding position in the international business world which we believe will more and more be hers. It is of the utmost importance that this position be not jeopardized, especially at a time when the overflowing abundance of our own natural resources and the skill, business energy, and mechanical aptitude of our people make foreign markets essential."

Roosevelt integrated that kind of expansion with ideological considerations and imperatives to create an all-inclusive logic and set of responsibilities which made peace itself the consequence of empire. In his mind, at any rate, it was America's "duty toward the people living in barbarism to see that they are freed from their chains, and we can free them only by destroying barbarism itself." Thus, he concluded, "peace cannot be had until the civilized nations have expanded in some shape over the barbarous nations."

The inherent requirements of economic expansion coincided with such religious, racist, and reformist drives to remake the world. The reason for this is not difficult to perceive. As they existed, the underdeveloped countries were poor, particularistic, and bound by traditions which handicapped business enterprise. They were not organized to link up with the modern industrial system in a practical and efficient manner. It was economically necessary to change them *in certain ways and to a limited degree* if the fruits of expansion were to be harvested. As with the missionaries, therefore, the economic and political leaders of the country decided that what was good for Americans was also good for foreigners. Humanitarian concern was thus reinforced by hard-headed economic requirements.

The administrations of Theodore Roosevelt understood this relationship between economic expansion and overseas reform, and explicitly integrated it into the strategy of the Open Door Policy. It was often commented upon in dispatches and policy statements concerning China and Latin America. In his famous Corollary to the Monroe Doctrine, for example, Roosevelt (who thought of the Open Door Policy as the Monroe Doctrine for Asia) stressed the need for reforms and asserted the right and the obligation of the United States to see that they were made—and honored. . . .

The integration of these elements was carried forward, and given classic expression in rhetoric, style, and substance, in the diplomacy of President Woodrow Wilson and Secretary of State [William Jennings] Bryan. Both men were leaders of the secular American reform movement, and both brought to their conduct of foreign affairs a religious intensity and righteousness that was not apparent in earlier administrations and that has not been matched since their time. As Protestants imbued with a strong sense of Anglo-Saxon self-consciousness, they personified the assertive idealism that complemented and reinforced the economic drive for markets. . . .

By the time of World War I, therefore, the basic dilemma of American foreign policy was clearly defined. Its generous humanitarianism prompted it to improve the lot of less fortunate peoples, but that side of its diplomacy was undercut by two other aspects of its policy. On the one hand, it defined helping people in terms of making them more like Americans. This subverted its ideal of self-determination. On the other hand, it asserted and acted upon the necessity of overseas economic expansion for its own material prosperity. But by defining such expansion in terms of markets for American exports, and control of raw materials for American industry, the ability of other peoples to develop and act upon their own patterns of development was further undercut.

The Pursuit of Interests and a Balance of Power

NORMAN A. GRAEBNER

For the Founding Fathers, no less than for European statesmen, the central task of diplomacy was that of limiting the behavior of the ambitious to what they regarded acceptable. What preserved Europe's remarkable stability, despite its continuing wars, was the existence of an equilibrium or balance of power. Nations checked

From Norman A. Graebner, "Tradition: The Founding Fathers and Foreign Affairs," an address for Convocation Ceremony at the University of Virginia, Fall 1987. The White Burkett Miller Center for Public Affairs, Charlottesville, VA, pp. 6–12. Reprinted by permission.

the recurrent selfishness of others with the counterchecks composed of opposing combinations of power. The Founding Fathers discovered early that the European equilibrium would be the essential source of American security. Even as colonists the American people achieved major victories over Europe's two most powerful countries by managing to throw British power against France to drive the French from the North American Continent, and then, within twenty years, to drive the British out of the thirteen colonies by utilizing the power of France. Thereafter John Adams and Thomas Jefferson, representing the young Republic in London and Paris respectively, understood clearly that as long as Britain and France, occupying the two poles of the European equilibrium, remained strong and antagonistic toward the other, the United States was safe. Neither London or Paris would permit the other to interfere in American affairs to the detriment of the European equilibrium. Thomas Boylston Adams, one of the sons of John Adams, expressed this truth in October, 1799: "It must always happen, so long as America is an independent Republic or nation, that the balance of power in Europe will continue to be of the utmost importance to her welfare. The moment that France is victorious and Britain with her allies depressed, we have cause for alarm ourselves. The same is true when the reverse of this happens."

None of the nation's early leaders matched Thomas Jefferson in his persistent concern for the European equilibrium. During his years as minister to France he commented often and brilliantly on Europe's shifting balance of power and its significance for European and Atlantic stability. With the outbreak of the Napoleonic wars after 1803, with the full might of Napoleon's France confronting that of Britain and the rest of Europe, Jefferson feared a victory of either France or Britain over the other. After Napoleon's triumph at Austerlitz in 1806 Jefferson, as President, considered an alliance with Britain. Soon British insolence forced him back into a posture of neutrality, although he continued to believe that the French emperor endangered the balance of power and thus the security of the United States. . . .

Even as the United States entered its war against England in 1812, Jefferson believed that Napoleon, now America's informal ally, had grown too powerful and hoped that Britain, although the declared enemy of the United States, would find an opportunity for reducing its great rival. Jefferson wrote on that occasion: "We especially ought to pray that the powers of Europe may be so poised and counterpoised among themselves, that their own security may require the presence of all their forces at home, leaving the other quarters of the globe in undisturbed tranquility." Throughout the war it mattered less to Jefferson whether Britain or France triumphed in Europe than that the European equilibrium remained intact. He no more than the Adamses would entrust American security to the Atlantic alone.

If the pursuit of precisely defined and limited interests in a carefully balanced world of sovereign nations established the outlines of American foreign policy, the Founding Fathers faced powerful impediments to their closely calculated approach to world affairs. From the beginning the American people displayed a profound propensity to involve themselves in external affairs far beyond either their interests or their effective power. The French Revolution quickly taught President Washington and his Federalist advisers that the country's republican ideology and revolutionary zeal, unleashed by the American Revolution itself, could readily encourage Americans to make other people's causes their own. When Washington attempted to maintain the official neutrality of the United States in the burgeoning war between France and the allied powers led by Britain, his political opponents accused him of ignoring the cause of liberty. Only with difficulty did the Washington administration prevent the country from mounting a futile crusade in behalf of the French.

Alexander Hamilton rushed to the defense of the Washington administration with a series of brilliant essays, published in 1793 and 1794 under the names "Pacificus" and "Americanus." These writings constituted the most pervading examination of the diplomatic principles guiding the young Republic to come from the pen of any of the nation's early leaders. The country's pro-French legions had anchored their demands for a strong national allegiance to France on the assumptions that the United States must be faithful to its treaty obligations, show gratitude for previous assistance, and underscore its affinity for republican institutions in a monarchial world. Hamilton attacked these notions head on. He argued in "Pacificus" that the country's first obligation was to itself. Without sea power the United States carried no obligation even to the French islands in the West Indies. There could be no balance, enjoying the sanction of common sense, between the damage that the United States would inflict on itself by opposing Britain and the advantages that it might bring to France. "All contracts," wrote Hamilton, "are to receive a reasonable construction. Self-preservation is the first duty of a Nation; and though in the performance of stipulations relating to war, good faith requires that the *ordinary hazards* of war should be fairly encountered, . . . yet it does not require that *extraordinary* and *extreme* hazards should be run. . . ." From engaging in a naval war with Great Britain, without a navy or coastal fortifications, he concluded, "we are dissuaded by the most cogent motives of self-preservation, no less than of interest." . . .

Throughout his second term Washington was dismayed by the intense partisanship which too many Americans entertained toward the European belligerents. He stressed the necessity of greater attention to American interests in a letter to Patrick Henry: "My ardent desire is . . . to see that [the United States] *may be* independent of *all,* and under the influence of none. In a word, I want an *American* character, that the powers of Europe may be convinced we act for *ourselves* and not for *others*. . . ." In his Farewell Address Washington explained why foreign attachments endangered the nation's wellbeing: "The Nation, which indulges toward another an habitual hatred, or an habitual fondness, is in some degree a slave. It is a slave to its animosity or its affection, either of which is sufficient to lead it astray from its duty and its interests." Sympathy for favored countries, Washington warned, assumed common interests which seldom existed and enmeshed a people in the enmities of others without justification.

John Quincy Adams, ultimately the greatest of all American diplomatists, assigned himself the special task to warn the nation against unnecessary and unpromising involvements in the affairs of others. When pro-French pressures mounted against the Washington administration in 1793, Adams wrote in his "Marcellus" essays: "As men, we must undoubtedly lament the effusion of human blood, and the mass of misery and distress which is preparing for the great part of the civilized world; but as the citizens of a nation at a vast distance from the continent of Europe, . . . disconnected from all European interests and European politics, it is our duty to remain, the peaceable and silent, though sorrowful spectators of the sanguinary scene." In December 1817, as secretary of state, John Quincy Adams complained to his father that Latin America, then in revolution against Spain, had replaced France as the great external source of discord in the United States. "The republican spirit of our country" he wrote, "not only sympathizes with people struggling in a cause, . . . but it is working into indignation against the relapse of Europe into the opposite principle of monkery and despotism. And now, as at the early stage of the French Revolution, we have ardent spirits who are for rushing into the conflict, without looking to the consequences."

For John Quincy Adams it was improper for the American people or their government to judge the right or wrong in the behavior of other countries, especially when the practices regarded as abhorrent in no way endangered the interests of the United States, and those condemning the alleged evils had no intention of underwriting their sentiments with policies designed to effect the desired changes. When in 1821 enthusiasts, with no attention to means, sought to launch a crusade to save the Greeks from Turkish oppression, Adams again admonished his fellow Americans in his noted July 4 address of that year. "Wherever the standard of freedom and Independence has been or shall be unfurled," he declared, "there will [America's] heart, her benedictions and her prayers be. But she goes not abroad, in search of monsters to destroy. She is the well-wisher to the freedom and independence of all. She is the champion and vindicator only of her own." . . .

It was not strange that the Founding Fathers, facing recurrent pressures for foreign involvements which they opposed, fostered isolationism. But their isolationism was never that of Tom Paine who found his assurances of peace and non-involvement in world politics in the broad Atlantic and the civilizing quality of commerce. The Founding Fathers, in expanding the concept of geographical isolation into a fundamental element of national policy, never regarded the Atlantic a sure defense against reluctant involvements in defense of distant interests. Washington's Farewell Address, the ultimate prescription for American isolationism, was scarcely an isolationist document at all. Nowhere did Washington's recognition of distance and oceans as significant sources of security and power vary from Britain's reliance on the English Channel as a protection against continental encroachments on its freedom of action. What country did not seek to maximize its physical advantages in its contests with others? Washington emphasized America's separation from Europe, not because the Atlantic freed the United States from the traditional rules of international behavior, but because the Atlantic was a special asset worth exploiting in the design of external policy. . . .

This sampling of the thought of the Founding Fathers on foreign affairs cannot render full justice to their voluminous writings, but it demonstrates the quality of mind and felicity of expression that established their place in history. It reveals as well that no aspect of international life escaped them. No less than Europe's leading analysts they recognized the rules of conduct that enabled sovereign states to thrive in a world without law. They adapted the established principles of modern diplomacy to the peculiar needs and advantages of the American republic. The Founding Fathers assumed that foreign policies emanated from government itself. For them it mattered only that officials seek the best ideas available, whatever their origins. They acknowledged the astuteness that generations of experience had provided the leading governments of Europe, and thus the wisdom of soliciting their advice on external issues. Understanding the nation's propensity to overextend its purposes abroad, the

Founding Fathers argued especially against the two fundamental tendencies toward overcommitment: partiality toward other people's quarrels and the inclination to enter foreign crusades beyond the country's means or real intentions. They condemned the use of popular phrases, capable of enlisting domestic and even foreign support but too vague to commit the United States or other countries to any specific course of action. The international system, they knew, responded to the interests of nations, not to generally accepted codes of international behavior. The United States would serve human society by pursuing its real interests, nothing more. If the precepts of the early republic regarding foreign affairs became lost to later generations, the tradition they embodied remains an illustrious element in the nation's heritage, one to be recalled and pondered by those who seek direction in this complex and troubled world.

Gender, Expansionism, and Imperialism

ANDREW ROTTER

Gender, or gendering, is not a static idea but a transnational process: it is the assignment of certain characteristics based on prevailing ideas of masculinity and femininity to a people and nation by another people and nation. Masculinity and femininity are not, in this view, biologically determined categories but culturally and socially conditioned ideas. Nations and the people who constitute them become "gendered," and this affects the policies that other nations pursue toward them.

Gender, like discourses of race, class, and religion, is rooted in systems of power. It does not simply and innocently describe circumstances: rather, it helps to shape the world according to the wishes of those who control (in this case) United States foreign policy. Although power is a fluctuating commodity, and although those who exercised it in the realm of foreign policy were not of course the same people in 1898 as were around in 1824, it is possible to describe them at both times as an elite group who were exclusively white, and predominantly male, well born, and Protestant. They saw the world in light of their own experience, and hoped to remake it according to their own principles and prejudices. In terms of gender, one can say of them that they believed that, while women had certain desirable qualities, only men were sufficiently logical, assertive, disciplined, and strongminded to exert power properly. . . .

Until recently, the history of United States foreign relations has not generally been viewed as susceptible to gender analysis. That has now changed. Historians and scholars of cultural studies have shown that gender analysis can explain how people understand themselves and why they perceive others as they do, and that these understandings and perceptions contribute to policymaking. While diplomats and policymakers are seldom explicit about their gendered reasons for doing what they do, they live, like all of us, in a wider world of symbols, rituals, and images—in others words, in culture. Their spoken, written, and body language often reveals their feelings about gender, even if inadvertently. Men who face challenges to their masculinity (however that is defined) may act more boldly or rashly than circumstances would seem to require. Women who sense that foreign policy has taken on a

---

This essay was prepared specifically for this book and is copyrighted by Andrew Rotter, 2003.

harshness that needs (in their view) softening might seek to influence policymakers to behave with more compassion, generosity, or subtlety, all allegedly feminine qualities. . . . A decision made to dominate others chiefly for economic or strategic reasons may also have a basis in gender, though we must be careful to avoid what is called the "overdetermination" of decisions. Equally likely, gender relations might be used to justify a decision made for other reasons—that is, to make the domination of one nation by another seem as allegedly natural as the domination of a woman by a man. . . .

Let us [turn] to the case of U.S. expansionism, 1800–1900. As George Washington suggested, effeminacy was, in the virtuous years of the early republic, associated with luxury, corruption, and vice. Even more than Washington, James Madison and Thomas Jefferson worried that all small republics eventually developed over time, evolving from agricultural to industrial as their population densities increased and arable land was taken up. Here is what they believed: that if contained within limited borders, the United States would become dependent on foreign trade, especially in the kinds of effeminate fripperies for which the European countries had become notorious. Culturally sophisticated as Europe might be, its nations were overpopulated and overripe, rotting from within as the sweet corruptions of luxury ate away their moral foundations. The courts of Europe, particularly that of Bourbon France before the Revolution, served to warn Americans of the sort of decadence that could set in as a nation developed over time. Men in wigs, perfume, and silk, leading lives of luxury and effeminate foolishness, were a specter haunting any nation that stagnated after the fashion of Europe.

Was there a way out? Perhaps. Writing in defense of the newly drafted Constitution in 1788, James Madison advised his fellow Americans to "extend the sphere" in order to incorporate more interests into the polity, thereby preventing domination by a single faction or an easily formed majority. In spatial terms, of course, Madison sought more land. The Madisonian/Jeffersonian prescription, as [the historian] Drew McCoy has described it, was to cheat development through time by pursuing expansion across space, into the North American hinterland. If a bottled-up nation would become a manufacturing nation, a people left free to roam the land at will would remain virtuous farmers, and the greater the expanse of territory the greater the number of farmers there would be. And if the nation had a vigorous foreign trade, which both Madison and Jefferson endorsed, its farmers would have to work so hard to satisfy demand that they could not possibly grow lazy and effeminate. Clearing the land and preparing it with the plow, caring for livestock, sowing and harvesting, building and maintaining houses and barns, hunting and trapping, and protecting the homestead against Indians—this was men's work, most felt. Jeffersonian virtue bore the masculine gender.

At the same time, there was to be a polite side to landed expansion. It would not do to admit too freely the brutishness of life and work on the frontier; expansionism, after all, was a means to secure what Americans saw as virtue, and was itself a virtuous enterprise. Women approved the westward movement, domesticated it, and sanctified it with their higher virtue. Morally elevated women, most insisted, were healers, sent to rid reputedly primitive others of disease. Others pointed out that they were good Christians—women attended church more regularly than men in the nineteenth century—and thus well suited for missionary work among the Indians.

The Manifest Destiny enacted predominantly by American men carried with it what [the American studies scholar] Amy Kaplan has called "manifest domesticity," whereby women, "positioned at the center of the home, play[ed] a major role in defining the contours of the nation and its shifting borders with the foreign." Unwilling to accept that they were making a landed empire, Americans distinguished their efforts from those of Europeans, whose emerging empires were tainted by greed and had no regard for the welfare of their subjects. American expansionism, undertaken in the name of progress and accompanied by feminine highmindedness, was to be as benign as it was inevitable.

In these ways did a gendered foreign policy emerge from the recesses of the self, from the psychology, that is, of those who promoted expansionism. But U.S. policy was impelled as well by gendered perceptions of others. Let it be said that ideas based on gender often overlapped with those involving race. It was easiest to imagine as others those who were most different from selves, so if we assume that expansionist policymakers were almost always white men, women (or effeminate men) and those with dark skins were most likely to be reckoned as foreign. . . . Native Americans and Mexicans, and ultimately Cubans, Puerto Ricans, and Filipinos, were deemed by policymakers self-evidently captious or mischievous, requiring a strong, masculine hand for discipline. Or they were judged weak— actual or potential victims of others—and thereby required a strong and benevolent masculine hand for protection. Common to both conceptions, of course, was an American sense of superiority that rendered U.S. passivity unthinkable in a wider world of threats and opportunities.

U.S. relations with Mexico in the second quarter of the nineteenth century provided both of these. In 1819, Spanish authorities invited Americans to settle the northern Mexican province of Texas, with the condition that they convert to Catholicism and generally behave themselves. Instead, the settlers became only nominal Catholics and, worse, brought slaves with them, an anathema to the Mexican government that became independent in 1823. The Mexicans tried to crack down, prompting an indignant response by the Texans and their supporters in Washington. Texas would be free, the rebellious Sam Houston told his fellow settlers, because the humiliations of Mexican rule created a "situation . . . peculiarly calculated to call forth all your manly energies." The Texans' revolt, beginning in 1836, played out in a series of masculine melodramas: the heroic and suicidal stand at the Alamo; the outrage of Goliad, at which the patently unmanly Mexican leader Santa Anna (even his name seemed effeminate) killed unarmed American prisoners; and the triumphantly climactic battle at San Jacinto, during which the Americans exhibited masculine cunning, courage, and finally magnanimity in their decision to release the captured Santa Anna.

Houston hoped for annexation by the United States; Texas, he said, having been liberated by men, now presented itself "as a bride adorned for her espousals." Marriage became a leading metaphor of annexation. It legitimated expansion by making both parties to territorial union seem honest and their arrangement consensual. The metaphor could work against expansionism too, or at least against hasty annexation of foreign lands, especially if the intended bride was darker skinned than the groom. This was the case after 1846, when Mexico, never reconciled to the loss of Texas (or at least so much of it), went to war with the United States. The Americans won the battles and took the territory, but there were some objections. President Zachary Taylor worried that annexationists would "drag California into the Union before her wedding garment has yet been cast about her person." California was added to the union anyway. The debate was more vigorous over whether to annex all of Mexico, and it was inflected by gender. Those favoring annexation argued that Mexico could be a "sister republic," and especially that Mexican women craved the protection and affection of North American men. Opponents claimed that Mexican men, who would become voters in U.S. elections if added to the union, were insensible, uncouth, and indolent, and as a result made Mexico indigestible by a "civilized race." A Boston poet summed up the dilemma in 1846:

> The Spanish maid, with eye of fire,
> At balmy evening turns her lyre
> And, looking to the Eastern sky,
> Awaits our Yankee chivalry
> Whose purer blood and valiant arms,
> Are fit to clasp her budding charms.
>
> The *man*, her mate, is sunk in sloth—
> To love, his senseless heart is loth:
> The pipe and glass and tinkling lute,
> A sofa, and a dish of fruit;
> A nap, some dozen times by day;
> Sombre and sad, and never gay.

In the end, there was compromise: the United States annexed only Mexican territory north of the Rio Grande.

Expansion on the land continued through the nineteenth century, despite the considerable distraction of fratricidal sectional conflict. The increase in manufacturing following the Civil War seemed ominously to indicate that the Jeffersonians had at last run out of time and space, that Americans were now bottled up and agrarian virtue was a fleeting memory. The superintendent of the census appeared to confirm this fear in 1890 when he assembled figures showing that the West was settled, no longer an open frontier. Expansionist energies now turned outward. As [the historian] Kristin Hoganson has argued, the economic shocks and psychic frustrations of the 1890s drove American men to seek foreign markets and adventures, a quest that, if successful, would keep them from "idleness and dissipation" at home and allow them "to meet the basic male obligation of providing for their families" as trade grew and the economy improved. In a world of empires, in which even small European states had navies and colonies, it seemed unmanly to linger at home. Indeed, American men were exhorted to act boldly by the likes of Alfred Thayer Mahan, who demanded of his confreres "manly resolve" not "weakly sentiment," and Theodore Roosevelt, who in 1899 preached the virtues of "the strenuous life" and expressed admiration for "the man who embodies victorious effort . . . who has those virile qualities necessary to win in the stern strife of actual life." These exhortations reached the ears of men worried about the growing feminization of social and cultural life and even politics, wherein advocates of woman suffrage were making progress. Thus were male selves prepared, by a combination of expansionist history and current anxieties, for an aggressive foreign policy.

The condition of others also prompted a searching look abroad. For decades, the people of Cuba, near neighbors of the North Americans, had chafed under Spanish rule. In 1895 the Cubans rebelled; they were met with Spanish repression. There were atrocities by both sides in the rebellion, but most Americans sympathized with the Cubans, and they made clear their sympathies in gendered words and images. They depicted Spanish men as devious, cruel, and rapacious; Cuba, wrote one commentator, was a "country that Spain has never loved, but has always wished to hold in bondage for lust and brutality." It followed that Cuba was rendered a woman, courageous and resourceful in her way but finally helpless to fend off the determined advances of the Spanish interloper. Only Uncle Sam (and we are back to selves here), tough and virile and yet sufficiently avuncular as to seem unthreatening to respectable lady Cuba, claimed the ability to drive the interloper off. A "pusillanimous cad," jeered an editorial in the *New York World*, would turn his back on a woman in distress (Cuba), while "a *man* would interfere." When President William McKinley equivocated over whether to go to war against Spain in 1898, cartoonists depicted him as a man without a spine, or as a woman, complete with apron and bonnet.

McKinley did declare war, of course, and Spain quickly proved no military match for the disorganized but potent American military. It was, according to Secretary of State John Hay, "a splendid little war," in which the United States dispatched Spanish forces in Cuba, Puerto Rico, and the Philippines. The Cubans, plucky though they might have been in rebellion, were in North American eyes clearly unready to govern themselves. Señoritas in distress now rescued by heroic North American men (self-described), their fate was submission to kind but firm male control. So too were Puerto Ricans "feminized and infantilized" by North Americans, as [the historian] Eileen J. Findlay has written, subject to "the United States' virile, fatherly imperial rule." . . .

Cuba and Puerto Rico were small islands close to the United States, and North Americans could (and did) argue that extending to them the blessings of protection was no less natural a process than buying Louisiana or taking California. No such claim was possible for grabbing the Philippines. Halfway around the world and remote from the United States in history and culture, the Philippines promised to test the proposition that U.S. political institutions could jump water. The McKinley administration decided they could. For one thing, Filipinos were, like Indians, Mexicans, and Cubans, alleged to be racially inferior to white Americans, and thus incapable of looking after themselves. They were supposedly childish too, and thus incapable of looking after themselves. And they were—and the conclusion was once more supposed to be obvious—feminized or effeminate, too weak to fend off enemies and too lightheaded to forge their own political system. A previous generation of Americans had likened their absorption of others' lands to a marriage, as if the policy was mutual. Imperialists made the same case for taking control of the Philippines. "For better for worse, for richer or poorer, the Philippines have become subject to the jurisdiction of the United States," declared one writer. . . .

Let us close with a play—one that reminds us that gendered image-making is a two-way street, even where differences in power are apparent. The play, written in Tagalog, is called *Hindi Pa Aco Patay (I Am Not Yet Dead)*; its Filipino author is Juan Matapang Cruz. The villain of the piece is Macamcam (in English, "avaricious"), who represents the American colonial government in the Philippines. He wants to marry the beautiful Karangalan ("dignity," the offspring of the motherland), but she loves Tangulan ("protector"), a Filipino patriot, and therefore refuses Macamcam's lascivious overtures. The "American" bribes a Filipino collaborator ("the shameless one") to kidnap Karangalan. Tangulan comes to rescue her, and challenges Macamcam to a duel. Macamcam gets the better of it and Tangulan falls, apparently dead. But as the coerced wedding proceeds, Tangulan suddenly reappears and announces, "I am not yet dead!" The Americans are thwarted, Filipino nationalism is triumphant, and the Filipino audience, presumably, roars its approval. Thus are discourses of gender used to subvert as well as dominate. And yet, it is worth noting that, while playwright Cruz in the end gives the Filipinos power over the Americans, thus inverting the reality on the ground, gender roles in the play remain standard issue: men lust and fight and crave power, but the good ones finally save women from terrible fates.

The Adaptable Power of Racism

MICHAEL L. KRENN

The longevity of racism, particularly in terms of its role in U.S. foreign policy, is not difficult to understand. Throughout the years, racism has demonstrated remarkable adaptability to the needs of American diplomacy, incredible resiliency in the face of challenges, and undeniable power which, on occasion, has actually overridden the needs of U.S. foreign policy. The use of a few examples from America's past should suffice to prove these points.

Racism has never been a static element in American foreign policy. Instead, it has shown a truly amazing ability to adapt to the specific needs of U.S. diplomacy at different times in the nation's history. During the days of Manifest Destiny, racism quickly came to the aid of the arguments for territorial expansion. It seemed perfectly natural, indeed inevitable, that the white race would overrun and displace the weaker races. In this particular instance, the weaker race was the "mongrel" mixture of the Mexicans, and most Americans expressed little doubt (and less sympathy) when it came to the question of seizing Texas, the New Mexico territory, and California. The Mexicans—backward, lazy, stupid, and completely incapable of self-improvement—simply had to give way to the march of progress. It was, after all, the destiny of the Anglo-Saxon race.

Half a century later Americans were once again bent on expansion. This time, however, the goal was markets not territory. And now the people in these faraway lands were not to be displaced or annihilated, for they would provide both labor to extract the mineral and agricultural wealth demanded by the American market and consumers for American products. American racial thought, now in the thrall of social Darwinism, again served as a bulwark for U.S. expansion, subtly adapting itself to the new demands of American diplomacy. Now the goal of U.S. policy was couched in terms of "uplift" and civilization." It was painfully obvious that the peoples of Cuba, the Philippines, and other territories on which the American flag

The Adaptable Power of Racism from Michael L. Krenn, *The Color of Empire: Race and American Foreign Relations,* Potomac Books, Inc., 2006, pp. 103–107. Reprinted by permission of Potomac Books, Inc.

was planted were incapable of progress toward a civilized society if left to their own devices. They must be "freed" from the control of the inefficient (and racially suspect) Spaniards so that Yankee ingenuity could work its wonders on their primitive societies. [The U.S. exhibit at the 1904 World's Fair in St. Louis] made the point in dramatic fashion. At the Philippine Reservation visitors could see for themselves the choice before the American nation: leave the natives to their barbaric savagery or raise them to an acceptable level of civilization. Miraculously, this was also part of the destiny of the Anglo-Saxon race.

Racism has also proven itself nearly invulnerable to attacks from a variety of directions. Early in its development, for instance, the concept of race had to fend off challenges from religion. How could there be different races if God created man in his own image—and in one place? Such was the resilience of racial thinking, however, that it easily withstood these theological assaults. Racism turned the Bible against itself, arguing that the Tower of Babel story explained the diversity of mankind, that the dispersion of the human race to far-off corners of the world resulted in different kinds of people who had adapted to their new environments. Eventually, those who strongly supported racial theories simply dispensed with the pretense of monogenesis and argued that in contrast to the Biblical story of creation there had, in fact, been any number of creations. Early nineteenth-century science put the final nail in the coffin by "proving" the diversity of mankind; going further, they even suggested that the differences resulted in a hierarchy of races ranging from the strongest and most civilized (the Anglo-Saxon) to the weakest and most degraded (sometimes black, sometimes Native American).

Yet, when science turned against racism in the 1920s and 1930s with the new emphasis on culture instead of biology as an explanation for human differences and when the horrors of the Nazi regime signaled the death knell of scientific racism, racial thinking mutated once again. Like a virus, racism insinuated itself into the debates on culture and "modernization" in the 1950s and 1960s. The differences between Western society and "traditional" societies were no longer discussed in terms of skin color or cranial capacity but rather in terms of different cultural norms. Traditional societies just needed to be nudged into the "stages of economic growth." Much of this thinking, however, was racist thinking in sheep's clothing. Modernization theory still posited the same general thinking that lay behind American imperialism in the late nineteenth century: that traditional (i.e., nonwhite) societies were hopelessly and helplessly behind the modern (i.e., white) world. Only through the infusion of Western ideas into these cultures could they ever hope to move beyond their stagnant, backward status. In short, modernization depended on the acceptance of white leadership and the superiority of white culture. It was a rather remarkable feat. In the space of two hundred years, racism had beaten both religion and science to a standstill.

Finally, there is the undeniable power of racism. [R]ace is [not] the only determinant of U.S. foreign policy. But to deny race's role in American diplomacy is to have an incomplete understanding of the nature of America's international relations. And in some cases, the power of racism has been overwhelming—even when its power runs contrary to what would appear to be the goals of U.S. policy. Let us take but two examples. In 1919 the United States met with the other victorious Allied powers at Versailles to bring an official end to World War I and chart the future of the world. When Japan surprised many of the delegates by putting forward a resolution for international racial equality, the moment seemed propitious for the United States to rather easily gain the respect and possibly friendship of a growing power in the Far East. The resolution itself was rather innocuous and its application to the international scene was never spelled out in any specifics. The United States, therefore, seemed to have little to lose by supporting the resolution. Relations with the Japanese had always been somewhat tense, and it was undeniable that Japan had become a major player in the diplomatic jousting in Asia. President Woodrow Wilson, however, could not break free from the stranglehold of racism. His own personal views on the inferiority of other races, the powerful strains of racism running through his own nation, and the pressure applied by his Anglo-Saxon allies to thwart any attempt to introduce racial equality into the international arena led Wilson to squash the resolution even after it passed by an overwhelming majority.

Four decades later the United States confronted a strange turn of events. Its racism had been turned back upon it by communist propaganda that consistently homed in on racial injustices inside the "leader of the free world." America's "Achilles' heel," as the race problem was referred to, was steadily losing the nation prestige among both friends and foes. The U.S. commitment to the ideals it consistently professed—equality, justice, and democracy—suffered blow after blow as incidents of racism multiplied, highlighted by the ugly scenes coming out of Little Rock [, Arkansas,] in 1957, [when white students and parents violently resisted school desegregation.] The people of the world, particularly in Asia, Africa, and Latin America, were left to wonder whether America's rhetoric had any basis in reality. To confront this international public relations nightmare, the United States embarked on a truly novel approach to propaganda in 1958. America decided to admit to the world at the World's Fair in Brussels that it suffered from race problems, while at the same time suggesting that it was making progress in solving those problems and looked forward to the day when the United States would have a completely integrated society. It was a brave but ultimately futile gesture. The forces of racism in America immediately mounted a counterattack and found a receptive audience in President Dwight D. Eisenhower. Despite evidence that indicated that the "Unfinished Business" exhibit was having a positive impact on the world's perception of the United States, the American government first revised and then simply scrapped the section on segregation. Even in the heat of the Cold War, racism proved more powerful than national interest.

Given the history of racism in American foreign policy, what can we surmise about the future? The adaptability, resiliency, and power of racism suggest that we have not seen the end of its pernicious effects on the nation's international relations. Talk about the growing interdependence of nations and the increasing "smallness" of our world brought about by greater communication and transportation is not altogether comforting, for proximity and contact with other peoples has not often resulted in greater sympathy or understanding from Americans. Suggestions that diversity, multiculturalism, political correctness, and acceptance now dominate the intellectual climate of our nation are welcome, but racism has taken on challengers before and always come out on top. Efforts to increase Americans' knowledge of the world around them are laudable and altogether necessary. To argue that such knowledge in and of itself will lead to greater understanding and appreciation of other cultures only partially allays the fear that race will continue to impact America's relations with the world. Unless the United States is willing to forcefully and consistently come to grips with the role of race in its own society and come face to face with the damage that racism has left in its wake, it seems likely that race and racism will continue to haunt us at home and abroad.

Culture, National Identity, and the "Myth of America"

WALTER L. HIXSON

Foreign policy flows from cultural hegemony affirming "America" as a manly, racially superior, and providentially destined "beacon of liberty," a country which possesses a special right to exert power in the world. Hegemonic national identity drives a continuous militant foreign policy, including the regular resort to war.

Having internalized this Myth of America, a majority, or at least a critical mass, of Americans have granted spontaneous consent to foreign policy militancy over the sweep of U.S. history. While specific foreign policies often provoke criticism, to be sure, national identity contains such criticism within secure cultural boundaries. Only by gaining a better understanding of the cultural construction of foreign policy and national identity can we hope to forge a new hegemony, a more equitable society, and a commitment to cooperative internationalism. . . .

Cultural analysis illuminates the remarkable continuity of U.S. foreign policy flowing from a distinctive national identity. Despite breathtaking socioeconomic and technological change—from royal charters to multinational corporations, from powder muskets to bunker-busting nuclear warheads—foreign policy has proven remarkably continuous. This seemingly ahistorical argument for continuity flows from a powerful identity of imperial nationalism. In the U.S. historiographic tradition, as [the American Studies Scholar Amy] Kaplan observes, most historians make the mistake "of viewing empire as a twentieth-century aberration, rather than as part of an expansionist continuum." Diplomatic history has long been plagued by relative neglect of pre–World War II and especially pre-twentieth-century studies. . . .

Only by locating the analysis within modernity can we fully grasp the continuity of U.S. foreign policy. Euro-American history emerged within the broader frame of modernity, which defined itself in contrast with others, perceived as primitive or backward. Modernity may be defined as a worldview emanating from Enlightenment rationalism in the sixteenth, seventeenth, and eighteenth centuries and exported globally from Europe through imperial expansion. Through Enlightenment principles white male elites understood and shaped their world within a universe they perceived as being ordered. Religious cosmologies remained deeply embedded in culture, to be sure, yet increasingly in the Age of Reason empowered European men sought to direct the forces of history rather than live in the shadow of an omnipotent God. At the same time, Europeans achieved a global reach, as revolutionary advances in shipbuilding and navigation enabled them to

Hixson, Walter L., "Culture, National Identity, and the 'Myth of America'" from *The Myth of American Diplomacy: National Identity and U.S. Foreign Policy* (New Haven: Yale University Press, 2008), pp. 1–2, 5, 7–8, 12–15, 305–306. Reprinted by permission of Yale University Press.

fan out across the seas to Africa, the Americas, and Asia. An Atlantic world community linked four continents, as Europeans set out to discover, map, classify, and conquer the natural world.

Gradually weakened by these forces of modernity, the structured order of the ancien régime, anchored by centralized church authority, monarchy, and aristocracy, imploded in a process that culminated in the U.S., French, and Latin American revolutions. Modernity required masses of people to define a new identity, to relocate themselves in a world in which conditions had undergone profound change. At this point, *culture* began to replace the *structure* of the ancien régime in establishing a foundation for the new modern world. Culture comprised the realm in which shared values and political meanings were digested, contested, constructed, and affirmed.

Modernity comprised a rational and reasoned worldview that Europeans came to view as the only legitimate path to progress. Modern international relations (foreign policy) evolved as technology enabled Westerners to transport their culture and way of life, which they equated with progress, under God, onto foreign shores. . . .

Colonialism and imperialism thus flowed from the aggressive expansion of a western European worldview that apotheosized its way of life as ordered, reasoned, and providentially sanctioned. By implication, those peoples of the world who lived under divergent worldviews were viewed as unreasoned, unenlightened, and unchosen and thus subject to various forms of control and domination. When this effort at domination provoked resistance, modernists "externalized and projected" the violent disorder onto "the non-Western other, thus helping to stimulate the desire to penetrate, police and control, while at the same time validating a narcissistic Western identity.". . .

Scholars analyze nations as products of the "invention of tradition" and as "imagined communities." Nationalism evolved in an effort to unite common territories and pull together ethnic, regional, linguistic, and otherwise segmented communities. If nations are invisible, intangible, and fundamentally imagined, they therefore must be represented symbolically and in a manner reflecting the distinctiveness of a particular culture. Understanding the behavior of a state requires analysis extending beyond merely invoking the named community, as if what it represents reflects an ontological status, a universally accepted state of being. Thus one cannot fully grasp the foreign policy of the United States without examining the nation's identity.

As they "settled" a putatively virgin land, the early Euro-American communities and then the United States had to be more fully imagined, had to do more to invent their traditions than most. [The historian] Louis Hartz long ago argued that "American exceptionalism" stemmed from the absence of the structure of the ancien régime—the centuries of European religious, monarchical, and aristocratic order. U.S. nationalism assumed overdetermined characteristics that created community bonds in the absence of those traditions undergirding the modern European nations. "If all states are 'imagined communities,' devoid of ontological being apart from the many practices that constitute their reality," [the political scientist] David Campbell notes, "then [the United States] is the imagined community par excellence."

"America" became particularly dependent on representation to produce consent behind national identity.

I argue that foreign policy plays a profoundly significant role in the process of creating, affirming, and disciplining conceptions of national identity. As Campbell puts it, U.S. foreign policy is "global in scope yet national in legitimation." Only by analyzing the mutually reinforcing relationship between the domestic and the foreign, under the canopy of national identity, can we glean a clearer understanding of the functioning of power both at home and abroad. . . .

By their cultural production of otherness and hierarchy, racial and gendered perceptions underscore the critical linkages between foreign policy and domestic life. Ethnic cleansing of Indians and the enslavement of Africans fueled capitalism and freedom for white men. Likewise, exaltation of masculinity, the strenuous life, and "Be all you can be" brought young men into the military while at the same time empowering masculine virtues in invidious contrast with soft and sentimental characteristics ascribed to women. Foreign policy reinforced heterosexuality as well by linking campaigns against homosexuals, dubbed lavender boys, with anti-Communist containment or through the ongoing purges of gays and lesbians from the military.

Under U.S. national identity, foreign policy militancy and domestic cultural hegemony thus proved mutually reinforcing. The primacy of foreign policy, national security, and homeland security emphasized the traditional role of males as protectors of vulnerable women and children. The masculine virtues of assertiveness, preparedness, militancy, and technological know-how enabled the nation to emerge as the world's dominant nuclear power and arms merchant. Advocacy of peaceful and cooperative internationalism could be feminized as the purview of squaw men, pantywaists, and wimps.

Analysis of religion, like race and gender, "historicizes a connection between domestic culture and foreign policy," as Seth Jacobs observes. Like the myth of a classless society, Myth of America identity fosters the illusion that in the United States freedom from religion prevails alongside freedom of religion. Religious faith permeates U.S. history and culture and carries profound domestic and foreign policy implications. . . .

Manifest Destiny, as myriad scholars have explicated, thus applies to far more than the Mexican War as a trope sanctifying the nation's mission of boundless expansion. Religious faith profoundly influenced foreign policy, and especially war, as the United States confronted a procession of "heathen" enemies, "godless Communists," and "evildoers" in a continuous history of violent conflict. . . . Much of the public viewed these apocalyptic struggles as divinely sanctioned reflections of national destiny. Victory in war, even the ultimate resolution of a bitter Civil War, affirmed the guiding hand of Providence. A critical mass of citizenry thus "continually reaffirmed . . . the conviction that America is a nation called to special destiny by God". . . .

War—like nothing else—forges emotional bonds of unity, loyalty, and patriotism that powerfully reaffirm Myth of America identity. War spurred nation building and brought cathartic relief in the contexts of taming the frontier, Manifest Destiny, overseas imperialism, world war, the Cold War, and wars on terror. Although not all wars were popular, particularly when they became prolonged and inconclusive, they nearly always served to reaffirm national identity and cultural hegemony and to promote campaigns of countersubversion. . . .

Regenerative war intensified the bonds between the people and the abstraction of the nation. The promise of the nation, as the "beacon of liberty" for all mankind, inspired massive external violence. . . . War became associated with heroism and consensus as the nation came together like a "band of brothers" in the life-and-death struggles with evil enemy-others. By making the ultimate sacrifice, the nation's war dead sanctified the Myth of America. They gave their lives that we might live, and such sacrifice could only be honored, not called into question.

While most Americans honored their obligation to support the troops, antiwar protesters subverted national identity. Advocates of peaceful internationalism thus find themselves policed, stigmatized as unpatriotic, and often incarcerated in a continuous series of countersubversive campaigns. War thus repeatedly functioned to reinforce cultural hegemony, diverting resources and attention away from peace internationalism and domestic inequalities, which might otherwise empower reform. Over the course of U.S. history, a succession of wars gradually erected a heavily militarized warfare and national security state. . . .

The point of emphasizing the constructed nature of national identity and foreign policy is to deconstruct the knowledge. Such analysis illuminates the ways in which knowledge and power are established, affirmed, disciplined, and policed against counterhegemonic challenges. Cultural analysis connects domestic identity and foreign policy, which too often are treated as being discrete rather than mutually dependent. . . .

Understanding derives not only from gleaning new knowledge, but also from unpacking and dispensing with some of the old. "Truths" must be interrogated and often delegitimated. I argue that the Myth of America and the pathologically violent foreign policy it inspires cannot remain unchallenged. The costs are too high, the consequences too great, both at home and abroad, to remain acquiescent. The hope is that broader public understanding of the constructedness of Myth of America identity can begin the process of trying to change it. Culture is organic, and societies are therefore susceptible to change, as the histories of Germany, Japan, South Africa, the Soviet Union, and many other nations and civilizations demonstrate.

FURTHER READING

Michael Adas, *Dominance by Design* (2006)
"American Military History: A Roundtable," *Journal of American History,* 93 (March 2007), 1116–1185.
Fred Anderson and Andrew Cayton, *The Dominion of War* (2004)
William H. Becker and Samuel F. Wells Jr., eds., *Economics and World Power* (1984)
Gail Bederman, *Manliness and Civilization* (1995)
James T. Campbell et al., eds., *Race, Nation, and Empire in American History* (2007)
Jerald A. Combs, *American Diplomatic History: Two Centuries of Changing Interpretaions* (1982)

"Diplomatic History Today: A Roundtable," *Journal of American History,* 95 (March 2009), 1053–1091.

James Fallows, *More Like Us* (1989)

"Foreign Relations in the Early Republic: Essays from a SHEAR Symposium," *Journal of the Early Republic,* 14 (1994), 453–495

Lloyd C. Gardner, ed., *Redefining the Past: Essays in Diplomatic History in Honor of William Appleman Williams* (1986)

John Lewis Gaddis, *Surprise, Security, and the American Experience* (2004)

Kenneth J. Hagan and Ian J. Bickerton, *Unintended Consequences: The United States at War* (2007)

Michael P. Hamilton, ed., *American Character and Foreign Policy* (1986)

David C. Hendrickson, *Union, Nation, Or Empire* (2009)

Joan Hoff, *A Faustian Foreign Policy from Woodrow Wilson to George W. Bush* (2008)

Michael J. Hogan, *Path to Power* (2000)

——— and Thomas G. Paterson, eds., *Explaining the History of American Foreign Relations* (2004)

Kristin L. Hoganson, *Fighting for American Manhood: How Gender Politics Provoked the Spanish-American and Philippine-American Wars* (1998)

Ole Holsti, *Public Opinion and American Foreign Policy* (1996)

Gerald Horne, *The Deepest South* (2007)

Michael H. Hunt, *The American Ascendancy* (2007)

———, *Ideology and U.S. Foreign Policy* (1987)

Robert Kagan, *Dangerous Nation* (2006)

Amy Kaplan, *The Anarchy of Empire in the Making of U.S. Culture* (2002)

——— and Donald Pease, eds., *Cultures of United States Imperialism* (1993)

Paul Kennedy, *The Rise and Fall of the Great Powers* (1987)

Richard Kluger, *From Sea to Shining Sea* (2007)

Annette Kolodny, *The Lay of the Land: Metaphor as Experience and History in American Life and Letters* (1975)

Paul A. Kramer, "Empires, Exceptions, and Anglo-Saxons: Race and Rule Between the British and United States Empires, 1880–1910," *Journal of American History,* 88 (2002), 1315–1353

Walter LaFeber, "Liberty and Power: U.S. Diplomatic History, 1750–1945," in Susan Porter Benson et al., eds., *The New American History* (1997)

Christopher Lasch, "William Appleman Williams on American History," *Marxist Perspectives,* 1 (1978), 118–126

James E. Lewis Jr., *The American Union and the Problem of Neighborhood* (1998)

Seymour Martin Lipset, *American Exceptionalism* (1996)

Charles S. Maier, *Among Empires* (2006)

Thomas J. McCormick, "Drift or Mastery?" *Reviews in American History,* 10 (1982), 318–330

Richard A. Melanson, "The Social and Political Thought of William Appleman Williams," *Western Political Quarterly,* 31 (1978), 392–409

Walter A. McDougall, *Freedom Just Around the Corner* (2004)

Peter Novick, *That Noble Dream: The "Objectivity" Question and the American Historical Progression* (1988)

Walter Nugent, *Habits of Empire* (2008)

Stephen E. Pelz, "A Taxonomy for American Diplomatic History," *Journal of Interdisciplinary History,* 19 (1988), 259–276

Andrew Preston, "Bridging the Gap between the Sacred and the Secular in the History of American Foreign Relations," *Diplomatic History,* 30 (November 2006), 783–812

Eric Rauchway, *Blessed Among Nations* (2006)

John Carolos Rowe, *Literary Culture and U.S. Imperialism* (2000)

David Ryan, *U.S. Foreign Policy in World History* (2000)

Arthur M. Schlesinger Jr., *War and the American Presidency* (2004)

Joan W. Scott, *Gender and the Politics of History* (1988)

Robert Shaffer, "Race, Class, Gender, and Diplomatic History," *Radical History Review,* 70 (1998), 156–168

Richard Slotkin, *Regeneration Through Violence* (1973)

"Symposium: Responses to Charles S. Maier, 'Marking Time,'" *Diplomatic History,* 5 (1981), 353–371

William O. Walker, *National Security and Core Values in American History* (2009)

Ted Widmer, *Ark of the Liberties* (2008)

"William Appleman Williams: A Roundtable," *Diplomatic History,* 25 (Spring 2001), 275–316

William Appleman Williams, *Empire as a Way of Life* (1980)

Molly M. Wood, " 'Commanding Beauty' and 'Gentle Charm': American Women and Gender in the Early Twentieth Century Foreign Service," *Diplomatic History,* 31 (June 2007), 505–530.

CHAPTER 2

The Origins of American Foreign Policy in the Revolutionary Era

Americans were once proud members of the British Empire. For more than 150 years, that membership brought good profit at low cost and protection against the French in North America. But in the 1760s, after victory in the French and Indian War, Britain began to impose new taxes and regulations that shattered the relationship. In 1776, the American colonials chose independence through revolution. They selected that dangerous course not only because of perceived British perfidy but also owing to their own New World sense of themselves as different from—indeed, superior to—the Old World of monarchy, relentless international rivalry, and corrupt institutions.

Geographic isolation from Europe helped to spawn such notions of exceptionalism, as did the American doctrine of mission and God-favored destiny that the Puritans had etched on American memory. Colonials from New England to Georgia had, moreover, become accustomed to making their own decisions, governing themselves at the local level in what one historian has tagged "island communities," and expanding their landholdings and commerce without much interference from the British crown and Parliament. Yet when Americans declared independence and then worked to gain and preserve it in a doubting and hostile world, they felt compelled to appeal for help from Europe, particularly France. They became conspicuously uneasy about calling on the decadent Old World to save their fresh New World experiment, because the linkage so violated what some scholars have labeled American "isolationism." At the same time, however, American leaders saw in their new treaties and nationhood the opportunity to reform traditional world politics to ensure the country's safety and prosperity.

As children of empire, early national leaders naturally dreamed of a new and ever-expanding American empire. They recognized the obstacles to expansion: Native Americans, European powers, and their own sectional and political differences. In fact, many of the nation's founders thought that internal squabbling and the absence of a strong central government threatened not just expansionism but also independence itself. A persuasive argument for the Constitution, ratified in 1789, *was that it would permit the new United States to devise coherent and respected foreign relations.*

Historians have debated the relative importance of isolationism, expansionism, imperialism, and idealism as characteristics of early American foreign relations. And they have wondered to what extent American leaders understood and exercised power in eighteenth-century world affairs. But they have agreed that Americans ardently claimed that their upstart republic held a unique international position that would transform the world community. Why Americans came to think so is explained by the documents and essays in this chapter.

DOCUMENTS

John Winthrop, the first governor of Massachusetts Bay, defined the Puritan mission in a lay sermon of June 1630 (Document 1), which he delivered aboard ship off the New England coast. Document 2, from John Adams's autobiography, summarizes his views of 1775. This prominent Massachusetts attorney and politician makes the case for ties with France, cautions against entanglement in Europe's wars, and urges neutrality for the future. Thomas Paine, who had moved from England to Philadelphia just two years before independence was declared, invigorated the revolutionary spirit with his popular 1776 tract *Common Sense* (Document 3), wherein he demanded severance from the British Empire. The Declaration of Independence of July 4, 1776, Document 4, outlined colonial grievances against the mother country. Its eloquent defense of "unalienable rights" captured imaginations across the world and was soon echoed by revolutionaries in Europe. The two treaties with France that followed in 1778, the Treaty of Amity and Commerce and the Treaty of Alliance (Document 5), provided not only for alliance but also for principles that would govern foreign commerce. The pivotal treaty, the Treaty of Peace (Document 6), providing for American independence, was signed in Paris on September 3, 1783, and ratifications were exchanged on May 8, 1784.

The new nation struggled to defend its interests and its honor under the decentralized government established by the Articles of Confederation. Alexander Hamilton, John Jay, and James Madison—all of whom served in diplomatic and military positions during the confederation era—combined in 1787 and 1788 to publish the *Federalist Papers,* arguing for strengthening the federal union through adoption of the newly drafted constitution. In Document 7, an excerpt from *Federalist Paper No. 4*, former Secretary for Foreign Affairs John Jay surveys the nation's commercial and security interests in a hostile world and articulates the advantages of stronger union. Document 8 presents those parts of the U.S. Constitution of 1789 that cover the making and execution of foreign policy.

DOCUMENT 1

Governor John Winthrop Envisions
a City Upon a Hill, 1630

Now the only way to avoid this shipwreck and to provide for our posterity is to follow the Counsel of Micah: to do justly, to love mercy, to walk humbly with our God. We must be knit together in this work as one man, we must entertain each other in brotherly

Reprinted by permission of the publisher from *The Journal of John Winthrop, 1630–1649,* Abridged Edition, edited by Richard S. Dunn, James Savage, and Laetitia Yeandle, pp. 9–11, Cambridge, Mass.: The Belknap Press of Harvard University Press, Copyright © 1996 by the President and Fellows of Harvard College and Massachusetts Historical Society.

affection, we must be willing to abridge ourselves of our superfluities for the supply of others' necessities, we must delight in each other, mourn together, labor and suffer together, always having before our eyes our Commission and Community in the work. So shall we keep the unity of the Spirit in the bond of peace. The Lord will be our God and delight to dwell among us, so that we shall see much more of His wisdom, power, goodness, and truth than formerly we have been acquainted with. We shall find that the God of Israel is among us, when ten of us shall be able to resist a thousand of our enemies, when He shall make us a praise and glory, that men shall say of succeeding plantations: the Lord make it like that of New England. For we must consider that we shall be as a City upon a Hill, the eyes of all people are upon us; so that if we shall deal falsely with our God in this work we have undertaken, and so cause Him to withdraw His present help from us, we shall be made a story and a by-word through the world. We shall open the mouths of enemies to speak evil of the ways of God and all professors for God's sake; we shall shame the faces of many of God's worthy servants, and cause their prayers to be turned into Curses upon us till we be consumed out of the good land where we are going. And to shut up this discourse with that exhortation of Moses, that faithful servant of the Lord in his last farewell to Israel, Deut. 30, Beloved, there is now set before us life and good, death and evil, in that we are commanded this day to love the Lord our God, and to love one another, to walk in His ways and to keep His Commandments and His Ordinance and His laws, and the Articles of our Covenant with Him that we may live and be multiplied, and that the Lord our God may bless us in the land where we go to possess it. But if our hearts shall turn away so that we will not obey, but shall be seduced and worship (serve) other Gods, our pleasures, and profits, and serve them; it is propounded unto us this day, we shall surely perish out of the good land whither we pass over this vast Sea to possess it:

> Therefore let us choose life,
> that we, and our seed,
> may live; by obeying His
> voice, and cleaving to Him,
> for He is our life, and
> our prosperity.

DOCUMENT 2

John Adams of Massachusetts Explains French Interest in American Independence and Cautions Against Alliance, 1775

Some gentlemen doubted of the sentiments of France; thought she would frown upon us as rebels, and be afraid to countenance the example. I replied to those gentlemen, that I apprehended they had not attended to the relative situation of France and England; that it was the unquestionable interest of France that the British Continental Colonies should be independent; that Britain, by the conquest of Canada and her naval triumphs during the last war, and by her vast possessions in America and the East Indies, was exalted to a height of power and preëminence that France must envy and could not endure.

This document can be found in Charles Francis Adams, ed., *The Works of John Adams, Second President: With a Life of the Author,* Vol. II, Boston: Charles C. Little and James Brown, 1850, pp. 504–506.

But there was much more than pride and jealousy in the case. Her rank, her consideration in Europe, and even her safety and independence, were at stake. The navy of Great Britain was now mistress of the seas, all over the globe. The navy of France almost annihilated. Its inferiority was so great and obvious, that all the dominions of France, in the West Indies and in the East Indies, lay at the mercy of Great Britain, and must remain so as long as North America belonged to Great Britain, and afforded them so many harbors abounding with naval stores and resources of all kinds, and so many men and seamen ready to assist them and man their ships; that interest could not lie; that the interest of France was so obvious, and her motives so cogent, that nothing but a judicial infatuation of her councils could restrain her from embracing us; that our negotiations with France ought, however, to be conducted with great caution, and with all the foresight we could possibly obtain; that we ought not to enter into any alliance with her, which should entangle us in any future wars in Europe; that we ought to lay it down, as a first principle and a maxim never to be forgotten, to maintain an entire neutrality in all future European wars; that it never could be our interest to unite with France in the destruction of England, or in any measures to break her spirit, or reduce her to a situation in which she could not support her independence. On the other hand, it could never be our duty to unite with Britain in too great a humiliation of France; that our real, if not our nominal, independence, would consist in our neutrality. If we united with either nation, in any future war, we must become too subordinate and dependent on that nation, and should be involved in all European wars, as we had been hitherto; that foreign powers would find means to corrupt our people, to influence our councils, and, in fine, we should be little better than puppets, danced on the wires of the cabinets of Europe. We should be the sport of European intrigues and politics; that, therefore, in preparing treaties to be proposed to foreign powers, and in the instructions to be given to our ministers, we ought to confine ourselves strictly to a treaty of commerce; that such a treaty would be an ample compensation to France for all the aid we should want from her. The opening of American trade to her, would be a vast resource for her commerce and naval power, and a great assistance to her in protecting her East and West India possessions, as well as her fisheries; but that the bare dismemberment of the British empire would be to her an incalculable security and benefit, worth more than all the exertions we should require of her, even if it should draw her into another eight or ten years' war.

🌐 D O C U M E N T   3

The Patriot Thomas Paine Demands Severance from the British Empire, 1776

I have heard it asserted by some, that as America has flourished under her former connection with Great Britain, the same connection is necessary towards her future happiness, and will always have the same effect. Nothing can be more fallacious than this kind of argument. We may as well assert that because a child has thrived upon milk, that it is never to have meat, or that the first twenty years of our lives is to become a precedent for the next twenty. But even this is admitting more than is true;

This document comes from Thomas Paine, *Common Sense* (Philadelphia, Robert Bell, 1776). It can also be found in Merrill Jensen, ed., *Tracts of the American Revolution, 1763–1776* (Indianapolis: Bobbs-Merrill, 1967), pp. 400–446.

for I answer roundly, that America would have flourished as much, and probably much more, had no European power taken any notice of her. The commerce by which she hath enriched herself are the necessaries of life, and will always have a market while eating is the custom of Europe.

But she has protected us, say some. That she hath engrossed us is true, and defended the continent at our expense as well as her own, is admitted; and she would have defended Turkey from the same motive, *viz.* for the sake of trade and dominion.

Alas! we have been long led away by ancient prejudices and made large sacrifices to superstition. We have boasted the protection of Great Britain, without considering, that her motive was *interest* not *attachment;* and that she did not protect us from *our enemies* on *our account;* but from *her enemies* on *her own account,* from those who had no quarrel with us on any *other account,* and who will always be our enemies on the *same account.* Let Britain waive her pretensions to the continent, or the continent throw off the dependence, and we should be at peace with France and Spain, were they at war with Britain. The miseries of Hanover's last war ought to warn us against connections. . . .

But Britain is the parent country, say some. Then the more shame upon her conduct. Even brutes do not devour their young, nor savages make war upon their families; wherefore, the assertion, if true, turns to her reproach; but it happens not to be true, or only partly so, and the phrase *parent* or *mother country* hath been jesuitically adopted by the king and his parasites, with a low papistical design of gaining an unfair bias on the credulous weakness of our minds. Europe, and not England, is the parent country of America. This new world hath been the asylum for the persecuted lovers of civil and religious liberty from *every part* of Europe. Hither have they fled, not from the tender embraces of the mother, but from the cruelty of the monster; and it is so far true of England, that the same tyranny which drove the first emigrants from home, pursues their descendants still.

In this extensive quarter of the globe, we forget the narrow limits of three hundred and sixty miles (the extent of England) and carry our friendship on a larger scale; we claim brotherhood with every European Christian, and triumph in the generosity of the sentiment. . . .

Much hath been said of the united strength of Britain and the colonies, that in conjunction they might bid defiance to the world. But this is mere presumption; the fate of war is uncertain, neither do the expressions mean any thing; for this continent would never suffer itself to be drained of inhabitants, to support the British arms in either Asia, Africa or Europe.

Besides, what have we to do with setting the world at defiance? Our plan is commerce, and that, well attended to, will secure us the peace and friendship of all Europe; because it is the interest of all Europe to have America a free port. Her trade will always be a protection, and her barrenness of gold and silver secure her from invaders. . . .

Europe is too thickly planted with kingdoms to be long at peace, and whenever a war breaks out between England and any foreign power, the trade of America goes to ruin, *because of her connection with Britain.* The next war may not turn out like the last, and should it not, the advocates for reconciliation now will be wishing for separation then, because neutrality in that case would be a safer convoy than a man of war. Every thing that is right or reasonable pleads for separation. The blood of the slain, the weeping voice of nature cries,' Tis TIME TO PART. Even the distance at which the Almighty hath placed England and America is a strong and natural proof that the authority of the one over the other, was never the design of heaven. . . .

Small islands not capable of protecting themselves are the proper objects for government to take under their care; but there is something absurd, in supposing a Continent to be perpetually governed by an island. In no instance hath nature made the satellite larger than its primary planet; and as England and America, with respect to each other, reverse the common order of nature, it is evident that they belong to different systems. England to Europe: America to itself. . . .

In almost every article of defence we abound. Hemp flourishes even to rankness, so that we need not want cordage. Our iron is superior to that of other countries. Our small arms equal to any in the world. Cannon we can cast at pleasure. Saltpeter and gunpowder we are every day producing. Our knowledge is hourly improving. Resolution is our inherent character, and courage has never yet forsaken us. Wherefore, what is it that we want? Why is it that we hesitate? From Britain we can expect nothing but ruin. If she is once admitted to the government of America again, this continent will not be worth living in. Jealousies will be always arising; insurrections will be constantly happening; and who will go forth to quell them? Who will venture his life to reduce his own countrymen to a foreign obedience? The difference between Pennsylvania and Connecticut, respecting some unlocated lands, shows the insignificance of a British government, and fully proves that nothing but continental authority can regulate continental matters. . . .

I shall conclude these remarks, with the following timely and well-intended hints. We ought to reflect, that there are different ways by which an independency may hereafter be effected; and that *one* of those *three,* will, one day or other, be the fate of America, *viz.* By the legal voice of the people in Congress; by a military power; or by a mob: It may not always happen that our soldiers are citizens, and the multitude a body of reasonable men; virtue, as I have already remarked, is not hereditary, neither is it perpetual. Should an independency be brought about by the first of those means, we have every opportunity and every encouragement before us, to form the noblest, purest constitution on the face of the earth. We have it in our power to begin the world over again. A situation, similar to the present, hath not happened since the days of Noah until now. The birthday of a new world is at hand, and a race of men, perhaps as numerous as all Europe contains, are to receive their portion of freedom from the events of a few months. The reflection is awful, and in this point of view, how trifling, how ridiculous, do the little paltry cavilings of a few weak or interested men appear, when weighed against the business of a world.

🌐 D O C U M E N T   4

The Declaration of Independence, 1776

When, in the course of human events, it becomes necessary for one people to dissolve the political bonds which have connected them with another, and to assume, among the powers of the earth, the separate and equal station to which the laws of nature and of nature's God entitle them, a decent respect to the opinions of mankind requires that they should declare the causes which impel them to the separation.

We hold these truths to be self-evident: That all men are created equal; that they are endowed by their Creator with certain unalienable rights; that among these are life, liberty, and the pursuit of happiness; that, to secure these rights, governments are

This document can be found in *United States Code, 1994 Edition* (Washington, D.C.: U.S. Government Printing Office, 1995), I, xli–xlii.

instituted among men, deriving their just powers from the consent of the governed; that whenever any form of government becomes destructive of these ends, it is the right of the people to alter or to abolish it, and to institute new government, laying its foundation on such principles, and organizing its powers in such form, as to them shall seem most likely to effect their safety and happiness. Prudence, indeed, will dictate that governments long established should not be changed for light and transient causes; and accordingly all experience hath shown that mankind are more disposed to suffer, while evils are sufferable, than to right themselves by abolishing the forms to which they are accustomed. But when a long train of abuses and usurpations, pursuing invariably the same object, evinces a design to reduce them under absolute despotism, it is their right, it is their duty, to throw off such government, and to provide new guards for their future security. Such has been the patient sufferance of these colonies; and such is now the necessity which constrains them to alter their former systems of government. The history of the present King of Great Britain is a history of repeated injuries and usurpations, all having in direct object the establishment of an absolute tyranny over these states. To prove this, let facts be submitted to a candid world.

He has refused his assent to laws, the most wholesome and necessary for the public good.

He has forbidden his governors to pass laws of immediate and pressing importance, unless suspended in their operation till his assent should be obtained; and, when so suspended, he has utterly neglected to attend to them.

He has refused to pass other laws for the accommodation of large districts of people, unless those people would relinquish the right of representation in the legislature, a right inestimable to them, and formidable to tyrants only.

He has called together legislative bodies at places unusual, uncomfortable, and distant from the depository of their public records, for the sole purpose of fatiguing them into compliance with his measures.

He has dissolved representative houses repeatedly, for opposing, with manly firmness, his invasions on the rights of people.

He has refused for a long time, after such dissolutions, to cause others to be elected; whereby the legislative powers, incapable of annihilation, have returned to the people at large for their exercise; the state remaining, in the mean time, exposed to all the dangers of invasions from without and convulsions within.

He has endeavored to prevent the population of these states; for that purpose obstructing the laws for naturalization of foreigners; refusing to pass others to encourage their migration hither, and raising the conditions of new appropriations of lands.

He has obstructed the administration of justice, by refusing his assent to laws for establishing judiciary powers.

He has made judges dependent on his will alone, for the tenure of their offices, and the amount and payment of their salaries.

He has erected a multitude of new offices, and sent hither swarms of officers to harass our people and eat out their substance.

He has kept among us, in times of peace, standing armies, without the consent of our legislatures.

He has affected to render the military independent of, and superior to, the civil power.

He has combined with others to subject us to a jurisdiction foreign to our constitution, and unacknowledged by our laws, giving his assent to their acts of pretended legislation:

For quartering large bodies of armed troops among us;

For protecting them, by a mock trial, from punishment for any murders which they should commit on the inhabitants of these states;

For cutting off our trade with all parts of the world;

For imposing taxes on us without our consent;

For depriving us, in many cases, of the benefits of trial by jury;

For transporting us beyond seas, to be tried for pretended offenses;

For abolishing the free system of English laws in a neighboring province, establishing therein an arbitrary government, and enlarging its boundaries, so as to render it at once an example and fit instrument for introducing the same absolute rule into these colonies;

For taking away our charters, abolishing our most valuable laws, and altering fundamentally the forms of our governments;

For suspending our own legislatures, and declaring themselves invested with power to legislate for us in all cases whatsoever.

He has abdicated government here, by declaring us out of his protection and waging war against us.

He has plundered our seas, ravaged our coasts, burned our towns, and destroyed the lives of our people.

He is at this time transporting large armies of foreign mercenaries to complete the works of death, desolation, and tyranny already begun with circumstances of cruelty and perfidy scarcely paralleled in the most barbarous ages, and totally unworthy the head of a civilized nation.

He has constrained our fellow-citizens, taken captive on the high seas, to bear arms against their country, to become the executioners of their friends and brethren, or to fall themselves by their hands.

He has excited domestic insurrection among us, and has endeavored to bring on the inhabitants of our frontiers the merciless Indian savages, whose known rule of warfare is an undistinguished destruction of all ages, sexes, and conditions.

In every stage of these oppressions we have petitioned for redress in the most humble terms; our repeated petitions have been answered only by repeated injury. A prince, whose character is thus marked by every act which may define a tyrant, is unfit to be the ruler of a free people.

Nor have we been wanting in our attentions to our British brethren. We have warned them, from time to time, of attempts by their legislature to extend an unwarrantable jurisdiction over us. We have reminded them of the circumstances of our emigration and settlement here. We have appealed to their native justice and magnanimity; and we have conjured them, by the ties of our common kindred, to disavow these usurpations, which would inevitably interrupt our connections and correspondence. They, too, have been deaf to the voice of justice and of consanguinity. We must, therefore, acquiesce in the necessity which denounces our separation, and hold them, as we hold the rest of mankind, enemies in war, in peace friends.

We, therefore, the representatives of the United States of America, in General Congress assembled, appealing to the Supreme Judge of the world for the rectitude of our intentions, do, in the name and by the authority of the good people of these colonies, solemnly publish and declare, that these United Colonies are, and of right ought to be, FREE AND INDEPENDENT STATES; that they are absolved from all allegiance to the British crown, and that all political connection between them and the state of Great Britain is, and ought to be, totally dissolved; and that, as free and independent states, they have full power to levy war, conclude peace, contract alliances, establish commerce, and do all other acts and things which independent states may of right do. And for the support of this declaration, with a firm reliance on the protection of Divine Providence, we mutually pledge to each other our lives, our fortunes, and our sacred honor.

🌐 D O C U M E N T   5

Treaties with France Enlist an Ally, 1778
Treaty of Amity and Commerce

Article 2.   The most Christian King, and the United States engage mutually not to grant any particular Favour to other Nations in respect of Commerce and Navigation, which shall not immediately become common to the other Party, who shall enjoy the same Favour, freely, if the Concession was freely made, or on allowing the same Compensation, if the Con[c]ession was Conditional. . . .

Article 19.   It shall be lawful for the Ships of War of either Party & Privateers freely to carry whithersoever they please the Ships and Goods taken from their Enemies, without being obliged to pay any Duty to the Officers of the Admiralty or any other Judges; nor shall such Prizes be arrested or seized, when they come to and enter the Ports of either Party. . . .

Article 25.   . . . And it is hereby stipulated that free Ships shall also give a freedom to Goods, and that every thing shall be deemed to be free and exempt, which shall be found on board the Ships belonging to the Subjects of either of the Confederates, although the whole lading or any Part thereof should appertain to the Enemies of either, contraband Goods being always excepted. It is also agreed in like manner that the same Liberty be extended to Persons, who are on board a free Ship, with this Effect, that although they be Enemies to both or either Party, they are not to be taken out of that free Ship, unless they are Soldiers and in actual Service of the Enemies.

Article 26.   This Liberty of Navigation and Commerce shall extend to all kinds of Merchandizes, excepting those only which are distinguished by the name of contraband; And under this Name of Contraband or prohibited Goods shall be comprehended, Arms, great Guns, Bombs with the fuzes, and other things belonging to them, Cannon Ball, Gun powder, Match, Pikes, Swords, Lances, Spears, halberds, Mortars, Petards, Granades Salt Petre, Muskets, Musket Ball, Bucklers, Helmets, breast Plates,

This document can be found in Hunter Miller, ed., *Treaties and Other International Acts of the United States of America* (Washington, D.C.: U.S. Government Printing Office, 1931), II, 3–29.

Coats of Mail and the like kinds of Arms proper for arming Soldiers, Musket rests, belts, Horses with their Furniture, and all other Warlike Instruments whatever. These Merchandizes which follow shall not be reckoned among Contraband or prohibited Goods, that is to say, all sorts of Cloths, and all other Manufacturers woven of any wool, Flax, Silk, Cotton or any other Materials whatever; all kinds of wearing Apparel together with the Species, whereof they are used to be made; gold & Silver as well coined as uncoin'd, Tin, Iron, Latten, Copper, Brass Coals, as also Wheat and Barley and any other kind of Corn and pulse; Tobacco and likewise all manner of Spices; salted and smoked Flesh, salted Fish, Cheese and Butter, Beer, Oils, Wines, Sugars and all sorts of Salts: & in general all Provisions, which serve for the nourishment of Mankind and the sustenence of Life; furthermore all kinds of Cotton, hemp, Flax, Tar, Pitch, Ropes, Cables, Sails, Sail Cloths, Anchors and any Parts of Anchors; also Ships Masts, Planks, Boards and Beams of what Trees soever; and all other Things proper either for building or repairing Ships, and all other Goods whatever, which have not been worked into the form of any Instrument or thing prepared for War by Land or by Sea, shall not be reputed Contraband, much less such as have been already wrought and made up for any other Use; all which shall be wholly reckoned among free Goods: as likewise all other Merchandizes and things, which are not comprehended and particularly mentioned in the foregoing enumeration of contraband Goods: so that they may be transported and carried in the freest manner by the Subjects of both Confederates even to Places belonging to an Enemy such Towns or Places being only excepted as are at that time beseiged, blocked up or invested.

Treaty of Alliance

Article 1.   If War should break out betwan [F]rance and Great Britain, during the continuence of the present War betwan the United States and England, his Majesty and the said united States, shall make it a common cause, and aid each other mutually with their good Offices, their Counsels, and their forces, according to the exigence of Conjunctures as becomes good & faithful Allies.

Article 2.   The essential and direct End of the present defensive alliance is to maintain effectually the liberty, Sovereignty, and independance absolute and unlimited of the said united States, as well in Matters of Gouvernement as of commerce. . . .

Article 5.   If the united States should think fit to attempt the Reduction of the British Power remaining in the Northern Parts of America, or the Islands of Bermudas, those Contries or Islands in case of Success, shall be confederated with or dependant upon the said united States.

Article 6.   The Most Christian King renounces for ever the possession of the Islands of Bermudas as well as of any part of the continent of North america which before the treaty of Paris in 1763, or in virtue of that Treaty, were acknowledged to belong to the Crown of Great Britain, or to the united States heretofore called British

This document can he found in Hunter Miller, ed., *Treaties and Other International Acts of the United States of America* (Washington, D.C.: U.S. Government Printing Office, 1931), II, 35–41.

Colonies, or which are at this Time or have lately been under the Power of The King and Crown of Great Britain.

Article 7.   If his Most Christian Majesty shall think proper to attack any of the Islands situated in the Gulph of Mexico, or near that Gulph, which are at present under the power of Great Britain, all the said Isles, in case of success, shall appertain to the Crown of france.

Article 8.   Neither of the two Parties shall conclude either Truce or Peace with Great Britain, without the formal consent of the other first obtain'd; and they mutually engage not to lay down their arms, until the Independence of the united states shall have been formally or tacitly assured by the Treaty or Treaties that shall terminate the War. . . .

Article 11.   The two Parties guarantee mutually from the present time and forever, against all other powers, to wit, the united states to his most Christian Majesty the present Possessions of the Crown of [F]rance in America as well as those which it may acquire by the future Treaty of peace: and his most Christian Majesty guarantees on his part to the united states, their liberty, Sovereignty, and Independence absolute, and unlimited, as well in Matters of Government as commerce and also their Possessions, and the additions or conquests that their Confederation may obtain during the war, from any of the Dominions now or heretofore possessed by Great Britain in North America, conformable to the 5th & 6th articles above written, the whole as their Possessions shall be fixed and assured to the said States at the moment of the cessation of their present War with England.

🌐 *D O C U M E N T   6*

Treaty of Peace Secures American Independence, 1783

Article 1st.   His Britannic Majesty acknowledges the said United States, viz. New-Hampshire, Massachusetts Bay, Rhode-Island & Providence Plantations, Connecticut, New York, New Jersey, Pennsylvania, Delaware, Maryland, Virginia, North Carolina, South Carolina & Georgia, to be free sovereign & Independent States; that he treats with them as such, and for himself his Heirs & Successors, relinquishes all Claims to the Government Propriety & Territorial Rights of the same & every Part thereof. . . .

Article 3d.   It is agreed that the People of the United States shall continue to enjoy unmolested the Right to take Fish of every kind on the Grand Bank and on all the other Banks of New-foundland, also in the Guiph of St. Lawrence, and at all other Places in the Sea where the Inhabitants of both Countries used at any time heretofore to fish. And also that the Inhabitants of the United States shall have Liberty to take Fish of every Kind on such Part of the Coast of New-foundland as British Fishermen shall use, (but not to dry or cure the same on that Island) And also on the Coasts Bays & Creeks of all other of his Britannic Majesty's Dominions in America,

This document can be found in Hunter Miller, ed., *Treaties and Other International Acts of the United States of America* (Washington, D.C.: U.S. Government Printing Office, 1931), II, 151–156.

and that the American Fishermen shall have Liberty to dry and cure Fish in any of the unsettled Bays Harbours and Creeks of Nova Scotia, Magdalen Islands, and Labrador, so long as the same shall remain unsettled but so soon as the same or either of them shall be settled, it shall not be lawful for the said Fishermen to dry or cure Fish at such Settlement, without a previous Agreement for that purpose with the Inhabitants, Proprietors or Possessors of the Ground.

Article 4th.   It is agreed that Creditors on either Side shall meet with no lawful Impediment to the Recovery of the full Value in Sterling Money of all bona fide Debts heretofore contracted.

Article 5th.   It is agreed that the Congress shall earnestly recommend it to the Legislatures of the respective States to provide for the Restitution of all Estates, Rights and Properties which have been confiscated belonging to real British Subjects. . . . And that Persons of any other Description shall have free Liberty to go to any Part or Parts of any of the thirteen United States and therein to remain twelve Months unmolested in their Endeavours to obtain the Restitution of such of their Estates Rights & Properties as may have been confiscated. . . .

And it is agreed that all Persons who have any Interest in confiscated Lands, either by Debts, Marriage Settlements, or otherwise, shall meet with no lawful Impediment in the Prosecution of their just Rights.

Article 6th.   That there shall be no future Confiscations made nor any Prosecutions commenc'd against any Person or Persons for or by Reason of the Part, which he or they may have taken in the present War, and that no Person shall on that Account suffer any future Loss or Damage, either in his Person Liberty or Property; and that those who may be in Confinement on such Charges at the Time of the Ratification of the Treaty in America shall be immediately set at Liberty, and the Prosecutions so commenced be discontinued.

Article 7th.   There shall be a firm and perpetual Peace between his Britannic Majesty and the said States and between the Subjects of the one, and the Citizens of the other, wherefore all Hostilities both by Sea and Land shall from henceforth cease: All Prisoners on both Sides shall be set at Liberty, and his Britannic Majesty shall with all convenient speed, and without causing any Destruction, or carrying away any Negroes or other Property of the American Inhabitants, withdraw all his Armies, Garrisons & Fleets from the said United States, and from every Port, Place and Harbour within the same: leaving in all Fortifications the American Artillery that may be therein: And shall also Order & cause all Archives, Records, Deeds & Papers belonging to any of the said States, or their Citizens, which in the Course of the War may have fallen into the Hands of his Officers, to be forthwith restored and deliver'd to the proper States and Persons to whom they belong.

Article 8th.   The Navigation of the River Mississippi, from its source to the Ocean shall for ever remain free and open to the Subjects of Great Britain and the Citizens of the United States.

DOCUMENT 7

Federalist No. 4: In Union There is Strength, 1787

It is too true, however disgraceful it may be to human nature, that nations in general will make war whenever they have a prospect of getting anything by it; nay, that absolute monarchs will often make war when their nations are to get nothing by it, but for purposes and objects merely personal, such as a thirst for military glory, revenge for personal affronts, ambition, or private compacts to aggrandize or support their particular families or partisans. These and a variety of other motives, which affect only the mind of the sovereign, often lead him to engage in wars not sanctified by justice or the voice and interests of his people. But, independent of these inducements to war, which are most prevalent in absolute monarchies, but which well deserve our attention, there are others which affect nations as often as kings; and some of them will on examination be found to grow out of our relative situation and circumstances.

With France and with Britain we are rivals in the fisheries, and can supply their markets cheaper than they can themselves, notwithstanding any efforts to prevent it by bounties on their own or duties on foreign fish.

With them and with most other European nations we are rivals in navigation and the carrying trade; and we shall deceive ourselves if we suppose that any of them will rejoice to see it flourish; for, as our carrying trade cannot increase without in some degree diminishing theirs, it is more their interest, and will be more their policy, to restrain than to promote it.

In the trade to China and India, we interfere with more than one nation, inasmuch as it enables us to partake in advantages which they had in a manner monopolized, and as we thereby supply ourselves with commodities which we used to purchase from them.

The extension of our own commerce in our own vessels cannot give pleasure to any nations who possess territories on or near this continent, because the cheapness and excellence of our productions, added to the circumstance of vicinity, and the enterprise and address of our merchants and navigators, will give us a greater share in the advantages which those territories afford than consists with the wishes or policy of their respective sovereigns.

Spain thinks it convenient to shut the Mississippi against us on the one side, and Britain excludes us from the Saint Lawrence on the other; nor will either of them permit the other waters which are between them and us to become the means of mutual intercourse and traffic. . . .

The people of America are aware that inducements to war may arise out of these circumstances, as well as from others not so obvious at present, and that whenever such inducements may find fit time and opportunity for operation, pretenses to color and justify them will not be wanting. Wisely, therefore, do they consider union and a good national government as necessary to put and keep them in *such a situation* as, instead of *inviting* war, will tend to repress and discourage it. That situation consists in the best possible state of defense, and necessarily depends on the government, the arms, and the resources of the country.

This document can be found in Clinton L. Rossiter, ed., *The Federalist Papers* (New York, Signet Classics, 2003), pp. 40–44.

As the safety of the whole is the interest of the whole, and cannot be provided for without government, either one or more or many, let us inquire whether one good government is not, relative to the object in question, more competent than any other given number whatever.

One government can collect and avail itself of the talents and experience of the ablest men, in whatever part of the Union they may be found. It can move on uniform principles of policy. It can harmonize, assimilate, and protect the several parts and members, and extend the benefit of its foresight and precautions to each. In the formation of treaties, it will regard the interest of the whole, and the particular interests of the parts as connected with that of the whole. It can apply the resources and power of the whole to the defense of any particular part, and that more easily and expeditiously than State governments or separate confederacies can possibly do, for want of concert and unity of system. It can place the militia under one plan of discipline, and, by putting their officers in a proper line of subordination to the Chief Magistrate, will, in a manner, consolidate them into one corps, and thereby render them more efficient than if divided into thirteen or into three or four distinct independent bodies. . . .

Leave America divided into thirteen or, if you please, into three or four independent governments—what armies could they raise and pay—what fleets could they ever hope to have? If one was attacked, would the others fly to its succor and spend their blood and money in its defense? Would there be no danger of their being flattered into neutrality by specious promises, or seduced by a too great fondness for peace to decline hazarding their tranquillity and present safety for the sake of neighbors, of whom perhaps they have been jealous, and whose importance they are content to see diminished. Although such conduct would not be wise, it would, nevertheless, be natural. The history of the states of Greece, and of other countries, abounds with such instances, and it is not improbable that what has so often happened would, under similar circumstances, happen again.

But admit that they might be willing to help the invaded State or confederacy. How, and when, and in what proportion shall aids of men and money be afforded? Who shall command the allied armies, and from which of them shall he receive his orders? Who shall settle the terms of peace, and in case of disputes what umpire shall decide between them and compel acquiescence? Various difficulties and inconveniences would be inseparable from such a situation; whereas one government, watching over the general and common interests and combining and directing the powers and resources of the whole, would be free from all these embarrassments and conduce far more to the safety of the people.

But whatever may be our situation, whether firmly united under one national government, or split into a number of confederacies, certain it is that foreign nations will know and view it exactly as it is; and they will act towards us accordingly. If they see that our national government is efficient and well administered, our trade prudently regulated, our militia properly organized and disciplined, our resources and finances discreetly managed, our credit re-established, our people free, contented, and united, they will be much more disposed to cultivate our friendship than provoke our resentment. If, on the other hand, they find us either destitute of an effectual government (each State doing right or wrong, as to its rulers may seem convenient), or split into three or four independent and probably discordant republics or confederacies, one inclining to Britain, another to France, and a third to Spain, and perhaps played off against each other by the three, what a poor, pitiful figure will America make in their eyes! How liable would she become not only to their contempt, but to their outrage; and how soon would dear-bought experience proclaim that when a people or family so divide, it never fails to be against themselves.

PUBLIUS

DOCUMENT 8

Foreign Policy Powers in the Constitution, 1789

Article I.   *Section 8.* The Congress shall have power

To lay and collect taxes, duties, imposts, and excises, to pay the debts and provide for the common defense and general welfare of the United States; but all duties, imposts and excises shall be uniform throughout the United States;

To borrow money on the credit of the United States;

To regulate commerce with foreign nations, and among the several States, and with the Indian tribes;

To establish an uniform rule of naturalization, and uniform laws on the subject of bankruptcies throughout the United States;

To coin money, regulate the value thereof, and of foreign coin, and fix the standard of weights and measures; . . .

To define and punish piracies and felonies committed on the high seas and offenses against the law of nations;

To declare war, grant letters of marque and reprisal, and make rules concerning captures on land and water;

To raise and support armies, but no appropriation of money to that use shall be for a longer term than two years;

To provide and maintain a navy;

To make rules for the government and regulation of the land and naval forces;

To provide for calling forth the militia to execute the laws of the Union, suppress insurrections, and repel invasions;

To provide for organizing, arming, and disciplining the militia, and for governing such part of them as may be employed in the service of the United States, reserving to the States respectively the appointment of the officers, and the authority of training the militia according to the discipline prescribed by Congress;

To exercise exclusive legislation in all cases whatsoever, over such district (not exceeding ten miles square) as may, by cession of particular States, and the acceptance of Congress, become the seat of government of the United States, and to exercise like authority over all places purchased by the consent of the legislature of the State, in which the same shall be, for erection of forts, magazines, arsenals, dock-yards, and other needful buildings;—and

To make all laws which shall be necessary and proper for carrying into execution the foregoing powers, and all other powers vested by this Constitution in the government of the United States, or in any department or officer thereof. . . .

This document can be found in *United States Code, 1994 Edition* (Washington, D.C.: U.S. Government Printing Office, 1995), I, lv–lx.

Section 10.   No State shall enter into any treaty, alliance, or confederation; grant letters of marque and reprisal; coin money; emit bills of credit; make anything but gold and silver coin a tender in payment of debts; pass any bill of attainder, ex post facto law, or law impairing the obligation of contracts, or grant any title of nobility.

No State shall, without the consent of Congress, lay any imposts or duties on imports or exports, except what may be absolutely necessary for executing its inspection laws: and the net produce of all duties and imposts, laid by any State on imports or exports, shall be for the use of the treasury of the United States; and all such laws shall be subject to the revision and control of the Congress.

No State shall, without the consent of Congress, lay any duty of tonnage, keep troops or ships of war in time of peace, enter into any agreement or compact with another State, or with a foreign power, or engage in war, unless actually invaded, or in such imminent danger as will not admit of delay. . . .

Article II.   *Section 2.* The President shall be commander in chief of the army and navy of the United States, and of the militia of the several States, when called into the actual service of the United States; he may require the opinion, in writing, of the principal officer in each of the executive departments, upon any subject relating to the duties of their respective offices, and he shall have power to grant reprieves and pardons for offenses against the United States, except in cases of impeachment.

He shall have power, by and with the advice and consent of the Senate, to make treaties, provided two-thirds of the Senators present concur; and he shall nominate, and by and with the advice and consent of the Senate, shall appoint ambassadors, other public ministers and consuls. . . .

Article III.   *Section 1.* The judicial power of the United States shall be vested in one Supreme Court, and in such inferior courts as the Congress may from time to time ordain and establish. . . .

Section 2.   The judicial power shall extend to all cases, in law and equity, arising under this Constitution, the laws of the United States, and treaties made, or which shall be made, under their authority;—to all cases affecting ambassadors, other public ministers and consuls;—to all cases of admiralty and maritime jurisdiction;—to controversies to which the United States shall be a party;—to controversies between two or more States;—*between a State and citizens of another State;*—between citizens of different States;—between citizens of the same State claiming lands under grants of different States, and between a State, or the citizens thereof, and foreign states, citizens or subjects.

In all cases affecting ambassadors, other public ministers and consuls, and those in which a State shall be party, the Supreme Court shall have original jurisdiction. . . .

Article IV.   *Section 3.* The Congress shall have power to dispose of and make all needful rules and regulations respecting the territory or other property belonging to the United States; and nothing in this Constitution shall be so construed as to prejudice any claims of the United States, or of any particular State. . . .

Article VI. This Constitution, and the laws of the United States which shall be made in pursuance thereof; and all treaties made, or which shall be made, under the authority of the United States, shall be the supreme law of the land; and the judges in every State shall be bound thereby, anything in the Constitution or laws of any State to the contrary notwithstanding.

E S S A Y S

Historians have striven to identify the bedrock principles of American foreign policy and the attitudes of the founders toward the outside world. In the first essay, Lawrence S. Kaplan, long a professor of history at Kent State University, examines America's treaty of alliance with France, signed in 1778. He concludes that the young nation's diplomats disdained international commitments and begrudgingly accepted a political and military alliance with Paris only when it became essential to winning independence from Great Britain. According to Kaplan, the nation's founders were isolationist rather than internationalist in outlook, and they believed that revolutionary ideals and the national interest would be best served by steering clear of the European powers. The isolationist strain, Kaplan suggests, remained a prominent feature of American foreign policy well into the twentieth century.

In the second essay, Robert Kagan, a senior associate at the Carnegie Endowment for International Peace, rejects the isolationist label. Kagan describes the revolution's leaders as "practical idealists" who espoused a nationalism based on universal republican principles, yet expertly played power politics to defend their young republic. The founders embraced the French alliance in order to wrestle independence from Britain. Once free, they relied on shrewd diplomacy and military prowess to advance U.S. territorial and commercial interests and stave off hostile native tribes, North Africa's Barbary pirates, and threatening European powers. According to Kagan, the pursuit of a vigorous, expansionist foreign policy spurred the former colonists to replace in 1789 the decentralized federal government of the Articles of Confederation with the Constitution, which granted Congress and the president greater diplomatic and military authority.

The Treaty of Alliance with France and American Isolationism

LAWRENCE S. KAPLAN

Isolationism has always held an elusive quality for American diplomatic historians. The term itself is no older than the 1920s, and fittingly is identified with a revulsion against the entanglements of world war. This rejection of Europe was undergirded by an earlier religious image of a New World arising out of the failure of the Old, sitting apart on its transatlantic hill. These Calvinist expectations of a New Jerusalem in turn received reinforcement from the secular thought of the Enlightenment, which contrasted the simple, egalitarian, free society of eighteenth-century America with the complex, class-ridden, war-plagued societies of Europe. As a consequence of this bifurcated vision of the world Washington's Farewell Address of 1796 became an enduring symbol of America's isolation. His message was directed against the French alliance of 1778, the first and only entangling political commitment to Europe the United States made until the framing of the North Atlantic Treaty in 1949.

For all but a few ideologues tied either to the mother country or to the wilderness, isolationism meant a freedom to enjoy access to all ports interested in receiving American products. It meant further a freedom from subservience to any foreign power, of the kind which had forced them into the service of a maternal economy or of dynastic wars in the past. Finally, it extended to a self-image of virtue and innocence that would be protected by advancing principles of peaceful relationships among nations.

The alliance with France violated these conceptions of America's position in the world. Conceivably, the potential contradiction between the profession of isolationism and the making of alliance lies in confusion over the meaning of "alliance." It may be resolved, according to [the scholar] Felix Gilbert, by accepting an eighteenth-century understanding of alliances which embrace both commercial agreements and military obligations. There were no genuine distinctions between a treaty of commerce and a treaty of alliance. So when the Founding Fathers spoke of a foreign alliance as a desideratum, they could reconcile their wish for a commercial connection with refusal of political bonds. There is evidence enough in the language used by policymakers during the life of the twenty-three year alliance to buttress this thesis. Both the French and Americans intertwined the provisions of the treaty of amity and commerce with the claims of the treaty of alliance in the 1790s. And the model treaty of 1776 lumped political and commercial considerations together.

But there is also abundant evidence that the men who framed foreign policy during the Revolution recognized clearly the distinctions between the two kinds of treaties. They wanted France to be obligated in the Model Treaty without cost to themselves. They failed to entice the French under these terms, and they knew they failed. If they accepted political and military entanglement it was because they felt they had no choice. The most they could do would be to limit the potential damage subservience to France's national interest would have. . . .

That a successful defiance of England would require the help of Europe was understood even before separation was made official. The Continental Congress established a five-man Committee of Secret Correspondence on 19 November 1775, "for the sole purpose of corresponding with our friends in Great Britain, Ireland, and other parts of the world." Since the voices of America's friends in and out of Parliament had either been stilled or had turned away from the colonies, the "other parts of the world" became an immediate object of attention. The most notable part was France, England's familiar enemy, which had been periodically testing colonial discontent for ten years to see how it might be turned to its own advantage.

The French Court's interest was not ephemeral. [Charles Gravier Comte de] Vergennes, the foreign minister, welcomed the dispatch of Silas Deane, a former delegate to the Congress from Connecticut and merchant connected with Robert Morris's firm in Philadelphia. It was not coincidental that Morris was a member of the committee which presented the Model Treaty of 1776. Deane was joined by Arthur Lee, the committee's agent in London and colonial agent from Massachusetts. He was the brother of Richard Henry Lee, another member of the Committee of Secret Correspondence. The scene was set then both for the supply of munitions, weapons, and equipment to the colonies by indirect means from the French and Spanish Crowns which permitted a vital and massive infusion of energy to the colonial war effort and an opportunity for fiscal confusion and personal profit for the American agents involved in the transactions. In all these dealings the substance was commerce, not politics; trade, not military obligations.

The function France was performing should have fitted perfectly the message of Thomas Paine in his *Common Sense,* when he expressed a few months later that "the true interest of America is to steer clear of Europe's contentions, which she never can do while, by her dependence on Britain, she is made the makeweight in the scale of British politics." More than this, he asserted that "Our plan is commerce, and that, well attended to, will secure us the peace and friendship of Europe." It also reflected the thinking of John Adams who had been the prime mover in the summer of 1776 in drawing up a model treaty. His Plan of 1776 operated on the assumption that Europe would sue for America's trade and would promote America's independence to secure this advantage as well as to weaken British colonial power. France was the vital cog in the plan that would serve the war effort but without the price of entangling reciprocal obligations. Adams's language could not be plainer: "I am not for soliciting any political connection, or military assistance, or indeed, naval from France. I wish for nothing but commerce, a mere marine treaty with them."

As a consequence of a confidence bordering on truculence the American treaty plan of 1776 elaborated on liberal ideas of international law and freedom of the seas, ideas appealing to the philosophers of France and to the naval competitors of the great seapower of the day. More controversial in tone was the self-denial Article 9 would impose on the French, forcing the king to promise that "he shall never invade, nor, under any pretense, attempt to possess himself of any of the territories of the mainland which had been French or Spanish in the past." Almost grudgingly it seemed, the French would be permitted to keep whatever West Indian possessions they acquired by virtue of joining the Americans.

Such euphoria as this plan reflected dissipated rapidly in 1776. The war went badly for American arms and American morale. While the surreptitious aid given by the French and Spanish was substantial, it did not produce the desired effects on the war effort. As a result, the demands on France moved from commercial support to military assistance to a promise of reciprocal political and military obligation, in return for open adherence to the war. It was the Americans, and not the French, who became the suitor for an alliance. An increasingly nervous awareness that the world was not so well ordered as the Paine scenario had implied informed the advice given the ministers in France by the Committee of Secret Correspondence and its successor, the Committee of Foreign Affairs. Deane and Lee, joined by Franklin late in 1776, were permitted to relax the requirements for French aid. They were to assure the French of no future allegiance to Britain, of no trade advantages to any other power greater than to the French benefactor, and an additional agreement to make no termination of war, should the French enter it, without full notice to the French partner.

As American confidence in its own power weakened, the commissioners' importunities became more frantic. The American distress abroad was compounded by the rivalry between Arthur Lee and his family on the one side, with Silas Deane, supported by Franklin, on the other. While this controversy ultimately became a major cause célèbre in the Continental Congress, ruining both Deane's and Lee's careers, it is worth noting that their position on the French alliance differed in no significant way before the treaty was made. Both men were willing to offer promises along with vague threats to move the French from their cautious stance. Deane warned the French that without sufficient help the Americans would be forced to reunite with the British. An independent America, on the other hand, would make France a successor to Britain in the domination of world commerce. Arthur Lee pursued a different tactic when he appealed to the French to witness America standing up to Britain and serving them by striking out at Britain's pretensions. "We are left like Hercules in his cradle, to strangle the serpent that annoys all Europe."

The French foreign office listened and bided its time. Port officials returned British prizes Americans brought too openly into French cities. There was no acknowledgement of the declaration of American independence, even as supplies and soldiers found their way to America from France. It required the victory at Saratoga in the fall of 1777, and more important, signs of British accommodation to America's early war aims before France was willing to make an alliance formally and accept the price of war for its pains. And when the treaty was finally concluded, the brave words of Adams and Paine were forgotten. Not only did the United States reassure the French about the termination of the war and about commercial benefits, but a specific entanglement was made in Article 11, which was not to be found in the Model Treaty, in the form of mutual guarantees "from the present time and forever, to wit, the united states to his most Christian Majesty the present Possessions of the Crown of France in America as well as those which it may acquire by the future. Treaty of peace. . . ." Thus the commissioners made an agreement which bound the United States for an indefinite future to the defense of a foreign power's territory in America, a sure guarantee of involvement in the European balance of power in any subsequent quarrel between Britain and France.

The American response was one of relief and gratitude. The Congress considered the treaty officially on 4 May 1778, and ratified it two days later with little commentary beyond directing the commissioners "to present the grateful acknowledgements of this Congress to his most Christian majesty for his truly magnanimous conduct respecting these States in the said generous and disinterested treaties." The only question raised by the commissioners concerned the mutual prohibitions of duties on exports between the United States and the French West Indies. These articles were removed.

The appreciation was genuine and appropriate. France's decision for alliance was a decision for war with Britain, and it confirmed American independence, if not victory on the battlefield. Given the turmoil of the Congress, the divisions within the new nation, and the uncertainties of the military results, France gave the United States a remarkable gift—that of a successful conclusion to the Revolution. It agreed to renounce its concerns with former colonies in the New World, and to maintain "effectually the liberty, Sovereignty, and independance absolute and unlimited of the said United States, as well in Matters of gouvernment as in commerce." In the short run the benefits outweighed any debits.

Generous as the French were, their interest in the success of the United States was always subordinated to their greater interests in their financial status, maintenance of the monarchical principle, and cultivation of their more important alliance with Spain. If America could achieve its objectives in war without clashing with France's other concerns, the French ally would gladly be of service, as long as the paternal guidance of His Most Christian Majesty would govern American behavior. But when it became apparent first to the new peace commission abroad—John Adams, John Jay, and Benjamin Franklin—and then to the Congress that France was prepared to accept less than the borders the United States wanted or the fisheries New England demanded, the relationship soon became uneasy. From the French side came charges of ingratitude as Minister [Conrad Alexandre] Gerard was caught up on the side of Deane in the Lee-Deane dispute, and as his successor had to pursue French interests by influencing public opinion through the subsidized journalism of Thomas Paine and Hugh Henry Brackenridge.

American restiveness was more openly expressed. A generalized anti-Gallican and anti-Catholic sentiment had its center in New England, but its vibrations were felt throughout the states. Friends of France like Jefferson were sorely disappointed over the quality of French military assistance. Distrust over the purposes of French aid was widespread from the beginnings of the alliance, as secret negotiations among the European powers between 1778 and 1782 evoked suspicions first of French disinterest in America's transappalachian ambitions, and then of the ally's collaboration with the British and Spanish in an attempt to confine the United States to the Atlantic littoral. These suspicions were justified, and most of the French *arrières pensées* ["ulterior motives"] about America were exposed before the war ended. Even more open were the pressures exerted by French officials in America to bend Congress's policies to France's wishes. [Chevalier de la] Luzerne, in the best manner of a patron chiding a client for his errors, made Congress revise its instruction to the American commission abroad from a general statement that the commission be guided by "the advice and opinion of the French peace negotiators" to a more specific mandate that it "undertake nothing in the negotiations for peace or truce without their knowledge and concurrence." Since the Court disliked John Adams, his appointment was broadened to include first two and then four commissioners.

But ironically as the war drew to a close, the Congress became more compliant rather than more resistant to French designs. The explanation for docility was not in the venality of politicians on the payroll, even though that roll was long, illustrious and well padded. It lies more in the increasing awareness of the fragility of the Confederation and in the psychological and financial drain of the long war with Britain. To men such as Robert R. Livingston, the first secretary for foreign affairs of the Confederation, and Robert Morris, its superintendent of finances from 1781 to 1783, there was no substitute for French support in this period.

Morris, in his critical capacity as finance minister, reveals this dependence clearly. Buoyed by the Franco-American victory at Yorktown, he expressed his surprise to Franklin in December 1781, that the United States made so many purchases in Holland. "If everything else were equal the generous conduct of France towards us has been such that I cannot but think every possible preference ought to be given to the manufacturers of that nation." Whether this sentiment reflected the state of his personal investments more than the national is less material than the importance he gave to the continuing French financial support. At the same time he recognized the price of this support. A few months later, after Congress heeded his advice, he had second thoughts about the relationship and urged merchants to draw upon Spanish and Dutch creditors rather than on Frenchmen exclusively. In July 1782, he lamented that France had not granted all aid as loan rather than a gift because "I do not think the weight of the debt would be so great as the weight of an obligation is generally found to be." No matter how assiduously Morris may have been pursuing his private welfare, he understood the public's as well.

As for Livingston, he was alarmed at the freewheeling behavior of the commissioners who wandered over Europe denouncing the ally, dickering with the enemy, and ignoring the will of the Congress. Jay, prodded by Adams, had exposed a secret French memorandum which presumably would have ended the war, with the British and Spanish sharing territory between the mountains and the Mississippi; while Franklin concluded a separate agreement with the British which left the French no alternative but to accept. Jay's letter chafing at Congressional fetters discomfited Livingston. Jay insisted on the Americans accepting British terms if they were appropriate: "we are under no obligation to persist in the war to gratify this court. But can it be wise to instruct your commissioners to speak only as the French minister shall give them utterance?" . . .

Embarrassed as Congress was over this issue, it is questionable if its fears were essentially military or political in nature. The American delegates were neither as naive nor as dependent as the French had hoped. Their problem was fiscal, and the one response they feared most was the rupture of the pipeline of credits and supplies from France to the American economy. Morris raised the question in January 1783, when he informed Congress of a multi-million livre gap between American commitments and American credits, and asked if he should take the risk of France refusing to honor bills. Congress decided to move on the assumption that even if peace came quickly, "France would prefer an advance in our favor to exposing us to the necessity of resorting to G.B. for it; and that if the war sd. continue the necessity of such an aid to its prosecution would continue." In short, Congress displayed much the same kind of *Realpolitik* Franklin showed to Vergennes when the latter had upbraided the American diplomat for faithlessness to the alliance. Franklin replied by asking for more funds from the French to repair the damaged ties. The major difference was that Americans at home found it less politic to rub French sensibilities quite as raw as Americans abroad were prepared to do. Ultimately a committee was appointed to consider application for more loans on the grounds that the monies used for the army's disbanding would leave a sense of gratitude to the French among ex-soldiers. The alternative, as the French were subtly reminded, was internal convulsions among unpaid veterans which would not serve France's interests. So much for American subservience to the claims of the alliance.

The treaty lost much of its significance to both parties after the war ended. France had too many other problems plaguing its society in the 1780s to place any priority on its American investment. With few immediate benefits on the horizon, subsidies to American journalists were no longer necessary, even if they could have been afforded. France's complaisance over America's inability to repay its debts reflects the comfort the government was able to take in a weak and divided nation that had only France to turn to for support, no matter how attenuated the relationship should become. . . .

Even as he sought French assistance, [minister to France Thomas] Jefferson recognized the dangers of entanglement. France's failure, after the Revolution, to liberalize American commerce with the West Indies or its earlier unwillingness, as guarantor of the Peace of Paris, to help Americans push the British out of the Northwest posts or to defend American shipping in the Mediterranean against Barbary pirates might have evoked stronger reactions from Americans. If they did not, a subliminal recognition of a counterpart guarantee to French possessions may have checked their anger. There was an underlying uneasiness over the French relationship experienced by American leaders of every persuasion. They agreed that the weakness of the Confederation required drastic remedies to cope with a hostile world. Madison and Jefferson, as well as Jay and Morris, believed that France as well as Spain and Britain was part of that world. . . .

Although the alliance survived, it lacked vitality. When its implications were considered, they frightened American statesmen. The language of the Constitutional Convention and of the Federalist Papers tells the feelings of the framers about entangling alliances, and it tells also of the continuing consensus of future Jeffersonians and Hamiltonians. Francophilism had no constituents in the Convention at Philadelphia in 1787, as far as political ties were concerned. Within the Confederation the differences in foreign affairs had never been between proponents and antagonists of alliance; rather, they were between xenophobes hoping to remove all foreign connections and nationalists who wanted central power to manage those connections better. Monroe and Elbridge Gerry [(Massachusetts delegate to the Constitutional Convention)] belonged to the former category in this period; their answer was to reduce a foreign establishment which would, in turn, minimize foreign relations. Gerry looked upon the French edict discriminating against American trade in the West Indies as symbolic of American impotence in international relations. The only solution for the United States was withdrawal.

No such pessimism dominated the Convention and the defenders of the Constitution. While the Federalist Papers—particularly Jay's early contribution—hypothecated the consequences of the dissolution of the Confederation and the subsequent intervention of foreign powers, they also cited the Constitution as the instrument to dissuade hostile Europeans from intervening. Not the French alliance, but American internal power, will save the nation. If alliance was mentioned, it was pejoratively. Jay wrote in Federalist number Five that if the nation broke into rival units, it is likely that "each of them should be more desirous to guard against foreign dangers by foreign alliances, than to guard against foreign dangers by alliances between themselves. . . . How many conquests did Romans and others make in the character of allies? . . ."

The record of the first few years of the Federal Union in which Jefferson and Hamilton shared power in the Cabinet discloses no significant shift in sentiment over the French alliance. . . .

[President] Jefferson pointedly agreed with George Logan, a devoted Pennsylvania peace seeker, [in March 1801] that the United States ought to join no confederacies, even when they pursued laudable goals of freeing the seas for neutral trade: "It ought to be the very first object of our pursuits to have nothing to do with the European interests and politics." This is American isolationism.

Revolutionary Internationalists Engage a Harsh World

ROBERT KAGAN

The Declaration of Independence was . . . America's first foreign policy document. To win foreign support—and, above all, French support—in the war against Britain, the colonists needed to demonstrate their final and irrevocable commitment to fight for their independence. In practical terms, the Declaration provided the international legal basis for France to lend support if it chose. It declared America a sovereign nation, and with that sovereignty came the legal right and ability to form alliances and establish terms of trade with other nations. The United States would "assume among the powers of the earth, the separate and equal station to which the Laws of Nature and of Nature's God entitle them." The Declaration proclaimed that as "free and independent states," the new "united States of America . . . have full Powers to levy War, conclude Peace, contract Alliances, establish Commerce, and to do all other Acts and Things which Independent States may of right do." Some historians have suggested that the Declaration of Independence and the Revolution were an "act of isolation, a cutting of the ties with the Old World, the deed of a society which felt itself different from those which existed on the other side of the Atlantic." Americans did believe they were different, but the purpose of the Declaration was the opposite of isolation. It was to create the legal basis necessary to form alliances with European powers. American independence, from the first, depended on successful diplomacy to secure foreign support. Foreign policy was not merely the "shield of the republic," as [the journalist] Walter Lippmann would later call it. Americans did not form a nation and then embark on a foreign policy to protect and further its interests. They began a foreign policy in order to establish themselves as a nation.

At America's birth, therefore, foreign policy and national identity were intimately bound together, and they would remain so for the next two centuries. Every nation's foreign policy reflects the national idea, however that idea may be defined and redefined over time. Most nationalisms are rooted in blood and soil, in the culture and history of a particular territory. But in the case of the United States, the Declaration of Independence and the Revolution produced a different kind of nationalism, different from that of other nations, and different, too, from the type of British imperial nationalism to which Americans had paid their allegiance before the Revolution. Americans were now tied together not by common ancestry, common history, and common land but by common allegiance to the liberal republican ideology. The principles of the Declaration transcended blood ties and national boundaries. Indeed, it was "only by transcending the English heritage and broadening it beyond the confines of historical-territorial limitation" that Americans were able to "establish their distinctive political existence."

This new universalistic nationalism inevitably shaped Americans' attitudes toward the world, toward their own place and role in that world, and toward what twentieth-century thinkers would call their national interest. The classic definition of national interest—the defense of a specific territory and promotion of the well-being of the people who live on it—was not perfectly suited to a nationalism that rested on a universalist ideology. Americans from the beginning were interested not only in protecting and advancing their material well-being; they also believed their own fate was in some way tied to the cause of liberalism and republicanism both within and beyond their borders. William Appleman Williams once commented, with disapproval, that Americans believe their nation "has meaning . . . only as it realizes natural right and reason throughout the universe." This observation, though exaggerated, contained an important kernel of truth. The new nation, and its new foreign policy, had moved from a British imperial worldview to a universalistic worldview. The British imperial vision that had shaped American thinking in the decades before the Revolution linked imperial expansion, and the resulting material benefits that came to the British people, with the advancement of civilization. This idea persisted in the United States after independence, especially as Americans marched across the continent over the course of the nineteenth century. But the Revolution added a new element, the hope for republican transformation in other lands, even those where Americans had no intention of settling or making money, as a matter of moral and ideological principle. . . .

The statesmen of the founding era were not unfamiliar with the ways of power politics, however. They were idealists in the sense that they were committed to a set of universal principles, the defense and promotion of which they believed would improve the human condition as well as further American interests. But they were practical idealists. In their moment of weakness they employed the strategies of the weak. They viewed alliances as necessary but dangerous. They denigrated so-called power politics and claimed an aversion to war and military power, all realms in which they were far inferior to the European great powers. They extolled the virtues of commerce, where Americans competed on a more equal plane. They appealed to international law as the best means of regulating the behavior of nations, knowing that they had no other means of constraining the great empires of Britain and France. They adjusted themselves to an unhappy reality that they knew to be very much at odds with their aspirations. . . .

They did not, for instance, oppose alliances as a matter of principle. They feared unequal alliances that threatened to undermine their sovereignty and make them slaves to the stronger power. They were also wary of making commitments to another power that they could not in safety fulfill. But they were not shy about seeking foreign entanglements when they needed them. Indeed, their very first significant utterance on the subject of foreign policy, the resolution introduced in Congress by Richard Henry Lee one month before the Declaration of Independence, declared it "expedient forthwith to take the most effectual measures for forming foreign Alliances."

Although some Americans, like John Adams, were wary at first of becoming too dependent on a powerful France, they quickly found themselves pleading for a greater entanglement than the French themselves were willing to undertake. Nor did Americans hope to forge a purely commercial relationship with France, as some historians have argued, even at the start. In early 1776 Arthur Lee, the Americans' "secret correspondent" in London, begged Pierre-Augustin Caron de Beaumarchais, the playwright and vigorous champion of the American cause in France, to "consider above all things that we are not transacting a mere mercantile business, but that politics is greatly concerned in this affair." . . .

Once concluded in 1778, the French alliance struck even conservative Americans as a godsend. John Adams abandoned his caution and embraced the alliance as "a Rock upon which we may safely build." He even hoped the alliance would be permanent: "The United States, therefore, will be for ages the natural bulwark of France against the hostile designs of England against her, and France is the natural defense of the United States against the rapacious spirit of Great Britain against them." Americans did try to set the terms of the alliance so that they would be required to do as little as possible in return for French assistance. This was not because they had a different sense of what "alliance" meant or because they hoped to establish a new system of international relations that transcended power politics. They simply recognized that France's main interest was in striking a blow at the British Empire: the French helped the Americans, but only because it was in their interests to help. They asked only that the United States not make a separate peace with Britain without consultation, which is precisely what the Americans eventually did. By 1782 Adams and his colleagues had abandoned the French "rock" and preferred amicable relations with both European powers. But it was not "a hankering after isolation" that made Americans resist entering traditional military and political alliances with European powers. At a time when the United States was too weak to defend itself from Indian marauders, it was difficult to imagine it coming to the aid of anyone in a major European conflict. "We have neither troops nor treasury nor government," [Alexander] Hamilton soberly noted in 1787. It was this reality that shaped American behavior, not utopian dreams about humanity. . . .

Few Americans believed they could fundamentally change their world, or somehow evade the realities of power politics, by such devices as promoting an international system of free trade. The celebration of what [the French philosopher] Montesquieu called "sweet commerce" was a staple of Enlightenment thinking on both sides of the Atlantic, and John Adams and others looked to a distant future in which trade could be a solvent of international conflict. But although they may have dreamed, they were under no illusions about their harsh, mercantile world. They were not even faithful apostles of free trade. As British colonials they had been full participants in the mercantilist system; "its acts of trade and navigation had both hindered and helped them." Exporters of raw materials such as tobacco benefited from a large and secure British market. Exporters of manufactured goods generally found ways to skirt the regulations. After independence different segments of the American economy were affected differently by the British restrictions. While tobacco growers suffered, most farmers were not much affected one way or the other. Merchant importers "had not liked the bonds of the Empire when a part of it, but they had enjoyed its privileges, and after the war was over many of them did not think they could survive without them."

Nor could many Americans believe that trade among nations necessarily made for global harmony and peace. They knew that competition for trade produced wars as often as "sweet commerce" prevented them. On this Hamilton and [Thomas] Jefferson were agreed. "Has commerce hitherto done anything more than change the objects of war?" Hamilton asked. "Is not the love of wealth as domineering and enterprising a passion as that of power or glory?" If Jefferson had his way, Americans would "practice neither commerce nor navigation" but would "stand with respect to Europe precisely on the footing of China. We should thus avoid wars, and all our citizens would be husbandmen." Americans knew that whatever their own preferences might be, the world in which they lived was inhospitable to any notion of free trade. Trade restrictions were a fact of life. Adams may have hoped that "[t]he increasing liberality of sentiment among philosophers and men of letters, in various nations," might lead to "a reformation, a kind of protestantism, in the commercial system of the world." But he was not surprised that governments had not followed the philosophers' advice, insisting instead on short-term self-aggrandizement. "National pride is as natural as self-love," Adams noted. "It is, at present, the bulwark of defense to all nations.". . .

Finally, there was the American attitude toward war and the possession of the tools of war. Americans tend to think of themselves as a people reluctant to go to war and believe that, especially in the early years of the republic, they differed in this respect from the warlike Europeans. But "[t]he legend of Americans rejecting European attitudes toward war because of their wilderness experience and their idealistic ambitions is . . . built upon myth rather than reality." They had spent more than half of the three decades from 1754 to 1784 embroiled in full-scale war. Early American leaders did not believe they had suddenly entered a new era of peace. Hamilton claimed that "the fiery and destructive passions of war reign in the human breast with much more powerful sway than the mild and beneficent sentiments of peace." Nor did Americans want to abandon war or the threat of war as tools to pursue their goals. Jefferson, so often characterized as the most idealistic in his aversion to power, was as quick as anyone to reach for the sword in instances where he believed it would work. In the 1780s, infuriated by the attacks of the Barbary powers against American traders in the Mediterranean, he concluded it would be necessary for the United States to open the sea-lanes by force: "We ought to begin a naval power, if we mean to carry on our own commerce." If the Barbary rulers refused to leave American traders in peace, Jefferson insisted he "preferred war" as less expensive than the continued payment of tribute. A naval victory in the Mediterranean would "have the defense of honor, procure some respect in Europe, and strengthen the government at home." John Jay also favored using force against the Barbary powers and proposed building a naval squadron of five forty-gun ships to patrol the sea-lanes. "The great question is whether we shall wage war or pay tribute. I, for my part, prefer . . . war." In July 1787 William Grayson proposed forming an alliance with European powers "to maintain a permanent naval force that would guard the Mediterranean for peaceful shipping." Hamilton was not alone in recognizing, one hundred years before the influential naval strategist Alfred Thayer Mahan, that the promotion and protection of American commerce overseas would require naval power with a global reach. The revolutionary generation, which had forged a nation by means of war with the British Empire, "assumed that war was normal, even inevitable, in human affairs."

Americans had many other occasions to contemplate war, only to be caught up short by the impossibility of actually waging it. John Adams, engaged in futile efforts in London to gain British evacuation of the northern forts, wrote a friend that if the posts were not evacuated the United States should "declare war directly and march one army to Quebec and another to Nova Scotia." When Spain closed off the Mississippi in 1784, westerners cried for war and talked of raising ten thousand troops to march on New Orleans. George Rogers Clark launched an attack on

Spanish subjects at Vincennes. Jefferson wrote from Paris that war might indeed be preferable to an unfavorable settlement, and John Jay agreed that the United States would be justified in going to war to vindicate its navigation rights. All this talk of war was empty. Neither during the Confederation era nor afterward did the United States have the strength to fight any of the great powers, even in North America. To pick a fight with one would open the United States to blackmail by the others. A fight with Spain in the South would mean the danger of British pressure in the North. A fight with Great Britain in the North would open vulnerabilities to Spanish pressure in the South. . . .

There were those who did flirt with utopianism, at least rhetorically. Thomas Paine, the author of *Common Sense*, arguably the most influential political tract ever written, did make the case for both isolationism and an international peace founded on commerce. In his narrowly focused, brilliant piece of revolutionary propaganda, designed to convince the colonists to sever their ties with their king and their beloved British Empire, Paine argued that every problem troubling Americans was the fault of the crown and that merely throwing off monarchical rule would produce a heaven on earth. He declared that all the wars fought in history were the product of dynastic quarrels, and that all the wars fought on the North American continent had been started by the kings and queens of England pursuing their own selfish ends. Americans had only to wrest themselves from the crown, and they would enjoy peace with the entire world. "Our plan is commerce," Paine declared, "and that, well attended to, will secure us the peace and friendship of all Europe; because it is the interest of all Europe to have America a free port. Her trade will always be a protection, and her barrenness of gold and silver secure her from invaders."

An excited populace may well have found Paine's visions of postmonarchic utopia compelling, if only for a moment, before returning to the more difficult world that surrounded them on all sides. But *Common Sense* was not a founding document of American foreign policy. Paine did not conduct American foreign relations after 1776, and those who did—Jay, Adams, Washington, Hamilton, Jefferson, and others—did not consult *Common Sense* for guidance or cite it to justify their policies. . . .

Americans believed the world would be a better and safer place if republican institutions flourished and if tyranny and monarchy disappeared. They believed, from Thomas Jefferson to Alexander Hamilton, that free peoples were less likely to make war, especially against other free peoples. They believed commerce tended, on the whole, to draw nations closer together and reduce the likelihood of conflict. . . .

In time, Americans imagined, they would help create such an international order. They would play a beneficial role in the world by leading mankind toward a better future. But that time had not yet come. Whatever revolutions Americans hoped their own rebellion might inspire around the world—and they did entertain such hopes—they were too weak to lend a hand to such struggles. . . .

In 1787 the general sense of national insecurity and the apparent helplessness of the young United States to defend and advance its interests and principles in a hostile world became what one historian has called the "major drive wheel" in the movement for increased central government power that culminated in the drafting and ratification of the American Constitution. The loose government structure established to prosecute the Revolutionary War under the Articles of Confederation had proved inadequate to the tasks of war and to preserving national security after the war. As in the colonial era, weak central government and uncooperative state governments plagued the effective conduct of military and diplomatic affairs. Maintaining unity and raising funds during the war had been hard enough. In peacetime, those problems grew unmanageable. The states refused to provide the money for an army to challenge British control of the forts or Spanish control of the Mississippi, or to defend settlers on the frontier from Indian attack. The government could not raise money for a navy to protect merchant sailors in the Mediterranean. Nor would the states unite behind a common policy of retaliatory trade restrictions that might force the British government to lessen its own. At the same time, the states also refused to abide by the terms of the Anglo-American treaty. Some refused to make good on debts to British loyalist creditors, for instance—and the British used this refusal as a pretext to delay withdrawal of British forces from U.S. territory. . . .

Not surprisingly, the leading American nationalists and Federalists in 1787 were generally men of experience in military and international affairs. James Madison, John Jay, Alexander Hamilton, Henry Knox, and George Washington—all these defenders of stronger central government had served in diplomatic and military positions at home and abroad, where the weaknesses of the Confederation had been most obvious. Thomas Jefferson, sitting in Paris, shared Anti-Federalist concerns about a strong central government, but he ultimately supported the constitution drafted by his fellow Virginian. The Federalist Papers, written to persuade Americans of the necessity of a new constitution, began with a series of essays on foreign policy by John Jay, who had charge of foreign affairs through most of the Confederation period. As Madison soothingly tried to explain to the Anti-Federalist critics, the operations of the national government would always be "most extensive and important in times of war and danger; those of the state government in times of peace and security." . . .

The national strength they sought was necessary not just to meet present dangers. The leaders of the United States were also trying to safeguard the future, to keep the doors open to expansion, progress, and prosperity, to fulfill the promise of greatness, and to ensure the survival and the spread of republican freedom. . . .

[T]he Anti-Federalists did not significantly differ from the Federalists on the fundamental principles of foreign policy, which is one reason they "rarely discussed foreign affairs" when attacking the proposed Constitution. Most favored territorial and commercial expansion. Indeed, many from the southern states were at least as eager to expand American power, influence, and territorial control as their Federalist opponents. Prominent Anti-Federalists like Virginia's James Monroe were powerful advocates of westward and southward expansion. Patrick Henry and other Virginians reviled the agreement John Jay negotiated with Spain [in 1789], which denied the United States navigation rights on the Mississippi, as an antisouthern conspiracy by northern merchants under the insidious influence of Great Britain. Southern Anti-Federalists warned that under the new Constitution, which required that all treaties be approved by two-thirds of the Senate. the North could always block settlement of new western lands by vetoing treaties with Indians and other foreign powers. . . .

Most Anti-Federalists shared the Federalist conviction that the United States, if governed correctly, had a great destiny before it. Charles Pinckney might argue that the "great end of Republican Establishments" was to make people "happy at home"; that "[w]e mistake the object of our government, if we hope or wish that it is to make us respectable abroad"; and that "[c]onquest or superiority among other powers is not or ought not ever to be the object of a republican system." But the Anti-Federalists, for the most part, did not deny that "respectability" abroad was important. They simply denied that it could be achieved only at the expense of the states' sovereign independence. The Massachusetts Anti-Federalist James Winthrop, writing as "Agrippa," proclaimed as proudly as Adams or [Benjamin] Franklin that human history had never "produced an instance of rapid growth in extent, in numbers, in art, and in trade, that will bear any comparison with our own country. . . . Two-thirds of the continental debt has been paid since the war, and we are in alliance with some of the most respectable powers of Europe. The western lands, won from Britain by the sword, are an ample fund for the principal of all our public debts; and every new sale excites that manly pride which is essential to our national virtue." All this "happiness," Winthrop declared, "arises from the freedom of our institutions and the limited nature of our government."

The debate between Federalists and Anti-Federalists was the first of what would over the next two centuries be a recurring battle between nationalists on one side and localists and advocates of states' rights against the federal government on the other. This debate would often be characterized as an argument over the proper course of American foreign policy, a debate between isolationism and internationalism, between America as exemplar to the world and America as active shaper of the world, and sometimes, most crudely, as America the "republic" versus America the "empire." But in the 1780s as later, the foreign policy dimension of the debate was inseparable from the argument over governance at home. In the end, the Anti-Federalists lost out to the forces of nationalism that had been rising up even before the Revolution and that crested after independence. The struggle between nationalism and localism throughout American history has been won, more often than not, by the nationalists, and the first great nationalist victory was the federal Constitution itself. It was the Constitution that enabled the young United States to begin conducting the kind of vigorous, expansionist foreign policy its drafters supported.

FURTHER READING

David Armitage, *The Declaration of Independence: A Global History* (2007)
Bernard Bailyn, *To Begin the World Anew* (2003)
H. W. Brands, *The First American: The Life and Times of Benjamin Franklin* (2002)
William R. Casto, *Foreign Affairs and the Constitution* (2006)
Thomas E. Chavez, *Spain and the Independence of the United States* (2002)
Francis D. Cogliano, *Revolutionary America* (1999)
John E. Crowley, *The Privileges of Independence* (1993)
Jonathan R. Dull, *A Diplomatic History of the American Revolution* (1985)
Marc Egnal, *A Mighty Empire: The Origins of the American Revolution* (1988)
J.H. Elliot, *Empires of the Atlantic World* (2006)
Joseph S. Ellis, *American Creation* (2007)
Joseph Ellis, *The Founding Brothers* (2001)
"Essays Commemorating the Treaty of Paris in 1783," *International History Review* (1983)
John Ferling, *Almost a Miracle* (2007)
David M. Fitzsimmons, "Tom Paine's New World Order," *Diplomatic History,* 19 (1995),
    569–582
Thomas Fleming, *The Perils of Peace* (2007)

"Foreign Relations in the Early Republic: Essays from a SHEAR Symposium," *Journal of the Early Republic,* 14 (1994), 453–495

Felix Gilbert, *To the Farewell Address: Ideas of Early American Foreign Policy* (1961)

Mary A. Giunta, *Documents of the Emerging Nation* (1998)

Eliga H. Gould and Peter S. Onuf, *Empire and Nation* (2005)

Patrick Griffin, *American Leviathan* (2007)

John Lamberton Harper, *American Machiavelli* (2004) (on Hamilton)

David C. Hendrickson, *Peace Pact* (2003)

Ronald Hoffman and Peter J. Albert, *Peace and the Peacemakers: The Treaty of 1783* (1986)

Reginald Horsman, *The Diplomacy of the New Republic* (1985)

Daniel J. Hulsebosch, *Constituting Empire* (2005)

James H. Huston, *John Adams and the Diplomacy of the American Revolution* (1980)

Walter Isaacson, *Benjamin Franklin* (2003)

Frank Lambert, *The Barbary Wars* (2005)

Walter LaFeber, "Foreign Policies of a New Nation," in William A. Williams, ed., *From Colony to Empire* (1972), pp. 9–37

Peggy Liss, *Atlantic Empires: The Network of Trade and Revolution, 1713–1826* (1983)

Frederick W. Marks III, *Independence on Trial: Foreign Affairs and the Making of the Constitution* (1973)

David McCollough, *John Adams* (2001)

Robert Middlekauf, *Benjamin Franklin* (1996)

Edmund S. Morgan, *Benjamin Franklin* (2002)

Craig Nelson, *Thomas Paine* (2006)

Peter S. Onuf and Nicholas Onuf, *Federal Union, Modern World* (1993)

Bradford Perkins, *The Creation of a Republican Empire, 1776–1865* (1993)

H. M. Scott, *British Foreign Policy in the Age of the American Revolution* (1990)

Matthew Spalding and Patrick J. Garrity, *A Sacred Union of Citizens* (1996)

Reginald C. Stuart, *United States Expansionism and British North America, 1775–1871* (1988)

"Symposium: Early U.S. Foreign Relations," *Diplomatic History*, 22 (1998), 63–120

Robert W. Tucker and David C. Henrickson, *The Fall of the First British Empire* (1982)

William Earl Weeks, "New Directions in the Study of Early American Foreign Relations," *Diplomatic History,* 17 (1993), 73–96

John Edward Wilz, "American Isolationism: Its Colonial Origins," *Amerikastudien/American Studies,* 21 (1976), 261–280

Jay Winik, *The Great Upheaval* (2007)

Gordon S. Wood, *The Americanization of Benjamin Franklin* (2005)

CHAPTER
3

The Great Debate of the 1790s

The peace with Britain ending the American Revolution, and the alliance with France that helped achieve independence, presented the United States with its first diplomatic problems as a new nation. Through the 1780s and into the early 1790s, the British refused to leave fortified posts on American soil and to negotiate a commercial treaty to protect American foreign trade. The 1778 alliance with France became an encumbrance in 1792–1793 when the French Revolution entered a stormy stage that initiated war between republican France and monarchical Europe. Conservative Americans recoiled from what they identified as the excesses of republicanism. Alexander Hamilton, Federalist party leader and secretary of the treasury in the administration of George Washington, especially denounced France and urged better relations with Great Britain as a bastion of order and as America's chief trading partner. In contrast, James Madison and Thomas Jefferson led a faction called the Republican party. While they disapproved the violence that swept France, they applauded the French Revolution as a notable triumph for freedom from tyranny and for the ideas expressed in the American Revolution. They argued also that the United States, because its foreign trade was so dependent on the British, was compromising its sovereignty by favoring Great Britain. The Republicans urged commercial sanctions to force concessions from Britain.

Jay's Treaty of 1794, signed with Britain, defused Anglo-American tensions, especially over the occupied forts, but it ignited a heated debate at home and further contributed to the formation of political parties. Although the debate seemed to pit admirers of France against friends of England, the issues transcended simple attachments to either nation. Americans confronted questions of peace and war, independence, alliances with other nations, military preparedness, trade principles and the rights of neutrals, domestic economic policies, and the relationship between federal power and states' rights. George Washington tried to cool political passions and summarize American diplomatic principles in his farewell address of 1796. But debate persisted, and not until 1800 did France and the United States temper their relations after two years of quasi-war on the high seas by signing an agreement terminating the 1778 alliance. Like other great debates in the history of American foreign relations, that of the 1790s illuminated profound questions and helped Americans to define their future.

🌎 *D O C U M E N T S*

At stake in the 1790s, many Americans thought, was the very survival of the fledgling American republic. After France and Britain went to war in February 1793, President Washington received the unanimous support of his cabinet to proclaim U.S. neutrality on April 28. He also asked Secretary of the Treasury Alexander Hamilton and Secretary of State Thomas Jefferson for advice on relations with France: Should the minister from the republic of France be received? Was the United States still bound by the 1778 alliance with France? As Documents 1 and 2 reveal, the competitive cabinet members gave strikingly different answers (Jefferson's statement is dated April 28; Hamilton's, May 2).

Document 3, Jay's Treaty, negotiated by Chief Justice of the Supreme Court John Jay and signed on November 19, 1794, became the focal point for vigorous public debate. James Madison, a member of Congress from Virginia, denounced Jay's Treaty as a pro-British, Federalist document; he preferred imposing restrictions (his "Commercial Propositions") on trade with Britain, as he wrote on April 20, 1795 (Document 4). On June 22, Jay's Treaty passed the Senate by the necessary two-thirds vote of 20–10. The political storm that the treaty kicked up is revealed in Document 5, a fiery resolution of September 28, 1795, passed by a Democratic-Republican society in South Carolina. More than forty such organizations in the United States considered themselves protectors of political liberty against the privilege of a powerful elite. They denounced secretly negotiated treaties and British trade restrictions and demanded alliance with France against Britain. Alexander Hamilton returned the volley with a series of twenty-eight essays in defense of Jay's Treaty published in two New York newspapers in 1795 and 1796 under the pen name of "Camillus." In "Defense No. 2," reprinted here as Document 6, Hamilton defended the administration's conciliatory stance toward Britain. Financial or trade reprisals, he argued, would have produced a war for which the young republic was ill-prepared—especially given that Jay's mission had secured several key objectives, including British evacuation of posts in the U.S. western territories.

Believing that the political factionalism engulfing the United States threatened the wellbeing of the nation, George Washington addressed this danger in his farewell address of September 17, 1796. This statement (Document 7), written mostly by Hamilton, spoke not only to the turmoil in domestic politics but also to the appropriate posture for the United States in international relations. Many scholars have interpreted Washington's warning against "permanent alliances" as a declaration of isolationism that guided U.S. foreign policy until the Cold War following World War II.

🌎 *D O C U M E N T   1*

Secretary of State Thomas Jefferson
Defends the Treaty with France, 1793

I proceed, in compliance with the requisition of the President, to give an opinion in writing on the general Question, Whether the U.S. have a right to renounce their treaties with France, or to hold them suspended till the government of that country shall be established? . . .

I consider the people who constitute a society or nation as the source of all authority in that nation, as free to transact their common concerns by any agents they think proper,

---

This document can be found in the Papers of George Washington, Library of Congress, Washington, D.C. It can also be found in John Catanzariti, ed., *The Papers of Thomas Jefferson* (Princeton: Princeton University Press, 1992), XXV, 608–618.

to change these agents individually, or the organization of them in form or function whenever they please: that all the acts done by those agents under the authority of the nation, are the acts of the nation, are obligatory on them, & enure to their use, & can in no wise be annulled or affected by any change in the form of the government, or of the persons administering it. Consequently the Treaties between the U.S. and France, were not treaties between the U.S. & Louis Capet, but between the two nations of America & France, and the nations remaining in existence, tho' both of them have since changed their forms of government, the treaties are not annulled by these changes. . . .

Compacts then between nation & nation are obligatory on them by the same moral law which obliges individuals to observe their compacts. There are circumstances however which sometimes excuse the non-performance of contracts between man & man: so are there also between nation & nation. When performance, for instance, becomes *impossible*, non-performance is not immoral. So if performance becomes *self-destructive* to the party, the law of self-preservation overrules the laws of obligation to others. . . .

But Reason, which gives this right of self-liberation from a contract in certain cases, has subjected it to certain just limitations.

The danger which absolves us must be great, inevitable & imminent. Is such the character of that now apprehended from our treaties with France? What is that danger. . . . Obligation is not suspended, till the danger is become real, & the moment of it so imminent, that we can no longer avoid decision without forever losing the opportunity to do it. . . .

The danger apprehended, is it that, the treaties remaining valid, the clause guaranteeing their West India islands will engage us in the war? But does the Guarantee engage us to enter into the war in any event?

Are we to enter into it before we are called on by our allies? Have we been called on by them?—Shall we ever be called on? Is it their interest to call on us?

Can they call on us before their islands are invaded, or imminently threatened?

If they can save them themselves, have they a right to call on us?

Are we obliged to go to war at once, without trying peaceable negotiations with their enemy?

If all these questions be against us, there are still others behind.

Are we in a condition to go to war?

Can we be expected to begin before we are in condition?

Will the islands be lost if we do not save them? Have we the means of saving them?

If we cannot save them are we bound to go to war for a desperate object?

Will not a 10 years forbearance in us to call them into the guarantee of our posts, entitle us to some indulgence?

Many, if not most of these questions offer grounds of doubt whether the clause of guarantee will draw us into the war. Consequently if this be the danger apprehended, it is not yet certain enough to authorize us in sound morality to declare, at this moment, the treaties null. . . .

But the reception of a Minister from the Republic of France, without qualifications, it is thought will bring us into danger: because this, it is said, will determine the continuance of the treaty, and take from us the right of self-liberation when at any time hereafter our safety would require us to use it. The reception of the Minister at all (in favor of which Col. [Alexander] Hamilton has given his opinion, tho reluctantly as he confessed) is an acknowlegement of the legitimacy of their government: and if the qualifications meditated are to deny that legitimacy, it will be a curious compound which is to admit & deny the same thing. But I deny that the reception of a Minister has any thing to do with the treaties. There is not a word, in either of them, about sending ministers. This has been done between us under the common usage of nations, & can have no effect either to continue or annul the treaties.

But how can any act of election have the effect to continue a treaty which is acknowledged to be going on still? For it was not pretended the treaty was void, but only voidable if we chuse to declare it so. To make it void would require an act of election, but to let it go on requires only that we should do nothing, and doing nothing can hardly be an infraction of peace or neutrality.

But I go further & deny that the most explicit declaration made at this moment that we acknowlege the obligation of the treaties could take from us the right of non-compliance at any future time when compliance would involve us in great & inevitable danger.

I conclude then that few of these sources threaten any danger at all; and from none of them is it inevitable: & consequently none of them give us the right at this moment of releasing ourselves from our treaties.

D O C U M E N T   2

Secretary of the Treasury Alexander Hamilton Urges Voiding the Treaty with France, 1793

Are the United States bound, by the principles of the laws of nations, to consider the treaties heretofore made with France, as in present force and operation between them and the actual governing powers of the French nation? or may they elect to consider their operation as suspended, reserving also a right to judge finally whether any such changes have happened in the political affairs of France as may justify a renunciation of those treaties?

It is believed that they have an option to consider the operation of those treaties as suspended, and will have eventually a right to renounce them, if such changes shall take place as can *bona fide* be pronounced to render a continuance of the connections which result from them disadvantageous or dangerous.

There are two general propositions which may be opposed to this opinion: 1st. That a nation has a right, in its own discretion, to change its form of government—to abolish one, and substitute another. 2d. That *real* treaties (of which description those in question are) bind the NATIONS whose governments contract, and continue in force notwithstanding any changes which happen in the forms of their government.

The truth of the first proposition ought to be admitted in its fullest latitude. But it will by no means follow, that because a nation has a right to manage its own concerns as it thinks fit, and to make such changes in its political institutions as itself judges best calculated to promote its interests—that it has therefore a right to involve other nations, with whom it may have had connections, *absolutely* and

This document can be found in the Alexander Hamilton Papers, Library of Congress, Washington, D.C. It can also be found in Harold C. Syrett, ed., *The Papers of Alexander Hamilton* (New York: Columbia University Press, 1992), XXV, 608–618.

unconditionally, in the consequences of the changes which it may think proper to make. This would be to give to a nation or society not only a power over its own happiness, but a power over the happiness of other nations or societies. It would be to extend the operation of the maxim much beyond the *reason* of it, which is simply, that every nation ought to have a right to provide for its own happiness. . . .

All general rules are to be construed with certain reasonable limitations. That which has been just mentioned must be understood in this sense, that changes in forms of government do not of course abrogate *real* treaties; that they continue absolutely binding on the party which makes the change, and will bind the other party, unless, in due time and for just cause, he declares his election to renounce them; that in good faith he ought not to renounce them, unless the change which happened does really render them useless, or materially less advantageous, or more dangerous than before. But for good and sufficient cause he may renounce them.

Nothing can be more evident than the existing forms of government of two nations may enter far into the motives of a real treaty. . . .

Two nations may form an alliance because each has confidence in the energy and efficacy of the government of the other. A revolution may subject one of them to a different form of government—feeble, fluctuating, and turbulent, liable to provoke wars, and very little fitted to repel them. Even the connections of a nation with other foreign powers may enter into the motives of an alliance with it. If a dissolution of ancient connections shall have been a consequence of a revolution of government, the external political relations of the parties may have become so varied as to occasion an incompatibility of the alliance with the Power which had changed its constitution with the other connections of its ally—connections perhaps essential to its welfare.

In such cases, reason, which is the touchstone of all similar maxims, would dictate that the party whose government had remained stationary would have a right, under a *bona-fide* conviction that the change in the situation of the other party would render a future connection detrimental or dangerous, to declare the connection dissolved.

Contracts between nations as between individuals must lose their force where the considerations fail.

A treaty *pernicious* to the state is of itself void, where no change in the situation of either of the parties takes place. By a much stronger reason it must become *voidable* at the option of the other party, when the voluntary act of one of the allies has made so material a change in the condition of things as is always implied in a radical revolution of government.

🌐 *D O C U M E N T   3*
_____

Jay's Treaty, 1794

Article II.   His Majesty will withdraw all His Troops and Garrisons from all Posts and Places within the Boundary Lines assigned by the Treaty of Peace to the United States. This Evacuation shall take place on or before the first Day of June One thousand seven hundred and ninety six. . . .

_____

This document can be found in Hunter Miller, ed., *Treaties and Other International Acts of the United States of America* (Washington, D.C.: U.S. Government Printing Office, 1931), II, 245–264.

Article III.   It is agreed that it shall at all Times be free to His Majesty's Subjects, and to the Citizens of the United States, and also to the Indians dwelling on either side of the said Boundary Line freely to pass and repass by Land, or Inland Navigation, into the respective Territories and Countries of the Two Parties on the Continent of America (the Country within the Limits of the Hudson's Bay Company only excepted) and to navigate all the Lakes, Rivers, and waters thereof, and freely to carry on trade and commerce with each other. But it is understood, that this Article does not extend to the admission of Vessels of the United States into the Sea Ports, Harbours, Bays, or Creeks of His Majesty's said Territories; nor into such parts of the Rivers in His Majesty's said Territories as are between the mouth thereof, and the highest Port of Entry from the Sea, except in small vessels trading bona fide between Montreal and Quebec, under such regulations as shall be established to prevent the possibility of any Frauds in this respect. Nor to the admission of British vessels from the Sea into the Rivers of the United States, beyond the highest Ports of Entry for Foreign Vessels from the Sea. The River Mississippi, shall however, according to the Treaty of Peace be entirely open to both Parties. . . .

Article VI.   Whereas it is alleged by divers British Merchants and others His Majesty's Subjects, that Debts to a considerable amount which were bónâ fide contracted before the Peace, still remain owing to them by Citizens or Inhabitants of the United States. . . . It is agreed that in all such Cases where full Compensation for such losses and damages cannot, for whatever reason, be actually obtained had and received by the said Creditors in the ordinary course of Justice, The United States will make full and complete Compensation for the same to the said Creditors. . . .

Article XII.   His Majesty Consents that it shall and may be lawful, during the time hereinafter Limited, for the Citizens of the United States, to carry to any of His Majesty's Islands and Ports in the West Indies from the United States in their own Vessels, not being above the burthen of Seventy Tons, any Goods or Merchandizes, being of the Growth, Manufacture, or Produce of the said States, which it is, or may be lawful to carry to the said Islands or Ports from the said States in British Vessels, and that the said American Vessels shall be subject there to no other or higher Tonnage Duties or Charges, than shall be payable by British vessels, in the Ports of the United States; and that the Cargoes of the said American Vessels shall, be subject there to no other or higher Duties or Charges than shall be payable on the like Articles, if imported there from the said States in British vessels.

And His Majesty also consents that it shall be lawful for the said American Citizens to purchase, load and carry away, in their said vessels to the United States from the said Islands and Ports, all such articles being of the Growth, Manufacture or Produce of the said Islands, as may now by Law be carried from thence to the said States in British Vessels, and subject only to the same Duties and Charges on Exportation to which British Vessels and their Cargoes are or shall be subject in similar circumstances.

Provided always that the said American vessels do carry and land their Cargoes in the United States only, it being expressly agreed and declared that during the Continuance of this article, the United States will prohibit and restrain the carrying any Meolasses, Sugar, Coffee, Cocoa or Cotton in American vessels, either from

His Majesty's Islands or from the United States, to any part of the World, except the United States, reasonable Sea Stores excepted. Provided, also, that it shall and may be lawful during the same period for British vessels to import from the said Islands into the United States, and to export from the United States to the said Islands, all Articles whatever being of the Growth, Produce or Manufacture of the said Islands, or of the United States respectively, which now may, by the Laws of the said States, be so imported and exported. And that the Cargoes of the said British vessels, shall be subject to no other or higher Duties or Charges, than shall be payable on the same articles if so imported or exported in American Vessels. . . .

Article XIII.   His Majesty consents that vessels belonging to the citizens of the United States shall be admitted and hospitably received in all the seaports and harbors of the British territories in the East Indies. And that the citizens of the said United States may freely carry on a trade between the said territories and the said United States, in all articles of which the importation or exportation respectively, to or from the said territories shall not be entirely prohibited. . . . But it is expressly agreed that the vessels of the United States shall not carry any of the articles exported by them from the said British territories to any port or place, except to some port or place in America. . . . It is also understood that the permission granted by this article is not to extend to allow the vessels of the United States to carry on any part of the coasting trade of the said British territories. . . .

Article XIV.   There shall be between all the dominions of His Majesty in Europe and the territories of the United States a reciprocal and perfect liberty of commerce and navigation. . . .

Article XV.   It is agreed, that no other or higher Duties shall be paid by the Ships or Merchandize of the one Party in the Ports of the other, than such as are paid by the like vessels or Merchandize of all other Nations. Nor shall any other or higher Duty be imposed in one Country on the importation of any articles, the growth, produce, or manufacture of the other, than are or shall be payable on the importation of the like articles being of the growth, produce or manufacture of any other Foreign Country. Nor shall any prohibition be imposed, on the exportation or importation of any articles to or from the Territories of the Two Parties respectively which shall not equally extend to all other Nations. . . .

Article XVIII.   In order to regulate what is in future to be esteemed Contraband of war, it is agreed that under the said Denomination shall be comprized all Arms, and Implements serving for the purposes of war . . . as also Timber for Shipbuilding, Tar or Rosin, Copper in Sheets, Sails, Hemp, and Cordage, and generally whatever may serve directly to the equipment of Vessels, unwrought Iron and Fir planks only excepted, and all the above articles are hereby declared to be just objects of Confiscation, whenever they are attempted to be carried to an Enemy. . . .

Article XXIV.   It shall not be lawful for any Foreign Privateers (not being Subjects or Citizens of either of the said Parties) who have Commissions from any other Prince or State in enmity with either Nation, to arm their Ships in the Ports of either of the said Parties, nor to sell what they have taken, nor in any other manner to exchange the same, nor shall they be allowed to purchase more provisions than shall be necessary for their going to the nearest Port of that Prince or State from whom they obtained their Commissions.

🌎 D O C U M E N T   4

Virginia Senator James Madison Proposes Commercial Restrictions Against Britain, 1795

What were the Commercial Propositions? They discriminated between nations in treaty, and nations not in treaty, by an additional duty on the manufactures and trade of the latter; and they reciprocated the navigation laws of all nations, who excluded the vessels of the United States, from a common right of being used in the trade between the United States, and such nations.

Is there any thing here that could afford a cause, or a pretext for war, to Great Britain or any other nation? If we hold at present the rank of a free people; if we are no longer colonies of Great Britain; if we have not already relapsed into some dependence on that nation, we have the self-evident right, to regulate our trade according to our own will, and our own interest, not according to her will or her interest. This right can be denied to no independent nation. It has not been, and will not be denied to ourselves, by any opponent of the propositions.

If the propositions could give no right to Great Britain to make war, would they have given any color to her for such an outrage on us? No American Citizen will affirm it. No British subject, who is a man of candor, will pretend it; because he must know, that the commercial regulations of Great Britain herself have discriminated among foreign nations, whenever it was thought convenient. They have discriminated against particular nations by name; they have discriminated, with respect to particular articles by name, by the nations producing them, and by the places exporting them. . . .

Great Britain is a commercial nation. Her power, as well as her wealth, is derived from commerce. The American commerce is the most valuable branch she enjoys. It is the more valuable, not only as being of vital importance to her in some respects, but of growing importance beyond estimate in its general character. She will not easily part with such a resource. She will not rashly hazard it. She would be particularly aware of forcing a perpetuity of regulations, which not merely diminish her share; but may favour the rivalship of other nations. If anything, therefore, in the power of the United States could overcome her pride, her avidity, and her repugnancy to this country, it was justly concluded to be, not the fear of our arms, which, though invincible in defence, are little formidable in a war of offence, but the fear of suffering in the most fruitful branch of her trade, and of seeing it distributed among her rivals.

If any doubt on this subject could exist, it would vanish on a recollection of the conduct of the British ministry at the close of the war in 1783. It is a fact which

This document can be found in *Political Observations* (pamphlet). Rare Books Division, Library of Congress, Washington, D.C. It can also be found in Thomas A. Mason et al., eds., *The Papers of James Madison* (Charlottesville: University Press of Virginia, 1985), XV, 516, 519–520, 529.

has been already touched, and it is as notorious as it is instructive, that during the apprehension of finding her commerce with the United States abridged or endangered by the consequences of the revolution, Great-Britain was ready to purchase it, even at the expence of her West-Indies monopoly. It was not until after she began to perceive the weakness of the federal government [under the Articles of Confederation], the discord in the counteracting plans of the state governments, and the interest she would be able to establish here, that she ventured on that system to which she has since inflexibly adhered. Had the present federal government, on its first establishment, done what it ought to have done, what it was instituted and expected to do, and what was actually proposed and intended it should do; had it revived and confirmed the belief in Great-Britain, that our trade and navigation would not be free to her, without an equal and reciprocal freedom to us, in her trade and navigation, we have her own authority for saying, that she would long since have met us on proper ground. . . .

[T]he friends of commercial measures, if consistent, will prefer these measures, as an intermediate experiment between negociation and war. They will persist in their language, that Great-Britain is more dependent on us, than we are on her; that this has ever been the American sentiment, and is the true basis of American policy; that war should not be resorted to, till every thing short of war has been tried; that if Great-Britain be invulnerable to our attacks, it is in her fleets and armies; that if the United States can bring her to reason at all, the surest as well as the cheapest means, will be a judicious system of commercial operations; that here the United States are unquestionably an overmatch for Great-Britain.

🌐 *D O C U M E N T   5*

A Democratic-Republican Society
Blasts Jay's Treaty, 1795

The Franklin, or Republican Society of Pendleton county, having by the watchful vigilance of their standing committee, on a most pressing question, been called together to give their opinion on a public measure—a right they will not tamely relinquish, nor resign but with their lives!—having taken into consideration the ruinous treaty *proposed* and signed by John Jay, the American ambassador, with his Britannic majesty—a treaty, as detestable in its origin, as contemptible in its event!—a treaty which can never be enforced but by the bayonet!—having fully weighed it in all its articles—and taking into view, that when the complaints of a brave and powerful people are observed to increase in proportion to the wrongs they have suffered!—when, instead of sinking into submission, they are roused to resistance! the time must come at which every inferior consideration will yield to their security—to the general safety of the empire! . . .

Resolved, That on the appointment of John Jay as an *extraordinary* ambassador to Britain, we were *led to believe* that our rights would have been vindicated with firmness, a reparation of our wrongs obtained!—On the contrary, *even after the signing of a treaty of amity*, our flag is the *common* sport of Britain, and our sailor fellow-citizens and property at their mercy.

This document can be found in the *City Gazette* (Charleston), October 28, 1795. It can also be found in Philip S. Foner, ed., *The Democratic Republican Societies, 1790–1800* (Westport, CT: Greenwood Press, 1976), pp. 400–409.

Resolved, That we were induced by *profession* to believe our administration sympathized in the cause of an ally [France], wrestling for liberty—a great and regenerated people, who cherish in their utmost purity those sacred principles which have laid the foundation of our *freedom in the blood of our dearest citizens!*—but that ally has been treated with *insincerity, even at the moment our inveterate enemy, and the foe of human happiness, has been invited to our bosom! and when British tyranny and baseness can leave not a doubt on a single unprejudiced mind that we are about to give that nation* A FOOTING IN LAW AMONG US WHICH WILL BE CONVERTED TO OUR RUIN! . . .

Resolved, That so far as is depending on his own integrity and good wishes to the United States, we are still willing to behold in Washington THE SAME GOOD AND GREAT MAN! But, is it not possible, at least respecting Jay's treaty, that he may have been wrongly advised? . . .

Resolved, That we view with surprize the industry used not to disclose the articles of Mr. Jay's treaty—AFFECTING *and* PRACTISING *all the secrecy of* MONARCHY, *so opposite to open and republican principles.*—Will it, dare it be contended, that the people have no right to ask, nay, to *demand* information on the posture of their affairs?—Secrecy robs them of this right, and makes *twenty* greater than the *whole*. Is this republicanism?—is this liberty?—Monarchs and conclaves make a *trade of secrecy—it suits their designs*—but neither monarchs nor conclaves are, as yet, in unison with the sentiments, nor the wishes of the American people. There is no authorized secrecy in *our* government, and to infer such a right from the practices of other nations, is a prostitution of republican principles. The constitution of the United States gives to the president and Senate the power of making treaties, but it communicates no ability to hatch those things in darkness. A treaty! which is to be the supreme-law-of-the-land! and yet the people not to be informed of the terms of this law until binding upon them! until the opportunity for amendment is past!—Secrecy and mystery marked the conception, birth, and parentage of this lump of abortion and deformity. . . .

Resolved, That by the article regarding the West-India trade, nothing can be more evident than that Britain mediated to wrest from America the carrying trade, an immense share of which she has lately possessed, as appears by the astonishing increase of our seamen and shipping; but we trust 'twill never be forgotten that the protection of a free carrying trade was one of the primary objects for which the federal government was established.—Let not, then, our national government have the discredit of doing any thing by which the limits of our navigation may be fettered—Let us not concur with the British ministry in eminently promoting the British commerce at the expense of our own!—Not satisfied with the innumerable depradations on our shipping, the British government wants their real destruction by this insidious article, confining our vessels to seventy tons, mere boats, whilst they reserve to themselves the right of navigating in any size vessels they please, in the same pursuit of trade. By this deceptive article, we *alone* granted—have been prevented from exporting in our own bottoms any articles of West-India produce, and even of *cotton*, an article of our own growth, and becoming a very important one in this and the sister state of Georgia (even in our own district)—while the vessels of *Britain*, and *every other* nation, would be at liberty to export from American ports every article of West-India, and some of our own produce, to all parts of the world. . . .

Resolved, finally, That the vice-moderator, the corresponding secretary, and secretary of the society, do sign the foregoing resolutions—and that they be generally printed, as expressive of our abhorrence and detestation of a treaty—which gives to the English government more power over us a[s] states, than it ever claimed over us as colonies—and which, if Britain had been left to her generosity, *she would have been ashamed to propose!*—a treaty, involving in its pusilanimity, stupidity, ingratitude, and TREACHERY!—to blast the rising grandeur of our common country—of our infant empire!

🌐 D O C U M E N T 6

Hamilton Defends Jay's Treaty, 1795

In this crisis two sets of opinions prevailed; one looked to measures which were to have a compulsory effect upon Great Britain—the sequestration of British debts and the cutting off of intercourse wholly or partially between the two countries—the other to *vigorous preparation* for war and *one more effort* of negotiation by a solemn mission to avert it.

That the latter was the best opinion no truly sensible man can doubt, and it may be boldly affirmed that the event has entirely justified it.

If measures of coercion and reprisal had taken place, war in all human probability would have followed. . . .

Few nations can have stronger inducements than the U States to cultivate peace. Their infant state in general—their want of a marine in particular to protect their commerce—would render war in an extreme degree a calamity. It would not only arrest our present rapid progress to strength and prosperity, but would probably throw us back into a state of debility and impoverishment from which it would require years to emerge. Our trade, navigation, and mercantile capital would be essentially destroyed. Spain being an associate with Great Britain, a general Indian war would probably have desolated the whole extent of our frontier. Our exports obstructed, agriculture would have seriously languished. All other branches of industry must have proportionally suffered. Our public debt, instead of a gradual diminution, must have sustained a great augmentation and drawn with it a large increase of taxes and burdens on this people.

But this perhaps was not the worst to be apprehended. It was to be feared that the war would be conducted in a spirit which would render it more than ordinarily calamitous. There are too many proofs that a considerable party among us is deeply infected with those horrid principles of Jacobinism which, proceeding from one excess to another, have made France a theater of blood and which notwithstanding the most vigorous efforts of the national representation to suppress it keeps the destinies of France to this moment suspended by a thread. It was too probable that the direction of the war if commenced would have fallen into the hands of men of this description. The consequences of this even in imagination are such as to make any virtuous man shudder.

This document can be found at Online Library of Liberty, Alexander Hamilton, The Camillus Essays, "The Defence, No. 2," 25 July 1795, http://oll.libertyfund.org.

It was therefore in a peculiar manner the duty of the Government to take all possible chances for avoiding war. The plan adopted was the only one which could claim this advantage. . . .

It cannot escape an attentive observer that the language which in the first instance condemned the mission of an envoy extraordinary to Great Britain, and which now condemns the treaty negotiated by him, seems to consider the U States as among the first rate powers of the world in point of strength and resource and proposes to them a conduct predicated upon that condition.

To underrate our just importance would be a degrading error. To overrate it may lead to dangerous mistakes.

A very powerful state may frequently hazard a high and haughty tone with good policy, but a weak state can scarcely ever do it without imprudence. The last is yet our character, though we are the embryo of a great empire. It is therefore better suited to our situation to measure each step with the utmost caution; to hazard as little as possible; in the cases in which we are injured to blend moderation with firmness; and to brandish the weapons of hostility only when it is apparent that the use of them is unavoidable.

It is not to be inferred from this that we are to crouch to any power on earth or tamely to suffer our rights to be violated. A nation which is capable of this meanness will quickly have no rights to protect, no honor to defend.

But the true inference is that we ought not lightly to seek or provoke a resort to arms. . . .

If we can avoid war for ten or twelve years more, we shall then have acquired a maturity which will make it no more than a common calamity and will authorize us on our national discussions to take a higher and more imposing tone. . . .

Should we be able to escape the storm which at this juncture agitates Europe, our disputes with Great Britain terminated, we may hope to postpone war to a distant period. This at least will greatly diminish the chances of it. For then there will remain only one power with whom we have any embarrassing discussion. I allude to Spain and the question of the Mississippi; and there is reason to hope that this question by the natural progress of things and perseverance in an amicable course will finally be arranged to our satisfaction without the necessity of the *dernier* resort.

The allusion to this case suggests one or two important reflections. How unwise was it to invite or facilitate a quarrel with Great Britain at a moment when she and Spain were engaged in a common cause, both of them having besides controverted points with the U States! How wise will it be to adjust our differences with the most formidable of those two powers and to have only to contest with one of them.

This policy is so obvious that it requires an extraordinary degree of infatuation not to be sensible of it, and not to view with favor any measure which tends to so important a result.

This cursory review of the motives which may be supposed to have governed our public councils in the mission to Great Britain serves not only to indicate the measures then pursued but to warn us against a prejudiced judgment of the result which may in the end defeat the salutary purposes of those measures.

I proceed to observe summarily that the objects of the mission, contrary to what has been asserted, have been substantially obtained. What were these? They were principally—

I.   to adjust the matters of controversy concerning the inexecution of the Treaty of Peace and especially to obtain restitution of our Western posts.

II.   to obtain reparation for the captives and spoliations of our property in the course of the existing war. . . .

The provisions with regard to commerce were incidental and auxiliary—some provisions on this subject were of importance to fix for a time the basis on which the commerce of the two countries was to be carried on, that the merchants of each might know what they had to depend upon—that sources of collision on this head might be temporarily stilled if not permanently extinguished—that an essay might be made of some plan conciliating as far as possible the opinions and prejudices of both parties—and laying perhaps the foundation of further and more extensive arrangements. Without something of this kind, there would be constant danger of the tranquillity of the two countries being disturbed by commercial conflicts.

D O C U M E N T   7

President George Washington Cautions Against Factionalism and Permanent Alliances in His Farewell Address, 1796

I have already intimated to you the danger of parties in the State, with particular reference to the founding of them on geographical discriminations. Let me now take a more comprehensive view, and warn you in the most solemn manner against the baneful effects of the spirit of party generally.

This spirit, unfortunately, is inseparable from our nature, having its root in the strongest passions of the human mind. It exists under different shapes in all governments, more or less stifled, controlled, or repressed; but in those of the popular form it is seen in its greatest rankness and is truly their worst enemy.

The alternate domination of one faction over another, sharpened by the spirit of revenge natural to party dissension, which in different ages and countries has perpetrated the most horrid enormities, is itself a frightful despotism. But this leads at length to a more formal and permanent despotism. The disorders and miseries which result gradually incline the minds of men to seek security and repose in the absolute power of an individual, and sooner or later the chief of some prevailing faction, more able or more fortunate than his competitors, turns this disposition to the purposes of his own elevation on the ruins of public liberty.

Without looking forward to an extremity of this kind (which nevertheless ought not to be entirely out of sight), the common and continual mischiefs of the spirit of party are sufficient to make it the interest and duty of a wise people to discourage and restrain it.

It serves always to distract the public councils and enfeeble the public administration. It agitates the community with ill-founded jealousies and false alarms; kindles the animosity of one part against another; foments occasionally riot and insurrection. It opens the door to foreign influence and corruption, which find a facilitated access to the government itself through the channels of party passion. Thus the policy and the will of one country are subjected to the policy and will of another. . . .

This document can be found in James D. Richardson, ed., *A Compilation of the Messages and Papers of the Presidents* (New York: Bureau of National Literature, 1897), I, 210–211, 213–215.

Observe good faith and justice toward all nations. Cultivate peace and harmony with all. Religion and morality enjoin this conduct. And can it be that good policy does not equally enjoin it? It will be worthy of a free, enlightened, and at no distant period a great nation to give to mankind the magnanimous and too novel example of a people always guided by an exalted justice and benevolence. . . .

In the execution of such a plan nothing is more essential than that permanent, inveterate antipathies against particular nations and passionate attachments for others should be excluded, and that in place of them just and amicable feelings toward all should be cultivated. The nation which indulges toward another an habitual hatred or an habitual fondness is in some degree a slave. It is a slave to its animosity or to its affection, either of which is sufficient to lead it astray from its duty and its interest. Antipathy in one nation against another disposes each more readily to offer insult and injury, to lay hold of slight causes of umbrage, and to be haughty and intractable when accidental or trifling occasions of dispute occur.

Hence frequent collisions, obstinate, envenomed, and bloody contests. The nation prompted by ill will and resentment sometimes impels to war the government contrary to the best calculations of policy. The government sometimes participates in the national propensity, and adopts through passion what reason would reject. At other times it makes the animosity of the nation subservient to projects of hostility, instigated by pride, ambition, and other sinister and pernicious motives. The peace often, sometimes perhaps the liberty, of nations has been the victim.

So, likewise, a passionate attachment of one nation for another produces a variety of evils. Sympathy for the favorite nation, facilitating the illusion of an imaginary common interest in cases where no real common interest exists, and infusing into one the enmities of the other, betrays the former into a participation in the quarrels and wars of the latter without adequate inducement or justification. It leads also to concessions to the favorite nation of privileges denied to others, which is apt doubly to injure the nation making the concessions by unnecessarily parting with what ought to have been retained, and by exciting jealousy, ill will, and a disposition to retaliate in the parties from whom equal privileges are withheld; and it gives to ambitious, corrupted, or deluded citizens (who devote themselves to the favorite nation) facility to betray or sacrifice the interests of their own country without odium, sometimes even with popularity, gilding with the appearances of a virtuous sense of obligation, a commendable deference for public opinion, or a laudable zeal for public good the base or foolish compliances of ambition, corruption, or infatuation.

As avenues to foreign influence in innumerable ways, such attachments are particularly alarming to the truly enlightened and independent patriot. How many opportunities do they afford to tamper with domestic factions, to practice the arts of seduction, to mislead public opinion, to influence or awe the public councils! Such an attachment of a small or weak toward a great and powerful nation dooms the former to be the satellite of the latter. Against the insidious wiles of foreign influence (I conjure you to believe me, fellow-citizens) the jealousy of a free people ought to be *constantly* awake, since history and experience prove that foreign influence is one of the most baneful foes of republican government. But that jealousy, to be useful, must be impartial, else it becomes the instrument of the very influence to be avoided, instead of a defense against it. Excessive partiality for one foreign nation and excessive dislike of another cause those whom they actuate to see danger only on one side, and serve to veil and even second the arts of influence on the other. Real patriots who may resist the intrigues of the favorite are liable to become suspected and odious, while its tools and dupes usurp the applause and confidence of the people to surrender their interests.

The great rule of conduct for us in regard to foreign nations is, in extending our commercial relations to have with them as little *political* connection as possible. So far as we have already formed engagements let them be fulfilled with perfect good faith. Here let us stop.

Europe has a set of primary interests which to us have none or a very remote relation. Hence she must be engaged in frequent controversies, the causes of which are essentially foreign to our concerns. Hence, therefore, it must be unwise in us to implicate ourselves by artificial ties in the ordinary vicissitudes of her politics or the ordinary combinations and collisions of her friendships or enmities.

Our detached and distant situation invites and enables us to pursue a different course. If we remain one people, under an efficient government, the period is not far off when we may defy material injury from external annoyance; when we may take such an attitude as will cause the neutrality we may at any time resolve upon to be scrupulously respected; when belligerent nations, under the impossibility of making acquisitions upon us, will not lightly hazard the giving us provocation; when we may choose peace or war, as our interest, guided by justice, shall counsel.

Why forego the advantages of so peculiar a situation? Why quit our own to stand upon foreign ground? Why, by interweaving our destiny with that of any part of Europe, entangle our peace and prosperity in the toils of European ambition, rivalship, interest, humor, or caprice?

It is our true policy to steer clear of permanent alliances with any portion of the foreign world, so far, I mean, as we are now at liberty to do it; for let me not be understood as capable of patronizing infidelity to existing engagements. I hold the maxim no less applicable to public than to private affairs that honesty is always the best policy. I repeat, therefore, let those engagements be observed in their genuine sense. But in my opinion it is unnecessary and would be unwise to extend them.

Taking care always to keep ourselves by suitable establishments on a respectable defensive posture, we may safely trust to temporary alliances for extraordinary emergencies.

Harmony, liberal intercourse with all nations are recommended by policy, humanity, and interest. But even our commercial policy should hold an equal and impartial hand, neither seeking nor granting exclusive favors or preferences; consulting the natural course of things; diffusing and diversifying by gentle means the streams of commerce, but forcing nothing; establishing with powers so disposed, in order to give trade a stable course, to define the rights of our merchants, and to enable the Government to support them, conventional rules of intercourse, the best that present circumstances and mutual opinion will permit, but temporary and liable to be from time to time abandoned or varied as experience and circumstances shall dictate; constantly keeping in view that it is folly in one nation to look for disinterested favors from another; that it must pay with a portion of its independence for whatever it may accept under that character; that by such acceptance it may place itself in the condition of having given equivalents for nominal favors, and yet of being reproached with ingratitude for not giving more. There can be no greater error than to expect or calculate upon real favors from nation to nation. It is an illusion which experience must cure, which a just pride ought to discard.

🌎 E S S A Y S

Scholars have long agreed that the foreign policy debates of the 1790s were crucial to the revolutionary generation's struggle to define national purpose and identity. They have nonetheless found ample room for disagreement regarding the diplomacy of the early republic. Who had the better case, James Madison and Thomas Jefferson's Republicans or Alexander Hamilton and George Washington's Federalists? How did each side define the national interest?

In the first essay, John Lamberton Harper of the Bologna Center of The Johns Hopkins University commends the Washington administration's treaty with Britain (Jay's Treaty) as a prudent measure that preserved the lucrative commerce with England, bolstered U.S. treasury finances, and kept the United States from pursuing a "disastrous war" with the former mother country. He highlights Alexander Hamilton's role in planning, instructing, and selling the Jay mission, outdueling the pro-French Republicans, and pursuing a far-sighted plan to reestablish the Anglo-American system of interdependent trade and finance that had made the colonies prosper prior to 1776.

The second essay by Peter S. Onuf and Leonard J. Sadosky of the University of Virginia, paints a sympathetic portrait of Jefferson and Madison. Republican opposition to Federalist diplomacy, the authors assert, arose only partly from ideological sympathy for Revolutionary France. It was also based on a concern that the Washington administration sought to restrict Congress' role in treaty making, and Jefferson's reading of the national interest, especially his belief in free trade as a vehicle for economic independence in the Atlantic system.

Hamilton and Jay's Treaty: Triumph of Prudence and Logic

JOHN LAMBERTON HARPER

[Alexander] Hamilton had begun to consider the prospect of an Anglo American war even before the shocking news from the West Indies [(on November 6, 1793 a British order in council prohibited neutral powers from transporting French colonial products)]. In "Americanus No.1," published in a Philadelphia paper, he dismissed the Republican line that the Jacobin cause was the cause of liberty and that the United States could help France. The depredations of U.S. privateers and the loss of trade would make a war "seriously distressing" to Britain, but could not have a decisive impact. U.S. action could not "arrest her career or overrule those paramount considerations [of national interest] which brought her into her present situation." In a second piece, Hamilton spelled out the consequences of war for the United States. "All who are not wilfully blind must see and acknowledge that this country at present enjoys an unexampled state of prosperity." The war-related boom in U.S. trade and shipping had become a key Federalist argument against Madison's program of anti-British retaliation. But American commerce would be "in a great

John Lamberton Harper, "Hamilton and Jay's Treaty: Triumph of Prudence and Logic" from *American Machiavelli: Alexander Hamilton and the Origins of U.S. Foreign Policy* (New York: Cambridge University Press, 2007), pp. 132–139, 164–167. Reprinted with the permission of Cambridge University Press.

degree annihilated by a war." Added to this was the fact that nine tenths of federal revenues were derived from commercial duties. "To abandon public Credit would be to renounce an essential mean of carrying on the war, besides the sacrifice of the public Creditors and the disgrace of a National bankruptcy."

Hamilton also debunked the popular Republican argument that France's enemies planned to attack the United States. Many Britons, "not improbably a majority, would see in the enterprise a malicious and wanton hostility against Liberty," unless, that is, the United States were foolish enough to thrust itself into the war. "Once embarked, Nations sometimes prosecute enterprises which they would not otherwise have dreamt of. The most violent resentment would no doubt in such case be kindled against us for what would be called a wanton and presumptuous meddling on our part." In effect, Hamilton postulated a kind of strategic standoff between Britain and the United States. Neither side could reduce the other, nor provide much help to its hypothetical allies. If either were misguided enough to provoke the other, it would end up doing serious damage to *itself*. Barring a spiral of reckless, perverse behavior, the premises for a settlement were at hand.

Hamilton's first instinct upon hearing of the November order-in-council was to try to shape the president's reaction. He could well imagine Washington's sense of outrage. Indeed, Washington shared a widespread perception that Britain was trying to provoke war with the United States. Hamilton tried to influence him much as he had during earlier crises: by taking a position that contained more backbone than that of his opponents but also offered greater hope for conciliation. He immediately (March 8, 1794) suggested fortifying the main ports, raising twenty thousand auxiliary troops, and vesting the president with the power to impose an embargo on exports. As an additional thought, it might "also deserve consideration whether the Executive ought not to take measures to form some concert of the Neutral Powers for common Defense." Hamilton's logic echoed Washington's in a recent address to Congress: "If we desire to avoid insult, we must be able to repel it; if we desire to secure peace, one of the most powerful instruments of our rising prosperity, it must be known, that we are at all times ready for War." Soon after, Federalist Congressman Theodore Sedgwick of Massachusetts introduced resolutions resembling Hamilton's advice.

On March 10, a caucus of Federalist senators from sea-faring states, Oliver Ellsworth of Connecticut, George Cabot and Caleb Strong of Massachusetts, and Rufus King of New York, met in King's Philadelphia office to devise a similar program. It contained a key suggestion absent from Hamilton's memo: "an Envoy extraordinary should be sent to England to require satisfaction for the loss of our Property, and to adjust those points which menaced a War between the two Countries." On March 12, Ellsworth called on the president and suggested that Hamilton should be the man. It may be that this idea had originated with Hamilton: declining to nominate himself, he had it done by his friends. But it is equally possible that Ellsworth and company acted on their own. Washington (according to King), "was at first reserved—finally more communicative and apparently impressed with Ellsworth's representation." Washington did, however, express doubts concerning Hamilton. The treasury secretary "did not possess the general confidence of the Country." Painfully aware of Republican loathing of Hamilton, Washington hesitated to make him the top choice.

This was even more the case after House investigators pounced on the revelation that Hamilton had deposited in the Bank of the United States a portion of funds earmarked by a 1790 statute for the repayment of European loans. Hamilton reminded the president that he had received verbal permission to do this. But following the advice of [Secretary of State Edmund] Randolph, and lacking documentation, Washington declined to confirm Hamilton's story. Nor did he immediately make up his mind about the peace mission. On March 26, he endorsed a joint resolution of Congress calling for a thirty-day embargo on ships leaving U.S. ports. (He advised his estate manager at Mount Vernon "to grind no more wheat until you hear further from me.") Federalists saw an embargo as preferable to continued British confiscation of U.S. ships and to truly provocative proposals like federal government sequestration of debts owed by private U.S. citizens to British creditors.

Washington's decision in favor of the mission can be traced to several factors. On March 28, news arrived that the November 6 order had been superseded by the more liberal policy of January 8 [(reinstating commerce between French colonies and U.S. ports in non-contraband products)]. Through a private source, King [now, U.S. minister to London] learned that [British Prime Minister William] Pitt had responded to the complaints of London merchants about the wholesale condemnation of U.S. cargoes by promising "the most ample compensation." London, typically, had not foreseen the American reaction to its initial move. On April 3, a message from [Secretary of War] Thomas Pinckney arrived containing reassuring words from [Britain's] Foreign Secretary Grenville about the future treatment of U.S. ships. News had also arrived of the French recapture of Toulon, thanks to the artillery tactics of Napoleon Bonaparte, on December 19. If, as Washington suspected, the British had been planning war with the United States, they must be having second thoughts.

Hamilton's attempt to resolve the crisis came in the form of a long, unsolicited letter to Washington. . . . The letter is one of the most cogent and penetrating, even if least known, of Hamilton's career. For whatever reason, Washington did make up his mind the day after he received it.

Hamilton identified three parties on the U.S. side, one in favor of military preparations but not reprisals (such as the sequestration of debts and a total cutoff of trade) pending a good-faith effort to gain reparations and a settlement, one calling for reprisals in order to provoke hostilities, and one favoring reprisals on the assumption that London would climb down to avoid war. Hamilton did not need to name names: the latter two parties were, respectively, the hotheaded Republicans represented in the antiadministration press and in the French-style "Democratic Societies" that had sprung up . . . and the more moderate Republicans led by Madison in the House. Hamilton reminded Washington that wars more often proceeded "from angry and perverse passions than from cool calculations of Interest." If this was true for the British, why, he asked, echoing "The Federalist No. 6," don't we admit it about ourselves?

Those two parties were driven, in effect, by the old "Virginia syndrome." "In hostility with Britain they seek the gratification of revenge upon a detested enemy with that of serving a favourite friend. . . . Those even of them who do not wish the extremity of war consider it as a less evil than a thorough and sincere accommodation" with the British. Yet it would be a mistake to assume that the country at large would back a war begun before a sincere effort had been made to avoid it, while a war with the country divided could "scarcely end in any thing better than an inglorious and disadvantageous peace." It would be equally incorrect to think that Britain was intent on war or that France enjoyed the upper hand. As Hamilton wrote the president, "To you, Sir, it is unnecessary to urge the extreme precariousness of the events of War. . . . This Country ought not to set itself afloat upon an ocean so fluctuating so dangerous and so uncertain but in a case of absolute necessity."

Britain's recent conciliatory behavior (Hamilton might have mentioned as well the underlying strategic standoff) suggested that the moment was "peculiarly favourable" to attempt a settlement. The three American parties now ostensibly agreed on a peace mission. Those who truly favored its success wished to give Britain an honorable way out. Those who did not wanted reprisals first and then negotiations. But it was obvious that Britain could not settle under such pressure "without renouncing her pride and dignity." And anyone who understood Britain's psychology could see that "she would be less disposed to receive the law from us than from any other nation—a people recently become a nation, not long since one of her dependencies, and as yet, if a Hercules—a Hercules in the cradle." The wise course was to negotiate while taking defensive measures rather than to antagonize one's negotiating partner at the outset while neglecting to prepare for war. "'Tis as great an error for a nation to overrate itself as to underrate itself"—especially one as dependent on British credit and British-generated revenues as the United States. "'Tis our error to overrate ourselves and to underrate Great Britain." This was a reference to Republican bravado born out of recent French victories: "We forget how little we can annoy how much we may be annoyed." In closing, Hamilton urged the president to make a clear and immediate choice between defensive steps and a peace mission unhampered by prior reprisals, on one hand, and coercion accompanied by a pro forma demand for redress, on the other. There was no middle course.

It was a meticulously argued attempt to prevent a costly, unnecessary war brought on by a combustible mix of American resentment and British pride. In a dramatic coda to the letter, Hamilton stated that he was taking himself out of the running as a possible envoy. He was aware of Washington's feelings, of the "collateral obstacles which exist," and assured the president that he would be completely satisfied with the choice of someone else. He did not let the occasion pass, however, to add that there was only one other person (someone he knew Washington was already considering) "in whose qualifications for success there would be thorough confidence," namely Chief Justice John Jay. Washington had been leaning in favor of the mission, but it was probably this letter that clinched the decision. Its sobering logic and call for prudence were incontestable. It also spared Washington the embarrassment of having to veto Hamilton. Though temporarily estranged from him and doubtful of his political suitability, Washington was sensitive to Hamilton's feelings. Before the April 14 letter, he must have felt reluctant to deny him something that he knew the younger man both wanted and deserved. Hamilton had taken Washington off the hook.

On the morning of April 15, Washington offered the envoyship to Jay. Hamilton, Strong, Ellsworth, Cabot, and King met with Jay the same afternoon. Jay agreed, writing his wife, "No appointment ever operated more unpleasantly upon me; but the public considerations which were urged, and the manner in which it was pressed, strongly impressed me with a conviction that to refuse it would be to desert my duty." The Senate approved the appointment on April 19, 1794. . . .

Hamilton did not dictate Jay's marching orders as is often suggested. Their preparation was a collective effort. . . . The Federalist conclave of Hamilton, King, Cabot, and Ellsworth laid out guidelines on the evening of April 21. Compensation for the spoliations in the West Indies, the explosive question of the moment, must come first [(due to the November order and an earlier June order that listed food-stuffs as wartime contraband)]. If Britain agreed to this, and to execute the peace treaty, the U.S. government should be willing to compensate Britain for losses to its creditors dating from the war. Jay himself played an active part in these discussions.

Hamilton's contribution emerges from a comparison of two late-April memoranda (requested by Washington) with Jay's official instructions. The first priority was "indemnification for the depredations . . . according to a rule to be set-tled." The "desirable" rule was obviously that only contraband, narrowly defined to exclude provisions (e.g., wheat), be subject to confiscation. But the United States would have to be flexible, insisting, for example, only that provisions be exempt when going to a port not actually blockaded and that, when seized, they be paid for at full value. "In the last resort," he was willing to accept British policy as laid down on January 8, 1794, in effect prohibiting American involvement in the direct trade between France and its colonies but allowing it between the colonies and U.S. ports. With respect to the peace treaty, he foresaw an exchange of British withdrawal from the posts and indemnification for abducted slaves in return for U.S. indemnifica-tion of British creditors. Hamilton's main desiderata in a commercial treaty were access by relatively small U.S. ships (sixty to eighty tons) to the British West Indies, to Britain's European dominions on the same basis as other foreigners, and to the British East Indies. If it proved necessary to accept a short-term treaty maintaining the status quo in order to gain satisfaction for the spoliations and the execution of the peace treaty, such a deal would be "consistent with the interests of the UStates."

Jay's instructions, drafted by Randolph and signed on May 6, 1794, incorpo-rated Hamilton's main points but were not identical to the above-cited memoranda. Indeed, Hamilton later described Jay's instructions as "a crude mass" but said that "the delicacy of attempting too much reformation in the work of another head of Department, the hurry of the moment, & a great Confidence in the person to be sent" had prevented his trying to change them. The top priority was compensation for injuries resulting from the order of June 8, 1793, on the grounds that provisions could not generally be considered contraband and from those resulting from the November 6, 1793, order on the further grounds that U.S. ships had been entrapped and their cargoes summarily condemned. Here, the instructions were somewhat vaguer than Hamilton had been as to the "rule" to be insisted on. The second priority was the peace treaty. Jay was to resolve the questions of British debts and the posts, but once again the instructions were less clear than in Hamilton's memoranda. They said nothing about indemnifying British creditors. They did not suggest, nor did they forbid, Jay's eventual approach: to agree to disagree rather than insist on winning the argument over who had first violated the treaty.

If the two main points were accomplished, Jay was free to discuss a commercial treaty. The instructions contained a long list of "desirable" but not necessarily "expected" objects: "free ships make free goods," "provisions never to be contraband, except in the strongest possible case, as the blockade of a port," and "in case of an Indian war, none but the usual supplies in peace shall be furnished." The status quo, plus access to the West Indies for ships of a certain size (left unspecified) "would afford an acceptable basis of [a] treaty"—but there must be no treaty that did *not* satisfy this demand. The instructions bore Randolph's own stamp in at least two places. Jay was authorized to sound out the ministers of Russia, Denmark, and Sweden in London on the possibility of joining an armed neutrality in defense of neutral rights. (Hamilton had not pursued the idea after his mention of it to Washington of March 8.) Second, Jay was to reject any British attempt to "detach" the United States, making it clear that we would "not derogate from our treaties and engagement" to the French.

Other than this last proviso, and the one on the West Indies, the instructions left Jay considerable leeway. He was to "consider the ideas, herein expressed, as amounting to recommendations only, which in your discretion you may modify, as seems most beneficial to the United States." Arguably, this reflected Hamilton's influence: it allowed him to steer Jay through a set of informal instructions—a "few loose observations" on strategic priorities—that he sent him the same day. As important as the objects of the mission were, Hamilton warned Jay, "it will be better to do nothing than to do any thing which will not stand the test of the severest scrutiny and especially which may be construed into the relinquishment of a substantial right or interest." The "*mere appearance* of indemnification" was not enough. But in his eagerness to settle, Hamilton repeated that he was willing "in the last resort" to accept the January 8, 1794, order-in-council as the "line" deciding who should be indemnified and governing future behavior.

Looking to the future, Hamilton was prepared to suggest that if Jay could settle the peace treaty issues and secure a "truly beneficial" commercial treaty, he might even drop the demand for indemnification and let the United States government pay off the aggrieved American merchants. Above all, Jay should open British eyes to the fact that America was an indispensable supplier of the British West Indies (now expanding in size through conquest) and of Britain itself, as well as the largest (and constantly growing) consumer of British goods. "How unwise then in G Britain to suffer such a state of things to remain exposed to the hazard of constant interruption & derangement by not fixing on the basis of a good treaty the principles on which it should continue?" Opening the Mississippi was an "object of immense consequence" politically and commercially to the United States, and the British could share in the benefits. As an added incentive, Hamilton proposed that Jay offer something not in his instructions: a U.S. prohibition of the sequestering of private debt.

One view of this private letter is that Hamilton, "to preserve peace and national credit" was "willing in the face of British sea power, to acquiesce in a complete reversion or suspension of the liberal principles incorporated in the American treaties with France, Sweden, Holland, and Prussia" (namely "free ships make free goods" and a narrow definition of contraband). This is technically true but misleading and a little disingenuous. For one thing, Hamilton supported the current goals, if not the methods, of British sea power. Principles *were* involved, but at a practical level the choice was between a disastrous war to uphold the right of American shippers to their windfall profits and a peace preserving a still-immensely lucrative commerce. . . . [I]t was absurd to think that the United States was acting from a position of strength. If ever appeasement was called for, this was the time.

Hamilton, moreover, had in mind something greater than trying to preserve peace and federal revenues—"a whole new Anglo-American system." It was a system not unlike the kind of unrestricted interdependency that had existed before 1776 and that might have been restored had Lord Shelburne [the conciliatory former British Prime Minister] and the West Indian planters prevailed in 1782–83. . . .

Hamilton had the right man for the job. No one was more associated with the vision of a liberal Anglo-America than John Jay and, aside from John Adams, no one had had more diplomatic experience. It is probable that the leeway in his orders was there because Jay had insisted that it be there. On a well-known occasion, he had patently ignored his government's instructions [(In Paris (1783), Jay, Adams, and Franklin made agreements with the British without French approval, contrary to instructions)]. He had no regrets about having done so, but it was an episode he preferred not to repeat. . . .

If Hamilton's most important contribution to the prevention of war was his little-known letter to Washington in April 1794, the Jay treaty ratification fight prompted his most sustained literary effort since "The Federalist," the "Camillus" essays. Hamilton composed twenty-eight of them, Rufus King the remaining ten. He wrote the first ("The Defense No. 1," signed. "Camillus," appeared in a New York paper on July 22, 1795) during a week when he had refused to duck in the face of his own unpopularity. Defending the treaty at an outdoor meeting in lower Manhattan on Saturday, July 18, he was reportedly struck on the forehead by a stone. . . .

Hamilton's first essay set out the motives of the Jay treaty's opponents: "the vanity and vindictiveness of human nature," in particular, the animosity aroused by the success of the federal system, old-fashioned demagoguery and political ambition, continuing resentment of Britain, and misguided enthusiasm for France. "From the combined operation of these different causes, it would have been a vain expectation that the treaty would be generally contemplated with candor and moderation." In "The Defense No. 2," he repeated his argument that it would have been folly to retaliate against Britain *before* negotiations and that peace was the path to national strength. "A very powerful state may frequently hazard a high and haughty tone with good policy, but a weak State can scarcely ever do it without imprudence. The last is yet our character, though we are the embryo of a great empire."

Another maxim was that "Nations, no more than individuals, ought to persist in error, especially at the sacrifice of their peace and prosperity; besides nothing is more common in disputes between nations, than each side to charge the other with being the aggressor or delinquent." Hamilton defended Jay's decision to compromise rather than persist in Jefferson's futile and erroneous argument that complete blame for the [1783] peace treaty violations lay with the British. He took up the British arguments on the slaves and the posts, concluding that they had considerable merit. . . . [In addition,] the American failure to implement Article 5 [(requiring state legislatures to compensate British subjects whose property had been seized)] was at least contemporaneous with the British failure to order a withdrawal from the posts. Jay, "because he did not mistake strut for dignity and rudeness for spirit, because he did not by petulance and asperity enlist the pride of the British Court against the success of his mission . . . is represented as having humiliated himself and his nation." Anticipating Theodore Roosevelt's famous motto [(to walk softly and carry a big stick)], Hamilton continued: "It is forgotten that mildness in the *manner* and *firmness* in the *thing* are most compatible with true dignity, and almost always go farther than harshness and stateliness."

Because Republicans railed against the treaty's failure to deal with the impressment of American seamen, Hamilton pointed out:

> Everybody knows that the safety of Great Britain depends on her Marine. This was never more emphatically the case, than in the war in which she is now engaged. Her very existence as an independent power seems to rest on a maritime superiority. In this situation can we be surprised that there are difficulties in bringing her to consent to any arrangement which would enable us by receiving her seamen into our employment to detach them from her service?

Hamilton dismissed the Republican view that French victories had weakened Britain to the point that it was ready to make significant concessions. He painted the picture of a defiant John Bull, still possessed of "an immense credit" and triumphant on the seas. The British government possessed "as much vigour" and had "as much national support as it perhaps ever had at any former period of her history."

Among those impressed was Jefferson himself. His view of the Jay treaty episode, as stated in a letter to [his former neighbor and political ally] Philip Mazzei, was that "Men who were Sampsons in the field and Solomons in the council [namely Washington] . . . have had their heads shorn by the harlot England." In September 1795, he urged Madison to take up his pen: "Hamilton is really a colossus to the antirepublican party–without numbers, he is a host within himself. They have got themselves into a defile, where they might be finished; but too much security on the Republican part, will give time to his talents and indefatigableness to extricate them." Madison, remembering that he had not done brilliantly in his 1793 tussle with "Pacificus," turned down the request.

In essay after essay, Hamilton defended the treaty's provisions on the posts, U.S.–Canada trade arrangements, compensation for British creditors, U.S. merchants and British ship owners (the latter for losses to illegal privateers), and the ban on the sequestering of private debt. He even had something nice to say about the notorious Article 12. Britain's Navigation Laws had been breached and it could be "strongly argued that the precedent of the privilege gained was of more importance than its immediate extent." Discussing the treaty's failure to uphold "free ships make free goods," he took pleasure in recalling Jefferson's 1793 sermon on the subject to Genêt. Article 18 contained an admittedly "unpleasant" element, the illiberal definition of contraband, but did not worsen things compared to the situation before the treaty. And "in a war in which it was more than ordinarily possible that the independent existence" of Britain might depend on its naval superiority, it was idle to expect it to give up the right to seize food and naval stores.

Hamilton's final three efforts as Camillus appeared within a week of each other in early 1796. Reminding readers that under the Constitution treaties became "the supreme law of the land," he dismissed the view that the treaty was unconstitutional because the Constitution gave Congress the "power to regulate commerce with foreign nations." That was equivalent to saying that "all the objects upon which the legislative power may act in relation to our Country are excepted out of the power to make treaties." Such a notion was absurd. In the final essay, he challenged Madison, a key member of the 1787 convention who was now preparing to attack the treaty in the House of Representatives, to deny that the framers had intended to give broad and binding treaty-making powers to the executive. Camillus concluded (January 9, 1796) on a note that suggested lingering feelings of betrayal and bitterness toward his former collaborator:

> It is really painful & disgusting to observe sophisms so miserable as those which question the constitutionality of the Treaty retailed to an enlightened people and insisted upon with so much seeming fervency & earnestness. It is impossible not to bestow on sensible men who act this part—the imputation of hypocrisy.

Should their doctrines be adopted, "There would be no security at home, no respectability abroad."

By the time Camillus took this parting shot, Hamilton, though theoretically retired, was once again playing a central role in the administration. In November, the president had him prepare his seventh annual address to Congress, delivered on December 8, 1795. Rather than answer, or even acknowledge, criticisms leveled at his conduct, Washington caught the Republicans off guard by emphasizing the positive. Never had he met the legislators "at any period when more than at present the situation of our public affairs has afforded just cause for mutual congratulation; and for inviting you to join with me in profound gratitude to the Author of all good for the numerous and extraordinary blessings we enjoy." He cited the victorious end of the Indian war, consolidated by the Treaty of Greenville (August 3, 1795), a preliminary peace with the Algerines [(North African pirates)], and news of the imminent treaty with Spain opening the Mississippi. Washington mentioned the Jay treaty next, almost in passing, before a discussion of the orderly and prosperous state of domestic affairs. The speech did not end the treaty controversy, but it was, as [the historian and Hamilton biographer Jame Thomas] Flexner writes, "a brilliant stroke."

Jefferson's Blend of Realism and Idealism

PETER S. ONUF AND LEONARD J. SADOSKY

The key issue in American political economy throughout Jefferson's age was to determine how the new nation would fit into the Atlantic economy. Well into the antebellum era, the staple producers who dominated the economy depended on export markets. This meant that all Americans, directly or indirectly, were subject to the vagaries of a collapsing European diplomatic system. It followed logically that the first great national political parties—the Federalists and the Republicans of the "first party system"—emerged out of conflicts over foreign policy issues. The federal government's diplomatic stance toward Britain, the former metropolis, and France, its revolutionary ally, potentially affected every region and interest in the union. Americans anxiously calculated the relative impact of these conflicting policy orientations. In doing so, they learned to suspect the motives of at least some of their countrymen. This growing consciousness of difference stood in uneasy counterpoint to the revolutionary republican assumption of a transcendent harmony of interests. Convinced that the enlightened pursuit of private interest should draw Americans together, not drive them apart, Federalists and Republicans alike were quick to interpret disagreements over policy as fundamental threats to the nation's survival. Projecting the most malign motives on to their opponents, paranoid partisans came close to destroying the union they professed to cherish.

The ideological ferment of the French revolutionary era made conflicts over political economy seem extraordinarily portentous, with the future of western civilization hanging in the balance. But it would be mistaken to conclude that the escalating, increasingly hysterical rhetoric of the 1790s was much ado about very little. The status of the United States as an independent nation was fundamentally problematic, and not simply because this "new order for the ages" was such a radical departure from European constitutional forms. The most significant fact about these former British colonies was that their respective economies were so imperfectly integrated with each other and, by contrast, so closely tied to Europe and particularly to Britain.... For example, in 1799, the British Empire received over a third of the total dollar value of American exports, while it was the source for 47 percent—almost half—of the value of everything that Americans imported that year. Britain remained the United States' leading conduit to continental markets; as they had been before 1776, British capital and credit continued to be critical to the operation of the Atlantic commercial system as a whole, and American engagement with this system in particular. Revolutionary Americans were precocious nationalists, anticipating modern conceptions of the nation or "people" as the foundation of legitimate authority. But the economic foundations of American nationhood were not yet in place, and could only be glimpsed in the conflicting designs of the opposing parties for the continent's future development. Simply put, American economy and polity were not yet fully integrated. In the short run any systematic effort to bridge the gap would necessarily draw the United States into closer political alliance with one or the other of the metropolitan powers; either alignment would underscore Americans' continuing dependence on Europe and thus the incompleteness and insufficiency of their revolution....

Throughout the 1790s, debates about how the federal government should conduct diplomacy in the Atlantic states system [also] often turned into questions about the structure of the federal union. This was the case in 1793, as Revolutionary France went to war with nearly all of Europe in the aftermath of the execution of Louis XVI. When the French National Convention dispatched a minister, Edmond Genêt, to the United States, the Washington administration was forced to decide whether to receive him and thus recognize the French Republic. Washington's cabinet was divided on the matter, with secretary of state Jefferson arguing for recognition and secretary of the treasury Hamilton arguing against. Revolutionary change in France raised controversial questions in the law of nations, most notably whether the Franco-American treaties of 1778 remained in effect after Louis's death. Did the French nation continue to exercise its sovereignty through the new republican regime? A related issue also polarized the cabinet. Jefferson and Hamilton agreed that the United States should steer clear of the European wars, whatever the language of the French treaty, but they divided over how this neutrality should be constitutionally determined and promulgated. Hamilton believed that a decision on neutrality hinged on the interpretation of a treaty, and therefore fell solely to the executive. Jefferson thought Congress should play the decisive role, "as the Executive cannot decide the question of war on the affirmative side, neither ought it to do so on the negative side." Washington decided on a compromise of sorts, recognizing Genêt and the treaties but unilaterally issuing the Proclamation of Neutrality on 22 April 1793.

Debate over the Proclamation simmered throughout the summer of 1793. It was largely a debate about means, not ends. Both Federalists and Republicans saw an Atlantic states system erupting into war and concluded that it was in the interest of the United States to remain neutral. But Republicans worried that the administration's responses to the transformation of the European system would transform the carefully balanced structures of the American states system. Conflicting partisan perspectives were fully elaborated in a polemical exchange between Hamilton (writing as "Pacificus") and Madison ("Helvedius"). Hamilton insisted that the ability to declare neutrality was part of the President's executive powers. "The legislative department is not the *organ* of intercourse between the United States and foreign nations," he asserted, "it is charged neither with *making* nor *interpreting* treaties." Because the neutrality proclamation simply stated and clarified, but did not in itself effect any change in the nation's situation, it fell well within the power of the President to execute the laws. Madison disagreed fundamentally. . . . Pacificus's thinly-veiled agenda was to use plausible arguments about the interpretation of treaties to justify a dangerous concentration of power in the executive branch. . . . The clear language of the Constitution left no doubt about where the disputed power lay. Because of far-reaching implications of the treaty power, any ambiguity on this point was intolerable. "A treaty is not an execution of laws," Madison insisted, but "is, on the contrary, to have itself the force of a *law*," for indeed, the Constitution made any treaty "the supreme law of the land." As a result, treaties "have sometimes the effect of changing not only the external laws of the society, but operate also on the internal code." Here was the ultimate source of Republican fears about the course of Federalist diplomacy. An enterprising president and his minions could corrupt the Senate, depriving the legislature of its legitimate role in conducting foreign policy. Once the executive gained the upper hand, he could then make law, altering the delicate constitutional balance the Convention had struggled to establish and endangering the residual sovereignty of the state-republics. The machinery which would keep the spheres of the republican political cosmos separate and distinct was in danger.

These were the concerns that shaped the Republican response to the Jay Treaty two years later. The commercial treaty that John Jay negotiated with Britain in 1794 and 1795 became a subject of national controversy when it was ratified by the Senate and made public. To secure commercial reciprocity (equal trade restrictions on both sides) with Great Britain itself, Jay had allowed trade with the British West Indies to remain closed; he had also abandoned the principle of "free ships, free goods," acceding to the British "Rule of 1756," which stipulated that a trade not open to a neutral in peacetime could not be opened in time of war. The Jay Treaty also failed to stop either the British practice of seizing contraband from neutral ships or the impressment of sailors from American ships. Republican critics concluded that the administration had betrayed the principles of the model treaty of 1776 by accepting limitations on American sovereignty and limiting the commercial choices available to American producers.

Historians have exaggerated Jefferson's Anglophobia and love for Revolutionary France in explaining his opposition to the Jay Treaty. Jefferson was most disturbed by the prospect that the treaty would alter power relationships within both the Atlantic and American states systems. The treaty's abandonment of neutral rights, a key principle in Jefferson's understanding of the law of nations, was particularly upsetting. From the Republican perspective, American independence and sovereignty in the Atlantic system were inextricably linked. Favoring the commerce of one nation over another could reduce American producers to dependency; the sovereignty of dependent states and their ability to assert their rights under the law of nations was radically, perhaps fatally, compromised.

At the same time, the Jay Treaty promised to alter the shape of the relations between sovereignties within the American states system. Writing to Madison in late 1795, Jefferson cast the problem in the starkest terms: the Federalists' campaign for the treaty was "the boldest act they have ever ventured to undermine the constitution" and thus destroy the union. "For it is certainly an attempt of a party which finds they have lost their majority in one branch of the legislature to make a law by the aid of the other branch, and of the executive, under color of a treaty, which shall bind up the hands of the adverse branch from ever restraining the commerce of the patron-nation." This was the same specter Madison had raised in the "Helvidius" essays. The quest of particular interests for commercial advantage in the Atlantic trading system jeopardized the structure of the American union. If the administration party could use diplomacy to subvert the federal legislative process, how could the state-republics be safe from unconstitutional encroachments? . . .

Jefferson envisioned dismantling the mercantilist regimes that inhibited free trade and entangled the New World in the never-ending cycle of European wars. Given Britain's maritime dominance and its determination, as set forth in Orders in Council limiting American participation in the lucrative West Indies carrying trade, Jefferson's conception of commercial freedom reflected a markedly anti-British bias that sustained the bitter animosity of the revolutionary war years. More direct trade with the European continent, where a large proportion of American exports were ultimately consumed, would guarantee Americans a fairer return for their contributions to world trade. In practice, this meant that France, the great continental power, would emerge as a counterweight to Britain, bidding up staple prices in free competition for American goods. Jefferson thus tilted toward France well before the French Revolution established the ideological affinity of the "sister republics" in their global struggle against the reactionary forces of the old regime. His diplomatic orientation was overdetermined, combining revolutionary animosity to the former metropolis and radical republican aspirations for world transformation with a more concrete sense of the new nation's interests—and particularly those of staple-exporting planters like Jefferson himself—in the Atlantic economy.

Jefferson's free-trade vision, and its corollary, the rights of neutral, noncombatant powers like the United States to continue to trade freely during wartime, epitomized the anti-mercantilist, anti-metropolitan thrust of his revolutionary republicanism. Had it been possible to implement such a regime, it was undoubtedly true that a wide array of interest groups from every part of the union would have been its beneficiaries. Jefferson thus always assumed that the enlightened pursuit of self-interest would reinforce the commitment of patriotic Americans to secure their economic as well as political independence; conversely, opposition to his political economy could only signify insufficient patriotism and continuing subservience to the old metropolis. Free trade would mean higher prices for agricultural products, but the expanding volume of commerce would also benefit the shipbuilders and merchants of the "eastern" states. In effect, Jefferson and his Republican colleagues thought that independent Americans could have it both ways, enjoying continuing access to the markets, capital, and credit the British Empire had formerly afforded them while gaining free, direct access to the rest of the world. Ironically, the free-trade vision was appealing to Americans precisely because of their experience with it in the empire. Because it was so obviously in Britain's own interest to sustain a free trade with the United States after independence—approximately a third of British exports, primarily manufactured goods, were sent to the colonies before the war—Jefferson was convinced that the Americans had a strong bargaining position in extracting commercial concessions. He interpreted the Federalist administration's unwillingness to assume a more aggressive diplomatic posture against Britain as a revealing indication of their counter-revolutionary bad faith. Advocates of the new federal Constitution had promised that American diplomats would be able to negotiate commercial treaties on more favorable terms. But instead of a commercial accord with Britain that would help initiate the free-trade millennium, John Jay's mission to England in 1794 led to an agreement that seemed to confirm American subservience to the mother country's political and economic interests.

FURTHER READING

Harry Ammon, *The Genet Mission* (1973)

Joyce Appleby, *Capitalism and a New Social Order: The Republican Vision of the 1790s* (1984)

————, *Inheriting the Revolution* (2000)

Doron S. Ben-Atar, *The Origins of Jeffersonian Commercial Policy and Diplomacy* (1993)

Irving Brant, *James Madison,* 6 vols. (1941–1961)

Gerald H. Clarfield, *Timothy Pickering and the American Republic* (1981)

Francis D. Cogliano, *Revolutionary America* (1999)

Jerald A. Combs, *The Jay Treaty* (1970)

Noble E. Cunningham, *Thomas Jefferson v. Alexander Hamilton* (2000)

Alexander DeConde, *Entangling Alliance: Politics and Diplomacy Under George Washington* (1958)

————, *The Quasi War* (1966)

John Patrick Diggins, *The Portable John Adams* (2004)

Stanley Elkins and Eric McKitrick, *The Age of Federalism* (1993)

Joseph J. Ellis, *American Sphinx* (on Jefferson) (1996)

———— *Founding Brothers* (2000)

Tod Estes, *The Jay Treaty Debate* (2006)

John Ferling, *Adams v. Jefferson* (2004)

James A. Field, "1789–1820: All Economists, All Diplomats," in William H. Becker and Samuel F. Wells Jr., eds., *Economics and World Power* (1984), pp. 1–54

James Thomas Flexner, *The Young Hamilton* (1997)

James Grant, *John Adams* (2005)

Don Higginbotham, *George Washington* (2002)

Peter P. Hill, *Napoleon's Troublesome Americans* (2005)

Lawrence S. Kaplan, *Alexander Hamilton: Ambivalent Anglophile* (2002)

Roger G. Kennedy, *Burr, Hamilton, and Jefferson* (1999)

James J. Kirschke, *Gouverneur Morris* (2005)

Walter LaFeber, "Jefferson and an American Foreign Policy," in Peter S. Onuf, ed., *Jeffersonian Legacies* (1993), pp. 370–391

David McCollough, *John Adams* (2001)

Forrest McDonald, *Alexander Hamilton* (1979)

———, *The Presidency of George Washington* (1979)

Melanie Randolph Miller, *Envoy to the Terror* (2004) (on Gouverneur Morris)

Conor Cruise O'Brien, *The Long Affair: Thomas Jefferson and the French Revolution* (1996)

Peter S. Onuf, *Jefferson's Empire* (2000)

Bradford Perkins, *The Creation of a Republican Empire, 1776–1865 (1993),* vol. 2 of *The Cambridge History of American Foreign Relations*

Merrill D. Peterson, *Thomas Jefferson and the New Nation* (1970)

Norman K. Risjord, *Jefferson's America* (2002)

Marie Jeanne Rossignol, *The Nationalist Ferment: The Origins of U.S. Foreign Policy, 1792–1812* (2004)

Scott A. Silverstone, *Divided Union* (2004)

Robert A. Rutland, *James Madison* (1987)

James Roger Sharp, *American Politics in the Early Republic* (1993)

James R. Sofka, "The Jeffersonian Idea of National Security," *Diplomatic History*, 21 (1997), 519–544

Walter Stahr, *John Jay* (2005)

Darren Staloff, *Hamilton, Adams, and Jefferson* (2007)

William Stinchcombe, *The XYZ Affair* (1981)

William Earl Weeks, "New Directions in the Study of Early American Foreign Relations," *Diplomatic History,* 17 (1993), 73–96

CHAPTER
4

The Louisiana Purchase

Behind the negotiations in Paris that produced the April 30, 1803, treaty whereby France sold the vast Louisiana Territory to the United States lay years of American interest in and anxiety over Louisiana and its port of New Orleans at the mouth of the Mississippi River. When Spain closed access to the mighty Mississippi in 1784, the vital water route down which western farmers shipped their goods to market, many Americans demanded war. But negotiations followed and through Pinckney's Treaty, signed in 1795, U.S. farmers and traders gained the "right of deposit"—the right to store goods destined for export—at New Orleans. Spanish control of the waterway nonetheless continued to cast doubt over the nation's future territorial expansion. Concern mounted in 1800 when word leaked that Spain had secretly transferred Louisiana to France, and that the right of deposit was again jeopardized. The administration of Thomas Jefferson intensified pressure on France to sell New Orleans to the United States. The French astounded American diplomats by offering to sell all of Louisiana. The "noble bargain," as French minister of foreign affairs Talleyrand called it, was consummated in a few days.

Through the purchase, the United States doubled in size, receiving 828,000 square miles of frontier land lacking precise boundaries. Napoleon Bonaparte's asking price for this substantial piece of his empire had been only $15 million, or just three cents an acre. Even before completion of the purchase, Jefferson astutely recruited his twenty-nine-year-old private secretary, Captain Meriwether Lewis, to lead an expedition across the expansive and largely uncharted domain to the Pacific Ocean.

Historians differ over the extent to which external and internal factors facilitated the purchase of Louisiana. Some have argued that the United States was simply lucky that it benefited from Napoleon's troubles with Great Britain and the prospect of war in Europe. The outbreak in 1791 of slave revolt on the island of Saint-Domingue (Santo Domingo and later Haiti), a colonial possession of the French, and France's decade-long inability to suppress it, also led Napoleon to jettison his transatlantic empire. Others have stressed America's long imperial interest in the territory and constant beseeching of France. In other words, the purchase came to pass in part because Napoleon realized that Americans, moving west, threatened someday to overrun the territory. Whether Americans profited from Europe's turmoil or their own devices, they had added immensely to what Jefferson envisioned as an "empire of liberty"—an expansive republic in which virtuous, white, yeoman farmers would reap the benefits of land, prosperity, and racial privilege.

🌐 D O C U M E N T S

Haiti's slave revolt of the 1790s, led by the former slave Toussaint L'Ouverture, helped set into motion events that led to the Louisiana Purchase. Delighted to strike a blow at France during the undeclared Quasi-War with France (1798–1800), and responsive to northern, antislavery forces, President John Adams lent support to Toussaint's insurgency. But the Haitian example fed fears of a similar, violent uprising in the American South. When the slaveholder Thomas Jefferson became president in 1801, he pulled back on U.S. backing for General Toussaint, who was captured by French forces and executed the following year, prior to the establishment of an independent Haitian Republic. Document 1, a letter written on July 17, 1801, by U.S. consul to Saint-Domingue, Tobias Lear, to Secretary of State James Madison, reports Toussaint's angry accusation that white racism accounted for Jefferson's failure to send a letter formally introducing the newly appointed American envoy. The French failed to suppress the revolution, a setback that prompted the French leader to abandon his dream of a revitalized empire in the Americas, and to sell Louisiana. Haiti became an independent republic in 1804, but the United States refused to grant diplomatic recognition until 1862, on the eve of the Emancipation Proclamation.

In Document 2, a letter of April 18, 1802, to American minister to France Robert R. Livingston, President Jefferson expresses alarm over the fate of Louisiana and the American export trade after he learned of Spain's cession of the territory to France. Document 3, from the 1830 recollections of the French official François Barbe Marbois, presents First Consul Napoleon Bonaparte's explanations to his advisers in April 1803 as to why Louisiana should be sold to the United States. In an April 13, 1803, letter to Secretary of State James Madison, Document 4, Livingston recounts the steps leading to the Louisiana Purchase. Jefferson's rival, Alexander Hamilton, published a stinging critique of the president's policies on July 5, 1803. This selection, reprinted as Document 5, first appeared in the *New-York Evening Post*. In it, Hamilton maintains that the American acquisition of Louisiana owed more to good fortune than to skillful diplomacy. Hamilton thus initiated a debate that even today continues among scholars. Document 6 is a letter of instruction written by President Jefferson to Captain Meriwether Lewis on June 20, 1803, just prior to the launching of the two-year Lewis and Clark expedition that explored the geography, botany, native peoples, and commercial potential of the newly purchased territory.

🌐 D O C U M E N T   1

Haitian General Toussaint L'Ouverture
Bristles at U.S. Racism, 1801

I have the pleasure to inform you that I arrived here on the 4th, instant, after a passage of 21 days from the Capes. We met with no Cruisers, and saw but three or four Vessels of any kind on our passage.

On my arrival I delivered your letter to [my predecessor, U.S. Consul] Dr. [Edward] Stevens, and received from him every mark of polite attention. He went with me to General Toussaint Louverture, to whom he introduced me as the person who was to succeed him in his Office. I handed my Commission to the General, who asked me if I had not a letter for him from the President, or from the Government. I told him I had not, and explained the reason, as not being customary in missions of this kind, where

This document can be found at http://thelouvertureproject.org.

I should be introduced by my Predecessor, and exhibit my Commission as an evidence of my Appointment. He immediately returned my Commission without opening it, expressing his disappointment and disgust in strong terms, saying that his Colour was the cause of his being neglected, and not thought worthy of the Usual attentions. I explained to him, with temper and candour, the nature of the Appointment as not requiring those particular introductions which are given to Diplomatic Characters, and assured him of the President's respect & consideration. He became more cool—said he would consider the matter, and desired me to see him at 9 o'clock the next morning. I went accordingly, and found with him Genl. Moyese [Moïse] and Genl. Christolphe. [Christophe], two of the principal Generals. He repeated the observations which he had made the Evening before, and added, that it must hurt him in the eyes of his Chief Officers, when it was found that he was not thot. [(thought)] worthy of having a letter from the President of the Governmt. I gave the same explainations wh. [(which)] I had offered before. He appeared to be much hurt; but after some further conversation, said, that, notwithstanding the mortification he felt, he would give an evidence of his sincere desire to preserve harmony and a good understanding with the United States, by received me, and giving me all the countenance and protection, in the execution of my Office, which I could desire. I left my Commission with him to be translated and recorded, and received it back the same evening. Since that time I have had no cause to complain of a want of attention. . . .

I have not been long enough here to form a correct opinion of the state of things in this Island. The General in Chief expresses, on all occasions, his strong wishes for a friendly intercourse with the United States.

A new and important Symbol Aera has commenced here. A Constitution has been formed for the Government of this Island, by Deputies called together for that purpose by the General in Chief. It was read in public, with great parade, on the 7th instant. The papers which I send you will shew the Addresses which preceded and followed the reading. It is not yet printed from the public. It declares Genl. [(General)] Toussaint Louverture Governor for life, with the power of naming his successor. It is to be submitted to the French Republic for approbation; but in the meantime, it is to have effect here in the Island.

I shall have the honor of writing to you more fully in a few days, by the Brig Neptune, in which I came out, and which returns directly to Alexandria. By that time I hope to get a Copy of the Constitution which I shall forward to you. The consequence of which I expect will be to drain this market, which is at present full, and create a demand in this place. With the highest respect & sincere Attachment I have the honor to be Sir, Your most obedient Servant.

🌐 *D O C U M E N T   2*

President Thomas Jefferson Assesses the French Threat in New Orleans, 1802

The cession of Louisiana, and the Floridas by Spain to France, works most sorely on the United States. On this subject the Secretary of State has written to you fully, yet I cannot forbear recurring to it personally, so deep is the impression it

This document can be found in Jefferson to Livingston, 18 April 1802, Thomas Jefferson Papers, Series 1, Reel # 26, Manuscripts Division, Library of Congress.

makes on my mind. It completely reverses all the political relations of the United States, and will form a new epoch in our political course. Of all nations of any consideration, France is the one which, hitherto, has offered the fewest points on which we could have any conflict of right, and the most points of a communion of interests. From these causes, we have ever looked to her as our *natural friend,* as one with which we never could have an occasion of difference. Her growth, therefore, we viewed as our own, her misfortunes ours. There is on the globe one single spot, the possessor of which is our natural and habitual enemy. It is New Orleans, through which the produce of three-eighths of our territory must pass to market, and from its fertility it will ere long yield more than half of our whole produce, and contain more than half of our inhabitants. France, placing herself in that door, assumes to us the attitude of defiance. Spain might have retained it quietly for years. Her pacific dispositions, her feeble state, would induce her to increase our facilities there, so that her possession of the place would be hardly felt by us, and it would not, perhaps, be very long before some circumstance might arise, which might make the cession of it to us the price of something of more worth to her. Not so can it ever be in the hands of France: the impetuosity of her temper, the energy and restlessness of her character, placed in a point of eternal friction with us, and our character, which, though quiet and loving peace and the pursuit of wealth, is high-minded, despising wealth in competition with insult or injury, enterprising and energetic as any nation on earth; these circumstances render it impossible that France and the United States can continue long friends, when they meet in so irritable a position. They, as well as we, must be blind if they do not see this; and we must be very improvident if we do not begin to make arrangements on that hypothesis. The day that France takes possession of New Orleans, fixes the sentence which is to restrain her forever within her low-water mark. It seals the union of two nations, who, in conjunction, can maintain exclusive possession of the ocean. From that moment, we must marry ourselves to the British fleet and nation. We must turn all our attention to a maritime force, for which our resources place us on very high ground; and having formed and connected together a power which may render reinforcement of her settlements here impossible to France, make the first cannon which shall be fired in Europe the signal for the tearing up any settlement she may have made, and for holding the two continents of America in sequestration for the common purposes of the United British and American nations. This is not a state of things we seek or desire.

DOCUMENT 3

Napoleon Bonaparte, First Consul of France, Explains the Need to Sell Louisiana to the United States, 1803

I know the full value of Louisiana, and I have been desirous of repairing the fault of the French negotiator who abandoned it in 1763. A few lines of a treaty have restored it to me, and I have scarcely recovered it when I must expect to lose

This document can be found in Barbé Marbois, *The History of Louisiana* (Philadelphia: Carey & Lea, 1830), 263–264, 274–275, 276, 312.

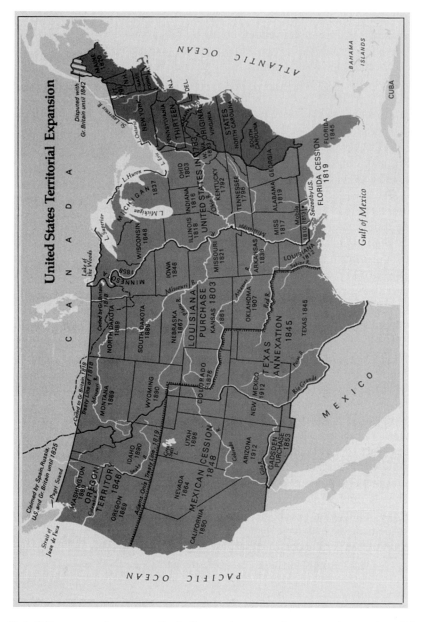

United States Territorial Expansion

it. But if it escapes from me, it shall one day cost dearer to those who oblige me to strip myself of it than to those to whom I wish to deliver it. The English have successively taken from France, Canada, Cape Breton, Newfoundland, Nova Scotia, and the richest portions of Asia. They are engaged in exciting troubles in St. Domingo. They shall not have the Mississippi which they covet. Louisiana is nothing in comparison with their conquests in all parts of the globe, and yet the jealousy they feel at the restoration of this colony to the sovereignty of France, acquaints me with their wish to take possession of it, and it is thus that they will begin the war. They have twenty ships of war in the Gulf of Mexico, they sail over those seas as sovereigns, whilst our affairs in St. Domingo have been growing worse every day since the death of [General Charles Victor Emmanuel] Leclerc [in Santo Domingo]. The conquest of Louisiana would be easy, if they only took the trouble to make a descent there. I have not a moment to lose in putting it out of their reach. I know not whether they are not already there. It is their usual course, and if I had been in their place, I would not have waited. I wish, if there is still time, to take from them any idea that they may have of ever possessing that colony. I think of ceding it to the United States. I can scarcely say that I cede it to them, for it is not yet in our possession. If, however, I leave the least time to our enemies, I shall only transmit an empty title to those republicans whose friendship I seek. They only ask of me one town in Louisiana, but I already consider the colony as entirely lost, and it appears to me that in the hands of this growing power, it will be more useful to the policy and even to the commerce of France, than if I should attempt to keep it. . . .

Irresolution and deliberation are no longer in season. I renounce Louisiana. It is not only New Orleans that I will cede, it is the whole colony without any reservation. I know the price of what I abandon, and I have sufficiently proved the importance that I attach to this province, since my first diplomatic act with Spain had for its object the recovery of it. I renounce it with the greatest regret. To attempt obstinately to retain it would be folly. I direct you to negotiate this affair with the envoys of the United States. Do not even await the arrival of Mr. [James] Monroe: have an interview this very day with Mr. [Robert] Livingston; but I require a great deal of money for this war, and I would not like to commence it with new contributions. For a hundred years France and Spain have been incurring expenses for improvements in Louisiana, for which its trade has never indemnified them. Large sums, which will never be returned to the treasury, have been lent to companies and to agriculturists. The price of all these things is justly due to us. If I should regulate my terms, according to the value of these vast regions to the United States, the indemnity would have no limits. I will be moderate, in consideration of the necessity in which I am of making a sale. But keep this to yourself. I want fifty millions [about $9,375,000] and for less than that sum I will not treat. . . .

Perhaps it will also be objected to me, that the Americans may be found too powerful for Europe in two or three centuries: but my foresight does not embrace such remote fears. Besides, we may hereafter expect rivalries among the members of the Union. The confederations, that are called perpetual, only last till one of the contracting parties finds it to its interest to break them, and it is to prevent the danger, to which the colossal power of England exposes us, that I would provide a remedy. . . .

This accession of territory . . . strengthens for ever the power of the United States; and I have just given to England a maritime rival, that will sooner or later humble her pride.

DOCUMENT 4

Robert R. Livingston, American Minister to France, Recounts the Paris Negotiations, 1803

By my letter of yesterday, you learned that the Minister [of the Treasury] had asked me whether I would agree to purchase Louisiana &c. On the 12th, I called upon him to press this matter further. He then thought proper to declare that his proposition was only personal, but still requested me to make an offer; and, upon declining to do so, as I expected Mr. Monroe the next day, he shrugged up his shoulders, and changed the conversation. Not willing, however, to lose sight of it, I told him I had been long endeavoring to bring him to some point; but, unfortunately, without effect: that I wished merely to have the negotiation opened by any proposition on his part; and, with that view, had written him a note which contained that request, grounded upon my apprehension of the consequence of sending General [Jean Baptiste Jules] Bernadotte without enabling him to say a treaty was begun. He told me he would answer my note, but that he must do it evasively, because Louisiana was not theirs. I smiled at this assertion, and told him I had seen the treaty recognizing it; that I knew the Consul had appointed officers to govern the country, and that he had himself told me that General Victor was to take possession; that, in a note written by the express order of the First Consul, he had told me that General Bernadotte was to treat relative to it in the United States, &c. He still persisted that they had it in contemplation to obtain it, but had it not. I told him that I was very well pleased to understand this from him, because, if so, we should not commit ourselves with them in taking it from Spain, to whom, by his account, it still belonged; and that, as we had just cause of complaint against her, if Mr. Monroe concurred in opinion with me, we should negotiate no further on the subject, but advise our Government to take possession. He seemed alarmed at the boldness of the measure, and told me he would answer my note, but that it would be evasively. I told him I should receive with pleasure any communication from him, but that we were not disposed to trifle; that the times were critical, and though I did not know what instructions Mr. Monroe might bring, I was perfectly satisfied that they would require a precise and prompt notice; that I was very fearful, from the little progress I had made, that my Government would consider me as a very indolent negotiator. He laughed, and told me that he would give me a certificate that I was the most importunate he had met with. . . .

I told him that the United States were anxious to preserve peace with France; that, for that reason, they wished to remove them to the west side of the Mississippi; that we would be perfectly satisfied with New Orleans and the Floridas, and had no disposition to extend across the river; that, of course, we would not give any great sum for the purchase; that he was right in his idea of the extreme exorbitancy

State Papers and Correspondence Bearing Upon the Purchase of the Territory of Louisiana. U.S. House of Representatives, 57th Congress, 2nd Session, Doc. No. 431, pp. 159–163. Washington, D.C.: Government Printing Office, 1903.

of the demand, which would not fall short of one hundred and twenty-five millions; that, however, we would be ready to purchase, provided the sum was reduced to reasonable limits. He then pressed me to name the sum. I told him that this was not worth while, because, as he only treated the inquiry as a matter of curiosity, any declaration of mine would have no effect. If a negotiation was to be opened, we should (Mr. Monroe and myself) make the offer after mature reflection. This compelled him to declare, that, though he was not authorized expressly to make the inquiry from me, yet, that, if I could mention any sum that came near the mark, that could be accepted, he would communicate it to the First Consul. I told him that we had no sort of authority to go to a sum that bore any proportion to what he mentioned; but that, as he himself considered the demand as too high, he would oblige me by telling me what he thought would be reasonable. He replied that, if we would name sixty millions, and take upon us the American claims, to the amount of twenty more, he would try how far this would be accepted. I told him that it was vain to ask anything that was so greatly beyond our means; that true policy would dictate to the First Consul not to press such a demand; that he must know that it would render the present Government unpopular, and have a tendency, at the next election, to throw the power into the hands of men who were most hostile to a connection with France; and that this would probably happen in the midst of a war. I asked him whether the few millions acquired at this expense would not be too dearly bought?

He frankly confessed that he was of my sentiments; but that he feared the Consul would not relax. I asked him to press this argument upon him, together with the danger of seeing the country pass into the hands of Britain. I told him that he had seen the ardor of the Americans to take it by force, and the difficulty with which they were restrained by the prudence of the President; that he must easily see how much the hands of the war party would be strengthened, when they learned that France was upon the eve of a rupture with England. He admitted the weight of all this: "But," says he, "you know the temper of a youthful conqueror; everything he does is rapid as lightning; we have only to speak to him as an opportunity presents itself, perhaps in a crowd, when he bears no contradiction. When I am alone with him, I can speak more freely, and he attends; but this opportunity seldom happens, and is always accidental. Try, then, if you can not come up to my mark. Consider the extent of the country, the exclusive navigation of the river, and the importance of having no neighbors to dispute you, no war to dread." I told him that I considered all these as important considerations, but there was a point beyond which we could not go, and that fell far short of the sum he mentioned. . . .

I speak now without reflection, and without having seen Mr. Monroe, as it was midnight when I left the Treasury Office, and is now near 3 o'clock. It is so very important that you should be apprized that a negotiation is actually opened, even before Mr. Monroe has been presented, in order to calm the tumult which the news of war will renew, that I have lost no time in communicating it. We shall do all we can to cheapen the purchase; but my present sentiment is that we shall buy. Mr. Monroe will be presented to the Minister to-morrow, when we shall press for as early an audience as possible from the First Consul. I think it will be necessary to put in some proposition to-morrow: the Consul goes in a few days to Brussels, and every moment is precious.

Hamilton Debunks Jefferson's Diplomacy, 1803

At length the business of New-Orleans has terminated favorably to this country. Instead of being obliged to rely any longer on the force of treaties, for a place of deposit, the jurisdiction of the territory is now transferred to our hands and in future the navigation of the Mississippi will be ours unmolested. This, it will be allowed, is an important acquisition; not, indeed, as territory, but as being essential to the peace and prosperity of our Western country, and as opening a free and valuable market to our commercial states. This purchase has been made during the period of Mr. Jefferson's presidency, and will, doubtless, give éclat to his administration. Every man, however, possessed of the least candor and reflection will readily acknowledge that the acquisition has been solely owing to a fortuitous concurrence of unforeseen and unexpected circumstances, and not to any wise or vigorous measures on the part of the American government.

As soon as we experienced from Spain a direct infraction of an important article of our treaty [of 1795], in withholding the deposit of New Orleans, it afforded us justifiable cause of war, and authorized immediate hostilities. Sound policy unquestionably demanded of us to begin with a prompt, bold, and vigorous resistance against the injustice; to seize the object at once. And having this vantage ground, should we have thought it advisable to terminate hostilities by a purchase, we might then have done it on almost our own terms. This course, however, was not adopted. . . .

On the part of France, the short interval of peace had been wasted in repeated and fruitless efforts to subjugate St. Domingo; and those means which were originally destined to the colonization of Louisiana had been gradually exhausted by the unexpected difficulties of this ill-starred enterprise.

To the deadly climate of St. Domingo, and to the courage and obstinate resistance made by its black inhabitants, are we indebted for the obstacles which delayed the colonization of Louisiana till the auspicious moment when a [prospective] rupture between England and France gave a new turn to the projects of the latter, and destroyed at once all her schemes as to this favorite object of her ambition.

It was made known to Bonaparte that among the first objects of England would be the seizure of New-Orleans, and that preparations were even then in a state of forwardness for that purpose. The First Consul could not doubt that, if an English fleet was sent thither, the place must fall without resistance. It was obvious, therefore, that it would be in every shape preferable that it should be placed in the possession of a neutral power. And when, besides, some millions of money, of which he was extremely in want, were offered him to part with what he could no longer hold, it affords a moral certainty that it was to an accidental state of circumstances, and not to wise plans, that this cession, at this time, has been owing. We shall venture to add that neither of the ministers through whose instrumentality it was effected will ever deny this, or even pretend that, previous to the time when a rupture was believed to be inevitable, there was the smallest chance of inducing the First Consul, with his ambitious and aggrandizing views, to

---

This document can be found in the *New York Evening Post,* July 5, 1803. It can also be found in Harold C. Syrett, ed., *The Papers of Alexander Hamilton* (New York: Columbia University Press, 1979), XXVI, 129–136.

commute the territory for any sum of money in their power to offer. The real truth is, Bonaparte found himself absolutely compelled, by situation, to relinquish his darling plan of colonizing the banks of the Mississippi. And thus have the government of the United States, by the unforeseen operation of events, gained what the feebleness and pusillanimity of its miserable system of measures could never have acquired.

D O C U M E N T   6

Jefferson Instructs Captain Meriwether Lewis on Exploration, 1803

The object of your mission is to explore the Missouri river, & such principal stream of it, as, by it's course & communication with the waters of the Pacific Ocean, may offer the most direct & practicable water communication across this continent, for the purposes of commerce.

Beginning at the mouth of the Missouri, you will take observations of latitude & longitude, at all remarkable points on the river, & especially at the mouths of rivers, at rapids, at islands & other places & objects distinguished by such natural marks & characters of a durable kind, as that they may with certainty be recognized hereafter. The courses of the river between these points of observation may be supplied by the compass, the log-line & by time, corrected by the observations themselves. The variations of the compass too, in different places, should be noticed.

The interesting points of portage between the heads of the Missouri & the water offering the best communication with the Pacific Ocean should also be fixed by observation, & the course of that water to the ocean, in the same manner as that of the Missouri. . . .

The commerce which may be carried on with the people inhabiting the line you will pursue, renders a knolege of these people important. You will therefore endeavor to make yourself acquainted, as far as a diligent pursuit of your journey shall admit,

> with the names of the nations & their numbers;
> the extent & limits of their possessions;
> their relations with other tribes or nations;
> their language, traditions, monuments;
> their ordinary occupations in agriculture, fishing, hunting, war, arts, & the implements for these;
> their food, clothing, & domestic accommodations;
> the diseases prevalent among them, & the remedies they use;
> moral & physical circumstances which distinguish them from the tribes we know;
> peculiarities in their laws, customs & dispositions;
> and articles of commerce they may need or furnish, & to what extent.

And considering the interest which every nation has in extending & strengthening the authority of reason & justice among the people around them, it will be useful to

This document can be found in Jefferson to Lewis, 20 June 1803. Thomas Jefferson Papers, Series 1, Reel # 28, Manuscipts Division, Library of Congress.

acquire what knolege you can of the state of morality, religion & information among them, as it may better enable those who endeavor to civilize & instruct them, to adapt their measures to the existing notions & practises of those on whom they are to operate.

Other object worthy of notice will be

the soil & face of the country, it's growth & vegetable productions; especially those not of the U.S.

the animals of the country generally, & especially those not known in the U.S.

the remains and accounts of any which may [be] deemed rare or extinct;

the mineral productions of every kind; but more particularly metals, lime stone, pit coal & salpetre; salines & mineral waters, noting the temperature of the last, & such circumstances as may indicate their character.

Volcanic appearances.

climate as characterized by the thermometer, by the proportion of rainy, cloudy & clear days, by lightening, hail, snow, ice, by the access & recess of frost, by the winds prevailing at different seasons, the dates at which particular plants put forth or lose their flowers, or leaf, times of appearance of particular birds, reptiles or insects. . . .

In all your intercourse with the natives treat them in the most friendly & conciliatory manner which their own conduct will admit; allay all jealousies as to the object of your journey, satisfy them of it's innocence, make them acquainted with the position, extent, character, peaceable & commercial dispositions of the U.S. of our wish to be neighborly, friendly & useful to them, & of our dispositions to a commercial intercourse with them; confer with them on the points most convenient as mutual emporiums, & the articles of most desireable interchange for them & us. If a few of their influential chiefs, within practicable distance, wish to visit us, arrange such a visit with them, and furnish them with authority to call on our officers, on their entering the U.S. to have them conveyed to this place at public expense. If any of them should wish to have some of their young people brought up with us, & taught such arts as may be useful to thcm, we will receive, instruct & take care of them. Such a mission, whether of influential chiefs, or of young people, would give some security to your own party. Carry with you some matter of the kinepox, inform those of them with whom you may be of it' efficacy as a preservative from the small-pox; and instruct & incourage them in the use of it. This may be especially done wherever you winter. . . .

Should you reach the Pacific ocean [One full line scratched out, indecipherable. . . .] inform yourself of the circumstances which may decide whether the furs of those parts may not be collected as advantageously at the head of the Missouri (convenient as is supposed to the waters of the Colorado & Oregon or Columbia) as at Nootka sound or any other point of that coast; & that trade be consequently conducted through the Missouri & U.S. more beneficially than by the circumnavigation now practised.

On your arrival on that coast endeavor to learn if there be any port within your reach frequented by the sea-vessels of any nation, and to send two of your trusty people back by sea, in such way as shall appear practicable, with a copy of your notes. And should you be of opinion that the return of your party by the way they went will be eminently dangerous, then ship the whole, & return by sea by way of Cape Horn or the Cape of good Hope, as you shall be able.

ESSAYS

The historiographical debate over the Louisiana Purchase revolves around President Thomas Jefferson's decisionmaking and the deliberateness of American policy. Did the Jefferson administration follow a coherent strategy that persuaded Napoleon Bonaparte to sell Louisiana? Or, was the United States simply the beneficiary of France's bad luck? Robert W. Tucker of The Johns Hopkins University and David C. Hendrickson of Colorado College argue in the opening essay that Jefferson sought territorial expansion but opposed the use of military force either unilaterally or bilaterally. Jefferson thus pursued a risky policy of conquest without war. Tucker and Hendrickson conclude that external factors—Napoleon's ill-fated attempt to quell the black slave rebellion in Saint Domingue and the imminence of war in Europe between France and Britain—prodded Napoleon to sell Louisiana to the United States.

Joseph J. Ellis of Mount Holyoke College takes a different approach in the second essay. He agrees that external factors in Europe and the Caribbean played into America's hands, but he praises Jefferson and his minister to France Robert Livingston for their patience and "diplomatic deftness." The steady application of pressure on France to sell New Orleans and western Florida, along with the timely leaking of a possible alliance with Great Britain, placed the United States in position to exploit Napoleon's failure to put down a slave insurrection and restore French rule to the colony of Santo Domingo. The "noble bargain" not only gave the United States ownership of vast new lands but also reinforced a providential sense of American destiny as a continental empire.

Jefferson's Risky Diplomacy of Watching and Waiting

ROBERT W. TUCKER AND DAVID C. HENDRICKSON

On September 28, 1801, the Secretary of State forwarded a letter of instructions to the newly appointed Minister to France [Robert Livingston], then awaiting passage to Bordeaux. The minister's attention was directed to the information that a "transaction" had likely been concluded between France and Spain involving "the mouth of the Mississippi, with certain portions of adjacent territory." The impending change of neighbors, Madison wrote Livingston, "is of too momentous concern not to have engaged the most serious attention of the Executive." Livingston was instructed to take up the subject with the French government and to express the anxiety of the United States over the prospects and consequences of the rumored transfer of territory. The "tendency of a French neighborhood," the government in Paris was to be delicately reminded, must "inspire jealousies and apprehensions which may turn the thoughts of our citizens towards a closer connexion with her rival, and possibly produce a crisis in which a very favorable part of her dominions would be exposed to the joint operations of a naval and territorial power." Should, however, Livingston find the cession a fait accompli, or virtually so, he was to make every effort to preserve those rights of trade and navigation then obtaining between the United States and Spain. Additionally, he was to see whether France could not be induced to cede the Floridas—or at least West Florida—to this country, assuming these territories to be included in the cession. Such cession by France would at once prove that nation's good will and serve to reconcile the United States to an arrangement so much "disrelished" by them. But should the Floridas neither have been ceded to France nor their cession contemplated by France, efforts were to be made to dispose Paris in favor of "experiments on the part of the United States, for obtaining from Spain the cession in view."

Thus France was to be warned that a return to the Mississippi valley could result in an alliance between this country and England, an alliance that might well result at some future date in France being driven altogether from North America. But the threat was to remain less than explicit, lest it unnecessarily arouse the French and thereby jeopardize American rights in the use of the river. Alternatively, France might be induced to give part of the territories ceded to it in order to gain the good will of this country. The cession of West Florida to the United States would reconcile the latter to the French presence elsewhere, while relieving France of spoliation claims by American citizens. On the other hand, if Spain still possessed the Floridas, France might nevertheless be disposed to assist us in obtaining these lands in return for our favorable disposition toward its presence here. How France might undertake this role was not elaborated.

These instructions, drawn up at the outset of the Louisiana crisis, form a succinct summary of the principal features of Jeffersonian diplomacy, not only in the Louisiana crisis but also in the subsequent efforts to obtain the Floridas. Essentially the same considerations, but with greater urgency, were pressed by Jefferson in his famous letter to Livingston in April 1802. Although once our "natural friend," Jefferson wrote, in possessing New Orleans France must become "our natural and habitual enemy." By doing so, he warned, France must seal its own fate, for in taking New Orleans it would not only force America into alliance with Great Britain but require the United States "to turn all our attention to a maritime force, for which our resources place us on very high grounds." When war broke out again in Europe, the United States would seize the opportunity to tear up any settlement France had made, and would then hold "the two continents of America in sequestration for the common purposes of the united British and American nations." In such a contest of arms, France would immediately lose New Orleans. "For however greater her force is than ours compared in the abstract, it is nothing in comparison of ours when to be exerted on our own soil." . . .

While the French never succeeded in taking possession of New Orleans, save in a formal sense and even then only for the briefest of periods, until the time Napoleon decided to sell the colony American diplomacy had to prepare against that day. How serious were the American efforts and what effect did they have on the French? The first question can be answered with greater assurance than the second. To characterize the American efforts to propitiate Great Britain as serious is to take no little liberty with that term. It may be argued, of course, that the propitiation of British power was virtually impossible during the period England was at peace with France, that there was no incentive the Jefferson administration could hold out that would tempt London to jeopardize the peace by allying England with the United States in opposing French plans of empire in North America. Even so, the question concerning the nature of the American efforts to enlist British support would remain. At best, those efforts must be characterized as halfhearted and without real significance. Given the outlook of Republicans, this was understandable. If an alliance was almost by definition an illicit relationship, an alliance with Great Britain represented for Jefferson and his political associates something approaching a state of mortal sin. Perhaps this explains why Jefferson and Madison appear to have thought of an alliance with England not as a product of the union of political wills but as something that resulted from a kind of political immaculate conception. Whereas the benefits of alliance were desired, the act that produced those benefits was not. For that act meant, if it meant anything, that benefits had to be apparent on both sides.

There is no evidence that Jefferson ever seriously considered the prospect of an alliance from this perspective. His strategy was not directed to the end of actually concluding an alliance with Great Britain. Instead, it was one of appearing to be moving in this direction, with the expectation—or hope—that the object of this strategic feint would be persuaded that the appearance foreshadowed the reality. Thus the story of Jefferson's alliance diplomacy during the Louisiana crisis is a story of attempts to pressure the French into yielding by threatening that the United States would ally itself with England against France. On occasion, the French were told that Great Britain was eager to conclude an alliance with this country. None of these threats reflected a discernible reality in the sense that the American government was, in fact, prepared to enter into an alliance or that the English were disposed to offer one. Instead, it was the threat that formed the sole reality of this diplomacy.

There is one apparent exception to this pattern and even it is not quite clear. In April 1803, when the crisis had moved close to its denouement, the President, with the support of a majority of his cabinet, decided that if the French proved intractable in the negotiations then in progress in Paris, [Special Envoy James] Monroe and Livingston should be instructed to enter into discussions with the British government "to fix principles of alliance." The instructions Madison wrote to the two envoys were based, in the main, on the supposition that "Great Britain and France are at peace, and that neither of them intend at present to interrupt it." In this situation, the instructions read, if the French government should either "meditate hostilities" or force the United States to initiate a war by closing the Mississippi, Monroe and Livingston were to communicate with the British government and "invite its concurrence in the war." It was to be made clear to Great Britain that although war depended on the choice of the United States alone, our choice of war in turn depended on Britain undertaking to participate in it. At the same time, Madison emphasized, the certainty of our choice of war "should not be known to Great Britain who might take advantage of the posture of things to press on the United States disagreeable conditions of her entering the war." . . . Monroe and Livingston were to conduct these negotiations with England if France, by denying free navigation of the Mississippi, made war inevitable. If, however, navigation was not disputed but the deposit alone was denied, the envoys were to make no explicit engagement, leaving to Congress the decision between war or further procrastination.

The instructions were addressed to a contingency that had already been excluded by France: closure of the Mississippi to navigation by the United States. The French had earlier undertaken to abide by Spain's obligations to this country once they succeeded to Louisiana. These obligations included the right of navigation and of deposit. In this context, what is significant about the instructions was not so much that they provided for situations that were very unlikely to arise but what they had to say about the nature of the administration's alliance diplomacy. For the alliance Monroe and Livingston were to conclude was an alliance Great Britain could not be expected to make. The instructions simply brushed aside the experience of the preceding year and a half. Although assuming that England was neither at war nor intending to enter upon war, the envoys were nevertheless to conclude an alliance the real value of which to Britain was apparent only if the nation were at war. But if that were to occur—if, the instructions read, war has "actually commenced, or its approach be certain"—the American ministers were to avail themselves of this change of circumstances "for avoiding the necessity of recurring to Great Britain, or, if the necessity cannot be avoided, for fashioning her disposition to arrangements which may be the least inconvenient to the United States." In brief, they were either to make no alliance or to make one that would carry virtually no obligations for the United States.

Even if it is concluded that the alliance diplomacy of the Jefferson administration had no solid basis and that it rested on little more than a kind of incantation, it does not follow that the party to whom it was primarily addressed was unaffected. Whether this diplomacy was "real" or not, the result, after all, was what mattered. Did it impress the French sufficiently to lead them, when taken together with other considerations, to draw back or substantially alter a course they were otherwise intent on taking? . . .

If Jefferson's alliance diplomacy was to affect French behavior, it was desirable—even imperative—that it do so during that critical period when France was moving militarily to occupy Louisiana and to build up the defenses of the colony. In the French plan this was the period when France would be at peace with England. The French calculation was that England would not break the peace over Louisiana. The calculation was sound. The English in entering into peace negotiations with France had deliberately put aside the issue of Louisiana in deference to Paris. That issue could not attract Great Britain into responding to the alliance diplomacy of the United States, and the French appreciated this very well.

It was only if the peace broke down for other reasons that this diplomacy could evoke a British response. Indeed, in the event that peace broke down, the English did not need Jefferson's encouragement to prompt them to strike at France's colonial efforts both at sea and on land. Then this diplomacy would be directed to restraining England's efforts rather than to eliciting them and for fear that otherwise these efforts might pave the way for subsequent claims. It is quite true that when peace visibly began to break down, Napoleon was at pains to see that the United States did not ally itself with Great Britain. The abandonment of Louisiana readily accomplished that. Still, Napoleon did not abandon Louisiana because he was affected by Jefferson's alliance diplomacy, but for quite different reasons. Having once decided to abandon the colony, however, he did so in a manner he considered would best serve his interests. Not the least of those interests was the creation of a power in the New World that might in time provide a serious challenge to the maritime power of England.

The question of Jefferson's alliance diplomacy is closely related to that of the President's use of the threat of war. The prevailing view among historians is that Jefferson was quite willing to use military power in pursuit of his diplomatic aim and that he effectively threatened France with war should it claim New Orleans.

Whether or not this view is well taken depends in no small measure on determining what constitutes a meaningful threat of force. The persuasion that Jefferson was quite willing to use military power is, in part at least, dependent on the fact—or what is so claimed—that he seriously threatened war. Did he?

A serious threat of war has the quality of imminence, if not of immediacy, and is dependent on the occurrence of a specified event. The significance of the temporal element is apparent. The longer the period of time that is entertained, the greater the possibility that changing circumstances may alter the will of the party making the threat. The element of specificity in defining the conditions or circumstances productive of war is also important. The more vague or ambitious the conditions, the more difficult it is for a threat of war to serve as a deterrent (and that, presumably, is its principal purpose). Jefferson's threat of war satisfied neither of these conditions. Indefinite in time and vague in circumstance, his threats to use force were all of a contingent and hypothetical nature, dependent on future developments that were likely to put the French at sufficient disadvantage as to make the prospect of this country resorting to force against them a credible one. But these were not the kinds of threats likely to command Napoleon's respectful attention. He might be deterred by a meaningful threat of force in the here and now. He could not be deterred by a hypothetical threat addressed to circumstances in which he already knew that his empire would be put at risk.

There is one apparent exception to this pattern of Jeffersonian threats and it is to be found in the famous letter of April 18, 1802. Although clearly containing a threat of war, the threat was contingent on an alliance with Great Britain. The letter contrasts markedly with the official instructions Madison wrote at the time to Livingston. In the latter, Livingston was directed to state that "a mere neighborhood could not be friendly to the harmony which both countries have so much an interest in cherishing; but if a possession of the mouth of the Mississippi is to be added to the other causes of discord, the worst events are to be apprehended." These threats of war, contingent and hypothetical though they were, undoubtedly reached the French, for as early as the beginning of 1802, Jefferson had told the French Chargé that a French occupation of New Orleans would lead to a rupture between the United States and France, an alliance between the United States and Great Britain, and, eventually, a war between this country and the occupant of New Orleans.

While Jefferson was voicing this to [French Chargé d'affaires Louis André] Pichon, however, his minister in Paris was assuring the French government that "as long as France conforms to the existing treaties between us and Spain, the government of the United States does not consider herself as having any interest in opposing the exchange." Madison's letter to Livingston of May 1, 1802, represented an abrupt change from the assurances the American minister had been giving the French, and Jefferson's private letter to Livingston amounted to an even more radical shift in policy.

The shift was more apparent than real, however, for it was not otherwise attended by a hardened diplomatic position. On the contrary, having delivered themselves privately and officially of hard-line positions, Jefferson and Madison seemed content to let matters rest. The impression was thereby given of a government that was not to be taken at its word, when that word was bellicose. This impression would have been confirmed had adversaries only been able to read the letter Jefferson wrote

in October 1802 to Livingston. Having told Livingston in April that the closest possible relationship must be formed between this country and England, in October the
President had again seen "all the disadvantageous consequences of taking a side"
between France and Great Britain. While acknowledging that we may yet be forced
into taking sides by a "more disagreeable alternative," in that event, Jefferson insisted, "we must countervail the disadvantages by measures which give us splendor
and power, but not as much happiness as our present system." And after insisting
in the spring of 1802 that war must be the inevitable result of a French occupation
of New Orleans, Jefferson insisted in the fall of that year that "no matter at present
existing between them and us is important enough to risk a break of peace,—peace
being indeed the most important of all things for us, except the preserving an erect
and independent attitude." . . .

It was not the appearance of French forces in New Orleans that formed the *casus
belli* for the administration, but the denial of free navigation of the Mississippi. This
position is apparent in the general instructions March 2, 1803, given Monroe and
Livingston. The American commissioners were to try to buy New Orleans and the
Floridas. They might offer close to ten million dollars for this as well as guaranteeing France commercial privileges. The commissioners, if pressed, might also offer
as an inducement a guarantee of the west bank of the Mississippi. But if France
refused to sell any of its territory under any conditions, the two envoys were to
secure the right of deposit, and hopefully to improve on the old right. Should even
the right of deposit be denied, Monroe and Livingston were to be guided by instructions specially adapted to the case.

The conclusion of Henry Adams that the instructions "offered to admit the French
without condition" is difficult to resist. The same must be said of the instructions
Madison subsequently wrote Monroe and Livingston on April 18. Unaware that
Napoleon had decided to sell Louisiana to the United States, Madison drafted
the April instructions primarily to provide for the eventuality that France "should
be found to meditate hostilities or to have formed projects which will constrain the
United States to resort to hostilities." But war was to be judged inevitable only in the
event that France "should avow or evidence a determination to deny to the United
States the free navigation of the Mississippi." If France should not dispute the right
of navigation and instead only deny deposit, the envoys were advised that "it will be
prudent to adapt your consultations to the possibility that Congress may distinguish
between the two cases, and make a question how far the latter right may call for an
instant resort to arms, or how far procrastination of that remedy may be suggested
and justified by the prospect of a more favorable conjuncture." . . .

At the same time, the administration took certain measures, including limited
preparation, for the possibility of armed conflict. These measures were taken against
the background of a military policy that had reduced the army from an authorized
strength of 5,500 to 3,300 regulars. In his second annual message, on December 15,
1802, Jefferson had declared that no change in the nation's military establishment
was "deemed necessary" and had contented himself with recommending to the Congress a "review" of the militia with the purpose of giving it "those improvements of
which you find it susceptible." Two weeks before, the Secretary of War had ordered
the reenlistment of every valuable soldier whose period of service was expiring, a
step, however, that added nothing to the existing force.

Beginning early in 1803, several measures were taken along the Mississippi frontier to increase the defensive capability of fortified positions there. Of these posts, the largest and most important was Fort Adams, situated on the Mississippi River just above the border with Spain. It was Fort Adams that constituted the principal defensive bulwark against an offensive thrust from New Orleans, just as it was this post that would have provided the base for an assault on New Orleans. In March 1803, Fort Adams had a force of seven companies. In the same month two additional companies were ordered there. Since the companies were in all likelihood under strength, the size of the force at this critical post probably numbered no more than six hundred men. Elsewhere, the distribution of forces both along the southern frontier, where they would face the French, as well as on the northern frontier, where they faced the British, inevitably meant that the army was stretched very thin.

How significant were the various measures taken to improve the readiness of the forces in the western posts and what do they indicate about Jefferson's intentions? Judged by the view that Jefferson himself seemed to have taken of his administration's efforts, they do not appear to have been more than of modest significance. Certainly, they scarcely seem to have been of such character as to have "left nothing to chance" in a showdown with Napoleon's forces. . . .

During the early winter of 1802–3, the expectation persisted that a French force would eventually be sent to New Orleans. There were no plans to contest its arrival by military means. Nor did the American government intimate, let alone declare, that the attempt by France to occupy New Orleans would be regarded by this country as a *casus belli*. It is true that by late winter, American authorities entertained strong doubt that the French would in fact attempt the military occupation of Louisiana. But this doubt was not the result of the preparatory military measures taken by the administration. It arose instead from the repeated failure of the French to mount an expedition because of the continuing demands of the Santo Domingo campaign as well as from the growing realization that war would soon be renewed between France and England. . . .

As late as the spring and early summer of 1802, the prospects for Napoleon's scheme of empire seemed quite bright to its architects. In fact, the stage was already being set for the disaster that would overtake the French by the late summer of that year. Napoleon had badly underestimated the requirements of the campaign on Santo Domingo, as the American Consul on the island had noted before his expulsion. The expedition sent out under [General Charles Victor Emmanuel] Leclerc was not nearly of the size that was needed to ensure against defeat. But to men who held the blacks in contempt, as did Napoleon and Leclerc, the prospect of defeat at their hands was not to be credited. Besides, Leclerc had waged a determined and ruthless campaign, one that by April had left French forces in control of all the principal towns and ports of the island. Although the French had paid a very heavy price in casualties for their successes, this did not appear to detract from what they saw as a victory. . . .

The optimism . . . did not last long. In July [1802], the storm suddenly broke over Leclerc's head. The French commander had been prudent enough not to attempt the immediate implementation of Napoleon's order restoring slavery. But rumors that slavery had been restored on Guadeloupe soon reached Santo Domingo, where they aroused the blacks to a fury that persisted until independence, and freedom, had been achieved. By July, Leclerc's forces were weakened by an outbreak of yellow fever that grew in violence as the summer progressed. By late summer, a badly depleted force was clearly on the defensive. Before Paris could respond to Leclerc's frantic calls for reinforcements, he too had succumbed to yellow fever in November 1802. Only with a new force of ten thousand troops did his successor, [Comte de] Rochambeau, manage to launch a new offensive that kept the French in the field as an effective fighting force.

Even if Jefferson was endowed with an unusual degree of prescience, it is unreasonable to assume that he clearly foresaw the various difficulties that would beset French plans. Certainly the disastrous decision to restore slavery on the island could not have been counted on. Nor was there reason to expect that yellow fever would strike with the intensity that it did. Jefferson might have hoped that the black rebels of Santo Domingo would continue indefinitely to consume French forces until Napoleon abandoned his colonial ambitions in the New World, but he could not prudently *count* on this outcome. Nor did he. As it turned out, the demands imposed by Santo Domingo, formidable though they were, could not preclude Napoleon from sending a force to occupy Louisiana. He might well have done so in the fall of 1802 and very nearly did so in the winter of 1803, only to be blocked from acting by unusual weather. For Jefferson, the expected difficulties on Santo Domingo provided time; but true deliverance from peril, he thought, lay elsewhere.

The central hope of Jefferson's Louisiana diplomacy was that Britain and France would again go to war. Had the French succeeded in occupying New Orleans, a renewed European war, which would have immediately isolated what forces France had deployed in the Western Hemisphere, might have allowed the United States to seize New Orleans at little cost. Or the United States might have acted in concert with Britain. Whether Jefferson would have employed force even under such favorable circumstances remains uncertain; he clearly hoped that the prospect of such an event would induce Napoleon to sell New Orleans to the United States, or at least to return Louisiana to Spain.

As events turned out, Jefferson's best hopes were realized. Napoleon did not succeed in sending an occupation force to New Orleans. By the time the weather permitted the departure of the military expedition, the English had blockaded it. Although still formally at peace with France, it was already apparent to the government in London that the die had been cast for a renewal of the hegemonic struggle. With the imminent renewal of the war, Napoleon had little to lose by getting what he could for Louisiana. Once at war, Louisiana could easily be taken from him by England and he doubtless thought that this loss was more than likely. By selling Louisiana to the United States, he would be able to finance a part of the coming war. Abandoning Louisiana, it is true, meant abandoning his grand plan of empire in the West. But that plan could not survive renewal of the war with England, and Napoleon appreciated this only too well. . . .

[Negotiation] was, indeed, Jefferson's true policy: to conquer without war or, if this proved impossible, to conquer without a costly war. If war was the nemesis that threatened to destroy everything the Republicans had achieved and still hoped to achieve, Jefferson's unwillingness to face squarely the prospect of war with France and to make serious preparations for it was surely understandable. At the same time, his policy involved considerable risk. It did so in the first instance because it was prepared to accept for the time being a French military presence in New Orleans.

Once this force was there, its removal might well have proven to be a difficult task. There was no way of knowing how large this presence might ultimately become. Nor was the size the principal consideration. Instead, it was the commitment itself. Once New Orleans was occupied by French forces, it was reasonable to expect that the nature of the crisis would be transformed. With the military occupation, the French commitment in Louisiana would have deepened.

Second, Jefferson's policy involved risk because it gambled with the sentiments of the western people. The argument that time would work increasingly against the French by virtue of numbers alone necessarily assumed that these numbers could always be counted on to support the American government's cause. This assumption was at odds, though, with the view that the very presence of a foreign power in the Mississippi valley would raise the specter of secession. Earlier, Jefferson himself had given expression to this dread prospect; he had done so in circumstances that were far less ominous than those faced in Louisiana. Moreover, even if in the long run time did work against the French, there might still be an enormous price to pay before the demographic fact worked its inevitable way. And once it had done so, it might still have left a legacy of disunion in its wake.

The purchase of Louisiana has often been regarded as one of the greatest triumphs of American diplomacy. Half of a continent was gained without war. The gauge of Jefferson's success has been measured almost as much in the means as in the end. Foremost among the means, presumably, was a brilliant diplomacy the central feature of which was to play for time. For time, Jefferson quickly sensed, was the great enemy of Napoleon's design. In time, the terrible cost of the ill conceived campaign on Santo Domingo would become apparent to all and would operate to constrain even a Napoleon. In time, the struggle between England and France, implacable adversaries as they were, was bound to be renewed. And in time, the American position in the Mississippi valley could only become stronger. The essence of Jefferson's strategy was to wait for these developments, to play for time until they could work their expected result. In this, historians have generally concluded, Jefferson was right. He used conditioning circumstances to his great advantage, just as he used to his advantage the threat of forming an alliance or of going to war. And this capitalizing on circumstances, it is argued, testified above all to his insight and skill rather than to his good fortune.

The favorable assessment of Jefferson's statecraft has often been further underlined by comparing it with the course of action recommended at the time by Alexander Hamilton. Two options, Hamilton declared, were open to the United States: "First, to negotiate and endeavor to purchase, and if this fails to go to war. Secondly, to seize at once on the Floridas and New-Orleans, and then negociate," a course of action that required an immediate increase in the army and militia as well as the full cooperation and support of Great Britain. For this counsel, the leading Federalist opponent of Jefferson has since been criticized. Hamilton's advice, this criticism runs, would have involved us in a war with both France and Spain, a war for which we were utterly unprepared. In this war, we could not count on the support of Great Britain, then at peace with France. Hamilton was too intelligent not to realize that the course he advocated could result only in disaster. This being the case, critics have concluded, it represented little more than a political maneuver made to embarrass the administration of the day.

Clearly, Hamilton's advice was intended to put the administration in an unfavorable light. Was this advice so manifestly misguided, however, that it does not warrant serious consideration? A positive response can scarcely be supported by pointing out that Hamilton's position rested on the assumption that France would never sell. Whatever his hopes might have been, Jefferson was often as skeptical of the chances for purchase as was Hamilton. But Jefferson stopped well short of accepting the proposition that in the event efforts to purchase failed, the alternative was war. The President did not accept Hamilton's first course. The war that for Jefferson would result from the failure of purchase negotiations was not a war in the here and now, as it undoubtedly was for Hamilton. Instead, it was a war projected into the future and one that was dependent on the fulfillment of certain conditions. The immediate prospect and reality for Jefferson was not war but palliating and enduring until these conditions were met. But this course, to repeat, carried its own risks. It meant allowing a French occupation of New Orleans. And it meant relying on the cooperation and help of the British.

In the circumstances of the winter of 1803, prudence dictated Hamilton's course rather than Jefferson's. The immediate war proposed by Hamilton surely involved considerable risks. The seizure of New Orleans and the Floridas would likely have resulted in naval hostilities with France and Spain, hostilities for which the country was unprepared. Nor could the United States count on the help of England; short of war between France and England, such assistance was always uncertain. At the same time, the risks entailed by Hamilton's course did not include a French military force in New Orleans, a risk that Jefferson's course could not avoid taking. Moreover, Hamilton might well have calculated, in February 1803, that Great Britain and France were bound to go to war in the reasonably near future. If this calculation is not seen as unjustified in assessing Jefferson's diplomacy, there is no apparent basis for deeming it unjustified in considering Hamilton's proposal.

At the same time, these differences between Jefferson and Hamilton reflected a deeper and more significant difference separating the two men. Hamilton's proposal stemmed from an outlook which assumed that time might work against us, that we could not entrust our fortunes to the contingencies of circumstance, and that we had to resolve immediately to take our fate into our own hands as far as this was at all possible. By contrast, Jefferson's diplomacy reflected an outlook which assumed that time was on our side, that something would turn up to favor our fortunes, and that far more harm than good would result from an impatience to bring matters to a head. The difference, of course, was one of temperament. Yet it was also one that reflected sharply different attitudes toward force and the justification for its use.

Patience, Deft Diplomacy, and Continental Empire

JOSEPH J. ELLIS

The story of the Louisiana Purchase has as many twists and turns as the Mississippi itself, and the biggest challenge in retelling it is to avoid getting caught in the diplomatic backwaters, where clerks chatter endlessly about minutiae. But just as sure as the Gulf of Mexico is the final destination of the Mississippi, the story of the Purchase flows inevitably toward a providential sense of American destiny as a continental empire, what Jefferson, with unintentional irony, called "an empire of liberty." . . .

At least on the face of it, this triumphal tone seems wholly justified. For $15 million—the rough equivalent of $260 million today—the United States doubled its size, adding what is now the American mid-west to the national domain, all the land from the Mississippi to the Rocky Mountains and the Canadian border to the Gulf of Mexico. At less than 4 cents an acre, the Purchase became the most lucrative real estate transaction in American history, easily besting the purchase of Manhattan for $24. Without quite knowing it, the United States had acquired the most fertile tract of land of its size on the planet, making it self-sufficient in food in the nineteenth century and the agrarian superpower in the twentieth. . . .

Spain remained the only European power blocking American expansion to the Pacific, and Spain was not so much a threatening power as a convenient presence, in effect a holding company awaiting an American takeover at the appropriate time. Although the term "manifest destiny" had not yet been coined, the Purchase made the idea itself another one of those self-evident Jeffersonian truths. A colossal and fully continental American empire was now almost inevitable. If the Mississippi ends at New Orleans and the Gulf of Mexico, the story of the Purchase (at least its triumphal version) ends at the Pacific. . . .

Unfortunately, the various versions of the story have all been driven by the simplistic urge to assign credit to one person or another. Most of Jefferson's biographers describe his management of the diplomacy as a tour de force, on a par with his inspirational role as author of the magic words of the Declaration of Independence. Other historians claim that Napoleon was the major player, that he, rather impetuously, "threw the province" at Jefferson and the American negotiators, that they "caught it and held it, and share between them equally—whatever credit there was." Alexander Hamilton, not one disposed to acknowledge Jefferson's brilliance, insisted that the story of the Purchase was really a tale about dumb luck. "Every man possessed of the least candor and reflection," observed Hamilton, "will readily acknowledge that the acquisition has been solely owing to the fortuitous concurrence of unforeseen and unexpected circumstances, and not to any wise or vigorous measures on the part of the American government."

Though blatantly partisan, Hamilton's assessment does have the virtue of its anti-Jefferson prejudices, for it calls attention to the multiple ingredients in the diplomatic equation beyond any single player's control. In that sense the Louisiana Purchase was like the perfect storm in which European clouds, Caribbean winds, and North America's prevailing westerlies converged in one place at one time. Jefferson's genius was to seize that time, to recognize that acquiring an empire required an imperial president. Given the peaceful way the Purchase occurred, it might be more accurate to think of it as the perfect calm, and of Jefferson's greatest diplomatic talent as the patience to stand still while history formed around him. . . .

Although Jefferson never traveled further west than the Natural Bridge in the Shenandoah Valley, he shared with most Virginians, including Washington, the keen sense that Europe was the past and the American west was the future. The portico at Monticello faced west, just as the piazza at Mount Vernon faced the Potomac, which both men misguidedly believed to be the providentially placed water route over the Alleghenies into the interior, linking with the Ohio and then flowing into the Mississippi Valley. (The Mississippi, of course, was the mother lode, as Madison once put it, "the Hudson, the Delaware, the Potomac, and all the navigable rivers of the Atlantic states, formed into one stream.") This early version of "Potomac fever" proved to be a hallucination—providence had somehow failed to provide a navigable water route from the Atlantic coast to the interior—but this inconvenient fact did little to deflect the westward flow of Jefferson's thinking, which, as it turned out, was even more grandiose than Washington's.

A few months after he took office, Jefferson shared his vision with James Monroe, then serving as governor of Virginia: "It is impossible not to look forward to distant times," Jefferson observed, "when our rapid multiplication will . . . cover the whole northern, if not the southern continent with a people speaking the same language, governed in similar forms, and by similar laws; nor can we contemplate with satisfaction either blot or mixture on that surface." By "blot or mixture" Jefferson did not mean Native Americans, who could be assimilated if only they abandoned their tribal mores for the more confined space required by farming. (If they refused to do so, well, that was their choice, for which they must suffer the tragic consequences.) The prospective blots were the blacks, who could not be assimilated and must be shipped back to Africa or to some location in the West Indies, where, in Jefferson's view, "nature seems to have formed these islands, to become the receptacle of the blacks transplanted into this hemisphere." It seems safe to say, then, that Jefferson's pre-Purchase view of the American west was breathtakingly bold, presumptively imperialistic, and thoroughly racist.

This Jeffersonian vision depended upon two crucial assumptions. At the time of his election, the census of 1800 revealed a total population of slightly more than five million, with about 500,000 residing west of the Alleghenies. Jefferson assumed that the western population would steadily swell and move the frontier gradually but inexorably forward to the Mississippi and beyond. Unlike Washington, he did not believe that this wave of settlers could or should be managed by the federal government. It was like a force of nature that must be allowed its own momentum. The lands to the west did not need to be conquered by armies, but rather occupied by settlers. In that sense, it was demography that made American destiny so manifest. The only role for government was to stay out of the way and allow the wave to roll westward.

The second assumption was that the only European power with a substantial presence on the North American continent would be Spain. A map of the Spanish Empire in the Western Hemisphere in 1800 made Spain's colonial empire appear gigantic, including Florida, the Gulf Coast, and all the land west of the Mississippi to the Pacific, not to mention Mexico and much of South America. But the map was deceptive in its grandeur because Spain was a hollowed-out imperial power, in decline since the defeat of the Spanish Armada in 1588.

By 1800 the treasury in Madrid was empty, the Spanish army and navy were harmless pretenders, and the once proud diplomatic corps was adept only at posturing. "Spain is the most proper European nation," observed one American diplomat, "to possess a great empire with insignificance." Jefferson concurred: "We consider her possession of the adjacent country as the most favorable to our interests," he remarked, "and should see with extreme pain any other nation substituted for them." His only fear was that the Spanish Empire was so weak that it would abandon its American colonies "before our population can be sufficiently advanced to gain it from them piece by piece." Spain was like an elderly mother hen, sitting the nest until the Americans arrived to relieve her.

Jefferson's continental calculus was confounded by a message he received from Secretary of State Madison only three weeks after the inauguration. The American ambassador to Great Britain, Rufus King, reported reliable rumors circulating in London that Spain had signed a secret treaty, ceding fully half of her North American colonies to France. If true, this transformed the entire strategic chemistry in North America by replacing the most feeble European nation with what had become under Napoleon the most potent military power on earth. For several months Jefferson monitored reports from Europe, most of which tended to confirm that Napoleon fully intended to reestablish the French Empire in America. Jefferson could only hope they were untrue. "I am willing to hope," Jefferson sighed, "as long as anybody will hope with me."

By the spring of 1803, all such hoping had become a sentimental extravagance, since the secret treaty ceding Louisiana to France had become the worst-kept secret in Europe. (Talleyrand, true to his duty and his reputation for duplicity, denied all the rumors as outrageous fabrications.) By April of 1803 Jefferson had decided that the time for hoping had ended and the time for action had begun.

Pushing the quite capable Madison aside, Jefferson chose to become his own secretary of state. "I cannot forbear recurring to it personally," he explained to Robert Livingston, the American minister in Paris, "so deep is the impression it makes on my mind." For the simple truth was that the French occupation of Louisiana would be an unmitigated calamity for the United States, constituting the greatest threat to American destiny since the Revolutionary War: "It completely reverses all the political relations of the United States and will form a new epoch in our political course. . . . There is on the globe one single spot, the possessor of which is our natural and habitual enemy. It is New Orleans." Spanish control of New Orleans was not threatening, since—Spain being Spain—the outcome of a conflict was certain. But French possession was another matter altogether. "From that moment," wrote Jefferson, "we must marry ourselves to the British fleet and nation."

This was an extraordinary statement coming from Jefferson, whose entire career as minister to France, secretary of state, and leader of the Republican opposition to the Jay Treaty had consistently favored France over Great Britain as America's most reliable European ally. But he was prepared to reverse himself once France became a threatening presence on the North American continent and a formidable challenge to America's demographic destiny.

Jefferson then made an extremely shrewd observation. On the face of it, a war with France was a suicidal venture, given the enormous discrepancy in military and economic resources. But all such assessments were irrelevant and misleading, "for however greater her force is than ours, compared in the abstract, it is nothing compared to ours, when to be exerted on our own soil." If Napoleon attempted to establish a French Empire in America by force of arms, he would encounter the same dilemma as the British in the War for Independence, marching hither and yon among a hostile population over a space even more immense. Livingston was instructed to apprise the French that if they attempted to occupy the Louisiana Territory, they would suffer the same fate as the British, for space and numbers were both on the American side. . . .

Jefferson practiced what has come to be called "back-channel diplomacy" by soliciting the assistance of a prominent French aristocrat, Pierre Samuel Du Pont de Nemours, to carry Livingston's instructions back to Paris and then to quietly disseminate within the corridors of power the same threatening message conveyed to Livingston. "If France proceeds to possess New Orleans," Jefferson told Du Pont, "we must marry ourselves to the British fleet and nation." Though this had the clear ring of an ultimatum, Jefferson wanted Du Pont—and eventually Napoleon—to know that he regarded war with France as a last resort. "You know how much I value peace," he explained, "and how unwillingly I should see any event take place that would render war a necessary recourse."

Jefferson was utterly sincere on this score, since war, even a successful war, would completely destroy his domestic agenda of debt reduction and minimalist government. And an alliance with Great Britain would contradict every foreign policy principle he had ever championed. (It did not help that he regarded the entire British nation as the epicenter for global tyranny.) Indeed, it is entirely possible that Jefferson's war threat was actually a bold bluff. (We can never know, because Napoleon never called it.) The preferred alternative for both sides, Jefferson informed Du Pont and Livingston, was a diplomatic resolution of the crisis. The United States was prepared to offer $6 million for the purchase of New Orleans and West Florida (the Gulf Coast from modern-day Pensacola to New Orleans). If Napoleon accepted this offer, the United States was, albeit reluctantly, prepared to accept French possession of the entire Louisiana Territory west of the Mississippi.

This was a huge concession. It is likely, though not certain, that Jefferson regarded any French presence in Louisiana as temporary. Once the advancing wave of American population reached the Mississippi, or, as Jefferson put it, "once we have planted such a population on the Mississippi as will be able to do their own business," the French position would become untenable because the Americans could mobilize an overwhelming force "without the necessity of marching men from the shores of the Atlantic 1500 or 2000 miles hither." Again, space, and more specifically space that was "peopled," was a unique and incalculable strategic advantage that Jefferson was prepared to exploit. But such scenarios all lay in the future. For now, the immediate crisis required a peaceful resolution. It was now in the hands of our man in Paris, Robert Livingston.

When Livingston presented his credentials to the French court, he was asked if he had ever been to Europe. He responded that he had not, and Napoleon purportedly said, "You have come to a very corrupt world." As a five-year veteran of the Parisian court scene, Jefferson worried that Livingston would come off as the innocent American, lost within the intrigues of the French salon set and the sinister plottings of the inscrutable Talleyrand. . . .

[He] need not have worried. It was true that Livingston was no confidence man in the European diplomatic mode, but he was a man of supreme confidence who could more than hold his own in sessions with Talleyrand, who found him strangely immune to duplicity, the kind of animal who could not be trapped because he always kept himself out of range. . . .

Livingston's first achievement was to confirm that the rumors were in fact true, that Spain had signed a secret treaty ceding the Louisiana Territory to France in return for several duchies in northern Italy, including Parma and Tuscany. (The more precise term is "retrocede," since France had once claimed the territory and even named it after the French king.) Talleyrand was the mastermind of the deal, which envisioned the recovery of the French Empire in North America, a place where French debtors, criminals, and derelicts could be shipped, much like Great Britain subsequently regarded Australia, and a permanent barrier, what Talleyrand called "a wall of brass," to block American expansion or any British effort at reestablishing a dominant presence on the American continent. Finally, Louisiana would become the granary or breadbasket for the highly lucrative French colonies in the Caribbean, chiefly Santo Domingo and Guadeloupe.

It was a vision of Gallic grandeur in the Western Hemisphere appropriately Napoleonic in scope. But in order for the vision to be realized, Livingston reported, the French plan for its implementation needed to work like clockwork. The first ingredient in the plan, maintaining secrecy about the treaty, had already proven impossible. The second ingredient called for the dispatch of a massive French expeditionary force of over 25,000 troops to Santo Domingo, where they would crush the ongoing slave insurrection under the charismatic ex-slave Toussaint L'Ouverture and restore slavery to the island. Then, the third ingredient: the French troops would sail to New Orleans, garrison the city, occupy the west bank of the Mississippi, and present the Americans with a military fait accompli before they had time to mobilize. The man entrusted with the command of the expeditionary force was Charles Leclerc, one of France's ablest officers, who also happened to be Napoleon's brother-in-law. All this Livingston reported in code to Madison and Jefferson two months before Leclerc departed France.

One might think that, upon hearing such news, Jefferson would have called for a substantial increase in the American army and a mobilization of the state militias. But he did neither. In fact, his budget requests for 1803 called for a *reduction* in the size of the army. He was prepared to run a high-stakes gamble against the odds that the French troops would get mired down in Santo Domingo and never make it to New Orleans. "What has been called a surrender of Toussaint to Leclerc," he predicted," I suspect will in reality be a surrender of Leclerc to Toussaint." This proved to be an extraordinarily shrewd wager, but at the time it appeared to resemble a dangerous brand of wishful thinking.

In the messy way that history happens, the congested diplomatic situation became even more complicated when a midlevel Spanish functionary in New Orleans declared the port closed to all American shipping. When news of this unexpected and startling development reached Washington in January of 1803, it produced a firestorm of protests against Jefferson's aversion to military action. Senator James Ross of Pennsylvania demanded a call-up of fifty thousand militia, who would then march upon and seize New Orleans. Even Jefferson's Republican supporters, not to be outdone, urged the raising of eighty thousand troops and then to "hold them in readiness to march at a moment's warning." Hamilton argued that there were two options: "Negociate and endeavor to purchase, and if this fails, go to war, or to seize at once on the Floridas and New Orleans, and then negociate." The latter option, he believed, was demonstrably preferable, but required energy and decisiveness, and "for this, alas, Jefferson is not destined."

Still regarding war as a last resort, hopeful that the French troops in Santo Domingo would never reach Louisiana, and convinced that Madrid would soon overrule the decision to close the port of New Orleans to American commerce, Jefferson refused to move. But he did budge. He announced the decision to send James Monroe as his special emissary to join Livingston in Paris. Monroe, who was a former ambassador to France, would be given complete discretionary power to negotiate the purchase of New Orleans and the Floridas. This did not satisfy the saber rattlers in Congress, but it did answer critics who charged the president with the equivalence of criminal negligence in his response to events thus far. . . .

If he failed to make headway in Paris, Monroe was to proceed across the Channel to London and negotiate an alliance with Great Britain. And those instructions should be leaked to the French press in order to enhance his diplomatic leverage with Talleyrand and Napoleon.

Meanwhile, back in Paris, Livingston was busy doing some leaking of his own. He distributed a memorandum to midlevel diplomats designed to expose the ludicrous lie that no secret treaty with Spain existed. He also revealed that France's scheme to recover its North American empire was common knowledge throughout the capitals of Europe. Livingston then raised questions about the feasibility of the French plan, suggesting that it would drive the United States into the arms of Great Britain, that Louisiana would prove indefensible in the next round of the Napoleonic Wars, and instead of a strategic asset would turn out to be an economic and military albatross. Livingston's leaks received reinforcement when the French press reported the extremely bellicose debates in the United States Senate—Livingston might have leaked these too—indicating that any putative French garrison in New Orleans would be confronted with a massive American military response.

This was deft diplomacy of the highest order, but for the moment it made no difference because, as Livingston explained, Talleyrand remained obstinately wedded to the fiction that there was no secret treaty with Spain, so there was really nothing to negotiate. . . .

Because the entire plan for reestablishing France's presence in the Western Hemisphere depended upon Leclerc's success in restoring French control over Santo Domingo, Napoleon assured that Leclerc's expedition enjoyed massive military superiority—a first wave of 25,000 troops, to be followed by a second wave of the same size if necessary. Leclerc's instructions were also brutally explicit. Upon landing his force, he should proclaim his support for Toussaint L'Ouverture and the black insurrectionaries, who had managed to seize control of the island and declare their own emancipation under the banner of "Liberty, Equality, Fraternity." Once securely ensconced and once Toussaint was convinced that Leclerc was an ally, Leclerc should unleash a war of annihilation. A thousand bloodhounds from Jamaica would be provided to hunt down every black rebel, who should be hanged, drowned, decapitated, burned alive over coals, or, for ultimate dramatic effect, crammed in the backside with gunpowder and exploded. Then the infamous Code Noir, institutionalizing all these barbarities, should be restored and the entire black population returned to slavery. When this rather gory mission was accomplished—Napoleon estimated it would take six weeks—Leclerc should transport his troops to New Orleans, where he would soon be reinforced sufficiently to stave off all challenges to the French Empire in America.

The first part of the scheme worked pretty much as planned. Toussaint and the rebel leaders allowed Leclerc's force to land without opposition, though there were divisions in the rebel camp about the wisdom of this act of trust. Toussaint paid the ultimate price for trusting Leclerc, captured at a supposedly secure meeting, then shipped off to a dungeon on the Swiss border, where he died from starvation and exposure within the year. Before departing Santo Domingo, Toussaint warned Leclerc that his capture would make no appreciable difference in the outcome, because the French had no idea what they were up against.

Events soon proved Toussaint's point. Once the black population of Santo Domingo realized that Napoleon's plan called for their reenslavement, Leclerc's mission became impossible. It was a matter of numbers. The black population, two-thirds of African birth and all former slaves, totaled 500,000. (There were another 30,000 mulattoes and 30,000 whites.) This meant that Leclerc's army, even at its high point of nearly 40,000 troops, was outnumbered more than ten to one. Leclerc could not believe it when hundreds of black prisoners strangled themselves to death rather than return to slavery. Women and children laughed at their executioners as they burned to death. Meanwhile, Leclerc's army was virtually annihilated by a combination of black reprisals, yellow fever, and malaria. . . .

As the earthly embodiment of the all-or-nothing style, Napoleon immediately recognized that the debacle in Santo Domingo changed everything. In April of 1803 he apprised Talleyrand of his intention to sell the entire Louisiana Territory: "I renounce Louisiana," he declared. "It is not only New Orleans that I will cede, it is the whole colony without any reservation. I know the price of what I abandon. . . . I renounce it with the greatest regret. But to attempt obstinately to retain it would be folly." When warned by his advisors that his decision was likely to establish the foundation for a rising American empire, Napoleon dismissed the warning as too farsighted: "In two or three centuries the Americans may be found too powerful for Europe . . . but my foresight does not embrace such remote fears." His immediate problem was gearing up for war with the current colossus, Great Britain. . . .

The big decision had been made, and the only question that remained, best left to the diplomatic accountants, was how much money could be extracted from the Americans. Napoleon indicated that he would be satisfied with 50 million livres, or $12.5 million.

Livingston was the only American in Paris who could make the big decision for the United States. Monroe had just landed in France, carrying full diplomatic authority, but it would take him several days to reach Paris, so Livingston decided to act on his own before Napoleon changed his mind. "The field open to us is infinitely larger than our instructions contemplated," he wrote to Madison, but the opportunity "must not be missed." Although the ultimate cost was sure to be much larger than he was authorized to spend, Livingston presumed that the sale of western land would yield revenues that more than made up the difference. He had to either exceed his instructions or allow the opportunity to pass. By the time Monroe arrived in Paris, Livingston had already committed the United States. All that remained was haggling over the price. On May 5, 1803, both sides agreed to the sale of the entire Louisiana Territory for 80 million francs, or $15 million. Napoleon got more than he expected and the Americans got an unexpected empire. Word of the Purchase reached Washington on July 3, 1803, so the celebration the following day coincided with the anniversary of American independence, thereby enhancing the prevalent sense of destiny in the air.

🌐 F U R T H E R   R E A D I N G

Stephen Ambrose, *Undaunted Courage* (1996) (on Meriwether Lewis)

Joyce Appleby, *Thomas Jefferson* (2003)

Lance Banning, *The Jeffersonian Persuasion* (1978)

Madison Smartt Bell, *Toussaint Louverture* (2007)

Albert H. Bowman, "Pichon, the United States, and Louisiana," *Diplomatic History* 1 (1977): 257–270

Frank W. Brecher, *Negotiating the Louisiana Purchase* (2006) (on Robert Livingston)

Noble E. Cunningham Jr., *In Pursuit of Reason: The Life of Thomas Jefferson* (1987)

George Dangerfield, *Chancellor Robert R. Livingston of New York, 1746–1813* (1960)

Alexander DeConde, *This Affair of Louisiana* (1976)

Laurent DuBois, *Avengers of the New World* (2004) (on Haiti)

Joseph J. Ellis, *American Sphinx* (1997) (on Jefferson)

Robert B. Holtman, ed., *Napoleon and America* (1988)

Robert M. Johnstone Jr., *Jefferson and the Presidency* (1978)

Lawrence S. Kaplan, *"Entangling Alliances with None": American Foreign Policy in the Age of Jefferson* (1987)

———, *Thomas Jefferson: Westward the Course of Empire* (1998)

Jon Kukla, *A Wilderness So Immense* (2003)

James W. Lewis, *The American Union and the Problem of Neighborhood* (1998)

Drew R. McCoy, *The Elusive Republic* (1980)

Forrest McDonald, *The Presidency of Thomas Jefferson* (1976)

Dumas Malone, *Jefferson the President* (1970)

Robert J. Miller, *Native America, Discovered and Conquered* (2006)

Peter S. Onuf, *Jefferson's Empire* (2000)

——— and Leonard J. Sadosky, *Jeffersonian America* (2001)

Bradford Perkins, *The Creation of a Republican Empire, 1776–1865* (1993)

Merrill D. Peterson, *Thomas Jefferson and the New Nation* (1970)

Norman K. Risjord, *Thomas Jefferson* (1994)

Malcolm J. Rohrbough, *The Trans-Appalachian Frontier* (1978)

Thomas P. Slaughter, *Exploring Lewis and Clark* (2003)

James R. Sofka, "The Jeffersonian Idea of National Security," *Diplomatic History* 21 (1997): 519–544

Paul A. Varg, *Foreign Policies of the Founding Fathers* (1970)

Marvin R. Zahniser, *Uncertain Friendship* (1975)

C H A P T E R
5

The War of 1812

🌐

In 1803, Europe exploded in war. As Britain and France battled furiously, the United States again became ensnarled in Europe's troubles. Through the Napoleonic Decree of November 1806, France declared the Continental System, designed to close Europe to British products and to force neutrals to cease trading with Britain. In response, Britain issued a series of Orders in Council, first on November 11, 1807, intended to blockade France and curb neutral commerce with Napoleon's nation. Trampling on neutral rights in these ways, both European powers seriously hampered U.S. foreign trade. Similarly insulting to the United States was the British practice of impressment: boarding American ships to seize sailors who had allegedly deserted from the Royal Navy. Americans also charged that British agents were stirring up Indian resistance to American settlers in the Northwest Territory. In fact, the Shawnee chieftain Tecumseh, who passionately struggled to preserve Indian lands, had sounded out the British regarding an alliance in order to contain U.S. expansionism.

Presidents Thomas Jefferson and James Madison retaliated against the European powers by launching their own commercial warfare, initiating restrictive measures to persuade the belligerents to respect U.S. neutrality and commerce. But nothing quieted the tempest; instead, the crosscurrents of decrees, orders, acts, and agreements emanating from both sides of the Atlantic only exacerbated the international rivalries. In the end, unable to sustain peace, the United States chose war—a war, some have suggested, that ranks as the second war for independence.

Why did the United States go to war in 1812? Historians debate several factors, including the defense of American national honor in the face of impressment and violations of neutral rights, injury to U.S. commerce and consequent fears of economic depression, removal of the Indians from the advancing white frontier, hunger for land and for conquest (especially of Canada), politics (Republicans' eagerness to strengthen their power), and the deeply felt need of Americans to revitalize and unify themselves during a time of wrenching domestic transformation and foreign threat. Other questions have likewise provoked differing scholarly perspectives: Did the United States, for example, wait too long to claim its rights and defend itself against humiliating assaults on its sovereignty? Was the War of 1812 a necessary war? Could it have been avoided? Were national leaders—Jefferson, Madison, and others—up to the task? Did they foolishly cling to a policy of commercial coercion that failed? Did policymakers have alternatives? Finally, what were the consequences of the War of 1812?

DOCUMENTS

In late June 1807, the British warship *Leopard* fired on, boarded, and seized sailors from the U.S. warship *Chesapeake*. In Document 1, a July 6 letter from Secretary of State James Madison to fellow Virginian and diplomat James Monroe, the future president expresses American outrage toward Britain. Responding to the Napoleonic Decree of 1806 and the British Orders in Council the following year, both of which disrupted neutral trade, the United States issued the Embargo Act of December 1807 (Document 2), by which it hoped to protect American vessels from capture, avoid disputes over neutral rights that might lead to war, and persuade belligerents to back down by denying them the benefits of American commerce. In a speech on January 19, 1809, Document 3, Federalist member of Congress from Massachusetts Josiah Quincy tries to calm calls for war by pointing out the United States's vulnerability to attack and questioning the assumption that Americans could seize Canada. Document 4, the Non-Intercourse Act of March 1, 1809, replaced the Embargo Act and freed American ships to trade with all other nations except Britain and France and promised renewed trade with either belligerent once neutral rights received appropriate respect.

As the Atlantic crisis escalated, Indian relations along the frontier also worsened. In a speech to Indiana's territorial governor, William Henry Harrison, on August 20, 1810, reprinted here as Document 5, the Shawnee chieftain Tecumseh denounces the U.S. government's practice of negotiating fraudulent land cessions and warns that he will seek British assistance in resisting further encroachment on Indian lands. The Shawnee leader, who with his brother "The Prophet" called for the revival of traditional Indian culture and Indian federation against white expansion, aligned with the British in the ensuing war and was killed in October 1813 at the Battle of the Thames. "War hawk" Henry Clay, a Republican member of Congress from Kentucky, delivered a thumping anti-British speech on December 31, 1811, Document 6. On June 1 of the following year, President Madison asked Congress to deliberate on the question of war. His message, Document 7, lists America's grievances. Document 8 is former President Thomas Jefferson's prediction, made in a private letter of August 4, 1812, that the United States would easily conquer Canada.

DOCUMENT 1

Secretary of State Madison Protests British Impressment of Americans from the *Chesapeake,* 1807

The documents herewith inclosed . . . explain the hostile attack with the insulting pretext for it, lately committed near the Capes of Virga. [Virginia] by the British ship of war the Leopard on the American frigate the Chesapeake. [One] is a copy of the Proclamation issued by the President interdicting [*sic*], in consequence of that outrage, the use of our waters and every other accommodation, to all British armed ships.

This enormity is not a subject for discussion. The immunity of a National ship of war from every species and purpose of search on the high seas, has never been contested by any nation. G. B. would be second to none in resenting such a violation of her rights, & such an insult to her flag. . . .

But the present case is marked by circumstances which give it a peculiar die. The seamen taken from the Chesapeake had been ascertained to be native Citizens of the U. States; and this fact was made known to the bearer of the demand, and doubtless,

---

This document can be found in the U.S. Department of State Records, National Archives, Washington, D.C. It can also be found in Gaillard Hunt, ed., *The Writings of James Madison* (New York: G. P. Putnam's Sons, 1908), VII, 454–455, 456, 458.

communicated by him to his commander previous to the commencement of the attack. It is a fact also, affirmed by two of the men with every appearance of truth that they had been impressed from American vessels into the British frigate from which they escaped, and by the third, that having been impressed from a British Merchant ship, he had accepted the recruiting bounty under that duress, and with a view to alleviate his situation, till he could escape to his own Country. Add that the attack was made during a period of negociation, & in the midst of friendly assurances from the B. Governmt.

The printed papers herewith sent will enable you to judge of the spirit which has been roused by the occasion. It pervades the whole community, is abolishing the distinctions of party, and regarding only the indignity offered to the sovereignty & flag of the nation, and the blood of Citizens so wantonly and wickedly shed, demands in the loudest tone, an honorable reparation.

With this demand you are charged by the President. The tenor of his proclamation will be your guide in reminding the British Govt. of the uniform proofs given by the U. S. of their disposition to maintain faithfully every friendly relation . . . till at length no alternative is left but a voluntary satisfaction on the part of G. B. or a resort to means depending on the United States alone. . . .

The exclusion of all armed ships whatever from our waters is in fact so much required by the vexations and dangers to our peace experienced from their visits, that the President makes it a special part of the charge to you, to avoid laying the U. S. under any species of restraint from adopting that remedy. Being extended to all Belligerent nations, none of them could of right complain; and with the less reason, as the policy of *all* nations has limited the admission of foreign ships of war into their ports, to such numbers as being inferior to the naval force of the Country, could be readily made to respect its authority & laws. . . .

The President has an evident right to expect from the British Govt. not only an ample reparation to the U. S. in this case, but that it will be decided without difficulty or delay. Should this expectation fail, and above all, should reparation be refused, it will be incumbent on you to take the proper measures for hastening home according to the degree of urgency, all American vessels remaining in British ports; using for the purpose the mode least likely to awaken the attention of the British Government. Where there may be no ground to distrust the prudence or the fidelity of Consuls, they will probably be found the fittest vehikles for your intimations. It will be particularly requisite to communicate to our public ships in the Mediterranean the state of appearances if it be such as ought to influence their movements.

All negociation with the British Govt on other subjects will of course be suspended untill satisfaction on this be so pledged & arranged as to render negociation honorable.

DOCUMENT 2

The Embargo Act Forbids U.S. Exports, 1807

Be it enacted by the Senate and House of Representatives of the United States of Amer-ica in Congress assembled, That an embargo be, and hereby is laid on all ships and vessels in the ports and places within the limits or jurisdiction of the United States,

This document can be found in *Public Statutes at Large of the United States* (Boston: Little, Brown, and Company, 1861), II, 451–453.

cleared or not cleared, bound to any foreign port or place; and that no clearance be furnished to any ship or vessel bound to such foreign port or place, except vessels under the immediate direction of the President of the United States: and that the President be authorized to give such instructions to the officers of the revenue, and of the navy and revenue cutters of the United States, as shall appear best adapted for carrying the same into full effect: *Provided*, that nothing herein contained shall be construed to prevent the departure of any foreign ship or vessel, either in ballast, or with the goods, wares and merchandise on board of such foreign ship or vessel, when notified of this act.

Sec. 2.   And be it further enacted, That during the continuance of this act, no registered, or sea letter vessel, having on board goods, wares and merchandise, shall be allowed to depart from one port of the United States to any other within the same, unless the master, owner, consignee or factor of such vessel shall first give bond, with one or more sureties to the collector of the district from which she is bound to depart, in a sum of double the value of the vessel and cargo, that the said goods, wares, or merchandise shall be relanded in some port of the United States, dangers of the seas excepted, which bond, and also a certificate from the collector where the same may be relanded, shall by the collector respectively be transmitted to the Secretary of the Treasury. All armed vessels possessing public commissions from any foreign power, are not to be considered as liable to the embargo laid by this act.

DOCUMENT 3

Massachusetts Federalist Josiah Quincy Denounces Calls for War, 1809

Again, sir, you talk of going to war against Great Britain, with, I believe, only one frigate, and five sloops of war, in commission! And yet you have not the resolution to meet the expense of the paltry, little navy, which is rotting in the Potomac. Already we have heard it rung on this floor, that if we fit out that little navy our Treasury will be emptied. If you had ever a serious intention of going to war, would you have frittered down the resources of this nation, in the manner we witness? You go to war, with all the revenue to be derived from commerce annihilated; and possessing no other resource than loans or direct or other internal taxes? You! a party that rose into power by declaiming against direct taxes and loans? . . . The general resources of our country are as well known in Europe as they are here. But we are about to raise an army of fifty thousand volunteers. For what purpose? I have heard gentlemen say "we can invade Canada." But, sir, does not all the world, as well as you, know that Great Britain holds, as it were, a pledge for Canada? And one sufficient to induce you to refrain from such a project, when you begin seriously to weigh all the consequences of such invasion? I mean that pledge which results from the defenceless state of your seaport towns. For what purpose would you attack Canada? For territory? No. You have enough of that. Do you want citizen refugees? No. You would be willing to dispense with them. Do you want plunder? This is the only hope an invasion of Canada can offer you. And is it not very doubtful whether she could not,

This document can be found in *Annals of the Congress of the United States,* 12th Congress, 1st Session (Washington, D.C.: Gales and Seaton, 1853), 1114.

in one month, destroy more property on your seaboard, than you can acquire by the most successful invasion of that Province? Sir, in this state of things, I cannot hear such perpetual outcries about war, without declaring my opinion concerning them.

DOCUMENT 4

The Non-Intercourse Act
Replaces the Embargo Act, 1809

Sec. 3.   That from and after the twentieth day of May next, the entrance of the harbors and waters of the United States and the territories thereof be, and the same is hereby interdicted to all ships or vessels sailing under the flag of Great Britain or France, or owned in whole or in part by any citizen or subject of either. . . . And if any ship or vessel sailing under the flag of Great Britain or France . . . [should] arrive either with or without cargo, within the limits of the United States or the territories thereof, such ship or vessel, together with the cargo, if any, which may be found on board, shall be forfeited, and may be seized and condemned in any court of the United States or the territories thereof. . . .

Sec. 11.   That the President of the United States be, and he hereby is authorized, in case either France or Great Britain shall so revoke or modify her edicts, as that they shall cease to violate the neutral commerce of the United States, to declare the same by proclamation; after which the trade of the United States, suspended by this act, and by the [embargo] . . . may be renewed with the nation so doing.

DOCUMENT 5

Shawnee Chief Tecumseh Condemns U.S.
Land Grabs and Plays the British Card, 1810

Since the peace [the Treaty of Fort Wayne, 1809] was made you have kill'd some of the Shawanese, Winebagoes Delawares and Miamies and you have taken our lands from us and I do not see how we can remain at peace with you if you continue to do so. You have given goods to the Kickapoos for the sale of their lands to you which has been the cause of many deaths amongst them. You have promised us assistance but I do not see that you have given us any.

You try to force the red people to do some injury. It is you that is pushing them on to do mischief. You endeavor to make destructions, you wish to prevent the Indians to do as we wish them to unite and let them consider their land as the common property of the whole you take tribes aside and advise them not to come into this measure and until our design is accomplished we do not wish to accept of your invitation to go and visit the President.

Document 4 can be found in *Public Statutes at Large of the United States* (Boston: Little, Brown, and Company, 1861), II, 528–533.

Document 5 can be found in Logan Esarey, ed., *Messages and Letters of William Henry Harrison* (Indianapolis: Indiana Historical Commission, 1922), VII, 463–469. It can also be found in David R. Wrone and Russell S. Nelson, *Who's the Savage: A Documentary History of the Native North American* (Greenwich: Fawcett Publishers, 1973), 218–221.

The reason I tell you this is—You want by your distinctions of Indian tribes in allotting to each a particular track of land to make them to war with each other. You never see an Indian come and endeavor to make the white people do so. You are continually driving the red people when at last you will drive them into the great lake where they can't either stand or work. . . .

This land that was sold and the goods that was given for it was only done by a few. . . . If you continue to purchase of them [land from the chiefs] it will produce war among the different tribes and at last I do not know what will be the consequence to the white people. . . .

We shall have a great council at which all the tribes shall be present when we will show to those who sold that they had no right to sell the claim they set up and we will know what will be done with those chiefs that did sell the land to you. I am not alone in this determination it is the determination of all the warriors and red people that listen to me.

I now wish you to listen to me. If you do not it will appear as if you wished me to kill all the chiefs that sold you this land. I tell you so because I am authorized by all the tribes to do so. I am at the head of them all. I am a Warrior and all the Warriors will meet together in two or three moons from this. Then I will call for those chiefs that sold you the land and shall know what to do with them. If you do not restore the land you will have a hand in killing them. . . .

I wish you would take pity on all the red people and do what I have requested. If you will not give up the land and do cross the boundary of your present settlement it will be very hard and produce great troubles among us. How can we have confidence in the white people when Jesus Christ came upon the earth you kill'd and nail'd him on a cross, you thought he was dead but you were mistaken. . . .

Everything I have said to you is the truth the great spirit has inspired me and I speak nothing but the truth to you. In two moons we shall assemble at the Huron Village (addressing himself to the Weas and Pottawatomies) where the great belts of all the tribes are kept and there settle our differences.

I hope you will confess that you ought not to have listened to those bad birds who bring you bad news. I have declared myself freely to you and if you want any explanation from our Town send a man who can speak to us.

If you think proper to give us any presents and we can be convinced that they are given through friendship alone we will accept them. As we intend to hold our council at the Huron village that is near the British we may probably make them a visit. Should they offer us any presents of goods we will not take them but should they offer us powder and the tomahawk we will take the powder and refuse the Tomahawk.

🌐 *D O C U M E N T   6*

Kentucky Republican Henry Clay Articulates U.S. Grievances Against Britain, 1811

What are we to gain by war, has been emphatically asked? In reply, he would ask, what are we not to lose by peace?—commerce, character, a nation's best treasure, honor! If pecuniary considerations alone are to govern, there is sufficient motive for

This document can be found in *Annals of the Congress of the United States,* 12th Congress, 1st Session (Washington, D.C.: Gales and Seaton, 1853), 599–602.

the war. Our revenue is reduced, by the operation of the belligerent edicts, to about six million of dollars, according to the Secretary of the Treasury's report. The year preceding the embargo, it was sixteen. . . .

He had no disposition to swell, or dwell upon the catalogue of injuries from England. He could not, however, overlook the impressment of our seamen; an aggression upon which he never reflected without feelings of indignation, which would not allow him appropriate language to describe its enormity. Not content with seizing upon all our property, which falls within her rapacious grasp, the personal rights of our countrymen—rights which forever ought to be sacred, are trampled upon and violated. The Orders in Council were pretended to have been reluctantly adopted as a measure of retaliation. The French decrees, their alleged basis, are revoked. England resorts to the expedient of denying the fact of the revocation, and Sir William Scott, in the celebrated case of the Fox and others, suspends judgment that proof may be adduced of it. And, at the moment when the British Ministry through that judge, is thus affecting to controvert that fact, and to place the release of our property upon its establishment, instructions are prepared for Mr. [Augustus John] Foster [British minister] to meet at Washington the very revocation which they were contesting. And how does he meet it? By fulfilling the engagement solemnly made to rescind the orders? No, sir, but by demanding that we shall secure the introduction into the Continent of British manufactures. England is said to be fighting for the world, and shall we, it is asked, attempt to weaken her exertions? If, indeed, the aim of the French Emperor be universal dominion (and he was willing to allow it to the argument), what a noble cause is presented to British valor. But, how is her philanthropic purpose to be achieved? By scrupulous observance of the rights of others; by respecting that code of public law, which she professes to vindicate, and by abstaining from self-aggrandizement. Then would she command the sympathies of the world. What are we required to do by those who would engage our feelings and wishes in her behalf? To bear the actual cuffs of her arrogance, that we may escape a chimerical French subjugation! We are invited, conjured to drink the potion of British poison actually presented to our lips, that we may avoid the imperial dose prepared by perturbed imaginations. We are called upon to submit to debasement, dishonor, and disgrace—to bow the neck to royal insolence, as a course of preparation for manly resistance to Gallic invasion! What nation, what individual was ever taught, in the schools of ignominious submission, the patriotic lessons of freedom and independence? Let those who contend for this humiliating doctrine, read its refutation in the history of the very man against whose insatiable thirst of dominion we are warned. . . .

He contended that the real cause of British aggression, was not to distress an enemy but to destroy a rival. A comparative view of our commerce with England and the continent, would satisfy any one of the truth of this remark. . . . It is apparent that this trade, the balance of which was in favor, not of France, but of the United States, was not of very vital consequence to the enemy of England. Would she, therefore, for the sole purpose of depriving her adversary of this commerce, relinquish her valuable trade with this country, exhibiting the essential balance in her favor—nay, more; hazard the peace of the country? No, sir, you must look for an explanation of her conduct in the jealousies of a rival. She sickens at your prosperity, and beholds in your growth—your sails spread on every ocean, and your numerous seamen—the foundations of a Power which, at no very distant day, is to make her tremble for naval superiority.

DOCUMENT 7

President Madison Urges Congress to Declare War on Great Britain, 1812

Without going back beyond the renewal in 1803 of the war in which Great Britain is engaged, and omitting unrepaired wrongs of inferior magnitude, the conduct of her Government presents a series of acts hostile to the United States as an independent and neutral nation.

British cruisers have been in the continued practice of violating the American flag on the great highway of nations, and of seizing and carrying off persons sailing under it, not in the exercise of a belligerent right founded on the law of nations against an enemy, but of a municipal prerogative over British subjects. British jurisdiction is thus extended to neutral vessels in a situation where no laws can operate but the law of nations and the laws of the country to which the vessels belong. . . .

The practice, hence, is so far from affecting British subjects alone that, under the pretext of searching for these, thousands of American citizens, under the safeguard of public law and of their national flag, have been torn from their country and from everything dear to them; have been dragged on board ships of war of a foreign nation and exposed, under the severities of their discipline, to be exiled to the most distant and deadly climes, to risk their lives in the battles of their oppressors, and to be the melancholy instruments of taking away those of their own brethren. . . .

British cruisers have been in the practice also of violating the rights and the peace of our coasts. They hover over and harass our entering and departing commerce. To the most insulting pretensions they have added the most lawless proceedings in our very harbors, and have wantonly spilt American blood within the sanctuary of our territorial jurisdiction. The principles and rules enforced by that nation, when a neutral nation, against armed vessels of belligerents hovering near her coasts and disturbing her commerce are well known. When called on, nevertheless, by the United States to punish the greater offenses committed by her own vessels, her Government has bestowed on their commanders additional marks of honor and confidence.

Under pretended blockades, without the presence of an adequate force and sometimes without the practicability of applying one, our commerce has been plundered in every sea. . . .

Not content with these occasional expedients for laying waste our neutral trade, the cabinet of Britain resorted at length to the sweeping system of blockades, under the name of orders in council, which has been molded and managed as might best suit its political views, its commercial jealousies, or the avidity of British cruisers.

To our remonstrances against the complicated and transcendent injustice of this innovation the first reply was that the orders were reluctantly adopted by Great Britain as a necessary retaliation on decrees of her enemy proclaiming a general blockade of the British Isles at a time when the naval force of that enemy dared not issue from his own ports. . . .

This document can be found in the Annals of the Congress of the United States, 12th Congress, 1st session (Washington, D.C.: Gales and Seaton, 1853). 1714–1719. It can also be found in Gaillard Hunt, ed., *The Writings of James Madison* (New York: G. P. Putnam's Sons, 1908), VII, 454–455, 456, 458.

Abandoning still more all respect for the neutral rights of the United States and for its own consistency, the British Government now demands as prerequisites to a repeal of its orders as they relate to the United States that a formality should be observed in the repeal of the French decrees nowise necessary to their termination nor exemplified by British usage, and that the French repeal, besides including that portion of the decrees which operates within a territorial jurisdiction, as well as that which operates on the high seas, against the commerce of the United States should not be a single and special repeal in relation to the United States, but should be extended to whatever other neutral nations unconnected with them may be affected by those decrees. . . .

Anxious to make every experiment short of the last resort of injured nations, the United States have withheld from Great Britain, under successive modifications, the benefits of a free intercourse with their market, the loss of which could not but outweigh the profits accruing from her restrictions of our commerce with other nations. And to entitle these experiments to the more favorable consideration they were so framed as to enable her to place her adversary under the exclusive operation of them. To these appeals her Government has been equally inflexible, as if willing to make sacrifices of every sort rather than yield to the claims of justice or renounce the errors of a false pride. Nay, so far were the attempts carried to overcome the attachment of the British cabinet to its unjust edicts that it received every encouragement within the competency of the executive branch of our Government to expect that a repeal of them would be followed by a war between the United States and France, unless the French edicts should also be repealed. Even this communication, although silencing forever the plea of a disposition in the United States to acquiesce in those edicts originally the sole plea for them, received no attention. . . .

In reviewing the conduct of Great Britain toward the United States our attention is necessarily drawn to the warfare just renewed by the savages on one of our extensive frontiers—a warfare which is known to spare neither age nor sex and to be distinguished by features peculiarly shocking to humanity. It is difficult to account for the activity and combinations which have for some time been developing themselves among tribes in constant intercourse with British traders and garrisons without connecting their hostility with that influence and without recollecting the authenticated examples of such interpositions heretofore furnished by the officers and agents of that Government.

Such is the spectacle of injuries and indignities which have been heaped on our country, and such the crisis which its unexampled forbearance and conciliatory efforts have not been able to avert. . . .

Whether the United States shall continue passive under these progressive usurpations and these accumulating wrongs, or, opposing force to force in defense of their national rights, shall commit a just cause into the hands of the Almighty Disposer of Events, avoiding all connections which might entangle it in the contest or views of other powers, and preserving a constant readiness to concur in an honorable reestablishment of peace and friendship, is a solemn question which the Constitution wisely confides to the legislative department of the Government. In recommending it to their early deliberations I am happy in the assurance that the decision will be worthy the enlightened and patriotic councils of a virtuous, a free, and a powerful nation.

Having presented this view of the relations of the United States with Great Britain and of the solemn alternative growing out of them, I proceed to remark that the communications last made to Congress on the subject of our relations with France will have shewn that since the revocation of her decrees, as they violated the neutral rights of the United States, her Government has authorized illegal captures by its privateers and public ships, and that other outrages have been practiced on our vessels and our citizens. It will have been seen also that no indemnity had been provided or satisfactorily pledged for the extensive spoliations committed under the violent and retrospective orders of the French Government against the property of our citizens seized within the jurisdiction of France. I abstain at this time from recommending to the consideration of Congress definitive measures with respect to that nation, in the expectation that the result of unclosed discussions between our minister plenipotentiary at Paris and the French Government will speedily enable Congress to decide with greater advantage on the course due to the rights, the interests, and the honor of our country.

🌎 D O C U M E N T   8

Former President Jefferson Predicts the Easy Conquest of Canada, 1812

I see, as you do, the difficulties and defects we have to encounter in war, and should expect disasters if we had an enemy on land capable of inflicting them. But the weakness of our enemy there will make our first errors innocent, and the seeds of genius which nature sows with even hand through every age and country, and which need only soil and season to germinate, will develop themselves among our military men. Some of them will become prominent, and seconded by the native energy of our citizens, will soon, I hope, to our force add the benefits of skill. The acquisition of Canada this year, as far as the neighborhood of Quebec, will be a mere matter of marching, and will give us experience for the attack of Halifax the next, and the final expulsion of England from the American continent. Halifax once taken, every cockboat of hers must return to England for repairs. Their fleet will annihilate our public force on the water, but our privateers will eat out the vitals of their commerce. Perhaps they will burn New York or Boston. If they do, we must burn the city of London, not by expensive fleets or congreve rockets, but by employing an hundred or two Jack-the-painters, whom nakedness, famine, desperation and hardened vice, will abundantly furnish from among themselves. We have a rumor now afloat that the orders of council are repealed. The thing is impossible after [Foreign Secretary] Castlereagh's late declaration in Parliament, and the re-construction of a [Spencer] Percival ministry.

I consider this last circumstance fortunate for us. The repeal of the orders of council would only add recruits to our minority, and enable them the more to embarrass our march to thorough redress of our past wrongs, and permanent security for the future. This we shall attain if no internal obstacles are raised up. The exclusion of their commerce from the United States, and the closing of the Baltic against it,

---

This document can be found in H. A. Washington, *The Writings of Thomas Jefferson* (Washington, D.C.: Taylor & Maury, 1854), VI, 75–76.

which the present campaign in Europe will effect, will accomplish the catastrophe already so far advanced on them.

ESSAYS

In the opening essay, Garry Wills of Northwestern University roundly critiques the Republican policy of commercial coercion, initiated on Secretary of State James Madison's advice during the Jefferson presidency and stubbornly pursued through the outbreak of war in 1812. Wills argues that Madison was naive to believe that commercial pressure would coerce Great Britain to halt the impressment of U.S. sailors and that the fourth president became easy prey for both British and French diplomats, who "suckered" him into believing they would honor America's neutral rights. At the same time, Madison failed to restrain U.S. militia attacks on western Indian tribes, which ultimately sought refuge and alignment with the British. As tensions with the British and Indians grew, Madison manipulated a reluctant Congress to support war. The president also undertook an ill-fated gambit of seizing Canada in the hope of denying its products to the British empire—one last futile effort at commercial warfare to force a settling of all of America's grievances.

The second essay, Walter L. Hixson of the University of Akron attributes the public's enthusiasm for the war to the American psyche—people's hopes and fears. Identifying cultural anxieties generated by the young nation's shift to a market economy and the growth of southern slavery during the early nineteenth century, Hixson finds that a divided nation undertook a war as a way to affirm the nation's manliness; revive its sagging, revolutionary patriotism; and revitalize its republican character. The "patriotic war," according to Hixson, ultimately accelerated the trend toward liberal capitalism, spawned an enlarged defense establishment, and reaffirmed a national identity—or an imagined "Myth of America"—that rallied ordinary citizens behind a foreign policy of forceful, Anglo-Saxon expansionism.

Economic Coercion and the Conquest of Canada: Madison's Failed Diplomacy

GARRY WILLS

The superpowers of the day, France and England, were . . . locked in the death grip of the Napoleonic wars. The foreign ministers the United States had to deal with—men like Talleyrand in France, Canning and Castlereagh in England, Godoy in Spain—were playing for high stakes in Europe, and the devious Napoleon was manipulating them all. The United States was a marginal player, sometimes no more than a distraction, in this showdown—though [James] Madison thought it was the key to the whole situation. Only the government that allied itself with America, he believed, could hope to prevail. As early as 1793 he had dreamed of solving the world's problems by using American commerce as a weapon of peaceful coercion: "In this attitude of things, what a noble stroke would be an embargo? It would probably do as much good as harm at home, and would force peace on the rest of the

---

world, and perhaps liberty along with it." It was a dream he would labor to make real as secretary of state. . . .

So [President Thomas] Jefferson proposed a Madisonian embargo. Congress passed the bill [the Embargo Act of December 1807]. Some legislators thought it was a way of buying time to come up with other measures, meanwhile keeping our ships at home to avoid danger. Some thought it was itself a preparation for war ([Treasury Secretary Albert] Gallatin hoped it was). Many did not believe Jefferson meant to maintain it indefinitely (it would go on for fifteen months). Defiance of it began immediately and escalated, as did Jefferson's determination to support it with force. The exports of America were barely a fifth in 1808 of what they had been in 1807. The depression this caused led to outright defiance of the law, which Jefferson grimly mobilized troops to enforce. He called on the regular army, on inspectors, on informers to wage war on smugglers. . . .

Madison was still saying that Congress must "make the Embargo proof against the frauds which have evaded it, which can be done with an effect little apprehended abroad"—that is, Congress could become even more draconian in punishment, without alerting other nations to the degree of resistance being mounted. But in fact the French and British already knew how unpopular the embargo was at home—they learned this not only from their representatives in America, but from smugglers who succeeded in evading the patrols and took their products abroad. Foreign governments professed satisfaction that the policy was hurting America more than it did them. John Armstrong, United States minister to France, wrote of the embargo, "Here it is not felt, and in England . . . it is forgotten."

Finally, Congress could take no more. Against the urgings of Madison, it voted to end the embargo. As a kind of gratuitous insult to Jefferson, the date of its expiration was set for the day he would be leaving office. [Congress replaced the Embargo Act with the Non-Intercourse Act in March 1809.] . . .

It seemed for a time that Madison would be blessed, early in his first term, with the kind of fortunate break that Jefferson enjoyed with the Louisiana Purchase. Shortly after his inauguration in March 1809, the British representative in Washington, David Erskine, reported that his government was ready to lift the Orders in Council that denied America neutral trading rights with other countries and their colonies. On April 19, the president used an authority given him by Congress to lift the nonintercourse act with whichever country, England or France, first removed its own trade barriers against the United States. Though the proclamation was not to take effect until June 10 (to allow time for promulgating its new trade terms over the ocean and back), six hundred ships left American shores during that interval, confident of free entry by June.

Even Madison's Federalist enemies, along with dissidents in his own party, now vied with each other to praise him. The wisdom of the embargo was retrospectively vindicated. England had been forced to truckle and Madison rubbed in his victory, telling Erskine that the captain of the British ship that had fired with insufficient warning on the USS *Chesapeake* should be handled "with what is due from His Britannic Majesty to his own honor"—a suggestion that the king had been dishonorable to that point. . . .

While the nation was rejoicing at this vindication of neutral trading rights, Madison, following Jefferson's example, left Washington for a summer break at his own plantation. While he was there, news began to trickle in from British newspapers that England was *not* lifting its Orders in Council. Erskine had exceeded his instructions, omitting three conditions for England's repeal of the Orders, including a continued right of the British to intercept and board American ships. Erskine was instantly recalled in disgrace, and it was announced that Francis James Jackson, a man notorious for war crimes, was being sent to replace him. The national euphoria over the end of conflict with England gave way to anger, disbelief, a desire to punish England, and a sense that Madison had been gulled.

How had the misunderstanding arisen? As [the historian Robert] Rutland puts it, "Madison heard what he wanted to hear." Not for the last time, Madison leaped at what he thought *should* be true before he could verify that it was true. He had predicted all along that England could not stand up to commercial pressure from America. [British foreign secretary George] Canning's instructions to Erskine tried to excuse British interception of American ships bound for France by saying that this was merely executing Americans' own laws, since Congress had forbidden ships to trade with France in response to Napoleon's Berlin decree against neutrals. Canning's supposed "concession" was a denial of American sovereignty over its own ships, and Madison had taken it as a matter for future discussion, not a hard condition for suspending the Orders in Council. Erskine let the misinterpretation stand, in his eagerness to strike an agreement.

It was mere wishful thinking for Madison, like Jefferson before him, to think that the British would give up the right to intercept American ships and to press back into service runaway British sailors. The 1806 treaty that James Monroe had negotiated in London was rejected by President Jefferson because it did not require an end to impressments at sea. But Monroe had good reasons for giving up on that condition. The British navy could not survive if it let its seamen escape to American ships, where they were better paid and flogged less often. The Napoleonic struggle had made control of the sea both difficult and necessary for England. Their press gangs at home had already forced British citizens by the thousands into service. . . .

In the search of American ships for British deserters, some ex-seamen who had become American citizens were taken. In fact, Americans with accents reflecting immigration were taken, too. The United States government was naturally angered by this; but it refused to take steps that would have prevented it. American ships could have refused to hire British subjects. The government could have issued certificates allowing employment only to American seamen. British deserters could have been quarantined in ports. But American merchants did not want any of these steps taken. They depended too heavily on British seamen. When Gallatin surveyed the overseas commercial trade in 1807, he found that roughly nine thousand British seamen were engaged in it—over a third of the overseas crews working under the American flag. Excluding these workers "would materially injure our navigation." Madison, as secretary of state, passed on these findings to President Jefferson, with a covering comment: "I fear that the number of British seamen may prove to be rather beyond our first estimate." Jefferson responded by calling off any efforts to check the employment of non-Americans: "Mr. Gallatin's estimate of the number of foreign seamen in our employ renders it prudent I think to suspend all propositions respecting our non-employment of them . . . our best course is to let the negotiation take a friendly nap."

The merchants whose vessels were being stopped preferred that invasion of their rights to the drying up of their work pool. But so long as the United States made no concessions on this employment of deserters, it was idle to suppose that England would give up seagoing impressments . . . yet Madison for years maintained the naive belief that the English, under pressure, would rather give up impressment (that is, give up their fleet) than give up American trade. . . .

With the failure of the great British breakthrough, Madison was back where he began—or, rather, he was worse off than before. The embargo had failed. The non-intercourse provision that followed had not only failed, but was about to expire. What could be substituted for it, if anything? What would Congress let the president try next? Gallatin, without much hope for his own new proposal, had Nathaniel Macon, as chairman of the proper committee, submit a plan to the House of Representatives on December 19, 1809. It would exclude British and French ships, but not British or French goods carried by other vessels. It was an attempt to keep some revenue from duties while maintaining the opposition to violators of our neutrality. The House and Senate took some things from Macon's bill, added some things to it, and then rejected it on March 16, 1810, just after the end of Madison's first year in office. It was time to start all over again.

Macon submitted another bill as chairman, which became known as Macon's Bill Number 2, though he was neither the author nor a supporter of it. This turned the old nonintercourse logic upside down. The former said that trade was banned with the great powers' ships until one or other power recognized America's neutral rights, upon which trade would be *resumed* with it. Macon Number 2 said that trade would be resumed with both until one recognized neutrality, upon which it would be *withdrawn* from the other. This was a weird form of reverse blackmail, saying in effect, "We will be nice to you both until one is nice in return, upon which we will turn nasty toward the other."

Though the bill was called "miserable feeble puff" at the time, it gave rise to more wishful thinking on Madison's part. His hopes for accord with England had been based on his belief that England could not do without American commerce. His hope for accord with France was that Napoleon wanted America as an ally against England, a role that Madison was willing to play if that could be done without actually going to war with England. His expectations were unrealistic on both grounds—that Napoleon needed our alliance, and that he would purchase it without obliging us to join with him in war. The mere willingness to entertain offers from Napoleon was an affront to the British, who had an ideology resembling America's in the Cold War. England felt that it was defending the free world against the international tyranny of Bonapartism, their equivalent of Bolshevism. Anyone who was not with them in that struggle was against them; and small nations could be pushed around on the way to getting at the real enemy. Madison's mistake was to take each British shove as proving that America was the main enemy, not merely a little obstacle in the way. . . .

Napoleon responded to Macon Number 2 on August 2, 1810. He promised to repeal his former bans on neutral trade (the Berlin and Milan decrees) on November 1, so long as America had imposed nonintercourse with England by then. He made this assurance in a letter issued by his foreign secretary, the Duc de Cadore. When this was delivered to our minister in France, John Armstrong, there had been no discussion of what other measures besides the Berlin and Milan decrees might be observed by

Napoleon. He had in fact issued the Decree of Rambouillet in March, which absorbed Holland and authorized the confiscation of American and other ships in all the harbors of his empire. He had no intention of reversing this policy. The mention of Berlin and Milan was a ruse to trap America into conflict with England. And it worked. Thanks to the provincialism and naivete that had been relatively harmless in his prior roles, Madison had been suckered again. . . . By the time Madison discovered that Napoleon was not observing the terms of Macon Number 2, the bill had done its work. A momentum toward war with England had been accelerated, and would become irreversible, even after England (unlike France) *did* meet the terms of Macon Number 2. . . .

The prospects for war were strengthened by news from the West, of a clash with Indians manufactured by the governor of the Indiana Territory, William Henry Harrison, who was disturbed by the organizing genius of a Shawnee religious leader, the Prophet, and his warrior brother, Tecumseh. Harrison had negotiated eight Indian treaties for Jefferson, and the Shawnee brothers were uniting people to prevent any further bargaining away of their lands. (They were thought to have murdered some chiefs who signed the treaties.) Like most western governors, Harrison had trouble calling up, organizing, and paying the Indiana militia. He wanted regular troops, and Madison's weak secretary of war, William Eustis, gave him some, ordering that they be used only for defensive purposes. But it was easy for Harrison to take any clash with Indians as an attack calling for a "defensive" counteroffensive. That is what he did while Tecumseh was away in the South organizing the Creek tribes. Harrison took the opportunity to march his troops to Prophetstown on the Tippecanoe River. He camped near the town on November 7, 1811, and left his camp without early morning lookouts, though that is the time when Indians often attacked. They did so in this case, inflicting and taking heavy casualties. The Indians withdrew when they ran out of ammunition, and Harrison marched into Prophetstown, which had been abandoned overnight. The Prophet had escaped.

Harrison, under criticism from his own men, rushed a self-serving announcement of victory to Washington, and Madison reported it as such on December 18, saying it had brought peace to the frontier. Actually, it brought greater worries—the Prophet and Tecumseh were still active—and more demand for troops from other uneasy governors. When reports began to reach Washington contradicting Harrison's account, Secretary Eustis told Madison it would be bad for military morale to investigate them—though Madison showed his distrust of Harrison in later dealings with him. The legend of Tippecanoe lived on unchallenged, and became a basis for Harrison's successful presidential campaign in 1840.

On November 5, shortly before news of Tippecanoe reached Washington, Madison sent to Congress the message he and Monroe had conceived at [the president's Virginia plantation] Montpelier, one that Gallatin tried to soften. It said that British actions "have the character as well as the effect of war" and, in conveying "my deep sense of the crisis in which you are assembled," expressed confidence that "Congress will feel the duty of putting the United States into an armor and attitude demanded by the crisis and corresponding with the national spirit and expectations." As a follow-up he had the secretary of war ask that ten thousand regular troops be raised. It has often been thought that Madison had war thrust upon him by a Congress controlled by "war hawks" from the West. But Congress was hesitant and doubtful, unwilling to vote for the taxes that would make war preparation a reality. It made some war moves that were actually meant to evade the issue. . . .

Some have thought that Madison shilly-shallied his way into war, dragged by others, stalled by doubts. Rutland claims he was little more than a leaf riding the surface of a torrent. . . . But Madison created some of the pressures that worked on the public and himself. His readiness, for instance, to seize on the unconfirmed evidence of French cooperation came from his determination to have a showdown with England, to work out his commercial strategy to its logical conclusion. . . .

In fact, the maneuvering toward war gave Madison an opportunity to use his old collaborative methods, working with a more public partner. Here his partner was Monroe—and, at one remove, Henry Clay [of Kentucky], who was working Congress up to a declaration of war. A good example of Madison's indirect approach was the way he timed the release of dispatches from England, selected for their intransigence, to create indignation in Congress. . . .

Another means Madison used to ratchet up the war spirit was a new embargo, planned by Madison, Monroe, and Clay, and presented to Congress on March 11 [and passed later that month]. . . .

That such background maneuverings were necessary to heat Congress toward a declaration of war became clear when Madison finally asked for that declaration, on June 1 (just before everyone's summer departure from the fetid city). Though the House, under Clay's leadership, quickly passed the declaration (seventy-eight to forty-five), it was a close-run matter in the Senate, which took two weeks of secret session to pass the measure by a vote of eighteen to thirteen. The vote in both houses was purely partisan, no Federalist voting for the war, several Clintonian Republicans [followers of New Yorkers George and DeWitt Clinton] voting against it. Madison gave five reasons for going to war with England: 1) impressment, 2) blockades preventing safe departure from the American coast, 3) blockades preventing safe arrival at other shores, 4) confiscation of neutral trade at sea, and 5) the incitement of Indian hostility in the Northwest. The four maritime violations were not new, and were overlapping as he listed them. The Indian hostility was caused more from American expansion than British instigation (the Indians fled to the British from campaigns like that at Tippecanoe), but this grievance had to be listed, in order to bring Henry Clay's western constituents into the effort. Madison, far from being pushed into war by a bellicose Congress, had to drag his own hesitant party into it, past the determined obstruction of the Federalists. What had made Madison, the former pacifist, become a "war hawk"? One thing—Canada.

[The historian] J. C. A. Stagg has shown how important Canada was in Madison's own war thinking. All through the 1790s, Madison had downplayed the commercial importance of Canada. To advance and defend his plan for the embargo, he had to say that the bulk of England's trade from North America could come only from the United States. Canada's exports were insufficient to make up for an American embargo. When the embargo was canceled, however, Madison performed one of those drastic reversals that mark his career. All of a sudden, Canada became vital to British survival. The United States could now subdue England by taking over Canada and denying *its* products to the empire. This switch was partly based on some real changes in the world situation. Napoleon had cut off much of England's supplies from Europe, so it did depend more on Canada for certain goods, especially for the vast amounts of timber the British fleet required. Madison could not know—though he might have allowed for the possibility—that this situation would be rapidly altered, as it was in 1812, right after Madison went to war, when Napoleon met repulse in both Russia and Spain, and England's old markets were opening up to them again.

But ideology had more to do with Madison's analysis than did the course of events. He found in the new assessment of Canada a way to maintain his idée fixe of three decades, that England could be tamed by commercial pressure. Now the pressure would come after a conquest of Canada—but that initial easy victory would actually *prevent* full-scale war. Britain, feeling helpless without Canadian timber, would finally grant America its rights as a neutral nation. He had changed his estimate of Canada to avoid changing his basic concept. As Stagg puts it, "Madison's decision to wage war for Canada was not basically inconsistent with the diplomacy of peaceful commercial restriction he had advocated prior to 1812."

The initial war aim, therefore, was to conquer Canada in 1812, before England could reinforce its troops or deploy the fleet to assist them. That schedule had two even closer deadlines built into it—enough progress should have been made by November to assure Madison's re-election, and enough of Canada should be in American hands by December to allow setting up defensible winter quarters there. As a minimum, Montreal should be taken, so the winter pause could be devoted to assembling resources for taking Quebec. As it turned out, no part of Canada was taken in 1812. Rather, Canada conquered the Michigan Territory. The United States had rushed into a war without military staff organization, supply depots, or a credit system worked out for dealing with military contractors. William Eustis, the secretary of war, spent much of his time looking at catalogues for supplying shoes and uniforms. . . .

Why did America go to war? And why with England rather than with France? French seizures of American shipping were not as common as English harassment, but they were, in principle, the same violations of sovereignty. But Americans had never been the subjects of France. There was special humiliation in any submission exacted by a former master. The new war promised to conclude the unfinished business of the Revolution. Impressment, exclusion from markets, smugglers' ties with Canada, Indian ties with British agents in the West—all these made some chafe as if they were still under the thumb of King George. But none of this would have justified the war unless an easy target seemed to offer itself. England's military force was deeply engaged in the war with Napoleon, which left its western remnant of empire exposed. Canada, it was thought, could be seized before England had the time or spare men and ships to rush aid to it. Once taken, it could be used as a bargaining chip for settling all American grievances, to be restored under terms if at all.

The Patriotic War

WALTER L. HIXSON

Westward expansion powerfully affirmed national perceptions of providential destiny and manly empire, but the European powers remained contemptuous of the new republic. As the Napoleonic wars roiled the waters of the Atlantic, menacing trade and freedom of the seas in the process, neutral rights won little respect from France and even less from Great Britain, which for years had boarded U.S. vessels at will,

---

Hixson, Walter L., "The Patriotic War," from *The Myth of American Diplomacy: National Identity and U.S. Foreign Policy* (New Haven: Yale University Press, 2008), pp. 48–52. Reprinted by permission of Yale University Press.

hanged alleged deserters, and impressed seamen into the British navy. When the British *Leopard* assaulted the *Chesapeake* just twelve miles off the Norfolk coast in 1807, righteous anger erupted.

The ongoing campaign of humiliation directly impinged on manliness and national honor. As patriotic indignation reached feverish levels, [President Thomas] Jefferson remained reluctant to choose war and its attendant risks, costs, and accumulation of centralized state power. Desperate for a solution, Jefferson implemented the Embargo (1807), cutting off trade with the European powers, presumably to instruct them on their dependence on the U.S. market, long a republican panacea. The initiative proved disastrous, as the Embargo crippled shipping and commerce, especially in New England, and heightened rather than quelled popular anxiety. In the West, where an influential new constituency arose in the expanding white republic, Henry Clay of Kentucky and other War Hawks decried the "shameful degradation" to which the decadent European powers subjected the new nation. Men who had "tamed the frontier" through violent conquest over Indians and nature would not back down against any external foe.

A pervasive discourse of manliness demanded a violent response against the English bully, known as John Bull. In an era in which men still satisfied affairs of honor through the *code duello*, the nation, too, could maintain its masculine dignity only by responding to the challenge. "Americans of the present day will prove to the enemy and to the World," South Carolina's John C. Calhoun declared, "that we have not only inherited the liberty which our fathers gave us, but also the will and power to maintain it."

Arriving with some reluctance at the same conclusion, James Madison, Jefferson's successor, decided that an address to Congress outlining Great Britain's affronts to neutral rights represented the appropriate protocol to seek a declaration of war. Madison ignited a seventeen-day debate that culminated, despite widespread opposition from the New England Federalists hurt most by the Embargo, in an affirmative vote of 79–49 in the House but only 19–13 in the Senate. Much as Jefferson had feared, the decision for war proved reckless, premature, and very nearly disastrous. Unbeknownst to Washington, London withdrew the orders-in-council that targeted U.S. shipping on the eve of the conflict. As John Quincy Adams later wrote of the war, "Its principal cause and justification was removed at precisely the moment when it occurred."

Although the central government had been strengthened under the Constitution, the nation went to war stunningly ill-prepared: it possessed an inadequate army, appropriated woefully insufficient federal funding, confronted an angry enemy aided by revanchist Indian allies, and faced strident internal opposition from the Federalists. The nation thus went "tail foremost" into a war that quickly became an "exercise in frustration, ineptness, and survival." The United States suffered a series of defeats, including another ill-conceived imperial thrust into Canada, which once again rejected the bayonet-point invitation, as it did during the Revolutionary War, to join the empire of liberty. With Napoleon's abdication in April 1814 and Britain assured of victory in Europe, the United States suffered humiliation that summer when British forces conducted a punitive expedition into Washington, sacked the city, and burned the presidential mansion, forcing James and Dolly Madison to flee into the countryside with a portrait of George Washington and a few other priceless possessions.

Exhausted from the Napoleonic wars and as usual preoccupied with wider domestic and imperial concerns, Britain settled for a peace accord with the United States. On January 8, 1815, before word of the Peace of Ghent reached U.S. shores, the Tennessee militia leader Andrew Jackson obliterated British invaders in the battle of New Orleans. U.S. forces had rallied to record battlefield successes on Lake Erie, the River Thames, at Plattsburg, and Baltimore, none of which could compare, however, with New Orleans, in which Britain paid for a foolhardy assault against entrenched positions with seven hundred dead and some two thousand additional casualties to twenty-one for the United States. The ringing victory invigorated manly national identity, giving rise to an "era of good feelings" and to the irrepressible political phenomenon of Jackson himself.

Underrated in its significance and innocuously labeled in historical discourse as the War of 1812, the second conflict with Britain is best understood as a patriotic war whose primary significance was an emotional reaffirmation of national identity. Calling the conflict the Second War for Independence offers little clarity insofar as the ultimate existence of the nation had never really been in doubt. The term *Patriotic War* underscores the essence of the conflict, which reflected the *domestic* drives inherent in national identity.

Like many subsequent conflicts fought ostensibly over foreign policy, state violence responded to internal psychic anxieties. The Patriotic War offered relief from a wrenching domestic transition while creating cultural space for the reaffirmation of national identity. The war had been reactionary, in a pure sense of the word, as it served to revive the flagging emotions of Revolutionary era patriotism. The culminating triumph in New Orleans created in Jackson the first national military hero since the venerable Washington. The war powerfully stimulated the imagined community, offering a usable past of a culminating ringing victory that overshadowed the lack of preparedness, myriad defeats, and the war's relative international insignificance as a sideshow to the epic struggle for Europe.

The Patriotic War, in short, offered rebirth, regeneration, and gave rise to good feelings at home. [The historian] Steven Watt notes that the "wartime fusion of revitalized national strength, liberal individualism, and godly affirmation of the republic surfaced everywhere in peace commemorations by Republican enthusiasts." Francis Scott Key immortalized the nation's destiny to endure, that through the "perilous fight" the Stars and Stripes yet waved "o'er the land of the free and the home of the brave." Editorial writers proudly proclaimed America's arrival "in the first rank of nations" after a "triumph of virtue over vice, of republican men and republican principles over the advocates and doctrines of Tyranny." Commemorations repeatedly invoked discourses of patriotic destiny "under God." "No nation, save Israel of old," exalted one writer, "hath experienced such great salvations" of liberty and national vindication.

Myth of America identity increased the power of the army and the state while marginalizing opponents of militant nationalism. Just as the Revolutionary War targeted loyalists, and the Quasi War the Republicans, the Patriotic War demonized the New England Federalists as virtual traitors in the nation's midst. The dominant patriotic discourse exploited the Hartford Convention (1814) to destroy the Federalists as a force in national politics, entrenching a one-party state in its wake. The Federalist call at Hartford for changes in the "national compact," including reconsideration of the proslavery Constitution, now appeared subversive and un-American.

The discursive regime, reinvigorated by foreign war, thus further ensconced and fatally sanctioned the expansion of slavery. The number of slaves doubled between 1800 and 1820 and continued increasing despite the end of the international slave trade in 1808, as the national economy became more rather than less dependent on the plantation system.

The Patriotic War flowed from psychic anxieties associated with the nation's transition from a seaboard republic presided over by a wig-wearing, knee-breeched national gentry to a more sprawling "frontier" nation rising around a dominant ethos of market capitalism and an egalitarian mythology of the common man. The entrepreneurial energy unleashed by the Revolution and fueled by the mass of land seized from Indians brought a sharply rising population, flourishing agriculture, commerce, ambition and opportunity, massive social and geographic mobility, and a culture of acquisitiveness. Such sweeping social change produced disorder and anxiety that coalesced in a cathartic foreign policy context. By focusing energies and emotions on the vanquishing of external foes, the national community could accommodate itself to destabilizing changes associated with rapid cultural transformation while at the same time disparaging as subversive the critics of militant nationalism.

Confirming the fears of classical republicanism, the Patriotic War spawned the U.S. warfare state, giving rise to a nation that would maintain a powerful "defense" establishment and employ state violence to perpetuate its own cultural imaginary. Preparing for war and *choosing* war thus inhered in national identity. The good feelings that arose in the war's aftermath foreshadowed similar anxiety-assuaging responses to the "splendid" imperial burst in 1898, the "good war" in 1945, and victory in the Cold War in 1991.

Another legacy flowing from national identity was the association between foreign war and domestic economic growth, as reflected in the Market Revolution that unfolded in the decade after the conflict. The war spurred nascent industry through government purchasing and investment in manufacturing. After the Napoleonic wars, economic dislocations in Europe brought sharply rising demand for U.S. food and grain. British mills drove a ceaseless demand for cotton, as U.S. farm output soared and new states in the South and Midwest entered the Union. From the Revolution to the end of the Patriotic War, the nation thus transitioned from a localized agrarian republic to a complex economy, with myriad interregional and broadened international connections. Dramatic population growth, stable and supportive government, individual ambition, Protestant anxieties, and a culture of acquisitiveness coalesced in a liberal capitalist society.

The discourse of wartime triumph, combined with the economic boom, reaffirmed the destiny and superiority of the white republic over war-plagued Europe, a continent characterized by "regal turpitude and unmanly subjection." Unlike the European monarchies and class-based social system, liberal capitalism "offered ordinary people an escape from the self-denying virtue of their superiors" thereby fostering support among white men for an ostensibly free republican government. Proud citizens viewed the United States as a land of enterprise, hard work, nascent industry, and opportunity for the common man. "No quality has so marked the character of American social life as individual aspiration," [the historian] Joyce Appleby notes, "turning the United States into a magnet for immigrants and a wellspring of hope for the adventurous." Hegemonic patriotic discourse silenced oppositional voices.

🌐 *F U R T H E R   R E A D I N G*

Lance Banning, *The Sacred Fire of Liberty: James Madison and the Founding of the Federal Republic* (1995)
Walter R. Borneman, *1812* (2004)
Richard Buel Jr., *America on the Brink* (2006)
Gregory E. Dowd, *A Spirited Resistance* (1992) (on American Indians)
R. David Edmunds, *The Shawnee Prophet* (1983)
Clifford L. Egan, *Neither Peace nor War: Franco-American Relations, 1803–1812* (1983)
Richard J. Ellings, *Embargoes and World Power* (1985)
Kenneth J. Hagan, *This People's Navy* (1991)
Ronald L. Hatzenbuehler and Robert L. Ivie, *Congress Declares War* (1983)
Donald R. Hickey, *Don't Give Up the Ship!* (2006)
——, *The War of 1812* (1989)
Peter P. Hill, *Napoleon's Troublesome Americans* (2005)
Reginald Horsman, *The Causes of the War of 1812* (1962)
A. J. Langguth, *Union 1812* (2007)
Jon Latimer, *1812* (2007)
Frederick C. Leiner, *The End of Barbary Terror* (2006)
Dumas Malone, *Jefferson the President* (1970–1974)
John C. Niven, *Henry Clay* (1991)
Bradford Perkins, *The Creation of a Republican Empire* (1993)
Robert V. Remini, *The Battle of New Orleans* (1999)
——, *Henry Clay* (1991)
Robert A. Rutland, *James Madison* (1987)
——, *The Presidency of James Madison* (1990)
——, ed., *The James Madison Encyclopedia* (1992)
J. C. A. Stagg, "Between Black Rock and a Hard Place: Peter B. Porter's Plan for an Invasion of Canada," *Journal of the Early American Republic*, 19 (1999), 385–422
——, *Mr. Madison's War* (1983)
John Sugden, *Tucumseh: A Life* (1998)
Bruce Vandervort, *Indian Wars of Mexico, Canada, and the United States* (2006)
Anthony F. C. Wallace, *Jefferson and the Indians* (2001)
Steven Watts, *The Republic Reborn* (1987)
Richard White, *The Middle Ground* (1991) (on American Indians)

The Monroe Doctrine

*In the early 1820s, events at home and abroad posed new threats to the
well-being of the young American nation. Although the Missouri Compromise
of 1820 calmed an immediate political crisis over slavery, it left a bitter legacy
that eventually would produce a civil war. Meanwhile, Spanish colonies in Latin
America, under such leaders as the legendary Simón Bolívar, were rebelling
against Spain. North Americans cheered their southern neighbors for breaking
the chains of their imperial master. Yet, judging Latin Americans inferior because
they were Catholics of mixed blood, and predicting that they could not create the
democratic institutions necessary to sustain their newfound independence, the
United States refrained from overtly supporting the new nations that emerged.
Secretary of State John Quincy Adams, moreover, feared that if the United States
extended formal diplomatic recognition to the new governments, Spain might
renege on the Transcontinental Treaty (1819) that had added the Floridas to the
U.S. empire. While Adams urged delay, Henry Clay of Kentucky, like Adams a
contender for the presidency, demanded U.S. recognition. In 1822, the Monroe
administration finally recognized the states of Argentina, Chile, Gran Colombia,
Mexico, and Peru. Spain fumed and plotted, intent on restoring its empire. What
would the United States do, contemporaries wondered, if Europe's Holy Alliance
(Russia, Spain, Austria, and France) sent military forces to destroy the new Latin
American governments?*

*On December 2, 1823, President James Monroe gave his annual message to
Congress. He stated principles that drew on the past and became guides for American
diplomacy in the future. He declared that the Western Hemisphere was no longer
open to European colonization, that the Old and New Worlds were so different
that the United States would abstain from European wars, and that the European
powers should not intervene forcefully in the Americas. Monroe designed these
three points—noncolonization, two spheres, and nonintervention—to warn the
monarchies of Europe against crushing the new Latin American states and to deter
Russia from encroaching on the Pacific coast.*

*Great Britain, which had profited commercially from the breakup of the
Spanish mercantile system and therefore did not welcome a restoration of Spanish
rule in South America, approached the United States with the idea of issuing a
joint declaration of opposition to Europen intervention. North Americans, who
also realized economic benefits from the dismantling of the Spanish Empire, shared*

British worries about the European threat. Monroe's "doctrine" constituted the independent U.S. answer to the European menace.

Historians rank the Monroe Doctrine as a cardinal and lasting statement of
American foreign policy. The traditional interpretation holds that the Monroe
Doctrine represented a defense of American ideals, security, and commerce—an
affirmation of the national interest. More critical scholars have placed the Monroe
Doctrine within the American expansionist tradition and have pointed out that
the declaration may have meant "hands-off" for the Europeans, but it permitted
"hands-on" for the United States. Others have argued that domestic American
politics, especially the presidential ambitions of the principal policymakers, and the
pressure of public opinion helped shape a key decision: to reject the British overture
in favor of a unilateral American proclamation.

D O C U M E N T S

A major architect of the Monroe Doctrine, Secretary of State John Quincy Adams,
welcomed Latin America's break from Spain, but he hesitated to extend diplomatic
recognition to the new governments. One of his fears was that recognition might
ensnare the United States in Latin American–European crises and, by dangerously enlarging U.S. commitments abroad, might undermine the nation at home. In Document 1,
a July 4, 1821, speech, Adams explains his hesitation and warnings.

Document 2 is British foreign secretary George Canning's appeal of August 20,
1823. In this letter to Richard Rush, American minister in London, Canning asks
the United States to join Great Britain in a declaration against possible European
intervention to restore Latin American states to Spanish rule. President James Monroe
consulted not only his cabinet but also former presidents Thomas Jefferson and
James Madison about Canning's proposal. In a letter of October 24, included here as
Document 3, Jefferson advised Monroe to cooperate with Britain. Document 4, from
Adams's diary, is an account of the cabinet discussion of November 7. Adams argued
successfully against an Anglo-American declaration. Document 5 is the president's
annual message to Congress on December 23, 1823—the Monroe Doctrine.

U.S. intent toward the newly independent Latin American republics remained
a point of contention during the years immediately following Monroe's message.
In Document 6, a July 2, 1824, letter to Secretary Adams from José Maria Salazar,
Colombia's minister to the United States, the Colombian government asks for
clarification of the Monroe Doctrine: Exactly how did the United States intend to
resist European intervention? Adams later evasively replied that the president would
consult with Congress and talk with the Europeans. Having succeeded Monroe to
the presidency in 1825, Adams announced the U.S. intention to attend the Panama
Congress called by the new Latin American states to promote hemispheric cooperation. On April 6, 1826, Republican Representative William L. Brent of Louisiana
delivered a speech to his congressional colleagues, included here as Document 7,
opposing legislation that would have barred the U.S. mission from joining
deliberations on Cuba's colonial status. The Washington rumor mill had it that the
White House supported plans advanced by the newly established republics
of Mexico and Colombia to foment a slave rebellion in Cuba against Spain.
Brent, a pro-slavery Adams ally, countered that the proposed restrictions on hemispheric talks would actually hinder the administration's efforts to maintain the
status quo and protect U.S. interests in Cuba. U.S. delegates ultimately attended

the conference, which approved continued Spanish rule in Cuba. Document 8, from the pen of Juan Bautista Alberdi, a prominent Argentine intellectual who wrote prolifically on political topics in the 1840s and 1850s, considers the Monroe Doctrine a self-interested U.S. effort to separate the Western Hemisphere from Europe and deny Spanish America true independence.

D O C U M E N T   1

Secretary of State John Quincy Adams Warns Against the Search for "Monsters to Destroy," 1821

And now, friends and countrymen, if the wise and learned philosophers of the elder world, the first observers of nutation and aberration, the discoverers of maddening ether and invisible planets, the inventors of Congreve rockets and Shrapnel shells, should find their hearts disposed to enquire what has America done for the benefit of mankind? Let our answer be this: America, with the same voice which spoke herself into existence as a nation, proclaimed to mankind the inextinguishable rights of human nature, and the only lawful foundations of government. America, in the assembly of nations, since her admission among them, has invariably, though often fruitlessly, held forth to them the hand of honest friendship, of equal freedom, of generous reciprocity. She has uniformly spoken among them, though often to heedless and often to disdainful ears, the language of equal liberty, of equal justice, and of equal rights. She has, in the lapse of nearly half a century, without a single exception, respected the independence of other nations while asserting and maintaining her own. She has abstained from interference in the concerns of others, even when conflict has been for principles to which she clings, as to the last vital drop that visits the heart. She has seen that probably for centuries to come, all the contests of that Aceldama the European world, will be contests of inveterate power, and emerging right. Wherever the standard of freedom and Independence has been or shall be unfurled, there will her heart, her benedictions and her prayers be. But she goes not abroad, in search of monsters to destroy. She is the well-wisher to the freedom and independence of all. She is the champion and vindicator only of her own. She will commend the general cause by the countenance of her voice, and the benignant sympathy of her example. She well knows that by once enlisting under other banners than her own, were they even the banners of foreign independence, she would involve herself beyond the power of extrication, in all the wars of interest and intrigue, of individual avarice, envy, and ambition, which assume the colors and usurp the standard of freedom. The fundamental maxims of her policy would insensibly change from *liberty* to *force*. . . .

This document can be found in, "An Address. Delivered at the Request of the Committee of Arrangement for Celebrating the Anniversary of Independence at Washington of the Fourth of July, 1821, Upon the Occasion of Reading the Declaration of Independence," by John Quincy Adams. Cambridge, Mass.: The University Press, 1821 (pamphlet).

She might become the dictatress of the world. She would be no longer the ruler of her own spirit. . . .

[America's] glory is not *dominion*, but *liberty*. Her march is the march of the mind. She has a spear and a shield: but the motto upon her shield is, *Freedom, Independence, Peace*. This has been her Declaration: this has been, as far as her necessary intercourse with the rest of mankind would permit, her practice.

● D O C U M E N T   2

British Foreign Secretary George Canning Proposes a Joint Declaration, 1823

Is not the moment come when our Governments might understand each other as to the Spanish American Colonies? And if we can arrive at such an understanding, would it not be expedient for ourselves, and beneficial for all the world, that the principles of it should be clearly settled and plainly avowed?

For ourselves we have no disguise.

1. We conceive the recovery of the Colonies by Spain to be hopeless.
2. We conceive the question of the recognition of them, as Independent States, to be one of time and circumstances.
3. We are, however, by no means disposed to throw any impediment in the way of an arrangement between them, and the mother country by amicable negotiation.
4. We aim not at the possession of any portion of them ourselves.
5. We could not see any portion of them transferred to any other Power, with indifference.

If these opinions and feelings are as I firmly believe them to be, common to your Government with ours, why should we hesitate mutually to confide them to each other; and to declare them in the face of the world?

If there be any European Power which cherishes other projects, which looks to a forcible enterprize for reducing the Colonies to subjugation, on the behalf or in the name of Spain; or which meditates the acquisition of any part of them to itself, by cession or by conquest; such a declaration on the part of your government and ours would be at once the most effectual and the least offensive mode of intimating our joint disapprobation of such projects.

It would at the same time put an end to all the jealousies of Spain with respect to her remaining Colonies—and to the agitation which prevails in those Colonies, an agitation which it would be but humane to allay; being determined (as we are) not to profit by encouraging it.

This document can be found in William R. Manning, ed., *Diplomatic Correspondence of the United States Concerning the Independence of the Latin-American Nations* (New York: Carnegie Endowment for International Peace, 1925), III, 1478–1479.

Do you conceive that under the power which you have recently received, you are authorized to enter into negotiation, and to sign any Convention upon this subject? Do you conceive, if that be not within your competence, you could exchange with me ministerial notes upon it?

Nothing could be more gratifying to me than to join with you in such a work, and, I am persuaded, there has seldom, in the history of the world, occurred an opportunity when so small an effort, of two friendly Governments, might produce so unequivocal a good and prevent such extensive calamities.

🌐 D O C U M E N T   3

Jefferson Advises President James Monroe
to Cooperate with Britain, 1823

The question presented by the letters you have sent me, is the most momentous which has ever been offered to my contemplation since that of Independence. That made us a nation, this sets our compass and points the course which we are to steer through the ocean of time opening on us. And never could we embark on it under circumstances more auspicious. Our first and fundamental maxim should be, never to entangle ourselves in the broils of Europe. Our second, never to suffer Europe to intermeddle with cis-Atlantic affairs. America, North and South, has a set of interests distinct from those of Europe, and peculiarly her own. She should therefore have a system of her own, separate and apart from that of Europe. While the last is laboring to become the domicile of despotism, our endeavor should surely be to make our hemisphere that of freedom. One nation, most of all, could disturb us in this pursuit; she now offers to lead, aid, and accompany us in it. By acceding to her proposition, we detach her from the bands, bring her mighty weight into the scale of free government, and emancipate a continent at one stroke, which might otherwise linger long in doubt and difficulty. Great Britain is the nation which can do us the most harm of any one, or all on earth; and with her on our side we need not fear the whole world. With her then, we should most sedulously cherish a cordial friendship; and nothing would tend more to knit our affections than to be fighting once more, side by side, in the same cause. . . .

But we have first to ask ourselves a question. Do we wish to acquire to our own confederacy any one or more of the Spanish provinces? I candidly confess, that I have ever looked on Cuba as the most interesting addition which could ever be made to our system of States. The control which, with Florida Point, this island would give us over the Gulf of Mexico, and the countries and isthmus bordering on it, as well as all those whose waters flow into it, would fill up the measures of our political well-being. Yet, as I am sensible that this can never be obtained, even with her own consent, but by war; and its independence, which is our second interest, (and especially its independence of England,) can be secured without it, I have no hesitation in abandoning my first wish to future chances, and accepting its independence,

This document can be found in H. A. Washington, ed., *The Writings of Thomas Jefferson* (Washington, D.C.: Taylor and Maury, 1854), VII, 315–317.

with peace and the friendship of England, rather than its association, at the expense of war and her enmity.

I could honestly, therefore, join in the declaration proposed, that we aim not at the acquisition of any of those possessions, that we will not stand in the way of any amicable arrangement between them and the Mother country; but that we will oppose, with all our means, the forcible interposition of any other power, as auxiliary, stipendiary, or under any other form or pretext, and most especially, their transfer to any power by conquest, cession, or acquisition in any other way. I should think it, therefore, advisable, that the Executive should encourage the British government to a continuance in the dispositions expressed in these letters, by an assurance of his concurrence with them as far as his authority goes; and that as it may lead to war, the declaration of which requires an act of Congress, the case shall be laid before them for consideration at their first meeting, and under the reasonable aspect in which it is seen by himself.

DOCUMENT 4

Adams Argues Against a Joint Anglo-American Declaration in the Cabinet Meeting of November 7, 1823

Cabinet meeting at the President's from half-past one till four. Mr. [John] Calhoun, Secretary of War, and Mr. [Samuel] Southard, Secretary of the Navy, present. The subject for consideration was, the confidential proposals of the British Secretary of State, George Canning, to R. Rush, and the correspondence between them relating to the projects of the Holy Alliance upon South America. There was much conversation, without coming to any definite point. The object of Canning appears to have been to obtain some public pledge from the Government of the United States, ostensibly against the forcible interference of the Holy Alliance between Spain and South America; but really or especially against the acquisition to the United States themselves of any part of the Spanish-American possessions.

Mr. Calhoun inclined to giving a discretionary power to Mr. Rush to join in a declaration against the interference of the Holy Allies, if necessary, even if it should pledge us not to take Cuba or the province of Texas; because the power of Great Britain being greater than ours to *seize* upon them, we should get the advantage of obtaining from her the same declaration we should make ourselves.

I thought the cases not parallel. We have no intention of seizing either Texas or Cuba. But the inhabitants of either or both may exercise their primitive rights, and solicit a union with us. They will certainly do no such thing to Great Britain. By joining with her, therefore, in her proposed declaration, we give her a substantial and perhaps inconvenient pledge against ourselves, and really obtain nothing in return.

This document can be found in Charles Francis Adams, ed., *Memoirs of John Quincy Adams Comprising Portions of His Diary from 1795 to 1848* (Philadelphia: J.B. Lippincott, 1875), VI, 177–179.

Without entering now into the enquiry of the expediency of our annexing Texas or Cuba to our Union, we should at least keep ourselves free to act as emergencies may arise, and not tie ourselves down to any principle which might immediately after-wards be brought to bear against ourselves.

Mr. Southard inclined much to the same opinion.

The President was averse to any course which should have the appearance of taking a position subordinate to that of Great Britain. . . .

I remarked that the communications recently received from the Russian Minister, Baron Tuyl, afforded, as I thought, a very suitable and convenient opportunity for us to take our stand against the Holy Alliance, and at the same time to decline the overture of Great Britain. It would be more candid, as well as more dignified, to avow our principles explicitly to Russia and France, than to come in as a cock-boat in the wake of the British man-of-war.

This idea was acquiesced in on all sides, and my draft for an answer to Baron Tuyl's note announcing the Emperor's determination to refuse receiving any Minister from the South American Governments was read.

🌎 *D O C U M E N T*　*5*

The Monroe Doctrine Declares the Western Hemisphere Closed to European Intervention, 1823

At the proposal of the Russian Imperial Government, made through the minister of the Emperor residing here, a full power and instructions have been transmitted to the minister of the United States at St. Petersburg to arrange by amicable negotia-tion the respective rights and interests of the two nations on the northwest coast of this continent. . . . In the discussions to which this interest has given rise and in the arrangements by which they may terminate the occasion has been judged proper for asserting, as a principle in which the rights and interests of the United States are involved that the American continents, by the free and independent condition which they have assumed and maintain, are henceforth not to be considered as subjects for future colonization by any European powers. . . .

It was stated at the commencement of the last session that a great effort was then making in Spain and Portugal to improve the condition of the people of those countries, and that it appeared to be conducted with extraordinary modera-tion. It need scarcely be remarked that the result has been so far very different from what was then anticipated. Of events in that quarter of the globe, with which we have so much intercourse and from which we derive our origin, we have always been anxious and interested spectators. The citizens of the United States cherish sentiments the most friendly in favor of the liberty and happiness of their fellow-men on that side of the Atlantic. In the wars of the European

---

This document can be found in James D. Richardson, ed., *A Compilation of the Messages and Papers of the Presidents* (New York: Bureau of National Literature, 1897), II, 778, 786–788.

powers in matters relating to themselves we have never taken any part, nor does it comport with our policy so to do. It is only when our rights are invaded or seriously menaced that we resent injuries or make preparation for our defense. With the movements in this hemisphere we are of necessity more immediately connected, and by causes which must be obvious to all enlightened and impartial observers. The political system of the allied powers is essentially different in this respect from that of America. This difference proceeds from that which exists in their respective Governments; and to the defense of our own, which has been achieved by the loss of so much blood and treasure, and matured by the wisdom of their most enlightened citizens, and under which we have enjoyed unexampled felicity, this whole nation is devoted. We owe it, therefore, to candor and to the amicable relations existing between the United States and those powers to declare that we should consider any attempt on their part to extend their system to any portion of this hemisphere as dangerous to our peace and safety. With the existing colonies or dependencies of any European power we have not interfered and shall not interfere. But with the Governments who have declared their independence and maintained it, and whose independence we have, on great consideration and on just principles, acknowledged, we could not view any interposition for the purpose of oppressing them, or controlling in any other manner their destiny, by any European power in any other light than as the manifestation of an unfriendly disposition toward the United States. In the war between those new Governments and Spain we declared our neutrality at the time of their recognition, and to this we have adhered, and shall continue to adhere, provided no change shall occur which, in the judgment of the competent authorities of this Government, shall make a corresponding change on the part of the United States indispensable to their security.

The late events in Spain and Portugal shew that Europe is still unsettled. Of this important fact no stronger proof can be adduced than that the allied powers should have thought it proper, on any principle satisfactory to themselves, to have interposed by force in the internal concerns of Spain. To what extent such interposition may be carried, on the same principle, is a question in which all independent powers whose governments differ from theirs are interested, even those most remote, and surely none more so than the United States. Our policy in regard to Europe, which was adopted at an early stage of the wars which have so long agitated that quarter of the globe, nevertheless remains the same, which is, not to interfere in the internal concerns of any of its powers; to consider the government *de facto* as the legitimate government for us; to cultivate friendly relations with it, and to preserve those relations by a frank, firm, and manly policy, meeting in all instances the just claims of every power, submitting to injuries from none. But in regard to those continents circumstances are eminently and conspicuously different. It is impossible that the allied powers should extend their political system to any portion of either continent without endangering our peace and happiness; nor can anyone believe that our southern brethren, if [left] to themselves, would adopt it of their own accord. It is equally impossible, therefore, that we should behold such interposition in any form with indifference.

Colombia Requests an Explanation of U.S. Intentions, 1824

My Government has seen with the greatest pleasure the Message of the President of the United States, a work very worthy of its author, and which expresses the public sentiments of the people over whom he presides: it cannot be doubted, in virtue of this document, that the Government of the United-States endeavours to oppose the policy and ultimate views of the Holy Alliance, and such appears to be the decision of Great Britain from the sense of the Nation, some acts of the Ministry, and the language of her Commissioners in Bogotá.

In such circumstances the Government of Colombia is desirous to know in what manner the Government of the United-States intends to resist on its part any interferences of the Holy Alliance for the purpose of subjugating the new Republics or interfering in their political forms: if it will enter into a Treaty of Alliance with the Republic of Colombia to save America in general from the calamities of a despotic system; and finally if the Government of Washington understands by foreign interference the employment of Spanish forces against America at the time when Spain is occupied by a French Army, and its Government under the influence of France and her Allies.

It appears that it is already in the situation intended by this declaration, since it [is] generally asserted that an expedition has sailed from Cadiz destined for the coasts of Peru composed of the Ship Asia and of some frigates and brigs; there is no doubt that Spain does not furnish this force by herself alone in her present state of despotism and anarchy, without an army, without a marine and without money. This Nation notwithstanding its spirit of domination would have ere now decided for peace had it not been assisted for war.

In the name of my Government therefore, and reposing on the sympathy of the United States, I request the said explanations which may serve for its government in its policy and its system of defence.

Representative William L. Brent Advocates Hemispheric Cooperation to Safeguard U.S. Slavery and Expansion, 1826

Mr. Chairman, there is *one subject* to be discussed at the Congress at Panama, in which I feel a deep interest, as being one of the Representatives of a Southern State. I allude to the condition of the Islands of Cuba and Porto Rico. If the amendment now before the committee should be adopted, our Ministers will be prevented from taking any part, or

---

Document 6 can be found in William R. Manning. ed., *Diplomatic Correspondence of the United States Concerning the Independence of the Latin-American Nations* (New York: Carnegie Endowment for International Peace. 1925), II, 1281–1282.

Document 7 can be found in Register of Debates in Congress, 19th Congress, 1st Session (Washington, D.C.: Gales and Seaton, 1826), II, 2062–2065.

making any remonstrance upon *that subject;* and for this reason, if for none other, I am opposed to that amendment. Sir, the condition of the Island of Cuba, in the neighborhood of the State of Louisiana, one of whose Representatives I am, excites my most lively anxieties. To the destiny of Cuba we are not indifferent. Our sympathies, our partiality for free and independent Governments, make us not indifferent to the condition of our fellow-men, the subjects of monarchy; under any other circumstances, and differently situated, we would hail with pleasure the independence of Cuba; but for reasons, Mr. Chairman, which you, as a Southern man, *feel*, and the nation know, I should look upon that event, as connected with our interests and with humanity, as one of the greatest evils which, in the existing state of things, could befal the Southern States, and particularly the State of Louisiana. I need not refer to the population of Cuba, to justify my fears. Sir, do you believe that if the Republics of the South were to unite to aid Cuba in her independence, that its liberty would be achieved, in peace and good feeling, between all, and without scenes of ruin, horror, and desolation, too painful to be portrayed? Would not the signal for its independence be the watchword for *another object?* And how could it be restrained? Where would be the armed force to stop the bloody torrent?

But, let us for a moment suppose, that the independence of Cuba should be effected without an attempt by a certain part of its population to attain the ascendency—is it not reasonable for us to suppose that part of its population, as in the other South American Republics, would all be declared free; and, if so, with the black population of Mexico on the frontier of Louisiana, and Hayti and Cuba for neighbors, what would be the condition of the Southern planters? Sir, the very thought of the consequences flowing from such a state of things, excites feelings too heart-rending to be dwelt upon for one moment. I must turn from them. . . .

It is said, by the opponents of the President, that he is hostile to our Southern interests: and, in their newspapers and speeches, here and elsewhere, it is insinuated that he wishes to send Ministers to Panama to form an alliance with the South American Republics, to aid the independence of Cuba, by which a vital blow would be given to the South. Sir, if I saw any thing like this, or that could make me believe it, I would be amongst the first men in the nation to raise my voice against his administration: for, no man has more Southern prejudices or jealousies than myself—I acknowledge it. How can it be otherwise? My ancestors, my nativity, my education, my habits, and my feelings and interests, were, and are, all Southern. If such were the sentiments of the present administration, I think gentlemen could find something like *facts* to support their attacks upon. I challenge them to do it. In what instance has such partiality been shown? In none. It exists alone in their animated, heated declarations. . . .

One thing is clear, and will be seen by the nation, from the correspondence between our Government with the different Powers in Europe, and with the South American Republics—that the present Administration always have been, and are still, doing all that can be done, to prevent the independence of Cuba, by the aid of the Republics of the South, for the reasons I have given, and also to prevent that island falling into the hands of any other Government than that of Spain. Should the latter event take place, it might be destructive to the interests of the West, and so materially injure the commerce of this country as to make it necessary for us to embark in a war, to protect both of those great interests. . . . It is every thing to the Western country, and all important to them, that it should never fall into the possession of any foreign Power, that could cramp or embarrass the free trade in the Gulf of Mexico. It is the key to that trade; and the Power that holds it, if formidable, can admit or exclude your trade, in that region, at its option. . . .

To contradict the assertions which have gone abroad in the public prints and otherwise, and have been repeated in this Hall, that, as regards Cuba, the Administration is friendly to the views of the South American Republics, and that this mission will lead to this Government's lending their aid in that way, to do an injury to the Southern interests, I must call the attention of the committee to the President's message, in which he discloses his views upon the subject, and clearly refutes the motives attempted to be attributed to him, and conclusively shows that the object of the Administration is, to prevent, if possible, a change in the condition of Cuba, in any manner whatsoever, and thereby to protect our interests, instead of destroying them.

D O C U M E N T   8

Juan Bautista Alberdi of Argentina Warns Against the Threat of "Monroism" to the Independence of Spanish America, n.d.

The revolution for independence has not eliminated the Europeanized civilization of the new world: it has only changed its form. What exists in America [North, Central, and South] continues to be an aspect of what exists in Europe. There is an intimate solidarity of interests and destinies among the peoples of both continents.

They are not two *worlds*, as the figurative expression goes; they are not two planets with beings of separate races, rather they are parts of one geographical and political world.

The seas bring peoples together rather than separating them.

Without the sea, Chile would have no communication with Europe. The idea of a land voyage of three thousand leagues is unheard of. The community of business interests is proof of the solidarity of interests and destinies of both continents. The doctrine attributed to Monroe, is a contradiction, the daughter of egoism. Even though the United States owes everything to Europe, it wants to isolate America from Europe, from any influence that does not emanate from the United States, which will make the United States the only custom house for the civilization of transatlantic origin. Monroe wanted to make his country the *Porto-Bello of American liberty*. . . . [(Porto Bello, on the isthmus of Panama, was one of the most important commercial centers in the Spanish empire—a symbol of Spanish control.)]

Although the *Monroe* [D]octrine is antithetical to the doctrines of the *Holy* Alliance in Spanish America, with regard to the America of Spanish origin, it is as ominous as the doctrines of the Holy Alliance. Both have as their objective the conquest of Spanish America: one for the benefit of *Spain*, the other for the benefit of the *United* States.

Both doctrines are the expression of two ambitions, the object of which is Spanish America.

This document can be found in Juan Bautista Alberdi, *La Doctrina de Monröe y la America Española*, ed. by Raimundo Rodriquez (Buenos Aires: Nuevo Meridión, 1987), 103–104, 117–118, 123–124. Translated from the Spanish by Miriam Biurci. The essay was probably written in the 1840s–1850s.

Between the colonial annexation of South America by a European nation and colonial annexation by the United States, what is the difference? Which is preferable for South America? As far as annexation is concerned, neither: independence is better. In other words, neither *monroism* nor *holy alliance*. But let us compare the results of these two annexations, the practical examples of which are Havana and Texas. Havana, though a colony, is Spanish. Texas, though free, has died for the Spanish race. *Havana* lives, even if it is enslaved; of *Texas*, the only thing left is the soil.

Thus, the colonial annexation by Europe is the conservation of the race and the species with loss of liberty. Annexation by the United States is the loss of the race and its being as it acquires liberty . . . as is well understood by the living, not by the dead. Between the two annexations, let the devil choose. . . .

Those who are not, in any respect, in agreement over the intervention of Europe, accommodate themselves to the idea of a *protectorate* by the *United States* over the entire American continent.

Apart from the absurdity of such a protectorate—due to its impracticality—it is not honorable to the independence of the South American republics, as any *protectorate* is not honorable, wherever it emanates from and whoever exercises it.

All *protectorates* are humiliating because they are the denial of the means to *independence*, from which is derived, in practice, the *right* to be.

E S S A Y S

In the first essay, James E. Lewis Jr. of Kalamazoo College portrays the Monroe Doctrine as a defensive initiative. The Monroe administration's recognition of the newly established Latin American states in early 1822 had arisen from the calculation that the nation's interests were tied to the creation of independent, republican states in the New World. Fearful of European intervention to reclaim lost empire, and suspicious of Britain's commitment to Latin American independence, Monroe spurned London's proposal for a joint Anglo-American statement against reconquest and instead issued a unilateral warning that asserted the existence of a distinct hemispheric political system and foreclosed the recolonization of the newly independent states. According to Lewis, the presidential proclamation, along with a round of diplomatic activity aimed to splinter the Holy Alliance, successfully kept conservative Europe at bay without involving the United States in a war for South American independence.

In the second essay, Piero Gleijeses of The Johns Hopkins School for Advanced International Studies downplays U.S. sympathy for Latin American independence and casts the Monroe Doctrine as an expression of expansionist fervor. Although the pronouncement declared the Western Hemisphere closed to further European colonization, it did not disavow U.S. claims to territory and hegemony. Gleijeses observes that congressional debate over U.S. attendance at the Inter-American, Panama Congress in 1826 revealed bipartisan opposition to the liberation of nearby Cuba where an African-Cuban slave uprising might threaten the legitimacy of slavery in the southern United States.

In the final essay, Ernest R. May of Harvard University studies the personal ambitions of policymakers in Washington, D.C. He maintains that because the European powers never intended to send forces to the New World (largely because they feared British resistance), domestic politics, especially the upcoming presidential election, must have determined the outcome of debates within the Monroe administration.

In Defense of the Nation and Hemispheric Republicanism

JAMES E. LEWIS JR.

In the eighteen months after [President James] Monroe and [Secretary of State John Quincy] Adams decided to recognize the new states [(in early 1822)], the tensions between their concerns for Europe's reaction and their anxieties about Spanish America's instability shaped policymaking. Initially, caution prevailed. . . . European war, Spanish American upheaval, and domestic divisions intensified both immediate and long-term dangers, even as they made the government less prepared to meet a crisis. But Monroe and Adams pressed ahead with their efforts to safeguard the United States against the dangers inherent in a Europeanized New World, calculating that the adoption of European principles and the formation of European ties in Spanish America represented the greater threat. As they sent the first ministers to the new states, they worked to settle the Spanish American governments into the diplomatic, political, and commercial habits that they considered essential to the well-being of the United States and the entire hemisphere. Only by following the North American model of political isolation, republican government, and liberal commerce could the Spanish American governments help to create a political system in the New World favorable to the interests of all of its states. In the summer of 1823, Monroe and Adams remained hopeful. They expected, as Monroe informed Jefferson, that "time . . . and the force of our example [would] gradually mature them, for the great trust deposited in their hands."

Early in the fall of 1823, the administration's hopes faced an unexpected check when news arrived from Great Britain that the Holy Alliance might try to carry its restoration of legitimate rule from Spain to Spanish America. The cabinet considered two questions—how to meet this threat and how to reply to a British invitation for a joint declaration against it. Passages in the president's annual message that later became known as the Monroe Doctrine answered these questions. Because of this doctrine's later significance, its origins have been examined in countless articles and books. Most of these accounts stress the factors that subsequently made it important: its unilateral assertion of the principle of noncolonization, of a warning against European interference in the New World, and of a pledge of abstinence from European affairs. By emphasizing these factors, these accounts portray the Monroe Doctrine as a bold step into the future with an extensive impact on policymaking. In doing so, however, they understate the degree to which the course adopted in the fall of 1823 was a tentative step governed by the significant policy decisions of the preceding two years. The Monroe Doctrine, as well as the larger response of which it was but one part, emerged naturally from the much more transformative recognition decision. Taken as a whole, moreover, this response appears more hesitant and flexible than the historiography suggests.

In October and November 1823, the administration received information through British and Russian sources of the potential threat from the Holy Alliance and of the British proposal for joint action. Dispatches from the minister to Great Britain,

Richard Rush, described discussions of the French invasion of Spain with British foreign minister George Canning. Warning that the Holy Alliance hoped to restore Spanish rule in the New World, Canning pressed Rush for a joint statement that disavowed any interest in acquiring Spanish colonies and declared an opposition to their resubjugation by any power except Spain. Such a statement, he argued, would defeat the Allies' plans before they matured. Rush recorded this and subsequent meetings in a series of letters that reached Washington on 9 October. When Adams returned to the capital two days later, he immediately discussed the letters with Monroe, [Secretary of War John C.] Calhoun, and Attorney General William Wirt. Not until the president returned from his Virginia plantations in early November, however, did the cabinet's deliberations begin in earnest. In the interim, meetings between Adams and Baron Hendrik de Tuyll van Serooskerken, the Russian minister, had heightened the fears about the Holy Alliance's designs. The cabinet agreed from the start that the answers to Rush's and de Tuyll's communications "must all be parts of a combined system of policy and adapted to each other." Over the next three weeks, it devised this "system of policy," deciding to decline the British offer and to assert the American position unilaterally.

American policymakers believed that it was their recognition of the new states that compelled them to respond to this crisis at all. Recognition made the United States, alone among the established nations of the world, committed in some form to an independent New World. Monroe, Adams, and Rush each noted that without this commitment the government might have dismissed the situation as a wholly European question. As Adams remarked to Monroe, recognition "had pledged us now to take ground which we had not felt at all bound to take five years ago," when the Great Powers met at Aix-la-Chapelle to discuss Spanish America. Then, he reminded Monroe, the administration "had not even thought of interfering." But, if an "over-hasty" recognition had provided the only reason to risk an otherwise unnecessary war, Monroe and Adams could have retreated from it easily. From Paris, one of the cabinet's informal agents, George W. Erving, strongly urged precisely this course in a letter that reached Washington during the cabinet discussions. After warning of the danger to Spanish America, Erving suggested "submit[ting] to the mortification of retracing our steps." Rather than risk war or join with Great Britain, the government could simply "abandon the colonies."

In the thinking of Monroe and Adams, however, the absolute necessity of responding arose less from recognition itself than from the reconceptualization of American interests that had led to recognition and continued to shape policymaking. Accepting that the well-being of the American union required a New World composed of independent, republican states increased the ways in which Europe could harm the United States and, thus, increased the threat of the Holy Alliance's plans. At times, the prospect of a direct attack on the United States worried the cabinet, particularly Monroe and Calhoun. In October, Monroe informed Madison that he had no doubt "of the alledged project of the allied powers" or that, "if they succeeded with the colonies[,] they would, in the next instance, invade us." But the indirect threat of a Europeanized New World proved equally alarming, particularly to Adams. Adams viewed any movement against Spanish America as unlikely and any attempt to restore Spanish rule as certain to fail. But even a failed attempt to reconquer the New World might initiate a chain of events with dire consequences for the United States. Once the Allies found it impossible to prop up Spain, they would abandon the pretense and seek dominion for themselves. "The ultimate result of their undertaking," Adams feared, "would be to recolonize [the new states], partitioned out among themselves." France would seize Mexico and Buenos Aires; Russia would grab the Pacific provinces, including California. In this situation, Great Britain would claim Cuba "for her share of the scramble." This fear of a repartition of the New World drove the cabinet to make a stand in support of the new states and in "opposition against the Holy Alliance."

The fact and the logic of recognition dictated not only the response to the Holy Alliance's plans, but also the answer to Canning's proposal for a joint statement. From the beginning, Rush stressed the disparity in the American and British positions and urged Canning to recognize the Spanish American states. During the second week of meetings, Rush even decided to join in a declaration on his own authority, *"if the recognition be made by Great Britain without more delay."* "Upon no other footing whatever" was joint action possible. Adams reiterated this point in a meeting with the British minister in early November. With Canning unwilling to join the United States on this ground, the cabinet decided in its first meeting "to decline the overture of Great Britain" and "to take [its own] stand against the Holy Alliance." While Monroe and Calhoun suggested giving Rush "a discretionary power" to cooperate with Canning in an emergency, it was not until *after* the president delivered his message in early December that the cabinet considered accepting the British offer. As long as Canning withheld recognition, any plan for a united response would "[rest] only upon a casual coincidence of interests," increasing the commitment of the United States, while leaving Great Britain "free to accommodate her policy to any of those distributions of power, and partitions of territory [that were] the ultima ratio" of European politics. Only a common insistence on Spanish American independence could insure that a joint policy would prevent the dangers that worried the cabinet.

Monroe and Adams also considered a unilateral declaration better suited to defeat the European threat and to promote the nation's hemispheric interests. By acting alone, they expected to take advantage of their unique position. Moving unilaterally, as Monroe explained to Madison, would have a "better effect with our southern neighbours, as well as with Russia & other allied powers," than cooperating with Great Britain. Rather than join Great Britain in erecting an Anglo-American barrier against the Holy Alliance, Monroe and Adams attempted to entice its leader, the Russian czar, into not moving at all. They kept the United States and Great Britain apart as a way to play upon the czar's fears of "any connection or concert between [them]" and to pry from him "some accomodation to prevent" an accord. Unilateral action would not only meet the threat from the Holy Alliance, but also prevent new ties between Spanish America and Great Britain. In an Anglo-American partnership, Monroe noted, the United States would rank as "a secondary party" and Great Britain would receive "the principal credit." Following the British lead or failing to act at all would show the Spanish Americans that Great Britain afforded the only "guarantee" of their independence, "throw[ing] them completely into her arms [and] mak[ing] them her Colonies instead of those of Spain."

As Monroe and Adams grappled with this critical situation in late 1823, the fact and the logic of the recognition decision of early 1822 controlled their response.

Having decided that an independent, republican, and liberal New World was essential to the United States, they could not view the plans of the Holy Alliance with equanimity. Even a failed effort to restore Spanish rule in the former colonies, Monroe and Adams now worried, might encourage new steps toward monarchy within each state or produce a partition among the European powers. Their new approach to Spanish America further dictated that their stand against the Holy Alliance take a unilateral form. Only by acting alone could the United States counteract the plans of the Holy Alliance without furthering the influence of Great Britain among the new states. At the same time, Monroe and Adams believed that it was only by acting alone that they could retain complete control over the extent of their commitment to the New World. Their response in the fall of 1823 encompassed many elements and retained great flexibility. The Monroe Doctrine itself—three paragraphs in the president's annual message to Congress—was only the most public component of a multifaceted policy. Monroe and Adams also used other diplomatic tools to accomplish their goals. Furthermore, they carefully monitored the message's reception in the United States and Europe for months, remaining willing to strengthen, to redefine, or to abandon their public stance as needed. In the end, however, they reinterpreted the message not because of the attitude of Congress or Europe, but because of the response of Spanish American states who tried to use it to claim new support.

Monroe's message to Congress of 2 December 1823 formed the centerpiece of the administration's unilateral response. With it, Monroe and Adams framed the recently developed view of the nation's interests as immutable principles. An early section of the message included, and made public for the first time, an idea that Adams had expressed to Rush the previous summer. "The American Continents," Adams had asserted in July, "henceforth [would] no longer be subjects of *colonization*." Two other paragraphs near the end of the message bore directly on the European situation and the British proposal. In the first, Monroe alerted the European powers that the United States would view "any attempt on their part to extend their system to any portion of this hemisphere as dangerous to our peace and safety." The United States would not "interfere" with Europe's "existing colonies." But, with respect to the states that it had already recognized, it "could not view any interposition for the purpose of oppressing them, or controlling in any other manner their destiny, . . . in any other light than as the manifestation of an unfriendly disposition toward [itself]." In the second, the president reaffirmed the long-standing principle of noninterference in Europe's "internal concerns." Though apparently written by Monroe, these paragraphs showed Adams's influence in the clarity with which they demarcated the political systems of the two hemispheres and the emphasis that they placed on keeping these systems separate. As Adams desired, Monroe's message "[made] an American cause" and declared a commitment to "adhere inflexibly to [it]."

But the president's message formed only one component of the administration's response. Monroe and Adams also worked through regular diplomatic channels to further their goals. A note to the Russian minister, instructions for the ministers to France and Chile, and three official letters to Rush in London were all coordinated to effect their goals and to retain their freedom to respond as needed if the public message produced a backlash. In late November, Adams previewed Monroe's message for de Tuyll in a confidential note that "was drawn to correspond exactly with

[it]." This note not only responded to de Tuyll's disclosures of Russian views, but also advanced the policy of separating the czar from France. Through a variety of appeals, it encouraged the czar to make "a formal disavowal of any dispositions unfriendly to the United States." When he delivered the note, moreover, Adams may have tried to heighten Russian interest by mentioning that "there had been communications between us and Great Britain also relating to South American."

Similarly, Monroe and Adams took advantage of the fact that the new ministers to Chile, Heman Allen, and France, James Brown, had not yet departed the United States when the crisis developed. Seizing an opportunity to inform the Spanish Americans of the Allied threat, the British proposal, and the American response, Monroe and Adams further delayed Allen's departure to allow him to read Rush's dispatches. Adams's new instructions to Allen, moreover, stressed that the states of the New World composed "a distinct *American* portion of the human race[,] . . . differing from Europe in the fundamental principles upon which their respective Governments are founded." To attack the European threat from another angle, Adams also prepared instructions for Brown that embodied the "sentiments" of the president's message and directed him to "[manifest], on proper occasions, the dispositions of this Country." At the same time, Brown was to "avoid any measure by which the Government might be prematurely implicated." These diplomatic representations supplemented the public message in the effort to defeat the threat to Spanish America. Monroe wanted to round out these efforts with a new letter to the minister to Russia, Henry Middleton, instructing him to work upon the czar's fears of an Anglo-American concert in order to separate him from the Holy Alliance on Spanish American issues. While he asked Adams to prepare the necessary instructions on a number of occasions in November and December 1823, Adams apparently never did so.

At the same time, the administration's instructions to Rush showed a continuing flexibility with respect to Canning's offer. Monroe, in particular, refused to abandon the possibility of a joint response in the future. He insisted that the instructions avoid an explicit refusal to cooperate, even if Canning still held back on recognition. The first letter provided Rush with a carefully worded reply to Canning; the second letter explained the reasons for that reply. In an emergency, the first noted, "a *joint* manifestation of opinion" might still be adopted "according to the principles of our Government, and in the forms prescribed by our Constitution." To Monroe, the message to Congress and the letters to Rush together met Canning's proposal "in full extent . . . & in the mode to give it the greatest effect." But a future crisis might still require a joint statement. When Washington newspapers reported that French troops were preparing to invade the former colonies just one day after the message was sent to Congress, Monroe, for the first time, suggested accepting the British proposal. He wanted Adams to instruct Rush to offer to "unite with the British govt, in measures, to prevent the interference of the allied powers." Within days, new reports proved these rumors false. Even so, Monroe had confidential instructions sent to Rush that left open the possibility of "a further concert of operations." When he wrote Rush privately two weeks later, the president explained that he saw the message as a mode of cooperating with Canning—one that seemed more likely to succeed precisely because "the first public act" had been taken by the United States rather than Great Britain.

Prepared to redefine their position as necessary, Monroe and Adams carefully observed the message's reception both at home and abroad. The bulk of the domestic reaction, in the press and in Congress, praised the stand taken against the Holy Alliance. In Congress, members of each house quickly sought ways to show their support for the administration's position. Senator James Barbour considered proposing "a resolution advising the President to Co-operate by treaty with Great Britain." Representative David Trimble informed Adams that he planned "to offer a Resolution ecchoing back the Sentiments of the President's message." Both Barbour and Trimble held off from these proposals. But, in late December, the House requested information about the designs of the Holy Alliance. From the administration's perspective, this interest came too early. Monroe and Adams wanted to learn the British and European reactions to the message before opening the question in Congress. Still, their concerns made them wary of dissuading congressional action entirely. Suspicious of European intentions and worried that British resolve required a "demonstration of a determination to resist," Monroe counseled "that we should be very guarded in the answer" to the call for papers. Hinting at the confidentiality of the dispatches, they withheld the correspondence and postponed any congressional action. In late January, Clay presented a resolution supporting the message, but it quickly became entangled in the debates over the Greek revolution. By the end of the session, "events and circumstances" made it seem unnecessary, and he never brought it to a vote.

Convinced that Congress would support their course, Monroe and Adams awaited news from Europe. They had known when they drafted the message in late November that Canning's interest in joint action had "much abated." Unable to account for this shift, they worried about the intentions of the European allies and the British minister. Over the next six weeks, letters from Paris and London reporting upon a series of October meetings between Canning and the French minister, the Prince de Polignac, removed much of the mystery and relieved much of the anxiety. But even this news failed to dispel the administration's fears entirely. They anxiously waited for letters from the ministers in Europe and from an agent who they sent to spy on an expected European congress. As late as May 1824, Adams thought that "the policy of Great Britain & of Continental Europe, with regard to South America, [was] not yet fully disclosed." Despite his early doubts about the Allies' intentions and the reassuring reports of recent months, he believed that prudence demanded "watch[ing] with unabating attention" new developments and remaining ready "to adapt our own measures in reference to them." A month later, Monroe suggested a new attempt at "detaching Russia, from any co-operation with Spain, or any other member of the holy alliance, against So. Am:." He was still pushing this tactic in late July, when the cabinet discussed a "confidential dispatch [to Middleton] respecting the affairs of South America." For the remainder of Monroe's presidency, the administration remained alert to European developments.

This intense concern for the domestic and European reactions to the message stands in stark contrast to the administration's casual disregard of the Spanish American reaction. Initially, Monroe and Adams had tried to involve the new states. In late November, Adams not only delayed Allen's departure, but also met with the Colombian minister, José María Salazar, to apprise them of the situation. Once they sent in the message, however, Monroe and Adams seemed uninterested in the Spanish American response. Over the next nine months, they were startled when Colombia and formerly Portuguese Brazil tried to use it to secure aid against the European powers, including Spain, and an alliance. But the cabinet had never viewed the message as a pledge of military support; the United States, Monroe had emphasized to Rush from the beginning, "are not bound to engage in war." As the European danger dissipated, the administration retreated steadily from any such implications. When Salazar requested support against French attempts to promote monarchy in Colombia in July 1824, Monroe and Adams demurred. Adams informed him that the message encompassed only "a deliberate and concerted system of the allied Powers to exercise force." Even then, American aid would require a vote of Congress and "a previous understanding" with Great Britain. In private, the cabinet simply accepted that Colombia would have "to maintain its own independence." Developments in Europe alone could prompt the administration to act on the vague promises of the message.

To understand the Monroe administration's response to the critical situation that it confronted in the fall of 1823, it is necessary to place the president's message—the Monroe Doctrine—in context. Looking beyond the fall of 1823, the larger context included the sweeping reevaluation of American interests at the time of the recognition decision in early 1822. Focusing on the crisis weeks themselves, the larger context included the other parts of the American response. The Monroe Doctrine provided only the most public and, in some ways, most blunt component of a complex policy. Monroe and Adams designed the confidential note to de Tuyll and the instructions to Brown to supplement the message in checking the Holy Alliance. They intended the instructions to Allen and the meeting with Salazar to maximize the benefits of the message's unilateral stand in Spanish America. And they used the letters to Rush to preserve a possibility of Anglo-American cooperation that the message seemed to foreclose. In the months after they sent the message to Congress, Monroe and Adams found it unnecessary to play most of the cards that they had carefully dealt themselves. When they redefined the message in the summer of 1824, they did so in response not to the dangerously hostile reaction in Europe that they had feared, but to the excessively favorable reaction in Spanish America that they seem never to have contemplated.

The Monroe Doctrine served its intended purposes. Canning's information and proposal caught Monroe and Adams in a delicate position, committed by recognition and, more importantly, by a reconceptualization of the nation's interests to an independent, republican, and liberal New World. Through the annual message, they effectively announced that the Holy Alliance could not scare them into abandoning this goal. At the same time, however, their multifaceted response to the Allied threat and the British offer showed great caution. "A war for South American independence, . . . under certain circumstances, might be expedient," Adams admitted to Clay on the day that the message went to Congress. But he still believed that any war would "necessarily plac[e] high interests of the different portions of the Union in conflict with each other, and thereby [endanger] the Union itself." As such, Monroe and Adams avoided raising the stakes prematurely, even as they tried to discover the advantages of their unique position. Although the danger was probably never as great as the cabinet, including Adams, feared, it seemed sufficient to merit a potentially risky declaration of the new view of the nation's hemispheric interests.

The Monroe Doctrine testified to the continuing belief that the greatest danger to the United States lay in the expansion of European influence, institutions, or principles in its expanded neighborhood.

Expansionist Ambition, Not Republican Ideals

PIERO GLEIJESES

It was the United States, not Great Britain, that first recognised the independence of the Spanish American states in 1822, three years before any European government. "This recognition", [the historian] Samuel Flagg Bemis has stated, "was the greatest assistance rendered by any foreign power to the independence of Latin America."

Was it? It meant no material benefit to the rebels. The US government . . . refused to provide any loans, US merchants . . . held to their "arithmetic" neutrality, and US volunteers . . . shunned the rebel armies. It is difficult to see how recognition facilitated Bolívar's victories over the next two years—victories that ended in the destruction of Spanish power in South America. Nor did US recognition influence the behaviour of the European powers, except Britain, which viewed the United States as its rival for the favour of the new states. The United Kingdom recognised the Latin American states in 1825. Perhaps in the absence of the US recognition she would have waited longer. Perhaps, but here, too, the same point applies: British recognition had no effect on the course of the war.

This is also true of the Monroe Doctrine of December 1823, which asserted that the hemisphere was closed to European colonisation and to the extension of Europe's political system. "This principle," Henry Clay later stated, "was declared in the face of the world at a moment when there was reason to apprehend that the allied Powers were entertaining designs inimical to the freedom, if not the Independence of the new Governments. There is ground for believing that the declaration of it had considerable effect in preventing the maturity, if not in producing the abandonment, of all such designs."

Clay was boasting. Insofar as France and Russia may have been tempted to intervene, it was the British fleet that restrained them (something that the most lucid member of Monroe's cabinet, John Quincy Adams, recognised fully). In August 1817 a memorandum by Foreign Secretary Robert Castlereagh informed France, Russia, Austria and Prussia, in unequivocal terms, "that Great Britain would allow no European interference except on such terms as she chose to dictate"—that is, that "force was not to be employed except by Spain herself." Then, at the Congress at Aix-la-Chapelle in late 1818, Castlereagh bluntly reminded Tsar Alexander that Britain forbade any threat of interference by any other power in the relations between Spain and her colonies.

Finally, in the fall of 1823, as Europe was awash with rumours of a projected Franco-Russian expedition to the new world, Castlereagh's successor, George Canning, reiterated that Britain would forcefully oppose any French military action in Spanish America and obtained from the French, in the Polignac memorandum, a pledge that no such action would be undertaken. . . .

Piero Gleijeses, "Expansionist Ambition, Not Republican Ideals" from *The Journal of Latin American Studies* 24 (October 1992): 487–502, 504–505. Copyright © 1992. Reprinted with the permission of Cambridge University Press.

What the Monroe doctrine did was to score a clear propaganda victory by arousing the hopes of several Spanish American leaders that the United States would come to their assistance against Spain and the Holy Alliance—a delusion of which they were quickly disabused by US officials. And Monroe's statement carried another message. As [the historian] Richard Van Alstyne has remarked:

> The Monroe Doctrine lowered—or purported to lower—a hypothetical curtain over the American continents . . . Its dogmas—all phrased, let us repeat, as " Thou shalt nots"— were assimilated into the catechism of American nationalism . . . But it is not these negatives that really count; it is the hidden positives to the effect that the United States shall be the only colonizing power and the sole directing power in both North and South America. This is imperialism preached in the bland manner, for the only restrictions placed on the directing power are those which it imposes upon itself. The Monroe Doctrine is really an official declaration fencing in the "western hemisphere" as a United States sphere of influence.

Monroe's words were an ominous portent of which some perceptive Spanish American leaders were immediately aware. . . .

Territorial expansion had been part of the mission of the United States from the very outset—expansion against the decaying Spanish empire, and expansion into the lands of the Spanish Americans. This drive was bound to affect US attitudes toward the independence of Spanish America: there was bound to be a difference between the US stance toward the independence of Chile or Buenos Aires, colonies too distant to be part of the imperial vision, and toward those colonies that were close to the United States.

Whatever may have been felt for the more distant South Americans, US feelings toward the Mexicans were not neighbourly. "To be candid the majority of the people of the whole nation as far as I have seen them want nothing but tails to be more brutes than the Apes," Stephen Austin wrote from Mexico in 1823. His views were echoed by many. "[They] look upon us . . . as inferiors," warned the Mexican minister in Washington. The stereotype was based, notes a scholar, "not so much on direct observation or experience with Mexicans, but was in large part an extension of negative attitudes toward Catholic Spaniards which Anglo Americans had inherited from their Protestant English forebears." Antipathy was bred by propinquity and fuelled by greed: the USA wanted Texas. And no one more than Henry Clay, that warm friend of Spanish American independence. When it came to the Mexicans— and Texas—his generosity lapsed into something less pristine: "The question was," he pleaded in an 1820 debate, "by whose race shall it [Texas] be peopled? In our hands it will be peopled by freemen. . . . In the hands of others, it may become the habitation of despotism and of slaves."

When praising the role of the United States on behalf of Spanish American independence, patriotic US scholars avoid discussion of Cuba. . . .

It was [Thomas] Jefferson who first cast his gaze toward Cuba, strategically situated and rich in sugar and slaves. In 1809 he even counselled President [James] Madison to prepare for a deal with Napoleon whereby France would give Cuba to the United States and receive a free hand in Spanish America in return. "That would be a price," he wrote, "and I would immediately erect a column on the southernmost limit of Cuba, and inscribe on it a *ne plus ultra* as to us in that direction."

The US desire to annex Cuba transcended sectional divisions. Southern and Northern statesmen united in greed. Adams' 1823 instructions to the US minister in Madrid illuminated both his and Monroe's dreams:

> Cuba, almost in sight of our shores, from a multitude of considerations has become an object of transcendent importance to the commercial and political interests of our Union. . . . it is scarcely possible to resist the conviction that the annexation of Cuba to our federal republic will be indispensable to the continuance and integrity of the Union itself.

But US dreams clashed with the sea that encircled the island—the sea and the British fleet. For Britain had made it clear that it would not tolerate Cuba's annexation to the United States, and the British fleet dominated the waves—facts that Jefferson in his impetuous longing had for a moment overlooked ("Cuba can be defended by us without a navy"), but which had troubled more sober US statesmen.

If the United States could not annex Cuba immediately, then it would wait until the fruit was ripe; time was on her side. In Adams' words, "there are laws of political as well as of physical gravitation; and if an apple severed by the tempest from its native tree cannot choose but fall to the ground, Cuba, forcibly disjoined from its own unnatural connection with Spain and incapable of self-support, can gravitate only towards the North American Union, which by the same law of nature cannot cast her off from its bosom."

Through the administrations of Jefferson, Madison, Monroe and Adams, no US official or congressman expressed any sympathy for those Cubans who sought the independence of their country. On this, there was no difference between "warm-hearted" Clay and "cool-headed" Adams. But President Adams and Secretary Clay did more than avert their eyes: they became active champions of Spanish rule in Cuba.

Angered by Spain's refusal to acknowledge their independence, and by her attempts to prolong the war, Colombia and Mexico considered launching an expedition to liberate Cuba and Puerto Rico, punishing Madrid and depriving her of bases from which to harass them. Overestimating both the strength of the threat and [the South American Patriot Simón] Bolívar's desire to free Cuba, the United States reacted with extreme wariness. "The success of the enterprise is by no means improbable," warned Clay, noting that "a large portion of the inhabitants of the islands is predisposed to a separation from Spain, and would therefore form a powerful auxiliary to the republican arms."

To avert the danger that Spain might lose Cuba, the United States turned to Europe. It sought to persuade Ferdinand of Spain to recognise the independence of Mexico and Colombia so that they would have little incentive to free Cuba and Puerto Rico. It also urged Russia, France and Britain to reason with Ferdinand. But France and Russia remained aloof, while Britain countered with an unwelcome proposal: it was not Colombia and Mexico, but the great powers that posed the greatest threat to Spain's control of Cuba—France, Britain and the United States should, therefore, pledge that they had no designs on the island.

To prevent the liberation of Cuba, the United States also turned to Colombia and Mexico. "I know, sir—the documents before us prove it—that we have been exhibiting the character of a *political busybody* in the Cabinets of . . . America," a US senator remarked. First the United States reasoned—to no avail. Then it urged, and finally it threatened: "The United States have too much at stake in the fortunes of Cuba, to allow them to see with indifference a war of invasion . . . The humanity of the United States . . . would constrain them, even at the hazard of losing the friendship, greatly as they value it, of Mexico and Colombia, to employ all the means necessary to their security."

US officials opposed the liberation of Cuba because they feared that it might become a second Haiti: that the slaves might take advantage of the conflict to seize power. They also feared that other powers, such as France or Britain, might take advantage of a weak, independent Cuba and occupy the island. But one wonders whether another consideration was not present: the independence movement in Cuba had strong democratic tendencies; it advocated both the abolition of slavery and equal rights for blacks and whites.

Had such a Cuban republic emerged, the fruit would never have ripened. For a democratic Cuba would bitterly resist annexation to a Jeffersonian America, where the blacks were slaves or outcasts and where enlighted whites sought to solve the race question by shipping blacks to Africa. (In Jefferson's words, neither "blot or mixture" could be tolerated in the United States.) This would have been the demise of the dream to annex Cuba and a threat to racial harmony, such as it was, in the United States.

While the Cuban issue was in the forefront of the worries of the US government, President Adams received, and accepted, the invitation to attend the Panama Congress organised by Bolívar. The Congress would consider issues of great importance to the United States, notably the Mexican and Colombian expedition to free Cuba and the place of Haiti among the nations of the Western Hemisphere. As Adams turned to the Senate to ask for confirmation of the two envoys he had selected, he expected swift approval. But there was nothing swift in the ensuing debate.

"Sir, I can see nothing around us but dark, lowering, portentous storms. I am opposed to this whole matter of Panama," Congressman John Floyd of Virginia cried out. His anguish was shared by a great many of his peers.

The anguish and the dark storms developed against the backdrop of the divisive presidential elections of 1824. In these elections Andrew Jackson had received only a plurality of electoral votes, followed by Adams, William Crawford and Clay. Therefore, the House had to choose among the first three. Clay, with votes to distribute, became the kingmaker. "I seemed to be the favorite of everybody. Describing my situation to a distant friend, I said to him, 'I am enjoying, whilst alive, the posthumous honors which are usually awarded to the venerated dead.'" As soon as he selected Adams, however, "the oil has been instantly transformed into vinegar." His subsequent appointment as Secretary of State aroused a storm of accusations and counteraccusations—"secret conclaves" had been held, and "cabals" had been entered "to impair the pure principles of our republican institutions . . . [and] to prostrate that fundamental maxim which maintains the supremacy of the people's will." Adams' presidency would be dominated by the cry against the corrupt bargain, and the struggle for the next presidential election began "within a matter of weeks—nay days"—of his election.

This bitter partisanship was fuelled by Adams' first presidential message:

> In a bold, courageous, statesmanlike, and politically inept assertion of the government's responsibilities to advance the intellectual and economic well-being of the country, Adams laid before Congress a program of public works of breathtaking magnitude, a program immediately denounced by the Radicals and Jacksonians as unconstitutional and visionary.

Included in Adams' message were his acceptance of the invitation to the Panama Congress and his request for Senate confirmation of the two envoys he had selected.

The ensuing debate was not memorable for its intellectual power, its originality or its wit. But it is the most detailed, the most lengthy debate on US policy toward Latin America during the latter's wars of independence—not only in the number of pages it occupies in the congressional records, but in the number of participants, both in the House and the Senate, and in the number of days that it consumed.

The debate touched on religious matters. In his message to the Senate, Adams had noted, "Some of the Southern Nations are, even yet, so far under the dominion of prejudice, that they have incorporated, with their political constitutions, an exclusive church, without toleration of any other than the dominant sect." The United States should go to Panama to help the Latins free themselves from "this last badge of religious bigotry and oppression.". . .

The debate also touched on the rights of Spain. Many of the critics worried that participation at the Panama Congress "would be cause of just complaint on the part of Spain." Not that they feared that "wretched, degraded, Spain" would respond by making war on the United States—she was too weak for that—but "Surely, Sir, we are not to be called upon to violate our neutral obligations towards Spain because Spain is weak." What would this say of the country's "sense of justice" "Will it comport with out character for candor and good faith?"

This sudden sensitivity was all the more touching because it was unexpected. (Indeed, some of the most sensitive souls were supporters of General Jackson, whose contempt for Spain was legendary.) One can sympathise with the wonderment of an administration supporter: "We have become suddenly alive to the claims of Spain. We have more than once invaded her territories. We have, during the whole contest, received the flags of the revolting Colonies in our ports. We have recognised their independence. . . . But now, taking lessons from prudence, and counsel from our fears, we cannot send Ministers to Panama, without violating the delicate relations of neutrality."

The religious sensitivity of the Latin Americans and the pride of old Spain were not momentous matters. But what about the other issues that attracted the pompous eloquence of Congress: the place of the United States in relation to the Latin American countries, the fate of Cuba and that of Haiti? . . .

Almost every speaker, on both sides of the aisle, referred to Cuba. Far more was said about Cuba alone than the rest of Latin America combined. This reflected Cuba's importance to the United States—"the most delicate, and vastly the most important point in all our foreign relations," in the words of a congressman from Massachusetts.

As opponents of the administration vented their anger at Adams, accusing him of preparing to betray America's sacred interests, as they droned on, relentlessly, one can sympathise with the exasperation of one of Adams' supporters: "It is strange, that, agreeing with the Executive in object, you should so differ in your opinion of the means!" If the critics were intransigent ("Cuba and Puerto Rico must remain as they are"), so, too, were the administration's supporters ("It is our interest and our duty to keep Cuba as it is"). And if the critics based their arguments on economic, strategic and humanitarian grounds, so too did the supporters. It was neither a partisan, nor a sectional question. Congressmen from the South and from the North, supporters and critics of the administration, rivalled each other in the luridness of their descriptions of the horrors that would befall the Cubans (that is, the whites in Cuba) if the Colombians and Mexicans were to liberate the island. All agreed that this would result in the freedom of the slaves—an intolerable proposition, even if it did not lead to a massacre of the whites. "Let us for a moment suppose," reasoned an administration supporter, "that the independence of Cuba should be effected without an attempt by a certain part of its population to attain the ascendancy—is it not reasonable for us to suppose that part of its population, as in the other South American Republics, would all be declared free; and, if so, with the black population of Mexico on the frontier of Louisiana, and Hayti and Cuba for neighbors, what would be the condition of the Southern planters?" . . .

Just as Cuba must remain under the Spanish yoke—until the fruit be ripe—so Haiti must remain a pariah. In the words of a senator from Georgia, "the intercourse which would result from such [diplomatic] relations would be productive of the most awful calamity—would introduce a moral contagion, compared with which, physical pestilence, in the utmost imaginable degree of its horrors, would be light and insignificant. . . . Is the emancipated slave, his hands yet reeking in the blood of his murdered master, to be admitted into their [Southern States] ports, to spread the doctrines of insurrection, and to strengthen and invigorate them, by exhibiting in his own person an example of successful revolt?" Of the many speakers who addressed the case of Haiti, not one advocated establishing diplomatic relations and not one accused the administration of such a sordid thought. . . .

[T]he debate was artificial. What divided the members of Congress was far less than what united them, and it was partisan bitterness, one surmises, that explains the venom of the dissensions, . . . As one historian notes, "the critics of the mission felt very little kinship with the Latin Americans. . . . The new republics 'differ from us in every particular,' announced [Democrat John M.] Berrien of Georgia, 'in language, religion, laws, manners, customs, habits, as a mass, and as individuals.' [Republican William Cabell] Rives of Virginia thought the cultural conflict so great as to preclude 'any cordial fraternity between us and them'." The point is well taken. But how much kinship, how much sympathy, did the supporters of the mission feel? Their expressions of sympathy for Latin America—which are echoed by most of the critics of the mission—are brief, perfunctory, devoid of warmth, except when expressing their opposition to any change in Cuba (barring annexation to the United States) and to accepting Haiti in the comity of nations. It is not an uplifting debate, it is not one in which ideas, dreams or ideals clash. This is why it is so shallow and repetitive, devoid of both the passion and sparks of generosity that mark the debates on Greece in 1824 and on the Indian Removal Bill in 1830. It ended, at long last, on 14 March in the Senate when Adams' envoys were confirmed and on 22 April in the House when the necessary funds were approved. "The Mission to Panama has been very ungraciously sent," remarked a US diplomat.

Great Britain accepted the invitation to attend the Panama Congress with far more dispatch and grace than did the United States. She, too, opposed the liberation of Cuba, but she kept her counsel, in order not to offend Colombia and Mexico, and left it to the United States to do the threatening.

Beyond the United States and Britain, however, a third country helped the rebels: Haiti, the pariah. The Haitian government alone provided direct aid to the Spanish Americans in their quest for independence. The aid was crucial, for it was given when the struggle for independence in Spanish America was at its nadir. "You are the greatest benefactor on the earth," Bolívar wrote to Haitian President Alexandre Pétion. "One day America will proclaim you her Liberator.". . .

For the reconquest of *Tierra Firme* [("dry land," a reference to the Isthmos of Panama)], he received no loans from Haiti—only gifts: six thousand rifles, a ship with twenty cannons and a few smaller vessels, an undisclosed amount of money and a printing press. In return, Pétion asked only that slavery be abolished in the lands Bolívar would liberate. . . .

Bolívar soon forgot his debt to Haiti, just as so many historians later forgot Haiti's contribution, waxing eloquent, instead, on the role of the United States or Britain.

Of the three countries that rendered assistance to the Spanish American rebels, Britain comes first in material terms, and Haiti comes first for the generosity of its contribution and its timing. US sympathy for Spanish American independence was shallow and warped by territorial greed. As the diplomatic correspondence and the debate on the Panama Congress show so well, the United States did more than oppose the transfer of Cuba to another power—it simply, bluntly and unequivocally opposed Cuban independence, just as it hungered for Texas.

Bolívar recognised the lack of a community of interests between the United States and Spanish America and the danger that the United States represented for his region. Instead of Monroe's north-south axis (excluding Europe from the New World), he sought an east-west axis, calling on the best of the Old World (Britain) to help Spanish America and protect her from both the United States and the Holy Alliance.

Bolivarianism and Monroeism were two opposite conceptions of Panamericanism. "Bolívar was in fact the originator of the Pan-American idea," a British official wrote in 1916, "but he probably did not contemplate the consummation of his policy under the aegis of the United States." Indeed, he did not. Panamericanism, as it has developed for the last hundred years, represents Monroe's victory and Bolívar's defeat.

Domestic Politics and Personal Ambitions

ERNEST R. MAY

Books on the [Monroe] Doctrine [have] analyzed the principles which had been announced: European powers should not help Spain regain her former colonies; European monarchies should not impose their ideology on nations in the New World; and there should be no future European colonization in the Americas. [The historian]

Reprinted by permission of the publisher from *The Making of the Monroe Doctrine* by Ernest R. May, pp. viii–x, 132–133, 181, 183–189, 255, Cambridge, Mass.: Harvard University Press, Copyright © 1975, 1992 by the President and Fellows of Harvard College.

Dexter Perkins made a convincing case that the dangers envisioned had been unreal. To the extent that statesmen on the continent contemplated aiding Spain, overturning American republics, or establishing new colonies in the Western Hemisphere, they were deterred by fear of Britain, not by concern about the United States.

It was clear from the record, however, that the American doctrine had been developed in large part because Monroe and his advisers faced issues which seemed to require decisions. They had an invitation to join Britain in resisting the alleged European threat to Latin America. Everyone recognized that acceptance would mean abandonment of the posture previously held and, as Monroe put it, entanglement "in European politicks, & wars." On the other hand, Monroe, and most of those whom he consulted, saw the offer as so advantageous that it should not be turned down. Except for the maxim that there should be no future colonization, the Monroe Doctrine expressed general agreement with British positions.

Coincidentally, the administration faced the question of whether to recognize or aid Greeks who were fighting for independence from the Ottoman Empire. There was loud public demand to do so. The argument for resisting this demand was again to avoid entanglement in European politics. Daniel Webster summarized a popular view, however, when he asked how the United States could defend liberty in Latin America and ignore the same cause in Europe.

In the upshot, the British alliance did not materialize, and the United States did not lead in recognizing Greece. These decisions, even more than the rhetoric that accompanied them, reaffirmed a policy of nonentanglement. But why?

The literature on the Monroe Doctrine did not answer this question—at least not to my satisfaction. Among those who knew of the British alliance overture, everyone except Secretary of State [John Quincy] Adams favored acceptance. Adams was the only member of the administration consistently to oppose recognition of Greece. Explaining why the outcomes were victories for Adams, [the historian Samuel Flagg] Bemis says simply that his "views by the force of their reason had prevailed over everybody." The same explanation appears in other accounts. In fact, however, there is no evidence that Adams changed anyone's opinion. His own diary records that his colleagues held much the same views at the end as at the beginning. Yet Adams got what he wanted.

When puzzling about what besides Adams's persuasive powers might have produced this outcome, I remembered what had struck me when poring through his manuscripts—the quantity of diary entries and especially correspondence that had to do with the approaching presidential election. It was a preoccupation in his house-hold. His wife characterized the coming contest as "a mighty struggle which arouses alike all the passions and most ardent feelings of mankind." And, as it happened, most of his rivals were in one way or another participants in the foreign debate. [Secretary of the Treasury] William H. Crawford and [Secretary of War] John C. Calhoun were fellow members of Monroe's cabinet. Henry Clay was the speaker of the house. Andrew Jackson, who had just begun to be talked of as a candidate, was a newly elected member of the Senate. None of the existing accounts of the Monroe Doctrine makes more than passing reference to the "mighty struggle" which filled the mind of Mrs. Adams. Yet the more I thought about it, the more I became convinced that the struggle for the presidency might provide a key to understanding why the foreign policy debates came out as they did.

In [my] book I explore three hypotheses. The first is that the positions of the various policymakers were largely determined by their ideas of national interest and their personal interplay—in other words, that Adams's convictions were more definite and firm and he more stubborn and forceful than the others. The second is that the outcomes are best understood as products of international politics. The hypothesis is that, in view of what other governments were doing, the range of options open to Americans was very narrow, and the choices actually made were those which would have been made in the same circumstances by almost any reasonable men. The third hypothesis is that the whole process was governed by domestic politics. The positions of the policymakers were determined less by conviction than by ambition. They had different stakes riding on the outcomes, and Adams had a greater stake than the others.

No one of these hypotheses seems to me inherently the more plausible. In a study of American foreign policy during and after World War II, I concluded that convictions about "lessons" of history were a controlling force. Examining in more detail the China policy of that period, I found the strength of character of Secretary of State [George C.] Marshall a critical determinant. In analyzing American policy during World War I, I was most impressed by the extent to which international politics constrained decision-makers in Washington. In the case of the Monroe Doctrine, however, my conclusion is that the outcomes are best explained in terms of domestic politics. . . .

The men who constructed the Monroe Doctrine were all deeply interested in the approaching presidential election. Indeed, it is not too much to say that this subject preoccupied most of them. Mrs. Adams's diary and letters testify that this was the case for her husband, and his own diary suggests the same. Calhoun's nonofficial correspondence for the period dealt with little else. The same is true of Crawford and Clay. We should therefore examine the stakes for which these men were competing and the strategies which they had adopted, for it seems likely that expectations and fears related to the election could well have influenced their reasoning about the pressing issues of foreign policy. . . .

Throughout, Clay's chief target was Adams. In the summer of 1822, probably with Clay's knowledge if not connivance, a document was issued that accused Adams of having truckled to the British during the peace negotiations [ending the War of 1812] at Ghent and having shown a willingness to sacrifice the interests of westerners to those of New England fishermen. The author was Jonathan Russell of Rhode Island who, along with Clay and Adams, had been a member of the delegation at Ghent. All the while, newspapers supporting Clay emphasized Adams's Federalist past, his possible pro-British inclinations, and the likelihood that he represented narrow sectional interests.

The logic of this campaign was self-evident. If Clay could make it appear that he alone was the nationalist candidate, he might rally to himself western and northern Republicans whose concern was to prevent the election of Crawford, the triumph of the Radicals, and the preservation of a southern dynasty.

Adams's strategy was partly dictated by these attacks from Clay, some of which were echoed by supporters of Crawford and Calhoun. He had the advantage of being the only prominent candidate who was not a slaveholder. He thus had some chance of capitalizing on the antislavery sentiment that had manifested itself in the North, parts of the West, and even parts of the South during the controversy of 1819–1820 over the admission of Missouri as a state. He had the disadvantages of being his father's son, a former Federalist, and a citizen of a state that was viewed as having interests adverse to those of many other states. Adams needed to establish his credentials as a Republican, a patriot, and a man with a national and not just sectional perspective. . . .

Like Clay, Adams set forth a foreign policy platform. He did so in 1821 in a Fourth of July speech delivered in Washington and subsequently published not only in pro-Adams newspapers but as a pamphlet. Much of his speech simply attacked Britain. [Pierre de] Poletica, then the Russian minister to the United States, characterized it as "from one end to the other nothing but a violent diatribe against England, intermingled with republican exaggerations." Also, however, the speech included a prophecy that colonialism would not survive anywhere. Giving more than an intimation of the forthcoming administration decision to recognize some of the Latin American republics, these passages answered Clay's implied accusation that Adams lacked sympathy for people struggling for independence. Also, Adams's speech countered Clay's appeal for a counterpoise to the Holy Alliance by calling in strident language for America to avoid involvement in European politics and to guard above all her own security and peace. "Wherever the standard of freedom or independence has been or shall be unfurled, there will her heart, her benedictions, and her prayers be," said Adams in the lines best to be remembered later. "But she goes not abroad in search of monsters to destroy. She is the well-wisher to the freedom and independence of all. She is the champion and vindicator only of her own."

Characterizing his speech variously as a direct reply to Clay's Lexington speech and as an address "to and for *man,* as well as to and for my country," Adams emphasized to various correspondents how plainly it demonstrated his hostility to the British. To a friendly Philadelphia editor, he wrote that he had meant to warn the British against yielding to their "malignant passions." To another prominent Phildelphian, he explained, "I thought it was high time that we should be asking ourselves, where we were in our relations with that country." Adams manifestly hoped that his Fourth of July oration would put to rest any suspicion that he was an Anglophile.

In the following year, when there appeared Jonathan Russell's indictment of his conduct at Ghent, Adams set aside all but the most imperative business and employed the better part of his summer composing a book-length answer. Being diligent enough and lucky enough to find the originals of some documents that Russell had misquoted and misused, Adams succeeded in demolishing Russell's case. The episode, had, however, demonstrated that the charge of partiality to Britain was a hydra he would have to fight as long as he remained a candidate, and thereafter he continually hacked at it. The *National Journal,* a newspaper started in Washington in November 1823 as a personal organ for Adams, asserted that independence of Britain and the rest of the Old World would remain the chord of its editorial policy.

In campaigning for the presidency, Adams faced problems that did not face Clay, for he was responsible for what happened as well as for what was said. Apparently, he felt that mere rhetoric would have little practical effect on the policies of other governments toward the United States. Otherwise he would not have drafted the notes and dispatches which Crawford criticized and Monroe fretfully modified nor would he have assailed Great Britain in a public speech. On the other hand, he showed keen concern lest the Monroe administration *do* something that would provoke anger or reprisals abroad. After recognition of the Latin American republics, he counseled Monroe to postpone actually sending envoys until reactions had been reported from London and the continental capitals. He fought in the cabinet against any encouragement of an independence movement in Cuba. The prospect that independence might be followed by American annexation, he argued, could lead the British to take preemptive action and seize the island. Similarly, though publicly declaring himself sympathetic with the Greeks, Adams was emphatic in cabinet in opposing any official encouragement. He protested even the proposal that a fact-finding commission be dispatched, as had been done early on for some of the Latin American states. Both the British and the Holy Allies, he warned, could take offense.

The contrast between the boldness of Adams's language and the cautiousness of his actions was due in part, of course, to differences between his role as candidate and his role as responsible statesman. But Adams's efforts to avoid actual trouble with England or the continental powers also served his interests as a candidate. In the first place, he had to be aware that any real trouble with a foreign nation would be blamed on him. If the trouble were with England, the result could be fatally to weaken Adams's base of support in the sea-dependent New England states and among Anglophiles and former Federalists who, while they were sure to deplore his campaign oratory, might nevertheless vote for him as a lesser evil. In the second place, Adams could not ignore the fact that, if war began to seem imminent, public attention would shift away from the accomplishments for which he could claim credit, such as the annexation of Florida, and focus instead on the probable demands of the conflict to come. Notice, publicity, and interest would go to Calhoun, the secretary of war, who had been a clamorous advocate of preparedness, or perhaps to the military hero, Jackson. Reasons of politics as well as reasons of state could have led Adams to the positions he took within the cabinet.

Adams's optimum strategy thus involved preserving relative tranquility in the nation's international relations while at the same time persuading the doubtful that he was as patriotic and anti-British as any dyed-in-the-wool Jeffersonian and as much a nationalist and as much a partisan of the frontiersmen as was Clay. It was not a strategy easily pursued, especially by a man who felt compelled to explain to a diary the highmindedness of his every action.

Calhoun's task was simpler despite the fact that he, too, held a responsible office. The basis for his campaign was an assumption that none of the other candidates could win. He discounted Clay on the ground that no westerner could receive the votes of the North and South. Crawford would fail, he believed, because his Georgia base and Virginian support would arouse hostility in northern states where electors were chosen by popular ballot and because his advocacy of states' rights would alienate people who wanted federal aid for canals, roads, and manufacturing establishments. Adams's disabilities were his identification with New England, his Federalist past, and his lack of experience on domestic issues. Calhoun thought that his own championing of internal improvements, a protective tariff, and frontier defense would capture some of Clay's constituents; his South Carolina background would bring him support in the South; and his nationalistic policies plus his Connecticut ties would allow him to win over some of Adams's partisans.

Calhoun's strategy thus involved out-Claying Clay on internal issues while seeking to chop away at Adams's credibility as a candidate. Through his Federalist allies, the newspapers established by his friends, and Pennsylvania organs controlled by the "Family Party," Calhoun advertised his positions and sounded the refrain that, if neither Clay nor Adams could win, then all opponents of Crawford and the Radicals should rally in his camp. At first, this campaign avoided direct attacks on either Clay or Adams. By 1823, however, Calhoun had become more confident. Late that summer, he directed a change in policy, writing confidentially to his lieutenants that they and the pro-Calhoun press should begin to emphasize policy differences with Adams and to call attention to the fact that Adams's onetime Federalism so compromised him that he would never win the votes of true Republicans outside New England and might even fail to win their votes there. Calhoun's strategy was thus in part complementary to Clay's. It aimed at discrediting Adams and driving him out of the race.

Crawford, too, had a simpler problem than Adams. He had to take blame or credit for what he did as secretary of the treasury, and he and his friends had continually to fight unfounded charges of misuse of funds or patronage. At least by 1823, however, he had less answerability for other activities of the administration, for it has become notorious that he opposed not only Adams and Calhoun but also Monroe on almost every domestic issue.

Crawford campaigned as, in effect, the leader of an old Jeffersonian party whose principles had been deserted by the Monroe administration. His managers branded all other candidates as actual or potential tools of the Federalists. They contended that the whole Missouri question had been gotten up by Federalists as a device for disrupting Republican unity, and they labeled the domestic programs espoused by Clay and Calhoun as Hamilton's programs in new disguise. They said and for the most part believed that, in any case, these two renegade Republicans would eventually drop out. The ultimate contest would be between Crawford and Adams. Hence they persistently voiced the theme that Adams, the ex-Federalist, was in fact the Federalist candidate.

Until late in 1823, there was no Jackson strategy, for Jackson himself was not yet committed to running, and the men urging him to do so took no action except to disparage other candidates and stimulate signs of the general's personal popularity.

As of the autumn of 1823, Adams was therefore the central figure in the presidential campaign. Clay, Calhoun, and Crawford were all concentrating on undermining him, and he was battling their efforts to tar him as a lukewarm friend of liberty, an Anglophile, a Federalist, and a candidate with a hopelessly narrow electoral base. In view of the small numbers of legislators and voters whose shifts in opinion could transform the prospects for 1824, the contest was carried on relentlessly by all parties.

Knowing the stakes and strategies of the candidates, a detached observer aware of the pressing foreign policy issues might well have made the following predictions:

- That Adams would oppose acceptance of the proffered informal alliance with England. Likely to get most of the credit or blame for anything the administration did in foreign affairs, he would be held to have been its author. Those voters disposed to worry about his possible Federalist or Anglophile proclivities might feel that their fears had been confirmed. Furthermore, Adams would be open to fresh attack from Clay for failing to maintain America's independence. The result would be to cost him important marginal votes in the West, erode his support in the Middle States, and perhaps even lose him influential backers in Vermont, New Hampshire, and Maine. Adams's political interests would be best served if the British offer were spurned.

- That Adams would also oppose actual recognition of Greece. In the first place, he was likely to fear trouble with the continental powers, producing the domestic effects that he had tried to avert by counseling Monroe to be forceful in language but cautious in deed. In the second place, he had to anticipate embarrassment from the fact that the logical person to be envoy or commissioner to Greece was Edward Everett of Harvard, who had composed the pro-Greek manifesto in the *North American Review,* made no secret of his desire to have the job, and expected Adams's help in getting it. Since Everett was a Federalist, Adams had reason to expect that the appointment would fuel Republican prejudices. On the other hand, to deny Everett the post would be to offend Federalists in New England and elsewhere who might otherwise go to the polls for Adams and who seemed almost certain to do so if Calhoun fell out of the race. It was in Adams's interest as a candidate that any change in American posture toward Greece be postponed until after the election.
- That Crawford and Calhoun and their adherents would favor both alliance with England and recognition of Greece if Adams could be made to seem the sponsor of these acts because of the harm they might work on his election prospects.
- That Calhoun would advocate these steps with special vehemence because they promised him the added benefit of arousing public concern about a possible war and hence turning public attention to his department and to the preparedness measures which he had all along been advocating.

The test of what was and what was not in the personal political interest of the various candidates would have yielded much more specific predictions than any test based on suppositions about their ideological positions or about conditions in the politics of other countries. Moreover, most of these predictions would have been right on the nose. . . .

In the instance of the Monroe Doctrine, the positions adopted by American policymakers seem to me to be best explained as functions of their domestic ambitions—Monroe's, to leave the presidency without being followed by recrimination and to be succeeded by someone who would not repudiate his policies; Adams's, Calhoun's, and Clay's, to become President; Jefferson's, [Albert] Gallatin's, and perhaps Madison's, to see Crawford succeed. Consistently with their fundamental beliefs, any of these men could have taken different positions. Adams, for example, could have reasoned just as easily as Jefferson that concert with England would guarantee America's independence, security, and peace. He actually said as much not long before the specific issues materialized. The processes producing the actual foreign policy decisions are better understood as bargaining encounters among men with differing perspectives and ambitions than as debates about the merits of different policies. And the outcomes are most explicable as ones that equilibrated the competing or conflicting interests of men with differing political assets.

This conclusion may seem cynical. It is not meant to be. For it is in fact an affirmation that foreign policy can be determined less by the cleverness or wisdom of a few policymakers than by the political structure which determines their incentives.

✪ *F U R T H E R   R E A D I N G*

Harry Ammon. *James Monroe* (1970)
_____, "Monroe Doctrine: Domestic Politics or National Decision?" *Diplomatic History* 5 (Winter 1981): 53–70
Samuel Flagg Bemis, *John Quincy Adams and the Foundations of American Foreign Policy* (1949)
Kinley J. Brauer, "1820–1860: Economics and the Diplomacy of American Expansionism." in William H. Becker and Samuel F. Wells Jr., eds., *Economics and World Power* (1984)
Edward P. Crapol. "John Quincy Adams and the Monroe Doctrine: Some New Evidence," *Pacific Historical Review* 48 (1974): 413–418
Noble E. Cunningham Jr., *The Presidency of James Monroe* (1996)
Michael F. Holt, *Political Parties and American Political Development from the Age of Jackson to the Age of Lincoln* (1992)
John J. Johnson, *A Hemisphere Apart* (1990)
Lawrence S. Kaplan, "The Monroe Doctrine and the Truman Doctrine: The Case of Greece." *Journal of the Early Republic* 13 (1993): 1–21
Howard Kushner. *Conflict on the Northwest Coast: American-Russian Rivalry in the Pacific Northwest, 1790–1867* (1975)
Walter LaFeber, ed., *John Quincy Adams and American Continental Empire* (1965)
Lester D. Langley, *The Americas in the Age of Revolution* (1996)
John E. Lewis Jr., *John Quincy Adams* (2001)
Gretchen Murphy, *Hemispheric Imaginings* (2005)
Paul C. Nagel, *John Quincy Adams* (1997)
Lynn Hudson Parsons, *John Quincy Adams* (1999)
Bradford Perkins, *Castlereagh and Adams* (1964)
Dexter Perkins, *A History of the Monroe Doctrine* (1955)
Robert V. Remini, *John Quincy Adams* (2002)
Greg Russell, *John Quincy Adams* (1995)
Norman E. Saul, *Distant Friends* (1991) (on U.S.-Russia)
Charles Sellers, *The Market Revolution: Jacksonian America*, 1815–1846 (1991)
William E. Weeks, *Building the Continental Empire* (1996)
_____, *John Quincy Adams and American Global Empire* (1992)

CHAPTER 7

Westward Expansion
and Indian Removal

*Americans' vast migration westward in the nineteenth century has often been
viewed as an inexorable movement into empty lands. In fact, of course, the rich
territory along the frontier had inhabitants—indigenous American peoples, the
Native Americans, or Indians. The story of expansion is thus also the story of Indian
decline—owing sometimes to European American diseases, sometimes to wars and
massacres, and sometimes to treaties, honored and unhonored.*

*The removal of the Indians that began in the early stages of European
settlement during the colonial period stemmed from a greed for land. Europeans
and Americans justified their land grabbing by claiming that Native American
cultures were inherently inferior to white culture. Indian religious customs,
communal land holding, subsistence economies, and decentralized tribal
governments seemed at odds with European American notions of legitimate social
and political organization.*

*After the 1780s, federal policy treated each tribe as a sovereign entity capable
of signing treaties with the U.S. government. Although federal officials dealt with
tribes as separate nations, they hoped the Indians would abandon their traditional
ways and become "Americanized." Many tribes and tribal factions did adopt aspects
of white culture, including European and American dress, English language,
Christian religion, private enterprise, and in some cases even slaveholding. But
as whites relentlessly pushed westward into the trans-Appalachian territory, they
clashed with Native American populations that held treaty-guaranteed lands and
resisted white encroachment. In the War of 1812, Indians in the Old Northwest, led
by the Shawnee chieftain Tecumseh, joined British soldiers to battle U.S. forces. Soon
these Indians were punished for their resistance to white advancement: The federal
government ordered them moved to the trans-Mississippi West. The Kickapoos, Sacs,
Foxes, Chippewas, Sioux, Potawatomies, Winnebagos, and others reluctantly trekked
to lands beyond the Mississippi River.*

*Whites' demands for land also squeezed out the tribes of the Southeast: the
Cherokees, Choctaws, Creeks, Seminoles, and Chickasaws. The first southern removals took place just prior to the War of 1812 and continued in the war's aftermath.*

In most cases, minority factions, rather than principal chiefs and their followers, signed treaties that ceded eastern lands to whites in exchange for land west of the Mississippi. The transactions often divided tribes between acculturated "progressive" factions, who accepted removal, and proud "traditionalists." By the 1820s, many Indians in the Southeast questioned the legitimacy of the treaties and resisted further removal. When the Cherokee Tribe established a sovereign republic in 1827 in an effort to clarify negotiating authority and forestall further cessions, land-hungry white Georgians began to pass discriminatory laws against Indians and lobbied the federal government to take action. In the Indian Removal Act of 1830, engineered by President Andrew Jackson, Congress authorized the removal of all eastern Indians to areas west of Iowa, Missouri, and Arkansas, by force if necessary.

Some tribes and tribal factions continued to fight for their rights. Some, such as the Seminoles, resorted to armed resistance. Others, such as the Cherokees, took their case to U.S. courts. In the end, the southeastern tribes lost their ancestral lands, although they clung to their culture and sense of identity. Indian removal culminated in the late 1830s in the Cherokee Trail of Tears, the name given to the tribe's long, painful trek to Oklahoma, in the course of which perhaps four thousand Cherokees died.

Why and how this tragedy of U.S. expansionism at the expense of Native Americans occurred is the subject of this chapter.

🌐 D O C U M E N T S

Representative Edward Everett, a member of the Whig Party from Massachusetts, became one of the most vocal and articulate opponents of Indian removal. Document 1, a speech he gave on May 19, 1830, during a House of Representatives debate over President Andrew Jackson's removal bill, warned that the Cherokees, who had adopted many of the trappings of Anglo-American life, would suffer a humanitarian catastrophe on the forced trek westward. Historians agree that the Indian Removal Act of May 28, 1830, reprinted here as Document 2, doomed Indians to immense hardship, despite the language in the legislation suggesting a fair "exchange" of lands. Document 3, an appeal of the Cherokee Nation issued on July 24, 1830, protests the removal policy and predicts it will bring calamity to native peoples. In his Second Annual Message to Congress on December 6, 1830, Document 4, President Jackson rebuts critics, arguing that "benevolent" removal would serve all parties.

The U.S. Supreme Court's ruling in *Cherokee Nation* v. *the State of Georgia* (1831), Document 5, stemmed from Georgia's passage of legislation that circumvented federal law and treaties dealing with the Cherokees as a separate nation. Counting the Indians as a "domestic dependent nation," the justices held that the Cherokees would have to redress their grievances elsewhere. The federal government negotiated a treaty in 1835 with a minority Cherokee faction known as the treaty party that provided an exchange of territory in the Southeast for a tract of land in northeastern Oklahoma. The last selection, Document 6, is a Cherokee memorial and protest, submitted to Congress by Principal Chief John Ross on June 22, 1836, denouncing fraudulent treaties that claimed to justify removal.

Indian Areas

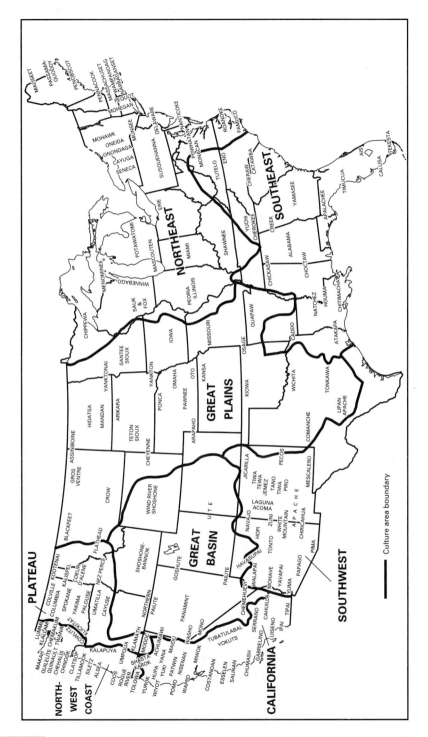

⊕ D O C U M E N T   1

Representative Edward Everett Decries Removal and the Inhumane Treatment of Indians, 1830

The people whom we are to remove are Indians, it is true; but let us not be deluded by names. We are legislating on the fate of men dependent on us for their salvation or their ruin. They are Indians, but they are not all savages; they are not any of them savages. They are not wild hunters. They are, at least some of the southern Indians are, a civilized people. They have not, in all their tribes, purged off every relic of barbarism, but they are essentially a civilized people. They are civilized, not in the same degree that we are, but in the same way that we are. I am well informed that there is probably not a single Cherokee family that subsists exclusively in the ancient savage mode. Each family has its little farm, and derives a part at least of its support from agriculture or some other branch of civilized industry. Are such men savages? Are such men proper persons to be driven from home, and sent to hunt buffalo in the distant wilderness? They are planters and farmers, tradespeople and mechanics. They have cornfields and orchards, looms and workshops, schools and churches, and orderly institutions. Sir, the political communities of a large portion of civilized and christian Europe might well be proud to exhibit such a table of statistics as I will read you. . . .

"A statistical table exhibiting the population of the Cherokee nation, as enumerated in 1824, agreeably to a resolution of the Legislative Council; also, of property, Etc. as stated.

Population,	–	–	–	–	–	15,560
Male negroes,	–	–	–	–	610⎫	
Female negroes,	–	–			667⎭	1,277
Grand total of males and females,			–	–		13,783
Total number of females,		–	–	–		6,900
Females over forty years of age,			–	–		782
Females from fifteen to forty years,			–	–		3,108
Females under fifteen years of age,			–	–		3,010
Total number of males,	–	–	–	–		6,883
Males over fifty-nine years of age,			–	–		352
Males from eighteen to fifty-nine years of age,			–	–		3,027
Males under eighteen years of age,			–	–		3,054
Add for those who have since removed into the nation from North Carolina, who were living in that State on reservations,			–	–		500. . . .

Such are the people we are going to remove from their homes: people, living, as we do, by husbandry, and the mechanic arts, and the industrious trades; and so much the more interesting, as they present the experiment of a people rising from barbarity into civilization. We are going to remove them from these their homes to a distant wilderness. Whoever heard of such a thing before? Whoever read of such project? Ten or fifteen thousand families, to be rooted up, and carried hundreds, aye, a thousand of miles into the wilderness! There is not such a thing in the annals of mankind. . . . Gentlemen, who favor the project, cannot have viewed it as

This document can be found in *Register of Debates in Congress,* 21st Congress, 1st Session (Washington, D.C., Gales and Seaton, 1830), VI, 1068–1074.

it is. They think of a march of Indian warriors, penetrating, with their accustomed vigor, the forest or the cane brake—they think of the youthful Indian hunter, going forth exultingly to the chase. Sir, it is no such thing. This is all past; it is a matter of distant tradition, and poetical fancy. They have nothing now left of the Indian, but his social and political inferiority. They are to go in families, the old and the young, wives and children, the feeble, the sick. And how are they to go? Not in luxurious carriages; they are poor. Not in stage coaches; they go to a region where there are none. Not even in wagons, not on horseback, for they are to go in the least expensive manner possible. They are to go on foot; nay, they are to be driven by contract. The price has been reduced, and is still further to be reduced, and it is to be reduced, by sending them by contract. It is to be screwed down to the least farthing, to eight dollars per head. . . . The imagination sickens at the thought of what will happen to a company of these emigrants, which may prove less strong, less able to pursue the journey than was anticipated. Will the contractor stop for the old men to rest, for the sick to get well; for the fainting women and children to revive? He will not; he cannot afford to. And this process is to be extended to every family, in a population of seventy-five thousand souls. This is what we call the removal of the Indians! . . .

Now let any gentleman think how he would stand, were he to go home, and tell his constituents that they were to be removed, whole counties of them—they must fly before the wrath of insupportable laws—they must go to the distant desert, beyond the Arkansas—go for eight dollars a head, by contract—that this was the policy of the Government—that the bill had passed—the money was voted—you had voted for it—and go they must.

Is the case any the less strong because it applies to these poor, unrepresented tribes, "who have no friends to spare?" If they have rights, are not those rights sacred—as sacred as ours—as sacred as the rights of any congressional district? Are there two kinds of rights, rights of the strong, which you respect because you must; and rights of the weak, on which you trample, because you dare? . . . We are going, in a very high-handed way, to throw these Indians into the western wilderness. I call upon every gentleman who intends to vote for the bill, to ask himself if he has any satisfactory information as to the character of that region. I say it is a *terra incognita*. It has been crossed, but not explored. . . .

Sir, General [William] Clark is your most experienced superintendent of Indian affairs; and his superintendency lies in this haunted Indian Canaan, beyond the Mississippi. Let us learn wisdom from the fate of the Shawnees and Delawares, who, in twenty years, have sunk from the possession of comfortable farms and competence, to abject, roving poverty. One statement more, from an official letter of General Clark, of March 1, 1826, and I leave this topic.

"The condition of many tribes west of the Mississippi, is the most pitiable that can be imagined. During several seasons in every year, they are distressed by famine, in which many die for the want of food, and during which the living child is often buried with the dead mother, because no one can spare it as much food as would sustain it through its helpless infancy. This description applies to the Sioux and Osages, and many others; but I mention those because they are powerful tribes, and live near our borders, and my official station enables me to know the exact truth. . . ."

This is the country to which the Indians are to be moved. This is the fertile region in which they are to be placed. This their prospect of improvement.

The worthy chairman of the [claims] committee [Jacksonian William McCoy of Virginia] told us of the causes of their degeneracy, seated in the nature or in the habit, the second nature, of the Indians. I admit the truth of the representation. I am sorry there is so much foundation for it. My hopes have never been over-sanguine of elevating the race to a high degree of civilization; although within a few years better hopes have been authorized, than ever before. But these causes of degeneracy exist. The Indians, it is said, suffer from the proximity of the whites, and the jealousy and hostility between them, and the conscious inferiority of the Indian. But this is not remedied west of Arkansas, they will have a white population crowding on them there. There is one already. . . . The Cherokees of Arkansas remained unmolested ten years. If the lands to which you remove them are what you describe them to be, you may as well push back the tide in the Bay of Fundy, as keep out the white population. Its progress onward is sure, and as surely will it push the Indians before it. This new wilderness which you parcel out to them, is not a permanent home. It is a mere halting place—a half-way house on the road to the desert.

🌎 D O C U M E N T   2

The Indian Removal Act Authorizes Transfer of Eastern Tribes to the West, 1830

An Act to provide for an exchange of lands with the Indians residing in any of the states or territories, and for their removal west of the river Mississippi.

Be it enacted by the Senate and House of Representatives of the United States of America, in Congress assembled, That it shall and may be lawful for the President of the United States to cause so much of any territory belonging to the United States, west of the river Mississippi, not included in any state or organized territory, and to which the Indian title has been extinguished, as he may judge necessary, to be divided into a suitable number of districts, for the reception of such tribes or nations of Indians as may choose to exchange the lands where they now reside, and remove there; and to cause each of said districts to be so described by natural or artificial marks, as to be easily distinguished from every other.

And be it further enacted, That it shall and may be lawful for the President to exchange any or all of such districts, so to be laid off and described, with any tribe or nation of Indians now residing within the limits of any of the states or territories, and with which the United States have existing treaties, for the whole or any part or portion of the territory claimed and occupied by such tribe or nation, within the bounds of any one or more of the states or territories, where the land claimed and occupied by the Indians, is owned by the United States, or the United States are bound to the state within which it lies to extinguish the Indian claim thereto.

And be it further enacted, That in the making of any such exchange or exchanges, it shall and may be lawful for the President solemnly to assure the tribe or

This document can be found in *Public Statutes at Large of the United States of America* (Boston: Little, Brown, 1850), IV, 411–412.

nation with which the exchange is made, that the United States will forever secure and guaranty to them, and their heirs or successors, the country so exchanged with them; and if they prefer it, that the United States will cause a patent or grant to be made and executed to them for the same: *Provided always*, That such lands shall revert to the United States, if the Indians become extinct, or abandon the same.

And be it further enacted, That if, upon any of the lands now occupied by the Indians, and to be exchanged for, there should be such improvements as add value to the land claimed by any individual or individuals of such tribes or nations, it shall and may be lawful for the President to cause such value to be ascertained by appraisement or otherwise, and to cause such ascertained value to be paid to the person or persons rightfully claiming such improvements. And upon the payment of such valuation, the improvements so valued and paid for, shall pass to the United States, and possession shall not afterwards be permitted to any of the same tribe.

And be it further enacted, That upon the making of any such exchange as is contemplated by this act, it shall and may be lawful for the President to cause such aid and assistance to be furnished to the emigrants as may be necessary and proper to enable them to remove to, and settle in, the country for which they may have exchanged; and also, to give them such aid and assistance as may be necessary for their support and subsistence for the first year after their removal.

And be it further enacted, That it shall and may be lawful for the President to cause such tribe or nation to be protected, at their new residence, against all interruption or disturbance from any other tribe or nation of Indians, or from any other person or persons whatever.

And be it further enacted, That it shall and may be lawful for the President to have the same superintendence and care over any tribe or nation in the country to which they may remove, as contemplated by this act, that he is now authorized to have over them at their present places of residence: *Provided*, That nothing in this act contained shall be construed as authorizing or directing the violation of any existing treaty between the United States and any of the Indian tribes.

And be it further enacted, That for the purpose of giving effect to the provisions of this act, the sum of five hundred thousand dollars is hereby appropriated, to be paid out of any money in the treasury, not otherwise appropriated.

🌐 *D O C U M E N T   3*

The Cherokee Nation Protests the Removal Policy, 1830

We are aware that some persons suppose it will be for our advantage to remove beyond the Mississippi. We think otherwise. Our people universally think otherwise. Thinking that it would be fatal to their interests, they have almost to a man sent their memorial to Congress, deprecating the necessity of a removal. This question was distinctly before their minds when they signed their memorial. Not an adult person can be found, who

This document can be found in the Address of the "Committee and Council of the Cherokee Nation in General Council Convened to the People of the U.S.," *Cherokee Phoenix and Indians' Advocate*, 24 July 1830, University of Nebraska-Love Library.

has not an opinion on the subject; and if the people were to understand distinctly, that they could be protected against the laws of the neighboring States, there is probably not an adult person in the nation, who would think it best to remove; though possibly a few might emigrate individually. There are doubtless many who would flee to an unknown country, however beset with dangers, privations and sufferings, rather than be sentenced to spend six years in a Georgia prison for advising one of their neighbors not to betray his country. And there are others who could not think of living as outlaws in their native land, exposed to numberless vexations, and excluded from being parties or witnesses in a court of justice. It is incredible that Georgia should ever have enacted the oppressive laws to which reference is here made, unless she had supposed that something extremely terrific in its character was necessary, in order to make the Cherokees willing to remove. We are not willing to remove; and if we could be brought to this extremity, it would be, not by argument; not because our judgment was satisfied; not because our condition will be improved—but only because we cannot endure to be deprived of our national and individual rights, and subjected to a process of intolerable oppression.

We wish to remain on the land of our fathers. We have a perfect and original right to claim this, without interruption or molestation. The treaties with us, and laws of the United States made in pursuance of treaties, guaranty our residence, and our privileges, and secure us against intruders. Our only request is, that these treaties may be fulfilled, and these laws executed.

But if we are compelled to leave our country, we see nothing but ruin before us. The country west of the Arkansas territory is unknown to us. From what we can learn of it, we have no prepossessions in its favor. All the inviting parts of it, as we believe, are preoccupied by various Indian nations, to which it has been assigned. They would regard us as intruders, and look upon us with an evil eye. The far greater part of that region is, beyond all controversy, badly supplied with wood and water; and no Indian tribe can live as agriculturists without these articles. All our neighbors, in case of our removal, though crowded into our near vicinity, would speak a language totally different from ours, and practice different customs. The original possessors of that region are now wandering savages, lurking for prey in the neighborhood. They have always been at war, and would be easily tempted to turn their arms against peaceful emigrants. Were the country to which we are urged much better than it is represented to be, and were it free from the objections which we have made to it, still it is not the land of our birth, nor of our affections. It contains neither the scenes of our childhood, nor the graves of our fathers.

🌎 *D O C U M E N T   4*

President Andrew Jackson
Defends Removal, 1830

It gives me pleasure to announce to Congress that the benevolent policy of the Government, steadily pursued for nearly thirty years, in relation to the removal of the Indians beyond the white settlements is approaching to a happy consummation. Two important tribes have accepted the provision made for their removal at the last

This document can be found in James D. Richardson, ed., *A Compilation of the Messages and Papers of the Presidents* (New York: Bureau of National Literature, 1897), III, 1082–1086.

session of Congress, and it is believed that their example will induce the remaining tribes also to seek the same obvious advantages.

The consequences of a speedy removal will be important to the United States, to individual States, and to the Indians themselves. The pecuniary advantages which it promises to the Government are the least of its recommendations. It puts an end to all possible danger of collision between the authorities of the General and State Governments on account of the Indians. It will place a dense and civilized population in large tracts of country now occupied by a few savage hunters. By opening the whole territory between Tennessee on the north and Louisiana on the south to the settlement of the whites it will incalculably strengthen the southwestern frontier and render the adjacent States strong enough to repel future invasions without remote aid. It will relieve the whole State of Mississippi and the western part of Alabama of Indian occupancy, and enable those States to advance rapidly in population, wealth, and power. It will separate the Indians from immediate contact with settlements of whites; free them from the power of the States; enable them to pursue happiness in their own way and under their own rude institutions; will retard the progress of decay, which is lessening their numbers, and perhaps cause them gradually, under the protection of the Government and through the influence of good counsels, to cast off their savage habits and become an interesting, civilized, and Christian community. These consequences, some of them so certain and the rest so probable, make the complete execution of the plan sanctioned by Congress at their last session an object of much solicitude.

Toward the aborigines of the country no one can indulge a more friendly feeling than myself, or would go further in attempting to reclaim them from their wandering habits and make them a happy, prosperous people. I have endeavored to impress upon them my own solemn convictions of the duties and powers of the General Government in relation to the State authorities. For the justice of the laws passed by the States within the scope of their reserved powers they are not responsible to this Government. As individuals we may entertain and express our opinions of their acts, but as a Government we have as little right to control them as we have to prescribe laws for other nations.

With a full understanding of the subject, the Choctaw and the Chickasaw tribes have with great unanimity determined to avail themselves of the liberal offers presented by the act of Congress, and have agreed to remove beyond the Mississippi River. Treaties have been made with them, which in due season will be submitted for consideration. In negotiating these treaties they were made to understand their true condition, and they have preferred maintaining their independence in the Western forests to submitting to the laws of the States in which they now reside. These treaties, being probably the last which will ever be made with them, are characterized by great liberality on the part of the Government. They give the Indians a liberal sum in consideration of their removal, and comfortable subsistence on their arrival at their new homes. If it be their real interest to maintain a separate existence, they will there be at liberty to do so without the inconveniences and vexations to which they would unavoidably have been subject in Alabama and Mississippi.

Humanity has often wept over the fate of the aborigines of this country, and philanthropy has been long busily employed in devising means to avert it, but its progress has never for a moment been arrested, and one by one have many powerful tribes disappeared from the earth. To follow to the tomb the last of his race and to tread on the graves of extinct nations excite melancholy reflections. But true philanthropy reconciles the mind to these vicissitudes as it does to the extinction of one generation to make room for another. In the monuments and fortresses of an unknown people, spread over the extensive regions of the West, we behold the memorials of a once powerful race, which was exterminated or has disappeared to make room for the existing savage tribes. Nor is there anything in this which, upon a comprehensive view of the general interests of the human race, is to be regretted. Philanthropy could not wish to see this continent restored to the conditions in which it was found by our forefathers. What good man would prefer a country covered with forests and ranged by a few thousand savages to our extensive Republic, studded with cities, towns, and prosperous farms, embellished with all the improvements which art can devise or industry execute, occupied by more than 12,000,000 happy people, and filled with all the blessings of liberty, civilization, and religion?

The present policy of the Government is but a continuation of the same progressive change by a milder process. The tribes which occupied the countries now constituting the Eastern States were annihilated or have melted away to make room for the whites. The waves of population and civilization are rolling to the westward, and we now propose to acquire the countries occupied by the red men of the South and West by a fair exchange, and, at the expense of the United States, to send them to a land where their existence may be prolonged and perhaps made perpetual. Doubtless it will be painful to leave the graves of their fathers; but what do they more than our ancestors did or than our children are now doing? To better their condition in an unknown land our forefathers left all that was dear in earthly objects. Our children by thousands yearly leave the land of their birth to seek new homes in distant regions. Does humanity weep at these painful separations from everything, animate and inanimate, with which the young heart has become entwined? Far from it. It is rather a source of joy that our country affords scope where our young population may range unconstrained in body or in mind, developing the power and faculties of man in their highest perfection. These remove hundreds and almost thousands of miles at their own expense, purchase the lands they occupy, and support themselves at their new homes from the moment of their arrival. Can it be cruel in this Government when, by events which it can not control, the Indian is made discontented in his ancient home to purchase his lands, to give him a new and extensive territory, to pay the expense of his removal, and support him a year in his new abode? How many thousands of our own people would gladly embrace the opportunity of removing to the West on such conditions! If the offers made to the Indians were extended to them, they would be hailed with gratitude and joy.

And is it supposed that the wandering savage has a stronger attachment to his home than the settled, civilized Christian? Is it more afflicting to him to leave the graves of his fathers than it is to our brothers and children? Rightly considered, the policy of the General Government toward the red man is not only liberal, but generous. He is unwilling to submit to the laws of the States and mingle with their population. To save him from this alternative, or perhaps utter annihilation, the General Government kindly offers him a new home, and proposes to pay the whole expense of his removal and settlement. . . .

May we not hope, therefore, that all good citizens, and none more zealously than those who think the Indians oppressed by subjection to the laws of the States, will unite in attempting to open the eyes of those children of the forest to their true condition, and by a speedy removal to relieve them from all the evils, real or imaginary, present or prospective, with which they may be supposed to be threatened.

⊕ *D O C U M E N T   5*

Cherokee Nation v. the State of Georgia:
The Supreme Court Refuses
Jurisdiction over Indian Affairs, 1831

Mr. Chief Justice [John] Marshall delivered the opinion of the Court:

This bill is brought by the Cherokee nation, praying an injunction to restrain the state of Georgia from the execution of certain laws of that state, which, as is alleged, go directly to annihilate the Cherokees as a political society, and to seize, for the use of Georgia, the lands of the nation which have been assured to them by the United States in solemn treaties repeatedly made and still in force.

If courts were permitted to indulge their sympathies, a case better calculated to excite them can scarcely be imagined. A people once numerous, powerful, and truly independent, found by our ancestors in the quiet and uncontrolled possession of an ample domain, gradually sinking beneath our superior policy, our arts and our arms, have yielded their lands by successive treaties, each of which contains a solemn guarantee of the residue, until they retain no more of their formerly extensive territory than is deemed necessary to their comfortable subsistence. To preserve this remnant, the present application is made.

Before we can look into the merits of the case, a preliminary inquiry presents itself. Has this court jurisdiction of the cause?

The third article of the constitution describes the extent of the judicial power. The second section closes an enumeration of the cases to which it is extended, with "controversies" "between a state or the citizens thereof, and foreign states, citizens, or subjects." A subsequent clause of the same section gives the supreme court original jurisdiction in all cases in which a state shall be a party. The party defendant may then unquestionably be sued in this court. May the plaintiff sue in it? Is the Cherokee nation a foreign state in the sense in which that term is used in the constitution?

The counsel for the plaintiffs have maintained the affirmative of this proposition with great earnestness and ability. So much of the argument as was intended to prove the character of the Cherokees as a state, as a distinct political society, separated from others, capable of managing its own affairs and governing itself, has, in the opinion of a majority of the judges, been completely successful. They have been uniformly treated as a state from the settlement of our country. The numerous treaties made with them by the United States recognize them as a people capable of maintaining the relations of peace and war, of being responsible in their political character for any violation of their engagements, or for any aggression committed on the citizens of the United States by any individual of their community. Laws have been enacted in the spirit of these treaties. The acts of our government plainly recognize the Cherokee nation as a state, and the courts are bound by those acts.

A question of much more difficulty remains. Do the Cherokee constitute a foreign state in the sense of the constitution?

This document can be found in Richard Peters, ed., *Report of Cases Signed and Adjudicated in the Supreme Court of the United States: January Term, 1832*, 5:15–20 (Philadelphia: Thomas Corsperthwait & Co., 1845).

The counsel have shown conclusively that they are not a state of the union, and have insisted that individually they are aliens, not owing allegiance to the United States. An aggregate of aliens composing a state must, they say, be a foreign state. Each individual being foreign, the whole must be foreign.

This argument is imposing, but we must examine it more closely before we yield to it. The condition of the Indians in relation to the United States is perhaps unlike that of any other two people in existence. In the general, nations not owing a common allegiance are foreign to each other. The term foreign nation is, with strict propriety, applicable by either to the other. But the relation of the Indians to the United States is marked by peculiar and cardinal distinctions which exist no where else.

The Indian territory is admitted to compose a part of the United States. In all our maps, geographical treaties, histories, and laws, it is so considered. In all our intercourse with foreign nations, in our commercial regulations, in any attempt at intercourse between Indians and foreign nations, they are considered as within the jurisdictional limits of the United States, subject to many of those restraints which are imposed upon our own citizens. They acknowledge themselves in their treaties to be under the protection of the United States; they admit that the United States shall have the sole and exclusive right of regulating the trade with them, and managing all their affairs as they think proper; and the Cherokees in particular were allowed by the treaty of Hopewell, which preceded the constitution, "to send a deputy of their choice, whenever they think fit, to congress." Treaties were made with some tribes by the state of New York, under a then unsettled construction of the confederation, by which they ceded all their lands to that state, taking back a limited grant to themselves, in which they admit their dependence.

Though the Indians are acknowledged to have an unquestionable, and, heretofore, unquestioned right to the lands they occupy, until that right shall be extinguished by a voluntary cession to our government; yet it may well be doubted whether those tribes which reside within the acknowledged boundaries of the United States can, with strict accuracy, be denominated foreign nations. They may, more correctly be denominated domestic dependent nations. They occupy a territory to which we assert a title independent of their will, which must take effect in point of possession when their right of possession ceases. Meanwhile, they are in a state of pupilage. Their relation to the United States resembles that of a ward to his guardian.

They look to our government for protection; rely upon its kindness and its power; appeal to it for relief to their wants; and address the president as their great father. They and their country are considered by foreign nations, as well as by ourselves, as being so completely under the sovereignty and dominion of the United States, that any attempt to acquire their lands, or to form a political connexion with them, would be considered by all as an invasion of our territory, and an act of hostility.

These considerations go far to support the opinion, that the framers of our constitution had not the Indian tribes in view, when they opened the courts of the union to controversies between a state or the citizen thereof, and foreign states.

In considering this subject, the habits and usages of the Indians, in their intercourse with their white neighbours, ought not to be entirely disregarded. At the time the constitution was framed, the idea of appealing to an American court of justice for an assertion of right or a redress of wrong, had perhaps never entered the mind of an Indian or of his tribe. Their appeal was to the tomahawk, or to the government. This was well understood by the statesmen who framed the constitution of the United States, and might furnish some reason for omitting to enumerate them among the parties who might sue in the courts of the union. Be this as it may, the peculiar relations between the United States and the Indians occupying our territory are such, that we should feel much difficulty in considering them as designated by the term foreign state, were there no other part of the constitution which might shed light on the meaning of these words. But we think that in construing them, considerable aid is furnished by that clause in the eighth section of the third article; which empowers congress to "regulate commerce with foreign nations, and among the several states, and with the Indian tribes."

In this clause they are as clearly contradistinguished by a name appropriate to themselves, from foreign nations, as from the several states composing the union. They are designated by a distinct appellation; and as this appellation can be applied to neither of the others, neither can the appellation distinguishing either of the others be in fair construction applied to them. The objects, to which the power of regulating commerce might be directed, are divided into three distinct classes—foreign nations, the several states, and Indian tribes. When forming this article, the convention considered them as entirely distinct. . . .

The court has bestowed its best attention on this question, and, after mature deliberation, the majority is of opinion that an Indian tribe or nation within the United States is not a foreign state in the sense of the constitution, and cannot maintain an action in the courts of the United States. . . .

If it be true that the Cherokee nation have rights, this is not the tribunal in which those rights are to be asserted. If it be true that wrongs have been inflicted, and that still greater are to be apprehended, this is not the tribunal which can redress the past or prevent the future.

The motion for an injunction is denied.

D O C U M E N T   6

Cherokee Chief John Ross Denounces
U.S. Removal Policy, 1836

[T]he United States solemnly guaranteed to said nation [Cherokee Nation] all their lands not ceded, and pledged the faith of the government, that "all white people who have intruded, or may hereafter intrude on the lands reserved for the Cherokees, shall be removed by the United States. . . ." The Cherokees were happy and prosperous under a scrupulous observance of treaty stipulations by the government of the United States, and from the fostering hand extended over them, they made rapid advances in civilization, morals, and in the arts and sciences. Little did they anticipate, that when taught to think and feel as the American citizen, and to have with him a common interest, they were to be *despoiled by their guardian*, to become strangers and wanderers in the land of their fathers, forced to return to the savage life, and to seek a new home in the wilds of the far west, and that without their consent. An instrument purporting to be a treaty with the Cherokee people, has recently been

This document can be found in the House Executive Document, #286, 24th Congress, 1st Session 1–2, June 22, 1836.

made public by the President of the United States, that will have such an operation if carried into effect. This instrument, the delegation aver before the civilized world, and in the presence of Almighty God, is fraudulent, false upon its face, made by unauthorized individuals, without the sanction, and against the wishes, of the great body of the Cherokee people. Upwards of fifteen thousand of those people have protested against it, solemnly declaring they will never acquiesce.

✎ E S S A Y S

In the first essay, Theda Perdue of the University of North Carolina, Chapel Hill, examines the origins and evolution of Indian removal. She emphasizes how Europeans and Americans from colonial times expropriated the lands of native peoples, whose cultures they denigrated. As the white population grew in the Southeast and the Cotton Kingdom expanded, state governments in that region increased pressure on tribes to sell their lands and remove to the West. A turning point arrived with Andrew Jackson's election to the presidency. The Indian Removal Act (1830) authorized the president, and provided him with funds, to negotiate exchanges of Indian territory in the East for federal lands in the West. Some southeastern tribes agreed to cede their lands, some resisted, and others—notably the Cherokee—splintered into pro-treaty and anti-treaty factions. For many, removal came about tragically at the hands of the U.S. military, along a bitter trail of tears and deprivation. Still, Perdue notes, many Native Americans struggled to adapt their economic and political systems to the assault and preserve their heritage.

In the second essay, Stuart Banner of Washington University Law School in St. Louis explores the climate of white opinion on removal policy. He differentiates between the legal debate that arose over whether the government had the right to force removal and a second debate over the wisdom of removal. According to Banner, U.S. law and legal precedent affirmed Indian land titles and blocked forcible removal, but the Jackson administration ardently supported state and local forces in the South and the West that ratcheted up the pressure on tribes to sell their lands and resettle in the West. Although some humanitarian groups opposed removal, others argued that it would protect indigenous tribes from annihilation. In the end, the division among Indian sympathizers allowed white land hunger to triumph over Indian rights. White racism further sealed the fate of indigenous tribes by allowing removal advocates to dismiss Indian opposition to removal as misguided and illegitimate.

The Origins of Removal and the Fate of the Southeastern Indians

THEDA PERDUE

When the United States government began implementing the removal policy in the early nineteenth century, five major Indian groups lived in the Southeast. The Chickasaws occupied territory in western Tennessee, northern Mississippi, and northwestern Alabama. The Choctaws, who spoke a language very similar to Chickasaw, lived to the south in central Mississippi and Alabama. East of the Choctaws was the Creek

From Theda Perdue, "The Trail of Tears," in Philip Weeks, ed., *The American Indian Experience, A Profile: 1524 to the Present*, pp. 96–115 (notes omitted). Copyright © 1988 Forum Press, Inc. (a.k.a. Harlan Davidson, Inc.). Reproduced by permission.

Confederacy of Alabama and Georgia. In northern Georgia, northwestern Alabama, eastern Tennessee, and southwestern North Carolina lay the Cherokee country, and in Florida lived the Seminoles, a tribe made up of disaffected Creeks, native Florida tribes, and runaway African slaves. While each of these tribes was a separate political entity with its own cultural peculiarities, they all participated in the same broad cultural tradition, just as Europeans were a part of "western civilization." At the time of European contact, this Indian culture was known as Mississippian. Interestingly, whites understood little about Mississippian culture. Perhaps self-interest clouded their view, but, for whatever reason, they often overlooked or distorted major cultural characteristics. As a result, the cultural inferiority and inadequacy which whites later used to justify removal frequently had not existed in the first place.

The basis of southeastern Indian culture for centuries before European contact was a dependence on agriculture. Native peoples began to cultivate squash and gourds about 1000 B.C., and in approximately 200 B.C. they cultivated corn and beans. While agriculture may have developed independently in the Southeast, it is likely that the concept as well as the crops originated elsewhere and that native traders or migrating tribes brought them into the region. Whatever the circumstances surrounding the introduction of farming, the broad fertile valleys of the Southeast, a long growing season, and an annual rainfall averaging from 40 to 64 inches made the Southeast admirably suited for an agricultural economy. By A.D. 700 this new Mississippian culture based on agriculture had begun to emerge. . . .

Indians were governed primarily by an ethic which sought to maintain harmony and balance in the community and the natural world. Because each individual accepted this responsibility and subordinated his own ambitions and desires to the welfare of all, tribes had no need for a king or other authoritarian form of government. Before the disruption of native life by European incursions, hereditary despots may have ruled some tribes, but by the late eighteenth century town councils made decisions after exhaustively discussing an issue and arriving at a consensus. There were leaders, of course, but they led only because their achievements commanded respect. Even in tribes such as the Creeks, who seem to have chosen chiefs from a particular clan, kinship was not necessarily a determinant of political power. This form of government appeared to Europeans to be fraught with uncertainty, and, in fact, some whites suggested that southern Indians had no genuine government at all.

Europeans, therefore, failed to understand a great deal about southern Indians. Over several centuries, native peoples had developed a complex culture characterized by permanent villages, an agricultural economy, political and social organizations which emphasized the community rather than the individual, a belief system aimed at preserving order and harmony in the world, and a ceremonial life which reflected the values and aspirations of the society. In the eighteenth century, however, the major southeastern tribes began to feel the pressure of European expansion. In this period they had extensive contact with three European powers—French, Spanish, and British—who were vying for control of the continent. The British triumphed, and this victory set in motion a series of events which culminated in the removal of the southern Indians from their ancient homeland. . . .

From the British perspective, the land did not really belong to the Indians. The British based their claim to North America on the discoveries of the Cabots and others who explored the New World under the auspices of the British Crown. People,

Indian Land Cessions, 1830–1839

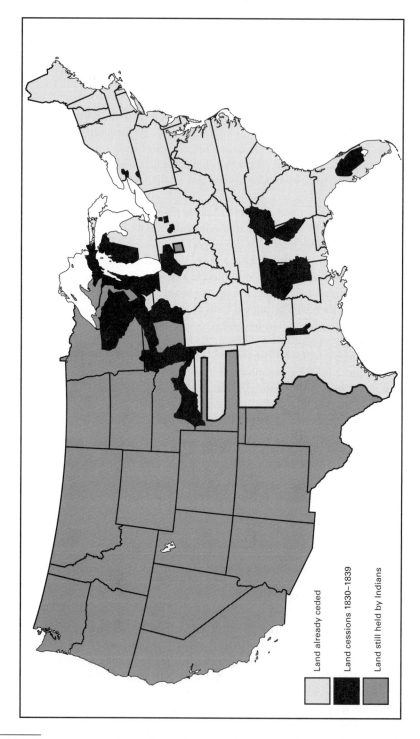

Land already ceded

Land cessions 1830–1839

Land still held by Indians

of course, lived in this "newfound" land, but the British insisted that the natives had only the right to occupy the land temporarily. This limited right of occupancy stemmed from the perception of Indian peoples as wandering hunters and gatherers who did not cultivate the soil or permanently inhabit a particular tract of land. Discovery entailed the right of preemption, that is, the right to possess the land when the Indians no longer occupied it. The immediate problem for the British was how to remove the Indians from tracts of land so that colonists could exercise their right of preemption. The solution lay in treaties whereby the Indians surrendered their right to live on the land. When the Indians relinquished their right of occupancy, the "civilized" nation which had discovered the land could then settle, put it to proper use, and establish legitimate ownership. The British, therefore, viewed Indian titles as transitory and European titles as genuine and permanent.

The British policy of acquiring specific tracts of land led to a formal distinction between Indian and British territory. Normally natives and colonists did not share tracts of land: if the British acquired the land, the Indians left and whites moved in. In one sense, this was the beginning of Indian removal. Although Indian enclaves existed in the colonies, the British tended to push the native peoples westward and to create a frontier, a boundary, between Indians and whites. In 1763 after the British victory in the French and Indian War, George III formalized the boundary and prohibited migration of British colonists beyond the crest of the Appalachians. The Crown and its colonial governments also carefully regulated intercourse between the colonies and the Indians by appointing agents and licensing traders. Therefore, the British regarded the Indians as sovereign for the purpose of negotiating treaties but they did not view native peoples living on land "discovered" by British subjects as permanently entitled to the land. When the United States achieved its independence, the new country inherited the British right of discovery and a well-established method for dealing with the native peoples who temporarily resided within that domain.

The Articles of Confederation, under which the United States was governed from 1779 to 1789, placed Indian relations within the province of Congress. Often at odds with the state governments, Congress nevertheless established an Indian policy which reserved for the federal government the right to regulate trade and travel with the Indian nations. The architects of early Indian policy clearly considered the tribes in the Northwest Territory and the old Southwest to be residing on United States land; that is, they believed that Indians only lived on land which actually was owned by the United States. Under the Articles of Confederation, the United States also set up a procedure for disposing of land once the Indians ceased to occupy it: U.S. agents surveyed tracts and then sold them at minimal price in order to encourage rapid white settlement and ultimate statehood. Even in its infancy, the nation prepared to move westward, and the justifications and machinery for dispossessing the Indians were well in place by the meeting of the Constitutional convention.

The Constitution of 1789 also reserved the conduct of Indian affairs to the federal government. The first chief executive under the Constitution, George Washington, delegated his authority to various cabinet officials. Indian affairs was under the secretary of war because the pacification of the Indians through negotiation or, if necessary, military defeat was a major concern. Henry Knox, Washington's secretary of war, advocated the British concept of proprietorship and their practice of purchasing the Indians' occupancy claims. He also maintained that the privilege of acquiring Indian land belonged exclusively to the federal government rather than to individuals or states. Overcoming opposition from Georgia and other states, Congress concurred with Knox and passed a series of laws called the Indian Trade and Intercourse Acts. Through these laws, the federal government established Indian boundaries, regulated trade with and travel in the Indian nations, controlled the liquor traffic, restricted the purchase of Indian land to the federal government, and provided funds for the education and "civilization" of the Indians.

The Indian policy established by the new nation reflects a dichotomy in American attitudes toward the Indians. On the one hand, white Americans wanted Indian land. They believed that they could make better use of that resource than the Indians and that they were the rightful owners. On the other hand, many Americans were committed to "civilizing" the Indians. They believed that Indians could be transformed culturally and assimilated into white society. While the specter of hunting grounds that could be opened to white occupancy after civilized Indians abandoned them no doubt accounts for much of the interest in Indian civilization, genuine altruism motivated many whites. Convinced that "savage" peoples could not compete with civilized ones and consequently were doomed to destruction, these individuals sought to save American Indians by civilizing them.

The federal government sought to promote civilization in two ways. First, federal agents lived among the Indians and introduced the principles of commercial agriculture, animal husbandry, and the domestic arts. Second, the federal government provided financial assistance to missionary societies willing to send people into this particular mission field. Such aid was compatible with the government's goals because most Protestants considered civilization and Christianity to be intrinsically linked, and a good Christian life was a civilized one. Similarly, the architects of federal Indian policy believed that civilization entailed not only an agricultural economy, a republican government, and an English education but also conversion to Christianity. . . .

Many southern Indians readily accepted the government's civilization program, which was aided considerably by the erosion of traditional culture in the eighteenth century. The descendants of white traders and Indian women already were accustomed to the white man's ways and capitalized on the material aspects of the program. Also many men who formerly had engaged in hunting and war found an avenue for self-fulfillment and an outlet for aggression in the individualistic economic system and acquisitive values which agents introduced. These men, whose ancestry was Indian, plus others of mixed ancestry became civilized, or at least they acquired that "love for exclusive property" on which Knox believed civilization rested. In the late eighteenth and early nineteenth centuries, leadership of the southern tribes fell increasingly to individuals who were well on their way to acculturation. These were the people with whom U.S. agents and treaty commissioners interacted most easily and comfortably. In some cases, more traditional Indians deferred to these progressives and looked to them as interpreters of U.S. policies and as mediators of culture. In other cases, however, government officials grossly overestimated the power of people who supported federal policies and failed to realize that they had little internal support.

Most federal officials viewed the civilization program as a means to an end: The real objective of U.S. Indian policy was the acquisition of Indian land. The United

States pressured southern Indians to relinquish "surplus" land in a variety of ways. The War Department authorized the construction of government-owned trading posts, or factories, and instructed traders to permit Indians to run up sizable accounts. Then authorities demanded payment in land. In 1802, for example, the federal government built a factory among the Chickasaws who within three years owed $12,000. They paid their debts by ceding their territory north of the Tennessee River. Treaty commissioners sent to negotiate land cessions bribed chiefs and exploited tribal factionalism. In the Cherokee removal crisis of 1806–1809, for example, the federal government took advantage of discord between the upper towns of eastern Tennessee and western North Carolina and the lower towns of Alabama and Georgia. Lower towns were more committed to civilization and ultimate assimilation into white society. Espousing the political fiction of tribal unity, federal officials negotiated land cessions and exchanges with lower town chiefs in the name of the entire tribe. They also lubricated the process by bribing lower town chiefs with the inclusion of secret treaty provisions appropriating funds to particularly cooperative chiefs. . . .

In response to these tactics, southern tribes began to devise ways of coping with incessant demands for their land. With the hearty approval of the civilizers, agents and missionaries, southern tribes began to adopt Anglo-American political institutions. The Cherokees, Creeks, Choctaws, and Chickasaws began to centralize their tribal governments, to formalize political processes and structures, to delegate authority to clearly designated chiefs, and to hold those chiefs accountable for their actions. Between 1808 and 1810 the Cherokees established a national police force, created an executive committee to transact tribal business between council meetings, and made murder a national crime (instead of a family matter) by abolishing blood vengeance. In 1829, they committed to writing a previously unwritten but well-known law making the cession of tribal land a capital offense. . . .

Among southern Indians, a significant number of people rejected or, perhaps more appropriately, ignored aspects of civilization. They preferred their traditional town councils to centralized governments, the lessons taught by elders and family to mission schools, and their own religion to Christianity. The persistence of traditional culture troubled missionaries and U.S. agents who mistakenly had believed that civilizing the Indians would be a fairly simple task. They feared for these recalcitrant savages whose days, they felt certain, were numbered by the onrush of civilization.

Some conditions in the Indian nations in the early nineteenth century seemed to confirm these fears. Exposure to civilization only further corrupted these savages. Equally distressing was the inability of others who acknowledged the virtue of civilization to resist the vices. Many Indians lived on credit, and their wants far exceeded their means. Some discovered a civilized way to avoid manual labor: they bought African slaves to work for them. Southern Indians also liked to gamble, and, although this had been an aboriginal practice, civilization introduced new contests such as horse racing on which they could wager. But most tragically, many Indians acquired a taste for alcohol. Faced with the weakening of cultural traditions, economic and political changes, and an uncertain future, they overindulged, and drunkenness became a serious problem.

The difficulties encountered by the civilization program soon led philanthropists to question how quickly and easily the southern Indians could be assimilated. These doubts opened the door for those who desired the Indians' land rather than their civilization. Reconciliation of these opposing positions came in the proposal to move the Indians beyond the reach of civilization where they could adjust more slowly and successfully to the problems which civilization brought. The Indians would be saved and their land could be opened for white settlement. The immediate problem, however, was where to send the Indians.

As a great advocate of assimilation, Thomas Jefferson had provided a solution: he had bought Louisiana. Jefferson apparently had not had Indian emigration in mind when he made the Louisiana Purchase in 1803, but his political opponents (and even some supporters) demanded to know exactly what he intended to do with this vast wilderness. Jefferson responded that the eastern Indians could now be moved west of the Mississippi and civilized at their own pace. The removal policy officially was born. . . .

The Jefferson administration succeeded only, however, in convincing the lower Cherokees to exchange land, and in 1810 about 1,000 Cherokees moved to Arkansas. Subsequent administrations followed the Jeffersonian model and arranged territorial exchanges. Another Cherokee emigration took place in 1817–1819 after a group of Cherokees (who received private reservations which could be sold at considerable profit) ceded land in the Southeast to compensate the federal government for additional land the Arkansas Cherokees had settled. In 1820, the Choctaws agreed to the Treaty of Doak's Stand, under which they relinquished one-third of their eastern domain for a larger tract in Arkansas. Because of protest from white residents of Arkansas, however, the treaty had to be renegotiated in Washington in 1825, and the Choctaws received a tract of land in what is today southeastern Oklahoma. In 1826, the Creeks grudgingly acceded to an exchange of land in Georgia for a tract north of the Choctaws so that the followers of [Chief] William McIntosh could emigrate.

The consequences of these exchanges were not exactly what Jefferson and other proponents of the removal policy had had in mind. Some Indians who moved west were the traditionalists for whom Jefferson originally had proposed removal. A surprisingly large number, however, were highly acculturated Indians. Some of these were escaping political enemies, but economics probably motivated most. Perhaps they hoped to capitalize on the westward movement, or they may simply have felt the same urge to go west as many white Americans. These progressives experienced little remorse in leaving their homeland, but the traditionalists who were the intended beneficiaries of removal felt a profound attachment to the land and refused to move. Those who still practiced traditional religion regarded their own territory as the center of the world and associated the West with death. In addition, their mythology incorporated familiar land forms. The Choctaws, for example, believed that they came originally from the Nanih Waiya mound in Mississippi, and the Cherokees thought that they could see and influence the future through the crystal forelock of the Uktena, a monster which lived in the high mountain passes of their country. Sacred medicine, which southern Indians used to cure physical and spiritual ills, came from native plants that did not necessarily grow in the Trans-Mississippi West. For these traditionalists, removal meant not only physical relocation but also spiritual reorientation. . . .

The slow pace of removal angered many southerners. As prices for cotton rose, the white population in the South grew, and as the Cotton Kingdom expanded, the desire for additional land suitable for cultivating cotton increased. Consequently, southern states began to demand that the federal government, which controlled Indian relations, liquidate Indian title to land within their borders. Georgia, in particular, insisted on federal compliance with the Compact of 1802. In this agreement, the state relinquished claims to the western land, which became Alabama and Mississippi, and the federal government promised to extinguish Indian land titles within the state at some unspecified time. In the 1820s, Georgians thought that the federal government had delayed long enough. Indian land promptly became a political issue. Constitutional changes in 1825 which provided for the direct election of governors (who previously had been elected by the state senate) contributed to the uproar. Politicians seized on Indian land as an issue with broad popular appeal. In 1826, Georgians rejoiced when the Creeks gave up their remaining land in the state and withdrew to Alabama. Then they turned their attention to the Cherokees.

In 1827, the Cherokees established a republican government with a written constitution patterned after that of the United States. Georgia interpreted this act to be a violation of state sovereignty and renewed demands for the extinction of Indian land titles. The state legislature enacted a series of laws intended to establish state control over the Cherokee country and to make life so miserable for the Indians that they would leave. The legislature extended Georgia law over the Cherokees and created a special militia, the Georgia Guard, to enforce state law in the Cherokee country. One legislative act prohibited Indians from mining gold which had been discovered in their territory. Other laws prevented Indians from testifying against whites in court and required all whites, including missionaries, to take an oath of allegiance to the state. The Georgia legislature enjoined the Cherokee council from meeting and leaders from speaking publicly against removal. Finally, legislators formulated plans for a survey and division of Cherokee lands in preparation for their distribution by lottery to whites. Other southern states soon followed Georgia's lead and extended oppressive state laws over their Indian populations.

President John Quincy Adams had little sympathy for southerners in their struggle for Indian lands, but in 1828 he was defeated by Andrew Jackson. Jackson brought to the office long experience fighting and negotiating with southern Indians. He made clear his intention to acquire and open to white settlement all Indian land in the Southeast. In his 1829 message to Congress, Jackson offered southern Indians two alternatives—they could become subject to the discriminatory laws of the states or move west and continue their own tribal governments. The president and most southerners believed that they should move. In 1830, Congress passed the Indian Removal Act, which authorized the president to negotiate exchanges of territory and appropriated $500,000 for that purpose. Under the proposed removal treaties, the federal government would compensate emigrants for improvements (such as houses, cleared and fenced fields, barns, orchards, ferries) and assist them in their journey west.

The Choctaws were the first tribe to remove under the provisions of the Indian Removal Act. In the fall of 1830, a group of Choctaw chiefs agreed to the Treaty of Dancing Rabbit Creek. In this treaty, the Choctaws ceded their land in the Southeast, but those who wished to remain in Mississippi (or could not pay their debts to citizens of the state) would receive fee simple title to individual allotments of land and become citizens of the state. The federal government promised those who removed reimbursement for improvements, transportation to the West, subsistence for one year after removal, and an annuity for the support of education and other tribal services. There was much dissatisfaction with the treaty, particularly among Choctaw traditionalists who did not want to go west under any condition. Opponents had little opportunity to protest formally because the U.S. government refused to recognize any chief as long as the Choctaws remained in Mississippi. Consequently, the Choctaws began preparations for their westward migration. . . .

The federal government made allotment a major feature of the treaties signed with the Creeks and Chickasaws in 1832. The Creek chiefs agreed to cede much of their land in Alabama and to permit some Creeks to receive the remainder in allotments. Land speculators descended on the Indians and once again defrauded many of them of their individual allotments. Evicted from their homes and farms, many Creeks still refused to go west. Tension between white intruders and foraging Indians escalated and finally erupted into violence. In 1836, the War Department responded by forcibly removing thousands of Creeks as a military measure. Although many Creeks died during their westward trek as a result of the sinking of a steamboat, disease, hunger, and exposure, about 14,500 finally assembled in their new nation in the west.

The Chickasaws avoided some of the suffering of the Creeks, but, once again, corruption and fraud characterized their removal. . . .

The scandal generated by allotment failed to temper Georgia's demands that the federal government extinguish Indian land titles within the state. The widespread suffering, however, did strengthen the Cherokees' resolve to resist removal negotiations. When Georgia courts sentenced two white missionaries to prison for their failure to take the oath of allegiance to the state, the Cherokees turned to the U.S. Supreme Court for redress of grievances. In *Worcester* v. *Georgia,* the Court enjoined Georgia from enforcing state law in the Cherokee Nation and ordered the release of the missionaries. The state refused to comply. Legal technicalities and Jackson's disinclination to interfere precluded federal enforcement of the decision. The missionaries remained in prison, and Georgians continued to harass the Cherokees.

A group of Cherokees began to consider negotiations when it became obvious that the Supreme Court decision would have little impact on the situation in the Nation. This group came to be known as the Treaty Party, and its leaders included Major [John] Ridge, who had fought with the United States in the War of 1812 and had risen to a prominent leadership role in the Nation, his New England–educated son John, and Elias Boudinot, editor of the bilingual newspaper *The Cherokee Phoenix*. Motivated at least as much by economic and political ambitions as by concern for the Cherokee people, the Treaty Party enjoyed little popular support. The vast majority of Cherokees supported Principal Chief John Ross in his steadfast opposition to removal. Nevertheless, the U.S. treaty commissioner met with about one hundred Treaty Party members in December 1835, and they negotiated the Treaty of New Echota. This treaty provided for the exchange of Cherokee territory in the Southeast for a tract of land in what is today northeastern Oklahoma. While the original document gave acculturated Cherokees such as those who signed the treaty preemption rights (that is, the right to stay in the East and come under state law), supplemental articles eliminated this provision. Therefore, no Cherokees received individual allotments; removal encompassed the entire tribe. Although fifteen thousand Cherokees, almost the total population, signed a petition protesting the treaty, the U.S. Senate ratified the document. In summer 1838, federal troops seized thousands of Cherokees and imprisoned them in stockades in preparation for their westward trek. As the death toll mounted, the [Martin] Van Buren administration, which had inherited the removal program, agreed to let the Cherokees conduct their own removal in the winter of 1838–1839. Despite this "humanitarian" gesture, four thousand Cherokees died enroute to their new home in the West.

The Cherokees had fought violation of their rights in the courts; the Seminoles resisted removal militarily. In 1832, the Seminoles signed a provisional removal treaty in which they agreed to go west if they found a suitable country. The next year, their agent conducted a delegation of Seminoles west in search of a relocation site and reportedly forced the delegation to sign a new treaty guaranteeing removal from Florida by 1837. Although the Seminoles signed under duress, the Senate ratified the treaty, and Jackson, who had fought the Seminoles in the War of 1812, ordered it enforced. Because many Seminoles once had been a part of the Creek confederacy, the U.S. government believed that the two tribes should reunite in the West. The Seminoles strenuously objected to this plan and demanded that their tribal integrity be preserved. Ignoring Seminole objections, the United States sent troops to Florida to round up the Indians for removal. In 1835, desperate Seminole warriors ambushed a company of soldiers, and the massacre sparked the Second Seminole War. Skillfully employing guerrilla tactics in the swamps of southern Florida and led by superb warriors such as Osceola, the Seminoles forced the United States to commit a total of forty thousand men, spend $30,000 to $40,000, and suffer substantial casualties over the next seven years. In attempting to defeat and remove the Indians, the government resorted to even more duplicitous means than bribing chiefs and exploiting tribal factionalism: commanders in the field, with approval from Washington, repeatedly captured Seminole warriors under flags of truce. Even after the official end of the war in 1842, soldiers continued to capture and deport bands of Indians until about three thousand resided in the West and only several hundred remained in the Florida Everglades.

Although remnants of all southern tribes continued to live in their ancient homeland, most occupied worthless land from which they barely eked out a subsistence. Because these Indians had little that whites wanted, the pressure to remove them diminished. In the 1840s and 1850s, state and federal governments turned their attention to other issues, in particular, the growing sectional conflict over slavery. Many white Americans quickly forgot about the southern Indians and their tragic removal. . . .

Following removal, the division between [Indian] traditionalists or conservatives and the highly acculturated progressives became more pronounced. Progressives reestablished centralized republican governments and written law codes, built schools, encouraged missionaries, and took advantage of the economic opportunities afforded by the new land. They grew corn, raised cattle, made salt, and engaged in trade. Some amassed fortunes. After the American Civil War, progressives tended to advocate the construction of railroads and the exploitation of natural resources such as timber, asphalt, coal, and oil. They did not oppose the influx of white railroad workers, loggers, and cowboys, and at the turn of the century most supported allotment of land to individuals, dissolution of tribal governments, and Oklahoma statehood.

Conservatives, on the other hand, shunned many of the political, economic, and cultural changes of the progressives. Civilization had not saved their homeland, and now they regarded it with misgivings and even disdain. After removal, conservatives found comfort in what they could preserve of their traditional practices. Family and town continued to be the fundamental relationships of these people who were content with a mere economic subsistence. They found outlets for aggression in the ball play and other traditional games. Medicine men and women still relied on plants and sacred formulas to cure disease, cast spells, and control the natural world. Many conservative communities built square grounds, or stomp grounds, where they performed all-night dances, celebrated [traditional ceremonies], and took medicine to cleanse themselves physically and spiritually. The rituals of the stomp ground reinforced their traditional values of kinship, purity, and balance. Some southern Indians even formed secret societies in an attempt to revitalize the culture which embodied these values. The Cherokee Kee-too-wah society, for example, encouraged the abandonment of the white man's way and a return to traditional customs and beliefs. When faced with allotment and statehood, some traditionalists resisted violently, but most simply withdrew to their families, communities, and stomp grounds. At best, however, these people held on to a remnant of a cultural tradition admirably suited to their native Southeast and dramatically transformed by a series of events which culminated in removal.

From the white perspective, removal accomplished its goals: the U.S. government "protected" thousands of Indians from the corrupting influence of civilization by moving them west and opened millions of acres of Indian land to white settlement. These successes can be charted in economic, political, and demographic terms, but the human cost is not so easily measured. Thousands died; others suffered permanent mental and physical impairment. Although some traditions survived, southern Indians experienced significant cultural modification and even transformation. All of this took place not according to the will of the Indians but by the dictates of white policymakers. Manipulated, exploited, and oppressed, the Indians did not have the power to direct their own course or to determine their own future. Perhaps the greatest tragedy of Indian removal is that white Americans used their power over Indians to inflict great suffering. They congratulated themselves on their humanitarianism and blithely sealed the fate of the southern Indians.

The Debate Over the Legality and Wisdom of Indian Removal

STUART BANNER

There were really two debates about Indian removal in the late 1820s and early 1830s. They were sometimes conflated by participants, but it will be useful to treat them separately because their outcomes were different. One was a *legal* debate, over whether the government had the right to *force* the Indians to exchange their land for land in the west. The Indians won this debate. As a legal matter, it was generally

Reprinted with permission of the publisher from *How the Indians Lost Their Land: Law and Power on the Frontier*, by Stuart Banner, pp. 201–214, Cambridge, Mass.: The Belknap Press of Harvard University Press, Copyright © 2005 by the President and Fellows of Harvard College.

accepted within the federal government and among lawyers that removal could be accomplished only by treaty. The other debate was over the *wisdom* of removal. What would be best for the eastern Indians: remaining where they were or moving west? This was a question on which Indians as well as whites were divided. Some concluded that they would be better off removing, while others determined to stay in place. Given the relative power of the two groups, it was white opinion that mattered, and in the end, after years of argument, the pro-removal position would prevail.

The result was an uneasy combination of conclusions—that removal was in the best interests of the Indians, but that it could be lawfully accomplished only if the Indians consented. This tension gave rise to the actual circumstances of removal. Southern state governments (and eventually the federal government) would gradually ratchet up the pressure on the tribes to sell, until it reached a point best described as extortion. . . .

Proponents of forced removal made two legal arguments, both of which were ahead of their time. One was articulated by the lawyer-turned-soldier Andrew Jackson as early as 1817, while he was fighting the Seminoles in Florida. "The wisdom of the Government has wisely provided, that the property of a Citizen can be taken for public use, on just compensation being made," Jackson pointed out, correctly, in a letter to the new president, James Monroe. This power of eminent domain was enshrined in the Fifth Amendment to the Constitution, which Jackson was paraphrasing in his letter. Why, Jackson wondered, shouldn't the same principle apply to the Indians? . . .

The answer to Jackson's question rested partly on history and partly on then-current law. For two hundred years, Anglo-American governments had normally obtained Indian land by contract, never by exercising the power of eminent domain. That principle had originated at a time when English settlers lacked the power to acquire the Indians' land without the Indians' consent, and when the Indians' unsold land was understood to be beyond the effective control of any European government. As Jackson's letter underscored, however, both of those conditions had changed. The federal government was strong enough to take at least some Indian land by eminent domain, and the land in question no longer seemed so far away—now some of it comprised islands of Indian territory within a sea of white-owned land. The historical rationale for the government's reluctance to take Indian land by eminent domain was growing weaker with the passage of time.

American lawyers of the era would have had two more objections to Jackson's suggestion, objections grounded not in history but in early nineteenth-century American law. Indian tribes were sovereign entities of a sort. Exactly what that sovereignty entailed was in dispute, but all agreed that Indian tribes had always governed themselves internally by their own laws. The United States had always respected that sovereignty by negotiating treaties with Indian tribes rather than regulating them directly. Most lawyers would accordingly have been more hesitant than Jackson to suggest that the federal government's power of eminent domain extended to the Indians' land. They would most likely have deemed the United States no more capable of taking Indian land than of taking land in Canada—both areas would have been understood to lie within the sovereignty of an entity other than the United States. Jackson was sharp enough to realize this. He knew he had to supplement his argument with the claim that the federal government was wrong to treat Indian tribes like sovereign states. "The Indians are subjects of the United States, inhabiting its territory and acknowledging its sovereignty," he argued to Monroe. "Then is it not absurd for the sovereign to negotiate by treaty with the subject[?]" On this point Jackson was ahead of his time. Later in the century, the law would catch up with him: Congress would put an end to the practice of holding treaties with Indian tribes and would begin regulating the tribes directly. In 1817, however, the tradition of obtaining land by treaty was too strong to dislodge.

Most lawyers would also have objected to Jackson's expansive reading of the "public use" requirement of the Fifth Amendment. Taking land from the Indians in order to build a highway, or a fort, or some such public project, might amount to a public use, they would have argued. But taking land from the Indians in order to distribute it to white farmers would not be a public use, most early nineteenth-century lawyers would probably have concluded; it would be merely the expropriation from one group of people for the benefit of another, a redistribution of wealth understood in the early nineteenth century to lie beyond the government's power of eminent domain. Here too Jackson was ahead of his time. In the twentieth century, as government became more explicitly redistributive, the conventional understanding of the public use requirement broadened, to include the redistribution of property from one group to another, so long as it was backed by a plausible public-spirited motive. In 1817, however, most lawyers would have considered Jackson's plan too much a private transfer to be within the government's power of eminent domain.

James Monroe was a lawyer too, but his response to Jackson revealed none of these doubts. "The view which you have taken of the Indian title to lands is new but very deserving of attention," Monroe began. "It has been customary to purchase the title of the Indian tribes," he recognized, but he agreed that the custom deserved rethinking, in light of what he saw as the Indians' misguided determination to retain their land and their traditional ways of life, a stubbornness that was only driving them to extinction. "A compulsory process seems to be necessary, to break their habits, & to civilize them, & there is much cause to believe, that it must be resorted to, to preserve them." If this was Monroe's private view, his public pronouncements adhered to the tradition of acquiring Indian land only with the Indians' consent. In his first annual message to Congress as president, delivered two months after he responded to Jackson, Monroe emphasized the twin goals of civilizing the Indians and obtaining the land east of the Mississippi they still retained. But he also emphasized the need to *purchase* the land. Throughout his administration, Monroe continued to resist demands from Georgians and others that the Indians' land be taken without their consent.

Whatever Monroe's true preferences were, the idea that the Indians' land could be taken by eminent domain was never put into practice, even when Andrew Jackson became president, and it seems never to have gained much support. Most white Americans probably agreed that the land could be put to better use by white farmers, but the notion of seizing it, even with compensation to the Indians, seemed too extravagant. As an anonymous contributor to the *North American Review* put it at the height of the removal controversy, "the United States would contend with a very ill grace for the doctrine, that unsettled lands may be seized by those, who need them for the purposes of cultivation." The doctrine had some troubling implications, because the federal government itself owned a vast amount of unproductive land. "How many millions of the people of France, Germany and Ireland might appropriate to themselves good farms in the States of Indiana, Illinois and Missouri? Why should they not take immediate possession?" The Indians and their supporters won this branch of the legal argument.

Advocates of forced removal had a second legal argument, one that was voiced more often. After the Supreme Court's decisions in *Fletcher* v. *Peck* and *Johnson* v. *M'Intosh*, there was no doubt that state governments were the fee simple owners of the unsold Indian land within their borders. The Indians, the Court had held, possessed only a "right of occupancy" in the land. Georgia's congressional delegation used these decisions to argue that the federal government had the right to remove the Indians from Georgia by force. "The Indians are simply occupants—tenants at will," they reasoned. *Tenants at will* was a term of property law, referring to tenants who could be removed at any time, at the landlord's pleasure. "If a peaceable purchase cannot be made in the ordinary mode," Georgia's congressmen argued, "nothing remains to be done but to order their removal.". . .

But this argument did not prevail either, because it was so inconsistent with two centuries of practice. The New England lawyer and reformer Jeremiah Evarts, one of the leading white opponents of removal, made the point as plain as possible in one of his widely read essays, published under the pseudonym "William Penn" in the Washington *National Intelligencer*: The law had never declared "that Indians are tenants at will," he pointed out. On the contrary, "the whole history of our negotiations with them, from the peace of 1783 to the last treaty to which they are a party, and of all our legislation concerning them, shows, that they are regarded as . . . possessing a territory, which they are to hold in full possession, till they voluntarily surrender it." In an 1829 memorial to Congress, the Cherokees made the same argument. "Your memorialists solemnly protest against being considered tenants at will," they insisted. "As we have never ceded nor forfeited the occupancy of the soil and the sovereignty over it, we do solemnly protest against being forced to leave it."

The law was thus on the side of the Indians. Despite the increasingly belligerent claims of Georgia and nearby states, there was never room to make a serious legal argument that the Indians could be removed by force. Even the Andrew Jackson administration would pursue removal in the form of treaties rather than simply using the army to force the Indians to move.

The other removal debate was about removal's wisdom. The Indians had the legal right to stay where they were, but was that a right they should exercise? Or would it be in their best interest to exchange their land for new land west of the Mississippi?

Some of the arguments advanced by the white proponents of removal were of course grounded in the interests of white settlers, not Indians. Government officials often noted that the pattern of Indian land purchasing had produced a jagged frontier, with scattered white settlements separated by intervening Indian territory. Defense against Indian attack, they repeatedly pointed out, would be far simpler and less expensive if whites and Indians each occupied a single contiguous territory, the two separated by a single line. Some of the other arguments in favor of removal were equally self-serving. Senator Thomas Buck Reed of Mississippi complained that "the Indian territory in Mississippi affords a complete sanctuary for debtors and vagabonds and criminals from every part of the Union." Richard Henry Wilde of Georgia thought removal appropriate simply because, in his view, whites would do better things with the land. "Are we to check the human course of happiness," he asked, "obstruct the march of science—stay the works of art, and stop the arm of industry, because they will efface in their progress the wigwam of the red hunter, and put out forever the council fire of his tribe?". . .

Other proponents of removal claimed to be friends of the Indian, but made arguments so patently disingenuous as to undermine the claim. When the General Assembly of Indiana, for example, sent a memorial to Congress praying that the federal government extinguish the Indian title of the two tribes remaining within the state, the Assembly suggested that the Indians would find the territory west of the Mississippi "so much better adapted to their wants and their habits" than Indiana, "where they now acquire but a precarious and scanty subsistence." One may wonder whether the Indiana Assembly would have been as solicitous of the Indians' well-being had the Indians not occupied land coveted by the state's white residents. On the floor of the Senate, John Elliott of Georgia provided a range of ostensibly humanitarian reasons the Indians ought to move west, but then undercut his own posture when, evidently warming to his subject, he began rhapsodizing over how much money the government would take in from selling all that land to settlers.

With all this thinly disguised self-interest floating around, it is perhaps easy to be cynical about the motives of *all* the white proponents of removal. No doubt many of those who argued for removal were not nearly as interested in the welfare of the Indians as they claimed to be. And given what we know, with the benefit of hindsight, about the long-term consequences of removal, it is easy to suspect that those consequences were intended by the whites who urged the Indians to move west. But in the 1820s and 1830s, as in all periods of American history, whites were not as monolithic in their motives or their opinions with respect to Indians as we sometimes implicitly accuse them of being. There were many white Americans who advocated removal because they genuinely believed it was in the hest interests of the Indians.

Proponents of removal began with the obvious truth that contact with white settlers had always proven disastrous for the Indians. "If ever one tribe of Indians has flourished" in close proximity to settlers, observed the Baptist missionary Isaac McCoy, "we will hope that the like may happen again. But if such an event has never occurred, we may confidently assure ourselves that it never will." Wherever whites settled in large numbers, most of the Indians eventually died or moved away. After two hundred years of such encounters, some tribes had been driven to extinction, and others were nearly there. Everyone knew that the white population of the United States was constantly increasing and that white settlement was pushing steadily westward. Barring a dramatic change in the federal government's Indian policy, the Indians' future looked dismal. James Barbour, the secretary of war under President John Quincy Adams, was just one of many who recognized the looming catastrophe. "Shall we go on quietly in a course, which, judging from the past, threatens their extinction?" he asked in a thoughtful 1826 memorandum recommending removal. Or was there something the government could do to save the Indians? . . .

The geography of the United States suggested a solution. Across the Mississippi River lay an enormous region about which little was known other than that it was very sparsely populated. It was generally agreed (incorrectly, as it turned out) that this territory was so big, and so remote, that it would not see substantial white settlement for a very long time, perhaps centuries. West of the Mississippi lay the only long-term answer to the inevitable humanitarian disaster—enough land, far enough from whites. The territory acquired in the Louisiana Purchase could be "a land of refuge, where this unhappy race may find rest and safety," declared Lewis Cass in the *North American Review* shortly before he became the administrator of removal as Andrew Jackson's secretary of war. For two hundred years, Indian policy had been a series of ad hoc, small-scale removals, and the Indian population had steadily diminished. For removal's proponents, the Indians' choice was either more of the same, which would lead to extinction, or the replacement of multiple small removals with one final, major, permanent removal that would be the Indians' only hope of survival. As [the commissioner of Indian affairs] Thomas McKenney explained to a pro-removal organization formed in 1829 by clergymen and laymen of the Reformed Dutch Church in Manhattan, "we believe if the Indians do not emigrate, and fly the causes, which are fixed in themselves, and which have proved so destructive in the past, they *must perish!*" His audience then included the same message in a memorial to Congress. The Indians "appear to us as if standing on the very verge of ruin," they declared. Removal west of the Mississippi would be "the only alternative left."

Religious organizations had long taken an active interest in the Indians' welfare, both in this life and the next, so it is not surprising that they were among the most vocal proponents of removal. The Baptists were particularly strong supporters. The *American Baptist Magazine* published repeated endorsements of removal. Local Baptist associations petitioned Congress to the same effect. Baptist advocates of removal were careful to remind readers that the Indians had the legal right to remain in place, and that removal would be legitimate only if the Indians voluntarily agreed to it. "Whether it is expedient for the Indians to remove," one explained, "is distinct from the question whether they possess a right to retain their lands." What the Indians *should* do, and what they could be *forced* to do, were two separate issues. "A man may think it for the good of the Cherokees themselves that they should follow their countrymen beyond the Mississippi," declared a Baptist correspondent calling himself "Roger Williams," in honor of the early defender of Indian property rights, "and yet feel grief and indignation at a violation of solemn treaties, or an attempt to force the Indians from their homes." Other religious organizations favoring removal emphasized the same distinction: the Indians would either move west of the Mississippi or face imminent destruction, but that was a choice only the Indians could make.

But what exactly was the humanitarian thing to do? Many thought removal was only likely to drive the Indians *toward* extinction. Heman Humphrey, the president of Amherst College, insisted that removal was nothing but a plan "to drive 70,000 unoffending people from the soil on which they were born, into distant wilds, where most of them will perish." Among well-meaning whites with the shared goal of protecting the Indians, there were two opinions about removal.

Opponents emphasized that removal would hardly be the clean operation implicitly envisioned by its supporters. "It is no slight task," one observed, "for a whole people, from helpless infancy to the decrepitude of age, to abandon their native land, and seek in a distant, and perhaps barren region, new means of support." Even if the logistics of mass migration could be managed, the Indians would only face more hardships once they arrived at their destination. No one could say for sure whether they would encounter other Indian tribes, who would be hostile to the new comers.

Nor was there any certainty that the land west of the Mississippi would be a sanctuary from white settlers for as long as the proponents of removal hoped. If the land was any good for farming, it would be coveted by whites soon enough. "If the lands to which you remove them are what you describe them to be," predicted Representative Edward Everett of Massachusetts, "you may as well push back the tide in the Bay of Fundy, as keep out the white population." If the land was unsuitable for farming, on the other hand, the Indians were being snookered into an unfair trade. Either way, argued a group of Massachusetts residents in a memorial to Congress, the concept of removal was "too visionary to require serious attention."

Perhaps the most commonly voiced objection to removal was that it was utterly inconsistent with the government's long-standing policy of helping the Indians along the path toward civilization. For decades, the federal government had urged tribes to live more like Anglo-Americans—to settle in permanent towns, to build churches and schools, to make long-term investments in farm animals and equipment. Some tribes, especially the Cherokees, had done just that, and were gradually adopting a lifestyle similar to that of their white neighbors. After the Indians had made so much progress toward civilization, opponents of removal wondered, how could the government turn around and advise the Indians to migrate westward into the wilderness? "How will these facts tell in history?", one asked. . . . The inconsistency between the goals of civilization and removal was not lost on the Cherokees. "Where have we an example in the whole history of man," wondered Elias Boudinot, editor of the *Cherokee Phoenix*, "of a Nation or tribe, removing in a body, from a land of civil and religious means, to a perfect wilderness, *in order to be civilized.*"

Because of arguments like these, for every religious group that favored removal, there was another urging the Indians not to accept the trade, and pleading with the federal government to protect the Indians in the east today rather than promising protection in the west tomorrow. The most urgent pleas came from missionaries resident among the Cherokees, who repeatedly predicted that removal would pose a far greater threat to the Indians' well-being than anything they might encounter at home. The religious organizations, like white humanitarian opinion generally, were divided over removal.

This division was important, because whenever Indian land policy was at issue, whites essentially divided into two camps. Many, particularly in the south and the west, were interested in obtaining the land and had little or no concern with the welfare of the Indians. Many others, particularly in the northeast, might loosely be called "humanitarians." Whatever their interest in acquiring the Indians' land, they were able to keep at least one eye on the Indians' well-being, and they had at least some desire to protect the Indians from the aggressions of white settlers. Such people often occupied important positions in the federal government. Henry Knox, the United States' first secretary of war, was such a person, as was Thomas McKenney, who was in charge of the federal government's relations with the

Indians between 1816 and 1830. These eastern humanitarians were the only significant political counterweight to the expansionists on the frontier. The state of relations between the United States and the Indian tribes at any given time normally reflected the balance of power between the two groups, and the extent to which easterners possessing nominal power were actually able to use that power to keep westerners under control.

Because the humanitarians were split over removal, they could not provide the ordinary counterweight to the southerners and westerners who advocated removal on expansionist grounds. Had the debate among whites over the wisdom of removal simply pitted expansionists against humanitarians, the outcome might have landed somewhere in the middle, as Indian policy so often did. The "middle" in this context would have been a continuation of the traditional piecemeal method of land acquisition that had prevailed for two centuries. But the debate over the wisdom of removal pitted some of the humanitarians on one side against strange bedfellows on the other—the rest of the humanitarians, joined by the expansionists. By 1830, if not earlier, it became clear that white opinion supported removal.

The result was an uncomfortable juxtaposition of outcomes. Most whites agreed that the Indians could not be removed against their will. But most also agreed that the Indians ought to exchange their land for land west of the Mississippi. And many within the latter group sincerely believed that such an exchange would be in the Indians' best interests, even if the Indians themselves had not yet realized as much. Many whites were thus of the view that they were justified in pressuring the Indians into voluntarily agreeing to remove.

This was partly a matter of assumed racial superiority. If Indians were less intelligent than whites, they might not perceive their own self-interest as clearly as whites did. Just as children could not make important decisions without guidance from adults, the Indians' own preferences about removal might be helped by guidance from whites.

But there was more at work than racial paternalism in the apparently widespread belief, especially among government officials, that they had no need to take the Indians' stated preferences at face value. At least as important was the general impression within the federal government that the opposition to removal expressed by tribal leaders did not reflect the views of the majority of tribe members. Cherokee and Creek chiefs consistently declined offers to remove, but federal officials were convinced that the chiefs were misrepresenting the wishes of their constituents in a desperate attempt to preserve their own status. "It is by no means unnatural for the chiefs of those tribes to oppose the going away of their people," Thomas McKenney assured Congress in his 1829 annual report. "In proportion to the reduction of their numbers does their power decrease; and their love of power is not less strong than other people's." The House Committee on Indian Affairs concluded in 1830 that the Cherokees were governed by an aristocracy of mixed-blood families that controlled the entire wealth of the tribe and spoke for the tribe in its dealings with the government, despite constituting no more than 5 percent of the tribe's population. The remaining nineteen of twenty Cherokees, the Committee found, "are the tenants of the wretched huts and villages in the recesses of the mountains and elsewhere, remote from the highways and the neighborhood of the wealthy and prosperous." These "common Indians" stood to gain from removal, the Committee believed, and would have already accepted the government's offer to remove, had their voices not been silenced and their preferences not dictated by the Cherokee aristocracy, who stood to lose their wealth and power if the tribe headed west. The parallel committee in the Senate agreed that the Cherokees' opposition to removal was in truth the view "of comparatively a few, who are either white men connected with the nations by marriage, or of those of mixed blood, born in the nation, who are well educated and intelligent, who have acquired considerable property." Most Cherokees, "the mass of the population, are as poor and degraded as can well be imagined," and would prefer to move west of the Mississippi, the Committee concluded, if the tribal leadership did not keep them in the dark as to the benefits of removal. Such views were self-serving but not without foundation. As Indian tribes acculturated to Anglo-American ways, wealth distribution within tribes was indeed becoming more unequal, and the interests of rich and poor tribe members were diverging more and more. Exacerbating the problem, in the view of some government officials, were the missionaries living among the Indians, who, more interested in maintaining their own positions than in helping the Indians, urged the Indians to resist the government's offers to remove.

This was the climate of white opinion in the late 1820s when removal first became a major national issue. Among those capable of influencing the federal government's Indian policy, it was generally understood that removal would be in the best interests of whites because it would open up new land to white settlement; that removal would also be in the best interests of the Indians because it was the only measure that would protect them from extinction; that the Indians could not be removed by force, but only by treaty; and that when Indians refused to agree to treaties of removal, the refusal did not have to be taken too seriously because it did not express the true preferences of most Indians.

This combination of beliefs was a recipe for extortion. It was only a matter of time before frontier state governments, answerable to white settlers bordering on Indian land, began ratcheting up the pressure on the nonselling tribes by threatening to make life considerably more difficult for Indians who refused to sell their land. That pressure, and the federal government's response to it, gave rise to the series of events that has come to be remembered as "removal."

🌐 F U R T H E R   R E A D I N G

William H. Anderson, *Cherokee Removal: Before and After* (1991)
John M. Belohlavek, *"Let the Eagle Soar!" The Foreign Policy of Andrew Jackson* (1985)
Robert F. Berkhofer Jr., *The White Man's Indian* (1978)
Ned Blackhawk, *Violence Over the Land* (2006)
H. W. Brands, *Andrew Jackson* (2006)
Andrew Burstein, *The Passions of Andrew Jackson* (2005)
Gregory E. Dowd, *A Spirited Resistance* (1992)
Richard Drinnon, *Facing West: The Metaphysics of Indian Hating and Empire Building* (1980)
John Ehle, *Trail of Tears* (1983)
Arrell M. Gibson, *The American Indian* (1980)
Arthur N. Gilbert, "The American Indian and United States Diplomatic History," *History Teacher,* 7 (1974–1975), 229–241

Michael D. Green, *The Politics of Indian Removal* (1982)

Claudia B. Haake, *The State, Removal, and Indigenous Peoples* (2007)

Stan Hoig, *White Man's Paper Trail* (2006)

Frederick E. Hoxie, ed., *Indians in American History* (1988)

Thomas N. Ingersoll, *To Intermix with Our White Brothers* (2005)

Gloria Jahoda, *The Trail of Tears* (1995)

Patrick J. Jung, *The Blackhawk War of 1832* (2007)

Barbara Alice Mann, *George Washington's War on Native Americans* (2005)

William G. McLoughlin, *Cherokee Renascence in the New Republic* (1986)

Calvin Martin, ed., *The American Indian and the Problem of History* (1987)

Jon Meacham, *The Lion* (2008) (on Andrew Jackson)

James H. Merrell, *Into the American Woods* (1999)

Steven Mintz, ed., *Native American Voices* (1995)

Celia E. Naylor, *African Cherokees in Indian Territory* (2008)

Sharlotte Neely, *Snowbird Cherokees* (1991)

Theda Perdue and Michael Green, eds., *The Cherokee Removal* (1995)

Francis P. Prucha, *The Great Father: The United States Government and the American Indians* (1984)

Robert V. Remini, *Andrew Jackson and His Indian Wars* (2001)

Michael Paul Rogin, *Fathers and Children: Andrew Jackson and the Subjugation of the American Indians* (1975)

Deborah A. Rosen, *American Indians and State Law* (2007)

Claudio Saunt, *A New Order of Things* (1999) (on the Creek Tribe)

John Sugden, *Tucumseh: A Life* (1998)

William E. Unrau, *The Rise and Fall of Indian Country* (2007)

Anthony F. C. Wallace, *Jefferson and the Indians* (2001)

———, *The Long, Bitter Trail* (1993)

Philip Weeks, *Farewell My Nation: The American Indian and the United States, 1820–1890* (1990)

Richard White, *The Middle Ground* (1991)

Sean Wilentz, *Andrew Jackson* (2001)

Thurman Wilkins, *Cherokee Tragedy: The Ridge Family and the Decimation of a People* (1986)

Mary E. Young, "The Cherokee Nation: Mirror of the Republic," *American Quarterly,* 33 (1981), 502–524

Manifest Destiny, Texas,
and the War with Mexico

The 1840s witnessed an expansionist surge that netted new territories for the United States. After the threat or use of force and much debate, the territories of Texas, Oregon, and California became part of the expanding American empire. From infancy the United States had been expansionist and had moved steadily westward, enlarging its territory, pushing out its boundaries, and removing Native Americans. In the 1840s, expansionism took a new name. A journalist proclaimed that it was the United States's "Manifest Destiny" to extend its reach to the Pacific Ocean. In 1846, Oregon joined the American empire, and President James K. Polk took the nation to war against Mexico.

The origins of the Mexican-American War (1846–1848) can be traced to Spain's decision in 1819 to allow North American colonists, led by Moses Austin and his son Stephen, to settle in the Mexican province of Texas. Lured by the availability of cheap, fertile land, the settlers—who included many slaveholding southern planters—swelled in number to more than 15,000 within a decade. Tensions flared between the colonists and the new, independent Mexico when the central government in Mexico City required Texans to accept membership in the Roman Catholic Church and to abolish slavery. In a further attempt to clamp down on the American migrants, Mexican president Antonio López de Santa Anna in 1830 abolished the province's legislature and marched his army into Texas. Led by the legendary Sam Houston, the indignant Texans rebelled in 1836. Although the rebels suffered a costly defeat at the Alamo mission in San Antonio, they regrouped and quickly secured Texan independence. The United States' annexation of the Lone Star Republic and the admission of Texas to the Union in 1845 soon sparked a new conflict. War broke out between the United States and Mexico along the disputed Texas border in 1846; and two years later, a defeated Mexico, in the Treaty of Guadelupe Hidalgo, transferred one-half of its national domain to the United States.

What explains this burst of territorial acquisitiveness? President Polk's ardent expansionism? A cumulative and traditional American expansionism? Idealism? Racism? Security concerns? Commercial interest? The answers vary, as the selections in this chapter indicate.

🌐 D O C U M E N T S

On December 12, 1835, the commander in chief of Texas's rebel army, Sam Houston, issued a proclamation to his fellow citizens. The pronouncement, Document 1, summarizes Texas's complaints against Mexican authorities and beseeches all Texans to join the struggle for independence. In Document 2, a memoir written in 1837, Mexico's Antonio López de Santa Anna defends his efforts to crush the Texas revolution. The colorful leader, renowned for leading the bloody assault in 1836 against badly outgunned rebels at the Alamo in San Antonio, disputes the legitimacy of Texan nationhood and condemns clandestine U.S. support for the uprising.

John L. O'Sullivan is credited with having popularized the idea of Manifest Destiny, which ultimately rationalized the United States' annexation of Texas and other territories. As the editor of the *Democratic Review,* he flamboyantly sketched an unbounded American future of democratic mission and territorial expansion. Document 3 is taken from his "The Great Nation of Futurity," published in 1839. James K. Polk became president in 1845. An avowed expansionist, he hungrily eyed Mexican lands and territories in the Southwest and he disputed boundaries with the British in the Northwest. Document 4, Polk's inaugural address of March 4, 1845, makes the case for the United States's absorbing Texas and Oregon. Document 5 is Polk's war message of May 11, 1846, in which the president presents U.S. grievances and asks Congress to declare war against Mexico.

The outbreak of the war, American territorial ambitions, and the ultimate U.S. triumph ignited considerable debate. In Document 6, the Wilmot Proviso, drafted by Representative David Wilmot of Pennsylvania, the author seeks to keep slavery out of any territory won from Mexico. Although the House passed this amendment to an appropriations bill in 1846 and again in 1847, the Senate turned it down, thereby exposing deep divisions over whether limits ought to be placed on expansion.

In Document 7, a speech delivered in the U.S. Senate on March 23, 1848, the leader of the Whig party, Daniel Webster of Massachusetts, denounces the acquisition of new territories as an abuse of executive power and an unconscionable act of aggression against Mexico. Webster predicts that the admission of new states from the former Mexican territories will alter the balance of power in the Senate between southern slaveholding and northern free states, disrupting the Union. The final selection, Document 8, is an excerpt from the collective views of a group of Mexican leaders, first translated into English and published in 1850. They portray the United States as an aggressive, expansionist power, condemn the annexation of Texas, and accuse Washington of having provoked war in 1846 by sending General Zachary Taylor's forces across the disputed Texas-Mexico border. Disarray in the Mexican government and politics, they acknowledged, eased the drive to acquire Texas.

🌐 D O C U M E N T   1

Commander Sam Houston Issues a Battle Cry for Texas Independence from Mexico, 1835

Your situation is peculiarly calculated to call forth all your manly energies. Under the Republican constitution of Mexico, you were invited to Texas, then a wilderness. You have reclaimed and rendered it a cultivated country. You solemnly swore to support the Constitution and its laws. Your oaths are yet inviolate. In accordance with them, you have fought with the [Mexican] liberals against those who sought to overthrow

---

This document can be found in *Texan and Emigrants Guide,* Nacogdoches, 2 January, 1836.

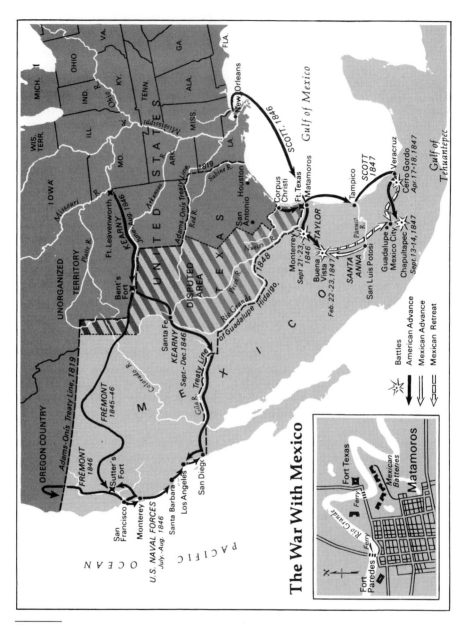

The War With Mexico

Thomas G. Paterson et al., *American Foreign Relations*, 6/e. Copyright © 2005 Wadsworth, Cengage Learning. Used with permission.

the Constitution in 1832 when the present usurper was the champion of liberal principles in Mexico. Your obedience has manifested your integrity. You have witnessed with pain the convulsions of the interior and a succession of usurpations. You have experienced in silent grief the expulsion of your members from the State Congress. You have realized the horrors of anarchy and the dictation of military rule. The promises made to you have not been fulfilled. Your memorials for the redress of grievances have been disregarded and the agents you have sent to Mexico have been imprisoned for years without enjoying the rights of trial agreeable to law. Your constitutional executive has been deposed by the bayonets of a mercenary soldiery while your State Congress has been dissolved by violence, and its members either fled or were arrested by the military force of the country. The federation has been dissolved, the Constitution declared at an end, and centralism has been established. . . .

The usurper dispatched a military force to invade the colonies and exact the arms of the inhabitants. The citizens refused the demand, and the invading force was increased. The question then was shall we resist the oppression and live free, or violate our oaths and bear a despot's stripes? The citizens of Texas rallied to the defense of their constitutional rights. They have met four to one and by their chivalry and courage, they have vanquished the enemy with a gallantry and spirit which is characteristic of the justice of our cause. . . .

Since our army has been in the field, a consultation of the people, by their representatives, has met and established a provisional government. This course has grown out of the emergencies of the country; the army has claimed its peculiar care. We were without law and without a constitutional head. The Provisional Executive and the General Council of Texas are earnestly engaged in their respective duties preparing for every exigency of the country and I am satisfied from their zeal, ability and patriotism, that Texas will have everything to hope from their exertions in behalf of the principles which we have avowed. . . .

Citizens of Texas, your rights must be defended. The oppressors must be driven from our soil. Submission to the laws and union among ourselves will render us invincible; subordination and discipline in our army will guarantee to us victory and renown. Our invader has sworn to extinguish us or sweep us from the soil. He is vigilant in his work of oppression and has ordered to Texas ten thousand men to enforce the unhallowed purposes of his ambition. His letters to his subalterns in Texas have been intercepted and his plans for our destruction have been disclosed. Departing from the chivalric principles of warfare, he has ordered arms to be distributed to a portion of our population for the purpose of creating in the midst of us a servile war. The hopes of the usurper were inspired by a belief that the citizens of Texas were disunited and divided in opinion and that alone has been the cause of the present invasion of our rights. He shall realize the fallacy of his hopes in the union of her citizens and their ETERNAL RESISTANCE to his plans against constitutional liberty. We will enjoy our birthright or perish in its defense. . . .

Let the brave rally to our standard.

🌐 *D O C U M E N T   2*

General Antonio López de Santa Anna Defends Mexican Sovereignty over Texas, 1837

Santa Anna, whether conqueror or conquered, whether free or in chains, yea, I swear it before the world, did not in Texas debase the Mexican name in which he glories and takes pride. . . .

This document can be found in Carlos E. Castañeda, ed., *The Mexican Side of the Texas Revolution, 1836* (Dallas: P. L. Turner Co., 1928), 5–8, 16–17.

[In] November, 1835, [I took] charge of a war from which I could have been excused, for the fundamental law of the country offered me a decorous excuse that my broken health made all the more honorable. Nevertheless, aware of the adverse circumstances I have expressed, I still desired to try to serve my country. In a few days I gathered six thousand men, clothed and equipped. At the cost of immense sacrifices, rising above obstacles that seemed insuperable, this force set out from San Luis towards the end of December, 1835. . . .

Let it be said now in order to avoid repetition: the war against Texas has been as just on the part of the Mexican government as the lack of the slightest attempt on the part of those who forced it upon Mexico has been to try to justify their action. Few of the colonists, properly speaking, have taken up arms in the struggle. The soldiers of [Colonel William Barret] Travis at the Alamo, those of [Captain James W.] Fannin at Perdido, the riflemen of Dr. [James] Grant, and [Sam] Houston himself and his troops at San Jacinto, with but few exceptions, were publicly known to have come from New Orleans and other points of the neighboring republic exclusively for the purpose of aiding the Texas rebellion without ever having been members of any of the colonization grants.

Some Mexicans, partisans of a former system of government, thought, perhaps in good faith, that the only effect of fanning the fire of war in Texas would be a political change in accord with their opinion. Their shortsighted ambition must be a terrible lesson to them as well as a source of eternal remorse. Too late, they now deplore having placed in jeopardy the integrity of our national territory.

Our country found itself invaded not by an established nation that came to vindicate its rights, whether true or imaginary; nor by Mexicans who, in a paroxysm of political passion, came to defend or combat the public administration of the country. The invaders were all men who, moved by the desire of conquest, with rights less apparent and plausible than those of [the Spanish conquistadors Hernán] Cortés and [Francisco de] Pizarro, wished to take possession of that vast territory extending from Béxar to the Sabine belonging to Mexico. What can we call them? How should they be treated? All the existing laws, whose strict observance the government had just recommended, marked them as pirates and outlaws. The nations of the world would never have forgiven Mexico had it accorded them rights, privileges, and considerations which the common law of peoples accords only to constituted nations.

🌎 D O C U M E N T   3

Democratic Publicist John L. O'Sullivan
Proclaims America's Manifest Destiny, 1839

The American people having derived their origin from many other nations, and the Declaration of National Independence being entirely based on the great principle of human equality, these facts demonstrate at once our disconnected position as regards any other nation; that we have, in reality, but little connection with the past history of any of them, and still less with all antiquity, its glories, or its crimes. On the contrary,

This document can be found in "The Great Nation of Futurity," *The United States Magazine and Democratic Review* VI (November 1839): 426–430. It can also be found in Norman A. Graebner, ed., *Manifest Destiny* (Indianapolis: Bobbs-Merrill Co., 1968), 15–21.

our national birth was the beginning of a new history, the formation and progress of an untried political system, which separates us from the past and connects us with the future only; and so far as regards the entire development of the natural rights of man, in moral, political, and national life, we may confidently assume that our country is destined to be the great nation of futurity.

It is so destined, because the principle upon which a nation is organized fixes its destiny, and that of equality is perfect, is universal. It presides in all the operations of the physical world, and it is also the conscious law of the soul—the self-evident dictates of morality, which accurately defines the duty of man to man, and consequently man's rights as man. Besides, the truthful annals of any nation furnish abundant evidence, that its happiness, its greatness, its duration, were always proportionate to the democratic equality in its system of government. . . .

What friend of human liberty, civilization, and refinement, can cast his view over the past history of the monarchies and aristocracies of antiquity, and not deplore that they ever existed? What philanthropist can contemplate the oppressions, the cruelties, and injustice inflicted by them on the masses of mankind, and not turn with moral horror from the retrospect?

America is destined for better deeds. It is our unparalleled glory that we have no reminiscences of battle fields, but in defence of humanity, of the oppressed of all nations, of the rights of conscience, the rights of personal enfranchisement. Our annals describe no scenes of horrid carnage, where men were led on by hundreds of thousands to slay one another, dupes and victims to emperors, kings, nobles, demons in the human form called heroes. We have had patriots to defend our homes, our liberties, but no aspirants to crowns or thrones; nor have the American people ever suffered themselves to be led on by wicked ambition to depopulate the land, to spread desolation far and wide, that a human being might be placed on a seat of supremacy.

We have no interest in the scenes of antiquity, only as lessons of avoidance of nearly all their examples. The expansive future is our arena, and for our history. We are entering on its untrodden space, with the truths of God in our minds, beneficent objects in our hearts, and with a clear conscience unsullied by the past. We are the nation of human progress, and who will, what can, set limits to our onward march? Providence is with us, and no earthly power can. We point to the everlasting truth on the first page of our national declaration, and we proclaim to the millions of other lands, that "the gates of hell"—the powers of aristocracy and monarchy—"shall not prevail against it."

The far-reaching, the boundless future will be the era of American greatness. In its magnificent domain of space and time, the nation of many nations is destined to manifest to mankind the excellence of divine principles; to establish on earth the noblest temple ever dedicated to the worship of the Most High—the Sacred and the True. Its floor shall be a hemisphere—its roof the firmament of the star-studded heavens, and its congregation an Union of many Republics, comprising hundreds of happy millions, calling, owning no man master, but governed by God's natural and moral law of equality, the law of brotherhood—of "peace and good will amongst men." . . .

Yes, we are the nation of progress, of individual freedom, of universal enfranchisement. Equality of rights is the cynosure of our union of States, the grand exemplar of the correlative equality of individuals; and while truth sheds its effulgence, we cannot retrograde, without dissolving the one and subverting the other. We must onward to the fulfilment of our mission—to the entire development of the principle of our organization—freedom of conscience, freedom of person, freedom of trade and business pursuits, universality of freedom and equality. This is our high destiny, and in nature's eternal, inevitable decree of cause and effect we must accomplish it. All this will be our future history, to establish on earth the moral dignity and salvation of man—the immutable truth and beneficence of God. For this blessed mission to the nations of the world, which are shut out from the life-giving light of truth, has America been chosen; and her high example shall smite unto death the tyranny of kings, hierarchs, and oligarchs, and carry the glad tidings of peace and good will where myriads now endure an existence scarcely more enviable than that of beasts of the field. Who, then, can doubt that our country is destined to be *the great nation* of futurity?

DOCUMENT 4

President James K. Polk Lays Claim to Texas and Oregon, 1845

I regard the question of annexation as belonging exclusively to the United States and Texas. They are independent powers competent to contract, and foreign nations have no right to interfere with them or to take exceptions to their reunion. Foreign powers do not seem to appreciate the true character of our Government. Our Union is a confederation of independent States, whose policy is peace with each other and all the world. To enlarge its limits is to extend the dominions of peace over additional territories and increasing millions. The world has nothing to fear from military ambition in our Government. While the Chief Magistrate and the popular branch of Congress are elected for short terms by the suffrages of those millions who must in their own persons bear all the burdens and miseries of war, our Government can not be otherwise than pacific. Foreign powers should therefore look on the annexation of Texas to the United States not as the conquest of a nation seeking to extend her dominions by arms and violence, but as the peaceful acquisition of a territory once her own, by adding another member to our confederation, with the consent of that member, thereby diminishing the chances of war and opening to them new and ever-increasing markets for their products.

To Texas the reunion is important, because the strong protecting arm of our Government would be extended over her, and the vast resources of her fertile soil and genial climate would be speedily developed, while the safety of New Orleans and of our whole southwestern frontier against hostile aggression, as well as the interests of the whole Union, would be promoted by it.

In the earlier stages of our national existence the opinion prevailed with some that our system of confederated States could not operate successfully over an extended territory, and serious objections have at different times been made to the

This document can be found in James D. Richardson, ed., *A Compilation of the Messages and Papers of the Presidents* (New York: Bureau of National Literature, 1897), V, 2230–2231.

enlargement of our boundaries. These objections were earnestly urged when we acquired Louisiana. Experience has shown that they were not well founded. The title of numerous Indian tribes to vast tracts of country has been extinguished; new States have been admitted into the Union; new Territories have been created and our jurisdiction and laws extended over them. As our population has expanded, the Union has been cemented and strengthened. . . .

None can fail to see the danger to our safety and future peace if Texas remains an independent state or becomes an ally or dependency of some foreign nation more powerful than herself. Is there one among our citizens who would not prefer perpetual peace with Texas to occasional wars, which so often occur between bordering independent nations? Is there one who would not prefer free intercourse with her to high duties on all our products and manufactures which enter her ports or cross her frontiers? Is there one who would not prefer an unrestricted communication with her citizens to the frontier obstructions which must occur if she remains out of the Union? Whatever is good or evil in the local institutions of Texas will remain her own whether annexed to the United States or not. None of the present States will be responsible for them any more than they are for the local institutions of each other. They have confederated together for certain specified objects. Upon the same principle that they would refuse to form a perpetual union with Texas because of her local institutions our forefathers would have been prevented from forming our present Union. Perceiving no valid objection to the measure and many reasons for its adoption vitally affecting the peace, the safety, and the prosperity of both countries, I shall on the broad principle which formed the basis and produced the adoption of our Constitution, and not in any narrow spirit of sectional policy, endeavor by all constitutional, honorable, and appropriate means to consummate the expressed will of the people and Government of the United States by the reannexation of Texas to our Union at the earliest practicable period.

Nor will it become in a less degree my duty to assert and maintain by all constitutional means the right of the United States to that portion of our territory which lies beyond the Rocky Mountains. Our title to the country of the Oregon is "clear and unquestionable," and already are our people preparing to perfect that title by occupying it with their wives and children. But eighty years ago our population was confined on the west by the ridge of the Alleghanies. Within that period—within the lifetime, I might say, of some of my hearers—our people, increasing to many millions, have filled the eastern valley of the Mississippi, adventurously ascended the Missouri to its headsprings, and are already engaged in establishing the blessings of self-government in valleys of which the rivers flow to the Pacific. The world beholds the peaceful triumphs of the industry of our emigrants. To us belongs the duty of protecting them adequately wherever they may be upon our soil. The jurisdiction of our laws and the benefits of our republican institutions should be extended over them in the distant regions which they have selected for their homes. The increasing facilities of intercourse will easily bring the States, of which the formation in that part of our territory can not be long delayed, within the sphere of our federative Union. In the meantime every obligation imposed by treaty or conventional stipulations should be sacredly respected.

D O C U M E N T 5

Polk Asks Congress to Declare War on Mexico, 1846

The strong desire to establish peace with Mexico on liberal and honorable terms, and the readiness of this Government to regulate and adjust our boundary and other causes of difference with that power on such fair and equitable principles as would lead to permanent relations of the most friendly nature, induced me in September last to seek the reopening of diplomatic relations between the two countries. . . . An envoy of the United States repaired to Mexico with full powers to adjust every existing difference. But though present on the Mexican soil by agreement between the two Governments, invested with full powers, and bearing evidence of the most friendly dispositions, his mission has been unavailing. The Mexican Government not only refused to receive him or listen to his propositions, but after a long-continued series of menaces have at last invaded our territory and shed the blood of our fellow-citizens on our own soil.

It now becomes my duty to state more in detail the origin, progress, and failure of that mission. . . . On the 10th of November, 1845, Mr. John Slidell, of Louisiana, was commissioned by me as envoy extraordinary and minister plenipotentiary of the United States to Mexico, and was intrusted with full powers to adjust both the questions of the Texas boundary and of indemnification to our citizens. . . .

Mr. Slidell arrived at Vera Cruz on the 30th of November, and was courteously received by the authorities of that city. But the Government of General [José Joaquín de] Herrera was then tottering to its fall. The revolutionary party had seized upon the Texas question to effect or hasten its overthrow. Its determination to restore friendly relations with the United States, and to receive our minister to negotiate for the settlement of this question, was violently assailed, and was made the great theme of denunciation against it. The Government of General Herrera, there is good reason to believe, was sincerely desirous to receive our minister; but it yielded to the storm raised by its enemies, and on the 21st of December refused to accredit Mr. Slidell upon the most frivolous pretexts. These are so fully and ably exposed in the note of Mr. Slidell of the 24th of December last to the Mexican minister of foreign relations, herewith transmitted, that I deem it unnecessary to enter into further detail on this portion of the subject.

Five days after the date of Mr. Slidell's note General Herrera yielded the Government to General [Mariano] Paredes without a struggle, and on the 30th of December resigned the Presidency. This revolution was accomplished solely by the army, the people having taken little part in the contest; and thus the supreme power in Mexico passed into the hands of a military leader. . . .

In my message at the commencement of the present session I informed you that upon the earnest appeal both of the Congress and convention of Texas I had ordered an efficient military force to take a position "between the Nueces [river] and the Del Norte [(the upper Rio Grande)]." This had become necessary to meet a threatened invasion of Texas by the Mexican forces, for which extensive military preparations had been made. The invasion was threatened solely because Texas had determined, in accordance with a solemn resolution of the Congress of the United States,

This document can be found in James D. Richardson, ed., *A Compilation of the Messages and Papers of the Presidents* (New York: Bureau of National Literature, 1897), VI, 2288–2292.

to annex herself to our Union, and under these circumstances it was plainly our duty to extend our protection over her citizens and soil.

This force was concentrated at Corpus Christi, and remained there until after I had received such information from Mexico as rendered it probable, if not certain, that the Mexican Government would refuse to receive our envoy.

Meantime Texas, by the final action of our Congress, had become an integral part of our Union. The Congress of Texas, by its act of December 19, 1836, had declared the Rio del Norte to be the boundary of that Republic. Its jurisdiction had been extended and exercised beyond the Nueces. The country between the river and the Del Norte had been represented in the Congress and in the convention of Texas, had thus taken part in the act of annexation itself, and is now included within one of our Congressional districts. Our own Congress had, moreover, with great unanimity, by the act approved December 31, 1845, recognized the country beyond the Nueces as a part of our territory by including it within our own revenue system, and a revenue officer to reside within that district has been appointed by and with the advice and consent of the Senate. It became, therefore, of urgent necessity to provide for the defense of that portion of our country. Accordingly, on the 13th of January last instructions were issued to the general in command of these troops to occupy the left bank of the Del Norte. This river, which is the southwestern boundary of the State of Texas, is an exposed frontier. From this quarter invasion was threatened; upon it and in its immediate vicinity, in the judgment of high military experience, are the proper stations for the protecting forces of the Government. . . .

The Army moved from Corpus Christi on the 11th of March, and on the 28th of that month arrived on the left bank of the Del Norte opposite to Matamoras, where it encamped on a commanding position, which has since been strengthened by the erection of fieldworks. A depot has also been established at Point Isabel, near the Brazos Santiago, 30 miles in the rear of the encampment. The selection of this position was necessarily confided to the judgment of the general in command.

The Mexican forces at Matamoras assumed a belligerent attitude, and on the 12th of April General Ampudia, then in command, notified General Taylor to break up his camp within twenty-four hours and to retire beyond the Nueces River, and in the event of his failure to comply with these demands announced that arms, and arms alone, must decide the question. But no open act of hostility was committed until the 24th of April. On that day General Arista, who had succeeded to the command of the Mexican forces, communicated to General Taylor that "he considered hostilities commenced and should prosecute them." A party of dragoons of 63 men and officers were on the same day dispatched from the American camp up the Rio del Norte, on its left bank, to ascertain whether the Mexican troops had crossed or were preparing to cross the river, "became engaged with a large body of these troops, and after a short affair, in which some 16 were killed and wounded, appear to have been surrounded and compelled to surrender." . . .

Upon the pretext that Texas, a nation as independent as herself, thought proper to unite its destinies with our own she has affected to believe that we have severed her rightful territory, and in official proclamations and manifestoes has repeatedly threatened to make war upon us for the purpose of reconquering Texas. In the meantime we have tried every effort at reconciliation. The cup of forbearance had been exhausted even before the recent information from the frontier of the Del Norte. But now, after reiterated menaces, Mexico has passed the boundary of the United States, has invaded our territory and shed American blood upon the American soil. She has proclaimed that hostilities have commenced, and that the two nations are now at war.

As war exists, and, notwithstanding all our efforts to avoid it, exists by the act of Mexico herself, we are called upon by every consideration of duty and patriotism to vindicate with decision the honor, the rights, and the interests of our country.

🌐 *D O C U M E N T   6*

The Wilmot Proviso Raises the Issue of Slavery in New Territories, 1846

Provided, That, as an express and fundamental condition to the acquisition of any territory from the Republic of Mexico by the United States, by virtue of any treaty which may be negotiated between them, and to the use by the Executive of the moneys herein appropriated, neither slavery nor involuntary servitude shall ever exist in any part of said territory, except for crime, whereof the party shall first be duly convicted.

🌐 *D O C U M E N T   7*

Massachusetts Senator Daniel Webster Protests the War with Mexico and the Admission of New States to the Union, 1848

The members composing the other House . . . [have] passed a resolution affirming that "the war with Mexico was begun unconstitutionally and unnecessarily by the Executive Government of the United States." I concur in that sentiment. I hold that to be the most recent, authentic expression of the will and the opinions of the people of the United States. There is another proposition, not so authentically announced hitherto, but in my judgment equally true—equally capable of demonstration—and that is, that this war was begun, has been continued, and is now prosecuted, for the great and leading purpose of the acquisition of new territory. . . . Every intelligent man knows that there is a strong desire in the heart of the Mexican citizen to retain the territories belonging to that republic. We know that the Mexican people part with their territory—if part they must—with regret, with pangs of sorrow. That we know. . . .

This war was waged for the purpose of creating new States, near the southern portion of the United States, out of Mexican territory, and with such population as might be found resident therein. I have opposed that project. I am against the creation of new States. I am against the acquisition of territory to form new States. . . .

But we think we must take territory. For the sake of peace, we must take territory! This is the will of the President! If we do not take it, we may fare worse! Mr. Polk will take no less! That is fixed upon! He is immovable! He has put down

---

Document 6 can be found in *Congressional Globe,* 29th Congress, 1st Session (August 8, 1846), 1217.

Document 7 can be found in *Congressional Globe,* 30th Congress, 1st Session (March 23, 1848), 530–535.

his foot! He had put it down, sir, on "fifty-four forty," [(America's northern-most claim along the Oregon-Canadian border)] but it didn't stay! I speak of the President of the United States as I speak of all Presidents, without disrespect; but I know no reason why his opinions, his will, his purpose declared to be fixed, should control us, any more than our purpose formed upon equally conscientious motives, and I may add, formed under as high responsibilities, should control him. . . .

I have found, sir, in the course of thirty years' experience, that whatever measure the Executive Government embraces and pushes, is quite likely to succeed. There is a giving way somewhere. If the Executive Government acts with uniformity, steadiness, entire unity of purpose, sooner or later it is quite apt enough—according to my construction of history, too apt—to effect its purpose. . . .

I never could, and I never should, bring myself to be in favor of the admission of any States into the Union as slaveholding States, and I might have added, any State at all. Now, as I have said, in all this I acted under the resolutions of the State of Massachusetts—certainly concurrent with my own judgment, so often repeated, and reaffirmed by the unanimous consent of all men of all parties; that I could not well go through the series of pointing out, not only the impolicy, but the unconstitutionality of such annexation. A case presented is this: If a State proposes to come into the Union, and to come in as a slave State; then there is an augmentation of the inequality in the representation of the people, which already exists—an inequality already existing, with which I do not quarrel, and which I never will attempt to alter, but shall preserve as long as I have a vote to give, or any voice in this Government, because it is a part of the original compact. Let it stand. But then there is another consideration of vastly more general importance even than that—more general, because it affects all the States, free and slaveholding; and it is, that if States formed out of territories thus thinly populated come into the Union, they necessarily, inevitably break up the relation existing between the two branches of the Government, and destroy its balance. They break up the intended relation between the Senate and the House of Representatives. If you bring in new States, any State that comes in must have two Senators. She may come in with fifty or sixty thousand people or more. You may have, from a particular State, more Senators than you have Representatives. Can anything occur to disfigure and derange the form of government under which we live more signally than that? . . .

Sir, we take New Mexico and California. Who is weak enough to think that there is an end? Why, do we not hear it avowed every day, that it is proper for us also to take Sonora and Tamaulipas, and other provinces or States of northern Mexico? Who thinks that the hunger for dominion will stop here of itself? Somebody has said that this acquisition is so mean, and lean, and unsatisfactory, that we shall seek no further. In my judgment, sir, you may believe that, if you can believe that a rapacious animal that has made one unproductive foray won't try for a better! . . .

I think I see a course adopted that is likely to turn the Constitution under which we live into a deformed monster—into a curse rather than a blessing—into a great frame of unequal government, not founded on popular representation, but founded in the grossest inequalities; and I think, if it go on—for there is danger that it will go on—that this government will be broken up.

Mexican Patriots Condemn U.S. Aggression, 1850

To explain then in a few words the true origin of the war, it is sufficient to say that the insatiable ambition of the United States, favored by our weakness, caused it. . . .

Texas has over the greater part of Mexico the advantage of inclosing within its borders, beautiful and navigable rivers, the only blessing wanting in almost all the other parts of our richly endowed country. Texas, by its fertility and riches, by its climate and position, possesses all the elements requisite for prosperity in agriculture, industry, commerce, and navigation.

The profit which would accrue from the possession of this land stimulated the United States to procure it at any price. . . .

A short time before the independence of Mexico, in the year 1819, the Spanish government granted to Moses Austin the requisite authority to form a colony in Texas. This concession was owing principally to the zeal that animated the King of Spain for the dissemination and protection of the Catholic religion. Moses Austin had represented his sect as disheartened and dispersed, and begged that these lands might be given to him as an asylum, where the immigrants could and would enter for the exercise of their faith.

Stephen Austin, the son and heir of Moses, continued the work commenced by his father, and made a beginning of a vast enterprise by colonizing, in 1820, between the Brasos and Colorado rivers. The emancipation of our Republic opened a wide door to immigration. They received with open arms the strangers who touched our soil. But the political inexperience of our national governors converted into a fountain of evils a benevolent and purely Christian principle. Immigration, which ought to have·equalized the laborious arms to agriculture, manufacture, and commerce, finally resulted in the separation of one of the most important states. It was this which involved us soon in actual, disastrous war. . . .

On the 12th April, 1844, the President of the United States made a treaty with Texas relative to the incorporation of that country into the Union. This treaty was not ratified by the Senate; the usurpation remained for the present suspended, which was soon, however, effected in a new way. . . .

At this time, more properly than before, it would have been exact justice to have immediately made war on a power that so rashly appropriated what by every title belonged to us. This necessity had increased to a point, that the administrations which had successively been intrusted with our affairs, upon consideration, had all agreed in the principle, that a decree of annexation should be viewed as a *casus belli*—a cause of war. . . .

At the close of the year 1844, a new revolution having overturned the government of General Santa Anna, intrusted in the interim to General [Antonio] Canaliso, elevated to power D. José Joaquin de Herrera, the President of the Council. . . .

The policy which this party [the Decembrists] pursued differed entirely from that observed by the former administrations. They acted upon the principle, in the firm belief that the Department of Texas had from the year 1830 been lost for ever; from which it was madness to suppose that our victorious eagles could be borne to

This document can be found in Ramón Alcarez et al., eds., *The Other Side: Or Notes for the History of the War Between Mexico and the United States,* trans. Albert C. Ramsey (New York: Wiley, 1850), 2, 9, 15–16, 23–24, 25, 26, 27–28, 29–30, 32.

the other side of the Sabine. They therefore decided on negotiation, and war on no account: for we were wanting in essentials the most indispensable. . . .

Notwithstanding . . . public clamor raised in opposition, [General Herrera's administration] persisted with firmness in the path proposed to be taken. To the end to open negotiations relating to this object, they formally asked and Congress passed a decree on the 17th May, 1845, conceding authority to it to hear the propositions which Texas had made, and to arrange or conclude a treaty which should be suitable and honorable to the Republic. The propositions presented were the four following: 1st. The independence of Texas was recognised. 2d. Texas agreed not to annex or subject herself to any other country. 3d. Limits and conditions were reserved for a final treaty. 4th. Texas was ready to submit the points in dispute about territories and other subjects to the decision of arbitrators. . . .

These preliminaries caused the belief that it would not be difficult to obtain a satisfactory arrangement. But the subsequent conduct of Texas finally resolved itself into annexation with the American Union. Whether it was owing to a breaking with this nation or because an arrangement was incompatible with the motions and revolutions it had against the government of the Decembristas, the negotiations were suspended, and soon this interesting question was left to the fate of arms. . . .

The year 1846 witnessed at its commencement new rules figuring in the political drama, having been elevated to power by another revolution. General [Mariano] Paredes pronounced in San Luis against Herrera. A few days were sufficient for this shameful revolution to become a triumph the most complete. Then Mr. Slidell renewed his suit, in considering that, although the old had been terminated by a refusal, still, as the business now went into new hands to be transacted, it was a favorable opportunity to see if he should meet in them a better disposition. The matter again underwent a revision in the council of the government, which repeated the reasons on which the former had been based, concluding with a renewal of the declaration that it could not admit Mr. Slidell further than Plenipotentiary *ad hoc* for the question of Texas. The government made this known to the Envoy, who now could do no more than ask for his passports, and withdraw from the Republic.

General Paredes, on the 21st of March of the same year, declared that peace not being compatible with the maintenance of the rights and independence of the nation, he should defend its territory. . . .

While the United States seemed to be animated by a sincere desire not to break the peace, their acts of hostility manifested very evidently what were their true intentions. Their ships infested our coasts; their troops continued advancing upon our territory, situated at places which under no aspect could be disputed. Thus violence and insult were united: thus at the very time they usurped part of our territory, they offered to us the hand of treachery, to have soon the audacity to say that our obstinacy and arrogance were the real causes of the war.

To explain the occupation of the Mexican territory by the troops of General [Zachary] Taylor, the strange idea occurred to the United States that the limits of Texas extended to the Rio Bravo del Norte. . . .

From the acts referred to, it has been demonstrated to the very senses, that the real and effective cause of this war that afflicted us was the spirit of aggrandizement of the United States of the North, availing itself of its power to conquer us. Impartial history will some day illustrate for ever the conduct observed by this Republic against all laws, divine and human, in an age that is called one of light, and which is, notwithstanding, the same as the former—one of *force and violence.*

E S S A Y S

Historians have extensively probed the roots of expansionism in the 1840s. In the first essay, Anders Stephanson of Columbia University examines the ideology of Manifest Destiny that guided American expansionism. Studying the writings of the Jacksonian newspaper editor John O'Sullivan, Stephanson concludes that a misguided and ethnocentric idealism, undergirded by a belief in American exceptionalism and Anglo-Saxon racism, contributed significantly to the quest for territory.

In the second essay, Thomas R. Hietala of Grinnell College in Iowa questions the role of ideology in American expansionism. Although Hietala acknowledges that the idea of Manifest Destiny served as a legitimizing myth, he concludes that hard-headed interests—especially a desire for western land, Pacific ports, and markets—motivated the Polk administration to use force to acquire territory and empire.

The Ideology and Spirit of Manifest Destiny

ANDERS STEPHANSON

"In *America,*" a foreign observer wrote from afar in 1848, "we have witnessed the conquest of Mexico and have rejoiced at it." The defeated nation hitherto had been "exclusively wrapped up in its own affairs, perpetually rent with civil wars, and completely hindered in its development." The best it could have hoped for in those circumstances was economic subjection to Britain. From a Mexican viewpoint, therefore, it was "an advance" now to be "forcibly drawn into the historical process" and "placed under the tutelage of the United States." Thus the opinion of Friedrich Engels.

Later in life, Engels would become more critical of such historical "advances." In this he was at one with his American contemporary Walt Whitman. The great poet, editor of the Democratic *Brooklyn Eagle* during the war, had found "miserable, inefficient Mexico" totally incompatible "with the great mission of peopling the New World with a noble race." I cite these two figures at the outset to indicate the political span of typical mid-nineteenth-century Western notions of progress. It is good to bear that range in mind when we now [turn] to John O'Sullivan and the ideology of Jacksonian expansionism, which he expressed better than anyone else. Not only did O'Sullivan coin the phrase "manifest destiny," but his political sallies formed a veritable summa of the arguments of this type. His journal, the *Democratic Review,* is in fact more interesting as a source here than the widely disseminated "penny press," which echoed the same sentiment but evinced less of the revealing ambivalence and ambiguity.

O'Sullivan, after consulting [Andrew] Jackson and [Martin] Van Buren, founded the *Review* in 1837 in order to give the Jacksonian movement intellectual and political presence in the domain of highbrow culture, which was then dominated by staid and conservative forces. Under his editorial guidance, the *Review* became the liveliest and most interesting journal of its kind. A whole constellation of future literary "greats" appeared in it. [Nathaniel] Hawthorne, a strong Democratic supporter, contributed from the start, but the new publication also opened its pages to Henry David Thoreau and Edgar Allan Poe, neither of whom was a Jacksonian. O'Sullivan mixed liberality of literary taste with a strongly polemical line, set by himself, in political affairs. It was the peculiar mixture of partisan politics and cultural openness that gave the journal its character. Though it never achieved great circulation, it was read by important people and became such a thorn in the side of conservatives that the *American Whig Review* was revamped in 1845 into a political counterpart.

Reduced to simple propositions, the views of O'Sullivan and his contemporaries now seem overblown and jejune. To maintain a sense for the rhetorical flavor (and of our historical distance from it), therefore, I shall make use of some extensive quotation.

O'Sullivan, as a good Jacksonian, spent the first years attacking the combined evils of consolidated government and banking aristocracy. Following Van Buren, he was also fully aware that he had "to stand aloof from the delicate and dangerous topic of Slavery and Abolition." In these early campaigns against what he typically called "delusive theories and fatal heresies," there was already a strongly destinarian conception of the United States:

> The last order of civilization, which is the democratic, received its first permanent existence in this country. . . . A land separated from the influences of ancient arrangement, peculiar in its position, productions, and extent, wide enough to hold a numerous people, admitting, with facility, intercommunication and trade, vigorous and fresh from the hand of God, was requisite for the full and broad manifestation of the free spirit of the new-born democracy. Such a land was prepared in the solitudes of the Western hemisphere.

As "the nation of human progress," with Providence in support and "a clear conscience unsullied by the past," the United States was obviously unstoppable in its "onward march." Others had better take heed:

> The far-reaching, the boundless future will be the era of American greatness. In its magnificent domain of space and time, the nation of many nations is destined to manifest to mankind the excellence of divine principles; to establish on earth the noblest temple ever dedicated to the worship of the Most High—the Sacred and the True.
>
> For this blessed mission to the nations of the world, which are shut out from the life-giving light of truth, has America been chosen; and her high example shall smite unto death the tyranny of kings, hierarchs, and oligarchs, and carry the glad tidings of peace and good will where myriads now endure an existence scarcely more enviable than that of beasts of the field.

Democracy was in fact nothing "but Christianity in its earthly aspect—Christianity made effective among the political relations of men" by elimination of "the obstacles reared by artificial life." History was a providential plan whose end was to be played out in the specially designed space of America, where Jacksonianism had made manifest and transparent the universal truth of democracy. The cause of humanity was identical with that of the United States; and that cause was "destined to cease only when every man in the world should be finally and triumphantly redeemed." In short, Christianity, democracy, and Jacksonian America were essentially one and the same thing, the highest stage of history, God's plan incarnate.

This would seem to leave the Democrats with nothing much to do except the administration of things and vigilant preservation of the sacred Origin. Yet O'Sullivan still saw need for battle against residual forces of corruption and enemies of truth. Culturally, there was also a tendency to ape European models, "bending the new to foreign idolatry, false tastes, false doctrines, false principles." However, as the very embodiment of historical truth, the people would see to the problem of false idols as well. His conclusion was indeed that the United States would not be led astray because it represented such a sharp break with the past. The "last order" in history was a completely new and completely *clean* civilization, free "from ancient arrangement" and so also free to choose destiny. "The scenes of antiquity" were of interest only as "lessons of avoidance." The future, and the future alone, was what mattered. (Herman Melville, after the Mexican War, put it more poetically: "The Past is a text-book of tyrants; the Future is the Bible of the Free.") The nation, then, was bound by nothing except its founding principles, the eternal and universal principles. It existed, as the "great nation of futurity," only in a perpetual present centered on projects and expectations.

Not much, however, was said about this "futurity," or about what the United States might actually do, other than being marvelous, to smite the tyrants of the world unto death. But gradually after [James K.] Polk's ascendency over Van Buren in 1844, the idea of acquiring boundless expanses of land became prominent. For this land would preserve in neo-Jeffersonian fashion the original moment of freedom as perpetual genesis, struggle, and appropriation. Expansion would afford the swelling masses of the future, the "men of simple habits and strong hands," the opportunity of carving out a properly independent American existence, away from the claws of "the great monopoly paper-coining machine." This utopian impulse was unthinkingly coupled in O'Sullivan, as in so many other Jacksonians, with one speculative scheme after another, in his case wholly without success.

Jacksonian virtue, he firmly believed, translated into a pacific posture vis-à-vis foreign powers. Since people and government were constitutionally identical and the people only wanted "freedom to trade," American foreign policy would always be marked by *"peace* and *good-faith."* In keeping with this concept, the *Review* followed an expansionist but pacific line, differing markedly from the many jingoistic elements within the party. War and blustering talk of national honor were inherently bad, peace and negotiation inherently good. The British, meanwhile, were singled out as particularly nasty exponents of the old anti-ethic of slaughter and conquest. In India and Afghanistan, they had engaged in "constant aggression, without any shadow of excuse or apology." Good thing, then, that the American system did not offer any "pretext of excuse for such wholesale oppression, robbery, and murder."

It is interesting to see this attitude come under pressure during the exciting but stressful sequence of Texas-Oregon-Mexico, which offered some evidence of both "pretexts" and "robbery," engineered by none other than a Jacksonian president. The least difficult question to face here was Oregon. As early as 1843 the *Review* took a maximalist stance, based on a critique of the "monopolistic" Hudson Bay Company. But when the issue heated up, the journal became a voice of moderation on the Democratic side, quietly suggesting extension along the forty-ninth parallel and carefully avoiding bellicose rhetoric. When one author indicated that war, while generally a bad thing, would finally liberate Americans from their cultural "thraldom" to Britain and cleanse "the political atmosphere," he was rebuked in an editorial note that declared war "an unmixed evil in its moral influences" that could never have any "benefits on the national spirit and character." War with the British, cads though they were, would ultimately be a great calamity.

In his short-lived popular paper the *Morning Star,* however, O'Sullivan maintained the original maximalism, while not calling for war. It was in this context that, on December 27, 1845, he proclaimed

> The right of *our manifest destiny* to overspread and to possess the whole continent which providence has given us for the development of the great experiment of liberty and federated self government. [Italics added]

Congress, at the time, was debating Oregon, and a member of the Whig opposition, in the course of denouncing the idea of "a universal Yankee nation," picked up the expression for ridicule, thus inadvertently helping to make it a staple of the political language of American history. But O'Sullivan and others had deployed the two words constantly. He had in fact used the expression six months earlier with regard to Texas annexation without any special notice.

The Oregon issue had barely been settled before the *Review,* in a sudden change of tone, published a lyrical ode to the coming fusion of England's manufacturing and American agriculture through the mechanism of free trade. The occasion was the repeal of the restrictive British corn laws and the commercial visions of American exports that this induced: "the Anglo-Saxon race" would be reunited (under American dominance) and prosperity ensue for all. The new economic theme articulated an underlying fact: powerful Britain, land of the Anglo-Saxons, was not Mexico. The two could not be conceived in the same frame.

A kind of geographical determinism originally governed O'Sullivan's views on Texas. Anyone, he said in April 1844, who "cast a glance over the map of North America" would see that Texas was "a huge fragment, artificially broken off" from its proper continental setting, a setting "symmetrically planned and adapted in its grand destiny" and duly "in the possession of the race sent there for the providential purpose." An impartial observer, therefore, would have to conclude that Texas "*must,* sooner or later, come together into one homogeneous unity" with the rest. Reading maps and spatial configurations in such a manner was common in the educated Western world of the nineteenth century. From a religious viewpoint, it was obvious that God had laid out the landscape with some intention in mind. From a rationalist perspective it was obvious that nature was not an accidental heap of materials but a system whose inner logic could be uncovered by scientific analysis. The two perspectives generally could indeed be reconciled in "natural theology": the real was rational and thus subject to inherent, natural laws, which in turn had been divinely engineered. In the United States, geographical rationalism had a most reputable pedigree. Jefferson had considered New Orleans a "natural" (hence rightful) possession of the United States, and his comprehension of the Floridas followed the same pattern. Henceforth, cartographically minded politicians would find various "natural borders" to invoke, depending on the historical moment: The St. Lawrence River, the Mississippi, the Rocky Mountains, Hudson Bay, the Gulf of Mexico, the Pacific, the North American continent, even the Sandwich Islands (Hawaii). By the 1850s, it was in fact possible to think of the Caribbean islands as "naturally" American on account of their being the natural, effluvial result of the Mississippi.

Having read his map, O'Sullivan was less sure how to make the natural occur in real life. He was still wedded to the principle of morally impeccable expansion and insisted, therefore, that Mexico must agree before Texas annexation could take place. Such a "poor neighbour" ought not to be bullied. But by early 1845, after his political switch to Polk, he was favoring immediate annexation, now finding the neighborly complaints "the most insolent farce ever attempted even by the bombastic absurdity of Mexican conceit and imbecility." Worse still was the "traitorous Anti-Americanism" at home that was attempting to depict annexation by "misrepresentation and sophism" as "an act of national rapacity, spoliation, and bad faith," whereas in fact the behavior of "our great, pacific and friendly Union" had been extraordinarily restrained. It was with great satisfaction, therefore, that he took note in mid-1845 of the congressional assent to annexation:

> Texas has been absorbed into the Union in the inevitable fulfillment of the general law which is rolling our population westward. . . . It was disintegrated from Mexico in the natural course of events, by a process perfectly legitimate on its own part, blameless on ours; and in which all the censures due to wrong, perfidy and folly, rest on Mexico alone.

He went on to predict that California would be the next candidate for annexation: "Already the advance guard of the irresistible army of Anglo-Saxon emigration has begun to pour down upon it, armed with the plough and the rifle, and marking its trail with schools and colleges, courts and representative halls, mills and meeting-houses." The reality was less idyllic. In 1848, when California did become American territory, the condition of its Hispanic population deteriorated markedly; and when "the irresistible army of Anglo-Saxon emigration" came marching in to pursue land, gold, and profits, it was as usual a genocidal catastrophe for the Indian population.

Once Texas had been secured, O'Sullivan was remarkably quick in speculating on the virtues of gobbling up all of Mexico, laying out before the war the parameters of what would turn into a heated debate only in late 1847. He assumed that the southern neighbor would "become an integral portion of these United States at some future period" but thought it not a good idea for the moment because "the entire Mexican vote would be substantially below our national average both in purity and intelligence." Inclusion might also give rise to consolidated rule from the federal center, always something to be dreaded. Still, the march was on and so an obvious dilemma had arisen: "Democracies must make their conquests by moral agencies. If these are not sufficient, the conquest is robbery." His solution was pacific penetration by *commercial means,* which would "beget a community of interest between us" while suitably instilling in the Mexicans "confidence and respect for our institutions." Americans would gain an outlet for their right to pursue their interest and Mexicans would learn the ways of the future in good time. Through the "moral" education emanating from commerce, then, "the whole of this vast continent is destined one day to subscribe to the Constitution of the United States," whereas "a sword drawn to hasten the event" would detract from its value.

He wrote this to stem a flood of enthusiastic annexationism within his own party in the wake of the Texas victory. There was already a danger, as he saw it, that the United States would "be obliged, in self-defense, to assume an aggressive attitude towards Mexico," in which case it would be exceedingly difficult to avoid "an end short of absolute subjugation." And on that note the matter rested. The *Review* remained conspicuously low-key when war actually did break out. Nothing substantial was in fact said on the subject of Mexico between October 1845 and February 1847. A certain unease about Polk's war was probably one reason; another, more prosaic, was that O'Sullivan sold the journal in 1846, and though he continued to write editorials now and then, the polemics about foreign affairs declined in frequency. He himself commenced a private campaign to persuade the administration to buy Cuba. Polk was won over to the idea, but the ensuing proposal to the Spanish government was rebuffed in no uncertain terms. O'Sullivan then shifted his focus to conquering the islands by conspiring with Cuban interests in the United States, but the ensuing expeditions failed and almost got him convicted of breaking American neutrality laws.

Apprehensions about the legitimacy of the war against Mexico were gone, in any event, when the *Review* resumed serious coverage in 1847. Racial inflections now marked the tone, and the narrative was framed around how constant had been the historical advance of the American "race of hardy pioneers." Thus "barbarism" and "the savages" were said to have given way naturally to "the intelligent and peaceful settler," a process that differed fundamentally and favorably from European models of military invasion. While Americans had shown "democratic energy and enterprise" in "driving back the Indians, or annihilating them as a race," the Spanish conquerors of Mexico had showed no such spirit of mission. But if Christianization, civilization, and cultivation of the land had been sadly lagging, change was now in the works because of "the descent of the northern race." Yet because "the degraded Mexican-Spanish" were in no state to receive the "virtues of the Anglo-Saxon race," there could be no talk of any "political union." That same degradation, however, also made peaceful "accommodation" impossible: the opponent was simply incapable of acting reasonably. The only feasible result of the war, therefore, was "the annihilation" of Mexico "as a nation." Americans were obliged to seize control of the country and "settle its affairs." What O'Sullivan had feared in 1845 had seemingly come to pass.

Yet the Mexican vanishing act, however the *Review* imagined it, could not occur in the near future for there were millions of them; and while one might envisage a time when "every acre of the North American continent" would be peopled "by citizens of the United States," the task of settling the affairs of Mexico was, on balance, fraught with danger to the true spirit of America. A drawn-out effort would stimulate domestic militarism and so create vested interests dominated by the Whigs. Better, then, to take California and New Mexico against proper payment and let time take care of the rest. Nothing, at any rate, was more important than keeping the millions of "proverbially indolent" out of the American "political family."

Thus the prospect of dilution of American purity caused the *Review* to shrink before the actual task of extensive rearrangement of Mexico's affairs. Earlier, O'Sullivan had in fact singled out "homogeneity" as *the* factor that would make the American empire a lasting one. Its territory would be enormous, but similarity of "laws and institutions" would nevertheless make it "compact"; and the people themselves would also "be homogeneous." Other empires, past and present, had fallen precisely because of their "dissimilar and hostile materials." Hence, while "England must fade" and "the colossus of Russia must crumble," the empire of freedom would remain.

And so, one is bound to say, it has happened. The United States would have to go through a wrenching civil war to achieve unity, and the ensuing American empire would eventually be anything but homogeneous in population. But it has lasted in no small measure because of its insistence on constitutional homogeneity, its refusal of any room for territorialized differences of any significance within its continental compass. The precondition of that success, on the other hand, lay in the contradictory process, expressed with unconscious irony above, of peaceable settlers engaged in lofty acts of annihilation. Peace and annihilation were seemingly two sides of the same coin. Meanwhile, the other two empires are now in fact gone, a century or so later than O'Sullivan probably expected but partly for the very reasons he indicated: heterogeneity and "hostile materials." His early notion, it should be added, of elevating Mexico to American standards through the blessings of free trade, achieving the manifest destiny through economic flows, has a certain late-twentieth-century ring to it.

It may be suitable, in view of the general content of the *Review*, to end this exposition in a literary vein with a sonnet by William Gilmore Simms, a leading southern intellectual. His poem appeared in early 1846 under the title "Progress in America":

> The adventurous Spaniard crack'd th' Atlantic's shell—
>   Though not for him to penetrate the core.
> The good old Norman stock will do as well,
>   Nay, better; a selected stock of old
>   With blood well-temper'd, resolute and bold;
> Set for a mighty work, the way to pave
>   For the wrong'd nations, and, in one great fold,
> Unite them, from old tyrannies to save!
> We do but follow out our destiny,
>   As did the ancient Israelite—and strive,
> Unconscious that we work at His decree,
>   By Whom alone we triumph as we live!

These heroic commonplaces of American chosenness expressed a spirit that was least of all "unconscious," as the poet paradoxically argued. Seldom has there been a more articulated, explicit awareness of working His decrees in every way.

Empire by Design, Not Destiny

THOMAS R. HIETALA

The recurring emphasis on material factors in the Democrats' speculations about the need for expansion raises some important questions about the purported idealism of both "Jacksonian Democracy" and manifest destiny. To O'Sullivan and other Democrats, previous territorial acquisitions had been indispensable to the success of the American political and economic system. And though the Jacksonians were convinced of the superiority of popular government, they were much less certain about its viability. Their ambitions for a continental empire represented much more than simple romantic nationalism: they demanded land because they regarded it as the primary prerequisite for republican government and for an economy and society based upon individual acquisitiveness, geographical and social mobility, and a fluid class structure. These beliefs—best expressed by O'Sullivan but articulated by other Democrats as well—were crucial to most Jacksonian policies, especially those promoting territorial and commercial expansion. To consider manifest destiny in the context of such principles of political economy is a way of making more comprehensible the sustained drive for empire in the 1840s.

Misconceptions about manifest destiny still influence Americans' impressions about their nation's history. Although the civil rights struggle and the Vietnam War have led many Americans to question several of the prevailing orthodoxies of United States history, popular attitudes about the country's past—the self-concept of Americans and their definition of their nation's role in world affairs—have shown a remarkable resiliency, despite the challenges of revisionist scholars. Prevailing ideas about westward expansion are inextricably linked to the values associated with American exceptionalism and mission, fundamental components of the Jacksonian creed. The persistence of manifest destiny ideology under radically different political, economic, and military realities since the 1840s attests to the significant impact these legitimizing myths of empire have had on popular beliefs about United States history. Since continental expansion gave birth to and nurtured so many nationalistic myths, a reevaluation of the historical circumstances that spawned them is an essential exercise in the reassessment of the American past. . . .

Jacksonians exalted the pioneer as the epitome of the common man, and they celebrated American expansion as an integral part of their mission to obtain a better nation and a better world based on individual freedom, liberalized international trade, and peaceful coexistence. The Democrats equated American progress with global progress and repeatedly argued that European oligarchs were actually opposing the interests of their own people by trying to discourage the expansion of the United States. Geographically and ideologically separated from Europe, the United States, under Jacksonian direction, tried to improve its democratic institutions, utilize the land's rich resources, and demonstrate to the world the superiority of a system allowing free men to compete in a dynamic society. Consequently, the impact of the pioneering process transcended the concerns of the frontiersmen. In forming "a more perfect union" on a continually expanding frontier, Americans thought that they were actually serving the cause of all mankind.

Such a melding of exceptionalism and empire permitted the Jacksonians the luxury of righteous denunciation of their critics at home and abroad. Their domestic foes could be paired with European monarchs as spokesmen for an old order of aristocracy, privilege, and proscription; American expansionism and the Jacksonian domestic program, on the other hand, represented the antithesis of traditional systems. Since territorial acquisitions and Democratic policies fostered opportunity and democracy, they liberated men from oppressive social and economic relationships. The Jacksonians' program promised so much for so little; no wonder messianic imagery appeared so frequently in their rhetoric.

Skeptical Whigs often challenged the Democrats' sincerity, however, sensing that the Jacksonians' motives for aggrandizement were more selfish than they usually admitted. The Democrats' rhetoric proved more resilient than the Whigs' trenchant criticisms of "manifest destiny," however, and so subsequent generations of Americans have underestimated the extent and the intensity of opposition to the policies behind expansionism in the 1840s, especially the Mexican War. . . .

The expansionism of the 1840s acquires a new significance, however, when it is considered within the context of the cultural, social, and political factors that motivated the Jacksonians to pursue a continental empire. In promoting the acquisition of new lands and new markets, the Democrats greatly exaggerated the extent of European hostility to the United States and refused to admit the duplicity and brutality behind their own efforts to expand their nation's territory and trade. By joining their concepts of exceptionalism and empire, the expansionists found a rationale for denying to all other nations and peoples, whether strong or weak, any right to any portion of the entire North American continent. If a rival was strong, it posed a threat to American security and had to be removed; if a rival was weak, it proved its inferiority and lent sanction to whatever actions were taken by pioneers or policy makers to make the territory a part of the United States.

The confusion surrounding expansion results in part from the ambivalence of the Jacksonians themselves, who demonstrated both compassion and contempt in their policies, depending on the racial and ethnic identities of the peoples to be affected by Democratic measures. Generous and humane toward impoverished Americans and poor immigrants from Europe, the Democrats showed far less concern for nonwhites whom they dispossessed or exploited in the process of westward expansion and national development. Removal, eclipse, or extermination—not acculturation and assimilation—awaited the Indians, blacks, and mixed-blood Mexicans on the continent. Despite occasional statements to the contrary, the expansionists regarded the incorporation of nonwhite peoples into the country as both unlikely and undesirable. Without hint of hypocrisy the Jacksonians sought lenient naturalization laws and opportunities for newcomers while strenuously defending policies to separate Indians and Mexicans from their lands and programs to relocate blacks to Africa and Central America. . . .

Jeffersonian ideology, especially its romantic agrarianism, its fear of industrialization, and its conviction that the United States had a natural right to free trade, contributed significantly to the ideology of manifest destiny. To the Jeffersonians and Jacksonians, American farms raised good republican citizens as well as corn, cotton, and wheat: cultivated fields produced virtuous, cultivated people. Whatever the realities of the late Jacksonian period, the expansionists insisted that agricultural societies fostered opportunity and political equality, the essential features of American uniqueness. Moreover, the neo-Jeffersonians contended that only industrial nations became international predators; agricultural countries were self-contained and did not need colonies or privileged markets. These misconceptions cloak some of the more unflattering aspects of antebellum economy and society: slavemasters, not sturdy yeomen, dominated the social and political life of the South; the country's most important export crops, cotton and tobacco, were produced by forced labor; Indians were cruelly dispossessed of their lands and often their culture to make room for American producers; "go-ahead" Americans frequently seemed more interested in land speculation schemes than in patient tilling of the soil; and the United States, like other empires, did prey upon other peoples and nations to augment its wealth, power, and security.

The fact that the United States acquired contiguous rather than noncontiguous territory makes American aggrandizement no less imperial than that of other empires of the mid-nineteenth century. The United States enjoyed several advantages that facilitated its enlargement and made it more antiseptic. Mexico's weakness, the inability of Indian tribes to unite and resist dispossession, the decline of France and Spain as colonizing powers in the New World, and geographical isolation from Europe all served the interests of the United States as it spread across the continent. In addition, the preference for an anticolonial empire embodied in the concept of a confederated Union also contributed to American success. But many Democrats wanted to venture beyond the continent, and had the party not become so divided during and after the Mexican War, the Polk administration probably would have taken steps to add Yucatán and Cuba to the United States, thereby extending the empire into the Caribbean.

The urge to expand beyond the continent was diminished by the fact that the continent itself was incredibly rich in resources. Those abundant resources provided the basis for unparalleled economic growth at home and power in relations with countries abroad. The expansionists regarded the nation's productivity as an irresistible weapon that could counterbalance the military strength of Europe. Here, again, an old Jeffersonian perception dating back to the 1790s came into play: the world desperately needed American commerce and would sacrifice a great deal to obtain it. Although the expansionists never had cause to drive the masses of Europe to starvation and revolution through an embargo on grain and cotton, their speculations on the subject showed them to be far more imperial than philanthropic in their attitudes toward their nation's wealth.

Distressed by many trends in American life, the Democrats formulated their domestic and foreign policies to safeguard themselves and their progeny for a potentially dismal future. They hoped to prevent domestic disturbances by acquiring additional territory and markets. Other measures were also devised to protect the country from various perils: the Democrats discouraged the growth of manufacturing and monopolistic banking, attempted to minimize the conflict over slavery, encouraged the sale and settlement of the national domain, and tried to discredit the efforts of dissidents to form third parties that might jeopardize the two-party system. . . .

Another myth of manifest destiny concerns the role of military power in American expansion. On May 11, 1846, President Polk informed Congress that "after reiterated menaces, Mexico has passed the boundary of the United States, has invaded our territory and shed American blood upon the American soil." War had begun, Polk observed, in spite of "all our efforts to avoid it." Much evidence, however, raises doubts about just how hard Polk tried to prevent war. Six weeks before Polk's war message, for example, Captain William S. Henry, a subordinate commander in [General Zachary] Taylor's army en route to the city of Matamoras, noted in his journal, "Our situation is truly extraordinary: right in the enemy's country (to all appearance), actually occupying their corn and cotton fields, the people of the soil leaving their homes, and we, with a small handful of men, marching with colors flying and drums beating, right under the very guns of one of their principal cities, displaying the star-spangled banner, as if in defiance, under their very nose." This army's purpose was not limited to the defense of Texas. It is true that the United States claimed the Rio Grande as the border; it is also true that the United States, in the person of James K. Polk, claimed that the nation had a "clear and unquestionable" title to Oregon up to 54° 40'. But the issue for the Polk administration was not the validity of various boundary claims, but rather the issue of whether military pressure could force Mexico to relinquish the disputed territory between the Nueces and Rio Grande, and the undisputed territories of New Mexico and California besides. The Democrats chose war to defend an unclear and questionable title in the Southwest but retreated from a supposedly clear and unquestionable title in the Northwest. The hypocrisy did not escape the Whigs. . . .

Polk . . . acted as imperially as any of his twentieth-century successors. Democratic process and an aggressive foreign policy were as incompatible in the mid-nineteenth century as in the twentieth, as congressional critics frequently noted. In late 1846, for example, Whig Garrett Davis pointed out that the founding fathers had "entrusted to the president the national shield," but they had intentionally given the national sword and "the entire war power" to Congress. "To make war is the most fearful power exerted by human government," Davis warned, a power too momentous to be placed in any one man's hands. That admonition was out of fashion for two decades after World War II, but Vietnam gave it new meaning. In the 1840s and in the 1960s, Congress was remiss in its responsibility to scrutinize how American military power was used, for what purposes, and under what pretenses. In both cases a scheming president misled Congress into sanctioning a wider war than anticipated. . . .

Orthodox historical "truths" possess considerable resiliency. By extolling the virtues and achievements of a self-conscious people, they appeal to nationalistic feeling, and through constant repetition they acquire an aura of unquestioned certainty over time. The idealism of westward expansion embodied in the concept of manifest destiny persists because it helps to reconcile American imperialism with an extremely favorable national image. The assumed benevolence and the supposedly accidental nature of American expansion are convenient evasions of the complexities of the past. In accepting the rhetoric of American mission and destiny, apologists for the expansionists of the 1840s have had to minimize or ignore much historical evidence. Perhaps more to the point, defenders of American exceptionalism and innocence have actually had to slight other crucial motives for expansion that the Democrats themselves often candidly admitted.

Though the phrase *manifest destiny* appears repeatedly in the literature of American foreign relations, it does not accurately describe the expansionism of the 1840s. It is one of many euphemisms that have allowed several generations of Americans to maintain an unwarranted complacency in regard to their nation's past, a complacency that has contributed in a fundamental way to the persistent quandary the United States has faced in trying to define a realistic role for itself in a world that seldom acts according to American precepts. Geographical isolation and a powerful exceptionalist ideology have insulated the United States from the complexities of culture and historical experience affecting other peoples, leaving Americans susceptible to myths and misconceptions at home and abroad. Often unaware of their own history, Americans frequently misunderstand foreign cultures and experiences as well. Myths and misconceptions often fill the void created by ignorance of history.

The expansionists of the 1840s should not be permitted to expropriate many of the best American ideals for their own purposes. . . . [They exploited] American exceptionalist ideology to ennoble their ambitions for riches and dominion. But rhetoric could not hide the chauvinism, aggressiveness, and design that were essential components of continental expansion. The United States used many tactics to expand its domain, and like other empires it created legitimizing myths to sanction that expansion. Some Americans, however, challenged the validity of those myths and condemned the conduct they excused. But critics of national policy seldom reach generations other than their own, for history—especially American history—often records only the dominant voices of the past. That the United States has changed dramatically since attaining its continental empire is obvious. That the American people have reassessed their basic assumptions about themselves, their national experience, and their approach to other nations is not so obvious.

🌎 *F U R T H E R   R E A D I N G*

Jeremy Adelman and Stephen Aaron, "From Borderlands to Borders: Empires, Nation-States, and the People in Between in North American History," *American Historical Review* 104 (June 1999): 814–841

Maurice G. Baxter, *One and Inseparable: Daniel Webster and the Union* (1984)

Paul H. Bergeron, *The Presidency of James K. Polk* (1987)

Albert Boime, *The Magisterial Gaze: Manifest Destiny in American Landscape Painting* (1991)

Walter R. Borneman, *Polk* (2008)

H. W. Brands, *Lonestar Nation* (2005)

Kinley Brauer, "The Great American Desert Revisited: Recent Literature and Prospects for the Study of American Foreign Relations, 1815–1861." *Diplomatic History* 3 (1989): 395–417

Charles H. Brown, *Agents of Manifest Destiny* (1980)

Richard Griswold del Castillo, *The Treaty of Guadalupe-Hidalgo* (1990)

Nathan J. Citino, "The Global Frontier: Comparative History and the Frontier-Borderlands Approach in American Foreign Relations" in *Explaining the History of American Foreign Relations*, ed. Michael J. Hogan and Thomas G. Paterson (2004), 194–211

Brian DeLay, "Independent Indians and the U.S.-Mexican War," *American Historical Review* (February 2007): 35–68

William Dusinberre, *Slavemaster President* (2007) (on Polk)

John Eisenhower, *So Far from God: The U.S. War with Mexico* (1989)

Will Fowler, *Santa Anna of Mexico* (2007)

William H. Goetzmann, *New Lands, New Men* (1987)

Laura E. Gómez, *Manifest Destinies* (2007)

Norman A. Graebner, *Manifest Destiny* (1968)

Amy Greenberg, *Manifest Manhood* (2005)

Neal Harlow, *California Conquered* (1982)

Sam W. Haynes, *James K. Polk and the Expansionist Impulse* (2002)

Timothy J. Henderson, *A Glorious Defeat* (2007)

Reginald Horsman, *Race and Manifest Destiny* (1981)

Albert L. Hurtado, *Intimate Frontiers* (1999) (on gender and culture)

Robert W. Johannsen. *To the Halls of Montezuma* (1985)

Howard Jones and Donald A. Rakestraw, *Prologue to Manifest Destiny* (1995)

Gary Clayton Anderson, *The Conquest of Mexico* (2005)

Amy Kaplan, *The Anarchy of Empire in the Making of U.S. Culture* (2002)

Ernest M. Lander Jr., *Reluctant Imperialists: Calhoun, the South Carolinians, and the Mexican War* (1980)

Thomas M. Leonard, *James K. Polk* (2000)

Robert E. May, *Manifest Destiny's Underworld* (2002) (on filibusters)

Aims McGuiness, *Path of Empire* (2007) (on Panama and U.S. gold rush)

Christopher Morris and Sam W. Haynes, eds., *Manifest Destiny and Empire* (1998)

Anna K. Nelson, *Secret Agents: President Polk and the Search for Peace with Mexico* (1988)

Gregory H. Nobles, *American Frontiers* (1997)

W. Dirk Raat, *Mexico and the United States* (1993)

Leonard L. Richards, *The Life and Times of Congressman John Quincy Adams* (1986)

Gregory Rodriguez, *Mongrels, Bastards, Orphans, and Vagabonds* (2007) (on Mexican immigration)

Jaime E. Rodriguez, *Down from Colonialism: Mexico's Nineteenth Century Crisis* (1983)

——— and Kathryn Vincent, *Myths, Misdeeds, and Misunderstandings* (1997) (on Mexican-U.S. relations)

Ramón Eduardo Ruíz, *Triumphs and Tragedies* (1992)

John Seigenthaler, *James K. Polk* (2001)

Robert L. Scheina, *Santa Anna* (2002)

Joel H. Silbey, *Storm Over Texas* (2006)

Paul A. Varg, *United States Foreign Relations, 1820–1860* (1979)

Josefina Vázquez and Lorenzo Meyer, *The United States and Mexico* (1985)

David J. Weber, *The Mexican Frontier, 1821–1846* (1982)

———, *"From Hell Itself": The Americanization of Mexico's Northern Frontier, 1821–1846* (1983)

Joseph Wheelan, *Invading Mexico* (2007)

Richard Bruce Winders, *Crisis in the Southwest* (2002) (on Texas)

CHAPTER 9

Expansion to the Pacific and Asia

Americans only began to learn about Asia firsthand (see map on p. 235) when the Empress of China *sailed from New York to China in 1784 to initiate a lucrative trade with the land of Confucianism. In the 1830s, merchants and sailors were joined by American Protestant missionaries intent on converting the Chinese to Christianity. Like their fellow Westerners from Europe, Americans who ventured to China in this era judged its civilization to be stagnant and immoral, yet also reformable. For their part, Chinese officials extolled China as the center of the universe and judged all foreigners as barbarians—confining visitors to one port: Canton. A clash of cultures ensued.*

When Chinese authorities cracked down on shippers who illicitly imported opium into their land, Britain sent its warships to keep the opium door open and to humble the Chinese. After suffering defeat in the Opium War of 1839–1842, the Chinese had to make concessions in a series of international agreements, including the Treaty of Wanghia (Wangxia) in 1844—the first treaty between China and the United States. This accord contained a most-favored-nation clause and opened five more "treaty ports" to American ships; the treaty also provided for extraterritoriality, meaning that Americans accused of crimes in China would be subject to American, not Chinese, law.

With the U.S. acquisition of the Pacific coast territories of Oregon and California in the 1840s, American interest in China intensified. Sino-American trade grew as grand clipper ships transported American cotton to China and Chinese tea to the United States. Despite their failure to win large numbers of converts, Protestant missionaries also extended their work. As China underwent the Taiping Rebellion (1851–1864) and its accompanying domestic upheaval, Britain and France invaded and forced China to grant more trading privileges and protection for missionaries. In the Treaty of Tientsin (Tianjin) of 1858, the United States once again benefited from European imperialism and gained access to several more ports for trade and missionary activity, as well as the right to station diplomats in the capital Beijing (Peking).

American commercial and missionary activities also expanded in the Hawaiian (or Sandwich) Islands. American traders and whalers had long stopped at the Pacific archipelago two thousand miles from the west coast, and missionaries found Hawai'i more hospitable than China. By midcentury, when Americans dominated the economic life of the islands, Washington was warning other nations that Hawai'i ranked as a special U.S. interest that they should not covet or molest.

Americans also hoped to penetrate isolated Japan. Fearful that contact with Western culture would undermine the traditional feudal order, the Japanese since the seventeenth century had largely sealed themselves off from the rest of the world. Other than selected Asians, only a few Dutch traders won commercial opportunities in Japan. Seeking to protect shipwrecked American sailors stranded on hostile Japanese shores, to gain trading rights, and to use Japan as a coaling station along the commercial route to China, U.S. officials determined to pry Japan open. Commodore Matthew C. Perry, backed by a fleet of warships, sailed into Edo (Tokyo) Bay on July 8, 1853. After deliberate delay and a contentious internal debate, the Japanese government signed a treaty on March 31, 1854, that provided for the protection of marooned sailors and the opening of two ports to U.S. trading vessels. A formal trade treaty followed five years later.

This chapter probes the encounters between Americans and Asians in the early to mid-nineteenth century. The documents and essays explore how various American agents—diplomats, merchants, and missionaries—interacted to define and expand U.S. interests in the region and to shape lasting perceptions and policies. The themes of expansionism and imperialism in all their forms are central.

🌐 D O C U M E N T S

Document 1 is a petition of May 25, 1839, to Congress from American merchants in Canton, China, during the First Opium War (1839–1842). The merchants appeal for official U.S. help to protect their interests. On March 16, 1840, Massachusetts Whig Caleb Cushing addressed the House of Representatives and roundly condemned reports from London that U.S. officials had joined "heart and hand" with the British government forcibly to win commercial privileges in China. In the fiery speech, reprinted as Document 2, Cushing contrasted American respect for the laws and practices of the Chinese empire with Britain's aggressive and high-handed approach, and asked the Committee on Foreign Affairs to disavow Anglo-American cooperation. Chinese officials downplayed distinctions between U.S. and other foreigners. Document 3, a statement from early 1841 by Juan Yüan, China's grand secretary, contemplates pitting "barbarians" against "barbarians" so that China can blunt increasing Western penetration. Chinese resistance failed to turn back British gunboats, and in 1842 the Chinese court signed the infamous Treaty of Nanking that granted British traders unrestricted access to five ports. In Document 4, dated May 8, 1843, U.S. Secretary of State Daniel Webster instructs Caleb Cushing on the goals of Cushing's mission to China to seek a treaty providing for advantageous trade terms equal to those of other nations (achieved in the Treaty of Wanghia, signed on July 3, 1844).

Having secured wider access to China's foreign trade, U.S. leaders scouted other opportunities in Asia. On July 14, 1851, in a letter to the American commissioner in Hawai'i (Document 5), Secretary Webster firmly states U.S. opposition to any European power's attempt to undermine Hawaiian independence—thus protecting U.S. interests on the islands. Document 6, dated November 5, 1852, written by C. M. Conrad of the Department of State and Secretary of the Navy John P. Kennedy, sets out the U.S. objectives that Commodore Matthew C. Perry should pursue in his mission to open Japan. Officials of the Japanese government disagreed over how to respond to Perry's demands for a treaty. In an 1853 memorial, Document 7, Ii Naosuke, *daimyo* or feudal lord of Hikone, advocates signing a treaty with the Americans in order to avoid a disastrous military confrontation and to buy time for strengthening the country's

China at Midcentury

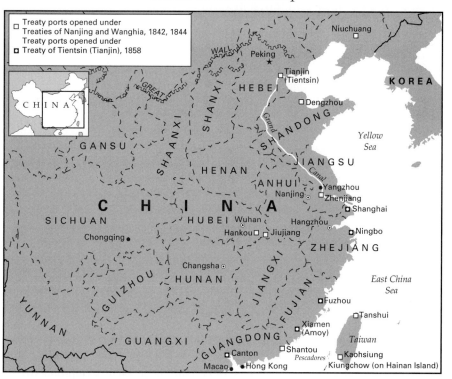

| | Treaty ports opened under Treaties of Nanjing and Wanghia, 1842, 1844 |
| | Treaty ports opened under Treaty of Tientsin (Tianjin), 1858 |

Reprinted from *The Search for Modern China* by Jonathan D. Spence. Copyright © 1990 by Jonathan D. Spence. Reprinted by permission of W. W. Norton & Company, Inc.

defenses. In Document 8, another 1853 memorial, Tokugawa Nariaki, *daimyo* of Mito, makes a forceful case against a treaty with Perry and for a policy of peace. Japan and the United States ultimately signed a treaty on March 31, 1854.

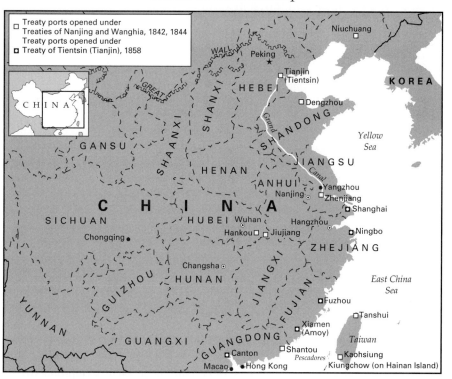 D O C U M E N T   1

American Merchants in Canton Plead for Protection During the Opium Crisis, 1839

That, upon the twenty-second day of March last, we were, in common with the resident foreigners of all nations [in Canton], made prisoners in our factories, and surrounded by armed men and boats; deprived of our servants, and cut off from all

This document can be found in U.S. House of Representatives, *Executive Documents,* 26th Congress, 1st Session, House Doc. No. 40, January 9, 1840, pp. 1–4.

communication with our ships at Whampoa, Lintin, and Macao; by which means, together with the threatened forfeiture of life if his arbitrary exactions were not complied with, a commissioner from the Imperial Government at Peking has succeeded in wresting from residents here upwards of twenty thousand chests of British owned opium, which may be valued at more than ten millions of dollars. We have, also, been threatened with severe but undefined penalties for refusing to sign a bond by which all concerned in a vessel that may hereafter be found bringing opium to China are required to be given up to the authorities for punishment by death. . . .

Edicts and proclamations have from time to time been promulgated, prohibiting the opium trade; but notwithstanding these, the highest officers in the province have not only connived at the smuggling or introduction of the drug by the Chinese, receiving a fee or duty varying from twenty to seventy dollars per chest, but they have been active participators therein; and it is a well-known fact, that a large amount of the opium delivered at Lintin has been delivered to boats belonging to, and bearing the flags of the Governor, the Hoppo, or collector of customs, and other high officers of the province. . . .

We have no wish to see a revival of the opium trade; on the contrary, before the adoption of the violent measures that have given occasion for the present memorial, we had, most of us, signed a voluntary pledge that, believing in the sincerity of this Government in their efforts to destroy the trade, we would in future abstain from dealing in the drug. We are alive to the fact, that during the last five years Great Britain and her Indian possessions have drawn from this empire thirty to thirty-five million dollars in gold and silver, and forty to forty-five millions of dollars in teas, raw silk, etc., in exchange for a drug which has been productive of much evil and of scarcely a single good to the Chinese; a drug, the introduction of which, we have reason to fear, has degraded the foreign character in the estimation of the better portion of the Chinese. And whether we view the subject in a moral and philanthropic light, or merely as a commercial question, we are extremely desirous to see the importation and consumption of opium in China entirely at an end.

We cannot, however, perceive the slightest ground for justification of the robbery committed upon British subjects here, nor for the detention of the persons, ships, and property of those who are entirely disconnected from the obnoxious trade. The measures of the Imperial Government should have been directed first against its own officers, who have been engaged and most active in the trade; but, taking advantage of the unprotected state of the foreign community of Canton, the commissioner has proceeded in his high-handed measures, regardless alike of the respect due to the representatives of foreign powers resident in Canton, and of the laws or customs and usages that have heretofore been observed and considered the chief guaranties for the safety of the foreign trade. . . .

We would, therefore, with all deference and respect, express our opinions that the United States Government should take immediate measures; and, if deemed advisable, to act in concert with the Governments of Great Britain, France, and Holland, or either of them, in their endeavors to establish commercial relations with this empire upon a safe and honorable footing, such as exists between all friendly powers; and by direct appeal to the Imperial Government at Peking, to obtain a compliance with the following among other important demands:

1st. Permission for foreign envoys to reside near the court at Peking, on the terms and with all the privileges accorded at other courts, through whom appeal may be made to the Imperial Government in cases of difficulty with the local authorities in the prosecution of our commercial pursuits.

2nd. The promulgation of a fixed tariff of duties on articles, both of import and export, from which no deviation shall be allowed under any pretext whatever.

3d. A system of bonding warehouses, or some regulations permitting the transhipment of such goods as it may be desirable to re-export for want of a market in China.

4th. The liberty of trading at other port or ports in China than that of Canton.

5th. Compensation for the losses caused by the stoppage of the whole legal trade of the port, and the consequent detention of vessels and property; with a guaranty against the recurrence of similar arbitrary acts, and security for the free egress from Canton, and other ports, of all persons not guilty of crimes or civil offences, at any and at all times.

6th. That until the Chinese laws are distinctly made known and recognised, the punishment for wrongs committed by foreigners upon the Chinese, or others, shall not be greater than is applicable to the like offence by the laws of the United States or England; nor shall any punishment be inflicted by the Chinese authorities upon any foreigner, until the guilt of the party shall have been fairly and clearly proved. . . .

In conclusion, we have but to express our candid conviction that the appearance of a naval force from the United States, England, and France, upon the coast of China, would, without bloodshed, obtain from this Government such acknowledgments and treaties as would not only place our commerce upon a secure footing, but would be mutually beneficial, and greatly increase the extent and importance of our relations with this empire.

⊛ D O C U M E N T   2

Massachusetts Representative Caleb Cushing Bellows: "God Forbid Cooperating with the British," 1840

I proposed a resolution, early in the session, calling on the Executive for information as to our relations with China, which resolution, being afterwards submitted to the Committee on Foreign Affairs, was by them reported to the House, and adopted; and to which the Executive has since responded, in a Message now in the procession of the House. My colleague [Mr. [Abbott] Lawrence [(MA)]] also presented a memorial from citizens of the United States in China, relative to the same matter.

This document can be found in *The Congressional Globe,* 26th Congress, 1st Session, (16 March 1840), pp. 274–275.

These papers are now under consideration in the Committee on Foreign Affairs. Meanwhile, I am somewhat disturbed to learn, through the intelligence brought by the Great Western, that these movements here are construed in England as indicating a disposition on the part of the American Government "to join heart and hand"—as the expression is in a paragraph of an English ministerial journal now before me—"to join heart and hand with the British Government, and endeavor to obtain commercial treaties from the authorities in China." Now, so far as regards myself, I wish to say that this is a great misconception, if it be not a wilful perversion, of what is contemplated here. I have, it is true, thought that the present contingency,—when the Americans at Canton, and they almost or quite alone, have manifested a proper respect for the laws and public rights of the Chinese empire, in honorable contrast with the ortrageous misconduct of the English there—and when the Chinese Government, grateful for the upright department of the Americans, has manifested the best possible feeling towards them—I have thought that these circumstances afforded a favorable opportunity to endeavor to put the American trade with China on a just and stable footing for the future. But, God forbid that I should entertain the idea of co-operating with the British Government in the purpose—if purpose it have—of upholding the base cupidity and violence, and high handed infraction of all law, human and divine, which have characterized the operations of the British, individually and collectively, in the seas of China. I disavow all sympathy with those operations. I denounce them most emphatically. And, though it is not competent for me to speak now of what has been done or is intended in the Committee on Foreign Affairs relative to this, yet thus much I may say, that, in that committee, and among all its members, I am confident there is but one spirit—and that is, to guard the interests and to maintain the honor of the United States. It is due to the Executive, also, that I should say that I have no reason to believe or suspect that the President or his Cabinet entertains any but the most proper views on this subject. At the same time, to close the door at once against all misunderstanding, and set the whole matter in a clear light, in order that the Chinese Government need not be misled into supposing that, while the Americans in Canton profess to act in good faith, and enjoy the benefits of it, any different purpose is entertained here, I put this question to the chairman of the Committee on Foreign Affairs—whether he himself, or, so far as he knows, the Executive of the United States, has any idea of making common cause with Great Britain in reference to the recent events in China?

Mr. PICKENS [(Francis Wilkinson Pickens, Chair of the House Foreign Affairs Committee)], in reply, said that, in reference to himself, it was very far from being the fact that he was disposed to make common cause with England in her designs in China—for the very first moment the subject was referred to the committee, and laid before them, that very point was made by himself, and he objected expressly to our appearing before the world, (as might be inferred from the expression in the memorial) of acting in concert with the British Government in regard to this matter. So far as the Executive was concerned, he had no authority for speaking; but he was induced to believe that no such fact of intended concert with Great Britian, as the gentleman directly referred in existed. He had no intention directly or indirectly to aid in forcing on the Chinese the odious traffic in opium. He (Mr. P.) believed that if we could prevail on China to abandon her policy of non intercourse with the world if we could prevail on her to enter into any arrangement that might have for its basis commercial relations which would place us on an equal footing with other powers, it would be all that was necessary. But of this he had little hopes, for it was known that China, from time immemorial, had been opposed to all treaties. Our only object (said Mr. P.) is to place our commerce with China on an equal footing with that of other nations, and to see that no advantage be taken of us.

Surely England does *not occupy a position at present* to command any sympathy or co-operation from us. He would for bear to touch upon those points that are now at *issue between* us, which may, in the progress of events, become of the deepest importance. It is not our policy to appear to act under her cover and co-operation. We will act upon our separate and independent interests, and our own views of policy.

Mr. CUSHING then said: I think the House for its indulgence, and the chairman of the Committee on Foreign Affairs, who has answered my question so satisfactorily; and I trust the idea will no longer be entertained in England, if she chooses to persevere in the attempt to coerce the Chinese by force of arms to submit to be poisoned with opium by whole provinces, that she is to receive aid or countenance from the United States in that nefarious enterprise.

D O C U M E N T   3

A Chinese Official Recommends Pitting American Barbarians Against British Barbarians, 1841

According to rumor, since [Imperial Commissioner] Ch'i-shan reached Canton, the barbarians have not yet become tractable and I worry about it day and night. I have long since been aware that of the countries trading at Canton, besides England, the United States is the largest and most powerful. In this country the ground is level and rice plentiful. The English barbarians look to her for supplies and do not dare antagonize her. But the American barbarians at Canton have always been peaceable, not obstinate like the English barbarians. If we treat the American barbarians courteously and abolish their customs duties, and also take the trade of the English barbarians and give it to the American barbarians, then the American barbarians are sure to be grateful for this Heavenly Favor and will energetically oppose the English barbarians. Moreover, the ships and cannon of the English barbarians have mostly been acquired by hire or seizure from other foreign states. If the American barbarians are made use of by us, then other countries will learn of it, and it will not be difficult to break them down. When the American barbarians have received (Imperial) Favor, the English barbarians will certainly not take it lying down. Probably one or two ports will be bombarded by them, but when their strength is expended and we have strengthened fortifications and purged the countryside, then we will meet them and it will not be hard to repel them. Still, this is a plan devised during sickness and I do not yet know whether or not it is practicable.

This document can be found in Earl Swisher, ed., *China's Management of the American Barbarians: A Study of Sino-American Relations, 1841–1861, with Documents* (New Haven: Far Eastern Association, Far Eastern Publications, 1953), p. 57.

🌐 *D O C U M E N T   4*

Secretary of State Daniel Webster Instructs Caleb Cushing on Negotiating with China, 1843

Occurrences happening in China within the last two years have resulted in events which are likely to be of much importance as well to the United States as to the rest of the civilized world. Of their still more important consequences to China herself, it is not necessary here to speak. The hostilities which have been carried on between that Empire and England, have resulted, among other consequences, in opening four important ports to English commerce, viz: Amoy, Ning-po, Shang-hai, and Fu-chow.

These ports belong to some of the richest, most productive, and most populous provinces of the Empire; and are likely to become very important marts of commerce. A leading object of the Mission in which you are now to be engaged, is to secure the entry of American ships and cargoes into these ports, on terms as favorable as those which are enjoyed by English merchants. It is not necessary to dwell, here, on the great and well known amount of imports of the productions of China into the United States. These imports, especially in the great article of tea, are not likely to be diminished. Heretofore they have been paid for in the precious metals, or, more recently, by bills drawn on London. At one time, indeed, American paper, of certain descriptions was found to be an available remittance. Latterly a considerable trade has sprung up in the export of certain American manufactures to China. To augment these exports, by obtaining the most favorable commercial facilities, and cultivating, to the greatest extent practicable, friendly commercial intercourse with China, in all its accessible ports, is matter of moment to the commercial and manufacturing, as well as the agricultural and mining, interests of the United States. It cannot be foreseen how rapidly, or how slowly, a people of such peculiar habits as the Chinese, and apparently so tenaciously attached to their habits, may adopt the sentiments, ideas, and customs of other nations. But if prejudiced and strongly wedded to their own usages, the Chinese are still understood to be ingenious, acute, and inquisitive. . . .

As your Mission has in view only friendly and commercial objects—objects, it is supposed, equally useful to both countries, the natural jealousy of the Chinese, and their repulsive feeling towards foreigners, it is hoped may be in some degree removed or mitigated by prudence and address on your part. Your constant aim must be to produce a full conviction on the minds of the Government and the people that your Mission is entirely pacific; that you come with no purposes of hostility or annoyance; that you are a messenger of peace, sent from the greatest Power in America to the greatest Empire in Asia, to offer respect and good will, and to establish the means of friendly intercourse. . . .

In regard to the mode of managing this matter [the *kowtow*], much must be left to your discretion, as circumstances may occur. All pains should be taken to avoid the giving of offence, or the wounding of the national pride; but, at the same time, you will be careful to do nothing which may seem, even to the Chinese themselves, to imply any inferiority on the part of your Government, or any thing less than perfect independence of all Nations. You will say that the Government of the United States

This document can be found in U.S. Congress, 28th Congress, 2nd Session, *Public Documents Printed by Order of the Senate of the United States* (Washington, D.C.: Gales and Seaton, 1845), Doc. No. 138, pp. 1–5. It can also be found in Kenneth E. Shewmaker et al., eds., *The Papers of Daniel Webster: Diplomatic Papers, Volume I, 1841–1843* (Hanover, N.H.: University Press of New England, 1983), pp. 922–926.

is always controlled by a sense of religion and of honor; that Nations differ in their religious opinions and observances; that you cannot do any thing which the religion of your own country, or its sentiments of honor, forbid; that you have the most profound respect for His Majesty the Emperor; that you are ready to make to him all manifestations of homage which are consistent with your own sense; and that you are sure His Majesty is too just to desire you to violate your own duty. . . . Taking care thus in no way to allow the Government or people of China to consider you as tribute bearer from your Government, or as acknowledging its inferiority, in any respect, to that of China, or any other Nation, you will bear in mind, at the same time, what is due to your own personal dignity and the character which you bear. . . .

It will be no part of your duty to enter into controversies which may exist between China and any European State; nor will you, in your communications, fail to abstain altogether from any sentiment, or any expression, which might give to other Governments just cause of offence. It will be quite proper, however, that you should, in a proper manner, always keep before the eyes of the Chinese the high character, importance, and power of the United States. You may speak of the extent of their territory, their great commerce spread over all seas, their powerful navy, every where giving protection to that commerce, and the numerous schools and institutions established in them, to teach men knowledge and wisdom. It cannot be wrong for you to make known, where not known, that the United States, once a country subject to England, threw off that subjection, years ago, asserted its independence, sword in hand, established that independence, after a seven years' war, and now meets England upon equal terms upon the ocean and upon the land. The remoteness of the United States from China, and still more the fact that they have no colonial possessions in her neighborhood, will naturally lead to the indulgence of a less suspicious and more friendly feeling, than may have been entertained towards England, even before the late war between England and China. It cannot be doubted that the immense power of England in India must be regarded by the Chinese Government with dissatisfaction, if not with some degree of alarm. You will take care to show strongly how free the Chinese Government may well be from all jealousy arising from such causes towards the United States. Finally, you will signify, in decided terms, and a positive manner, that the Government of the United States would find it impossible to remain on terms of friendship and regard with the Emperor, if greater privileges, or commercial facilities, should be allowed to the subject of any other Government, than should be granted to citizens of the United States.

D O C U M E N T   5

Webster Warns European Powers
Away from Hawai'i, 1851

This Government still desires to see the Nationality of the Hawaiian Government maintained, its independent administration of public affairs respected, and its prosperity and reputation increased.

This document can be found in *Senate Executive Documents,* 52nd Congress, 2nd Session, Doc. No. 77 (Washington, D.C.: Government Printing Office, 1893), pp. 95–97. It can also be found in Kenneth E. Shewmaker et al., eds., *The Papers of Daniel Webster: Diplomatic Papers, Volume 2, 1850–1852* (Hanover, N.H.: University Press of New England, 1987), pp. 275–277.

But while thus indisposed to exercise any sinister influence itself over the counsels of Hawaii, or to overawe the proceedings of its government by the menace, or the actual application of superior military force, it expects to see other powerful nations, act in the same spirit. It is therefore with unfeigned regret, that the President has read the correspondence, and become acquainted with the circumstances, occurring between the Hawaiian Government and M. [Louis Emile] Perrin the Commissioner of France at Honolulu.

It is too plain to be denied or doubted, that demands were made upon the Hawaiian Government, by the French Commissioner, wholly inconsistent with its character as an independent State, demands, which if submitted to in this case, would be sure to be followed by other demands, equally derogatory, not only from the same quarter, but probably also, from other States; and that could only end, in rendering the Islands and their government, a prey to the stronger commercial nations of the world. . . .

The Hawaiian Islands are ten times nearer to the United States, than to any of the powers of Europe. Five sixths of all their commercial intercourse is with the United States; and these considerations, together with others of a more general character, have fixed the course which the Government of the United States will pursue in regard to them. The annunciation of this policy, will not surprise the governments of Europe, nor be thought to be unreasonable by the nations of the civilized world; and that policy is, that while the government of the United States, itself faithful to its original assurance, scrupulously regards the independence of the Hawaiian Islands, it can never consent to see those Islands taken possession of by either of the great commercial powers of Europe; nor can it consent, that demands, manifestly unjust and derogatory, and inconsistent with a bona fide independence, shall be enforced against that government. . . .

The Navy Department will receive instructions to place, and to keep, the Naval Armament of the United States in the Pacific Ocean, in such a state of strength and preparation, as shall be requisite for the preservation of the honor and dignity of the United States, and the safety of the Government of the Hawaiian Islands.

DOCUMENT 6

Instructions to Commodore Matthew C. Perry for His Expedition to Japan, 1852

Recent events—the navigation of the ocean by steam, the acquisition and rapid settlement by this country of a vast territory on the Pacific [California], the discovery of gold in that region, the rapid communication established across the isthmus which separates the two oceans—have practically brought the countries of the east in closer proximity to our own; although the consequences of these events have scarcely begun to be felt, the intercourse between them has already greatly increased, and no limits can be assigned to its future extension. . . .

The objects sought by this government are—

1. To effect some permanent arrangement for the protection of American seamen and property wrecked on these islands, or driven into their ports by stress of weather.

This document can be found in U.S. Congress, 33rd Congress, 2nd Session, *Executive Documents Printed by Order of the Senate of the United States* (Washington, D.C.: Beverly Tucker, Senate Printer, 1855), Ex. Doc. 34, pp. 4–9.

2. The permission to American vessels to enter one or more of their ports in order to obtain supplies of provisions, water, fuel, &c., or, in case of disasters, to refit so as to enable them to prosecute their voyage.

It is very desirable to have permission to establish a depot for coal, if not on one of the principal islands, at least on some small uninhabited one, of which, it is said, there are several in their vicinity.

3. The permission to our vessels to enter one or more of their ports for the purpose of disposing of their cargoes by sale or barter. . . .

It is manifest, from past experience, that arguments or persuasion addressed to this people, unless they be seconded by some imposing manifestation of power, will be utterly unavailing.

You will, therefore, be pleased to direct the commander of the squadron [Perry] to proceed, with his whole force, to such point on the coast of Japan as he may deem most advisable, and there endeavor to open a communication with the government, and, if possible, to see the emperor in person, and deliver to him the letter of introduction from the President with which he is charged. He will state that he has been sent across the ocean by the President to deliver that letter to the emperor, and to communicate with his government on matters of importance to the two countries. That the President entertains the most friendly feeling towards Japan, but has been surprised and grieved to learn, that when any of the people of the United States go, of their own accord, or are thrown by the perils of the sea within the dominions of the emperor, they are treated as if they were his worst enemies. . . .

He will inform him of the usages of this country, and of all Christian countries, in regard to shipwrecked persons and vessels, and will refer to the case of the Japanese subjects who were recently picked up at sea in distress and carried to California, from whence they have been sent to their own country; and will state that this government desires to obtain from that of Japan some positive assurance, that persons who may hereafter be shipwrecked on the coast of Japan, or driven by stress of weather into her ports, shall be treated with humanity; and to make arrangements for a more extended commercial intercourse between the two countries. The establishment of this intercourse will be found a difficult, but, perhaps, not an impossible task.

The deep-seated aversion of this people to hold intercourse with Christian nations is said to be owing chiefly to the indiscreet zeal with which the early missionaries, particularly those of Portugal, endeavored to propagate their religion. The commodore will therefore say, that the government of this country, unlike those of every other Christian country, does not interfere with the religion of its own people, much less with that of other nations. It seems that the fears or the prejudices of the Japanese are very much excited against the English, of whose conquests in the east, and recent invasion of China, they have probably heard. As the Americans speak the same language as the English, it is natural that they should confound citizens of the United States with British subjects. Indeed, their barbarous treatment of the crews of the [U.S.] vessels . . . was partly occasioned by the suspicion that they were really English. . . .

Commodore Perry will, therefore, explain to them that the United States are connected with no government in Europe. That they inhabit a great country which lies directly between them and Europe, and which was discovered by the nations of Europe about the same time that Japan herself was first visited by them; that the portion of this continent lying nearest to Europe was first settled by emigrants from that country, but that its population has rapidly spread through the country until it has reached the Pacific ocean. . . .

If, after having exhausted every argument and every means of persuasion, the commodore should fail to obtain from the government any relaxation of their system of exclusion, or even any assurance of humane treatment of our shipwrecked seamen, he will then change his tone, and inform them in the most unequivocal terms that it is the determination of this government to insist, that hereafter all citizens or vessels of the United States that may be wrecked on their coasts, or driven by stress of weather into their harbors shall, so long as they are compelled to remain there, be treated with humanity; and that if any acts of cruelty should hereafter be practised upon citizens of this country, whether by the government or by the inhabitants of Japan, they will be severely chastised. In case he should succeed in obtaining concessions on any of the points above mentioned, it is desirable that they should be reduced into the form of a treaty, for negotiating which he will be furnished with the requisite powers. . . .

In his intercourse with this people, who are said to be proud and vindictive in their character, he should be courteous and conciliatory, but at the same time, firm and decided. He will, therefore, submit with patience and forbearance to acts of discourtesy to which he may be subjected, by a people to whose usages it will not do to test by our standard of propriety, but, at the same time, will be careful to do nothing that may compromit, in their eyes, his own dignity, or that of the country. He will, on the contrary, do everything to impress them with a just sense of the power and greatness of this country, and to satisfy them that its past forbearance has been the result, not of timidity, but of a desire to be on friendly terms with them.

DOCUMENT 7

Ii Naosuke, Feudal Lord of Hikone, Advocates Accommodation with the United States, 1853

Careful consideration of conditions as they are today . . . leads me to believe that despite the constant differences and debates into which men of patriotism and foresight have been led in recent years by their perception of the danger of foreign aggression, it is impossible in the crisis we now face to ensure the safety and tranquillity of our country merely by an insistence on the seclusion laws as we did in former times. Moreover, time is essential if we are to complete our coast defenses. Since 1609, when warships of over 500 *koku* [5,000 cubic feet ship capacity] were forbidden, we have had no warships capable of opposing foreign attack on our coasts with heavy guns. Thus I am much afraid that were the foreigners now to seize as bases such outlying islands as Hachijō-jima and Ōshima, it would be impossible for us to remain inactive, though without warships we should have no

From *Select Documents on Japanese Foreign Policy, 1853–1868,* translated and edited by W. G. Beasley, 1955, by permission of Oxford University Press.

effective means of driving them off. There is a saying that when one is besieged in a castle, to raise the drawbridge is to imprison oneself and make it impossible to hold out indefinitely; and again, that when opposing forces face each other across a river, victory is obtained by that which crosses the river and attacks. It seems clear throughout history that he who takes action is in a position to advance, while he who remains inactive must retreat. Even though the Shōgun's ancestors set up seclusion laws, they left the Dutch and the Chinese to act as a bridge [to the outside world]. Might this bridge not now be of advantage to us in handling foreign affairs, providing us with the means whereby we may for a time avert the outbreak of hostilities and then, after some time has elapsed, gain a complete victory?

I understand that the coal for which the Americans have expressed a desire is to be found in quantity in Kyūshū. We should first tell them, as a matter of expediency, that we also have need of coal, but that should their need of it arise urgently and unexpectedly during a voyage, they may ask for coal at Nagasaki and if we have any to spare we will provide it. Nor will we grudge them wood and water. As for foodstuffs, the supply varies from province to province, but we can agree to provide food for the shipwrecked and unfortunate. Again, we can tell them, of recent years we have treated kindly those wrecked on our coasts and have sent them all home. There is no need for further discussion of this subject, and all requests concerning it should be made through the Dutch. Then, too, there is the question of trade. Although there is a national prohibition of it, conditions are not the same as they were. The exchange of goods is a universal practice. This we should explain to the spirits of our ancestors. And we should then tell the foreigners that we mean in future to send trading vessels to the Dutch company's factory at Batavia [in contemporary Indonesia] to engage in trade; that we will allocate some of our trading goods to America, some to Russia, and so on, using the Dutch to trade for us as our agents; but that there will be a delay of one or two years because we must [first] construct new ships for these voyages. By replying in this way we will take the Americans by surprise in offering to treat them generally in the same way as the Dutch.

We must revive the licensed trading vessels [system] . . . , ordering the rich merchants of such places as Ōsaka, Hyōgo, and Sakai to take shares in the enterprise. We must construct new steamships, especially powerful warships, and these will load with goods not needed in Japan. For a time we will have to employ Dutchmen as masters and mariners, but we will put on board with them Japanese of ability and integrity who must study the use of large guns, the handling of ships, and the rules of navigation. Openly these will be called merchant vessels, but they will in fact have the secret purpose of training a navy. As we increase the number of ships and our mastery of technique, Japanese will be able to sail the oceans freely and gain direct knowledge of conditions abroad without relying on the secret reports of the Dutch. Thus we will eventually complete the organization of a navy. Moreover, we must shake off the panic and apprehensions that have beset us and abandon our habits of luxury and wasteful spending. Our defenses thus strengthened, and all being arranged at home, we can act so as to make our courage and prestige resound beyond the seas. By so doing, we will not in the future be imprisoning ourselves, indeed, we will be able, I believe, so to accomplish matters at home and abroad as to achieve national security.

DOCUMENT 8

Tokugawa Nariaki, Feudal Lord of Mito, Argues Against Peace, 1853

I propose to give here in outline the ten reasons why in my view we must never choose the policy of peace.

1. Although our country's territory is not extensive, foreigners both fear and respect us. That, after all, is because our resoluteness and military prowess have been clearly demonstrated to the world outside. . . . Despite this, the Americans who arrived recently, though fully aware of the Bakufu's [military government] prohibition, entered Uraga displaying a white flag as a symbol of peace and insisted on presenting their written requests. Moreover they entered Edo Bay, fired heavy guns in salute and even went so far as to conduct surveys without permission. They were arrogant and discourteous, their actions an outrage. Indeed, this was the greatest disgrace we have suffered since the dawn of our history. The saying is that if the enemy dictates terms in one's own capital one's country is disgraced. . . . Should it happen not only that the Bakufu fails to expel them but also that it concludes an agreement in accordance with their requests, then I fear it would be impossible to maintain our national prestige [*kokutai*]. That is the first reason why we must never choose the policy of peace.

2. The prohibition of Christianity is the first rule of the Tokugawa house [Japan's governing dynasty]. Public notices concerning it are posted everywhere, even to the remotest corner of every province. . . . The Bakufu can never ignore or overlook the evils of Christianity. Yet if the Americans are allowed to come again this religion will inevitably raise its head once more, however strict the prohibition; and this, I fear, is something we could never justify to the spirits of our ancestors. That is the second reason why we must never choose the policy of peace.

3. To exchange our valuable articles like gold, silver, copper, and iron for useless foreign goods like woollens and satin is to incur great loss while acquiring not the smallest benefit. The best course of all would be for the Bakufu to put a stop to the trade with Holland. By contrast, to open such valueless trade with others besides the Dutch would, I believe, inflict the greatest possible harm on our country. That is the third reason why we must never choose the policy of peace.

4. For some years Russia, England, and others have sought trade with us, but the Bakufu has not permitted it. Should permission be granted to the Americans, on what grounds would it be possible to refuse if Russia and the others [again] request it? That is the fourth reason why we must never choose the policy of peace.

5. It is widely stated that [apart from trade] the foreigners have no other evil designs and that if only the Bakufu will permit trade there will be no further difficulty. However, it is their practice first to seek a foothold by means of trade and then to go on to propagate Christianity and make other unreasonable demands. . . . That is the fifth reason why we must never choose the policy of peace.

6. Though the Rangakusha group may argue secretly that world conditions are much changed from what they were, Japan alone clinging to ideas of seclusion

From *Select Documents on Japanese Foreign Policy, 1853–1868,* translated and edited by W. G. Beasley, 1955, by permission of Oxford University Press.

in isolation amidst the seas, that this is a constant source of danger to us and that our best course would therefore be to communicate with foreign countries and open an extensive trade; yet, to my mind, if the people of Japan stand firmly united, if we complete our military preparations and return to the state of society that existed before the middle ages, then we will even be able to go out against foreign countries and spread abroad our fame and prestige. But if we open trade at the demand of the foreigners, for no better reason than that, our habits today being those of peace and indolence, men have shown fear merely at the coming of a handful of foreign warships, then it would truly be a vain illusion to think of evolving any long-range plan for going out against foreign countries. That is the sixth reason why we must never choose the policy of peace. . . .

9. I hear that all, even though they be commoners, who have witnessed the recent actions of the foreigners, think them abominable; and if the Bakufu does not expel these insolent foreigners root and branch there may be some who will complain in secret, asking to what purpose have been all the preparations of gun-emplacements. . . . That, I believe is because even the humblest are conscious of the debt they owe their country, and it is indeed a promising sign. Since even ignorant commoners are talking in this way, I fear that if the Bakufu does not decide to carry out expulsion, if its handling of the matter shows nothing but excess of leniency and appeasement of the foreigners, then the lower orders may fail to understand its ideas and hence opposition might arise from evil men who had lost their respect for Bakufu authority. It might even be that Bakufu control of the great lords would itself be endangered. That is the ninth reason why we must never choose the policy of peace.

10. There are those who say that since the expulsion of foreigners is the ancient law of the Shōgun's ancestors, reissued and reaffirmed in the Bunsei period [1818–1830], the Bakufu has in fact always been firmly resolved to fight, but that even so one must recognize that peace has now lasted so long our armaments are inadequate, and one cannot therefore tell what harm might be done if we too recklessly arouse the anger of the foreigners. In that event, they say, the Bakufu would be forced to conclude a peace settlement and so its prestige would suffer still further damage. Hence [it is argued], the Bakufu should show itself compliant at this time and should placate the foreigners, meanwhile exerting all its efforts in military preparations, so that when these preparations have been completed it can more strictly enforce the ancient laws. . . . I . . . believe that if there be any sign of the Bakufu pursuing the policy of peace, morale will never rise though preparations be pressed forward daily; and the gun-batteries and other preparations made will accordingly be so much ornament, never put to effective use. But if the Bakufu, now and henceforward, shows itself resolute for expulsion, the immediate effect will be to increase ten-fold the morale of the country and to bring about the completion of military preparations without even the necessity for issuing orders.

ESSAYS

Two selections analyze the opening of U.S. commercial and diplomatic relations with two of East Asia's oldest and most venerated kingdoms—both of which resisted Western influences. In the first essay, Macabe Keliher of Georgetown University traces the origins of U.S. policy toward China. Disagreeing with scholars who emphasize

Anglo-American cooperation in mid-nineteenth-century China, Keliher highlights the fierce competition that existed between British and U.S. merchants and political leaders. Rather than applauding Britain's victory in the Opium Wars that gave British traders special port privileges, an alarmed John Tyler administration appointed former Massachusetts representative Caleb Cushing to lead the first U.S. mission to China in 1843 and negotiate the first U.S. treaty with China (the Treaty of Wangxia, 1844). According to Keliher, Cushing's energetic advocacy of U.S.-Chinese economic relations anticipated the U.S. pursuit of an "open door" trade policy at the turn of the twentieth century.

In the second essay, Walter LaFeber, a long-time professor at Cornell University, examines Commodore Matthew Perry's opening of Japan in 1853 and the signing of the first U.S.-Japanese trade treaty in 1858. In this selection, taken from his award-winning book *The Clash: U.S.-Japanese Relations Throughout History,* LaFeber cites the credo of Manifest Destiny, the acquisition of west coast ports, dreams of an expanded trade with China, and the advent of steam-powered navigation as factors that propelled the United States across the Pacific. Although Washington sought diplomatic and trade ties, Japan's leaders accepted relations with the United States only after a contentious internal debate over the wisdom of contact with the West. Opening Japan to U.S. and foreign influence, LaFeber observes, accelerated that country's drive toward modernity and undermined its traditional feudal social order.

Anglo-American Rivalry
and the Origins of U.S. China Policy

MACABE KELIHER

In the spring of 1843, after a number of lively and often heated debates, the U.S. Congress approved funds for the first U.S. mission to China. President John Tyler spoke of the mission as one of great "magnitude and importance," and Secretary of State Daniel Webster called it "a more important mission than ever proceeded from this Country, and more important mission than any other, likely to succeed it, in our day." Indeed, this mission, led by former Congressman Caleb Cushing, resulted in the first U.S. treaty with China (the Treaty of Wangxia, 1844), which secured trading privileges for American merchants and opened a host of Chinese ports to serve as outlets for surplus American production. Contained within the treaty was also the first appearance of a most favored nation clause—inserted in order to assure the United States of the same privileges in China as might be granted any other nation.

Historians seeking the origins of the United States' China policy have, however, dismissed the Cushing mission and the Wangxia Treaty. They have instead placed the inception of U.S. China policy at the turn of the nineteenth century with the proclamation of the Open Door policy and the possession of the Philippines as means to access the China market. Working on the thesis that cooperation and comity existed between the United States and Britain, these scholars argue that prior to the Open Door policy the United States merely followed the lead set by Britain in China. . . .

In contrast to this conventional interpretation, this article argues that U.S. China policy—that is, active government participation in promoting its merchants'

Macabe Keliher, "Anglo-American Rivalry and the Origins of U.S. China Policy," from *Diplomatic History* 31 (April 2007): 227–228, 236–238, 241–250, 253–256. Copyright © 2007. Reprinted by permission of Blackwell Publishing Ltd.

interests in China and a positive role in the penetration of the China market—began more than a half century before the Open Door notes and was in fact reflected in the Treaty of Wangxia. This article also challenges the assumption of Anglo-American comity in China in the early and mid nineteenth century—something that even the purveyors of this view admit was an anomaly to the general antagonistic state of Anglo-American relations in this period. Indeed, . . . it was a bitter rivalry with Britain for markets and influence in the Pacific that forced U.S. politicians and bureaucrats to assume a positive role in East Asia in the early 1840s. For decades, American merchants in China had requested greater U.S. government presence, but these requests went ignored until Britain gained new and improved trading rights in the wake of the Opium War in 1842. These new rights by their rivals forced American politicians either to move to formalize trade relations with China and secure similar privileges, or to face the possibility of the loss of a potentially large market to the British. . . .

Early American trade with China has been well documented. Emerging from their newly won independence into a world devoid of the advantages of British colonial marketplaces, the now free American merchants were forced to find new markets. The profitable markets in the Atlantic and the East Indies remained restricted to subjects of the British Empire, which forced American merchants to go anywhere and everywhere else. As J. N. Reynolds, the diarist of the four-year voyage of the USS *Potomac* into the Pacific Ocean in the early 1830s, put it, "When the war of our revolution had been so gloriously terminated in establishment of our independence, that the maritime spirit and intelligence of our own merchants, no longer shackled by oppressive colonial restrictions, looked abroad to all parts of the globe." In 1784, the first American merchant ship—the *Empress of China*—reached Canton [Guangzhou] carrying ginseng and returning with black tea. The cost of the voyage came to around $120,000, while returns yielded an insubstantial $37,727. Although not profitable, it captured the imagination of the American merchant community, so that by the end of the decade American trade in Canton had become firmly established. . . . By 1801, at least fourteen American merchant ships took part in the fur trade, buying pelts from northwestern American Indians to shuttle to China and sell for high profits and returning to New York loaded with tea. High profits attracted more traders so that prior to the outbreak of the War of 1812, over forty American merchant ships frequented Canton each year, delivering almost $6 million worth of U.S. goods annually. . . .

U.S. trade with China resumed with increasing vigor after the lull due to British military activity against American merchants during the War of 1812. By the early 1830s, for example, over sixty U.S. ships visited Canton yearly, exchanging over US$8 million in trade annually. . . .

Despite this interest in the East, the U.S. government did not concern itself directly with China. Decades of American merchant and consular requests for government involvement and diplomatic action failed to elicit even a response from the State Department. This was in part due to the fact that the United States was still small and government resources limited—the government had not the funds to freely spend on diplomacy. But furthermore, a positive government role in the private sphere stood against the philosophical convictions of Americans who railed against monarchical control and the invasion of the state into the affairs of its citizens.

Yet there would come a point—indeed many points in time—in which the state needed to play a positive role not only to guarantee economic advantages for its subjects but also for the sake of its very own survival. . . .

As Americans' interaction and fascination with China grew, conflicts with the Chinese government arose which became more than just grievances, and actually hindered Americans conducting trade in China. There were no set taxes or duties in China, but rather a collection of fees that fluctuated arbitrarily. On top of these trade fees, items such as measurement duties for the size of the ship, a "cumshaw tax" in the form of extralegal fees and percentages to Chinese officials, and linguist and comprador fees also were paid out to the Chinese. For example, the owner of the ship *Lion* from New York had a fine of $2,000 charged to him in 1816 "by the Hoppo [the Western name for the Chinese official in charge of trade at Canton] for suspicion of smuggling on board ship," which his Chinese trade partner said he had better pay without complaint. On top of this, the Chinese government placed various restrictions on trade, such as the prohibition of ships carrying only specie, trading in opium, or the export of bullion or rice. And saltpeter—a key ingredient in the making of gunpowder—could only be sold to the government. Furthermore, the government put strict limitations on the movement of foreign merchants. This became a serious issue among all foreign merchants doing business in China, not just Americans, as they were confined to only the single port of Canton to trade and could not enter the cities, could not bring women, and were limited in the number of servants they employed. All this created a general feeling of inequality and resentment among all foreign merchants residing and doing business in China. . . .

From 1839 to 1842, Britain engaged China in what became known as the Opium War. Facing the same confining conditions of trade and movement in China as their American counterparts, Britain did not fail to press the case through military pressure when the opportunity presented itself. Acting on the "illegal" seizure of British opium bound for the China market, the British government demanded redress, and failing to get it, shelled Canton and sent gunboats north toward the Chinese capital. As part of the settlement of the war, signed in 1842 as the Nanjing Treaty, Britain secured for its merchants a host of trade privileges, including greater access to Chinese markets through the opening of more ports to British ships.

Cooperation between Britain and the United States in exploiting China was not a feature of the Anglo-American relationship during this war. In fact, American suspicion increased as Britain prepared for hostilities against China in 1839. Catching word of the impending British blockade of Canton in early 1840, U.S. Consul P. W. Snow wrote a stern letter to the senior officer commanding the British fleet: "I now enter my most solemn protests against the establishment of a blockade so illegal, and consequently, unjust. And I do hereby declare, in behalf of my Government, that I shall hold the Government of Great Britain responsible for any act of violence on citizens of the United States, or their property." Or Cushing, who took the floor in the House in March 1840 and decried not the behavior and attitude of the Chinese but rather British action, and who denounced rumors that the United States was "to join heart and hand with the British Government, and endeavor to obtain commercial treaties from the authorities in China." Such a disposition of cooperation, Cushing said, "is a great misconception. . . . God forbid that I should entertain the idea of co-operating with the British Government in the purpose—if purpose it have—of upholding the base cupidity and violence, and high handed infraction of all law, human and divine, which have characterized the operations of the British, individually and collectively in the seas of China."

Conflict between Britain and China did, however, provoke new calls for action by Americans in China. On the eve of British hostilities. American merchants sent a number of pressing letters to Washington politicians warning of a possible British monopoly and requesting immediate government diplomatic and naval support. The first of these letters, dated May 25, 1839, and signed by eight American merchants, recounts the beginnings of the Opium War then stirring between Britain and China, and how, as Western merchants, they had been caught in the middle. The merchants' letter relates how Chinese officials seized and destroyed British opium, made the Americans prisoners in their own factories, and threatened them with severe penalties for refusing to sign a bond prohibiting the trade of opium, the breaking of which would sentence the trader to death. Vexed at the "injustice of China to arbitrarily end opium trade and seize property," the merchants drew up a list of six demands for the U.S. government to press upon China. These demands included a minister in Beijing, fixed tariffs, a system of warehouses, opening of more ports, compensation for the loss of trade, and only the enactment of U.S. laws for American citizens. . . .

It was at this point, then, that U.S. politicians began to take an intense interest in the affairs of China and the rights of its merchants. Certainly trade with China had grown to a point at which it was "only exceeded by that of trade with Britain, France and Spain," as Congressman Cushing pointed out in 1840 in a letter to the secretary of state and copied to the president. Trade, and the facilitation of trade, did play a role in the U.S. decision to secure its own treaty with China. As Cushing said, "I feel strongly persuaded that the foremost . . . [illegible] . . . is to enter into relations with China." But Britain loomed large. When the House Committee on Foreign Affairs, on which Cushing sat as a leading Whig, passed a resolution on February 7, 1840, requesting all White House and Treasury reports on China, it also called for an investigation into British intentions in China. Thus, the British threat in combination with growing trade drew American attention to this issue. . . .

The next January (1841), as hostilities between China and Britain raged, President Martin Van Buren and Secretary of State John Forsyth held a special meeting with Peter Parker, a Protestant medical missionary who had lived in China since 1834. Parker had returned home for a visit and to argue the need for an official diplomatic treaty between the United States and China. He met later that month with Daniel Webster—who would become the secretary of state with the new administration in March—and explained "the expediency of improving the present unprecedented Crisis in the relation of this Government and China, to Send a *Minister Plenipotentiary, direct and without delay to the Court of Taou Kwang* [Daoguang, the emperor of China]." Parker met again with the highest echelons of the U.S. government before he returned to China, holding audience with President Tyler and Secretary Webster on September 14, 1841. Congressman John Quincy Adams, whom Parker visited after his meeting, wrote, "Dr. Parker said . . . he had seen the President, who assured him that he had his eye fixed upon China, and would avail himself of any favorable opportunity to commence negotiation with the Celestial Empire."

U.S. merchants cried vehemently in their letters, and politicians passed resolutions in Congress, yet still the U.S. government took no action to actively address the situation in China. Not until the British signed the first commercial treaty with China in August 1842 did the U.S. administration find itself in a position where it could no longer afford to remain diplomatically aloof from developments. This resulted in the president's special message to Congress, drafted by Webster, requesting funds to send to China what would become the Cushing mission. . . .

Caleb Cushing takes center stage in the formation of early U.S. China policy, if not stealing the show. As a representative in the U.S. Congress, he was one of the first politicians to argue for a U.S. government presence in China to protect the interests of American merchants. He was a close friend of both President Tyler and Secretary of State Webster, and served as an adviser to both men. The speeches and documents of the president and secretary of state in their own arguments for a China mission reflect the arguments and at times even wording of Cushing's private correspondence with each of them. It thus comes as no surprise to find Cushing leading the mission to China and his signature on the treaty beside his Chinese counterpart's.

As important an agent as Cushing was in the formation of U.S. China policy, we must view the man not as an individual subject who promoted and developed policy, but rather as the embodiment of the forces and attitudes that gave rise to the policy. Cushing represents both literally and figuratively the interests of Americans in China and their Anglophobic sentiment. As a U.S. congressman he represented the interests of his Massachusetts constituents, most of whom owed their wealth and prosperity to overseas trade. As the eldest son of a merchant family, he had personal ties with the China trade. His father had a trading establishment in Oregon, which . . . was poised to access the China market, and his cousin, J. P. Cushing, was head of Perkins and Company, one of the largest American merchant houses in China. Furthermore, Cushing, like many of his contemporaries, held the deep convictions of the moral supremacy of the United States and its destiny to expand to all quarters of the earth through the strength and character of its people, not the power of its government. Likewise, his bitter and often rapacious hatred of the British resounded the sentiments of most Americans. In Caleb Cushing, therefore, we find not an exception who bent the age to his will, but rather the embodiment of Americans' interests, ideologies, and desires through which America's China policy was articulated. . . .

Tyler admired Cushing's vast intellect, and constantly called on him asking for advice and comments on issues on everything from foreign affairs to the postal system in the northeastern United States. Cushing visited the White House frequently to meet with Tyler, often joining him for dinner with other distinguished guests. With Webster, Cushing had an even closer relationship. He would dine at Webster's home at least once a week, and between 1837 and 1843 Cushing lent Webster upward of $10,000 dollars with no mention of interest or date of repayment. Through these intimate relationships with the country's most powerful men, Cushing became integral in the formation of policy, and his views on China resonated with both the secretary of state and the president. For these policymakers the time had come to act; Cushing argued that the United States could no longer passively observe the China trade and hope that its merchants succeed. Now that the British had taken the initiative and gained an advantage in the Far East, the day was coming for a showdown in the Pacific between the old West and the new. "The British government," Cushing wrote to President Tyler on December 27, 1842, "has succeeded in forcing China to admit British vessels into five ports in the Chinese Empire and to cede to England in perpetual sovereignty a commercial depots . . . [illegible] . . . on the coast of China." If the United States did not act in the Far East, Cushing warned, the British would seize Japan and Hawaii, giving them control of the Pacific "to the immense future peril, not only of our territory possessions, but of all our vast commerce on the Pacific." Cushing recommended dispatching a mission to China to negotiate a commercial treaty for the United States. Three days later, in a special message to Congress, Tyler announced the Pacific Ocean and Hawaii within the U.S. sphere of influence, effectively extending the Monroe Doctrine to the Pacific, and asked Congress for funds for a commissioner to reside in China. . . .

The significance of the British treaty with China was not lost on Washington policymakers. Former Secretary of State, President, and now Chairman of the House Committee on Foreign Affairs, John Quincy Adams, took up the cause of pushing for official relations with China. Just months after his meetings with Peter Parker in 1841, for example, he delivered a speech before the Massachusetts Historical Society on the need to press China to allow diplomatic relations. And in the debates following Tyler's request, although he himself stood on the opposite side of the political divide from the president, Adams led the charge against Tyler's political enemies to secure the necessary funds for a mission for the purpose of "providing the means of future intercourse between the United States and the Government of China." The three-hour debate that ensued in the House on February 21, 1843, touched on the absolute economic necessity for the U.S. government to do all in its power to promote and expand trade with China. As South Carolina Congressman Isaac E. Holmes put it, "The trade of South America and Europe is fixed on an established basis. But, by the opening of intercourse with China, three hundred and twenty millions of people (hitherto shut out from the rest of the world) would be brought within the entire circle of commercial republics." The depression at the end of the 1830s weighed heavily on politicians' minds, and constant concern of a commodity glut forced them to think in terms of new and larger overseas markets. They knew very well that this put them in direct competition with Britain, a race, if you will, for the markets of the world. As Holmes articulated that day, "When England is advancing in this matter, and preparing to take to herself the exclusive benefits of the new state of things in China—is it wise for us to stand still until that nation should have arranged the treaties between herself and China, so as to exclude the United States from all advantages whatever?"

The House approved funds for the mission to China by a vote of ninety-six to fifty-nine, paving the way for what Secretary of State Webster likened to the most important mission in history. The details of the preparation for this mission, and the mission itself, have been thoroughly explored elsewhere. Here it is important to note two developments: that the mission's most vocal advocate, the British-hating Cushing, was chosen to lead the mission, and that the nature of the instructions to Cushing, which were composed by himself and Webster, pertained specifically to securing trading rights weighed in relation to Britain. Through an understanding of the Anglo-American rivalry of the day it becomes clear that the United States acted first and foremost to counter British influence and the perceived threat of British monopoly of markets in East Asia. Viewed in this way, the emphasis of the mission in Cushing's instructions shows not just the United States trying to gain most favored nation status but actively countering the threat of Great Britain:

> A leading object of the mission in which you are now to be engaged is to secure the entry of American ships and cargoes into these ports on terms as favorable as those which are enjoyed by English merchants. . . . It cannot be wrong for you to make known, where not known, that the United States, once a country subject to England, threw off that subjection years ago, asserted its independence, sword in hand, established that independence after a seven years' war, and now meets England upon equal terms upon the ocean and upon the land. . . .

Recognition of the role of Anglo-American rivalry should change the conventional understanding of the development of U.S.-China relations and lead us to revise our premises of Western penetration in China. We can no longer view the wars of aggression against China in the nineteenth century as acts of cooperation among Western powers who worked together to exploit China. Rather, a very real fear of the advantages the other power might secure shaped each country's foreign policy. This went to the very heart of the matter. If Britain secured privileges and monopolized the Pacific market, it would endanger the U.S. economy. This made a mission to China of immediate and utmost importance, just as those in the highest political offices in the United States articulated.

It was under these circumstances that the U.S. government came to establish an independent China policy that had remained unspoken since the beginnings of the Republic: the penetration of and facilitation of access to the China market, over which the U.S. economy would rise or fall. Americans consistently saw their future as one of expansion westward to the markets of East Asia, where the riches of China could be had and the clutches of the Old World discarded. The U.S. government formed domestic policy around this vision, and moved the nation westward in construction of a natural infrastructure to access this market. When the time came in Washington to enter into formal state-to-state relations the United States did so reluctantly, and only under threat of dire economic and political consequences if it remained mute. Here we find the origins of U.S. China policy—not at the turn of the nineteenth century—but born with the Republic and manifest with the Treaty of Wangxia.

The Origins of the U.S.-Japanese Clash

WALTER LAFEBER

[Americans were] propelled across the Pacific by their national credo of "manifest destiny," their growing desire to conquer Asian markets, and—paradoxically—a fear of deepening internal crisis. The slogan of "manifest destiny" had appeared in a feverishly expansionist Democratic Party newspaper in 1845 that demanded the conquering of Oregon, even if it meant war with Great Britain which also claimed the territory. The slogan came to mean that Americans ("with the calm confidence of a

Christian holding 4 aces," as frontier writer Mark Twain later phrased it) believed they had God-given rights to spread both their new political institutions and successful commerce across the continent, then into Latin America, and to uplift, among others, the benighted Europeans and Asians.

Driven by principle, Americans aimed also to gain profits. God and Mammon, the larger purpose and the individual's earthly success, were seldom far apart in mainstream American society. (In Japan, to the contrary, when a larger purpose— a Japanese manifest destiny—did emerge, it was seldom confused with individual acquisition.)

Between 1790 and 1853 at least twenty-seven U.S. ships (including three warships) visited Japan, only to be turned away. In 1832, as part of his epochal navigation of the Pacific, Edmund Roberts received orders from the Andrew Jackson administration to make a treaty with Japan, but he died before reaching the islands. Five years later, the *Morrison,* owned by Americans in Canton, tried to enter Japan with the excuse that it was returning shipwrecked Japanese sailors. The crew, however, hoped to Christianize Japanese as well as "trade a little." When shore cannon opened fire, the *Morrison* beat it back to China. In 1846, Commodore James Biddle, head of the newly created U.S. East Asia squadron, carried on heated talks with Japanese officials near Tokyo Bay, only to have them emphasize they had no interest in trading with him and that he need not try a second time. To demonstrate their point, when Biddle tried to force his way onto a Japanese ship a crew member knocked him down.

Meanwhile, U.S. whaling vessels worked the rich Japanese coastal waters and often (as in 1848) forced their shipwrecked sailors on the unkind mercies of Japanese villagers. Whaling became a metaphor for the American crossing of the last great frontier of the Pacific, and the hubris that compelled individuals to challenge those frontiers, when Herman Melville published *Moby-Dick* in 1851. (Later, when Commodore Matthew C. Perry wanted a writer to tell the story of how he opened Japan to the West, Nathaniel Hawthorne recommended Melville. Some 140 years later, Melville's work shaped both United States and Japanese literary studies.)

Japan moved into still sharper focus after 1840 when Shanghai was opened to trade. U.S. ship captains followed the shorter way from California to Shanghai via the north circle route that brought them close to Japan. The 1846–48 conquests of California ports, along with an accelerating industrial and agricultural economic revolution, opened a historic opportunity—but also a potential trap. The opportunity was noted by Secretary of the Treasury Robert Walker in 1848: "By our recent acquisitions in the Pacific, Asia has suddenly become our neighbor, with a placid intervening ocean inviting our steamships upon the track of a commerce greater than that of all Europe combined." In 1851, *Hunt's Merchant Magazine* warned that U.S. production was already furnishing "us with a potential danger: constantly augmenting capital that must seek for new channels of employment." The showdown, *Hunt's* believed, would be against the equally aggressive British and result, happily, in American control of "the whole Oriental trade."

But manifest destiny had its dark side. As vast new territory was rapidly annexed, bitter debate erupted between a pro-slave South and anti-slave North over which section would control the newly conquered West and its ports. When Congress passed the Compromise of 1850, the problem seemed resolved. But many, including Secretary of State Daniel Webster, feared the crisis had been only papered over. In 1850–51, Webster even resorted to blowing up a very minor problem with Austria into a diplomatic crisis so, as he later admitted, he could take American minds off internal dangers and put them on less divisive foreign problems. Webster, moreover, had long been a leader of the Whig Party, whose most powerful members included large mercantile houses deeply involved in international trade. During earlier debates over whether to annex Texas, Webster caught Whig foreign policy priorities perfectly when he proclaimed that one San Francisco was worth twenty Texases. Using U.S. ports as the springboards to Asia became a Websterian principle. As Secretary of State in 1843, he had written the instructions that led to the first U.S. trade treaty with China in 1844. In 1842, moreover, he had penned a declaration, duly announced by President John Tyler, that Hawaii was to be treated by other powers as a special U.S. reserve. Webster was creating the first American policy for the Pacific and China. Japan was next.

In May 1851, Webster heard from Captain John H. Aulick, who was to take command of the East Asia squadron, that the return of seventeen shipwrecked Japanese then in San Francisco might provide the opportunity for "opening commercial relations with Japan." The Secretary of State put Aulick in charge of the mission. Captain James Glynn, an experienced Asian hand, gave President Millard Fillmore and Aulick good advice: do not treat Japanese "as being less civilized than ourselves," do not get into arguments over treatment of U.S. sailors, and do focus only on obtaining a trade treaty. Moreover, Glynn shrewdly added, do not ask for exclusive U.S. privileges, but for access to Japan for all nations. Thus the powerful British will have reason to support, rather than oppose, the American demands.

On May 10, 1851, Webster drafted a letter from President Fillmore to the Japanese Emperor. Assuring the Emperor that Aulick was on no religious enterprise, the letter asked for "friendship and commerce," as well as help (especially coal) for ships that used the northern route to China. Of special interest, Webster's draft of the note emphasized recent U.S. triumphs on land and in technology:

> You know [Fillmore told the Emperor] that the United States of America now extend from sea to sea; that the great countries of Oregon & California are parts of the United States; and that from these countries, which are rich in gold & silver & precious stones, our steamers can reach the shores of your happy land in less than twenty days. . . .
>
> [These ships] must pass along the Coast of your Empire; storms & winds may cause them to be wrecked on your shores, and we ask & expect from your kindness & your greatness, kindness for our men. . . . We wish that our people may be permitted to trade with your people, but we shall not authorize them to break any laws of your Empire. . . .
>
> Your Empire has a great abundance of coal; this is an article which our Steamships, in going from California to China, must use.

Or, as Webster phrased it to Aulick, "The moment is near, when the last link in the chain of oceanic steam-navigation is to be formed," and "our enterprising merchants [should] supply [that] last link in that great chain, which unites all nations of the world." Such a dream propelled many powerful Americans westward across the Pacific after as well as before 1900.

The opening of Japan thus resulted from both the U.S. quest for China's trade and the technological breakthroughs (especially steam) of the 1840s. Japan, as Webster nicely phrased it to a friend, was the key because God had placed coal "in the depths of the Japanese islands for the benefit of the human family." Aulick, however, fumbled his chance to become famous. Charged with mistreating a Brazilian diplomat, Aulick was replaced by Fillmore with Commodore Matthew C. Perry. The commodore initially protested: he preferred commanding the U.S. Mediterranean squadron instead of trying to make yet another attempt to open Japan. Born in Rhode Island in 1794, Perry had served in the War of 1812 under his famous brother, Oliver Hazard Perry (who after one battle in 1813, issued the succinct, soon-to-be-famous announcement: "We have met the enemy, and they are ours"). By 1837 Matthew had risen through the ranks and commanded one of the first U.S. steam warships. During the Mexican War he won some fame for helping to conquer Vera Cruz. . . .

Perry's four ships, the *Susquehanna, Mississippi* (both the new steam type), *Plymouth,* and *Saratoga,* took the long traditional route along the Atlantic, around the Cape of Good Hope, through the Indian Ocean, then to Singapore, Hong Kong, and Shanghai, before approaching Japan. Then they returned briefly to the China coast and, finally, moved into Edo (Tokyo) Bay on July 8, 1853. The Dutch had warned the Shogun's government, the *bakufu,* that Americans were coming, but the Japanese were nevertheless surprised that Perry appeared so soon. Their surprise mounted when the commodore ignored low-level officials and insisted—pointedly as he stood beneath the cannons of his warship—on dealing only with *bugyo* (that is, someone given specific powers directly by the Shogun [Japan's military leader]). Their surprise changed into near horror when they further learned that President Fillmore's letter was addressed to the Emperor [the Shogun's only superior] as if Emperor Komei were a mere equal. The stunned *bakufu* decided to play for time by sending two *bugyo* to accept the letter on July 14. They also used their women to appease and distract the powerful. One U.S. officer recorded that "the inhabitants . . . by the most unmistakable signs invited our intercourse with their women." As the historian Ian Buruma explains, "The Americans had guns, the Japanese lifted their skirts." (A similar drama would be played out in late 1945.) Despite the diversion, Perry rightly feared that the Japanese might stall until he ran short of water and provisions; he would then have to sail away in disgrace. The commodore therefore declared he was departing for China, but promised to return a year later—with force—to receive the Japanese response.

The next move was up to Abe Masahiro, leader of the Shogun's council. A *daimyo* (and hence known and trusted by most other powerful lords of these more than one hundred fiefdoms), Abe was a gentle, well-liked man so shrewd that he had entered the council at age twenty-four in 1843. A politician who sometimes bent too easily and quickly to prevailing political winds, he carefully sounded out the *daimyo* about the proper response to Perry. These men divided. Some knew nothing of dangerous international situations in the western Pacific. But all seemed to agree that under no circumstances could Japan open its empire to foreign traders; their goods would upset the nation's internal order. But how to inform Perry of this when he returned with his warships? Some of the more powerful *daimyo* advised stalling while the *bakufu* built a modern military to deal with the commodore on Japanese terms. A number, indeed, were willing to go to war with the United States—after proper preparations.

These *daimyo* demonstrated a fascinating confidence that Japan could quickly match the West's military technology, as well as perhaps profit from that technology in international trade. ("We have reason to believe that the Americans and Russians have recently learned the art of navigation," a typically confident *daimyo* told Abe; "in what way would the keen and wise men of our empire appear inferior to the Westerners if they got into training from today?") Abe knew that the West, most immediately Perry, would not give Japan the needed time. Any doubt of that disappeared when Admiral [Evfimii] Putiatin . . . led his four Russian ships into Nagasaki harbor just after Perry left Edo. The convenient death of the Shogun gave Abe an excuse to put off Putiatin's demands for a treaty. At the same time, however, Abe removed a two-century rule against building large ships and named an admiral of the new Shogun's navy. A different Japan was beginning to stir.

Putiatin finally departed just before Perry reappeared on February 24, 1854. This time he brought seven impressive ships and sailed straight into sight of Edo— before the edgy Japanese talked him into moving some forty-five miles west to Kanagawa. As the *bakufu* examined the commodore's demands, the two sides demonstrated their friendship by exchanging gifts. Perry's legendary gifts included a telegraph machine, books, maps, and a miniature steam train that the Japanese delighted in operating. On the last day of March 1854, Perry and the Japanese signed a treaty of Kanagawa that contained a dozen provisions. The first promised eternal peace between Japan and America. Another clause opened to U.S. vessels two ports, Shimoda and Hakodate, where shipwrecked sailors could also be taken in. Americans could move around within a roughly fifty-mile radius of these two ports. The *bakufu* agreed to accept a U.S. consul in Japan. But—pointedly—nothing was stated explicitly about trade. Allowing entry into Japan's market was so complex, the Shogun's officials told Perry, that a decision required a great deal of time. The Japanese, in other words, had no intention of following the downhill slide of China into dependency on the wishes and products of foreigners.

After two centuries of dealing only with the Dutch, the 250-year-old Tokugawa Shogunate [the government of the Tokugawa family] opened itself—carefully, narrowly, and fearfully—to the recently born United States. In late 1854, the British, Russians, and Dutch issued successful demands for access to ports that would allow them to match Perry's victory. Again, however, the Europeans received no trading rights. (When Putiatin had to build a vessel to replace one of his Russian warships damaged at sea, the Japanese watched intently and soon afterward produced an exact copy.) The news of Perry's success reached the United States via the *Saratoga,* which made the fastest trip yet between Japan and America. The *New York Times* bragged that the United States had opened Japan to the West, and upstaged the Europeans as well, by using "peaceful diplomacy, to overcome obstacles hitherto considered insurmountable," despite "the sneers, the ridicule, and the contempt" of shortsighted European and American newspapers.

The *Times,* however, was also puzzled. The Japanese "seemed remarkably conversant with the affairs of the United States—knew all about the Mexican War, its occasion and results." Quite true. Even when Perry felt, in the words of a later historian, "like a combination Santa Claus and conjurer" as he demonstrated the toy railroad, the Japanese actually knew all about railways from the *Illustrated London News,* to which the Shogun himself regularly subscribed.

More important, the Japanese had kept up with American affairs since 1797 when officials discovered that the Dutch, short of their own ships, were sneaking U.S. vessels into Nagasaki under the Dutch flag. The Shogunate demanded information about these Americans. The Dutch responded with history lessons that featured the revolt against the British in 1776 (because, the Dutch emphasized, of cruel treatment by the British), the 1787 Constitution, the great George Washington ("a very capable general" whose name has been given to "a new city"), and Thomas Jefferson. The Dutch had supported the new nation in the 1770s, so the Shogun heard a pro-American version of the history. By the 1840s, Japanese used the Dutch to acquire good world geographies, as well as histories, and exploited their contacts with China, where U.S. missionaries were publishing material, to obtain fresh information. Then, too, a few Japanese who had lived in the United States returned home and, as one reported in 1851, announced that Americans were "lewd by nature, but otherwise well-behaved." Japan might have chosen isolation, but its people, including peasants, were about as well educated as the British (and more so than the general French population), and in reality they were not isolated. By 1839 one group of intellectuals was so active in learning from the Dutch and spreading the information that several committed suicide fearing their activities embarrassed their *daimyo* master in the eyes of the Shogun.

The tension illustrated by these suicides—the tension created between the seeking of outside news to protect Japan, yet the fear that spreading of such foreign influence could create disorder, perhaps civil war—shaped the background that foreigners such as Perry never understood. For two centuries, after all, the Tokugawa Shogun had assumed that the tightest relationship existed between foreign and domestic policies. The government had announced, on the basis of its bitter sixteenth-century experience, that Japan's survival and the maintenance of internal order required cutting off the inherently disorderly—and usually uncontrollable—affairs of the outside world. A powerful and influential argument was made by a scholar from the domain of Mito, two days travel from Edo. In 1825, Aizawa Seishisai wrote *New Proposals (Shinron).* His work had been triggered by a Shogunate decree that again, to Aizawa's great satisfaction, banned foreign ships. Aizawa warned that Japanese weakness "for novel gadgets" could "lure ignorant people" to the spell of "treacherous foreigners." The result, he concluded, would be the internal corruption and decay of Japanese society, or outright foreign conquest.

Aizawa had reason to worry. Not only were foreigners trying to penetrate Japan. Of equal importance, his own domain of Mito had long suffered from low agricultural production, natural disasters, and increased taxation. Famine and revolt threatened to spread. After 1750 especially, these economic problems, including natural disasters, forced the Shogun (who was living beyond his means anyway) to tax and borrow. The *daimyo* did the same, and thus the peasants and samurai paid and suffered even more exploitation. A new merchant class (*chonin*) meanwhile arose to provide goods for the nation's growing population—and also make loans to the once-proud samurai. The *chonin* began to break apart the feudal restrictions on trade, land transfer, and certain kinds of new production. Mito's changes and unrest encapsulated only a small case study of immense Japanese social problems by 1850.

The samurai, for example, became dissatisfied and restless as the Shogun turned them into bureaucrats. *Chonin* also grew restless; they wanted to rupture the feudal restraints of the *daimyo*. Thus even as Americans, Russians, and British approached from the outside, Tokugawa rule was being internally undermined by spreading frustrations as well as by a rising price inflation caused in part by the Shogun's own overspending.

An intense debate was therefore erupting just as Perry demanded entrance. By the mid-1850s, his appearance helped turn a central part of that debate into the highly dangerous question of how Japan must change in order to deal with "the barbarians." The shock of Perry's timing and success, moreover, transformed a once-restricted discussion into an explosive public argument. The political stakes rose dramatically as several fiefs that had never been fully controlled by the Shogun or the *bakufu* seized on the debate to challenge the *bakufu* and try to solve their growing economic crises by transforming themselves to make their own domains more efficient. The Shogunate began to endure exactly what it had long feared: opening Japan to foreign influences was helping undermine Tokugawa rule and destroying social harmony.

The clash between Japanese and American systems therefore occurred initially not in Manchuria in 1910, or China in the 1930s, or the international market of the 1980s. The clash came with the first appearance of Americans in Edo Bay during 1853–54. The Tokugawa rule had long been under attack. The Americans did not cause these fundamental economic and social problems that struck Japan, but they accelerated the problems and, of special note, created a new and more dangerous political environment in which the *bakufu* had to deal with the crises. For nothing less was happening than an assault on a centuries-old feudal structure that many Japanese assumed to be fundamental for their own happiness. Americans were the cutting edge of a new world, a world that had little use for feudal order; a world that valued social harmony less than individual acquisition; and a world that (unlike the Shogun's) saw its survival resting not on exclusion, but on a manifest destiny that required the opening of ports and markets everywhere.

Abe found himself trying to steer a weakening Japan around a radical turn in its history. He had to steer, moreover, as competing groups grabbed for control. On one side was the Shogun Iesada (1853–58) who, out of a sense for survival, wanted to exclude the Americans while building up military power at home. (The term *Shogun* could be translated as "barbarian-fighting general.") He was supported by his only superior, Emperor Komei (who ruled in 1846–67). Komei's ardent xenophobia merely moderated in the 1860s. On the other side were Ii Naosuke, a tough, powerful *daimyo* of Hikone, and Hotta Masayoshi, *daimyo* of Shimoda. They believed that increased contacts, even treaties, with foreigners were inevitable, so should be turned to advantage. Amid this power struggle, another more serious fight intensified: outlying areas, especially Choshu, in the extreme west, and Satsuma, in the far south, had never been fully integrated into Tokugawa, Japan. Led by Choshu, these areas began a major assault on the weakened *bakufu*'s powers. The challenges to the central government were supported by some intellectuals and political activists who saw the American Revolution as exemplifying the kind of radical change needed to replace the decaying Shogunate. Many of these writers wished to work with the Americans. But some (like Nakaoka Shintaro) thought the 1776 Revolution simply a splendid example of how to expel foreigners.

Abe and the Shogun thus not only had to deal with the Westerners but to develop a policy that stood the beliefs of two centuries on their head—that is, deal with foreigners without bringing about a war while reconciling the internal debates and facing down the Choshu-Satsuma challenge. All of this suddenly came to a head on August 21, 1856, when a U.S. consul, Townsend Harris, appeared at Shimoda. Harris announced that the Japanese must now sign a trade agreement with the United States. . . .

The key official who was to deal with Harris belonged to the . . . camp [which urged making a deal with the Americans]. Hotta Masayoshi, soon to be the most powerful member of the *bakufu*, was also one of the more moderate. Hotta had somehow gained extensive knowledge of "Dutch studies"—that is, events in the West. He wrote later in 1857 that "military power always springs from national wealth," and that such wealth could be found "principally in trade and commerce." Japan consequently had "to conclude friendly alliances . . . send ships to foreign countries everywhere and . . . copy the foreigners where they are at their best and so repair our own shortcomings." By March 1857, Hotta's approach led to the first substantive talks with Harris. The consul was plagued by cholera, little medical help, no news from U.S. ships on the China coast, and no assistance whatever from Washington. He nevertheless warned the Shimoda officials that he had been instructed to tell them that if they continued to delay, the President would ask Congress for the authority to use "arguments . . . they [the Japanese] could not resist." In June, Harris excitedly recorded that he had broken through. Shimoda officials agreed to a convention that opened Nagasaki to U.S. ships, allowed American residency and a vice consul at Hakodate, enabled Harris to move around Japan more freely, and settled the exchange rate for Japanese money at a more favorable level. But this agreement only prepared the way for the most difficult step: traveling to Edo and negotiating a full trade treaty with Hotta. . . .

On December 7, 1857, Harris had a brief, formal, historic meeting with the Shogun, who expressed pleasure with the consul's presence and declared, according to the interpreter, that "intercourse shall be continued forever." But detailed talks with officials on December 12 turned frustrating. Harris notably opened them by explaining two of the beliefs that drove U.S. policy, then and since: because of the technological breakthrough (of steam locomotion), "Japan would be forced to abandon her exclusive policy"; her wealth and happiness would grow most rapidly "when developed by the action of free trade." Otherwise the powers would "send powerful fleets" to force Japan open. Hotta thanked Harris for the thoughts, then added "that the Japanese never acted as promptly on business of importance as the Americans" because "many persons had to be consulted." Weeks dragged by. Harris began to complain . . . [of] the mysteries of the Japanese language: it "does not possess either singular or plural, has no relative pronoun, nor is the use of the antecedent known. . . . I never shall get to the bottom of the deceptions of the Japanese." (Later observers also helped explain Harris's frustration by noting that, having considerable mistrust of verbal skills, a Japanese preferred to communicate feeling indirectly and even without language. If these signals were communicated, the receiver, not the sender, was blamed for lacking sensitivity and intelligence if they were not picked up.)

Finally in March 1858, agreement was nearly complete, a result of Hotta's influence and ominous British and French warmaking in China, when again Japanese internal divisions stalled the talks. In June, Hotta carried the day. The treaty, signed initially on July 29, 1858, opened five ports to trade between then and 1863, including Nagasaki and Kanagawa (later Yokohama); allowed foreigners into Osaka and Edo; permitted a resident minister in Edo and a Japanese minister in Washington with each country's consuls at the other's open ports; protected Americans through extraterritoriality (that is, they would be tried only in American courts); and imposed an import and export tariff that was fixed extremely low so the Japanese could not manipulate it to keep out foreign goods. Americans could enjoy freedom of religion as well as own land for business, residential, and even religious purposes. (Later, in 1859, Harris tried to obtain a provision guaranteeing religious freedom for the Japanese themselves, but the *bakufu* quickly rejected it.) Oddly, one of the great U.S. diplomatic principles, that of most-favored-nation—that any trading rights Japan gave to one nation automatically went to others—was not included. (This omission was remedied in August when the British, using Harris's secretary and treaty, opened trade relations with Japan and obtained most-favored-nation rights.)

Of special significance was a provision in Article III:

> Americans may freely buy from Japanese and sell to them any articles that either may have for sale, without the intervention of any Japanese officers in such purchase or sale.

Not for the last time, Americans, with deep suspicions about state power, tried to remove that power as much as possible in their commerce with Japan. They enjoyed little success in this attempt. Nor could they become involved in Japan's internal commerce, for foreign traders were mostly confined to a residential area near the ports.

The Dutch and Russians as well as the British followed Harris into the Japanese market during August 1858. The American, meanwhile, followed up his triumph by having a physical breakdown that had been building since August 1856. Delirious for days, he was probably saved because the Shogun ordered Japan's best physicians to attend him. Harris nevertheless had his historic treaty and even a letter for President James Buchanan from the Shogun, the first letter sent by a Shogun to a foreign leader in 240 years.

Harris knew his demands had divided the *bakufu,* but he did not realize he was helping to destroy the 250-year-old Tokugawa rule itself. For his demands, coupled with the growing internal unrest, had led to a crisis and Hotta's removal in June 1858. He was replaced by Ii Naosuke (1815–1860), a powerful *daimyo* of Hikone. Tough, determined, relentless, Ii became a virtual dictator of the *bakufu.* Assuming power in mid-1858, he discovered that the Emperor, sitting in his majesty at Kyoto, feared the proposed treaty. "The American affair is a great sorrow to our divine land," he had told Hotta. The treaty "would disturb the ideas of our people and make it impossible to preserve lasting tranquility." Many *daimyo* sided with the Emperor. But most of them, Ii learned, believed the treaty to be inevitable. The alternative of war with the Western powers was unthinkable.

Ii, moreover, heard in July 1858 that British and French warships had finished their work in China and might be heading for Japan. He decided therefore to sign the treaty with Harris in July. The Emperor had not changed his mind, but he reluctantly went along out of fear that the Westerners would play on the divisions between his court in Kyoto and the Shogun in Edo. The rebels who hoped to keep out the "hairy barbarians" and weaken the Shogun never forgave Ii for easing the foreigners' entry into Japan. On March 3, 1860, eighteen samurai from the rebellious *daimyo* at Mito, assisted by Shinto priests, attacked Ii outside the Imperial Palace. Because it was raining, Ii's sixty guards had covered their sword hilts. Before they could uncover their swords, Ii lay dead and four guards were dying. The attackers were killed or captured, but the death of the decisive Ii left a power vacuum that soon proved fatal for the Shogun himself. Harris's treaty was already casting long shadows.

🌐 *F U R T H E R   R E A D I N G*

Suzanne Wilson Barnett and John K. Fairbank, eds., *Christianity in China: Early Protestant Writings* (1985)
Michael A. Barnhart and Edward Arnold, *Japan and the World Since 1868* (1995)
W. G. Beasley, *Japan Encounters the Barbarian* (1995)
Ellsworth C. Carlson, *The Foochow Missionaries, 1850–1880* (1974)
Paul A. Cohen, *China and Christianity* (1963)
Warren I. Cohen, *America's Response to China* (2000)
Peter Duus, ed., *The Japanese Discovery of America* (1997)
Patricia Buckley Ebrey, *Cambridge Illustrated History of China* (1996)
John K. Fairbank, *The United States and China* (1983)
———, *Trade and Diplomacy on the China Coast: The Opening of the Treaty Ports, 1842–1854* (1964)
Peter W. Fay, "The Protestant Mission and the Opium War," *Pacific Historical Review,* 40 (1971), 145–161
Wayne Flint and Gerald W. Buckley, *Taking Christianity to China* (1997)
Arrell Morgan Gibson, *Yankees in Paradise* (1993)
Jonathan Goldstein, *Philadelphia and the China Trade, 1682–1846* (1978)
Andrew Gordon, *A Modern History of Japan* (2003)
Edward V. Gulick, *Peter Parker and the Opening of China* (1973)
Paul Harris, *Nothing but Christ* (1999)
Joseph M. Henning, *Outposts of Civilization* (2000) (on Japan)
Curtis T. Henson Jr., *Commissioners and Commodores: The East India Squadron and American Diplomacy in China* (1982)
Michael H. Hunt, *The Making of a Special Relationship: The United States and China to 1914* (1983)
William R. Hutchinson, *Errand to the World: American Protestant Thought and Foreign Missions* (1987)
Donald D. Johnson, *The United States in the Pacific* (1995)
Phyllis Forbes Kerr, ed., *Letters from China* (1996)
Ralph S. Kuykendall, *The Hawaiian Kingdom* (1967)
Elizabeth L. Malcolm, "The *Chinese Repository* and Western Literature on China, 1800 to 1850," *Modern Asian Studies,* 7 (1973), 165–178
Stuart C. Miller, "The American Trader's Image of China, 1785–1840," *Pacific Historical Review,* 36 (1967), 375–395
———, *The Unwelcome Immigrant: The American Image of the Chinese, 1785–1882* (1969)
Samuel Eliot Morison, *"Old Bruin"* (1967) (on Perry)
Charles E. Neu, *The Troubled Encounter* (1975)
John Curtis Perry, *Facing West* (1994)
David Pletcher, *The Diplomacy of Involvement* (2001)
Murray A. Rubenstein, "The Wars They Never Wanted: American Missionaries' Use of *The Chinese Repository* before the Opium War," *American Neptune,* 58 (1988), 271–282
John Schroeder, *Matthew Calbraith Perry* (2001)
———, *Shaping a Maritime Empire: The Commercial and Diplomatic Role of the American Navy, 1829–1861* (1985)
Eileen P. Scully, *Bargaining with the State from Afar* (2001) (on China Treaty Port System)

Kenneth E. Shewmaker, "Forging the 'Great Chain': Daniel Webster and the Origins of
     American Foreign Policy Toward East Asia and the Pacific, 1841–1852," *Proceedings of
     the American Philosophical Society,* 129 (September 1985), 225–255
———— et al., eds., *The Papers of Daniel Webster* (1983–1987)
Jonathan Spence, *The Search for Modern China* (1990)
Merze Tate, *The United States and the Hawaiian Kingdom* (1965)
James C. Thomson et al., *Sentimental Imperialists* (1981)
John E. Van Sant, *Pacific Pioneers* (2000) (on Japanese pioneers)
Paul A. Varg, *New England and Foreign Relations, 1789–1850* (1983)
Peter Booth Wiley with Korogi Ichiro, *Yankees in the Land of the Gods* (1991) (on Perry)

The Diplomacy of
the Civil War

American expansionism faltered in the 1850s and 1860s when sectionalism bedeviled the nation. After Union and Confederate armies began to bloody themselves and ravage the countryside, expansionists on both sides worried more about their survival than about expanding empire. Southern diplomats busied themselves with winning European favor for their secession and independence. Northern diplomats threw their energy into preventing European interference. Whereas Confederate leaders worked to internationalize the conflict, Union leaders strove to contain the conflagration and to warn Europeans—including the French who occupied Mexico—against taking advantage of American weakness to extend their interests in the Western Hemisphere.

The competition centered on Britain. Jefferson Davis's Confederacy sought to woo the British with "King Cotton" diplomacy, believing that British industry was dependent on southern cotton exports and could be persuaded to back Confederate independence because of economic self-interest. Abraham Lincoln's Union tried to foil such arrangements with a blockade of southern ports, sparking controversy with London over maritime rights. Lincoln had tagged the rebellion a domestic insurrection. Under international law this denied the Confederacy status as a belligerent power. But the North's declaration of a blockade constituted an act of war and affected neutral powers. When London proclaimed neutrality, it implicitly acknowledged southern belligerency—including the rebel states' right to borrow and trade. The British building of war vessels, or "iron clads," for the Confederacy further angered unionists and sparked Anglophobia throughout the North. But Prime Minister Lord Palmerston's government stopped short of extending official diplomatic recognition to the rebel government, and it ultimately opted against a European mediation of the conflict—a move that also would have implied recognition.

Civil War diplomacy hinged on more than economic and legal factors. British public opinion divided over which side to favor. Devoted liberals, including many of Lancashire's textile workers, endured the cotton embargo because they sympathized with the North's antislavery stance. Their commitment grew following Lincoln's Emancipation Proclamation, issued on September 22, 1862. Conservatives tended to scorn northern democracy, felt a sense of kinship toward the South's class-based,

265

slave oligarchy, and perceived the emancipation of slaves as a northern attempt to incite race war. Lincoln's secretary of state William H. Seward attempted to intimidate British officials with rhetorical bluster, including threats of war if London granted recognition to the Confederacy. The administration, however, also made timely concessions to Britain's maritime interests.

Whether the British responded to northern diplomacy, southern ineptitude, the political influence of pro-American citizens, the political and cultural dynamics of race, or a cautious respect for northern military power is the stuff of debate among historians.

🌎 *D O C U M E N T S*

The South's faith in "King Cotton" is evident in Document 1, a speech given before the U.S. Senate by James H. Hammond of South Carolina on March 4, 1858. As Congress confronted "Bleeding Kansas" and southerners contemplated secession, Hammond thundered that "Cotton is king" and predicted that an independent South would be destined for greatness. Three years later, as fratricidal war approached, Secretary of State William H. Seward advised President Lincoln in Document 2, dated April 1, 1861, to take the drastic action of fighting either Spain or France so as to cause southern secessionists to rally around the flag and rejoin the Union. Lincoln discreetly buried the proposal and reminded his impertinent secretary that the president was in charge. Document 3 is President Lincoln's controversial proclamation of blockade, issued shortly after the outbreak of war on April 19, 1861. In Document 4, Seward instructs Ambassador Charles Francis Adams in England to warn the British not to deal with the Confederate commissioners in London—"fraternize with our domestic enemy"—unless they wish an Anglo-American war. In the fall of 1861, the prospect of a rupture in U.S. relations with Britain loomed when James Mason and another Confederate agent were boldly seized from the British vessel *Trent* by Captain Charles Wilkes of the U.S. Navy. The British howled in protest, while northerners cheered Wilkes for his audacity. In the end the agents were set free. On January 9, 1862, Senator Charles Sumner of Massachusetts made the best of it by slamming the Confederates, applauding Wilkes's noble if illegal act, and ribbing the British for finally endorsing a traditional American principle against boarding neutral ships. Sumner's comments are reprinted as Document 5.

The Lincoln administration feared that conservative European powers would exploit the crisis and extend their interests in the Western Hemisphere. When Great Britain, France, and Spain launched a joint military expedition against Mexico after the Mexican government suspended payments on foreign loans in July 1861, Napoleon III of France capitalized on the chaos and created a puppet regime in Mexico City, led by Maximilian of Austria. Secretary Seward warned, in a letter of March 3, 1862, to American ambassador Charles Francis Adams in Great Britain (Document 6), that Europeans could never install a monarchy in Mexico against the will of the Mexican people and the United States. A turning point in the war and in Anglo-American relations came in September 1862, when the Union army scored a battlefield victory at Antietam Creek near the village of Sharpsville, Maryland. President Lincoln took the opportunity on September 22 to issue the Emancipation Proclamation, which, when it took effect on January 1, 1863, declared slaves residing in rebel territory to be free. The proclamation was meant to add moral clarity to the North's war aims, encourage black slaves to enlist with Union forces, and undercut those in Britain who favored intervention. The famous edict is reprinted here as Document 7. British arms sales to the Confederacy nonetheless continued to draw the wrath of the Lincoln administration. Document 8 is Charles Francis Adams's firm protest to the British against their delivery of ram-equipped "iron clads" built at the Laird shipyards—and capable of inflicting serious damage on northern shipping—to the Confederate navy. "It would be superfluous in me to point out to your lordship that this is war," Adams wryly commented.

⊕ D O C U M E N T   1

South Carolina Senator James H. Hammond Thunders: "Cotton Is King," 1858

If we never acquire another foot of territory for the South, look at her. Eight hundred and fifty thousand square miles. As large as Great Britain, France, Austria, Prussia and Spain. Is not that territory enough to make an empire that shall rule the world? With the finest soil, the most delightful climate, whose staple productions none of those great countries can grow, we have three thousand miles of continental sea-shore line so indented with bays and crowded with islands, that, when their shore lines are added, we have twelve thousand miles. Through the heart of our country runs the great Mississippi, the father of waters, into whose bosom are poured thirty-six thousand miles of tributary rivers; and beyond we have the desert prairie wastes to protect us in our rear. Can you hem in such a territory as that? You talk of putting up a wall of fire around eight hundred and fifty thousand square miles so situated! How absurd.

But, in this territory lies the great valley of the Mississippi, now the real, and soon to be the acknowledged seat of the empire of the world. The sway of that valley will be as great as ever the Nile knew in the earlier ages of mankind. We own the most of it. The most valuable part of it belongs to us now; and although those who have settled above us are now opposed to us, another generation will tell a different tale. They are ours by all the laws of nature; slave-labor will go over every foot of this great valley where it will be found profitable to use it, and some of those who may not use it are soon to be united with us by such ties as will make us one and inseparable. The iron horse will soon be clattering over the sunny plains of the South to bear the products of its upper tributaries of the valley to our Atlantic ports, as it now does through the ice-bound North. And there is the great Mississippi, a bond of union made by Nature herself. She will maintain it forever.

On this fine territory we have a population four times as large as that with which these colonies separated from the mother country, and a hundred, I might say a thousand fold stronger. Our population is now sixty per cent greater than that of the whole United States when we entered into the second war of independence. It is as large as the whole population of the United States was ten years after the conclusion of that war, and our own exports are three times as great as those of the whole United States then. Upon our muster-rolls we have a million of men. In a defensive war, upon an emergency, every one of them would be available. At any time, the South can raise, equip, and maintain in the field, a larger army than any Power of the earth can send against her, and an army of soldiers—men brought up on horseback, with guns in their hands. . . .

This document can be found in *Selections from the Letters and Speeches of the Hon. James H. Hammond of South Carolina* (New York: John F. Trow and Co., 1866), pp. 311–312.

But the strength of a nation depends in a great measure upon its wealth, and the wealth of a nation, like that of a man, is to be estimated by its surplus production. You may go to your trashy census books, full of falsehoods and nonsense—they tell you, for example, that in the State of Tennessee, the whole number of house-servants is not equal to that of those in my own house, and such things as that. You may estimate what is made throughout the country from these census books, but it is no matter how much is made if it is all consumed. If a man possess millions of dollars and consumes his income, is he rich? Is he competent to embark in any new enterprises? Can he long build ships or railroads? And could a people in that condition build ships and roads or go to war without a fatal strain on capital? All the enterprises of peace and war depend upon the surplus productions of a people. They may be happy, they may be comfortable, they may enjoy themselves in consuming what they make; but they are not rich, they are not strong. It appears, by going to the reports of the Secretary of the Treasury, which are authentic, that last year the United States exported in round numbers $279,000,000 worth of domestic produce, excluding gold and foreign merchandise re-exported. Of this amount $158,000,000 worth is the clear produce of the South; articles that are not and cannot be made at the North. . . .

With an export of $220,000,000 under the present tariff, the South organized separately would have $40,000,000 of revenue. With one-fourth the present tariff, she would have a revenue with the present tariff adequate to all her wants, for the South would never go to war; she would never need an army or a navy, beyond a few garrisons on the frontiers and a few revenue cutters. It is commerce that breeds war. It is manufactures that require to be hawked about the world, and that give rise to navies and commerce. But we have nothing to do but to take off restrictions on foreign merchandise and open our ports, and the whole world will come to us to trade. They will be too glad to bring and carry us, and we never shall dream of a war. Why the South has never yet had a just cause of war except with the North. Every time she has drawn her sword it has been on the point of honor, and that point of honor has been mainly loyalty to her sister colonies and sister States, who have ever since plundered and calumniated her.

But if there were no other reason why we should never have war, would any sane nation make war on cotton? Without firing a gun, without drawing a sword, should they make war on us we could bring the whole world to our feet. The South is perfectly competent to go on, one, two, or three years without planting a seed of cotton. I believe that if she was to plant but half her cotton, for three years to come, it would be an immense advantage to her. I am not so sure but that after three years' entire abstinence she would come out stronger than ever she was before, and better prepared to enter afresh upon her great career of enterprise. What would happen if no cotton was furnished for three years? I will not stop to depict what every one can imagine, but this is certain: England would topple headlong and carry the whole civilized world with her, save the South. No, you dare not make war on cotton. No power on earth dares to make war upon it. Cotton is king. Until lately the Bank of England was king; but she tried to put her screws as usual, the fall before last, upon the cotton crop, and was utterly vanquished. The last power has been conquered. Who can doubt, that has looked at recent events, that cotton is supreme? When the abuse of credit had destroyed credit and annihilated confidence, when thousands of the strongest commercial houses in the world were coming down, and hundreds of millions of dollars of supposed property evaporating in thin air; when you came to a dead lock, and revolutions were threatened, what brought you up? Fortunately for you it was the commencement of the cotton season, and we have poured in upon you one million six hundred thousand bales of cotton just at the crisis to save you from destruction. That cotton, but for the bursting of your speculative bubbles in the North, which produced the whole of this convulsion, would have brought us $100,000,000. We have sold it for $65,000,000 and saved you. Thirty-five million dollars we, the slaveholders of the South, have put into the charity box for your magnificent financiers, your "cotton lords," your "merchant princes."

D O C U M E N T   2

Secretary of State William H. Seward Presents "Some Thoughts for the President's Consideration," 1861

I would demand explanations from *Spain* and France, categorically, at once.

I would seek explanations from Great Britain and Russia, and send agents into *Canada, Mexico* and *Central America,* to rouse a vigorous continental *spirit of independence* on this continent against European intervention.

> And if satisfactory explanations are not received from Spain and France,
> Would convene Congress and declare war against them
> But whatever policy we adopt, there must be an energetic prosecution of it.
> For this purpose it must be somebody's business to pursue and direct it incessantly.
> Either the President must do it himself, and be all the while active in it; or
> Devolve it on some member of his Cabinet. Once adopted, debates on it must end, and all agree and abide.
> It is not in my especial province.
> But I neither seek to evade nor assume responsibility.

D O C U M E N T   3

President Abraham Lincoln Proclaims a Blockade, 1861

Whereas an insurrection against the Government of the United States has broken out in the States of South Carolina, Georgia, Alabama, Florida, Mississippi, Louisiana, and Texas, and the laws of the United States for the collection of the revenue cannot be effectually executed therein conformably to that provision of the Constitution which requires duties to be uniform throughout the United States:

And whereas a combination of persons engaged in such insurrection, have threatened to grant pretended letters of marque to authorize the bearers thereof to

---

Document 2 can be found in John G. Nicolay and John Hay, eds., *Complete Works of Abraham Lincoln* (New York: Tandy Thomas Co., 1894), VI, pp. 234–236.

Document 3 can be found in James D. Richardson, ed., *A Compilation of Messages and Papers of the Presidents* (New York: Bureau of National Literature, 1900), VI, pp. 14–15.

commit assaults on the lives, vessels, and property of good citizens of the country lawfully engaged in commerce on the high seas and in waters of the United States:

And whereas an Executive Proclamation has been already issued, requiring the persons engaged in these disorderly proceedings to desist therefrom, calling out a militia force for the purpose of repressing the same, and convening Congress in extraordinary session, to deliberate and determine thereon:

Now, therefore, I, Abraham Lincoln, President of the United States, with a view to the same purposes before mentioned, and to the protection of the public peace, and the lives and property of quiet and orderly citizens pursuing their lawful occupations, until Congress shall have assembled and deliberated on the said unlawful proceedings, or until the same shall have ceased, have further deemed it advisable to set on foot a blockade of the ports within the States aforesaid, in pursuance of the laws of the United States, and of the law of Nations in such case provided. For this purpose a competent force will be posted so as to prevent entrance and exit of vessels from the ports aforesaid. If, therefore, with a view to violate such blockade, a vessel shall approach, or shall attempt to leave either [sic] of the said ports, she will be duly warned by the Commander of one of the blockading vessels, who will endorse on her register the fact and date of such warning, and if the same vessel shall again attempt to enter or leave the blockaded port, she will be captured and sent to the nearest convenient port, for such proceedings against her and her cargo as prize, as may be deemed advisable.

And I hereby proclaim and declare that if any person, under the pretended authority of the said States, or under any other pretense, shall molest a vessel of the United States, or the persons or cargo on board of her, such person will be held amenable to the laws of the United States for the prevention and punishment of piracy.

DOCUMENT 4

Seward Warns the British, 1861

This government considers that our affairs in Europe have reached a crisis, in which it is necessary for it to take a decided stand, on which not only its immediate measures, but its ultimate and permanent policy can be determined and defined. At the same time it neither means to menace Great Britain nor to wound the susceptibilities of that or any other European nation. That policy is developed in this paper. . . .

[U.S. minister in London George] Dallas, in a brief dispatch of May 2, tells us that [Foreign Minister] Lord John Russell recently requested an interview with him on account of the solicitude which his lordship felt concerning the effect of certain measures represented as likely to be adopted by the President. In that conversation the British Secretary told Mr. Dallas that the three representatives of the Southern Confederacy were then in London, that Lord John Russell had not yet seen them, but that he was not unwilling to see them unofficially. He further informed Mr. Dallas that an understanding exists between the British and French governments which would lead both to take one and the same course as to recognition. . . .

This document can be found in U.S. Department of State, *Papers Relating to the Foreign Relations of the United States, 1861* (Washington, D.C.: Government Printing Office, 1861), pp. 87–90.

Intercourse of any kind with the so-called commissioners is liable to be construed as a recognition of the authority which appointed them. Such intercourse would be none the less hurtful to us for being called unofficial, and it might be even more injurious, because we should have no means of knowing what points might be resolved by it. Moreover, unofficial intercourse is useless and meaningless if it is not expected to ripen into official intercourse and direct recognition. . . . You will, in any event, desist from all intercourse whatever, unofficial as well as official, with the British government, so long as it shall continue intercourse of either kind with the domestic enemies of this country. When intercourse shall have been arrested for this cause, you will communicate with this department and receive further directions. . . .

As to the blockade, you will say that by our own laws and the laws of nature, and the laws of nations, this government has a clear right to suppress insurrection. An exclusion of commerce from national ports which have been seized by insurgents, in the equitable form of blockade, is a proper means to that end. You will not insist that our blockade is to be respected, if it be not maintained by a competent force; but passing by that question as not now a practical or at least an urgent one, you will add that the blockade is now, and it will continue to be, so maintained, and therefore we expect it to be respected by Great Britain. You will add that we have already revoked the *exequatur* of a Russian consul who had enlisted in the military service of the insurgents, and we shall dismiss or demand the recall of every foreign agent, consular or diplomatic, who shall either disobey the Federal laws or disown the Federal authority.

As to the recognition of the so-called Southern Confederacy, it is not to be made a subject of technical definition. It is, of course, direct recognition to publish an acknowledgment of the sovereignty and independence of a new power. It is direct recognition to receive its ambassadors, ministers, agents or commissioners, officially. A concession of belligerent rights is liable to be construed as a recognition of them. No one of these proceedings will pass unquestioned by the United States in this case. . . .

As to the treatment of privateers in the insurgent service, you will say that this is a question exclusively our own. We treat them as pirates. They are our own citizens, or persons employed by our citizens, preying on the commerce of our country. If Great Britain should choose to recognize them as lawful belligerents, and give them shelter from our pursuit and punishment, the laws of nations afford an adequate and proper remedy. . . .

These positions are not elaborately defended now, because to vindicate them would imply a possibility of our waiving them.

We are not insensible of the grave importance of this occasion. We see how, upon the result of the debate in which we are engaged, a war may ensue between the United States and one, two, or even more European nations. War in any case is as exceptional from the habits as it is revolting from the sentiments of the American people. But if it come it will be fully seen that it results from the action of Great Britain, not our own; that Great Britain will have decided to fraternize with our domestic enemy either without waiting to hear from you our remonstrances and our warnings, or after having heard them. War in defence of national life is not immoral, and war in defence of independence is an inevitable part of the discipline of nations.

🌐 *D O C U M E N T   5*

Senator Charles Sumner Taunts John Bull Over the *Trent* Affair, 1862

Two old men and two younger associates, recently taken from the British mail packet *Trent* on the high seas by order of Captain Wilkes of the United States Navy, and afterwards detained in custody at Fort Warren, have been liberated and placed at the disposition of the British Government. This has been done at the instance of that Government, courteously conveyed, and founded on the assumption that the original capture of these men was an act of violence which was an affront to the British flag, and a violation of international law. This is a simple outline of the facts. But in order to appreciate the value of this precedent, there are other matters which must be brought into view.

These two old men were citizens of the United States, and for many years Senators. One was the author of the fugitive slave bill, and the other was the chief author of the filibustering system which has disgraced our national name and disturbed our national peace. Occupying places of trust and power in the service of their country, they conspired against it, and at last the secret traitors and conspirators became open rebels. The present rebellion, now surpassing in proportions and also in wickedness any rebellion in history, was from the beginning quickened and promoted by their untiring energies. That country to which they owed love, honor, and obedience, they betrayed and gave over to violence and outrage. Treason, conspiracy, and rebellion, each in succession, have acted through them. The incalculable expenditures which now task our national resources, the untold derangement of affairs not only at home but also abroad, the levy of armies almost without an example, the devastation of extended regions of territory, the plunder of peaceful ships on the ocean, and the slaughter of fellow-citizens on the murderous battle-field; such are some of the consequences proceeding directly from them. To carry forward still further the gigantic crime of which they were so large a part, these two old men, with their two younger associates, stole from Charleston on board a rebel steamer, and, under cover of darkness and storm, running the blockade and avoiding the cruisers in that neighborhood, succeeded in reaching the neutral island of Cuba, where, with open display and the knowledge of the British consul, they embarked on board the British mail packet the *Trent,* bound for St. Thomas, whence they were to embark for England, in which kingdom one of them was to play the part of embassador of the rebellion, while the other was to play the same part in France. The original treason, conspiracy, and rebellion of which they were so heinously guilty, were all continued on this voyage, which became a prolongation of the original crime, destined to still further excess, through their embassadorial pretensions, which, it was hoped, would array two great nations against the United States, and enlist them openly in behalf of an accursed slaveholding rebellion. While on their way, the embassadors were arrested by Captain Wilkes, of the United States steamer *San Jacinto,* an accomplished officer, already well known by his scientific explorations, who, on this occasion, acted without instructions from his Government. If, in this arrest, he forgot for a moment the fixed

This document can be found in *The Works of Charles Sumner* (Boston, MA: Lee and Shepard, 1873), pp. 169–218.

policy of the Republic, which has been from the beginning like a frontlet between the eyes, and transcended the law of nations, as the United States have always declared it, his apology must be found in the patriotic impulse by which he was inspired, and the British examples which he could not forget. They were the enemies of his country, embodying in themselves the triple essence of worst enmity—treason, conspiracy, and rebellion; and they wore a pretended embassadorial character, which, as he supposed, according to high British authority, rendered them liable to be stopped. . . .

If this transaction be regarded exclusively in the light of British precedents; if we follow the seeming authority of the British admiralty, speaking by its greatest voice; and especially if we accept the oft-repeated example of British cruisers, upheld by the British Government against the oft-repeated protests of the United States, we shall not find it difficult to vindicate it. The act becomes questionable only when brought to the touchstone of these liberal principles, which, from the earliest times, the American Government has openly avowed and sought to advance, and which other European nations have accepted with regard to the sea. Indeed, Great Britain cannot complain except by now adopting those identical principles; and should we undertake to vindicate the act, it can be done only by repudiating those identical principles. Our two cases will be reversed. In the struggle between Laertes and Hamlet, the two combatants exchanged rapiers; so that Hamlet was armed with the rapier of Laertes and Laertes was armed with the rapier of Hamlet. And now on this sensitive question a similar exchange has occurred. Great Britain is armed with American principles, while to us is left only those British principles which, throughout our history, have been constantly, deliberately, and solemnly rejected. . . .

Mr. President, let the rebels go. Two wicked men, ungrateful to their country, are let loose with the brand of Cain upon their foreheads. Prison doors are opened; but principles are established which will help to free other men, and to open the gates of the sea. Never before in her active history has Great Britain ranged herself on this side. Such an event is an epoch. *Novus sæclorum nascitur ordo.* To the liberties of the sea this Power is now committed. To a certain extent this cause is now under her tutelary care. If the immunities of passengers, not in the military or naval service, as well as of sailors, are not directly recognized, they are at least implied; while the whole pretension of impressment, so long the pest of neutral commerce, and operating only through the lawless adjudication of a quarter-deck, is made absolutely impossible. Thus is the freedom of the seas enlarged, not only by limiting the number of persons who are exposed to the penalties of war, but by driving from it the most offensive pretension that ever stalked upon its waves. To such conclusion Great Britain is irrevocably pledged. Nor treaty nor bond was needed. It is sufficient that her late appeal can be vindicated only by a renunciation of early, long-continued tyranny. Let her bear the rebels back. The consideration is ample; for the sea became free as this altered Power went forth upon it, steering westward with the sun, on an errand of liberation.

In this surrender, if such it may be called, our Government does not even "stoop to conquer." It simply lifts itself to the height of its own original principles. The early efforts of its best negotiators—the patriot trials of its soldiers in an unequal war—have at length prevailed, and Great Britain, usually so haughty, invites us to practice upon those principles which she has so strenuously opposed. There are victories of force. Here is a victory of truth. If Great Britain has gained the custody of two rebels, the United States have secured the triumph of their principles.

Seward Warns Europe Against Intervention in Mexico, 1862

We observe indications of a growing opinion in Europe that the demonstrations which are being made by Spanish, French, and British forces against Mexico are likely to be attended with a revolution in that country which will bring in a monarchical government there, in which the crown will be assumed by some foreign prince.

This country is deeply concerned in the peace of nations, and aims to be loyal at the same time in all its relations, as well to the allies as to Mexico. The President has therefore instructed me to submit his views on the new aspect of affairs to the parties concerned. He has relied upon the assurances given to this government by the allies that they were seeking no political objects and only a redress of grievances. He does not doubt the sincerity of the allies, and his confidence in their good faith, if it could be shaken, would be reinspired by explanations apparently made in their behalf that the governments of Spain, France, and Great Britain are not intending to intervene and will not intervene to effect a change of the constitutional form of government now existing in Mexico, or to produce any political change there in opposition to the will of the Mexican people. Indeed, he understands the allies to be unanimous in declaring that the proposed revolution in Mexico is moved only by Mexican citizens now in Europe.

The President, however, deems it his duty to express to the allies, in all candor and frankness, the opinion that no monarchical government which could be founded in Mexico, in the presence of foreign navies and armies in the waters and upon the soil of Mexico, would have any prospect of security or permanency. Secondly, that the instability of such a monarchy there would be enhanced if the throne should be assigned to any person not of Mexican nativity. That under such circumstances the new government must speedily fall unless it could draw into its support European alliances, which, relating back to the present invasion, would, in fact, make it the beginning of a permanent policy of armed European monarchical intervention injurious and practically hostile to the most general system of government on the continent of America, and this would be the beginning rather than the ending of revolution in Mexico.

These views are grounded upon some knowledge of the political sentiments and habits of society in America.

In such a case it is not to be doubted that the permanent interests and sympathies of this country would be with the other American republics. It is not intended on this occasion to predict the course of events which might happen as a consequence of the proceeding contemplated, either on this continent or in Europe. It is sufficient to say that, in the President's opinion, the emancipation of this continent from European control has been the principal feature in its history during the last century. It is not probable that a revolution in a contrary direction would be successful in an immediately succeeding century, while population in America is so rapidly increasing, resources so rapidly developing, and society so steadily forming itself upon principles of democratic American government. Nor is it necessary to suggest to the allies the improbability that European nations could steadily agree

This document can be found in U.S. Congress, *Executive Documents Printed by Order of the House of Representatives* (Washington, D.C.: Government Printing Office, 1862), Ex. Doc. 100, pp. 207–208.

upon a policy favorable to such a counter-revolution as one conducive to their own interests, or to suggest that, however studiously the allies may act to avoid lending the aid of their land and naval forces to domestic revolutions in Mexico, the result would nevertheless be traceable to the presence of those forces there, although for a different purpose, since it may be deemed certain that but for their presence there no such revolution could probably have been attempted or even conceived.

The Senate of the United States has not, indeed, given its official sanction to the precise measures which the President has proposed for lending our aid to the existing government in Mexico, with the approval of the allies, to relieve it from its present embarrassments. This, however, is only a question of domestic administration. It would be very erroneous to regard such a disagreement as indicating any serious difference of opinion in this government or among the American people in their cordial good wishes for the safety, welfare, and stability of the republican system of government in that country.

DOCUMENT 7

Lincoln Redefines the Union's War Aims: The Emancipation Proclamation, 1862–1863

Whereas on the 22nd day of September, A.D. 1862, a proclamation was issued by the President of the United States, containing, among other things, the following, to wit:

"That on the 1st day of January, A.D. 1863, all persons held as slaves within any State or designated part of a State the people whereof shall then be in rebellion against the United States shall be then, thenceforward, and forever free; and the executive government of the United States, including the military and naval authority thereof, will recognize and maintain the freedom of such persons and will do no act or acts to repress such persons, or any of them, in any efforts they may make for their actual freedom.

"That the executive will on the 1st day of January aforesaid, by proclamation, designate the States and parts of States, if any, in which the people thereof, respectively, shall then be in rebellion against the United States; and the fact that any State or the people thereof shall on that day be in good faith represented in the Congress of the United States by members chosen thereto at elections wherein a majority of the qualified voters of such States shall have participated shall, in the absence of strong countervailing testimony, be deemed conclusive evidence that such State and the people thereof are not then in rebellion against the United States."

Now, therefore, I, Abraham Lincoln, President of the United States, by virtue of the power in me vested as Commander-In-Chief of the Army and Navy of the United States in time of actual armed rebellion against the authority and government of the United States, and as a fit and necessary war measure for suppressing said rebellion, do, on this 1st day of January, A.D. 1863, and in accordance with my purpose so to do, publicly proclaimed for the full period of one hundred days from the first day above mentioned, order and designate as the States and parts of States wherein the people thereof, respectively, are this day in rebellion against the United States the following, to wit:

This document can be found at *http://www.archives.gov/exhibit_hall/featured_documents/emancipation_proclamation/transcript.html.*

Arkansas, Texas, Louisiana (except the parishes of St. Bernard, Palquemines, Jefferson, St. John, St. Charles, St. James, Ascension, Assumption, Terrebone, Lafourche, St. Mary, St. Martin, and Orleans, including the city of New Orleans), Mississippi, Alabama, Florida, Georgia, South Carolina, North Carolina, and Virginia (except the forty-eight counties designated as West Virginia, and also the counties of Berkeley, Accomac, Northampton, Elizabeth City, York, Princess Anne, and Norfolk, including the cities of Norfolk and Portsmouth), and which excepted parts are for the present left precisely as if this proclamation were not issued.

And by virtue of the power and for the purpose aforesaid, I do order and declare that all persons held as slaves within said designated States and parts of States are, and henceforward shall be, free; and that the Executive Government of the United States, including the military and naval authorities thereof, will recognize and maintain the freedom of said persons.

And I hereby enjoin upon the people so declared to be free to abstain from all violence, unless in necessary self-defence; and I recommend to them that, in all cases when allowed, they labor faithfully for reasonable wages.

And I further declare and make known that such persons of suitable condition will be received into the armed service of the United States to garrison forts, positions, stations, and other places, and to man vessels of all sorts in said service.

And upon this act, sincerely believed to be an act of justice, warranted by the Constitution upon military necessity, I invoke the considerate judgment of mankind and the gracious favor of Almighty God.

🌐 D O C U M E N T   8

Ambassador Charles Francis Adams
Protests the Iron Clads, 1863

At this moment, when one of the iron-clad vessels is on the point of departure from this kingdom, on its hostile errand against the United States, I am honored with the reply of your lordship to my notes of the 11th, 16th, and 25th of July, and of the 14th of August. I trust I need not express how profound is my regret at the conclusion to which her Majesty's government have arrived. I can regard it no otherwise than as practically opening to the insurgents free liberty in this kingdom to execute a policy described in one of their late publications in the following language:

"In the present state of the harbor defences of New York, Boston, Portland, and smaller northern cities, such a vessel as the Warrior would have little difficulty in entering any of these ports and inflicting a vital blow upon the enemy. The destruction of Boston alone would be worth a hundred victories in the field. It would bring such a terror to the 'blue-noses,' as to cause them to wish eagerly for peace, despite their overweening love of gain which has been so freely administered to since the opening of this war. Vessels of the Warrior class would promptly raise the blockade of our ports, and would even, in this respect, confer advantages which would soon repay the cost of their construction."

This document can be found in U.S. Department of State, *Foreign Relations of the United States, 1863* (Washington, D.C.: Government Printing Office, 1864), I, pp. 367–368.

It would be superfluous in me to point out to your lordship that this is war. No matter what may be the theory adopted of neutrality in a struggle, when this process is carried on in the manner indicated, from a territory and with the aid of the subjects of a third party, that third party to all intents and purposes ceases to be neutral. Neither is it necessary to show, that any government which suffers it to be done fails in enforcing the essential conditions of national amity towards the country against whom the hostility is directed. In my belief it is impossible that any nation, retaining a proper degree of self-respect, could tamely submit to a continuance of relations so utterly deficient in reciprocity. I have no idea that Great Britain would do so for a moment.

E S S A Y S

In the first essay, the Pulitzer Prize–winning Civil War historian James M. McPherson of Princeton University examines how the South's cotton diplomacy fell victim to British realpolitik. Confederate officials, McPherson argues, neglected to take into account that bumper cotton crops and record exports in previous years would undermine an economic embargo. Likewise, they underestimated Britain's growing economic ties to the industrializing North and the power of "King Corn." Most of all, McPherson emphasizes, London withheld diplomatic recognition and minimized its support for the Confederacy because the ministry of Lord [Viscount] Palmerston considered it in Britain's best interest to avoid war with the Union. Ever the realist, Palmerston backed away from intervention after the Union military victory at Antietam in September 1862.

The second essay, by Howard Jones of the University of Alabama, focuses on British mediation efforts in late 1862 and concludes that historians, including McPherson, have underestimated how close London came to intervention following Antietam. Jones argues that Lincoln's Emancipation Proclamation heightened rather than diminished the possibility of British action because it aroused fear of slave revolts, seemed to enlarge the threat to British economic interests, and raised concerns that a horrific race war might pull England and other nations into the conflict. From his extensive research in British archives, Jones concludes that Secretary of War George Cornwall Lewis emerged as the principal deterrent in the Palmerston ministry to an Anglo-French mediation proposal, which he opposed on the grounds that it would likely lead to war with the Union.

British Realpolitik Trumps "King Cotton"

JAMES M. McPHERSON

Cotton was the principal weapon of southern foreign policy. Britain imported three-quarters of its cotton from the American South. The textile industry dominated the British economy. "What would happen if no cotton was furnished for three years?" asked James Hammond of South Carolina in his famous King Cotton speech of 1858. "England would topple headlong and carry the whole civilized world with her, save the South." The inevitability of British intervention to obtain cotton became an article of faith in the South during 1861. A Charleston merchant told the London *Times* correspondent a few days after the surrender of Fort Sumter that "if those miserable Yankees try to blockade us, and keep you from our cotton," he said, "you'll just send their ships to the bottom and acknowledge us. That will be before autumn, I think." In July 1861 [Confederate] Vice President Alexander Stephens expressed certainty that "in some way or other [the blockade will] be raised, or there will be revolution in Europe. . . . Our cotton is . . . the tremendous lever by which we can work our destiny."

To ply this lever, southerners decided to embargo cotton exports. "The cards are in our hands," exulted the *Charleston Mercury,* "and we intend to play them out to the bankruptcy of every cotton factory in Great Britain and France or the acknowledgment of our independence." The *Memphis Argus* instructed planters to "keep every bale of cotton on the plantation. Don't send a thread to New Orleans or Memphis till England and France have recognized the Confederacy—not one thread." Although the Confederate government never officially sanctioned the embargo, so powerful was public opinion that it virtually enforced itself. Most of the 1860 crop had been shipped before the war began. The shipping season for 1861 would normally have begun in September, but despite the looseness of the blockade little cotton went out. In the spring of 1862 southerners planted about half their usual cotton acreage and devoted the rest of the land to food production. British imports of cotton from the South in 1862 amounted to about 3 percent of the 1860 level.

King Cotton diplomacy seemed promising at first. British and French officials exchanged worried views about the probable impact of a cotton famine. Textile magnates in Lancashire and Lyons talked of shutdowns. "England must break the Blockade, or Her Millions will starve," declared a newspaper speaking for textile workers in September 1861. In October, Prime Minister Viscount Palmerston and Foreign Minister Lord Russell agreed that "the cotton question may become serious by the end of the year. . . . We cannot allow some millions of our people to perish to please the Northern States." British and French diplomats discussed the possibility of joint action to lift the blockade.

But in the end several factors prevented such action. The first was Russell's and Palmerston's desire to avoid involvement in the war. "For God's sake, let us if possible keep out of it," said Russell in May 1861, while Palmerston quoted the aphorism: "They who in quarrels interpose, will often get a bloody nose." Even without Secretary of State Seward's bellicose warnings against intervention—which the British regarded as insolent blustering—Britain recognized that any action against the blockade could lead to a conflict with the United States more harmful to England's interest than the temporary loss of southern cotton. Our "true policy," Palmerston told Russell on October 18, was "to go on as we have begun, and to keep quite clear of the conflict." Napoleon III of France leaned toward intervention, but was unwilling to take any action without British cooperation.

If Britain took umbrage at Seward's "bullying," many Englishmen resented even more the Confederacy's attempt at economic blackmail. If southerners "thought they could extort our cooperation by the agency of king cotton," declared the *Times,* they had better think again. To intervene on behalf of the South "because they keep cotton from us," said Lord Russell in September 1861, "would be ignominious beyond measure. . . . No English Parliament could do so base a thing."

Because of British (and French) sensitivity on this issue, southern diplomats could not admit the existence of a cotton embargo. But this trapped them in a paradox, for how could they proclaim the blockade ineffective if no cotton was reaching Europe? In reply to a question on this matter by the French foreign minister in February 1862, the Confederate commissioner to Paris conceded that "although a very large proportion of the vessels that attempted to run the blockade . . . had succeeded in passing, the risk of capture was sufficiently great to deter those who had not a very adventurous spirit from attempting it." Fatal admission! Eight days later Foreign Minister Russell announced Britain's position on the blockade: "The fact that various ships may have successfully escaped through it . . . will not of itself prevent the blockade from being an effective one by international law" so long as it was enforced by a number of ships "sufficient really to prevent access to [a port] *or to create an evident danger of entering or leaving it."* By February the northern blockade certainly met this criterion. Another influence working against British acceptance of southern arguments about paper blockades was a desire not to create a precedent that would boomerang against British security in a future war. As the crown's solicitor general put it: Britain must resist "new fangled notions and interpretations of international law which might make it impossible for us effectively at some future day to institute any blockade, and so destroy our naval authority."

Southern expectations of foreign intervention to break the blockade were betrayed by a double irony: first, the "success" of the cotton embargo seemed only to prove the success of the blockade; and second, the huge cotton exports of 1857–60, instead of proving the potency of King Cotton, resulted in toppling his throne. Even working overtime, British mills had not been able to turn all of this cotton into cloth. Surplus stocks of raw cotton as well as of finished cloth piled up in Lancashire warehouses. The South's embargo thus turned out to be a blessing in disguise for textile manufacturers in 1861. Although the mills went on short time during the winter of 1861–62, the real reason for this was not the shortage of cotton but the satiated market for cloth. Inventories of raw cotton in Britain and France were higher in December 1861 than any previous December. The cotton famine from which the South expected so much did not really take hold until the summer of 1862. By then the Confederacy had scuttled its embargo and was trying desperately to export cotton through the tightening blockade to pay for imported supplies. By then, too, the stimulus of high prices had brought about an increase of cotton acreage in Egypt and India, which supplied most of Europe's cotton imports for the next three years.

The worst time of unemployment in the British textile industry occurred from the summer of 1862 to the spring of 1863. But the impact of this did not measure up to southern hopes or British fears. Even before the war, textiles had been losing their dominant role in the British economy. The war further stimulated growth in the iron, shipbuilding, armaments, and other industries. This offset much of the decline in textiles. The manufacture of woolen uniforms and blankets for American armies absorbed some of the slack in cotton manufacturing. A flourishing trade in war matériel with the North as well as blockade running to the South helped convince British merchants of the virtues of neutrality. Crop failures in western Europe from 1860 through 1862 increased British dependence on American grain and flour. During the first two years of the Civil War the Union states supplied nearly half of British grain imports, compared with less than a quarter before the war. Yankees exulted that King Corn was more powerful than King Cotton. And because Confederate commerce raiders drove much of the U.S. merchant marine from the seas, most of this expanded trade with the North was carried by British ships—another economic shot in the arm that helped discourage British intervention in the war.

By the second year of the conflict, Britain was willing to tolerate extraordinary northern extensions of the blockade. In April 1862, Union warships began seizing British merchant vessels plying between England and Nassau or Bermuda, on the grounds that their cargoes were destined ultimately for the Confederacy. The first ship so captured was the *Bermuda,* which was confiscated by a U.S. prize court. The navy bought her and put her to work as a blockade ship. This added insult to the injury that had already provoked a jingoistic response in Britain. But American diplomats cited British precedents for such seizures. During the Napoleonic wars the royal navy had seized American ships carrying cargoes to a neutral port with the intention of reexporting them to France. British courts had established the doctrine of "continuous voyage" to justify confiscation of contraband destined ultimately for an enemy port even if the voyage was broken by landing at a neutral port. When this chicken came home to roost in 1862, Whitehall could hardly repudiate its own precedent. . . .

Next to obtaining British intervention against the blockade, the main goal of Confederate foreign policy was to secure diplomatic recognition of the South's nationhood. In the quest for recognition, the Confederate State Department sent to Europe a three-man commission headed by William L. Yancey. As a notorious fireeater and an advocate of reopening the African slave trade, Yancey was not the best choice to win friends in antislavery Britain. Nevertheless, soon after the southerners arrived in London the British government announced an action that misled Americans on both sides of the Potomac to anticipate imminent diplomatic recognition of the Confederacy.

Lincoln had proclaimed the rebels to be insurrectionists. Under international law this would deny the Confederacy status as a belligerent power. But the North's declaration of a blockade constituted an act of war affecting neutral powers. On May 13 Britain therefore declared her neutrality in a proclamation issued by the Queen. This would seem to have been unexceptionable—except that it automatically recognized the Confederacy as a belligerent power. Other European nations followed the British lead. Status as a belligerent gave Confederates the right under international law to contract loans and purchase arms in neutral nations, and to commission cruisers on the high seas with the power of search and seizure. Northerners protested this British action with hot words; Charles Sumner later called it "the most hateful act of English history since Charles 2nd." But northern protests rested on weak legal grounds, for the blockade was a virtual recognition of southern belligerency. Moreover, in European eyes the Confederacy with its national constitution, its army, its effective control of 750,000 square miles of territory and a population of nine million people, was a belligerent power in practice no matter what it was in northern theory. As Lord Russell put it: "The question of belligerent rights is one, not of principle, but of fact."

Northern bitterness stemmed in part from the context and timing of British action. The proclamation of neutrality came just after two "unofficial" conferences between Lord Russell and the Confederate envoys. And it preceded by one day the arrival in London of Charles Francis Adams, the new United States minister. The recognition of belligerency thus appeared to present Adams with a *fait accompli* to soften him up for the next step—diplomatic recognition of southern nationhood. As Seward viewed it, Russell's meetings with Yancey and his colleagues were "liable to be construed as recognition." The South did so construe them; and the *Richmond Whig* considered the proclamation of neutrality "a long and firm [step] in exactly the direction which the people of the Southern States expected."

All spring Seward had been growing more agitated by British policy. When he learned of Russell's meetings with the rebel commissioners, he exploded in anger. "God damn them, I'll give them hell," he told Sumner. On May 21 Seward sent an undiplomatic dispatch to Adams instructing him to break off relations if the British government had any more dealings with southern envoys. If Britain officially recognized the Confederacy, "we from that hour, shall cease to be friends and become once more, as we have twice before been forced to be, enemies of Great Britain."

Lincoln had tried with only partial success to soften Seward's language. The president did compel Seward to allow Adams discretion to present the substance of this dispatch verbally rather than handing it intact to Lord Russell. After reading Seward's bellicose words, Adams decided that in this case discretion was indeed the better part of valor. Adams had been a superb choice for the London legation. His grandfather and father had preceded him there; Charles had spent much of his youth in the St. Petersburg and London legations. His reserve and self-restraint struck an empathic chord among Englishmen, who were offended by the braggadocio they attributed to American national character. Adams and Lord Russell took each other's measure at their first meeting, and liked what they saw. Adams concealed Seward's iron fist in a velvet glove. Equally urbane, Russell assured the American minister that Britain had no present intention of granting diplomatic recognition to the Confederacy. The foreign secretary conceded that he had twice met with the southern commissioners, but "had no expectation of seeing them any more."

Nor did he. It took some time for this message to sink into the minds of the southern envoys, who continued to send optimistic reports to Richmond. In September 1861, however, Yancey grew restless and he resigned. At the same time the Confederate government decided to replace the commissioners with ministers plenipotentiary in major European capitals. Richmond sent James Mason of Virginia to London and John Slidell of Louisiana to Paris.

By so doing the South unwittingly set in motion a series of events that almost brought Anglo-American relations to a rupture. The departure of Mason and Slidell from Charleston by blockade runner was scarcely a secret. The U.S. navy was embarrassed by its failure to intercept their ship before it reached Havana, where the diplomats transferred to the British steamer *Trent.* Captain Charles Wilkes decided to redeem the navy's reputation. A forty-year veteran now commanding the thirteen-gun sloop *U.S.S. San Jacinto,* Wilkes was a headstrong, temperamental man who fancied himself an expert on maritime law. Diplomatic dispatches could be seized as contraband of war; Wilkes decided to capture Mason and Slidell as the "embodiment of despatches." This novel interpretation of international law was never tested, for instead of capturing the *Trent* as a prize after stopping her on the high seas on November 8, Wilkes arrested Mason and Slidell and let the ship go on.

The northern public greeted Wilkes's act with applause; "the people," reported a journalist, "are glad to see John Bull taken by the horns." The House of Representatives passed a resolution lauding Wilkes. But after the first flush of jubilation, second thoughts began to arise. Few expected Britain to take this lying down. The risk of war sent the American stock market into a dive. Government bonds found no buyers. News from Britain confirmed fears of an ugly confrontation. The British expressed outrage at Wilkes's "impressment" of Mason and Slidell. The Union Jack had been flouted. The jingo press clamored for war. Prime Minister Palmerston told his cabinet: "You may stand for this but damned if I will." The cabinet voted to send Washington an ultimatum demanding an apology and release of the Confederate diplomats. Britain ordered troops to Canada and strengthened the western Atlantic fleet. War seemed imminent.

Although the Anglophobe press in America professed to welcome this prospect, cooler heads recognized the wisdom of Lincoln's reported words: "One war at a time." The Union army's capacity to carry on even that one war was threatened by an aspect of the *Trent* crisis unknown to the public and rarely mentioned by historians. In 1861, British India was the Union's source of saltpeter, the principal ingredient of gunpowder. The war had drawn down saltpeter stockpiles to the danger point. In the fall of 1861 Seward sent a member of the du Pont company to England on a secret mission to buy all available supplies of saltpeter there and on the way from India. The agent did so, and was loading five ships with 2,300 tons of the mineral when news of the *Trent* reached London. The government clamped an embargo on all shipments to the United States until the crisis was resolved. No settlement, no saltpeter.

This issue among others was very much on Lincoln's and Seward's minds during the tense weeks of December 1861. The problem was how to defuse the crisis without the humiliation of bowing to an ultimatum. Seward recognized that Wilkes had violated international law by failing to bring the *Trent* into port for adjudication before a prize court. In an uncharacteristic mood of moderation, Seward expressed a willingness to yield Mason and Slidell on the grounds that Wilkes had acted without instructions. Diplomatic hints had come from London that this face-saving compromise would be acceptable to the British. In a crucial Christmas day meeting, Lincoln and his cabinet concluded that they had no choice but to let Mason and Slidell go. Most of the press had reached the same conclusion, so release would not peril the administration's public support. Mason and Slidell resumed their interrupted trip to Europe, where they never again came so close to winning foreign intervention as they had done by being captured in November 1861. Their release punctured the war bubble. Du Pont's saltpeter left port and was soon turned into gunpowder for the Union army. . . .

The course of the war in the summer of 1862 revived Confederate hopes for European diplomatic recognition. Lee's offensives convinced British and French leaders that northern armies could never restore the Union. These powers contemplated an offer of mediation, which would have constituted de facto recognition of Confederate independence. Influential elements of British public opinion grew more sympathetic to the southern cause. The Palmerston government seemed to shut its eyes to violations of British neutrality by Liverpool shipbuilders who constructed rebel cruisers to prey on the American merchant marine. The long-awaited cotton famine finally took hold in the summer of 1862. Louis Napoleon toyed with the idea of offering recognition and aid to the Confederacy in return for southern cotton and southern support for French suzerainty in Mexico.

Of all these occurrences, the building of commerce raiders was the only one that generated tangible benefits for the Confederacy. Liverpool was a center of prosouthern sentiment. The city "was made by the slave trade," observed a caustic American diplomat, "and the sons of those who acquired fortunes in the traffic, now instinctively side with the rebelling slave-drivers." Liverpool shipyards built numerous blockade runners. In March 1862 the first warship that the southern agent James D. Bulloch had ordered was also nearing completion. The ship's purpose as a commerce raider was an open secret. . . .

At issue was the meaning of Britain's Foreign Enlistment Act, which forbade the construction *and* arming of warships in British territory for a belligerent power. Remaining within the letter of the law while violating its spirit, Bulloch took delivery of the ship without arms, sent it to the Bahamas, and transported the guns from England in another vessel. The sleek warship took on her guns at a deserted Bahamian Cay and began her fearsome career as the *Florida.* She destroyed thirty-eight American merchant vessels before the Union navy captured her by a subterfuge in the harbor of Bahia, Brazil, in October 1864.

The willingness of British officials to apply a narrow interpretation of the Foreign Enlistment Act encouraged Bulloch's efforts to get his second and larger cruiser out of Liverpool in the summer of 1862. . . . Once again bureaucratic negligence, legal pettifoggery, and the Confederate sympathies of the British customs collector at Liverpool gave Bulloch time to ready his ship for sea. When an agent informed him of the government's belated intention to detain the ship, Bulloch sent her out on a "trial cruise" from which she never returned. Instead she rendezvoused at the Azores with a tender carrying guns and ammunition sent separately from Britain. Named the *Alabama,* this cruiser had as her captain Raphael Semmes, who had already proved his prowess as a salt-water guerrilla on the now-defunct *C.S.S. Sumter.* For the next two years Semmes and the *Alabama* roamed the seas and destroyed or captured sixty-four American merchant ships before being sunk by the *U.S.S. Kearsarge* off Cherbourg in June 1864. . . .

In addition to the escape of the *Alabama* from Liverpool, another straw in the wind seemed to preview a southern tilt in British foreign policy. Henry Hotze, a Swiss-born Alabamian who arrived in London early in 1862, was an effective propagandist for the South. Twenty-seven years old and boyish in appearance, Hotze nevertheless possessed a suavity of manner and a style of witty understatement that appealed to the British upper classes. He gained entry to high circles on Fleet Street and was soon writing pro-Confederate editorials for several newspapers. Hotze also recruited English journalists to write for the *Index,* a small newspaper he established in May 1862 to present the southern viewpoint. Hotze did a good job in stirring up British prejudices against the bumptious Yankees. To liberals he insisted that the South was fighting not for slavery but for self-determination. To conservatives he presented an image of a rural gentry defending its liberties against a rapacious northern government. To businessmen he promised that an independent Confederacy would open its ports to free trade, in contrast with the Union government which had recently raised tariffs yet again. To the textile industry he pledged a resumption of cotton exports. . . .

The canker in this image of southerners as freedom-loving nationalists, of course, was slavery. One thing upon which Englishmen prided themselves was their role in suppressing the transatlantic slave trade and abolishing slavery in the West Indies. To support a rebellion in behalf of slavery would be un-British. To accept the notion that the South fought for independence rather than slavery required considerable mental legerdemain. But so long as the North did *not* fight for freedom, many Britons could see no moral superiority in the Union cause. If the North wanted to succeed in "their struggle [for] the sympathies of Englishmen," warned a radical newspaper, "they must abolish slavery."

But these issues of ideology and sentiment played a secondary role in determining Britain's foreign policy. A veteran of a half-century in British politics, Palmerston was an exponent of *Realpolitik.* When pro-southern members of Parliament launched a drive in the summer of 1862 for British recognition of the Confederacy, Palmerston professed not to see the point. The South, he wrote, would not be "a bit more independent for our saying so unless we followed up our Declaration by taking Part with them in the war." Few in Britain were ready for that. Palmerston would like more cotton, but it remained unclear just how diplomatic recognition would get it. Southerners believed that recognition would help the Confederacy by boosting its credibility abroad and strengthening the peace party in the North. They may have been right. But so far as Palmerston was concerned, the South could earn recognition only by winning the war: Britain must "know that their separate independence is a truth and a fact" before declaring it to be so. . . .

But as the summer wore on, Confederate victories seemed likely to fulfill Palmerston's criterion for recognition: establishment of southern nationhood as truth and fact. During 1861 most British observers had assumed as a matter of course that the North could never conquer so large an area and so militant a people. After all, if the Redcoats could not prevail over a much weaker nation in 1776, how could the Yankees expect to win? Union victories in the first half of 1862 had threatened this smug assumption, but [General Stonewall] Jackson and [General Robert E.] Lee—who became instant legends in Britain—revived and made it stronger than ever. Even some of the Union's staunchest friends came to share the *Times*'s conviction that "North and South must now choose between separation and ruin." The "useless butchery and carnage" had proved only that "nine millions of people, inhabiting a territory of 900,000 square miles, and animated by one spirit of resistance, can never be subdued." By September, according to the French foreign secretary, "not a reasonable statesman in Europe" believed that the North could win.

In both Whitehall and on the Quai d'Orsay a sentiment favoring an offer of mediation grew stronger as reports of new Confederate victories filtered across the Atlantic. By bringing the war to an end, mediation might prove the quickest and safest way to get cotton. A joint offer by several powers—Britain, France, Russia, and perhaps Austria and Prussia—would be most effective, for the North could not ignore the united opinion of Europe and even the bellicose Seward could scarcely declare war on all of them. A mediation proposal would be tantamount to recognition of Confederate independence. Rumors that such a move was afoot caused euphoria among southern diplomats and plunged the American legation into gloom. . . .

The European belief that defeat might induce Lincoln to accept mediation misjudged his determination to fight through to victory. "I expect to maintain this contest until successful, or till I die," Lincoln had said, and he meant it. Even after the setback at Second Bull Run, Seward told the French minister that "we will not admit the division of the Union . . . at any price. . . . There is no possible compromise." Such obstinacy compelled the proponents of mediation to pin their hopes on a Democratic triumph in the northern elections. Betraying a typical British misunderstanding of the American constitutional system, Foreign Minister Russell expected that Democratic control of the House would force Lincoln to change his foreign policy. "The Democratic party may by that time [November] have got the ascendancy," wrote Russell in October. "I heartily wish them success."

So did Robert E. Lee, as he invaded Maryland to conquer a peace. The fate of diplomacy rode with Lee in this campaign. The Federals "got a very complete smashing" at Bull Run, wrote Palmerston to Russell on September 14, "and it seems not altogether unlikely that still greater disasters await them, and that even Washington or Baltimore may fall into the hands of the Confederates. If this should happen, would it not be time for us to consider whether . . . England and France might not address the contending parties and recommend an arrangement upon the basis of separation?" Russell was ready and willing. On September 17—the very day of the fighting at Sharpsburg—he concurred in the plan to offer mediation, adding that if the North refused, "we ought ourselves to recognise the Southern States as an independent State." But even before reports of Antietam reached England (news required ten days or more to cross the Atlantic), Palmerston turned cautious. On September 23 he told Russell that the outcome of the campaign in Maryland "must have a great effect on the state of affairs. If the Federals sustain a great defeat, they may be at once ready for mediation, and the iron should be struck while it is hot. If, on the other hand, they should have the best of it, we may wait awhile and see what may follow." Having learned of Lee's retreat to Virginia, Palmerston backed off. "These last battles in Maryland have rather set the North up again," he wrote to Russell early in October. "The whole matter is full of difficulty, and can only be cleared up by some more decided events between the contending armies."

But Antietam did not cool the ardor of Russell and [Chancellor of the Exchequer William E.] Gladstone for recognition. They persisted in bringing the matter before the cabinet on October 28, despite Palmerston's repeated insistence that matters had changed since mid-September, "when the Confederates seemed to be carrying all before them. . . . I am very much come back to our original view that we must continue merely to be lookers-on till the war shall have taken a more decided turn." The cabinet voted Russell and Gladstone down. The French weighed in at this point with a suggestion that Britain, France, and Russia propose a six months' armistice— during which the blockade would be suspended. This so blatantly favored the South that pro-Union Russia quickly rejected it. The British cabinet, after two days of discussion, also turned it down.

Thus ended the South's best chance for European intervention. It did not end irrevocably, for the military situation remained fluid and most Britons remained certain that the North could never win. But at least they had avoided losing. Antietam had, in Charles Francis Adams's understatement, "done a good deal to restore our drooping credit here." It had done more; by enabling Lincoln to issue the Emancipation

Proclamation the battle also ensured that Britain would think twice about intervening against a government fighting for freedom as well as Union.

British Intervention: A Very Close Call

HOWARD JONES

In late 1862, the British government attempted to mastermind a European intervention in the American Civil War that would doubtless have assured southern independence. To date, historians have not adequately explained why that intervention never took place, though there is substantial agreement that a European involvement in the war would have had momentous consequences for the North, the South, and the European powers. If only the British had intervened in the Civil War, so say the most ardent proponents of the "Lost Cause," the Confederate States of America would have won independence and taken its rightful place among the community of nations. Such a dramatic move by England, they insist, would have encouraged France and other nations on the Continent to do the same. Diplomatic recognition of the Confederacy would have dealt the Union a devastating blow, for the monumental step would have undermined the Constitution by justifying secession and thereby safeguarded slavery and the entire southern way of life.

According to conventional accounts, the Battle of Antietam in September 1862 marked a major turning point in the war because it led to the Emancipation Proclamation and thereby blocked British intervention on the side of the slave-holding South. Pulitzer Prize–winning historian James M. McPherson insists that the battle "frustrated Confederate hopes for British recognition and precipitated the Emancipation Proclamation. . . . Thus ended the South's best chance for European intervention." . . .

Mythology has often taken the place of history, and nowhere is this more so than in the Union's crisis over British intervention in the Civil War. Contrary to the long-accepted view stated above, the truth is that these pivotal events of autumn 1862 actually *heightened* British interest in intervention. The reason is clear: the interventionists, led by Foreign Secretary Lord John Russell and Chancellor of the Exchequer William E. Gladstone, feared that emancipation would incite a wave of slave revolts that would grow into a race war and, combined with the escalating hostilities between North and South, ultimately pull England and other nations into the fiery conflict. As the intervention crisis built, however, a less-known figure assumed statesman-like status. Secretary for War George Cornewall Lewis emerged as the chief opposition leader to a British involvement that probably would have led to war between England and the Union. . . .

England intended its official position of neutrality to keep its people out of the war while permitting trade with both North and South. But given England's strategic positions in Canada and the West Indies, along with its growing commercial interests in the Atlantic, trouble was certain. From the beginning of the American conflict, the Palmerston ministry expressed concern over the Union's dissolution, whether or not secession was legal. The prime minister, ever pragmatic and realistic, voiced the sentiment of many in his country by insisting that southern separation was a *fait accompli*—especially after the Union army's disaster at Bull Run in the summer of 1861—and often lamented the North's stubborn unwillingness to make that admission. Russell, Palmerston's diminutive but headstrong foreign secretary, agonized over the trial of the Union and the harmful economic impact it had on England, and came to consider southern independence a fair price to pay for peace. For humanitarian as well as economic reasons, he joined Gladstone in calling for an intervention intended to end the war. As for slavery, Russell and others in England proposed a remedy: "One Republic to be constituted on the principle of freedom & personal liberty—the other on the principle of slavery & the mutual surrender of fugitives." . . .

Even though the British had several reasons for intervention, their most serious concern was the horror of the war, which was accentuated by a fear of slave insurrections in the South that would develop into a race war of national proportions. To the House of Lords in early 1862, Russell expressed his anxieties over this dire possibility. Numerous British observers dreaded the outbreak of servile war; not only would such an event disrupt the cotton economy for years, but a racial upheaval would rock the South and perhaps the entire republic once the chains of bondage were broken. Indeed, such a calamity could upset the entire commercial relationship with the United States—including the British importation of northern wheat. Yet this very crisis seemed to be developing almost in conjunction with the waning hopes of the Lincoln administration. As early as January 1862, in the midst of the *Trent* war scare with England, [British Minister Richard] Lyons alerted Russell that the American conflict was "rapidly tending towards the issue either of peace and a recognition of the separation, or a Proclamation of Emancipation and the raising of a servile insurrection." Russell was alarmed that the president should want "a war of emancipation." Yet out of desperation, the foreign secretary and others believed, Lincoln might instigate a servile war once he realized that he could not restore the Union by other means.

By the spring of 1862, the White House seemed prepared to take that momentous step. To counter the threat of intervention, Secretary of State William H. Seward inadvertently provided substance for England's deepest fear: he warned the London government that its involvement in American affairs could set off a slave revolt that would spawn a race war in the United States. In a dispatch meant for Russell's perusal, Seward wrote [U.S. Minister to Great Britain Charles Francis] Adams that before the fall of New Orleans to Union forces that previous April, Europe had speculated about an intervention that could only have benefited the South. Now, despite the Union victory, British interest in such a scheme had not abated. An intervention based on southern separation would guarantee a servile war disruptive to the economy and injurious to all European interests in America.

The British became instantly alarmed by the ensuing events of the summer. In late July, the chargé in Washington, William Stuart, reported that the Union had shifted its wartime objective to antislavery. He was correct. Lincoln had recently informed his cabinet of this decision, although agreeing with Seward to delay a public announcement until there was news of a northern victory on the battlefield. Otherwise, England might interpret emancipation as a last-ditch effort to win the war. To undercut the South, Stuart feared, the North seemed ready to instigate a slave uprising intended to break the back of the Confederate army by forcing its soldiers to return home to protect their families. These developments, along with Seward's warning regarding slave insurrections, deeply troubled Russell. Indeed, in his anxiety he misinterpreted Seward's note to mean that the Lincoln administration was prepared to stir up a slave rebellion in a desperate effort to ward off foreign intervention. So serious were Russell's fears that Stuart read Russell's dispatch to Seward and later gave him a copy to drive home the point. The possibility of a race war, Russell insisted, would "only make other nations more desirous to see an end of this desolating and destructive conflict."

The Union's move against slavery so repelled the British that it encouraged the very intervention that the Lincoln administration sought to prevent. Most British observers did not believe that the Union advanced emancipation as a moral and humanitarian measure. When the war began, they had been surprised when the White House emphasized that the conflict did not concern slavery. They failed to understand, as Lincoln did, that a war against slavery would alienate slaveowners in the loyal border states, as well as Unionists in the Confederacy, and that few northern males were prepared to fight a war on behalf of blacks. Even if Lincoln had legitimate concerns about the domestic political consequences of a war against slavery, the British complained that he took the side of his countrymen— including those outside the Republican Party as well as those within—who had condoned slavery by refusing to take a stand against it. The British now regarded emancipation as hypocrisy—a desperate effort to save the Union by encouraging the South's slaves to rebel and bring down the Cotton Kingdom from within. The only remedy to this demonic action, from England's perspective, was an intervention premised on southern separation. . . .

European mediation—and perhaps recognition—seemed imminent in mid-September 1862, when news arrived in London of another resounding Union defeat—again at Bull Run. The British must have experienced a feeling of *déjà vu* upon receiving word of the second major engagement at Bull Run. At long last, the Union stood on the brink of a convincing defeat that would force it to give up the ill-conceived attempt to subjugate the South. And how bittersweet that fate had cast its judgment for northern humiliation again at Bull Run. Surely, British observers noted with impatience, the Union would not tempt fate again. In France, Foreign Minister Edouard Thouvenel observed that no reasonable leader on the Continent thought the Union could win. But again European hopes turned into exasperation. In a reaction similar to that after First Bull Run, the Lincoln administration neither lost its resolve to win the war nor its resistance to intervention. Union spirits soared even as disaster threatened to follow a trail northward.

To many British observers, the second Union defeat at Bull Run had underlined the North's inability to subjugate the South and therefore justified a move toward ending the war on the basis of a separation. In London the *Times* and the *Morning Post* (which both usually expressed Palmerston's views) leaned toward recognition, whereas the *Morning Herald* made a broader appeal: "Let us do something, as we are Christian men." Whether "arbitration, intervention, diplomatic action, recognition of the South, remonstrance with the North, friendly interference or forcible pressure of some sort . . . , let us do something to stop this carnage." Palmerston thought the time for intervention was nigh. "The federals . . . got a very complete smashing," he wrote Russell on 14 September, "and it seems not altogether unlikely that still greater disasters await them, and that even Washington or Baltimore may fall into the hands of the Confederates. If this should happen, would it not be time for us to consider whether . . . England and France might not address the contending parties and recommend an arrangement upon the basis of separation?" If the mediation offer were rejected, he insisted, "we ought ourselves to recognize the Southern States as an independent State." . . .

The move toward British intervention had approached a climactic point by the late summer of 1862. Indeed, if Lee had not followed his success at Bull Run with an immediate march north, the South might have won a mediation followed by recognition. But the full impact of Second Bull Run had not yet settled on London when Lee decided to take the war into Maryland, inspiring hope among southern strategists of bringing about the intervention that, ironically, may have been already in their grasp.

Although both Palmerston and Russell had turned to mediation after Second Bull Run, the prime minister remained concerned about a Union refusal to cooperate. Consequently, the news of a southern advance northward made Palmerston hope that Lee might win again, thereby increasing the chances for Union acquiescence in a mediation. . . .

Palmerston nonetheless saw great difficulties in mediation. Even if both North and South accepted the offer, a question would develop whether "the fact of our meddling would not of itself be tantamount to an acknowledgment of the Confederacy as an independent State." More explosive would be the ramifications of a mediation that the South accepted and the North did not. For at least that reason alone, Palmerston believed, England and France must invite the Union's friend, Russia, to participate. With Russia involved, the North would be more likely to go along. Even if the Russians declined, as he knew was probable, England would have won credibility with them by extending the invitation. Admittedly, it was better not to have the Russians' involvement because of their avowed favor for the North. But in the interests of peace, he hoped that they would set aside the bitterness still lingering over the recent conflict with England and France in the Crimea and realize that the North's welfare (and that of everyone else) lay in calling off the war. . . .

While the Palmerston ministry prepared for mediation, Confederate and Union forces confronted each other on 17 September at Antietam, a creek lying outside the small village of Sharpsburg in Maryland that became the scene of the bloodiest single day's fighting in the Civil War. The South's first major effort to take the war into the North came to a sudden and brutal end in the course of a few hours as tens of thousands of soldiers engaged in deadly combat. By early evening, more than 24,000 Union and Confederate soldiers had been wounded or killed. Lee's army had sustained such heavy casualties that it limped back into Virginia on the evening of the following day, leaving Union general George B. McClellan's battered legions in possession of the battlefield.

News of Antietam reached London in late September, at first disappointing the ministry by demonstrating again the North's determination to win and yet, paradoxically, lending support to a mediation intended to stop this growing bloodbath. Given the heightened British interest in some course of action, it seems more than coincidental that the Earl of Shaftesbury, who was the son-in-law of Lady Palmerston and widely known to be under the prime minister's influence, should pass through Paris about 23 September (*before* news of Antietam had reached Europe) to offer assurances, according to Confederate minister John Slidell, that British recognition was no more than a few weeks away. The South's drive for independence, Shaftesbury explained, had won the support of Englishmen who opposed the North's imperial interests. Indeed, on September 30 (*after* Antietam's news reached Europe), Shaftesbury assured Slidell that the British attitude had not changed: "There is every reason to believe that the event so strongly desired of which we talked when I had the pleasure of seeing you in Paris is very close at hand." . . .

Antietam appeared to confirm the contemporary view that the American antagonists had become locked in a death grip that could be broken only by outside assistance. In Washington, Stuart interpreted the results at Antietam as a lethal stalemate. After the battle, he wrote Russell, McClellan had wanted to rest his army and, like the South, did not want the Potomac River behind him during this season of rain and swollen waters. The general had failed to achieve a victory because he refused to pursue the enemy. Antietam was therefore "as near a drawn Battle as could be, only that the Federals have since held the ground." Stuart persisted in his optimism. The war appeared to be moving toward a political revolution in the North that would carry the peace advocates to the front. Palmerston likewise thought the war had deadlocked, which was, he told Russell with some relief, "just the case for the stepping in of friends." . . .

Shortly after the Battle of Antietam came the president's preliminary proclamation of emancipation. On 22 September, timed as Seward had advised—in the immediate aftermath of a Union military victory—Lincoln announced that, as of 1 January 1863, all slaves in states still in rebellion were free. "No other step," he had recently told an antislavery delegation in Washington, "would be so potent to prevent foreign intervention." Lincoln thus recognized the acute inseparability of foreign and domestic affairs, as well as the integral relationship between diplomatic and military considerations. The proclamation was "a practical war measure," he explained in the *Chicago Tribune,* "to be decided upon according to the advantages or disadvantages it may offer to the suppression of the rebellion." Emancipation would convince Europe that "we are incited by something more than ambition."

British suspicions of the Union's ulterior motives in emancipation were not entirely off the mark: Lincoln intended that this wartime measure undermine slavery and thus tear down the South from within. But no evidence suggests that he envisioned a Nat Turner–style revolt. He spoke only of black service in the Union army, mass flight from the plantations, and, to those slaves who remained, encouragement to cease work. To alleviate concern over the unrest that the measure would foment among the slaves, Lincoln made two additions to the proclamation at Seward's request—that freedmen be urged "to abstain from all violence, unless in necessary self-defense," and that, "in all cases, when allowed, they labor faithfully for reasonable wages." Further, in the hundred days between the preliminary and final proclamations, Lincoln had agreed to delete passages misinterpreted by many as a call for insurrection—those declaring that the executive would not restrict blacks in their attempt to secure freedom and those referring to colonization and compensated emancipation. The proclamation, however, was certain to raise the slaves' cry for freedom while intensifying southern resistance to the Union and thereby necessitating a war of subjugation. . . .

News of the president's proclamation reached England in early October, causing British spokesmen on all sides of the American issue to envision additional atrocities in the war. Emancipation, Russell learned from Stuart, had infuriated the Confederate Congress in Richmond and caused "threats of raising the Black Flag and other measures of retaliation." A northern governor had called for the importation of the French guillotine, and if Lincoln and the Republicans stayed in power, Stuart warned, "we may see reenacted some of the worst excesses of the French Revolution." From the Foreign Office in London, Permanent Under-Secretary Edmund Hammond (who was pro-South) likewise treated the proclamation with disdain. Even Member of Parliament Richard Cobden, who staunchly opposed slavery, had reservations about using emancipation as a military weapon. In attempting to prevent separation and the establishment of a slave nation, the North would "half ruin itself in the process of wholly ruining the South." To seek victory with black cooperation would lead to "one of the most bloody & horrible episodes in history." The English view attracted support from across the Channel. That same month, the French informed the Palmerston ministry that the threat of a slave uprising provided another reason for their willingness to work with England in ending the American war. . . .

Palmerston, of course, was the central figure in a mediation decision, and if he had moved cautiously closer to taking such an action before Antietam, he now just as cautiously moved farther away. He remained confident that the South would accept mediation "upon the Basis of Separation," but, he assured Russell, the North would reject the offer because Antietam had deluded the Lincoln administration into believing that its war aims were attainable. The South had still not achieved a major battlefield success capable of compelling the North to accept mediation without demanding a war of revenge against England. The mediation offer "has been lately checked" by the Battle of Antietam, and England might have to wait another ten days for "future prospects." If the Union insisted on war with the mediating nation (or nations), it might be advisable to delay the offer until spring weather opened British communications to Canada and permitted the Royal Navy to operate along the Atlantic coast. Perhaps the only way to avert an Anglo-American conflict resulting from a mediation would be to avoid a unilateral recognition of the South. "If the acknowledgement were made at one and the same time by England, France and some other Powers, the Yankee would probably not seek a quarrel with us alone, and would not like one against a European Confederation." . . .

Russell, however, had become dissatisfied with Palmerston's hesitation and wanted to forge ahead without waiting for a Confederate military victory. The moment for action had come, he wrote the prime minister: "I think unless some miracle takes place this will be the very time for offering mediation, or as you suggest, proposing North and South to come to terms." A British proposal must make two points: that England recommended separation, and that it "shall take no part in the war unless attacked." Russell did not share Palmerston's concern that British acknowledgment of southern separation meant war with the Union. "My only doubt," he declared, "[was] whether we and France should stir if Russia holds back. Her separation from our move would ensure the rejection of our proposals." Yet he appeared willing to go ahead with France and without the Russians. Perhaps because of their likely absence, he suddenly became amenable to avoiding any mention of separation. . . .

Despite the long-standing belief that the Union victory at Antietam, followed by the preliminary proclamation of emancipation, had halted a move toward British intervention, the truth is that the coming of the battle only put on hold a mediation procedure well under way and then, when the results of the battle became known, encouraged Russell to depart from Palmerston's cautionary strictures to resume the move toward intervention. Union forces had turned back Lee's first major thrust into the North and earned them the right to claim a strategic victory. The administration in Washington had tried to take advantage of that outcome by announcing emancipation in an effort to preempt British intervention. But the battle and proclamation did not shake the interest of Russell, Gladstone, and numerous others outside the ministry in mediation. Antietam and the proclamation combined to raise the specter of a war of subjugation made even more horrible by a certain slave uprising. . . .

In preparation for an October cabinet meeting to discuss the interventionist issue, Russell wrote a memorandum to his colleagues urging support for an armistice. Gladstone had just delivered a fiery speech a few days before in Newcastle, leaving the erroneous impression that the ministry was on the verge of extending recognition to the South. In reality, he had spoken rashly and without authorization, but his action had inadvertently brought attention to the three greatest obstacles to such a move: how to step between the antagonists without becoming involved in the war, how to present a workable solution to the problem, and how to secure Russian participation. Russell, however, failed to grasp these complexities. Emancipation, he now argued in his memo, had authorized the Union armies to commit "acts of plunder, of incendiarism, and of revenge" that would destroy the South. The war must stop. . . .

Russell's most formidable opponent finally emerged in the person of Secretary for War Lewis, who had long been convinced that any form of British intervention would be a mistake. A gentle and unpretentious man, he was a philosopher-scholar of unquestionable integrity who commanded widespread respect because of his wisdom and devotion to justice and country. The American war had disturbed him from its beginning. He had never believed that military force could keep the Union intact. In January 1861, he had declared to a friend: "You may conquer an insurgent province, but you cannot conquer a seceding State." Secession, he confided to another friend, would lead to "arbitration of the sword." But Lewis staunchly opposed intervention— particularly before the Confederacy had proved its claim to nationhood. In a speech in Hereford followed by a memo sent to fellow cabinet members, Lewis insisted that the South had not yet established independence and warned that Russell's armistice proposal would not go to a "conclave of philosophers" but to the great mass of "heated and violent partizans" on both sides who bitterly opposed compromise. He agreed with Russell that Lincoln intended for emancipation to provoke a slave uprising in the South; but Lewis insisted that intervention meant war with the Union. Further, England as mediator had no peace terms to suggest. If any plan sanctioned slavery, the ministry would become its guarantor while alienating the North. If England called for abolition, the South would resist. Where would the boundary lie between North and South? How would England deal with the border states? With the territories? "The sword has not yet traced the conditions of a treaty recognizing the independence of the South."

Lewis's argument only temporarily delayed Russell's call for an armistice, for French emperor Napoleon III soon made a proposal of his own. Russell had postponed the cabinet meeting after his peace plan drew little support from his colleagues, and he found France preoccupied with European problems. But he remained firmly convinced that it was the moral responsibility of the combined powers of England, France, Russia, and perhaps even Austria and Prussia to stop the American war. Then, in late October, Napoleon revived Russell's flickering hopes by proposing an Anglo-French-Russian mediation offer that included a six-month armistice and a suspension of the Union blockade. But the emperor had more—much more—in mind. Privately to Slidell, Napoleon added a dangerous twist to the proposal that, based on Russell's recent abortive involvement with France in Mexico, would not have been surprising if known: Union rejection of the joint offer, the emperor declared, would provide "good reason for recognition" and, in words carrying an obvious reference to the use of force, "perhaps for more active intervention."

Lewis again led the opposition, this time with a second memo to the cabinet of 15,000 words and with a series of letters to the editor of the *Times* that his stepson-in-law, William Vernon Harcourt (later the first person to hold the Whewell Chair of International Law at Cambridge University), signed under the pseudonym of "Historicus." Lewis insisted (as did Harcourt) that intervention would cause war with the Union by allying England with the Confederacy in its drive for independence. Yet to achieve peace, Lewis admitted, international law permitted neutral nations to engage in "an avowed armed interference in a war already existing." But, he asked, would this approach be expedient and wise? The North remained powerful despite secession, and the European powers would have great difficulty in sending fleets and armies to the Potomac. How would they transport large armies across the Atlantic? How would Europe's wooden vessels fare against the North's ironclads? And even if Europe's great powers succeeded in forcing the North to recognize the South, new problems would arise at the peace table. The intervening nations would have to establish in Washington a "Conference of Plenipotentiaries of the Five Great Powers." What would be its makeup? . . .

Lewis's long memo killed the French proposal and prompted a decisive British turn away from intervention in the American war. On 11–12 November, the cabinet met and, after a bitter debate punctuated by Russell's revelation that Russia refused to participate, overwhelmingly rejected Napoleon's offer. Then, as time approached for implementing the Emancipation Proclamation, a curious change in British attitude became evident: public indignation over Lincoln's move unexpectedly eased with the slow realization that slavery's end was in sight. To the north of London, workers gathered in huge rallies beginning in December 1862, cheering the North and proclaiming the rights of workers everywhere. For weeks, Adams was besieged with petitions, resolutions, and letters from working groups (and emancipation societies), all supporting the president's action. More than a few British spokesmen remained infuriated with what they continued to regard as the Union's hypocrisy concerning slavery and only grudgingly joined the swelling flood of support for the North. The Emancipation Proclamation made that task easier. In only that sense did Lincoln's move against slavery have an important impact on England. . . .

Americans have little understanding of the important international repercussions of the battle for Fort Sumter. Indeed, the focus on America's domestic crisis after April 1861 has distorted the history of this era by sharply diminishing the role of diplomacy. Both from television—especially from the widely acclaimed PBS series by Ken Burns—and the numerous books on the military aspects of the war, one gains the impression that President Abraham Lincoln successfully defined this struggle as totally domestic in nature. Appearances belie reality. The president did not succeed in keeping the distinction clear between a rebellion and a war, and the result was that foreign and domestic problems meshed.

🌐 *F U R T H E R   R E A D I N G*

Stuart L. Bernath, *Squall Across the Atlantic* (1970)
Eugene H. Berwanger, *The British Foreign Service and the American Civil War* (1994)
R. J. M. Blackett, *Divided Hearts* (2001) (on British opinion)
Gabor S. Borrit, ed., *Why the Confederacy Lost* (1992)
Kinley J. Brauer, "The Slavery Problem in the Diplomacy of the American Civil War,"
    Pacific Historical Review, 46 (1977), 439–469
Charles S. Campbell, *From Revolution to Rapprochement* (1974)
Richard J. Carwardine, *Lincoln: A Life of Purpose and Power* (2003)
Lynn M. Case and Warren F. Spencer, *The United States and France: Civil War
    Diplomacy* (1970)
Robert Cook, *Civil War America* (2003)
David P. Crook, *The North, the South, and the Great Powers* (1974)
Coy F. Cross, *Lincoln's Man in Liverpool* (2007)
David H. Donald, *Lincoln* (1995)
———, ed., *Why the North Won the Civil War* (1996)
Norman B. Ferris, *Desperate Diplomacy: William H. Seward's Foreign Policy, 1861* (1977)
———, *The "Trent" Affair* (1977)
Philip S. Foner, *British Labor and the American Civil War* (1981)
Joseph A. Fry, *Dixie Looks Abroad* (2002)
Gary W. Gallagher, *The Confederate War* (1997)
Kenneth J. Hagan, *In Peace and War: Interpretation of American Naval History* (1978)
Alfred J. Hanna and Kathryn A. Hanna, *Napoleon III and Mexico* (1971)
Claude M. Hubbard, *The Burden of Confederate Diplomacy* (1998)
Brian Jenkins, *Britain and the War for Union,* 2 vols. (1974–1980)
Howard Jones, *Abraham Lincoln and a New Birth of Freedom* (1999)
———, *Union in Peril* (1992)
Doris Kearns, *Team of Rivals: The Political Genius of Abraham Lincoln* (2006)
C. Douglas Kroll, *Friends in Peace and War* (2007) (on U.S.-Russian relations)
Dean B. Mahin, *One War at a Time* (1999)
H. C. G. Matthew, *Gladstone* (1986)
Robert E. May, ed., *The Union, the Confederacy, and the Atlantic Rim* (1995)
James M. McPherson, *Trial by War* (2008) (on Lincoln)
Frank J. Merli, *The Alabama, British Neutrality, and the American Civil War* (2004)
Phillip E. Myers, *Caution and Cooperation* (2008) (on Anglo-American relations)
Nicholas Onuf and Peter Onuf, *Nations, Markets, and War* (2006)
Bradford Perkins, *From Sea to Sea, 1776–1865* (1993)
W. Dirk Raat, *Mexico and the United States* (1992)
Charles M. Robinson, *Shark of the Confederacy* (1995) (on the *Alabama*)
Norman E. Saul, *Distant Friends: The United States and Russia, 1763–1867* (1991)
Thomas D. Schoonover, *Dollars over Dominion* (1978) (on Mexico)
———, *Mexican Lobby* (1986)
Jay Sexton, *Debtor Diplomacy* (2005)
Warren F. Spencer, *The Confederate Navy in Europe* (1983)
Glyndon G. Van Deusen, *William Henry Seward* (1967)
Gordon H. Warren, *Fountain of Discontent* (1981) (on the *Trent*)
Stephen R. Wise, *Lifetime of the Confederacy* (1988) (on blockade runners)
Robert W. Young, *Robert Murray Mason* (1998)
Craig L. Symonds, *Lincoln and His Admirals* (2008)

CHAPTER 11

Becoming a World Power in the Late Nineteenth Century

Strife over slavery, the sectional contest, and the bloody Civil War cooled the expansionist fervor of the early nineteenth century. But once the national crisis had subsided, expansionists again took up the call. Secretary of State William H. Seward (1861–1869) became their leader, and under his guidance the United States acquired the immense territory of Alaska and the tiny Midway Islands. Congress blocked Seward's other imperial ambitions, but the United States nonetheless steadily pushed its territorial and commercial frontiers farther abroad and became a major participant in the great power struggles that eventually led to the First World War. In the late nineteenth century, it built a "new navy" and ordered its ships to distant lands, participated in international conferences and fairs, scolded Europeans that the Monroe Doctrine remained sacrosanct, and launched Pam Americanism to bring Latin America under the Eagle's wings. U.S.-made products appeared in foreign marketplaces, and investors' dollars drove in other American stakes overseas. At the same time, imported consumer goods became standard fare on shop shelves and in homes across the United States, America exchanged growing numbers of travelers and tourists with distant lands, and the nation became increasingly connected with other peoples and societies worldwide. All of this activity commenced before the United States' defeat of Spain in the war of 1898 and the subsequent seizure of Spain's colonies for inclusion in the U.S. empire.

Historians have studied why and how American foreign policy and expansion shifted during the late nineteenth and early twentieth centuries to become more coherent and sustained, even aggressive—moving the United States from a regional power to a world power. The role of economic factors has particularly drawn scholars' interests, for the faster pace of expansion coincided with the nation's transformation into a thriving industrial economy with an enlarged foreign trade. Some have argued that America's rapidly expanding industrial economy, especially its drive to increase foreign trade, made it a leading actor in the capitalist world system and a major political and military power. Others maintain that economics may explain the timing of the imperial surge, but the motivation for expansion sprang mainly from long-standing ideological and cultural assumptions that celebrated America's mission to extend—by force if necessary—the fruits of liberty and progress to weaker nations and peoples. Still others have emphasized the impediments to expansionism imposed by domestic politics, ineptitude, ignorance, and the American aversion to a powerful federal government.

The late nineteenth century stands as an age of great-power colonialism and growing international integration, when economic, technological, military, and cultural foces connected states, territories, and peoples as never before. Why did the United States seek a pivotal role in the process? Why did it return so vigorously in the post-Civil War years to expansionism and empire? Wherein lie the roots of modern America's rise to world power? These fundamental questions are the subject of this chapter.

D O C U M E N T S

In Document 1, a speech delivered in St. Paul, Minnesota, on September 18, 1860, future secretary of state William H. Seward downplays the impending sectional crisis and expounds on his dream of a U.S. hemispheric empire. Known for his soaring rhetoric, Seward counted Alaska, Canada, Mexico, and the Latin American nations among the acquisitions that would constitute a greater America. Following the Civil War, U.S. policymakers began to fine-tune their overseas agenda. The Dominican Republic attracted U.S. attention because of the political turmoil that rocked the island nation, its potential as a naval base, and its proximity to North America. President Ulysses S. Grant decided to annex the Caribbean country to the United States. In a message to Congress on May 31, 1870, Document 2, he made his case.

Even after the Senate rejected Grant's treaty of annexation, the nation's passion for expansionism accelerated late in the century. In 1881, Secretary of State James G. Blaine planned to hold a Pan American Conference, but he soon left office. In 1888, however, he returned as secretary and organized the first such conference, which met in Washington, D.C., from October 1889 to April 1890. Document 3, a congressional resolution calling for the conference, spells out Blaine's objectives. Captain Alfred T. Mahan, a professor at the Naval War College, wrote the widely circulated book *The Influence of Seapower upon History* (1890), from which Document 4 is drawn. Mahan advocated a strong U.S. Navy and the acquisition of overseas bases. The quest for naval outposts and economic opportunities generated conflict with other nations and peoples. Queen Lili'uokalani of Hawai'i, ousted in 1893 by a revolution engineered by American planters and lawyers eager for annexation of the Hawaiian Islands to the United States, later recalled that the event succeeded only because U.S. forces assisted the conspirators. The United States formally annexed Hawai'i in 1898, the year of the publication of her memoir, *Hawaii's Story by Hawaii's Queen*. Document 5 constitutes two of her formal protests against U.S. actions.

Document 6 sprang from a boundary dispute between Great Britain and Venezuela near British Guiana in South America. Determined to settle the crisis, Secretary of State Richard Olny sent an imperious message to London on July 20, 1895. He invoked the Monroe Doctrine and declared U.S. hegemony over the Western Hemisphere. Through the Treaty of Paris with Spain at the conclusion of war in 1898, the United States brought the former Spanish colonies of the Philippines, Guam, and Puerto Rico under its formal tutelage. The imperial cause served as a rallying point for Republicans that year in their successful bid to maintain control of the White House and the Congress in the fall elections. In Document 7, a speech delivered on September 16, 1898, Indiana's Republican candidate for the U.S. Senate, Albert J. Beveridge, proclaims Americans to be God's "chosen people" and urges his compatriots to rally around the flag and the Anglo-Saxon mission to pursue military bases, commercial supremacy, and empire. Beveridge rode the wave of patriotism to victory and went on to serve two terms in the Senate, where he distinguished himself as a leading spokesperson for empire.

Future Secretary of State William H. Seward Dreams of Hemispheric Empire, 1860

I find myself now, for the first time, on the highlands in the center of the continent of North America, equidistant from the waters of Hudson's bay and the gulf of Mexico, from the Atlantic ocean to the ocean in which the sun sets—here on the spot where spring up, almost side by side, and so near that they may kiss each other, the two great rivers of the continent, the one of which pursuing its strange, capricious, majestic, vivacious course through rapids and cascade, lake after lake, bay after bay, and river after river, till, at last, after a course of two thousand five hundred miles, it brings your commerce into the ocean midway to the ports of Europe, and the other, which meandering through woodland and prairie a like distance of two thousand five hundred miles, taking in tributary after tributary from the east and from the west, bringing together the waters from the western declivity of the Alleghanies and the torrents which roll down the eastern sides of the Rocky mountains, finds the Atlantic ocean in the gulf of Mexico. Here is the central place where the agriculture of the richest regions of North America must begin its magnificent supplies to the whole world. . . . This is then a commanding field; but it is as commanding in regard to the commercial future, for power is not to reside permanently on the eastern slope of the Alleghany mountains, nor in the seaports of the Pacific. . . . In other days, studying what might perhaps have seemed to others a visionary subject, I have cast about for the future the ultimate central seat of power of the North American people. I have looked at Quebec and at New Orleans, at Washington and at San Francisco, at Cincinnati and at St. Louis, and it has been the result of my best conjecture that the seat of power for North America would yet be found in the valley of Mexico; that the glories of the Aztec capital would be renewed, and that city would become ultimately the capital of the United States of America. But I have corrected that view, and I now believe that the last seat of power on the great continent will be found somewhere within a radius not very far from the very spot where I stand, at the head of navigation on the Mississippi river and on the great Mediterranean lakes. . . .

I have never until now occupied that place whence I could grasp the whole grand panorama of the continent, for the happiness of whose present people and of whose future millions of millions, it is the duty of an American statesman to labor. . . . I seem to myself to stand here on this eminence as the traveler who climbs the dome of St. Peter's in Rome. There, through the opening of that dome, he seems to himself to be in almost direct and immediate communication with the Almighty Power that directs and controls the actions and the wills of men, and he looks down with pity on the priests and votaries below who vainly try, by poring over beads and rituals, to study out and influence the mind of the Eternal. Standing here and looking far off into the northwest, I see the Russian as he busily occupies himself in establishing seaports and towns and fortifications, on the verge of this continent, as the outposts of St. Petersburg, and I can say, "Go on, and build up your outposts all

This document can be found in George E. Baker, ed., *The Works of William H. Seward*, Boston: Houghton Mifflin Company, 1884, IV, pp. 331–334.

along the coast up even to the Arctic ocean—they will yet become the outposts of my own country—monuments of the civilization of the United States in the northwest." So I look off on Prince Rupert's land and Canada, and see there an ingenious, enterprising and ambitious people, occupied with bridging rivers and constructing canals, railroads and telegraphs, to organize and preserve great British provinces north of the great lakes, the St. Lawrence, and around the shores of Hudson bay, and I am able to say, "It is very well, you are building excellent states to be hereafter admitted into the American Union." I can look southwest and see, amid all the convulsions that are breaking the Spanish American republics, and in their rapid decay and dissolution, the preparatory stage for the reorganization in free, equal and self-governing members of the United States of America. In the same high range of vision I can look down on the states and the people of the Atlantic coast of Maine and Massachusetts, of New York and Pennsylvania, of Virginia and the Carolinas, and Georgia, and Louisiana, and Texas, and round by the Pacific coast to California and Oregon. I can hear their disputes, their fretful controversies, their threats that if their own separate interests are not gratified and consulted by the federal government they will separate from this Union. I am able to say, "peace, be still." These subjects of contention and dispute that so irritate and anger and provoke and alienate you, are but temporary and ephemeral. . . .

It is under the influence of reflections like these that I thank God here to-day, more fervently than ever, that I live in so great a country as this, and that my lot has been cast in it, not before the period when political society was to be organized, nor yet in that distant period when it is to collapse and fall into ruin, but that I live in the very day and hour when political society is to be effectually organized throughout the entire continent.

🌐 D O C U M E N T   2

President Ulysses S. Grant Urges Annexation of the Dominican Republic, 1870

The doctrine promulgated by President Monroe has been adhered to by all political parties, and I now deem it proper to assert the equally important principle that hereafter no territory on this continent shall be regarded as subject of transfer to a European power.

The Government of San Domingo has voluntarily sought this annexation. It is a weak power, numbering probably less than 120,000 souls, and yet possessing one of the richest territories under the sun, capable of supporting a population of 10,000,000 people in luxury. The people of San Domingo are not capable of maintaining themselves in their present condition, and must look for outside support.

They yearn for the protection of our free institutions and laws, our progress and civilization. Shall we refuse them?

This document can be found in James D. Richardson, ed., *A Compilation of the Messages and Papers of the Presidents* (New York: Bureau of National Literature, 1897), IX, 4015–4017.

I have information which I believe reliable that a European power stands ready now to offer $2,000,000 for the possession of Samaná Bay alone. If refused by us, with what grace can we prevent a foreign power from attempting to secure the prize?

The acquisition of San Domingo is desirable because of its geographical position. It commands the entrance to the Caribbean Sea and the Isthmus transit of commerce. It possesses the richest soil, best and most capacious harbors, most salubrious climate, and the most valuable products of the forests, mine, and soil of any of the West India Islands. Its possession by us will in a few years build up a coastwise commerce of immense magnitude, which will go far toward restoring to us our lost merchant marine. It will give to us those articles which we consume so largely and do not produce, thus equalizing our exports and imports.

In case of foreign war it will give us command of all the islands referred to, and thus prevent an enemy from ever again possessing himself of rendezvous upon our very coast. . . .

San Domingo will become a large consumer of the products of Northern farms and manufactories. The cheap rate at which her citizens can be furnished with food, tools, and machinery will make it necessary that the contiguous islands should have the same advantages in order to compete in the production of sugar, coffee, tobacco, tropical fruits, etc. This will open to us a still wider market for our products. . . .

The acquisition of San Domingo is an adherence to the "Monroe doctrine"; it is a measure of national protection; it is asserting our just claim to a controlling influence over the great commercial traffic soon to flow from east to west by the way of the Isthmus of Darien; it is to build up our merchant marine; it is to furnish new markets for the products of our farms, shops, and manufactories; it is to make slavery insupportable in Cuba and Porto Rico at once and ultimately so in Brazil; it is to settle the unhappy condition of Cuba [in rebellion against Spain], and end an exterminating conflict; it is to provide honest means of paying our honest debts, without overtaxing the people; it is to furnish our citizens with the necessaries of everyday life at cheaper rates than ever before; and it is, in fine, a rapid stride toward that greatness which the intelligence, industry, and enterprise of the citizens of the United States entitle this country to assume among nations.

DOCUMENT 3

Congress Calls for a Pan American Conference, 1888

The Conference is called to consider—

First. Measures that shall tend to preserve and promote the prosperity of the several American States.

Second. Measures toward the formation of an American customs union, under which the trade of the American nations with each other shall, so far as possible and profitable, be promoted.

Third. The establishment of regular and frequent communication between the ports of the several American States and the ports of each other.

This document can be found in the U.S. Department of State, *Papers Relating to the Foreign Relations of the United States, 1888* (Washington, D.C.: Government Printing Office, 1889), p. 1658.

Fourth. The establishment of a uniform system of customs regulations in each of the independent American States to govern the mode of importation and exportation of merchandise and port dues and charges, a uniform method of determining the classification and valuation of such merchandise in the ports of each country, and a uniform system of invoices, and the subject of the sanitation of ships and quarantine.

Fifth. The adoption of a uniform system of weights and measures, and laws to protect the patent-rights, copyrights, and trade-marks of citizens of either country in the other, and for the extradition of criminals.

Sixth. The adoption of a common silver coin, to be issued by each Government, the same to be legal tender in all commercial transactions between the citizens of all of the American States.

Seventh. An agreement upon and recommendation for adoption to their respective Governments of a definite plan of arbitration of all questions, disputes, and differences, that may now or hereafter exist between them, to the end that all difficulties and disputes between such nations may be peaceably settled and wars prevented.

Eighth. And to consider such other subjects relating to the welfare of the several States represented as may be presented by any of said States which are hereby invited to participate in said Conference.

D O C U M E N T   4

Captain Alfred T. Mahan Advocates
a Naval Buildup, 1890

The influence of the government will be felt in its most legitimate manner in maintaining an armed navy, of a size commensurate with the growth of its shipping and importance of the interests connected with it. More important even than the size of the navy is the question of its institutions, favoring a healthful spirit and activity, and providing for rapid development in time of war by an adequate reserve of men and of ships and by measures for drawing out that general reserve power which has before been pointed to, when considering the character and pursuits of the people. Undoubtedly under this second head of warlike preparation must come the maintenance of suitable naval stations, in those distant parts of the world to which the armed shipping must follow the peaceful vessels of commerce. The protection of such stations must depend either upon direct military force, as do Gibraltar and Malta, or upon a surrounding friendly population, such as the American colonists once were to England, and, it may be presumed, the Australian colonists now are. Such friendly surroundings and backing, joined to a reasonable military provision, are the best of defences, and when combined with decided preponderance at sea, make a scattered and extensive empire, like that of England, secure; for while it is true that an unexpected attack may cause disaster in some one quarter, the actual superiority of naval power prevents such disaster from being general or irremediable. History has sufficiently proved this. England's naval bases have been in all parts of the world; and her fleets have at once protected them, kept open the communications between them, and relied upon them for shelter.

This document can be found in Alfred Thayer Mahan, *The Influence of Sea Power Upon History: 1660–1783* (Boston: Little, Brown and Company, 1890), pp. 82–83, 87.

Colonies attached to the mother-country afford, therefore, the surest means of supporting abroad the sea power of a country. In peace, the influence of the government should be felt in promoting by all means a warmth of attachment and a unity of interest which will make the welfare of one the welfare of all, and the quarrel of one the quarrel of all; and in war, or rather for war, by inducing such measures of organization and defence as shall be felt by all to be a fair distribution of a burden of which each reaps the benefit.

Such colonies the United States has not and is not likely to have. As regards purely military naval stations, the feeling of her people was probably accurately expressed by an historian of the English navy a hundred years ago, speaking then of Gibraltar and Port Mahon. "Military governments," said he, "agree so little with the industry of a trading people, and are in themselves so repugnant to the genius of the British people, that I do not wonder that men of good sense and of all parties have inclined to give up these, as Tangiers was given up." Having therefore no foreign establishments, either colonial or military, the ships of war of the United States, in war, will be like land birds, unable to fly far from their own shores. To provide restingplaces for them, where they can coal and repair, would be one of the first duties of a government proposing to itself the development of the power of the nation at sea. . . .

The question is eminently one in which the influence of the government should make itself felt, to build up for the nation a navy which, if not capable of reaching distant countries, shall at least be able to keep clear the chief approaches to its own. The eyes of the country have for a quarter of a century been turned from the sea; the results of such a policy and of its opposite will be shown in the instance of France and of England. Without asserting a narrow parallelism between the case of the United States and either of these, it may safely be said that it is essential to the welfare of the whole country that the conditions of trade and commerce should remain, as far as possible, unaffected by an external war. In order to do this, the enemy must be kept not only out of our ports, but far away from our coasts.

🌍 *D O C U M E N T   5*
_____

Queen Lili'uokalani Protests U.S. Intervention in Hawai'i, 1893, 1897

January 17, 1893

I, Liliuokalani, by the grace of God and under the constitution of the Hawaiian kingdom Queen, do hereby solemnly protest against any and all acts done against myself and the constitutional government of the Hawaiian kingdom by certain persons claiming to have established a Provisional Government of and for this kingdom.

That I yield to the superior force of the United States of America, whose Minister Plenipotentiary, His Excellency John L. Stevens, has caused United States troops

_____

This document can be found in Lili'uokalani, *Hawaii's Story by Hawaii's Queen* (Boston: Lothrop, Lee, & Shepard, 1898), pp. 354–356, 387–388.

to be landed at Honolulu, and declared that he would support the said Provisional Government.

Now, to avoid any collision of armed forces, and perhaps the loss of life, I do, under this protest and impelled by said forces, yield my authority until such time as the Government of the United States shall, upon the facts being presented to it, undo the action of its representative, and reinstate me in the authority which I claim as the constitutional sovereign of the Hawaiian Islands.

June 17, 1897

I, Liliuokalani of Hawaii, by the will of God named heir apparent on the tenth day of April, A.D. 1877, and by the grace of God Queen of the Hawaiian Islands on the seventeenth day of January, A.D. 1893, do hereby protest against the ratification of a certain treaty, which, so I am informed, has been signed at Washington by Messrs. Hatch, Thurston, and Kinney, purporting to cede those Islands to the territory and dominion of the United States. I declare such a treaty to be an act of wrong toward the native and part-native people of Hawaii, an invasion of the rights of the ruling chiefs, in violation of international rights both toward my people and toward friendly nations with whom they have made treaties, the perpetuation of the fraud whereby the constitutional government was overthrown, and, finally, an act of gross injustice to me.

Because the official protests made by me on the seventeenth day of January, 1893, to the so-called Provisional Government was signed by me, and received by said government with the assurance that the case was referred to the United States of America for arbitration.

Because that protest and my communications to the United States Government immediately thereafter expressly declare that I yielded my authority to the forces of the United States in order to avoid bloodshed, and because I recognized the futility of a conflict with so formidable a power.

Because the President of the United States, the Secretary of State, and an envoy commissioned by them reported in official documents that my government was unlawfully coerced by the forces, diplomatic and naval, of the United States; that I was at the date of their investigations the constitutional ruler of my people.

Because such decision of the recognized magistrates of the United States was officially communicated to me and to Sanford B. Dole, and said Dole's resignation requested by Albert S. Willis, the recognized agent and minister of the Government of the United States.

Because neither the above-named commission nor the government which sends it has ever received any such authority from the registered voters of Hawaii, but derives its assumed powers from the so-called committee of public safety, organized on or about the seventeenth day of January, 1893, said committee being composed largely of persons claiming American citizenship, and not one single Hawaiian was a member thereof, or in any way participated in the demonstration leading to its existence.

Because my people, about forty thousand in number, have in no way been consulted by those, three thousand in number, who claim the right to destroy the independence of Hawaii. My people constitute four-fifths of the legally qualified voters of Hawaii, and excluding those imported for the demands of labor, about the same proportion of the inhabitants.

Because said treaty ignores, not only the civic rights of my people, but, further, the hereditary property of their chiefs. Of the 4,000,000 acres composing the territory said treaty offers to annex, 1,000,000 or 915,000 acres has in no way been heretofore recognized as other than the private property of the constitutional monarch, subject to a control in no way differing from other items of a private estate.

Because it is proposed by said treaty to confiscate said property, technically called the crown lands, those legally entitled thereto, either now or in succession, receiving no consideration whatever for estates, their title to which has been always undisputed, and which is legitimately in my name at this date.

Because said treaty ignores, not only all professions of perpetual amity and good faith made by the United States in former treaties with the sovereigns representing the Hawaiian people, but all treaties made by those sovereigns with other and friendly powers, and it is thereby in violation of international law.

Because, by treating with the parties claiming at this time the right to cede said territory of Hawaii, the Government of the United States receives such territory from the hands of those whom its own magistrates (legally elected by the people of the United States, and in office in 1893) pronounced fraudulently in power and unconstitutionally ruling Hawaii.

Therefore, I, Liliuokalani of Hawaii, do hereby call upon the President of that nation, to whom alone I yielded my property and my authority, to withdraw said treaty (ceding said Islands) from further consideration. I ask the honorable Senate of the United States to decline to ratify said treaty, and I implore the people of this great and good nation, from whom my ancestors learned the Christian religion, to sustain their representatives in such acts of justice and equity as may be in accord with the principles of their fathers, and to the Almighty Ruler of the universe, to him who judgeth righteously, I commit my cause.

🌐 *D O C U M E N T   6*

Secretary of State Richard Olney Trumpets U.S. Hegemony During the Venezuela Crisis, 1895

That America is in no part open to colonization, though the proposition was not universally admitted at the time of its first enunciation [in 1823], has long been universally conceded. We are now concerned, therefore, only with that other practical application of the Monroe doctrine the disregard of which by an European power is to be deemed an act of unfriendliness towards the United States. The precise scope and limitations of this rule cannot be too clearly apprehended. It does not establish any general protectorate by the United States over other American states. It does not relieve any American state from its obligations as fixed by international law nor

This document can be found in the U.S. Department of State, *Papers Relating to the Foreign Relations of the United States, 1895* (Washington, D.C.: Government Printing Office, 1896), Part I, pp. 554–555, 558, 561–562.

prevent any European power directly interested from enforcing such obligations or from inflicting merited punishment for the breach of them. It does not contemplate any interference in the internal affairs of any American state or in the relations between it and other American states. It does not justify any attempt on our part to change the established form of government of any American state or to prevent the people of such state from altering that form according to their own will and pleasure. The rule in question has but a single purpose and object. It is that no European power or combination of European powers shall forcibly deprive an American state of the right and power of self-government and of shaping for itself its own political fortunes and destinies. . . .

Today the United States is practically sovereign on this continent, and its fiat is law upon the subjects to which it confines its interposition. Why? It is not because of the pure friendship or good will felt for it. It is not simply by reason of its high character as a civilized state, nor because wisdom and justice and equity are the invariable characteristics of the dealings of the United States. It is because, in addition to all other grounds, its infinite resources combined with its isolated position render it master of the situation and practically invulnerable as against any or all other powers.

All the advantages of this superiority are at once imperiled if the principle be admitted that European powers may convert American states into colonies or provinces of their own. The principle would be eagerly availed of, and every power doing so would immediately acquire a base of military operations against us. What one power was permitted to do could not be denied to another, and it is not inconceivable that the struggle now going on for the acquisition of Africa might be transferred to South America. If it were, the weaker countries would unquestionably be soon absorbed, while the ultimate result might be the partition of all South America between the various European powers. The disastrous consequences to the United States of such a condition of things are obvious. The loss of prestige, of authority, and of weight in the councils of the family of nations, would be among the least of them. Our only real rivals in peace as well as enemies in war would be found located at our very doors. Thus far in our history we have been spared the burdens and evils of immense standing armies and all the other accessories of huge warlike establishments, and the exemption has largely contributed to our national greatness and wealth as well as to the happiness of every citizen. But, with the powers of Europe permanently encamped on American soil, the ideal conditions we have thus far enjoyed can not be expected to continue. We too must be armed to the teeth, we too must convert the flower of our male population into soldiers and sailors, and by withdrawing them from the various pursuits of peaceful industry we too must practically annihilate a large share of the productive energy of the nation. . . .

Thus, as already intimated, the British demand that her right to a portion of the disputed territory shall be acknowledged before she will consent to an arbitration as to the rest seems to stand upon nothing but her own *ipse dixit.* She says to Venezuela, in substance: "You can get none of the debatable land by force, because you are not strong enough; you can get none by a treaty, because I will not agree; and you can take your chance of getting a portion by arbitration, only if you first agree to abandon to me such other portion as I may designate." It is not perceived how such an attitude can be defended nor how it is reconcilable with that love of justice and fair play so eminently characteristic of the English race. It in effect deprives Venezuela of her free agency and puts her under virtual duress. Territory acquired by reason of it will be as much wrested from her by the strong hand as if occupied by British troops or covered by British fleets. It seems therefore quite impossible that this position of Great Britain should be assented to by the United States, or that, if such position be adhered to with the result of enlarging the bounds of British Guiana, it should not be regarded as amounting, in substance, to an invasion and conquest of Venezuelan territory.

DOCUMENT 7

Indiana Republican Albert J. Beveridge Campaigns for Office and Empire, 1898

It is a glorious history our God has bestowed upon His chosen people; a history heroic with faith in our mission and our future; a history of statesmen who flung the boundaries of the Republic out into unexplored lands and savage wilderness: a history of soldiers who carried the flag across blazing deserts and through the ranks of hostile mountains, even to the gates of sunset; a history of a multiplying people who overran a continent in half a century. . . .

Have we no mission to perform, no duty to discharge to our fellow-man? Has God endowed us with gifts beyond our deserts and marked us as the people of His peculiar favor, merely to rot in our own selfishness, as men and nations must, who take cowardice for their companion and self for their deity—as China has, as India has, as Egypt has? . . .

Hawaii is ours; Porto Rico is to be ours; at the prayer of her people Cuba finally will be ours; in the islands of the East, even to the gates of Asia, coaling stations are to be ours at the very least; the flag of a liberal government is to float over the Philippines, and may it be the banner that Taylor unfurled in Texas and Fremont carried to the coast.

The march of the flag! In 1789 the flag of the Republic waved over 4,000,000 souls in thirteen states, and their savage territory which stretched to the Mississippi, to Canada, to the Floridas. The timid minds of that day said that no new territory was needed, and, for the hour, they were right. But Jefferson, through whose intellect the centuries marched; Jefferson, who dreamed of Cuba as an American state; Jefferson, the first Imperialist of the Republic—Jefferson acquired that imperial territory which swept from the Mississippi to the mountains, from Texas to the British possessions, and the march of the flag began! . . .

[Opponents of empire] tells us that we ought not to govern a people without their consent. I answer, The rule of liberty that all just government derives its authority from the consent of the governed, applies only to those who are capable of self-government. We govern the Indians without their consent, we govern our territories without their consent, we govern our children without their consent. How do they

---

From Albert J. Beveridge *The Meaning of the Times* (Freeport, N.Y.: Books for Libraries Press, 1898), (Bobbs, Merrill), pp. 47–49, 51–57.

know that our government would be without their consent? Would not the people of the Philippines prefer the just, humane, civilizing government of this Republic to the savage, bloody rule of pillage and extortion from which we have rescued them?

And, regardless of this formula of words made only for enlightened, self-governing people, do we owe no duty to the world? Shall we turn these peoples back to the reeking hands from which we have taken them? Shall we abandon them, with Germany, England, Japan, hungering for them? Shall we save them from those nations, to give them a self-rule of tragedy? . . .

And, now, obeying the same voice that Jefferson heard and obeyed, that Jackson heard and obeyed, that Monroe heard and obeyed, that Seward heard and obeyed, that Grant heard and obeyed, that Harrison heard and obeyed, our President to-day plants the flag over the islands of the seas, outposts of commerce, citadels of national security, and the march of the flag goes on! . . .

And so, while we did not need the territory taken during the past century at the time it was acquired, we do need what we have taken in 1898, and we need it now. The resources and the commerce of these immensely rich dominions will be increased as much as American energy is greater than Spanish sloth. In Cuba, alone, there are 15,000,000 acres of forest unacquainted with the ax, exhaustless mines of iron, priceless deposits of manganese, millions of dollars' worth of which we must buy, to-day, from the Black Sea districts. There are millions of acres yet unexplored.

The resources of Porto Rico have only been trifled with. The riches of the Philippines have hardly been touched by the finger-tips of modern methods. And they produce what we consume, and consume what we produce—the very predestination of reciprocity—a reciprocity "not made with hands, eternal in the heavens." . . .

The commercial supremacy of the Republic means that this Nation is to be the sovereign factor in the peace of the world. For the conflicts of the future are to be conflicts of trade—struggles for markets—commercial wars for existence. . . .

So Hawaii furnishes us a naval base in the heart of the Pacific; the Ladrones another, a voyage further on; Manila another, at the gates of Asia—Asia, to the trade of whose hundreds of millions American merchants, manufacturers, farmers, have as good right as those of Germany or France or Russia or England; Asia, whose commerce with the United Kingdom alone amounts to hundreds of millions of dollars every year; Asia, to whom Germany looks to take her surplus products; Asia, whose doors must not be shut against American trade. Within five decades the bulk of Oriental commerce will be ours. . . .

Wonderfully has God guided us. Yonder at Bunker Hill and Yorktown His providence was above us. At New Orleans and on ensanguined seas His hand sustained us. Abraham Lincoln was His minister and His was the altar of freedom the Nation's soldiers set up on a hundred battle-fields. His power directed Dewey in the East and delivered the Spanish fleet into our hands, as He delivered the elder Armada into the hands of our English sires two centuries ago. The American people can not use a dishonest medium of exchange; it is ours to set the world its example of right and honor. We can not fly from our world duties; it is ours to execute the purpose of a fate that has driven us to be greater than our small intentions. We can not retreat from any soil where Providence has unfurled our banner; it is ours to save that soil for liberty and civilization.

In the first essay, Robert Kagan of the Carnegie Endowment for International Peace emphasizes the influence of the Civil War experience on America's late nineteenth-century rise to world power. Kagan casts the Union's victory over the forces of secession and slavery as America's first experiment in ideological conquest and postwar nation-building. He argues that the North's triumph infused U.S. foreign policy in the decades that followed with a distinctive moral tone. Postwar Republican leaders limited the nation's territorial acquisitions to a handful of overseas naval bases, but vigorously pursued commercial and ideological activism. Proud of their own liberty and progress, U.S. officials categorized other nations and peoples as needing varying degrees of reform. This body of thought, Kagan advises, often led policymakers to judge international politics according to simplistic and ethnocentric civilizational standards.

In the second essay, Michael H. Hunt of the University of North Carolina at Chapel Hill highlights America's economic and political development to explain its ascendancy to world power after the Civil War. Rich in natural resources and a safe distance from Europe's wars, the nation exploited its technological prowess and its ability to attract foreign capital and migrant labor to achieve primacy in the international economy. To maximize growth, local, state, and federal governments built extensive transportation systems, minimized business regulation, and kept taxes low. Hunt dismisses the notion of America's ideological uniqueness, noting that U.S. officials, very much like their counterparts in Europe and Japan, increasingly adopted a posture of racial and male chauvinism as they looked outward in search of economic opportunities, military bases, and empire.

In the last essay, Fareed Zakaria, a political scientist and editor of *Newsweek's* international magazine, offers a different perspective. Although he agrees that America emerged from the Civil War a powerful, industrial nation, Zakaria argues that the country's weak central government, featuring a tiny military and ragtag foreign service, inhibited overseas expansion and dictated a relatively isolationist posture toward the world. Held in check by strong congressional leaders, America's embrace of global activism awaited the emergence of a more powerful state structure, including the rise of the modern presidency, during the 1890s and the early years of the new century.

The Civil War and the Creed of Civilizational Progress

ROBERT KAGAN

The impact of the Civil War on American foreign policy was . . . profound. The Civil War was America's second great moral war, but unlike the Revolution it was a war of conquest. The North liberated the oppressed segment of the South's population and subjugated the oppressors. It established a decadelong military occupation of the South's territory, abolished the despotic institution of slavery, and attempted to establish reformed political and economic systems that would prevent a return to the old ways.

The Civil War was America's first experiment in ideological conquest, therefore, and what followed was America's first experiment in "nation-building." When Grant accepted Lee's surrender, the South lay in ruins. The southern economy was destroyed, and an entire generation of men had been killed, maimed, or incapacitated. The Confederate government was vanquished, so the U.S. Army became "the sole source of law and order in occupied areas." Army provost marshals were de facto governors of southern civilians, regulating every aspect of life, from arresting suspected "rebels" to distributing food and clothing. During the war Lincoln had established loyalist governments in some of the occupied states, but even these were dependent on and subordinate to the military department commanders.

To the North, the defeated South was, in the argot of the twentieth century, an underdeveloped nation. Its underdevelopment, its backwardness, exemplified by the archaic institution of slavery, many northerners believed, had been responsible for the horrendous conflict that had almost destroyed the entire nation. Now the North, having subdued the rebellion and punished its leaders, had the task not only of standing the conquered land back on its feet, but of curing it of the evils that had led to war, which in turn meant dragging it forcibly into the modern world. . . .

For the generation that lived through it, the Civil War would forever remain the most important event of their lives. Theirs was, as Oliver Wendell Holmes, Jr., later said, a generation "touched by fire." Just as World War II cast its shadow over American foreign policy for a half century after its conclusion—President George H. W. Bush, elected in 1988, had served as a pilot in the war—so the Civil War's influence on Americans persisted well into the beginning of the twentieth century. President William McKinley, elected in 1896 and again in 1900, had served as a major in the Union army, and in the nine presidential elections between the end of the Civil War and the election of Theodore Roosevelt in 1904, every Republican presidential candidate except one had served as an officer in the Civil War.

A living symbol of the continuing fixation on the sectional conflict and the issues of slavery and black rights was Charles Sumner, the onetime scourge of the slave power who after the war helped lead the Radical cause from his perch as chairman of the Senate Foreign Relations Committee. Probably no member of Congress in American history ever wielded more influence over foreign policy. . . .

The foreign policy question to which Sumner devoted most of his energies during the Reconstruction era, and on which he repeatedly frustrated the designs of two administrations, was the settlement of outstanding claims against England from the Civil War—the so-called *Alabama* claims. Most Americans, even the more viscerally anti-British politicians, focused chiefly on gaining British compensation for the economic damage done by Confederate commerce raiders operating with impunity out of British ports. That constituted a sizable claim, eventually determined by a commission of arbitration to amount to over $15 million. Sumner cared more about justice than about compensation, however. He wanted to punish Britain for its pro-Confederate actions and sympathies during the Civil War. Had it not been for British sympathy with the South, he believed, the rebellion would have quickly collapsed. England's actions had prolonged the war, therefore, and exacerbated the suffering of the American people. But in Sumner's eyes, British sins were even greater than that. Once the leader of the worldwide antislavery crusade—the hope and inspiration of the American antislavery movement and of Sumner himself—the British government during the Civil War had sold its soul for cotton. By its "flagrant, unnatural departure from that anti-slavery rule which . . . was the avowed creed of England," Sumner charged, the British government had "opened the gates of war" and then fanned the flames of destruction. What kind of financial settlement could compensate for such a historic moral betrayal? Sumner toted up the cost at something in excess of $2 billion (more than $25 billion in today's dollars), but he was prepared to accept Canada in lieu of a cash payment.

Sumner's passion for the issues of slavery and black rights also shaped his views on what became in the decade after the Civil War the perennial question of Santo Domingo. Whether to annex Santo Domingo (later the Dominican Republic) to the United States or, less ambitiously, to lease Samana Bay as a port for American warships, became one of the biggest foreign policy controversies of the Reconstruction era. But the hullabaloo over Santo Domingo had little to do with strategic or economic considerations. Senior American naval officers wanted Samana Bay partly because Confederate raiders during the Civil War had revealed the nation's vulnerability to attacks against its commerce and hence the desirability of acquiring what Seward called "island outposts" in the Caribbean for both military and commercial reasons. Merchants and West Coast politicians who favored building a transisthmian canal to secure easier passage between the Atlantic and Pacific viewed the island outposts as useful for defending and supplying the ships that would carry American trade through a Nicaraguan or Panamanian passage. The Dominican leader of the time, who eagerly sought either annexation or protectorate status to defend against his Haitian neighbors, held a dubious plebiscite that allegedly registered popular support for annexation. In the United States President Andrew Johnson supported the acquisition, as did Seward. President Grant was enthusiastic; [Secretary of State] Hamilton Fish was much less so but willing to go along. . . .

Instead, Sumner managed to build enough opposition in the Senate to deny Grant the two-thirds majority required to pass the treaty. Some of this opposition was purely partisan, and so was some of the support. But what ultimately killed the proposal was a combination of lingering sectional animosities, disagreements over what to do with the South, and the question of race. The defeat revealed the subtle changes that had come to American attitudes about foreign policy, and particularly about territorial expansion, as a result of the long sectional crisis and the Civil War.

Race and racism were a significant factor for many opponents of annexation, though for a variety of different and sometimes contradictory reasons. A powerful bloc of political leaders simply opposed adding the darker-skinned population of Dominicans to the already large population of African-Americans. . . .

Sumner opposed annexation of Santo Domingo not because he wanted to keep blacks away from whites but because he wanted to keep whites away from blacks. He wanted to preserve one place in the hemisphere where blacks could rule themselves free from white domination. An "ordinance of Nature," he claimed, a "higher law" had set aside the island of Santo Domingo for the "colored race" as a place where blacks could live free. . . .

The northern Republicans who dominated American politics after the war, meanwhile, brought to the Congress, the White House, and the State Department a perspective significantly shaped by long years of opposing the slave power. To many leading northerners, the Civil War had been fought precisely to prevent the South from expanding its territory, from annexing Santo Domingo, and from buying or conquering Cuba, more of Mexico, and parts of Central America. Containment of the southern expansionist drive had been the unifying principle of the Republican Party at its founding. Opposing territorial manifest destiny, when it aimed southward, was an established Republican Party tradition. After the Civil War this strain of opposition to southern territorial expansion continued to influence Republican policies. Even in the 1880s Blaine would recall that the nation's territorial acquisitions prior to the Civil War had "all been in the interest of slavery."

As before the war, there were exceptions to Republican opposition to territorial expansion. Many who opposed expansion southward still looked longingly northward. [Missouri Senator Carl] Schurz saw in the northern territories "a magnificent field . . . for our ambition of aggrandizement" and mistakenly hoped, along with many others, that the Canadian people would happily choose annexation to the United States if given the opportunity. It "fills my soul with delight when I see events preparing themselves which will lead the whole continent north of us into our arms." With its white, predominantly Anglo-Saxon and Protestant population, Canada could be absorbed without injecting a tropical, dark-skinned poison into the nation's bloodstream. . . .

Some leading Republicans still wanted to acquire naval stations and "island outposts," such as Samana Bay, or a port in Haiti or the Danish West Indies, both for the protection of the American coastline and American shipping and for the defense of an eventual canal. When the era of Reconstruction passed, Republican policy makers would return to these plans again. The purchase or lease of naval stations from which to promote and defend commerce had always been considered by northern Whigs and Republicans to be morally superior to the southern desire for territory in which to implant slavery. Grant's plans for Santo Domingo had failed in part because they had crossed the line from seeking a harbor to annexing an entire foreign population and thereby had acquired an excessively southern flavor.

Finally, there was the question of Hawaii, which had long been an object of first Whig and then Republican ambitions in the antebellum years. In the 1840s the annexation of Hawaii had been blocked by the sectional struggle, partly because the Hawaiian population, fearing enslavement, had insisted on admission to the Union as a nonslave state. It was another measure of how much Republican policies after the Civil War continued to be shaped by prewar attitudes that the acquisition of Hawaii, despite its large, dark-skinned, "mongrel" population, remained high on the agenda of Blaine and most Republican leaders, even those who rejected expansion into the tropics south of the Rio Grande.

These exceptions did not prevent Republican leaders after the Civil War from insisting, and believing, that the Union victory had put an end to the nation's territorial expansionism and certainly to expansion by military conquest. Any island outposts would be acquired not by force of arms but by purchase or by voluntary annexation. . . .

The postwar turn away from territorial expansionism was no turn toward isolationism. Republican leaders envisioned an enormous increase in American influence, commercial, political, and moral. They believed the United States, purged of slavery and slave power imperialism, stood on a higher moral plane. The path was clear for the United States to play the role it had always been destined to play, as a great power—indeed, the greatest of world powers—wielding its benevolent influence across the globe. . . .

Americans did not embark on a positive "mission" to change the world after the Civil War. There was no grand strategy for global reform, nor any deliberate policy to remake any specific country in the liberal mold. But when events or their own actions brought Americans into contact with "great social and moral wrongs," they responded with protest, sometimes with diplomatic interference, and occasionally with force, depending on the circumstances. Even when the United States took no particular action at all to address perceived wrongs, Americans formed attitudes toward other countries and peoples that affected their judgment at critical moments. There is more to a nation's foreign policies than invasions and annexations or the acquisition of territory and markets. The attitudes that Americans developed toward the rest of the world provided the context in which they acted. And sometimes the actions came long after the attitudes were formed.

One example was the evolving American attitude toward tsarist Russia. During the Civil War most Union supporters had viewed Russia favorably, mistakenly believing the tsar had intervened on the Union's side when the Russian fleet, looking for a place to hide from the British and French, decided to put in at New York harbor. "God bless the Russians!" Navy Secretary Gideon Welles had exclaimed. Northern antislavery leaders had also developed a high opinion of Alexander II, the "Tsar Liberator" who freed the serfs two years before Lincoln freed the slaves.

Soon after the Civil War ended, however, this goodwill evaporated, and the reason had little to do with matters of commerce or security. When Russia sold Alaska in 1867, it backed out of the Western Hemisphere and for the next three decades posed less danger to perceived American interests than any of the other great powers. Yet from the 1860s onward a large number of Americans came to despise Russia on grounds that were moral, humanitarian, and ideological.

American hostility to the Russian government grew out of its treatment of its Jewish population. Starting in the 1860s Alexander II began enforcing old anti-Semitic regulations, and tsarist authorities, refusing to distinguish between Russian Jews and American Jews, abused and sometimes arrested the latter for doing proscribed business while in Russia. In the late 1860s the issue came to dominate Russian-American relations, thoroughly souring American attitudes toward the tsarist government over the next three decades. . . .

Americans applied this measuring stick to all nations and peoples that came into their line of sight. Sometimes their judgments about who measured up were dubious, their perceptions distorted by being refracted through the lens of America's own circumstances and experiences. For instance, Bismarck's Germany enjoyed overwhelming American support for a brief time during and just after the Franco-Prussian War of 1870–71. Northerners, Republicans, and the U.S. government they controlled were grateful for Prussia's pro-Union leanings during the Civil War and for German immigrants' contribution to the northern cause. It helped that Germany's opponent was France, since northerners hated France for its pro-southern sympathies (many southerners and Democrats took the opposite view, of course) and for attempting to implant a European monarch in Mexico. The French invasion force had departed only three years before the war with Prussia. It helped, too, that the ethnic German population in the United States outnumbered the French immigrants by fifteen to one and was a crucial Republican voting bloc in several states.

These factors would have weighed less in the scales had not many Americans also convinced themselves that Bismarck's newly unified Germany would be a beacon of liberalism in Europe. Its federal constitution looked on the surface to be much like the American federal constitution. Bismarck in the early years often allied himself with the German National Liberal Party, and Protestant America applauded his

Kulturkampf against the powers and privileges of the German Catholic church, while it lasted. One American observer happily declared that the prevailing "tendency in Europe" was toward "the American system of separating church and state." The U.S. minister in Berlin, the historian George Bancroft, predicted the new German Empire would be "the most liberal government on the continent of Europe." It was "the child of America," its very birth inspired by the Union victory. Hamilton Fish agreed that the Germans were copying the American Constitution and American-style liberalism, and President Grant in an address to Congress in February 1871 applauded "the adoption in Europe of the American system of union under the control and direction of a free people." German success could not "fail to extend popular institutions and to enlarge the peaceful influence of American ideas."

Many Americans viewed the Franco-German conflict not in geopolitical terms, as a struggle between great powers, but in ideological and civilizational terms, as a struggle between liberalism and tyranny, progress and reaction. If Germany was the alleged outpost of American-style liberty in Europe, Napoleon III's France was the exemplar of imperial despotism. . . .

American's high expectations for a liberal Germany were indeed severely disappointed over the coming decades, as the imagined promise of liberal constitutional government soon devolved into the reality of conservative rule under the ever-shifting Bismarck and the kaiser. The early caricature of a peaceful, progressive, liberty-loving Germany metamorphosed into a very different caricature, of "Kaiser Bill" and an "autocratic, militaristic, rude, presumptuous Germany." Nasty trade battles in the 1880s helped this transformation along, and by the 1890s many Americans hated and feared the kaiser's Germany as much as they hated and feared the tsar's Russia. In both cases American perceptions of these nations as somehow backward, hostile to progress, despotic, and therefore aggressive shaped their strategic judgment. They provided the ideological backdrop for the confrontation between the United States and Germany over the tiny islands of Samoa in the 1880s and cast in a more sinister light Germany's tentative and mostly feeble probes in the Caribbean. . . .

Americans made Manichean distinctions in Asia, too, and looked for signs that their model of political and economic progress was being emulated by others. They searched "to find in progressive Chinese and Japanese," and later in progressive Koreans, "an image of progressive Americans." By the late 1860s a sturdy consensus had formed around the proposition that the progressive force in Asia was Japan, while China was a bastion of backwardness and barbarism. The ancient Chinese civilization, with its confident sense of superiority and apparent lack of interest in the outside world, including the "modern" world of Europe and America, made it contemptible in the eyes of most Americans. . . .

Japan, on the other hand, appeared to be everything China was not. Beginning in the late 1860s, when the restoration of the Meiji emperor produced a determined effort to copy Western ways and institutions, Americans looked upon Japan as a model of progress in Asia. They admired its people's "eagerness to adopt new ideas." The fact that Americans took credit for "opening" Japan, with Admiral Oliver Hazard Perry's expedition in 1853, enhanced their paternalistic fondness. A memorandum prepared for congressional committees in 1872 explained that "the Japanese people not only desire to follow, as far as possible, in all educational and political affairs, the example of the Americans, but . . . they look upon them as their best friends, among the nations of the globe." A best-selling American travelogue in the 1870s reported that Westernization and modernization had "taken Japan out of the ranks of the non-progressive nations" and "out of the stagnant life of Asia." Japan's advancement toward civilization practically removed it from its racial category in American eyes. The Japanese were increasingly viewed less as true Asians than as honorary Anglo-Saxons, "more Western than Asian." Or rather, more American. With their "vigor, thrift, and intelligence," the Japanese were "a bright, progressive people—the Americans, so called, of Asia." The strikingly different ways Americans viewed Japan and China had much to do with seeing their own reflection in the former but not the latter: "Japan was, and China was not, becoming like America."

Americans viewed conflicts among the Asian nations much as they viewed European conflicts, as contests between progress and reaction. This perspective often outweighed narrow strategic calculations and was independent of economic calculations. Americans regarded China as weak and contemptible, and they recognized that Japan was a rising power destined to be a force in East Asia, where Americans also hoped someday to be a force. American interests were more likely to clash with a rising Japan than a prostrate China. Yet they rooted for Japan in the Sino-Japanese War of 1894–95, precisely because it was strong and progressive and China was backward and pitiful. To the American mind, it was China's backwardness that was threatening while Japan's modernization was reassuring. . . .

American attitudes toward European and Asian powers revealed how after the Civil War the ideas of progress and civilization provided organizing principles for American thinking about foreign relations. This view was inherited from the Enlightenment and enjoyed an old pedigree in America. The founding generation had shared the prevailing Enlightenment faith in liberal progress, as well as the popular belief that the seat of civilization had over the centuries traveled west, from ancient China to Rome to Great Britain and finally to America. . . . Thanks to the work of Charles Darwin and his popularizers, it also acquired the aura of scientific "truth" in an age when reverence for science was growing. [The sociologist] Herbert Spencer, whose work was probably more widely read in America than Darwin's, extended evolutionary theory to human societies and also provided a new gloss of scientific authority to the old Enlightenment idea, well articulated by [the historian] Edward Gibbon, that human societies progressed on a developmental continuum from savagery to barbarism to civilization and then eventually, like Rome, to decay. Darwin's theory of evolution presented a dire challenge to theologians—though some, like Josiah Strong, managed to blend Darwinism and Christianity in their worldview—but it fit well with American ideas of progress that were rooted not in religion but in the secular ideas of the Enlightenment.

This fusion of old and new theories about human progress produced what one historian has called an American "ideology of civilization." Americans evaluated other nations and their relationship to the United States according to where they stood on the continuum of progress. . . .

"Opening" other nations to commerce was in American interests, therefore, not only because there was money to be made but because in time commercial penetration would hasten the progress of backward peoples toward civilization. They would become more liberal, more commercial, and therefore less threatening to the United States and to the civilized world in general. The spread of civilization was important not so much to accept a "white man's burden" but because it would bring "order worldwide through the spread of morality and the reinforcement of virtue." For some Americans, like [Theodore] Roosevelt, civilizing the world's barbaric peoples was all the more urgent because, according to the same reigning evolutionary paradigm, advanced liberal commercial societies like the United States were in danger of losing the martial spirit necessary to defend themselves. The world had to be made safe for civilized peoples. . . .

This universalistic and moralistic belief in progress distinguished Americans from most other peoples around the world, even to some degree from the liberal British. The sharpest contrast was with the Chinese, with their ancient Confucian view of "an eternal political order." While the Americans' view of progress made them look expectantly to other cultures and societies, anticipating and hoping for their evolution toward civilization, the Chinese were secure in their belief in a fixed hierarchy of which they were at the summit. The difference between the American and the Chinese perspectives was the difference between a nation founded upon universal principles and a people who considered their own culture unique and not transferable to others. Americans considered the Chinese hopelessly backward and out of step with the spirit of the age. But in fact it was the American perspective that was the more unusual, the more distant from the general view of humanity at the time, and also the more revolutionary in its implications. Most of the nations and peoples in the world in the late nineteenth century actually stood closer to the Chinese view of eternal order than to the American view of eternal progress. Even Europeans, despite repeated revolutions and a growing movement toward liberalism in some countries, still had a more organic and fixed view of society and were less sure of the benefits of progress. Americans were by far the most extreme in their universalism and in their belief in the inevitability and desirability of change.

Even American optimism about progress was not unqualified, however. While backward societies could be led toward civilization by the more advanced nations, many believed there was a limit to how quickly this process could be accelerated. Civilization took time, even centuries. And this raised a conundrum for Americans. Were backward peoples capable of self-government? Many Americans in the latter part of the nineteenth century, as in the latter part of the eighteenth century, believed they were not. But just as before, this view clashed with the American belief in universal natural rights. . . .

The nineteenth-century belief that the United States was the advance agent of civilization and morally superior to all others coexisted, of course, with a pervasive domestic racism that was hardening into the apartheidlike system of Jim Crow in the South. As Americans condemned pogroms in Russia and Romania in the 1880s and '90s, hundreds of innocent blacks were lynched, mostly but not exclusively in the South, tortured, and killed, their dead bodies sometimes torn to pieces by crazed white mobs. On the West Coast it was Chinese immigrant workers who were savagely beaten and murdered in great numbers. . . .

Hypocrisy did not stand in the way of moralism, however. Many Americans were aware of their own nation's failings, but most nevertheless extolled what they regarded as its superior institutions and enlightened worldview. Those who did not share that worldview were to be assisted and converted, criticized and sanctioned, and in the case of the South militarily defeated and reconstructed. This powerful impulse to reform had its roots in the universalist ideology of the Declaration of Independence. But the Civil War gave birth to new and more potent aspirations. As William Seward insisted, the war had a "positive moral and political significance," producing what he and other leading Americans considered "a homogenous, enlightened nation, virtuous and brave, inspired by lofty sentiments to achieve a destiny for itself that shall, by its influence and example, be beneficent to mankind." Even in the age of Seward it was clear to foreign observers as well as to some Americans that their belief in progress, their constant evaluation and measurement of societies and civilizations against their own ideals, and their disapproval of those that refused to conform to the spirit of the age would upset the status quo if and when Americans accumulated sufficient power and influence and the desire to use them to shape the world more to their liking.

Economic Primacy, Righteous Nationalism, and an Activist State

MICHAEL H. HUNT

Conquering and securing a continent was an essential but hardly in itself sufficient condition to moving toward ascendancy. Americans needed to develop wealth if they were to cut a larger figure on the world stage. This they did with astonishing success over the course of the nineteenth century. . . .

Every available yardstick shows the U.S. economy outstripping the rest of the world between 1820 and 1913, itself a remarkable time of growing global trade and investment. Perhaps the prime yardstick of growth is gross domestic product (or GDP), the value of all goods and services produced by a country in a given year. The United States had achieved exceptional, sustained growth to judge from a GDP that was forty times greater by the early twentieth century than it had been a century earlier. By 1919 the United States was firmly established as the world's largest economy, accounting for nearly a fifth of all global production. Per capita GDP is another revealing yardstick. By taking population into account, this measurement tells us what each person within an economy would receive were the value of the output divided evenly. That figure grew fourfold between 1820 and 1913 even though there were ever more Americans to claim a share of the total output. They had become the wealthiest people on earth.

This high level of economic performance pushed the United States past Britain, the leading power of the day. As early as 1870 the United States had caught up in total output and by 1913 dwarfed the British economy by a margin greater than two to one. By that latter date, Americans had also surpassed British per capita income, which was the highest in Europe. Germany and France lagged behind at about two-thirds of the U.S. figure. In terms of manufacturing, a defining feature of advanced economic development at the time, Americans could boast special success. In 1860 they stood behind the leaders, Britain and France. By 1913 the U.S. manufacturing output was far in the lead; indeed it exceeded the combined output of the two industrial powerhouses of the day, Germany and Britain, and accounted for a third of the total world production. . . .

Table 1   Forging ahead: Yardsticks of U.S. economic expansion

	1820	1870	1913
total GDP (billions of 1990$)[a]	13	98	517
U.S. share of total world GDP (%)	2	9	19
per capita GDP (1990$)	1,257	2,445	5,301
population (millions)	10	40	98
exports (billions of 1990$)	.3	2.5	19.2

Source: Angus Maddison, *The World Economy: A Millennial Perspective* (Paris: Development Centre of the Organisation for Economic Co-operation and Development, 2001), 183, 185, 261, 263, 361.

[a]Expressing dollar figures in terms of the value of 1990 dollars creates what economists call "constant dollars" that can be compared across time. Otherwise, the effects of inflation would put the value of one year's GDP beyond comparison with that of another year, especially over long periods of time.

Foreign commentators and visitors at the end of the nineteenth century noted the striking if predictable results of relatively high levels of steady growth. Their accounts made the U.S. economy a byword around the world for speedy economic development, steady technological achievement, and rapidly rising affluence. That the country was already in the 1880s "a vast hive of industry" that had arrived at an "advanced position as a leader of nations" was a point that visitor after visitor repeated, no matter how otherwise critical they were of this bland, crass, soulless civilization without modesty or redeeming social or moral ideals. H. G. Wells came away from turn-of-the-century America convinced that "nowhere now is growth still so certainly and confidently *going on* as here. Nowhere is it upon so great a scale as here, and with so confident an outlook towards the things to come." A French visitor marveled at the "extraordinary intensity" that Americans devoted to their work, yielding them "great riches" and swiftly transforming open land into "populous and industrious districts."

What was true of European visitors was also true of East Asians on the lookout for models for their own development. A Japanese elite bent on making their country strong and modern looked with ill-concealed admiration at U.S. achievements, especially its devotion to technology and practical education. A Japanese who studied in the United States in the decade after the Civil War found Americans "a nervous, energetic, enterprising people" and their development of the continent a "stupendous undertaking." . . . The influential Chinese reformer and journalist, Liang Qichao, was equally impressed but also alarmed by his encounter in 1903 with what he described for readers at home as "the premier capitalist nation in the world.". . .

How did the United States manage this rapid and widely recognized economic ascent to a position of agricultural and industrial preeminence? An explanation begins with natural endowments—abundant fertile land and rich timber and mineral resources that accrued to settler societies as a prerogative of conquest. Americans, like South Africans and Australians, seized these valuable assets with little or no recompense. . . . They provided the bedrock for the U.S. economy well into the twentieth century, and even as late as 1914 nonindustrial goods were the main U.S. export.

To abundant, cheap resources must be added fortunate location and timing. The United States as a settler society was able to bring an entire continent rapidly into production and lay the enduring economic basis for U.S. global power because nineteenth-century Americans occupied a privileged place within a dynamic North Atlantic economy. They enjoyed a prolonged peace—a century of freedom from major conflict running from the end of the Napoleonic wars in 1815 to the onset of World War I in 1914. During that time liberal notions of free trade gained wide currency. They exercised especially strong appeal during the middle decades of the nineteenth century as Britain led in removing barriers to trade. The free-trade gospel spread to Europe and the United States and with the backing of gunboats to China and Japan. A backlash against free trade and toward stronger national protection from foreign competition took hold from the 1870s onward, driven by economic downturns, social unrest, and revived great-power rivalry. Even so, this trend did not erase the earlier gains toward greater international economic openness and specialization. Measured as a percentage of total world GDP, total world exports rose from 1 percent in 1820 to 5 percent in 1870 to 8.7 by 1913.

More than anything else, new technology drove economic integration in a calm, outward-looking North Atlantic world. New forms of transport and communication—trains and steamships as well as telegraph cables across land and under the ocean—deepened and tightened the connections among the parts of the international economy. The first cable crossed the North Atlantic in 1869. Freight costs on land and sea fell dramatically, while speed and convenience increased no less dramatically. Refrigeration, introduced in the late 1870s and early 1880s, made possible long-distance shipment of goods such as meat, dairy products, and fruit. Taken together, the machines exploiting steam and electricity had revolutionary implications perhaps greater than more recent and familiar innovations such as the telephone, the airplane, and the computer. Ingenious mechanical contraptions were critical to pushing world trade to a level in 1913 that would not be matched relative to total world output until several decades after World War II. . . .

Federal, state, and local government made signal contributions to the ensuing economic drive. Foremost were policies meant to shape a single national market. This effort began with the building of canals and roads early in the nineteenth century and continued into the age of steam and electricity. Railroads crisscrossed the country and by 1866 spanned the continent. Telegraph lines paralleled the tracks, creating what one inventor at the time described as "the nervous system of this nation and of modern society." These developments laid the basis for the continent-wide network of mass production and mass marketing that would soon establish the United States as the international economic leader.

Government policies contributed to economic growth in other ways. Taxes were low, with spending directed at critical infrastructure such as public education and transport. Regulations on economic activity stayed minimal. Resources in the public domain—whether land, mineral deposits, grazing rights, or timber—were available to exploit on attractive terms, including land grants to encourage westward settlement. Businesses gained the right to incorporate and thus to act freely as a kind of superindividual—accumulating resources under no more restraint than any real person and shedding employees during economic downturns without a second thought, all the while wielding political influence that no individual alone could match.

Beyond all this, the federal government provided patent protection to inventors and tariff protection to rising industries. To ensure an ample labor force, Washington followed a pro-immigration policy. Finally, a point easy to overlook, the federal government maintained political stability and national unity that allowed entrepreneurs to work in a predictable, stable setting. It resolutely crushed the southern attempt to destroy that unity.

Government measures themselves reflected the preferences of a settler society oriented toward growth. That society encouraged innovation and risk and chafed against the constraints imposed by informal social structures or formal political regulations common in Europe. Individuals shed local attachments that limited geographic mobility, rejected arrangements such as guilds that obstructed technological innovation and market access, and shook free from rigid class identities that put a brake on individual initiative. An inspired breed of independent inventors such as Alexander Graham Bell, Thomas A. Edison, and the Wright brothers epitomized the country's bias toward material creativity. Their labs set off what *Scientific American* in 1896 called "a gigantic tidal wave of human ingenuity and resource, so stupendous in its magnitude, so complex in its diversity, so profound in its thought, so fruitful in its wealth, so beneficent in its results, that the mind is strained and embarrassed in its effort to expand to a full appreciation of it." . . .

A long peace, new technology, and an integrated, rapidly developing continental market not only accounted for the striking U.S. economic growth rates but also raised the U.S. profile in international trade. . . . Between 1870 and 1913, exports increased at an annual average of 4.9 percent. By the eve of World War I, they were seventy-six times higher than in 1820, and only Britain and Germany were more heavily dependent on exports. Unlike these and other trading powerhouses, the U.S. output was still primarily oriented toward a large and rapidly growing home market. External commerce was relatively marginal. Exports from the 1870s to the eve of World War I—a time of burgeoning international trade—held steady at 6–7 percent of gross national product (GNP).

The core of U.S. foreign trade was unprocessed goods sent to Europe. . . .

Industrial exports [however] began to loom larger in the course of the nineteenth century, raising the U.S. great-power profile. This shift was in part due to the relative decline of agriculture, which had fallen from 41 percent of GNP in 1840 to 18 percent by 1900. Manufacturing together with mining and hand trades rose between those same dates from 17 to 31 percent. In absolute terms, agricultural productivity remained high even though the proportion of workers in that sector dropped from three-quarters in 1800 to less than a third in 1910. Farms were operating with growing efficiency. Mechanization, improved transport for crops, and fertilizers all made possible higher output with fewer hands. This shift in the domestic economy away from agriculture was mirrored in exports. Around 80 percent through much of the nineteenth century, agricultural products fell rapidly to just over half of total U.S. exports by the first years of the new century. By then manufacturing had risen rapidly so that it accounted for a quarter of the whole. . . .

A few firms began already in the 1850s to carve out a significant international position for themselves. The earliest overseas pioneers specialized in mass-produced machine tools, guns, reapers, and sewing machines. The Singer Manufacturing Company led the way by taking its patented sewing machine technology to European markets and creating an efficient system of general agents. They established offices first in London and then Hamburg, publicized the marvels of U.S. machinery, trained and supervised a local force, promoted installment purchases, and stayed in close touch with the home office. By 1874 more than half of Singer's total machine sales were abroad. To keep prices low and to circumvent national tariffs, Singer moved some of its production overseas. By the 1890s this multinational production, sales, and marketing system constituted (in the words of one of the company's pioneer executives) "a living moving army of irresistible power, peacefully working to conquer the world." . . .

The relative decline of agriculture in favor of industry transformed the labor force, shifting dependence from the African born and African descended to Europeans. In the early stages of American economic development, unfree labor—approximately 400,000 slaves introduced over the course of the eighteenth century—played a critical role in expanding production. Agricultural output in the South was heavily dependent on workers of African descent, 1.7 million by 1820 or nearly one in five of the total U.S. population. Industrialization created a fresh demand for labor that was only partially met by workers thrown out of the agricultural sector. Many new hands came from overseas. The railways and steamships that carried goods quickly and cheaply and the telegraph that supplied timely information for business also facilitated a major labor migration out of the European, Russian, and Asian countryside—in sum about 150 million people on the move in three great streams over long distances between the 1840s and the 1930s. Of the nearly 50 million Europeans who left their homeland between the 1840s and the onset of World War I, most headed toward the Americas—Argentina, Brazil, Canada, and above all the United States (the destination for two-thirds of these transplants). The net migration to the United States alone between 1870 and 1913 came to 15.8 million. The peak year was 1907 with 1.3 million arrivals. This influx, which made possible an extraordinary economic expansion, helped push the total work force from 14.7 million in 1870 to 38.3 million in 1913. . . .

Foreign capital as well as foreign labor fueled U.S. economic growth. But overall funds from overseas were less important to U.S. dynamism than repeated infusions of fresh labor. A high and increasing savings rate among Americans over the course of the nineteenth century made it possible to meet much of the demand for fresh investment from domestic sources. Gross savings climbed from about 14 percent in the 1840s to 23 percent in the years around 1890. European money did, however, make an important contribution, particularly in facilitating railway construction and economic restructuring during the 1830s and 1880–1896 when demand for fresh capital surged. London banks were especially important. About half of all British savings were directed abroad. . . .

What dependence there had been on foreign investors began to diminish around the turn of the century as U.S. money moving overseas began to exceed incoming foreign funds. By 1914 U.S. direct investments overseas had risen to $2.65 billion, with nearly one-half directed at extracting raw materials (mining or oil operations). Canada and Mexico were the favored destinations as U.S. investors helped integrate these neighbors into U.S. economy. By 1914 65 percent of U.S. investments were to be found in the Western Hemisphere. Europe was next (the destination for about 20 percent) thanks largely to the commitment of companies like Singer, General

Electric, Westinghouse, and Standard Oil to creating marketing networks there. While even as late as 1914 the United States was on balance still a net debtor on international accounts to the tune of about $2.5 billion, the trend line pointed to a reversal of that position in the near term. It was already easy to glimpse a financial colossus in the making. . . .

[A] righteous sense of historical destiny was not unique to the United States; it found its counterpart in many lands where people increasingly defined themselves in national terms. Like the elites in other countries engaged in this ideological enterprise, their American counterparts (predominantly of English descent) constructed elaborate explanations for their country's dominion and created glowing images of its destiny. Their constructs drew from European sources, especially from Britain, but had to accommodate to the peculiar circumstances of a settler society. The resulting nationalist notions came to circulate widely thanks to publicly funded education, public celebrations, religious sermons, memorials and monuments, and the propaganda of political parties. And as they gained in reach, they were to prove important—as a force for creating cultural coherence out of a multiplicity of ethnic identities, as a response to a world of jostling European nationalisms, and as both a justification and tool for a central government devoted to an ambitious agenda.

Nationalism in the U.S. case developed a special intensity as a result of its relationship to an ethnically diverse society created by early settlement patterns and subsequently maintained by repeated waves of labor migration. That society consisted notably of peoples from Africa forced into economic service, free labor drawn from an increasingly wide swath of Europe, and vestiges of a native population. Leading intellectuals and politicians in the Anglo community set about establishing their dominion. They created and propagated a definition of the nation that entirely excluded blacks (as well as women) from citizenship, incorporated Europeans in relation to their perceived whiteness (a standard that became more inclusive over time, beginning with Scots and Germans), and banished Indians to the realm of myths and to remote reservations. In the process, these lords of North America practiced what has come to be called "orientalism"—expressing their own sense of superiority by diminishing others as infantile, feminine, and barbarous. . . .

Having potential—whether technological or military and economic—is one thing; making use of it . . . is another. . . . The war with Spain [in 1898] whetted the national appetite for wider influence in regions under the imperialist onslaught and even for colonies. It proved a short step from joining in the European rivalries on the colonial periphery to intervening in Europe's first great war. Intervention in that war in turn gave rise to a plan, firmly linked to Woodrow Wilson's name, to replace the system of rival imperial states with one of American design—democratic, peaceful, and commercial. This succession of grand projects in turn helped launch the modern American state. . . .

Far-reaching technological advances that made possible both globalization and imperialism help explain this sudden stirring of U.S. power. Technology was raising industrial and agricultural productivity in national markets, nowhere more dramatically than in [President William] McKinley's America. New technology was also boosting the destructive potential of warfare on land and at sea as well as the costs of preparing for war. The Civil War had already demonstrated how telegraph, train, and steamships together made possible the rapid movement, dependable supply, and easy coordination of large, far-flung forces. More sophisticated armaments were coming in a rush—smokeless powder, torpedoes, mines, and breach-loading cannon with rifled barrels for greater long-range accuracy. Warships grew ever larger with bigger, more accurate guns and heavier armor. . . .

Finally, technology was broadening the vistas of ordinary people. In the United States cheap newspapers ("penny press") reached the mass market with sensational international reports of yesterday's Spanish military outrage in Cuba or the slaughter of American innocents doing God's work in China. . . .

This worldwide technological shakeup in the decades around the turn of the century gave rise to concerns that made [many U.S. officials] receptive to the idea of an American empire. Taken together, these concerns looked strikingly similar to those gripping colonially minded Europeans. Little wonder: American advocates of empire were fascinated witnesses to the new wave of European colonialism in Africa and Asia in the 1880s and 1890s, and they were especially influenced by the British example and British imperial ideology. . . .

From their observations American imperialists extracted four simple propositions to justify overseas conquest. First, empire would make Americans feel good about doing their duty. British commentators described formal colonial holdings as the ornaments of a modern, powerful state and the testing grounds of civilized peoples. If Britain could claim a quarter of the world as its domain and even tiny Belgium could boast a major African kingdom, why should Americans not share in the glory? As a superior people in command of an advanced civilization, Americans were no less suited to exercise dominion over peoples unfit to direct their own affairs. The United States was in the words of one of the most fervent supporters of . . . empire, Indiana senator Albert J. Beveridge, "a greater England with a nobler destiny." . . .

Second, empire looked easy. Advances in military technology had lowered the costs of fixing control over peripheral peoples. Europeans had already demonstrated how gunboats, well-organized logistical trains linking colony to metropole, and rapid-fire guns could subdue even the most distant and hostile lands. Small French forces had extinguished repeated outbreaks of resistance in Vietnam, while equally limited application of British power had quelled opposition in India and at a variety of points in Africa. Surely Americans, tested in a running battle with Native Americans across the continent, knew how to coerce obedience as well as Europeans. . . .

Third, empire also seemed to serve security. Cable and steam had made the world smaller, while an increasingly colonized periphery—Africa carved up, the Middle East staked out, the independent states of Southeast Asia gobbled up, China threatened on all sides, and Pacific islands annexed—hemmed Americans in. From the perspective of U.S. strategists these same developments provided potential foes, now possessed of greater mobility and firepower than ever, with bases to launch an attack across the once secure ocean approaches to North America. Fending off this danger required defense in depth—the control of Pacific and Caribbean outposts. These same outposts could also serve as coaling stations and bases of operation if the United States wished to enforce the Monroe Doctrine in Latin America and have a say in the future of a China undergoing a slow-motion collapse.

Finally, empire promised domestic benefits—something for everyone. Empire seemed an answer to the needs of a dynamic economy suffering from bouts of overproduction that plunged the country into painful economic downswings in the 1870s, in the 1880s, and with special severity in the 1890s. To provide an outlet for the increasing output of American farm and factory, so one popular argument went, the government would have to help open and protect foreign markets. This might mean gaining access to Europe, the richest of the foreign markets, but it also entailed asserting American interests in regions under colonial pressure where investments were substantial (such as Cuba) or where future prospects seemed bright (China). Industry and trade groups, diplomats, and even missionaries rhapsodized over the nearly boundless prospects for U.S. products in a gigantic China market but worried about Europeans barring the way. One business journal warned in late 1897 that "we stand at the dividing of the ways between gaining or losing the greatest market which awaits exploitation." Empire promised in addition to promote national unity. Americans were badly divided by the 1890s by the socially disruptive effects of rapid industrialization and urbanization, the disaffection created by gyrations in the economy, the political insurgency in the rural heartland ignited by low farm prices, the reaction against a rising tide of immigrants that made the country worrisomely heterogeneous, and the sectional bitterness left over from the Civil War. A single, unifying, stabilizing civic religion that made all Americans agents of progress abroad could help bridge or obscure these divisions.

State-Centered Realism: How a Weak U.S. Government Inhibited America's Rise to World Power

FAREED ZAKARIA

The strong are all the same, [the political scientist] Michael Mandelbaum writes: "They expand. They send their soldiers, ships, and public and private agents abroad. They fight wars, guard borders, and administer territories and people of different languages, customs, and beliefs far from their own capitals. They exert influence on foreigners in a variety of ways. . . . The strong do to others what others cannot do to them." Over the course of history, states that have experienced significant growth in their material resources have relatively soon redefined and expanded their political interests abroad, measured by their increases in military spending, initiation of wars, acquisition of territory, posting of soldiers and diplomats, and participation in great-power decision-making. [The historian] Paul Kennedy concludes that "there is a very clear connection between an individual Great Power's economic rise and fall and its growth and decline as an important military power (or world empire)." . . .

So common was this pattern that European statesmen viewed the state that did not turn its wealth into political influence as an anomaly. In the eighteenth century, they spoke in astonishment and scorn of "the Dutch disease, a malady that prevented a nation enjoying unequalled individual prosperity and commercial prowess from remaining a state of great influence and power." With greater wealth, a country could build a military and diplomatic apparatus capable of fulfilling its aims abroad; but its very aims, its perception of its needs and goals, all tended to expand with rising resources. As European statesmen raised under the great-power system understood so clearly, capabilities shape intentions.

In the second half of the nineteenth century, the United States was afflicted with the Dutch disease. While America emerged from the Civil War as a powerful industrial state, unquestionably one of the three or four richest nations in the world, its foreign policy was marked by a persistent reluctance to involve itself abroad. Many historians of the period have asked why America expanded in the 1890s. But for the political scientist, viewing the country's power and expansion in comparative perspective, the more puzzling question is why America did not expand more and sooner. The period 1865–1908, particularly before 1890, presents us with many instances in which the country's central decision-makers noticed and considered clear opportunities to expand American influence abroad and rejected them. Certainly, between the time when they get rich and when they acquire expansive political interests abroad, countries often experience a time lag, frequently because policymakers fail to perceive the shift in their country's relative economic position. But America's central decision-makers were well aware of its economic strength and proudly proclaimed it. Nevertheless, the country hewed to a relatively isolationist line, with few exceptions, until the 1890s—a highly unusual gap between power and interests, for it lasted some thirty years. The United States would thus seem to represent an exception to the historical record and a challenge to the great-power rule. . . .

The ultimate measure of international influence in the late nineteenth century, a time of colonial competition and imperialism, was political control over foreign lands. Between 1865 and 1890, the United States acquired forsaken Alaska and the tiny Midway Islands and gained basing rights in Samoa. During the same period, Britain and France each acquired over three million square miles of new colonies. The American army was tiny, with an active force of twenty-five thousand in 1890—ranking it fourteenth in the world after Bulgaria, even though by this date the United States was the richest nation in the world. The state of the American navy was so unusual for a country with long coastlines that it was an object of ridicule in Europe. (After touring America in 1890, Oscar Wilde had his "Canterville Ghost" react with surprise when told by an American that her country had "no ruins and no curiosities." "'No ruins! no curiosities!' replied the Ghost; 'you have your navy and your manners.'") The U.S. Navy was the smallest among the major powers, just behind that of Italy, and the Italian army, smallest among the European powers, was still eight times the size of America's; American industrial strength, however, was thirteen times that of Italy.

America's diplomatic apparatus was in even worse shape than its defenses. In all but a few important countries, the United States was represented by honorary ambassadors and ministers. The State Department itself was a tiny affair, housed in a few rooms and run by two assistant secretaries of state, a few junior officers, and a host of clerks. Messages between Washington and most other foreign capitals were few and far between. The United States attended hardly any international conferences, participated in no joint decision-making, and of course brokered no alliances. As a result, America was treated like a second-rank power, on a par with countries that possessed a fraction of its material resources. . . .

Historians have offered various explanations for American inactivity abroad in the second half of the nineteenth century that account for important aspects of

American behavior. But they often contradict widely accepted propositions regarding foreign policy in general and American foreign policy in particular. For example, some historians argue that America was war-weary in 1865 and therefore uninterested in imperialist ventures. Yet historians often note that nations expand their interests abroad after a war, translating their military strength into political influence, as many European statesmen expected the United States to do in 1865. . . .

The national security approach mirrors the views of some policymakers and explains expansion as a response to potential or existing threats from European powers. . . . [The scholar] Tony Smith concludes that while economic factors were clearly important, a better explanation for U.S. policy toward Latin America is preemptive imperialism, which sets policy "in a region of importance to the United States when a potentially hostile great power might create a sphere of influence for itself there." This approach . . . fails to appreciate that European behavior was viewed as benign in the 1870s and 1880s, then threatening in the 1890s in large part because the United States began to define its interests more broadly. The real question is why the United States adopted a more expansive definition of its interests and hence its security over that period.

Still other diplomatic historians maintain that domestic factors account for nineteenth-century American isolationism. There the agreement stops: some emphasize the American national character, others internal upheaval that distracted Americans from foreign affairs. But domestic trouble is often used, even by the same historians, to explain expansion as well. Revisionist historians have stressed the primacy of economic motivations in explaining American expansion. The severe recession of 1893 to 1897, one of the worst before the Great Depression, led, they argue, to fears of American "overproduction" and pressure for the acquisition of foreign markets. . . .

If domestic ills like depressions prevented the United States from expanding in the 1860s and 1870s, how could the very same factors have forced it to expand—in a form of "social imperialism"—during the 1890s? This contradiction, common in the literature, underscores the general problem with domestic politics arguments. Clearly, the United States was significantly more active in foreign affairs during the 1890s than in the two decades before. Many of the factors that allegedly explain American inactivity during the first period were just as strong during the second, yet American foreign policy was markedly different. Statesmen in both periods perceived distinct opportunities to expand; some of these resulted in formal attempts at expansion, while others did not. If explanations for nonexpansion in 1865–89 cannot be reversed to explain the expansion of 1890–1908, they must be considered suspect. . . .

In the past two decades, social scientists—primarily in the fields of comparative politics, American politics, and international political economy—have begun to assess the role of the state as an independent actor. . . . And modest studies have successfully layered a variable concerning the structure and power of the state onto systemic analysis. [The theory of] state-centered realism is an attempt at a marriage between this recently resuscitated tradition and the field of international security. . . . It recognizes that statesmen encounter not only pressures from the international system but also constraints that are the consequence of state structure, chiefly the degree to which national power can be converted into state power. . . . Thus state-centered realism predicts that *nations try to expand their political interests abroad when central decision-makers perceive a relative increase in state power.* . . .

The pattern of American foreign policy from the end of the Civil War to the close of Theodore Roosevelt's term as president largely confirms the predictions of state-centered realism: central decision-makers, which in the American case means the president and his closet advisers, expanded American influence abroad when they perceived increases in state power. The decades after the Civil War saw the beginning of a long period of growth in America's material resources. But this national power lay dormant beneath a weak state, one that was decentralized, diffuse, and divided. The presidents and their secretaries of state tried repeatedly to convert the nation's rising power into influence abroad, but they presided over a federal state structure and a tiny bureaucracy that could not get men or money from the state governments or from society at large. The president also had to contend with a state that impaired his ability to translate his administration's preferences into national policy; Congress could, and often did, prevent him from exercising his will. It refused to enact civil service and military reform, and the Senate rejected several annexation projects the executive branch had proposed. During this period, the power of the presidency was at a historic low: Andrew Johnson was impeached for daring to fire his secretary of war without congressional approval. Also, the unprecedented national debt after the Civil War fostered a pervasive sense of national bankruptcy and weakness that exacerbated this tension. America was an unusual great power—a strong nation but a weak state. . . .

William Henry Seward, who served as secretary of state from 1861 until 1869, greatly admired John Quincy Adams. Like Adams, he was a fervent believer in America's manifest destiny who had, as a staunch opponent of slavery, refused to sanction antebellum expansion that would have created slaveholding territories. . . . Throughout his political career, Seward advocated policies that strengthened the industrial economy, such as large investments in America's transportation infrastructure and the import of cheap foreign labor. He understood that a strong America would be active abroad and that it would annex territory whenever opportunities presented themselves. "All prosperous nations must expand," he argued. "That expansion will be in adjacent regions if practicable; if not it will then be made in those regions however distant, which offer the least resistance." . . .

Seward's plans for expansion were often cloaked in soaring, imprecise rhetoric. His vague, if uplifting, phrases could not serve as the basis for a coherent foreign policy: what did he mean when he said that "the borders of the federal republic shall be extended so that it shall greet the sun when he touches the tropics, and when he sends his gleaming rays towards the polar circle"? On several occasions, however, and in specific terms, he portrayed as inevitable the annexation of Alaska, Canada, and Mexico. Seward also spoke of the need for island bases in both the Pacific and the Caribbean to project American power abroad and to defend the country's interests. He was so confident of the continued continental growth of the United States that he even devoted serious consideration to the new location for the capital of this far-flung empire, deciding on Mexico City as the most strategically placed site.

If Seward's rhetoric was ambiguous, however, his actions were clear. From 1865 until the end of his term in 1869, Seward led vigorous American efforts to extend the country's borders on all these fronts and more. While not all of his "inquiries" can be deemed serious, he initiated at least some official steps toward expanding American political control in Alaska, Canada, Greenland, Iceland, Mexico, the Darien Islands,

Hawaii, the Danish West Indies, Santo Domingo, Haiti, Culebra, French Guiana, Tiger Island, Cuba, Puerto Rico, and St. Bartholomew. Of these, Alaska was his only success and, along with the unplanned acquisition of the Midway Islands, remained the only extension of American rule abroad for almost twenty years. . . .

[O]ne after another, Seward's various efforts failed, the vast majority for a single dominant reason: constant strife between Congress and the executive branch both over plans for Reconstruction of the South and over more general issues of authority. In the end, Seward had less to fear from the Democrats than from the Republicans who controlled Congress. In the postwar period, Congress took control of virtually all aspects of national government, opposing almost every proposal—domestic and foreign—put forward by the Johnson administration. The Senate Foreign Relations Committee was headed by Charles Sumner, the fiery abolitionist from Massachusetts, who regarded the executive branch's desire to control foreign policy as a "usurpation" of congressional power. . . .

Seward's repeated failures did not entirely crush the expansionists' hopes, for the election of Ulysses S. Grant in 1868 gave the cause another chance. An "instinctive expansionist," Grant had long been in favor of various plans, such as the 1854 Ostend Manifesto, that urged the acquisition of Cuba; and his secretary of state, the patrician Hamilton Fish, was also a strong proponent of American expansion. As the commanding general of what was, at its peak, the largest army in the world, Grant had a keen—perhaps even exaggerated—sense of American power. And given his immense popularity as the hero of the Civil War and Fish's friendship with Charles Sumner, Grant thought he would have less trouble than his predecessor with Congress. But personal friendship and respect could not alter the structural realities of the American government. This period in American history was marked by a "constant campaign" by the Senate "to establish itself as the dominant part of the government," a campaign that eventually succeeded. Against this backdrop of interbranch rivalry, Grant's chances of turning his foreign affairs preferences into national policy were slim. He nevertheless made several serious efforts during his term, the most ambitious of which—and the one he tried hardest to achieve—being ratification of the treaty annexing Santo Domingo.

Grant went after Santo Domingo for a simple reason: the opportunity arose, and the costs seemed low. . . . One historian has listed the president's motives as "grab," "glory," and "power." When Congress rejected a proposal in early 1869, supported by then–President Johnson, to establish a protectorate on the island, annexationists in America and Santo Domingo did not give up, and while Fish was not enthusiastic about the idea, Grant found it very appealing. After learning that the president of the Dominican Republic favored annexation and after receiving a positive report on the island from high-ranking naval officers, he sent a longtime aide, General Orville Babcock, there to prepare a report. Babcock did more than that, however: by September he returned to Washington with a protocol for the island's annexation. Grant was thrilled and, after formalizing matters through the consul, decided to present the treaty to the Senate. The key figure he had to persuade was Sumner, and so, on January 2, 1870, the president walked to the Foreign Relations Committee chairman's house on Lafayette Square to inform him of the treaty and to ask for his support. . . .

Emerging from that fateful meeting, Grant believed that Sumner had promised his support. But Sumner vehemently denied the president's claim, and relations between the two quickly worsened. The administration began to take the necessary steps to strengthen its case. It arranged with the Dominican government for a plebiscite, which showed strong local support for American rule, and Grant, who was increasingly obsessed by the issue, also took the unprecedented step of personally lobbying wavering senators. He argued that the island was rich in natural resources and strategically situated for both American commerce and the navy. But the administration soon realized that it lacked the two-thirds of the Senate required for ratification. The treaty's supporters let it lapse unconsidered on March 29, allowing Grant more time to lobby for his cause—which he did vigorously, making patronage appointments to satisfy the demands of borderline senators and modifying the new treaty to accommodate their concerns. But all of Grant's efforts were to no avail. Sumner was dead set against the project, and many Republicans broke with the president and followed Sumner's lead. On June 30, 1870, the treaty was defeated 28 to 28, with 16 abstentions.

Senators cited three chief reasons for the treaty's defeat: the financial costs of annexation, the problems of assimilating a nonwhite populace, and the executive branch's improper unilateral attempts to initiate foreign policy. But the last was clearly the most critical. One of the shrewdest journalists in the country, E. L. Godkin, explained that the Senate's chief motive was the desire to preserve its newly acquired paramount role in government and "to gratify on every possible occasion its mania for humiliating the President and guiding the lower House." . . .

The administration of Rutherford B. Hayes (1877–81) represented the nadir of American state power and hence the low point of the expansion of American influence; some historians have called it the "dead center" of late-nineteenth-century American foreign policy. Hayes was elevated to the White House without the legitimacy that a clear-cut electoral victory would have bestowed, a fact that congressional Democrats never forgot, and his tenure was marked by severe gridlock. With one exception, Hayes and Secretary of State William Evarts did not even consider involving the United States in international events. . . .

The one exception to this pattern of inactivity involved Samoa. In 1877 a tribal chief from Samoa journeyed to Washington to seek American annexation or at least protection of his island. He met with Frederick Seward, . . . assistant secretary of state . . . [who had long been] frustrated by the inability of the American government to fulfill his father's vision. Seward was delighted at this opportunity and, recognizing that Congress would simply dismiss either of the chief's preferred options, negotiated a treaty in which the United States would acquire a naval and coaling station at Pago Pago in return for Washington's "good offices" in the event of trouble between Samoa and any other nation. Strangely, the Senate approved the treaty unanimously in executive session, leaving no rationale on record to explain why, after rejecting a virtually identical treaty just six years earlier, it moved so quickly now. Even after the Senate ratified the treaty, however, the House of Representatives refused to allot any funds to build a coal yard at Pago Pago.

The Hayes administration marked a watershed in late-nineteenth-century American foreign policy. With its close, several powerful constraints on state power loosened, and the direction of foreign policy shifted slowly but discernibly. The minor opportunity was that for a period of two years (1881–83), the House of Representatives moved back into the hands of the Republican Party. The more important change regarded the most fungible source of power: money. By the early 1880s, American statesmen realized that, despite several tax cuts, the Treasury was still yielding surpluses, year after year. In 1880 the surplus passed $100 million. They could have reduced tariffs, thereby eliminating most of the surplus, but strong domestic constituencies—many of them Republican—favored protecting indigenous industries. Politicians searched for issues that the federal government could spend money on—"surplus financiering," in the words of its critics. Concerns over the national debt and fears of large government expenditures persisted among Democrats, but the large recurring surplus gradually altered even their views on government spending. As the decade wore on, Congress abandoned the assumption that the government could not afford to spend money outside of bare necessities, and it grew receptive to increased spending in certain areas, particularly the U.S. Navy. These surpluses combined with the professionalization of the bureaucracy and a less divided government to result in the rise of "the new navy." . . .

The 1880s and 1890s mark the beginnings of the modern American state, which emerged primarily to cope with the domestic pressures generated by industrialization. The exigencies of the growing national economy and the collapse of the congressional bid for supremacy gave the federal government a more centralized, less political, and rational structure. And as the only nationally elected officer of government, the president emerged with strengthened authority. This transformation of state structure complemented the continuing growth of national power, and by the mid-1890s the executive branch was able to bypass Congress or coerce it into expanding American interests abroad. America's resounding victory in the Spanish-American War crystallized the perceptions of increasing American power both at home and abroad. In keeping with the work of [the political scientists] Robert Jervis and Aaron Friedberg, this study confirms that statesmen's perceptions of national power shift suddenly, rather than incrementally, and are shaped more by crises and galvanizing events like wars than by statistical measures. Having defeated a European great power in battle, America expanded dramatically in the years that followed, and several goals that had been under contemplation for decades—the annexation of Hawaii and Samoa, for example—became reality within months. At the moment of its greatest strength and security, having driven Spain out of the Western Hemisphere and with only an accommodating Britain as a European presence in the Americas, the United States chose to fill the resulting vacuum by expanding its influence. Because of its now-recognized status as a great power, actual threats to American security decreased from then on, and this greater security bred greater activism and expansionism. When confronted by real threats, as it occasionally was both before and after 1898, the United States usually opted to contract its interests, rather than expand to counter the enemy. . . .

With the birth of the modern presidency under William McKinley came a symbiotic relationship between national executive power and foreign policy activism that has continued throughout the twentieth century. Theodore Roosevelt exploited the powers McKinley created and developed new ones as well, such as the routine use of executive agreements instead of treaties. The Progressive era further strengthened the American state—again primarily for domestic reasons—and the great beneficiaries of this new authority were the national government and the president. Long a believer in congressional government, Woodrow Wilson became a particularly expansionist and unilateralist chief executive in matters of foreign policy. . . .

During the late nineteenth century and the Progressive era that followed, the American state grew primarily in response to pressures generated by industrialization. In contrast to the European states, which developed largely to cope with external pressures, the American state came to the fore during a period that lacked rising threats, and the documentary record reflects no clear link between international pressures and the building of the American state. The two wars at either end of the period under study—the Civil War and the Spanish-American War—left only slight impressions on the American state. . . . National power can be converted into international influence, but the state first requires the mechanisms and institutions that make this conversion possible.

🌐 F U R T H E R   R E A D I N G

Helena G. Allen, *The Betrayal of Queen Liliuokalani* (1982)
Arjun Appadurai, *Modernity at Large* (1996)
William H. Becker, *Industry, Government, and Foreign Trade, 1893–1921* (1982)
Robert Beisner, *From the Old to the New Diplomacy* (1986)
Eric Breitbart, *A World on Display* (1997) (on World's Fairs)
John Brewer and Roy Porter, eds., *Consumption and the World of Goods* (1993)
Charles S. Campbell, *The Transformation of American Foreign Relations* (1976)
Edward Crapol, *James G. Blaine: Architect of Empire* (1999)
Philip Darby, *Three Faces of Imperialism* (1987)
Robert B. Davies, *Peacefully Working to Conquer the World* (1976) (Singer company)
Justus D. Doenecke, *The Presidencies of James A. Garfield and Chester A. Arthur* (1981)
Frederick C. Drake, *The Empire of the Seas* (1984)
Mona Domosh, *American Commodities in an Age of Empire* (2006)
James A. Field Jr., "American Imperialism," *American Historical Review,* 83 (1978), 644–668
David S. Foglesong, *The American Mission and the "Evil Empire"* (2007) (on Russia)
Gerald R. Gems, *The Athletic Crusade* (2006) (on sports and empire)
William Glade, "Latin America and the International Economy, 1870–1914," in Leslie Bethell, ed., *The Cambridge History of Latin America,* vol. 4, c. *1870 to 1930* (1986), 1–56
Kenneth J. Hagan, *American Gunboat Diplomacy and the Old Navy, 1877–1889* (1973)
———, *This People's Navy* (1991)
Robert Hannigan, *The New World Power* (2002)
Daniel R. Headrick, *The Invisible Weapon: International Communications and International Politics, 1851–1945* (1991)
David Healy, *James G. Blaine and Latin America* (2001)
David Held and Anthony McGrew, eds., *The Global Transformations Reader* (2000)
Kristin L. Hoganson, *Consumer's Imperium* (2007)
Paul S. Holbo, *Tarnished Expansion* (1983)
———, *Rutherford B. Hayes* (1995)
Michael H. Hunt, *Ideology and U.S. Foreign Policy* (1987)
Akira Iriye, *Cultural Internationalism and World Order* (1997)
Matthew Frye Jacobson, *Barbarian Virtues* (2000)
Rhodri Jeffreys-Jones, ed., *Eagle Against Empire* (1983)
Amy Kaplan, *The Anarchy of Empire in the Making of U.S. Culture* (2002)
Paul Kennedy, *The Samoan Tangle* (1974)

Paul A. Kramer, "Empires, Exceptions, and Anglo-Saxons: Race and Rule Between the British and United States Empires, 1880–1910," *Journal of American History,* 88 (March 2002), 1315–1353

Walter LaFeber, *The American Search for Opportunity, 1865–1913* (1993)

———, *The New Empire* (1998)

Mark Lamster, *Spalding's World Tour* (2007) (on baseball)

Jackson Lears, *Rebirth of a Nation* (2009) (on culture and expansionism)

Eric T. L. Love, *Race over Empire* (2004)

Daniel S. Margolies, *Henry Watterson and the New South* (2006) (on foreign trade)

Henry E. Mattox, *The Twilight of Amateur Diplomacy* (1989)

Frank Ninkovich, *The United States and Imperialism* (2000)

Thomas G. Paterson and Stephen G. Rabe, eds., *Imperial Surge* (1992)

David M. Pletcher, *The Diplomacy of Trade and Investment* (1998)

Serge Ricard, ed., *An American Empire* (1990)

———, ed., *La République Impérialiste* (1987)

Emily S. Rosenberg, *Spreading the American Dream* (1982)

John Carlos Rowe, *Literary Culture and U.S. Imperialism* (2000)

Ramón Eduardo Ruíz, *The People of Sonora and Yankee Capitalists* (1988)

Robert W. Rydell et al., *Fair America: World's Fairs in the United States* (2000)

Robert W. Rydell and Rob Kroes, *Buffalo Bill in Bologna* (2005)

William F. Sater, *Chile and the United States* (1990)

Norman E. Saul, *Concord and Conflict: The U.S. and Russia, 1867–1914* (1996)

Howard D. Schonberger, *The United States in Central America, 1860–1911* (1991)

Mark R. Schulman, *Navalism and the Emergence of American Sea Power, 1882–1893* (1995)

Robert Seager, *Alfred Thayer Mahan* (1977)

David Sheinin, *Searching for Authority* (1998) (on Pan Americanism)

Gene Edward Smith, *Grant* (2001)

Joseph Smith, *Illusions of Conflict: Anglo-American Diplomacy Toward Latin America, 1865–1896* (1979)

Tony Smith, *The Pattern of Imperialism* (1981)

Allison L. Sneider, *Suffragists in an Imperial Age* (2008)

Homer E. Socolofsky and Allan B. Spetter, *The Presidency of Benjamin Harrison* (1987)

Merze Tate, *The United States and the Hawaiian Kingdom* (1965)

Richard E. Welch, *The Presidencies of Grover Cleveland* (1988)

William Appleman Williams, *The Roots of the Modern American Empire* (1969)

———, *The Tragedy of American Diplomacy* (1962)

Marilyn B. Young, "The Age of Global Power," in Thomas Bender, ed., *Rethinking American History in a Global Age* (2002), pp. 274–292

Thomas W. Zeiller, *Ambassadors in Pinstripes* (2006) (on baseball)

C H A P T E R
12

The Spanish-American-Cuban-Filipino War

The United States reached a diplomatic crossroad in 1898 when it intervened in colonial rebellions in Cuba and the Philippines, both against Spain. Inspired by the leadership of the patriot José Martí and the cry "Cuba Libre," Cubans launched their revolt in 1895. By the end of the following year, rebel forces controlled two-thirds of the island's territory. Beleaguered Spanish officials tried to halt the deterioration of their imperial position by implementing the reconcentrado *policy, which uprooted the rural population and forced them into government-run concentration camps. The unsanitary conditions and high death rates in the camps and Spain's brutal repression of the Cuban rebels shocked people around the world, including many North Americans. U.S. businesses on the island, especially entrenched in the sugar industry, worried about their investment of some $50 million. The administration of William McKinley encouraged Spain to negotiate an end to the violence, but both Spaniards and Cubans proved intransigent. The publication in early February 1898 of a private letter written by the Spanish minister in Washington, D.C., Enrique Dupuy de Lôme, harshly critical of President McKinley's leadership, added fuel to the crisis. When the Maine exploded in Havana harbor on February 15, killing 266 crew members, many Americans instantly blamed Spanish authorities. Public clamor for war intensified. Impatient with revolutionary disorder so near the United States and thinking diplomacy unworkable, McKinley asked Congress in April 1898 for authority to take up arms against Spain.

Most scholars agree that the war with Spain marked a turning point in the history of U.S. foreign relations. After this brief war, a triumphant United States acquired from Spain new colonial possessions: the Philippines, Puerto Rico, and Guam. During the war, moreover, Washington annexed the Hawaiian Islands and Wake Island. Having established its hegemony in Latin America and secured colonial dependencies in Asia, the United States emerged as an important player in the vigorous, great-power rivalry for spheres of influence that reshaped international relations during the late nineteenth and early twentieth centuries.

Why did the United States decide to fight Spain? Did the war break out because humanitarian concerns, stimulated by a sensational press, demanded it?

331

Or, did it arise from a deliberate policy of expansionism? Did economic motives, and the uncertainties of the depression-plagued 1890s, drive the imperialist thrust? Did the navy push the United States toward war because it coveted strategic ports such as Manila in the Philippines? Did U.S. cultural constructions of race, class, and gender contextualize Cubans as incapable of forging their own nation—thus needing American guidance? Can we discover in the U.S. regime imposed on Cuba after the war—including military occupation and the Platt Amendment, which gave the United States the right to intervene in the island's internal affairs—the reasons for the U.S. intervention in the Spanish-Cuban War in the first place?

William McKinley's leadership has continued to puzzle historians, too. Was he a weak, ineffectual politician swept along by the winds of public opinion? Or, was he a calculating president who believed in expansion and empire and acted decisively? Did McKinley, once he had determined that Spain must depart Cuba, have viable alternatives to war, such as recognition of the rebels or delay until the rebels themselves triumphed? In brief, was war inevitable or avoidable? Grappling with these questions helps us to understand America's rise as a modern global power. As well, these questions speak to fundamental factors in why nations go to war.

🌎 D O C U M E N T S

José Martí, the political and intellectual leader of the Cuban independence movement, returned home in April 1895 from exile in the United States, hoping to direct the final stages of the rebellion. But Martí lost his life in a skirmish with Spanish troops on the morning of May 19, 1895. In his last letter, Document 1, he warns fellow rebel Manuel Mercado about U.S. imperialism and lashes out at those Cubans who advocated compromise with Spain or annexation to the "monster" of the north. In mid-December 1897, the Spanish minister to the United States, Enrique Dupuy de Lôme, sent a letter to a senior Spanish official that described President William McKinley as a weak, self-seeking politician. Intercepted by a rebel sympathizer and leaked to William Randolph Hearst's *New York Journal,* the de Lôme letter, reprinted here as Document 2, helped turn McKinley sour on Spain and galvanized support for Cuba. On March 17, 1898, as the crisis deepened, Senator Redfield Proctor of Vermont, an influential voice in McKinley's Republican Party, reported to the Senate on his recent trip to Cuba. In his speech, Document 3, Proctor condemned Spain's *reconcentrado* policy and dramatized the human suffering it had caused.

The McKinley administration sought a negotiated solution to the standoff, but attempts at arbitration in late March failed to take hold. Madrid agreed to end reconcentration, but it resisted U.S. mediation. Cuba's rebels demanded independence and spurned talks altogether. A chorus of voices in Congress, including members of McKinley's Republican Party, criticized the president's diplomatic efforts. Document 4, a political cartoon that appeared in Joseph Pulitzer's *New York World,* a competitor of Hearst's *New York Journal,* in April 1898, demonstrates that the press and the public often viewed the confrontation with Spain as a test of American manhood. The illustration depicts Cuba as a ravished woman, victimized by a brutalizing Spain—as Uncle Sam prepares to defend Cuba's feminine virtue. Document 5, a cartoon published the following month in the *New York Journal,* calls into question President McKinley's decisiveness and manhood by portraying the commander in chief as an old woman trying to sweep back popular pressures for war. Hopes for a peaceful settlement faded.

In his war message of April 11, 1898, Document 6, President McKinley explains why the United States must fight Spain.

U.S. intervention in the revolution immediately raised the issue of Cuba's postwar status. Would the island be granted independence, or would it become a dependent of the United States? Following negotiations with the McKinley administration, Congress on April 20, 1898, passed the Teller Amendment. The fourth article of that joint resolution, which appears as Document 7, disavowed any U.S. attempt to annex Cuba. After the war, the Platt Amendment, Document 8, nevertheless placed substantial restrictions on Cuba's independence. Written in Washington in 1901 and attached to Cuba's constitution in 1902, and included in the U.S.-Cuba Treaty signed May 22, 1903, it remained in force until it was abrogated in 1934.

D O C U M E N T   1

Cuban Nationalist José Martí Cautions Against Annexation to the United States, 1895

Now I can write, now I can tell you how tenderly and gratefully and respectfully I love you and that home [Cuba] which I consider my pride and responsibility. I am in daily danger of giving my life for my country and duty, for I understand that duty and have the courage to carry it out—the duty of preventing the United States from spreading through the Antilles as Cuba gains its independence, and from overpowering with that additional strength our lands of America. All I have done so far, and all I will do, is for this purpose. I have had to work quietly and somewhat indirectly, because to achieve certain objectives, they must be kept under cover; to proclaim them for what they are would raise such difficulties that the objectives could not be realized.

The same general and lesser duties of these nations—nations such as yours and mine that are most vitally concerned with preventing the opening in Cuba (by annexation on the part of the imperialists from there and the Spaniards) of the road that is to be closed, and is being closed with our blood, annexing our American nations to the brutal and turbulent North which despises them—prevented their apparent adherence and obvious assistance to this sacrifice made for their immediate benefit.

I have lived in the monster [the United States] and I know its entrails; my sling is David's. At this very moment—well, some days ago—amid the cheers of victory with which the Cubans saluted our free departure from the mountains where the six men of our expedition walked for fourteen days, a correspondent from the [*New York*] *Herald,* who tore me out of the hammock in my hut, told me about the annexationist movement. He claimed it was less to be feared because of the unrealistic approach of its aspirants, undisciplined or uncreative men of a legalistic turn of mind, who in the comfortable disguise of their complacency or their submission to Spain, halfheartedly ask it for Cuba's autonomy. They are satisfied merely that

This document can be found in Philip Foner, ed., Elinor Randall, trans., *Our America: Writings on Latin America and the Struggle for Cuban Independence* by José Martí, Monthly Review Press, 1977, 439–442. Copyright © 1977 by Monthly Review Press. Reprinted by permission of Monthly Review Foundation.

there be a master—Yankee or Spanish—to support them or reward their services as go-betweens with positions of power enabling them to scorn the hardworking masses—the country's halfbreeds, skilled and pathetic, the intelligent and creative hordes of Negroes and white men. . . .

I am doing my duty here. The Cuban war, a reality of higher priority than the vague and scattered desires of the Cuban and Spanish annexationists, whose alliance with the Spanish government would only give them relative power, has come to America in time to prevent Cuba's annexation to the United States, even against all those freely used forces. The United States will never accept from a country at war, nor can it incur, the hateful and absurd commitment of discouraging, on its account and with its weapons, an American war of independence, for the war will not accept annexation. . . .

The formation of our utilitarian yet simple government can still take two more months, if it is to be stable and realistic. Our spirit is one, the will of the country, and I know it. But these things are always a matter of communication, influence, and accommodation. In my capacity as representative, I do not want to do anything that may appear to be a capricious extension of it. I arrived in a boat with General Máximo Gómez and four others. I was in charge of the lead oar during a storm, and we landed at an unknown quarry on one of our beaches. For fourteen days I carried my rifle and knapsack, marching through bramble patches and over hills. We gathered people along the way. In the benevolence of men's souls I feel the root of my affection for their suffering, and my just desire to eliminate it. The countryside is unquestionably ours to the extent that in a single month I could hear but one blast of gunfire.

🌍 D O C U M E N T   2

Spanish Minister Enrique Dupuy de Lôme Criticizes President William McKinley, 1897

The situation here [in Washington, D.C.] remains the same. Everything depends on the political and military outcome in Cuba. The prologue of all this, in this second stage (phase) of the war, will end the day when the colonial cabinet shall be appointed and we shall be relieved in the eyes of this country of a part of the responsibility for what is happening in Cuba, while the Cubans, whom these people think so immaculate, will have to assume it.

Until then, nothing can be clearly seen, and I regard it as a waste of time and progress, by a wrong road, to be sending emissaries to the rebel camp, or to negotiate with the autonomists who have as yet no legal standing, or to try to ascertain the intentions and plans of this Government. The [Cuban] refugees will keep on returning one by one, and as they do so will make their way into the sheepfold, while the leaders in the field will gradually come back. Neither the one nor the other class had the courage to leave in a body and they will not be brave enough to return in a body.

This document can be found in John Bassett Moore. *A Digest of International Law* (Washington, D.C.: Goverment Printing Office, 1906), VI, 176–177.

The message has been a disillusionment to the insurgents, who expected something different; but I regard it as bad (for us).

Besides the ingrained and inevitable bluntness with which is repeated all that the press and public opinion in Spain have said about [Spanish governor-general Valeriano] Weyler, it once more shows what [President William] McKinley is, weak and a bidder for the admiration of the crowd, besides being a would-be politician who tries to leave a door open behind himself while keeping on good terms with the jingoes of his party.

Nevertheless, whether the practical results of it [the presidential message to Congress] are to be injurious and adverse depends only upon ourselves.

I am entirely of your opinions; without a military end of the matter nothing will be accomplished in Cuba, and without a military and political settlement there will always be the danger of encouragement being given to the insurgents by a part of the public opinion if not by the Government.

I do not think sufficient attention has been paid to the part England is playing.

D O C U M E N T   3

Senator Redfield Proctor Condemns Spain's *Reconcentrado* Policy, 1898

Outside Habana all is changed. It is not peace nor is it war. It is desolation and distress, misery and starvation. Every town and village is surrounded by a "trocha" (trench), a sort of rifle pit, but constructed on a plan new to me, the dirt being thrown up on the inside and a barbed-wire fence on the outer side of the trench. These trochas have at every corner and at frequent intervals along the sides what are there called forts, but which are really small blockhouses, many of them more like large sentry boxes, loopholed for musketry, and with a guard of from two to ten soldiers in each.

The purpose of these trochas is to keep the reconcentrados in as well as to keep the insurgents out. From all the surrounding country the people have been driven in to these fortified towns and held there to subsist as they can. They are virtually prison yards, and not unlike one in general appearance, except that the walls are not so high and strong; but they suffice, where every point is in range of a soldier's rifle, to keep in the poor reconcentrado women and children. . . .

There are no domestic animals or crops on the rich fields and pastures except such as are under guard in the immediate vicinity of the towns. In other words, the Spaniards hold in these four western provinces just what their army sits on. Every man, woman, and child, and every domestic animal, wherever their columns have reached, is under guard and within their so-called fortifications. To describe one place is to describe all. To repeat, it is neither peace nor war. It is concentration and desolation. This is the "pacified" condition of the four western provinces. . . .

All the country people in the four western provinces, about 400,000 in number, remaining outside the fortified towns when Weyler's order was made were driven into these towns, and these are the reconcentrados. They were the peasantry, many

---

This document can be found in *Congressional Record*, XXXI (March 17, 1898), Part 3, 2916–2917, 2919.

of them farmers, some landowners, others renting lands and owning more or less stock, others working on estates and cultivating small patches; and even a small patch in that fruitful clime will support a family. . . .

The first clause of Weyler's order reads as follows:

I ORDER AND COMMAND.

First. All the inhabitants of the country or outside of the line of fortifications of the towns shall, within the period of eight days, concentrate themselves in the towns occupied by the troops. Any individual who, after the expiration of this period, is found in the uninhabited parts will be considered a rebel and tried as such.

The other three sections forbid the transportation of provisions from one town to another without permission of the military authority, direct the owners of cattle to bring them into the towns, prescribe that the eight days shall be counted from the publication of the proclamation in the head town of the municipal district, and state that if news is furnished of the enemy which can be made use of, it will serve as a "recommendation."

Many, doubtless, did not learn of this order. Others failed to grasp its terrible meaning. Its execution was left largely to the guerrillas to drive in all that had not obeyed, and I was informed that in many cases the torch was applied to their homes with no notice, and the inmates fled with such clothing as they might have on, their stock and other belongings being appropriated by the guerrillas. When they reached the towns, they were allowed to build huts of palm leaves in the suburbs and vacant places within the trochas, and left to live, if they could.

Their huts are about 10 by 15 feet in size, and for want of space are usually crowded together very closely. They have no floor but the ground, no furniture, and, after a year's wear, but little clothing except such stray substitutes as they can extemporize; and with large families, or more than one, in this little space, the commonest sanitary provisions are impossible. Conditions are unmentionable in this respect. Torn from their homes, with foul earth, foul air, foul water, and foul food or none, what wonder that one-half have died and that one-quarter of the living are so diseased that they can not be saved? A form of dropsy is a common disorder resulting from these conditions. Little children are still walking about with arms and chest terribly emaciated, eyes swollen, and abdomen bloated to three times the natural size. The physicians say these cases are hopeless. . . .

I could not believe that out of a population of 1,600,000, two hundred thousand had died within these Spanish forts, practically prison walls, within a few months past from actual starvation and diseases caused by insufficient and improper food. My inquiries were entirely outside of sensational sources. They were made of our medical officers, of our consuls, of city alcaldes (mayors), of relief committees, of leading merchants and bankers, physicians, and lawyers. Several of my informants were Spanish born, but every time the answer was that the case had not been overstated. What I saw I can not tell so that others can see it. It must be seen with one's own eyes to be realized. . . .

I have endeavored to state in not intemperate mood what I saw and heard, and to make no argument thereon, but leave everyone to draw his own conclusions. To me the strongest appeal is not the barbarity practiced by Weyler nor the loss of the

Maine, if our worst fears [that the Spanish sank the vessel] should prove true, terrible as are both of these incidents, but the spectacle of a million and a half people, the entire native population of Cuba, struggling for freedom and deliverance from the worst misgovernment of which I ever had knowledge. But whether our action ought to be influenced by any one or all these things, and, if so, how far, is another question.

D O C U M E N T   4

"Peace—But Quit That": Uncle Sam Defends Cuba's Feminine Virtue, 1898

Courtesy of the Widener Library, Harvard University.

"Another Old Woman Tries to Sweep Back the Sea": Critics Lampoon McKinley as Indecisive and Unmanly, 1898

🌐 *D O C U M E N T* 6

McKinley Asks Congress to Authorize War on Spain, 1898

Obedient to that precept of the Constitution which commands the President to give from time to time to the Congress information of the state of the Union and to recommend to their consideration such measures as he shall judge necessary and expedient, it becomes my duty to now address your body with regard to the grave crisis that has arisen in the relations of the United States to Spain by reason of the warfare that for more than three years has raged in the neighboring island of Cuba. . . .

Document 5 is courtesy of the Widener Library, Harvard University.

Document 6 can be found in John Bassett Moore, *A Digest of International Law* (Washington, D.C.: Government Printing Office, 1906), VI. 211–223.

Our people have beheld a once prosperous community reduced to comparative want, its lucrative commerce virtually paralyzed, its exceptional productiveness diminished, its fields laid waste, its mills in ruins, and its people perishing by tens of thousands from hunger and destitution. . . .

Our trade has suffered, the capital invested by our citizens in Cuba has been largely lost, and the temper and forbearance of our people have been so sorely tried as to beget a perilous unrest among our own citizens, which has inevitably found its expression from time to time in the National Legislature, so that issues wholly external to our own body politic engross attention and stand in the way of that close devotion to domestic advancement that becomes a self-contained commonwealth whose primal maxim has been the avoidance of all foreign entanglements. . . .

The war in Cuba is of such a nature that, short of subjugation or extermination, a final military victory for either side seems impracticable. The alternative lies in the physical exhaustion of the one or the other party, or perhaps of both—a condition which in effect ended the ten years' war by the truce of Zanjon. The prospect of such a protraction and conclusion of the present strife is a contingency hardly to be contemplated with equanimity by the civilized world, and least of all by the United States, affected and injured as we are, deeply and intimately, by its very existence.

Realizing this, it appeared to be my duty, in a spirit of true friendliness, no less to Spain than to the Cubans, who have so much to lose by the prolongation of the struggle, to seek to bring about an immediate termination of the war. To this end I submitted on the 27th ultimo, as a result of much representation and correspondence, through the United States minister at Madrid, propositions to the Spanish Government looking to an armistice until October 1 for the negotiation of peace with the good offices of the President.

In addition I asked the immediate revocation of the order of reconcentration, so as to permit the people to return to their farms and the needy to be relieved with provisions and supplies from the United States, cooperating with the Spanish authorities, so as to afford full relief.

The reply of the Spanish cabinet was received on the night of the 31st ultimo. It offered, as the means to bring about peace in Cuba, to confide the preparation thereof to the insular parliament, inasmuch as the concurrence of that body would be necessary to reach a final result, it being, however, understood that the powers reserved by the constitution to the central Government are not lessened or diminished. As the Cuban parliament does not meet until the 4th of May next, the Spanish Government would not object for its part to accept at once a suspension of hostilities if asked for by the insurgents from the general in chief, to whom it would pertain in such case to determine the duration and conditions of the armistice. . . .

With this last overture in the direction of immediate peace, and its disappointing reception by Spain, the Executive is brought to the end of his effort. . . .

The grounds for . . . intervention may be briefly summarized as follows:

First. In the cause of humanity and to put an end to the barbarities, bloodshed, starvation, and horrible miseries now existing there, and which the parties to the conflict are either unable or unwilling to stop or mitigate. It is no answer to say this is all in another country, belonging to another nation, and is therefore none of our business. It is specially our duty, for it is right at our door.

Second. We owe it to our citizens in Cuba to afford them that protection and indemnity for life and property which no government there can or will afford, and to that end to terminate the conditions that deprive them of legal protection.

Third. The right to intervene may be justified by the very serious injury to the commerce, trade, and business of our people and by the wanton destruction of property and devastation of the island.

Fourth, and which is of the utmost importance. The present condition of affairs in Cuba is a constant menace to our peace and entails upon this Government an enormous expense. With such a conflict waged for years in an island so near us and with which our people have such trade and business relations; when the lives and liberty of our citizens are in constant danger and their property destroyed and themselves ruined; where our trading vessels are liable to seizure and are seized at our very door by war ships of a foreign nation: the expeditions of filibustering that we are powerless to prevent altogether, and the irritating questions and entanglements thus arising—all these and others that I need not mention, with the resulting strained relations, are a constant menace to our peace. . . .

In view of these facts and of these considerations I ask the Congress to authorize and empower the President to take measures to secure a full and final termination of hostilities between the Government of Spain and the people of Cuba, and to secure in the island the establishment of a stable government, capable of maintaining order and observing its international obligations, insuring peace and tranquillity and the security of its citizens as well as our own, and to use the military and naval forces of the United States as may be necessary for these purposes. . . .

The issue is now with the Congress. It is a solemn responsibility. I have exhausted every effort to relieve the intolerable condition of affairs which is at our doors. Prepared to execute every obligation imposed upon me by the Constitution and the law, I await your action.

Yesterday, and since the preparation of the foregoing message, official information was received by me that the latest decree of the Queen Regent of Spain directs General Blanco, in order to prepare and facilitate peace, to proclaim a suspension of hostilities, the duration and details of which have not yet been communicated to me.

This fact, with every other pertinent consideration, will, I am sure, have your just and careful attention in the solemn deliberations upon which you are about to enter. If this measure attains a successful result, then our aspirations as a Christian, peace-loving people will be realized. If it fails, it will be only another justification for our contemplated action.

D O C U M E N T   7

The Teller Amendment Disavows the U.S. Annexation of Cuba, 1898

The United States hereby disclaims any disposition or intention to exercise sovereignty, jurisdiction, or control over said island [Cuba] except for the pacification thereof, and asserts its determination when that is accomplished to leave the government and control of the island to its people.

This document can be found in John Bassett Moore, *A Digest of International Law* (Washington, D.C.: Government Printing Office, 1906), VI, 226.

D O C U M E N T   8

The Platt Amendment Restricts
Cuba's Independence, 1903

Article I.   The Government of Cuba shall never enter into any treaty or other compact with any foreign power or powers which will impair or tend to impair the independence of Cuba, nor in any manner authorize or permit any foreign power or powers to obtain colonization or for military or naval purposes, or otherwise, lodgment in or control over any portion of said island.

Article II.   The Government of Cuba shall not assume or contract any public debt to pay the interest upon which, and to make reasonable sinking-fund provision for the ultimate discharge of which, the ordinary revenues of the Island of Cuba, after defraying the current expenses of the Government, shall be inadequate.

Article III.   The Government of Cuba consents that the United States may exercise the right to intervene for the preservation of Cuban independence, the maintenance of a government adequate for the protection of life, property, and individual liberty, and for discharging the obligations with respect to Cuba imposed by the Treaty of Paris on the United States, now to be assumed and undertaken by the Government of Cuba. . . .

Article V.   The Government of Cuba will execute, and, as far as necessary, extend the plans already devised, or other plans to be mutually agreed upon, for the sanitation of the cities of the island, to the end that a recurrence of epidemic and infectious diseases may be prevented, thereby assuring protection to the people and commerce of Cuba, as well as to the commerce of the Southern ports of the United States and the people residing therein. . . .

Article VII.   To enable the United States to maintain the independence of Cuba, and to protect the people thereof, as well as for its own defense, the Government of Cuba will sell or lease to the United States lands necessary for coaling or naval stations, at certain specified points, to be agreed upon with the President of the United States.

E S S A Y S

In the first essay, Walter LaFeber of Cornell University disagrees with scholars who have portrayed U.S. entry into the war as an accident of history—a reaction to momentary, irrational impulses. He argues that the economic depression and domestic social crisis of the 1890s helped launch a search for foreign markets and overseas influence. Although William McKinley did not initially want war with Spain, the president concluded that he could best obtain his economic and expansionist goals through armed force. An astute politician, McKinley maneuvered through a minefield of domestic and international pressures and ultimately led the nation to war on his terms.

This document can be found in Charles I, Bevans, comp., *Treaties and Other International Agreements of the United States of America, 1776–1949* (Washington, D.C.: Government Printing Office for Department of State, 1971), VI, 1116.

In the second essay, Kristin Hoganson of the University of Illinois-Champaign/ Urbana analyzes an additional social crisis of the 1890s—the crisis in American manhood—to explain the decision for war. Threatened by the assertive, suffrage-seeking "New Woman" of the late nineteenth century, and having had no war to prove their manliness since the days of Lincoln, American jingoists, according to Hoganson, cast Cuba as a damsel in distress and Uncle Sam as her chivalrous male protector in order to make the case for U.S. intervention. Hoganson questions McKinley's decisiveness, and she concludes that the president only reluctantly succumbed to the drumbeat for war when he realized that gendered ideas about leadership made armed conflict politically necessary. But in the last selection, Louis A. Pérez, Jr. of the University of North Carolina at Chapel Hill claims that U.S. leaders had long desired to annex Cuba and that intervention came at a time when a rebel victory seemed imminent. Convinced that the Spanish could no longer hold back the tide of Cuban nationalism, and that Cuba's racially mixed population was incapable of self-government, Washington intervened and ultimately imposed the Platt Amendment to quell instability, protect U.S. interests, and assert U.S. hegemony.

Preserving the American System

WALTER LaFEBER

The "splendid little war" of 1898, as Secretary of State John Hay termed it at the time, is rapidly losing its splendor. . . . Over the past decade few issues in the country's diplomatic history have aroused academics more than the causes of the Spanish-American War, and in the last several years the argument has become not merely academic, but a starting point in the debate over how the United States evolved into a great power, and more particularly how Americans got involved in the maelstrom of Asian nationalism. The line from the conquest of the Philippines in 1898 to the attempted pacification of Vietnam in 1968 is not straight, but it is quite traceable, and if Frederick Jackson Turner was correct when he observed in the 1890s that "The aim of history, then, is to know the elements of the present by understanding what came into the present from the past," the causes of the war in 1898 demand analysis from our present viewpoint.

Historians have offered four general interpretations to explain these causes. First, the war has been traced to a general impulse for war on the part of American public opinion. This interpretation has been illustrated in a famous cartoon showing President William McKinley, in the bonnet and dress of a little old lady, trying to sweep back huge waves marked "Congress" and "public opinion," with a very small broom. The "yellow journalism" generated by the Hearst-Pulitzer rivalry supposedly both created and reflected this sentiment for war. A sophisticated and useful version of this interpretation has been advanced by [the historian] Richard Hofstadter. Granting the importance of the Hearst-Pulitzer struggle, he has asked why these newspaper titans were able to exploit public opinion. Hofstadter has concluded that psychological dilemmas arising out of the depression of the 1890s made Americans react somewhat irrationally because they were uncertain, frightened, and consequently open to exploitation by men who would show them how to cure their

---

Walter LaFeber, "That 'Splendid Little War' in Historical Perspective:" *Texas Quarterly.* 11 (1968), 89–98.

frustrations through overseas adventures. In other words, the giddy minds of the 1890s could be quieted by foreign quarrels.

A second interpretation argues that the United States went to war for humanitarian reasons, that is, to free the Cubans from the horrors of Spanish policies and to give the Cubans democratic institutions. That this initial impulse resulted within ten months in an American protectorate over Cuba and Puerto Rico, annexation of the Philippines, and American participation in quarrels on the mainland of Asia itself, is explained as accidental, or, more familiarly, as done in a moment of "aberration" on the part of American policymakers.

A third interpretation emphasizes the role of several Washington officials who advocated a "Large Policy" of conquering a vast colonial empire in the Caribbean and Western Pacific. By shrewd maneuvering, these few imperialists pushed the vacillating McKinley and a confused nation into war. Senator Henry Cabot Lodge, of Massachusetts, Captain Alfred Thayer Mahan, of the U.S. Navy, and Theodore Roosevelt, Assistant Secretary of the Navy in 1897–1898, are usually named as the leaders of the "Large Policy" contingent.

A fourth interpretation believes the economic drive carried the nation into war. This drive emanated from the rapid industrialization which characterized American society after the 1840s. The immediate link between this industrialization and the war of 1898 was the economic depression which afflicted the nation in the quarter-century after 1873. Particularly important were the 1893–1897 years when Americans endured the worst of the plunge. Government and business leaders, who were both intelligent and rational, believed an oversupply of goods created the depression. They finally accepted war as a means of opening overseas markets in order to alleviate domestic distress caused by the overproduction. For thirty years the economic interpretation dominated historians' views of the war, but in 1936 Professor Julius Pratt conclusively demonstrated that business journals did not want war in the early months of 1898. He argued instead the "Large Policy" explanation, and from that time to the present, Professor Pratt's interpretation has been pre-eminent in explaining the causes of the conflict.

As I shall argue in a moment, the absence of economic factors in causing the war has been considerably exaggerated. At this point, however, a common theme which unites the first three interpretations should be emphasized. Each of the three deals with a superficial aspect of American life; each is peculiar to 1898, and none is rooted in the structure, the bed-rock, of the nation's history. This theme is important, for it means that if the results of the war were distasteful and disadvantageous (and on this historians do largely agree because of the diverse problems which soon arose in the Philippines and Cuba), those misfortunes were endemic to episodes unique to 1898. The peculiarities of public sentiment or the Hearst-Pulitzer rivalry, for example, have not reoccurred; the wide-spread humanitarian desire to help Cubans has been confined to 1898; and the banding together of Lodge, Mahan, and Roosevelt to fight for "Large Policies" of the late 1890s was never repeated by the three men. Conspiracy theories, moreover, seldom explain history satisfactorily.

The fourth interpretation has different implications. It argues that if the economic was the primary drive toward war, criticism of that war must begin not with irrational factors or flights of humanitarianism or a few stereotyped figures, but with the basic structure of the American system.

United States foreign policy, after all, is concerned primarily with the nation's domestic system and only secondarily with the systems of other nations. American diplomatic history might be defined as the study of how United States relations with other nations are used to insure the survival and increasing prosperity of the American system. Foreign policymakers are no more motivated by altruism than is the rest of the human race, but are instead involved in making a system function at home. Secretary of State, as the Founding Fathers realized, is an apt title for the man in charge of American foreign policy.

Turning this definition around, it also means that domestic affairs are the main determinant of foreign policy. When viewed within this matrix, the diplomatic events of the 1890s are no longer aberrations or the results of conspiracies and drift; American policymakers indeed grabbed greatness with both hands. As for accident or chance, they certainly exist in history, but become more meaningful when one begins with [the British historian] J. B. Bury's definition of "chance": "The valuable collision of two or more independent chains of causes." The most fruitful approach to the war of 1898 might be from the inside out (from the domestic to the foreign), and by remembering that chance is "the valuable collision of two or more independent chains of causes."

Three of these "chains" can be identified: the economic crisis of the 1890s which caused extensive and dangerous maladjustments in American society; the opportunities which suddenly opened in Asia after 1895 and in the Caribbean and the Pacific in 1898, opportunities which officials began to view as poultices, if not cure-alls, for the illnesses at home; and a growing partnership between business and government which reached its nineteenth-century culmination in the person of William McKinley. In April 1898, these "chains" had a "valuable collision" and war resulted.

The formation of the first chain is the great success story of American history. Between 1850 and 1910 the average manufacturing plant in the country multiplied its capital thirty-nine times, its number of wage-earners nearly seven times, and the value of its output by more than nineteen times. By the mid-1890s American iron and steel producers joked about their successful underselling of the vaunted British steel industry not only in world markets, but also in the vicinity of Birmingham, England, itself. The United States traded more in international markets than any nation except Great Britain.

But the most accelerated period of this development, 1873–1898, was actually twenty-five years of boom hidden in twenty-five years of bust. That quarter-century endured the longest and worst depression in the nation's history. After brief and unsatisfactory recoveries in the mid-1880s and early 1890s, the economy reached bottom in 1893. Unparalleled social and economic disasters struck. One out of every six laborers was unemployed, with most of the remainder existing on substandard wages; not only weak firms but many companies with the best credit ratings were forced to close their doors; the unemployed slept in the streets; riots erupted in Brooklyn, California, and points in between, as in the calamitous Pullman Strike in Chicago: Coxey's Army of broken farmers and unemployed laborers made their famous march on Washington; and the Secretary of State, Walter Quentin Gresham, remarked privately in 1894 that he saw "symptoms of revolution" appearing. Federal troops were dispatched to Chicago and other urban areas, including a cordon which guarded the Federal Treasury building in New York City.

Faced with the prospect of revolution and confronted with an economy that had almost ground to a stop, American businessmen and political officials faced alternative policies: they could attempt to re-examine and reorient the economic system, making radical modifications in the means of distribution and particularly the distribution of wealth; or they could look for new physical frontiers, following the historic tendency to increase production and then ferreting out new markets so the surplus, which the nation supposedly was unable to consume, could be sold elsewhere and Americans then put back to work on the production lines.

To the business and political communities, these were not actually alternatives at all. Neither of those communities has been known historically for political and social radicalism. Each sought security, not new political experiments. Some business firms tried to find such security by squashing competitors. Extremely few, however, searched for such policies as a federal income tax. Although such a tax narrowly passed through Congress in 1894, the Supreme Court declared it unconstitutional within a year and the issue would not be resurrected for another seventeen years. As a result, business and political leaders accepted the solution which was traditional, least threatening to their own power, and (apparently) required the least risk: new markets. Secretary of the Treasury John G. Carlisle summarized this conclusion in his public report of 1894: "The prosperity of our people, therefore, depends largely upon their ability to sell their surplus products in foreign markets at remunerative prices."

This consensus included farmers and the labor movement among others, for these interests were no more ingenious in discovering new solutions than were businessmen. A few farmers and laborers murmured ominously about some kind [of] political and/or economic revolution, but Richard Hofstadter seems correct in suggesting that in a sense Populism was reactionary rather than radical. The agrarians in the Populist movement tended to look back to a Jeffersonian utopia. Historians argue this point, but beyond dispute is the drive by farmers, including Populists, for foreign markets. The agrarians acted out of a long and successful tradition, for they had sought overseas customers since the first tobacco surplus in Virginia three hundred and fifty years before. Farmers initially framed the expansionist arguments and over three centuries created the context for the growing consensus on the desirability of foreign markets, a consensus which businessmen and others would utilize in the 1890s.

The farmers' role in developing this theme in American history became highly ironic in the late nineteenth century, for businessmen not only adopted the argument that overseas markets were necessary, but added a proviso that agrarian interests would have to be suppressed in the process. Industrialists observed that export charts demonstrated the American economy to be depending more upon industrial than agrarian exports. To allow industrial goods to be fully competitive in the world market, however, labor costs would have to be minimal, and cheap bread meant sacrificing the farmers. Fully comprehending this argument, agrarians reacted bitterly. They nevertheless continued searching for their own overseas markets, agreeing with the industrialists that the traditional method of discovering new outlets provided the key to prosperity, individualism, and status.

The political conflict which shattered the 1890s revolved less around the question of whether conservatives could carry out a class solution than the question of which class would succeed in carrying out a conservative solution. This generalization remains valid even when the American labor movement is examined for its response to the alternatives posed. This movement, primarily comprised of the newly-formed American Federation of Labor, employed less than 3 per cent of the total number of employed workers in nonfarm occupations. In its own small sphere of influence, its membership largely consisted of skilled workers living in the East. The AFL was not important in the West or South, where the major discontent seethed. Although Samuel Gompers was known by some of the more faint-hearted as a "socialist," the AFL's founder never dramatized any radical solutions for the restructuring of the economy. He was concerned with obtaining more money, better hours, and improved working conditions for the Federation's members. Gompers refused, moreover, to use direct political action to obtain these benefits, content to negotiate within the corporate structure which the businessman had created. The AFL simply wanted more, and when overseas markets seemed to be a primary source of benefits, Gompers did not complain. As [the historian] Louis Hartz has noted, "wage consciousness," not "class consciousness" triumphed.

The first "chain of causes" was marked by a consensus on the need to find markets overseas. Fortunately for the advocates of this policy, another "chain," quite complementary to the first, began to form beyond American borders. By the mid-1890s, American merchants, missionaries, and ship captains had been profiting from Asian markets for more than a century. Between 1895 and 1900, however, the United States for the first time became a mover-and-pusher in Asian affairs.

In 1895 Japan defeated China in a brief struggle that now appears to be one of the most momentous episodes in the nineteenth century. The Japanese emerged as the major Asian power, the Chinese suddenly seemed to be incapable of defending their honor or existence, Chinese nationalism began its peculiar path to the 1960s, and European powers which had long lusted after Asian markets now seized a golden opportunity. Russia, Germany, France, and ultimately Great Britain initiated policies designed to carve China and Manchuria into spheres of influence. Within a period of months, the Asian mainland suddenly became the scene of international power politics at its worst and most explosive.

The American reaction to these events has been summarized recently by Professor Thomas McCormick: "The conclusion of the Sino-Japanese War left Pandora's box wide open, but many Americans mistook it for the Horn of Plenty." Since the first American ship sailed to sell goods in China in 1784, Americans had chased that most mysterious phantom, the China Market. Now, just at the moment when key interest groups agreed that overseas markets could be the salvation of the 1890s crisis, China was almost miraculously opening its doors to the glutted American factories and farms. United States trade with China jumped significantly after 1895, particularly in the critical area of manufactures; by 1899 manufactured products accounted for more than 90 percent of the nation's exports to the Chinese, a quadrupling of the amount sent in 1895. In their moment of need, Americans had apparently discovered a Horn of Plenty.

But, of course, it was Pandora's box. The ills which escaped from the box were threefold. Least important for the 1890s, a nascent Chinese nationalism appeared. During the next quarter-century, the United States attempted to minimize the effects of this nationalism either by cooperating with Japan or European powers to isolate and weaken the Chinese, or by siding with the most conservative groups within the nationalist movement. Americans also faced the competition of European and Japanese products, but they were nevertheless confident in the power of their newly-tooled industrial powerhouse. Given a "fair field and no favor," as the Secretary of State phrased the wish in 1900, Americans would undersell and defeat any competitors. But could fair fields and no favors be guaranteed? Within their recently-created spheres of influence European powers began to grant themselves trade preferences, thus effectively shutting out American competition. In 1897, the American business community and the newly-installed administration of William McKinley began to counter these threats.

The partnership between businessmen and politicians, in this case the McKinley administration, deserves emphasis, for if the businessman hoped to exploit Asian markets he required the aid of the politician. Americans could compete against British or Russian manufacturers in Asia, but they could not compete against, say, a Russian manufacturer who could turn to his government and through pressure exerted by that government on Chinese officials receive a prize railroad contract or banking concession. United States businessmen could only compete against such business-government coalitions if Washington officials helped. Only then would the field be fair and the favors equalized. To talk of utilizing American "rugged individualism" and a free enterprise philosophy in the race for the China market in the 1890s was silly. There consequently emerged in American policy-making a classic example of the business community and the government grasping hands and, marching shoulder to shoulder, leading the United States to its destiny of being a major power on a far-Eastern frontier. As one high Republican official remarked in the mid-1890s: "diplomacy is the management of international business."

William McKinley fully understood the need for such a partnership. He had grown to political maturity during the 1870s when, as one Congressman remarked, "The House of Representatives was like an auction room where more valuable considerations were disposed of under the speaker's hammer than in any other place on earth." Serving as governor of Ohio during the 1890s depression, McKinley learned firsthand about the dangers posed by the economic crisis (including riots in his state which he terminated with overwhelming displays of military force). The new Chief Executive believed there was nothing necessarily manifest about Manifest Destiny in American history, and his administration was the first in modern American history which so systematically and completely committed itself to helping businessmen, farmers, laborers, and missionaries in solving their problems in an industrializing, supposedly frontierless Ameriea. Mr. Dooley caught this aggressive side of the McKinley administration when he described the introduction of a presidential speech: "Th' proceedin's was opened with a prayer that Providence might r-remain undher th' protection iv th' administration."

Often characterized as a creature of his campaign manager Mark Hanna, or as having, in the famous but severely unjust words of Theodore Roosevelt, the backbone of a chocolate eclair, McKinley was, as Henry Adams and others fully understood, a master of men. McKinley was never pushed into a policy he did not want to accept. Elihu Root, probably the best mind and most acute observer who served in the McKinley cabinets, commented that on most important matters the President had his ideas fixed, but would convene the Cabinet, direct the members toward his own conclusions, and thereby allow the Cabinet to think it had formulated the policy. In responding to the problems and opportunities in China, however, McKinley's power to exploit that situation was limited by events in the Caribbean.

In 1895 revolution had broken out in Cuba. By 1897 Americans were becoming increasingly belligerent on this issue for several reasons: more than $50,000,000 of United States investments on the island were endangered; Spaniards were treating some Cubans inhumanely; the best traditions of the Monroe Doctrine had long dictated that a European in the Caribbean was a sty in the eye of any red-blooded Amerrican; and, finally, a number of Americans, not only Lodge, Roosevelt, and Mahan, understood the strategic and political relationship of Cuba to a proposed isthmian canal. Such a canal would provide a short-cut to the west coast of Latin America as well as to the promised markets of Asia. Within six months after assuming office, McKinley demanded that the island be pacified or the United States would take a "course of action which the time and the transcendent emergency may demand." Some Spanish reforms followed, but in January 1898, new revolts wracked Havana and a month later the "Maine" dramatically sank to the bottom of Havana harbor.

McKinley confronted the prospect of immediate war. Only two restraints appeared. First, a war might lead to the annexation of Cuba, and the multitude of problems (including racial) which had destroyed Spanish authority would be dumped on the United States. Neither the President nor his close advisers wanted to leap into the quicksands of noncontiguous, colonial empire. The business community comprised a second restraining influence. By mid-1897 increased exports, which removed part of the agricultural and industrial glut, began to extricate the country from its quarter-century of turmoil. Finally seeing light at the end of a long and treacherous tunnel, businessmen did not want the requirements of a war economy to jeopardize the growing prosperity.

These two restraints explain why the United States did not go to war in 1897, and the removal of these restraints indicates why war occurred in April 1898. The first problem disappeared because McKinley and his advisers entertained no ideas of warring for colonial empire in the Caribbean. After the war Cuba would be freed from Spain and then ostensibly returned to the Cubans to govern. The United States would retain a veto power over the more important policy decisions made on the island. McKinley discovered a classic solution in which the United States enjoyed the power over, but supposedly little of the responsibility for, the Cubans.

The second restraint disappeared in late March 1898, exactly at the time of McKinley's decision to send the final ultimatum to Madrid. The timing is crucial. Professor Pratt observed in 1936 that the business periodicals began to change their antiwar views in mid-March 1898, but he did not elaborate upon this point. The change is significant and confirms the advice McKinley received from a trusted political adviser in New York City who cabled on March 25 that the larger corporations would welcome war. The business journals and their readers were beginning to realize that the bloody struggle in Cuba and the resulting inability of the United States to operate at full-speed in Asian affairs more greatly endangered economic recovery than would a war.

McKinley's policies in late March manifested these changes. This does not mean that the business community manipulated the President, or that he was repaying those businessmen who had played vital roles in his election in 1896. Nor does it mean that McKinley thought the business community was forcing his hand or circumscribing his policies in late March. The opinions and policies of the President and the business community had been hammered out in the furnace of a terrible depression and the ominous changes in Asia. McKinley and pivotal businessmen emerged from these unforgettable experiences sharing a common conclusion: the nation's economy increasingly depended upon overseas markets, including the whole of China; that to develop these markets not only a business-government partnership but also tranquillity was required; and, finally, however paradoxical it might seem, tranquillity could be insured only through war against Spain. Not for the first or last time, Americans believed that to have peace they would have to wage war. Some, including McKinley, moved on to a final point. War, if properly conducted, could result in a few select strategic bases in the Pacific (such as Hawaii, Guam, and Manila) which would provide the United States with potent starting-blocks in the race for Asian markets. McKinley sharply distinguished between controlling such bases and trying to rule formally over an extensive territorial empire. In the development of the "chains of causes" the dominant theme was the economic, although not economic in the narrow sense. As discussed in the 1890s, business recovery carried most critical political and social implications.

Some historians argue that McKinley entered the war in confusion and annexed the Philippines in a moment of aberration. They delight in quoting the President's announcement to a group of Methodist missionaries that he decided to annex the Philippines one night when after praying he heard a mysterious voice. Most interesting, however, is not that the President heard a reassuring voice, but how the voice phrased its advice. The voice evidently outlined the points to be considered; in any case, McKinley numbered them in order, demonstrating, perhaps, that either he, the voice, or both had given some thought to putting the policy factors in neat and logical order. The second point is of particular importance: "that we could not turn them [the Philippines] over to France or Germany—our commercial rivals in the Orient—that would be bad business and discreditable. . . ." Apparently everyone who had been through the 1890s knew the dangers of "bad business." Even voices.

Interpretations which depend upon mass opinion, humanitarianism, and "Large Policy" advocates do not satisfactorily explain the causes of the war. Neither, however, does Mr. Dooley's famous one-sentence definition of American imperialism in 1898: "Hands acrost th' sea an' into somewan's pocket." The problem of American expansion is more complicated and historically rooted than that flippancy indicates. George Eliot once observed, "The happiest nations, like the happiest women, have no history." The United States, however, endured in the nineteenth century a history of growing industrialism, supposedly closing physical frontiers, rapid urbanization, unequal distribution of wealth, and an overdependence upon export trade. These historical currents clashed in the 1890s. The result was chaos and fear, then war and empire. In 1898 McKinley and the business community wanted peace, but they also sought benefits which only a war could provide. Viewed from the perspective of the 1960's, the Spanish-American conflict can no longer be viewed as only a "splendid little war." It was a war to preserve the American system.

Manhood, Chivalry, and McKinley's Reluctant Decision for War

KRISTIN L. HOGANSON

Why did *Cuba libre* strike such a powerful chord in the United States? The leading explanation offered by historians is that humanitarian sentiments and democratic principles of self-government underlay the broad backing commanded by the Cubans. This explanation clarifies why Americans sided with the Cuban revolutionaries over their Spanish opponents, but it does not account for the depth of Americans'commitment to the Cubans, for destitute and disfranchised residents of the United States failed to provoke a comparable outpouring of support. As one pro-labor essayist noted. "The poor in the tenement houses of our cities are in worse extremes than the down-trampled population of Cuba, but what patriot suggests war to free them?"

The sympathy extended to the Cubans seems particularly incongruous when race is added to the picture. In the late nineteenth century, white Americans frequently invoked racial beliefs to justify denying self-government to people of color. Why, then, were so many white Americans distraught over the Cubans' political status? Sen. Orville H. Platt (R, Conn.) drew attention to this incongruity when he pointed out that men who did not seem outraged at the news of a recent lynching in Texas (in which a man was covered with kerosene and burned to death on a public platform in the presence of seven thousand cheering witnesses) were now "shedding tears over the sad fate of Maceo [a mixed-race Cuban general]." Although there was some debate over the whiteness of the Cuban revolutionaries, it was quite clear that whatever they were, "Anglo-Saxons" they were not. Taken as a whole, the Cuban revolutionaries undoubtedly had more African blood than their Spanish rulers. Given the racial prejudices, poverty, and political injustice tolerated within the United States, it appears that something more than humanitarian sympathy and democratic principles lay behind the outpouring of support for the Cubans.

The key to the Cubans' appeal can be found in the numerous press accounts that treated them and their cause sympathetically: many of these portrayed the Cuban revolutionaries in chivalric terms. [The historians] Michael Hunt and Amy Kaplan have considered one aspect of this in their respective studies of U.S. foreign policy and romance novels. Both find that nineteenth-century Americans often viewed Cuba metaphorically, as a maiden longing to be rescued by a gallant knight. Strange though it may seem, this interpretation fit into a larger chivalric understanding of Cuban affairs, for favorable accounts also characterized the Cuban revolution as a heroic crusade that merited the fraternal assistance of American men. In their effort to cast the Cuban revolution in chivalrous terms, sympathizers did not stop at presenting it metaphorically—they also portrayed real Cuban men and women as if they were the protagonists of one of the adventure-filled romance novels that were so popular at the time. The tendency to depict Cuban revolutionaries as if they were the heroes and heroines of a chivalric drama helps explain why so many white

Americans were well-disposed toward the mixed-race Cubans. To many Americans, chivalric standards represented the highest ideals of manhood and womanhood. Hence, the Cubans' positive gender images deflected attention from negative racial stereotypes.

If it seems odd that Americans strongly sympathized with the Cubans, it seems especially odd that they insisted on viewing a national liberation movement in chivalric terms. They did so because of domestic concerns: sympathizers looked to the Cubans as models of gallantry because they feared that chivalric standards were endangered within the United States. Many of those who fretted about a decline in chivalry regarded the assertive [politically active and suffrage seeking] New Woman as evidence of that decline, for at the heart of chivalry was the juxtaposition of feminine vulnerability and masculine power. An essay in *Popular Science Monthly* illustrates this conviction: "We know that the tenderness, affection, and sympathy which are the essential grace and charm of womanhood, as well as the courage, disinterestedness, and chivalric sentiment which form the nobility of manhood, have sprung from that very relation of strong to weak, protector and protected, which have for ages subsisted among all the civilized races." In the chivalric paradigm. women were the protected, men the protectors. Women were, in the words of the antisuffragist Helen Kendrick Johnson, "the inspiring force," men, "the organizing and physical power." Because the chivalric paradigm enshrined men's monopoly on political power, women who pushed for a greater public role seemed to pose a fundamental challenge to the standard. . . .

Because American women seemed ever less inclined to assume the role of an appreciative audience for male exploits, aspiring American knights and women who preferred pedestals to politics turned to Cuban women as models of femininity. In contrast to activist American women, Cuban women often appeared to be ideal romantic heroines. Americans found evidence for this view in narratives that described Cuban women as natural "home-bodies" and "chaste spouses and slaves to duty." Those who fretted about assertive New Women were captivated by reports that Cuban women, "the most feminine and simple women in the world," spent their time worshiping their husbands rather than meddling in men's affairs. As the *New York Tribune* reported, "The 'New Woman' is altogether unknown in Havana. There is not even a woman's club there. In fact, in this regard the city is actually medieval." Their image as acquiescent, traditional women made Cuban women seem to be perfect feminine foils for assertive American women. . . .

Although some sensational tales of the Cuban revolution described Cuban Amazons who fought alongside men, the chroniclers of the Amazons were careful to note that it was only the exigencies of war that turned Cuban women into fighters: ordinarily they were extremely feminine. The author Nathan Green effusively described Cuban women's fury in battle but then depicted the women as pitiful wrecks as soon as the fighting was over. "While the fighting lasts they show no emotion," he wrote, "but when the last shot is fired, I have seen women throw themselves on the ground and give way to a delirium of grief.". . .

If the first reason for the chivalric paradigm's powerful appeal was apprehension about the assertive New Woman, the second had to do with American men. Those who bemoaned the decline in chivalry often held American men partially accountable, their logic being that if men had upheld their side of the chivalric pact, then women would not be so eager to enter public life. According to this line of thought, the seeming decline in gallantry reflected a deterioration in manly character. Rep. John S. Williams (D. Miss.) drew attention to men's failings when he exclaimed. "In this latter end of the nineteenth century, men seem to think not only that 'the age of chivalry has gone,' but that this magnificent piece of humanity that God has created and which we call man . . . is nothing but a miserable money-making machine. . . . Poetry goes out from him: imagination ceases to exist with him. Chivalry is dead; manhood itself is sapped.". . .

To men frustrated by the standardized routines of an ever more industrialized society, Cuban men represented adventure and male display. To those disturbed by the prospect of degeneracy in a world of civilized comforts, Cuban men stood for a hardier manhood. And, perhaps most important, to those concerned about the civic virtue that American democracy was thought to rest upon, Cuban men seemed ideal citizens: fraternal-minded men willing to sacrifice themselves for a noble cause. Recognizing the appeal of such chivalric attributes as respect for women, martial prowess, and honorable objectives, sympathetic authors did their best to make the revolutionaries' story appear, as one article put it, "more like the wonders of a romance than like the authentic annals of our time.". . .

According to the conventions of chivalric novels, only a fiend would deny such heroic men that which they so valiantly struggled to attain. Cuban sympathizers did not disappoint these expectations in their descriptions of the Spaniards. Their critical assessments of the "proud Castilians" led numerous American readers to conclude that Spanish men, once known for the chivalry, had degenerated since the days of Don Quixote. The author Stephen Bonsal contributed to the Spaniards' degenerate image in his book *The Real Condition of Cuba To-Day* (1897). "It is not alone in prowess or in success that Spanish arms have fallen since the days they fought the Moors," wrote Bonsal, ". . . The decay has been even more strongly marked in the decadence of their chivalry." The most glaring evidence of Spanish men's decadent chivalry was the atrocities they committed against helpless civilians. American publications commonly presented the Spanish-Cuban War as a war waged against noncombatants, primarily women and children. As Davis said in reference to the Spanish policy of reconcentration, "In other wars men have fought with men, and women have suffered indirectly because the men were killed, but in this war it is the women, herded together in towns like cattle, who are going to die, while the men, camped in the fields and mountains, will live."

If the shocking stories of starved and butchered civilians that frequently appeared in pro-Cuban newspapers left any doubts about the Spaniards' chivalry, stories that depicted the Spanish soldiers as sexual predators worked to put these doubts to rest. One chronicle said that during General Valeriano Weyler's command (Weyler was in charge of the Spanish forces in Cuba from 1896 to 1897), "women dared not leave their homes. In many cases they were dragged out by the Spanish and by the drunken rabble of the town, who had license given to them at the same time that protection was withdrawn from the homes." Similarly, the author James Hyde Clark maintained that licentious Spanish soldiers violated and then killed "scores of young women," and Green contended that Weyler used his women prisoners in orgies, forced women to dance naked before his troops, and raped daughters in front of their parents. Accounts of bestial Spanish rapists paralleled the contemporary image, assiduously promoted by white supremacists, of dark-skinned rapists. But gender and racial stereotypes were at odds with each other in these stories from Cuba, for it was the white, Germanic Weyler and his Spanish associates who apparently brutalized women and the mixed-race Cuban men who respected them. . . .

Building on the many stories of victimized Cuban women, writers who endorsed the Cuban cause characterized the colonial relation between Spain and Cuba as one of lustful bondage. These accounts portrayed the entire island as a pure woman who was being assaulted by Spain. One such narrative described Cuba as "a country that Spain has never loved, but has always wished to hold in bondage for lust and brutality." A drama on the Cuban revolution (presented in Yiddish to enthusiastic audiences in the Bowery) based its plot on this allegory: it featured a dastardly Spanish villain who tried to force himself on an attractive Cuban maiden. The political cartoons that depicted Cuba as a ravished woman also promoted the idea of rape as a metaphor for the Spanish colonial endeavor. To add to the drama of the story, sympathizers played on Cuba's sobriquet, Queen of the Antilles, in their pleas on behalf of the revolution. " 'Queen of the Antilles!' Beautiful Cuba! For ages she has writhed under the oppression of the haughty Castilian," exclaimed one pro-Cuban account. Picturing the Spaniards as unchivalrous ravishers made their power seem immoral and illegitimate—a challenge to the principles of chivalry, which held that true women should be venerated and protected. It made the Spanish presence in Cuba appear to be an insult to the honor of Cuban women and the Cuban men charged with protecting them. . . .

Although the seemingly chivalrous Cuban cause captured Americans' imaginations because of domestic concerns, the chivalric paradigm had powerful foreign policy implications. By casting the Cuban revolution in metaphorical terms, it helped Americans make the leap from sympathizing with individuals to opposing Spanish colonial power. By making Spanish power seem thoroughly corrupt, the paradigm suggested that humanitarian aid or limited political reforms were inadequate to settle the Cuban issue. It thus helped jingoes build their case for U.S. military intervention. This was no accident. The chivalric understanding of the Cuban revolution appealed to people who were not jingoes, but jingoes embraced chivalric imagery and metaphors with singular enthusiasm. They turned to the chivalric paradigm to deepen American's interest in Cuban affairs and to propose a course of action for the United States. . . .

To further implicate the United States in the unfolding Cuban drama, jingoes declared that the United States was more than a spectator—that it had a role in the romance. After the *New York Journal* reported that the Spaniards had strip-searched three Cuban women on an American vessel, jingoes called for recognition of Cuban belligerency, even for U.S. intervention, to end such unchivalrous deeds. Rep. David A. De Armond (D, Mo.) was one of the jingoes who pressed for a strong response. "Young ladies stripped and searched on board an American vessel by Spaniards, bearded, booted, and spurred!" he exclaimed in his plea for action. What made the strip-searches particularly offensive was not so much their effects on Cuban women—after all, the press reported more horrifying stories of rape and murder—but that they occurred on American ships. Jingoes presented them as insults to American men's ability to protect the honor of women. Senator Allen made this clear when, after describing the strip-search, he said he found it "absolutely humiliating" that the

Spanish could commit such atrocities while American leaders "sit idly and supinely here." Richard Harding Davis, the writer who broke the story, agreed. Even after admitting that a female detective, not male soldiers, had stripped the young women, he continued to regard it as a grave affront to American honor. The true issue, he said, was that the demonstration of Spanish power on the American ship undercut the dignity of the United States. Davis was so ashamed by the incident that he cited it as grounds for intervention in the Spanish-Cuban War.

As they voiced their outrage over the nation's reluctance to protect victimized Cuban women, jingoes were mindful of the sympathy shown by a number of American women for the beleaguered Cubans and particularly for Cuban women. The same interest in women's well-being that led thousands of American women to join temperance and purity crusades in the 1880s and 1890s contributed to American women's empathy for their Cuban "sisters." Women who sympathized with the Cubans made their sentiments known in a variety of ways, starting with letters to political leaders. A *Christian Herald* leaflet that implored mothers to "think of the wretchedness of these poor, heart-broken mothers of Cuba" motivated one woman to write her senator to urge him to do something to end the suffering on the island. Women also indicated their views from the galleries of Congress. Perhaps most noticeable were the members of the Daughters of the American Revolution (DAR), who applauded congressmen who made assertive speeches on Cuba. Some of the women who sympathized with the Cubans were in political leaders' own households. A handful of prominent political wives in the nation's capital made their sympathies clear by establishing the National Relief Fund in Aid of Cuba. Other political wives expressed their positive feelings for the Cubans more discreetly in Washington social functions. . . .

[But] by appealing to American men to take a stance in favor of chivalric principles, jingoes couched the Cuban issue as one for men to resolve. The emphasis they placed on brotherhood and male honor helped to keep women on the sidelines of the Cuban debate. The chivalric paradigm implied that American women should plead on behalf of their Cuban sisters but that they should not lead rescuing crusades, much less fraternal expeditions. These, it implied, were men's responsibility. Indeed, according to the paradigm, the Cuban issue was nothing less than a test of American manhood. If American men were truly chivalrous, they should enter the lists.

Significantly, when jingoes held up American men as knightly rescuers, they often wrote Cuban men out of the romance. They implied that intervening American men would take the place of Cuban men who were unable to protect Cuban women because they were at the front, had been killed, or lacked the ability to do so. By removing Cuban men from the picture, the rescue paradigm sketched a hierarchical relation between the United States and Cuba. Viewing relations with Cuba as a chivalric rescue implied that the maidenly Cubans would submit to American governance just as the heroines of chivalric novels voluntarily submitted to their heroic rescuers. The rescue paradigm thus lent itself to imperial ambitions for Cuba as well as to the jingoes' desire to foster chivalric relations between men and women. . . .

On the night of February 15, 1898, the U.S. battleship *Maine*, which had been sent to Havana to protect American citizens after an outbreak of riots, exploded and sank in Havana harbor. Two hundred and sixty-six men died in the disaster. President

[William] McKinley responded to the crisis by appointing a court of naval inquiry. The court's report, submitted on March 25, attributed the explosion to an external source. Although the commission admitted that it could not determine who was responsible, suspicion came to rest on Spain. Not only did Spain have a reputation for perfidy, but, to many Americans, it appeared that only the Spanish government had the technological capabilities to commit such an act. Americans were outraged at the thought of the Spaniards striking in the dark without giving the sleeping crew a chance to fight. "Splendid sport, indeed! How chivalric!" exclaimed one senator, who, well-versed in the chivalric paradigm for understanding the Spanish-Cuban war, interpreted the incident as yet another manifestation of Spanish treachery.

Americans who blamed the disaster on Spain regarded it as a challenge to American men, particularly because Spain refused to apologize or offer reparations and instead suggested that the men of the *Maine* were at fault. Sen. Richard R. Kenney (D, Del.) captured the leading sentiment of the day in his response to the supposed Spanish insult: "American manhood and American chivalry give back the answers that innocent blood shall be avenged, starvation and crime shall cease, Cuba shall be free. For such reasons, for such causes, American[s] can and will fight. For such causes and for such reasons we should have war.". . .

As he contemplated how to respond to the sinking of the *Maine,* McKinley faced a number of issues: humanitarian concerns, the interests of American businessmen in Cuba, the impact of a war on the entire American economy, and the potential for coaling stations and strategic bases. Added to these were concerns for his reputation and credibility as a leader and the implications of his image for his party. McKinley suffered the constraint of being a first-term president in a political system that valued a military style of manliness in its leaders. McKinley was deeply sensitive to public opinion. As he assessed the tenor of the war debate, he undoubtedly realized that his perceived cowardice in foreign affairs was undermining his credibility as a leader, that it threatened to sink his administration along with the *Maine.*

The president had good reason to be apprehensive about charges of cowardice because, regardless of his youthful Civil War record [(he had served as an Army officer)], he was not universally esteemed as a great military hero or a forceful leader. The up-and-coming Theodore Roosevelt was not alone in thinking that despite his military record, McKinley was "not a strong man" The sedate McKinley did not embody the new standards of active, athletic, aggressive manhood. He had never enjoyed hunting, and when he tried fishing once as president, in his frock coat and silk hat, he capsized the boat and ruined his shoes and pants. The clean-shaven McKinley was the only president between Andrew Johnson and Woodrow Wilson not to have a beard or mustache, signs of masculinity. . . .

Besides appearing physically soft, McKinley appeared to lack the independence central to manliness. His opponents ridiculed him as a puppet of Marcus A. Hanna, who had risen to the Senate after running McKinley's campaign. A joke of the time questioned whether Hanna would still be president if McKinley died. Detractors accused McKinley of being a tool of his Wall Street advisers. "Take my word for it," said Representative [William] Sulzer, "the American people will never consent to be governed by any man who is not big enough to own himself." McKinley seemed not only overly dependent on Hanna and other wealthy backers, but also incapable of managing his own finances. Nineteenth-century men were expected to provide for their families, but McKinley had gone bankrupt in 1893. Although his Republican biographers maintained that McKinley had handled his business failure in a "manly way," their praise was defensive. . . .

A calculating politician, McKinley no doubt realized that he needed to demonstrate he still had backbone lest he lose his ability to lead a political system that equated military valor and leadership. Highly conscious of public opinion, he surely knew that many American men thought war was necessary to defend American honor and avenge the dead sailors from the *Maine*. In Congress, Republicans and Democrats alike were citing their constituents' eagerness to fight. Rep. Joseph Wheeler (D, Ala.) announced that the "chivalrous men who fought in that terrible conflict from 1861 to 1865, and their equally noble sons, inspired as they are by the fame earned by their sires, all stand ready to place their lives and treasure on the altar of duty." . . .

Assurances that men were eager to fight made efforts to avoid war seem incongruous with manly sentiment. If the masses of American men wanted to fight, why didn't McKinley? A *New York Journal* cartoon that depicted McKinley in a bonnet and apron futilely trying to sweep back a stormy sea conveyed the spreading (and, to McKinley, threatening) conviction that if the president countered the will of American men, he would become as politically potent as a feebleminded old woman.

In addition to worrying about losing the respect of the masses of American men, McKinley worried about losing leadership to Congress. After McKinley's message of March 28, the *Washington Post* reported that the president was afraid he would not be able to prevent Congress from acting on its own. On March 30 the *Post* noted. "If the President desires to lead the procession . . . he will be accorded every opportunity of doing so. If not, the ranks will be closed and the President will be under the necessity of falling in behind." Congressmen underscored the point that the president must act or lose his stature as a leader. In a letter of April 4, Sen. Joseph B. Foraker (R, Ohio) said that Congress had been waiting for the president to take the lead on the war issue, to no avail. The president, said Foraker, "disappointed all of us very seriously with his message about the *Maine* disaster and we made up our minds that we would not wait on his any longer." "The responsibility is now on Congress," said Sen. Marion Butler (Pop., N.C.) on April 12. "We must remove the humiliation that is upon us as a nation."

As Congress grew increasingly restive, even the president's erstwhile supporters began to question the manliness of his policies. Senator [John C.] Spooner commented that "we have borne the methods of Spain in Cuba with patience approaching pusillanimity. We can tolerate it no longer." Republicans begged the administration to make war for party survival. McKinley could appear to exhibit backbone by searching for a peaceful settlement for a while, but he could not hold back indefinitely. He knew that if Congress took the initiative in pressing for war, he might not regain his stature as a leader. A president who reluctantly followed the ranks into war would find it difficult to regain the confidence of men who interpreted politics in terms of military metaphors.

It is difficult to determine the degree to which McKinley's need to maintain his manly image affected his decision to push for war because he did not record his reasoning. He wrote few letters, left almost no personal papers, and said little in conversation.

But friends believed that McKinley did not want war. They viewed him as a man who deeply desired peace. McKinley's associates were convinced that the president was pushed into war to satisfy Congress and public opinion. Senator [William E.] Chandler believed that the president advised delay because he was unwilling to give a war message to a Congress he knew would accept nothing else. Chandler attributed the president's increasingly bellicose attitude toward Spain to "the rising temper of the country and Congress especially." Although Chandler did not mention the aspersions on McKinley's manhood, these were an important component of the country's "rising temper." Placing the assaults on the president's manliness in the larger context of a political culture based on military manhood leads to the conclusion that the need to appear manly to an aggressive constituency helped make war seem politically necessary to the president.

On March 30 McKinley burst into tears as he told a friend that Congress was trying to drive the nation into war. He remembered the Civil War as a horrible conflict and had hoped that international arbitration would replace war as a means of settling international disputes. McKinley did not want war, but neither did he want to wreck his presidency. Aware of his growing reputation as a spineless leader and recognizing that Republican legislators would be unwilling to go along with a new peace initiative, McKinley drafted a message in early April that put the Cuban matter into the hands of the infamously bellicose Congress.

After McKinley delivered his message on April 11, jingoes continued to criticize him for his refusal to resoundingly cry for war. As one critic said, everybody except "the bankers and the ladies felt a sense of shame in reading the message of the President." Such calumny discouraged McKinley from seeking a last-minute solution to the crisis. On April 19 Congress submitted a resolution to the president authorizing him to intervene to end the war in Cuba. McKinley felt he had no choice but to sign, although he knew the resolution would surely lead to war. Spain immediately severed diplomatic relations with the United States. On April 22 the United States imposed a naval blockade of Cuba; on April 24 Spain declared war; and on April 25 McKinley asked Congress to declare war. Congress did so eagerly, predating the start of war to April 21.

McKinley's scanty personal records mean that arguments about his motives (gender-based or otherwise) ultimately must be based on conjecture. But even though McKinley did not record his rationale, the debate over his backbone shows that gendered ideas about leadership limited the range of politically viable options available to him. McKinley's backbone became a central issue in the debate over war because political activists, whether Republicans, Democrats, or Populists, believed that manly character mattered in politics. Men from across the country agreed that the character of the nation's leaders attested to the acceptability of their policies, and following the *Maine* disaster, increasing numbers of men demanded a militant leader. Aware of the links between manhood, military prowess, and political power (indeed, eager to take advantage of them in the campaign of 1896), McKinley reached the logical conclusion that war was politically imperative. His decision to join the jingoes was less a reflection of his courage or cowardice, strength or weakness, than an acknowledgement that the political system he operated in would not permit any other course of action.

Derailing Cuban Nationalism
and Establishing U.S. Hegemony

LOUIS A. PÉREZ JR.

[By 1898] Spanish sovereignty in Cuba was coming to an end, or so it appeared. And appearances influenced outcomes. Of course, whether Cubans would have actually gone on to defeat Spain, then or thereafter, or even at all, cannot be demonstrated. What can be determined and documented, however, is that all parties involved had arrived at the conclusion that the days of Spanish rule in Cuba were numbered. This was the perception that, in the end, served as the basis on which the vital policy decisions were made and actions were taken.

Spanish authorities openly predicted defeat in Cuba. "Spain is exhausted," former president Francisco Pi y Margall concluded. "She must withdraw her troops and recognize Cuban independence before it is too late." The failure of autonomy, the Madrid daily *El Nuevo Régimen* editorialized, left only one alternative: "Negotiate on the basis of independence." *La Epoca* reached a similar conclusion. "In reality," observed the Madrid daily, "Cuba is lost to Spain."

Cubans, too, sensed that the end was near. A new optimism lifted separatist morale to an all-time high. Never had they been so openly certain of triumph as they were in early 1898. "This war cannot last more than a year." [General] Máximo Gómez exulted in January 1898. "This is the first time I have ever put a limit to it." [Rebel president] Bartolomé Masó agreed: in a "Manifesto" to the nation he confidently proclaimed: "The war for the independence of our country is nearing the end." . . .

U.S. officials were also among those who concluded that the Spanish cause was hopeless. "Spain herself has demonstrated that she is powerless either to conciliate Cuba or conquer it," former U.S. minister to Spain Hannis Taylor wrote in late 1897; "her sovereignty over [Cuba] is . . . now extinct." Secretary of State John Sherman agreed: "Spain will lose Cuba. That seems to me to be certain. She cannot continue the struggle." Assistant Secretary of State William Day warned grimly that the end was imminent. "The Spanish Government," he observed, "seems unable to conquer the insurgents." In a confidential memorandum to the White House, Day went further: "To-day the strength of the Cubans [is] nearly double . . . and [they] occupy and control virtually all the territory outside the heavily garrisoned coastal cities and a few interior towns. There are no active operations by the Spaniards. . . . The eastern provinces are admittedly 'Free Cuba.' In view of these statements alone, it is now evident that Spain's struggle in Cuba has become absolutely hopeless. . . . Spain is exhausted financially and physically, while the Cubans are stronger.". . .

In early 1898 the McKinley administration contemplated the impending denouement with a mixture of disquiet and dread. If Spanish sovereignty was untenable. Cuban pretension to sovereignty was unacceptable. The Cuban insurrection threatened more than the propriety of colonial administration; it also challenged the U.S. presumption of succession, for in contesting Spanish rule Cubans were advancing the claim of a new sovereignty. For much of the nineteenth century, the United States had pursued the acquisition of Cuba with resolve, if without results. The success of

From *The War of 1898: The United States and Cuba in History and Historiography* by Louis A. Pérez. Copyright © 1998 by the University of North Carolina Press. Used by permission of the publisher.

the Cuban rebellion threatened everything. In 1898 Cuba was lost to Spain, and if Washington did not act, it would also be lost to the United States. The implications of the "no transfer" principle [of the Monroe Doctrine] were now carried to their logical conclusion. If the United States could not permit Spain to transfer sovereignty to another power, neither could the United States allow Spain to relinquish sovereignty to Cubans.

Opposition to Cuban independence was a proposition with a past, possessed of a proper history, one that served to form and inform the principal policy formulations of the nineteenth century. Only the possibility of the transfer of Cuba to a potentially hostile foreign country seemed to trouble the United States more than the prospect of Cuban independence. Cuba was far too important to be turned over to the Cubans. Free Cuba raised the specter of political disorder, social upheaval, and racial conflict: Cuba as a source of regional instability and inevitably a source of international tension. Many had long detected in the racial heterogeneity of the island portents of disorder and dissolution. "Were the population of the island of one blood and color," John Quincy Adams affirmed in 1823, "there could be no doubt or hesitation with regard to the course which they would pursue, as dictated by their interests and their rights. The invasion of Spain by France would be the signal for *their* Declaration of Independence." However, Adams continued, in "their present state . . . they are not competent to a system of permanent self-dependence." Secretary of State Henry Clay gave explicit definition and enduring form to U.S. opposition to Cuban independence. "The population itself. . . ." Clay insisted, "is incompetent, at present, from its composition and amount, to maintain self government." This view was reiterated several decades later by Secretary of State Hamilton Fish, who looked upon a population of Indians, Africans, and Spaniards as utterly incapable of sustaining self-government. . . .

Nor was the McKinley administration any more sympathetic to the prospects of Cuban independence. "I do not believe that the population is to-day fit for self-government," McKinley's minister to Spain, Stewart L. Woodford, commented in early March 1898. Woodford characterized the insurgency as "confined almost entirely to negroes," with "few whites in the rebel forces." Under the circumstances, he asserted, "Cuban independence is absolutely impossible as a permanent solution of the difficulty, since independence can only result in a continuous war of races, and this means that independent Cuba must be a second Santo Domingo." Several days later Woodford again invoked the specter of racial strife: "The insurgents, supported by the great majority of the blacks, and led by even a minority of enterprising and resolute whites, will probably be strong enough to prevent effective good government. . . . This would mean and involve continuous disorder and practical anarchy. . . . Peace can hardly be assured by the insurgents through and under an independent government." He concluded: "I have at last come to believe that the only certainty of peace is under our flag. . . . I am, thus, reluctantly, slowly, but entirely a convert to the early American ownership and occupation of the island.". . .

There was nothing further to be gained by delay. On the contrary, continued postponement could only benefit the Cubans. On April 11 McKinley forwarded his message to Congress. The portents of his purpose were clear: no mention of Cuban independence, nothing about recognition of the Cuban provisional government, not a hint of sympathy with Cuba Libre, nowhere even an allusion to the renunciation of territorial aggrandizement—only a request for congressional authorization "to take measures to secure a full and final termination of hostilities between the Government of Spain and the people of Cuba, and to secure in the island the establishment of a stable government, capable of maintaining order and observing its international obligations." The U.S. purpose in Cuba, McKinley noted, consisted of "forcible intervention . . . as a neutral to stop the war." The president explained: "The forcible intervention of the United States . . . involves . . . hostile constraint upon both the parties to the contest."

The war was thus directed against both Spaniards and Cubans, a means by which to neutralize the two competing claims of sovereignty and establish by force of arms a third one. . . .

News of McKinley's April 11 message to Congress, proposing intervention without recognition, immediately provoked hostile reactions from the Cuban leadership. "We will oppose any intervention which does not have for its expressed and declared object the independence of Cuba," [Cuban revolutionary party leader] Gonzalo de Quesada vowed. [Cuban legal counsel] Horatio Rubens released a statement bluntly warning the U.S. government that an intervention such as McKinley had proposed would be regarded as "nothing less than a declaration of war by the United States against the Cuban revolutionists." The arrival of a U.S. military expedition to Cuba under such circumstances. Rubens predicted, would oblige the insurgents to "treat that force as an enemy to be opposed, and, if possible, expelled." He added: "[T]he Cuban army will . . . remain in the interior, refusing to cooperate, declining to acknowledge any American authority, ignoring and rejecting the intervention to every possible extent. Should the United States troops succeed in expelling the Spanish; should the United States then declare a protectorate over the island—however provisional or tentative—and seek to extend its authority over the government of Cuba and the army of liberation, we would resist with force of arms as bitterly and tenaciously as we have fought the armies of Spain." The State Department, in fact, had dreaded this reaction. As early as March 24, [Assistant] Secretary [William] Day indicated that unless the United States recognized the Cubans, "or make some arrangement with them when we intervene, we will have to overcome both the Spaniards and Cubans."

The cause of Cuba Libre had wide support in Congress, and defenders of the Cuban cause mounted sustained efforts to secure recognition of Cuban independence. Seven days passed between the arrival of the president's message and the final war resolution on April 18, almost all of which were given to acrimonious debate and intense political maneuvering by the administration and its congressional supporters to defeat pro-independence resolutions. Compromise was reached when Congress agreed to forgo recognition of independence in exchange for McKinley's acceptance of a Joint Resolution in which Article Four, the Teller Amendment, served as a disclaimer of mischievous intentions. . . .

The Joint Resolution calmed Cuban misgivings. Persuaded that the intervention made common cause with separatist objectives, Cubans prepared to cooperate with their new allies. No matter that the United States refused to recognize the republic, as long as Washington endorsed the goals for which the republic stood. "It is true," [General] Calixto García conceded, "that they have not entered into an accord with our government; but they have recognized our right to be free and independent and that is enough for me." . . .

The question of Cuban independence, of course, had not been resolved. In the weeks and months that followed the cessation of hostilities, the McKinley administration moved determinedly to evade, circumvent, or otherwise nullify the purpose if not the purport of the Teller Amendment. Cubans were simply not ready to govern themselves, U.S. officials proclaimed after the war. "Self-government!" General William Shafter thundered in response to a reporter's question. "Why those people are no more fit for self-government than gunpowder is for hell." General Samuel Young insisted that "the insurgents are a lot of degenerates, absolutely devoid of honor or gratitude. They are no more capable of self-government than the savages of Africa." General William Ludlow agreed. "We are dealing here in Cuba," he reported to Washington, "with a relatively uninstructed population, whose sensibilities are easily aroused but who lack judgment, who are wholly unaccustomed to manage their own affairs, and who readily resort to violence when excited or thwarted. . . . The whole structure of society and business is still on too slender and tottering basis to warrant putting any additional strain upon it."

The implications were clearly drawn. The United States could hardly release Cuba into the family of nations so utterly ill-prepared for responsibilities in self-government. One cabinet member announced bluntly that President McKinley did not intend to expel Spain only to turn the island "over to the insurgents or any other particular class or faction." General Leonard Wood, the U.S. military governor of Cuba, articulated administration thinking succinctly. "When the Spanish-American war was declared," he insisted, "the United States took a step forward, and assumed a position as protector of the interests of Cuba. It became responsible for the welfare of the people, politically, mentally and morally."

The rationale to retain control over Cuba was established immediately after the war and found justification in the very congressional resolution that had promised independence. The Joint Resolution was reexamined and reinterpreted. Had not the Teller Amendment stipulated the necessity for "pacification"? Swift and striking, the new consensus formed around the proposition that "pacification" implied more than simply the cessation of hostilities. It also meant stability. "It is true," editorialized the *Philadelphia Inquirer,* "that the Congressional resolutions . . . set forth that we, as a nation, had no designs upon Cuba, and that our sole object was to free it. But these resolutions went further. They also declared it to be our intention to see to it that a stable government should he formed." The *New York Times* made a similar point, but with far more ominous implications: "The pledge we made by no means binds us to withdraw at once, nor does full and faithful compliance with its spirit and letter forbid us to become permanent possessors of Cuba if the Cubans prove to be altogether incapable of self-government. A higher obligation than the pledge of the resolution of Congress would then constrain us to continue our government of the island." The United States, insisted the *New York Tribune,* "is not repudiating, but is scrupulously and exactly fulfilling the obligation it assumed in the Act of Intervention. It did not then recognize the independence or sovereignty of the so-called Cuban Republic. It did not promise to establish that republic, or to put the insurgents in control of the island. It avowed the intention of pacifying the island." . . .

By 1901 the definition of pacification had undergone final transfiguration as an extension of U.S. interests. What circumstances would satisfy U.S. notions of "pacification," the *Philadelphia Inquirer* asked—and answered: "As soon as the Cubans show themselves able and ready to govern the Island in accordance with American principles of order, liberty, and justice, it is to be assumed that this Government will be ready to fulfill its pledge and relinquish control to them. It is not to be assumed that it will do so one day before that time." Leonard Wood was unequivocal. To end the occupation without having established prior control over Cuba, Wood predicted, would be tantamount to inviting European powers to occupy every harbor of the island. The United States demanded some definition of a "special relationship" as a precondition for the completion of "pacification," and hence compliance with "independence." And this "special relationship" necessarily required defining the terms by which the new government of Cuba would be obliged to act in a manner consistent with U.S. interests, even if this meant violating the spirit of the Teller Amendment. The United States, Secretary of War Elihu Root explained years later, insisted on "vitalizing the advice" to be offered to the Cuban government. "'Advice' meant, in this connection, more than the advice a man might give to his client; it meant 'enforceable advice,' like the advice which Great Britain might give to Egypt." Senator [Orville] Platt expressed his preference for "very much more stringent measures" but understood, too, that "when they concede to us the right of intervention and naval stations . . . that the United States gets an effective moral position, and which becomes something more than a moral position." Platt was categorical. "All that we have asked," he responded in defense of the amendment that would bear his name, "is that the mutual relations [between Cuba and the United States] shall be defined and acknowledged coincidentally with the setting up of Cuba's new government. In no other way could a stable government be assured in Cuba, and until such assurance there could be no complete 'pacification' of the island, and no surrender of its control."

The passage of the Platt Amendment in 1901 fulfilled the U.S. purpose. The new Cuban republic was to be shorn of all essential properties of sovereignty prior to its creation. The Cuban government was denied authority to enter into "any treaty or other compact with any foreign power or powers," denied, too, the authority to contract a public debt beyond its normal ability to repay, and obliged to cede national territory to accommodate a U.S. naval station. Lastly, Cubans were required to concede to the United States "the right to intervene" for the "maintenance of a government adequate for the protection of life, property and individual liberty." . . .

Acceptance of the Platt Amendment, Cubans were told, was the minimum condition for ending the military occupation. "We should . . . make our requests and desires known to Cuba," Representative [Townsend] Scudder insisted, "and thereafter, if necessary, these requests should be put in the form of an ultimatum. . . . The probability is that Cuba will yield; but if she does not do so readily, then our troops must remain until an absolute understanding is reached." Elihu Root was equally adamant. "Under the act of Congress they can never have any further government in Cuba, except the intervening Government of the United States until they have acted." Root pronounced. "No constitution can be put into effect in Cuba, and no government can be elected under it, no electoral law by the Convention can be put into effect, and no election held under it until they have acted upon this question." Root's point was unambiguous: "There is only one possible way for them to bring about the termination of the military government and make either the constitution or electoral law effective: that is to do the whole duty they were elected for."

Cubans eventually acquiesced. The choice before the assembly, delegate Manuel Sanguily understood, was limited independence or no independence at all. "Independence with restrictions is preferable to the [U.S.] military regime," he explained in casting his vote to accept the Platt Amendment. Enrique Villuendas agreed. "There is no use objecting to the inevitable," he conceded. "It is either annexation or a Republic with an amendment." The Platt Amendment was incorporated into the Cuban Constitution of 1901 as an appendix and subsequently ratified into fixed bilateral relations by way of the Permanent Treaty of 1903. . . .

The Platt Amendment thus brought the U.S. purpose in 1898 to a successful conclusion. National interests were guaranteed, not—to be sure—by way of the direct succession of sovereignty so long foreseen. On the other hand, neither did sovereignty pass to a third party. The United States went to war, as it always said it would, to prevent the transfer of sovereignty of Cuba, in this instance to the Cubans themselves.

🌐 *F U R T H E R   R E A D I N G*

Robert L. Beisner, *Twelve Against Empire* (1968)

_____, *From the Old to the New Diplomacy* (1986)

Jules Benjamin, *The United States and Cuba* (1977)

Warren I. Cohen, *America's Response to China* (2000)

A. B. Feuer, *America at War: The Philippines* (2002)

James A. Field Jr., "American Imperialism," *American Historical Review* 83 (1978): 644–688

Mark T. Gilderhus, *The Second Century: U.S.–Latin American Relations Since 1889* (2000)

Frank Golay, *Face of Empire: United States–Philippine Relations, 1898–1946* (1998)

Lewis L. Gould, *The Spanish-American War and William McKinley* (1983)

Michael H. Hunt, *The Making of a Special Relationship* (1993) (on China)

Gilbert M. Joseph, et al., eds., *Close Encounters of Empire* (1998)

Stanley Karnow, *In Our Image* (1989) (on the Philippines)

Paul A. Kramer, "Empires, Exceptions, and Anglo-Saxons: Race and Rule Between the British and United States Empires, 1880–1910." *Journal of American History* 88 (March 2002): 1315–1353

Walter LaFeber, *The American Search for Opportunity, 1865–1913* (1993)

_____, *The New Empire* (1998)

Paul R. McCartney, *Power and Progress* (2006)

Joyce Milton, The *Yellow Kids* (1989) (on journalism)

Ian Mugridge, *The View from Xanadu* (1995) (on William Randolph Hearst)

Ivan Musicant, *Empire by Default* (1998)

John L. Offner, *An Unwanted War* (1992)

Thomas G. Paterson, "United States Intervention in Cuba: Interpretations of the Spanish-American-Cuban-Filipino War." *History Teacher* 29 (May 1996): 341–361

Louis A. Pérez, *Cuba Between Empires* (1988)

_____, *Cuba and the United States* (1990)

_____, *On Becoming Cuban* (1999)

David M. Pletcher, *The Diplomacy of Trade and Investment* (1998)

Hyman Rickover, *How the Battleship "Maine" Was Destroyed* (1976)

James Carlos Rowe, *Literary Culture and U.S. Imperialism* (2000)

Michael Salmon, *The Embarrassment of Slavery* (2001) (on the Philippines)

Peggy Samuels and Harold Samuels, *Remembering the Maine* (1998)

Thomas Schoonover, *Uncle Sam's War of 1898 and the Origins of Globalization* (2004)

Lars Shoultz, *The Infernal Little Cuban Republic* (2009)

Allison L. Sneider, *Suffragists in an Imperial Age* (2008)

John Lawrence Tone, *War and Genocide in Cuba* (2006)

David Trask, *The War with Spain in 1898* (1981)

Richard E. Welch, *Response to Imperialism* (1979) (on the Philippines)

C H A P T E R

13

Empire and Ambition in Asia: China and the Philippines

Admiral George Dewey's victory over the Spanish flotilla in Manila Harbor in May 1898 propelled the United States to great power status in Asia, just as an imperial drama unfolded in China. The faltering Qing (Ching), or Manchu, dynasty suffered a crippling blow after Japan soundly defeated China in the Sino-Japanese War of 1894–1895. Expansionist nations France, Germany, Great Britain, Italy, and Russia joined Japan in imposing unequal treaties and establishing spheres of influence, usually around China's prosperous port cities. Although American exports to China totaled only $3 million by 1890, U.S. leaders and Yankee merchants had for decades dreamed of a lucrative trade with the heavily populated country, and Protestant missionaries had labored to convert the "heathen Chinee" to Christianity. Would China be closed to Americans—traders, missionaries, and diplomats alike? What did the future hold for the Philippines following the defeat of Spanish colonialism? What shape would U.S. influence in Asia take?

The administration of William McKinley initially intended to minimize the U.S. presence in both China and the Philippines. The United States did not participate in the rush for concessions in China, and in the Philippines President McKinley thought of annexing only the northern island of Luzon with its highly prized harbor at Manila as a U.S. naval base. By October 1898, however, the president decided that the entire archipelago should be annexed, and the Treaty of Paris, signed by Spain on December 10, 1898, ceded all of the Philippines to the United States. In China, the McKinley administration took a different approach. In 1899 and 1900, Secretary of State John Hay sent the imperial powers two formal diplomatic notes requesting that they respect China's territorial integrity and the principle of equal trade opportunity, a traditional U.S. doctrine. These missives became known as the Open Door policy, a strategy designed to protect U.S. commerce in China and simultaneously disavow imperial intent. The great powers did not reject the Open Door in principle, but at the same time made no specific commitments to uphold it.

America's growing presence in Asia did not go uncontested. The U.S. Senate on February 6, 1900, approved the Treaty of Paris, but a popular anticolonial insurgency, led by the Philippine patriot Emilio Aguinaldo, challenged U.S. authority. Both sides committed atrocities. Americans burned villages, tortured suspected insurgents—whom they often referred to as "gu-gus" or "niggers"—and U.S.

officials introduced their own variant of the reconcentration policy that they had roundly condemned in Spanish Cuba. Before the insurrection had been crushed, more than 5,000 Americans and over 200,000 Filipinos were dead, victims of combat and disease. Violence rocked China as well when the anti-Christian Boxer Rebellion killed missionaries and their converts and attacked the diplomatic quarter in Beijing in 1900. Washington dispatched 4,000 U.S. troops to join other foreign forces in North China to protect embassies, consulates, and religious missions.

Many Americans—including notables such as the writer Mark Twain, the philosopher William James, the businessman Andrew Carnegie, and Democratic presidential hopeful William Jennings Bryan—questioned U.S. military actions and denounced the acquisition of the Philippines. Anti-imperialists argued that an empire across the Pacific would undermine the United States' anticolonial tradition, be expensive to hold and defend, empower the president at Congress's expense, and incorporate within the republic "undesirable" non-Anglo-Saxon subjects. Imperialists countered that American intervention in Asia would ultimately increase trade opportunities, balance the European presence, and benefit Filipinos by giving them the blessings of liberty. Theodore Roosevelt, who had become president following McKinley's assassination in September 1901, formally declared on July 4, 1902, that the Philippine insurrection had been extinguished. To solidify U.S. rule, the governor-general of the Philippines and future U.S. president William Howard Taft advanced a policy of limited Philippine self-rule, strong trade links to the United States, and improvements in roads, health, and education. To counter China's instability and promote a balance of power in Asia, Roosevelt nurtured improved relations with Japan, which many in Washington viewed as a force for modernization in the region.

Washington boasted that American colonialism in the Philippines, and the principle of the Open Door, constituted a more benign foreign policy than that practiced by Europeans. Most historians acknowledge that Americans, imbued with the spirit of 1776, ruled the Philippines with an uneasy conscience and much preferred the doctrine of the Open Door to the imperial creed. But scholars also agree that U.S. policies in East Asia did not always carry a beneficial impact. To what extent did U.S. intervention nurture democracy and development? How did the racial thinking evident in U.S. governance of the Philippines influence American policies then and in the long term? To what extent did U.S. rule promote an exploitative dependency? Did the Open Door notes truly challenge the imperial powers in China? Or, were they yet another example of American expansionism, another effort to build an informal empire—in this case, through the penetration of a China market that many thought to be immense? In short, was the United States exceptional in its approach to Asia, or did it for the most part mimic the behavior of other great powers?

🌐 D O C U M E N T S

On February 4, 1899, fighting erupted between U.S. troops and Emilio Aguinaldo's nationalist forces. The next day, Aguinaldo issued a ringing proclamation, reprinted as Document 1, that reviewed Philippine grievances and urged Filipinos to rally around the anticolonial cause. With the approval of the Treaty of Paris still pending in the Senate, American critics of U.S. policy denounced war for overseas empire. The platform of the Anti-Imperialist League (October, 17, 1899) is Document 2. On November 21, 1899, President William McKinley defended his decision to colonize the Philippines to a delegation of visiting Methodist church leaders. In Document 3, McKinley's presentation portrays the United States as a reluctant imperialist and insists that his decision to retain the Philippines derived from Christian conscience.

The Great Powers in Asia, 1900

Because of the archipelago's obvious economic and strategic significance, historians remain skeptical about McKinley's story.

As American troops battled for possession of the Philippines, the McKinley administration tried to persuade the other great powers to tame their drive for empire in China. In Document 4, the two Open Door notes of September 1899 and March 1900, Secretary of State John Hay appealed to Great Britain and the other imperial powers to respect the principles of equal trade opportunity in China and the preservation of Chinese independence. The imperial powers did not reject the Open Door in principle, but at the same time made no specific commitments to uphold it. The Open Door notwithstanding, the outbreak of the Boxer Rebellion in early 1900 spurred President McKinley to send U.S. troops to Beijing to participate in a multinational force to contain the anti-Western and anti-missionary uprising. The nationalistic zeal of the Boxer movement is revealed in Document 5, a notice prepared by participants in the rebellion.

America's inconsistent advocacy of self-determination in Asia did not escape public scrutiny, especially as the Philippine insurrection ground on. In Document 6, excerpts of hearings before a U.S. Senate committee in April 1902, Corporal Daniel J. Evans, a veteran of the Philippine-American war, describes the "water cure"—a variant of water boarding and a form of torture—U.S. troops used against Philippine insurgents and civilians. Document 7 is a veteran's memoir of 1902 by Major Cornelius Gardner, recalling the difficulty of distinguishing rebels from civilians in the rural, guerrilla-style war and questioning the morality of the American venture. In Document 8, the first U.S. governor-general in the Philippines, William Howard Taft, lays out to U.S. senators in early 1902 plans to establish a civil government in the recently acquired colony. Articulating what later became known as the policies of "attraction" and "benevolent assimilation," the governor-general emphasized America's mission to teach the recently defeated Filipinos the benefits of legislative government. Skeptical of Philippine abilities, Taft voiced confidence that U.S. imperial rule would be strengthened, and the cause of liberty advanced, by granting "qualified suffrage" to educated elites in the indigenous Federal Party.

D O C U M E N T   1

Emilio Aguinaldo Rallies the Philippine People to Arms, 1899

By my proclamation of yesterday I have published the outbreak of hostilities between the Philippine forces and the American forces of occupation in Manila, unjustly and unexpectedly provoked by the latter.

In my manifest of January 8 [1899] last I published the grievances suffered by the Philippine forces at the hands of the army of occupation. The constant outrages and taunts, which have caused the misery of the people of Manila, and, finally the useless conferences and the contempt shown the Philippine government prove the premeditated transgression of justice and liberty.

I know that war has always produced great losses; I know that the Philippine people have not yet recovered from past losses and are not in the condition to endure others. But I also know by experience how bitter is slavery, and by experience I know that we should sacrifice all on the altar of our honor and of the national integrity so unjustly attacked.

I have tried to avoid, as far as it has been possible for me to do so, armed conflict, in my endeavors to assure our independence by pacific means and to avoid more costly sacrifices. But all my efforts have been useless against the measureless pride of the American Government and of its representatives in these islands, who have treated me as a rebel because I defend the sacred interests of my country and do not make myself an instrument of their dastardly intentions.

Past campaigns will have convinced you that the people are strong when they wish to be so. Without arms we have driven from our beloved country our ancient

This document can be found in Major-General E. S. Otis, *Report on Military Operations and Civil Affairs in the Philippine Islands, 1899* (Washington, D.C.: Government Printing Office, 1899), pp. 95–96.

masters, and without arms we can repulse the foreign invasion as long as we wish to do so. Providence always has means in reserve and prompt help for the weak in order that they may not be annihilated by the strong; that justice may be done and humanity progress.

Be not discouraged. Our independence has been watered by the generous blood of our martyrs. Blood which may be shed in the future will strengthen it. Nature has never despised generous sacrifices.

But remember that in order that our efforts may not be wasted, that our vows may be listened to, that our ends may be gained, it is indispensable that we adjust our actions to the rules of law and of right, learning to triumph over our enemies and to conquer our own evil passions.

D O C U M E N T   2

The Anti-Impeirialist League Defends Democracy Against Militarism, 1899

We hold that the policy known as imperialism is hostile to liberty and tends toward militarism, an evil from which it has been our glory to be free. We regret that it has become necessary in the land of Washington and Lincoln to reaffirm that all men, of whatever race or color, are entitled to life, liberty and the pursuit of happiness. We maintain that governments derive their just powers from the consent of the governed. We insist that the subjugation of any people is "criminal aggression" and open disloyalty to the distinctive principles of our Government.

We earnestly condemn the policy of the present National Administration in the Philippines. It seeks to extinguish the spirit of 1776 in those islands. We deplore the sacrifice of our soldiers and sailors, whose bravery deserves admiration even in an unjust war. We denounce the slaughter of the Filipinos as a needless horror. We protest against the extension of American sovereignty by Spanish methods.

We demand the immediate cessation of the war against liberty, begun by Spain and continued by us. We urge that Congress be promptly convened to announce to the Filipinos our purpose to concede to them the independence for which they have so long fought and which of right is theirs.

The United States have always protested against the doctrine of international law which permits the subjugation of the weak by the strong. A self-governing state cannot accept sovereignty over an unwilling people. The United States cannot act upon the ancient heresy that might makes right.

Imperialists assume that with the destruction of self-government in the Philippines by American hands, all opposition here will cease. This is a grievous error. Much as we abhor the war of "criminal aggression" in the Philippines, greatly as we regret that the blood of the Filipinos is on American hands, we more deeply resent the betrayal of American institutions at home. The real firing line is not in the suburbs of Manila. The foe is of our own household. The attempt of 1861 was to divide the country. That of 1899 is to destroy its fundamental principles and noblest ideals.

This document can be found in Frederic Bancroft, ed., *Speeches, Correspondence, and Political Papers of Carl Schurz* (New York: G. P. Putnam's Sons, 1913), VI, 77–79.

Whether the ruthless slaughter of the Filipinos shall end next month or next year is but an incident in a contest that must go on until the Declaration of Independence and the Constitution of the United States are rescued from the hands of their betrayers. Those who dispute about standards of value while the foundation of the Republic is undermined will be listened to as little as those who would wrangle about the small economies of the household while the house is on fire. The training of a great people for a century, the aspiration for liberty of a vast immigration are forces that will hurl aside those who in the delirium of conquest seek to destroy the character of our institutions.

We deny that the obligation of all citizens to support their Government in times of grave National peril applies to the present situation. If an Administration may with impunity ignore the issues upon which it was chosen, deliberately create a condition of war anywhere on the face of the globe, debauch the civil service for spoils to promote the adventure, organize a truth-suppressing censorship and demand of all citizens a suspension of judgment and their unanimous support while it chooses to continue the fighting, representative government itself is imperiled.

We propose to contribute to the defeat of any person or party that stands for the forcible subjugation of any people. We shall oppose for reelection all who in the White House or in Congress betray American liberty in pursuit of un-American ends. We still hope that both of our great political parties will support and defend the Declaration of Independence in the closing campaign of the century.

We hold, with Abraham Lincoln, that "no man is good enough to govern another man without the other's consent. When the white man governs himself, that is self-government, but when he governs himself and also governs another man, that is more than self-government—that is despotism. Our reliance is in the love of liberty which God has planted in us. Our defense is in the spirit which prizes liberty as the heritage of all men in all lands. Those who deny freedom to others deserve it not for themselves, and under a just God cannot long retain it."

We cordially invite the cooperation of all men and women who remain loyal to the Declaration of Independence and the Constitution of the United States.

🌐 D O C U M E N T   3

President McKinley Preaches His Imperial Gospel, 1899

Hold a moment longer! Not quite yet, gentlemen! Before you go I would like to say just a word about the Philippine business. I have been criticized a good deal about the Philippines, but don't deserve it. The truth is I didn't want the Philippines, and when they came to us, as a gift from the gods, I did not know what to do with them. When the Spanish War broke out [Admiral George] Dewey was at Hongkong, and I ordered him to go to Manila and to capture or destroy the Spanish fleet, and he had to; because, if defeated, he had no place to refit on that side of the globe, and if the

This document can be found in James Rusling, "Interview with President William McKinley," *The Christian Advocate* (January 22, 1903), p. 17. It can also be found in Charles S. Olcott, *William McKinley* (Boston: Houghton Mifflin Company, 1916), II, 109–111.

Dons were victorious they would likely cross the Pacific and ravage our Oregon and California coasts. And so he had to destroy the Spanish fleet, and did it! But that was as far as I thought then.

When I next realized that the Philippines had dropped into our laps I confess I did not know what to do with them. I sought counsel from all sides—Democrats as well as Republicans—but got little help. I thought first we would take only Manila; then Luzon; then other islands perhaps also. I walked the floor of the White House night after night until midnight; and I am not ashamed to tell you, gentlemen, that I went down on my knees and prayed Almighty God for light and guidance more than one night. And one night late it came to me this way—I don't know how it was, but it came: (1) That we could not give them back to Spain—that would be cowardly and dishonorable; (2) that we could not turn them over to France and Germany— our commercial rivals in the Orient—that would be bad business and discreditable; (3) that we could not leave them to themselves—they were unfit for self-government— and they would soon have anarchy and misrule over there worse than Spain's was; and (4) that there was nothing left for us to do but to take them all, and to educate the Filipinos, and uplift and civilize and Christianize them, and by God's grace do the very best we could by them, as our fellow-men for whom Christ also died. And then I went to bed, and went to sleep, and slept soundly, and the next morning I sent for the chief engineer of the War Department (our map-maker), and I told him to put the Philippines on the map of the United States (pointing to a large map on the wall of his office), and there they are, and there they will stay while I am President!

DOCUMENT 4

The Open Door Notes Call for Equal Trade Opportunity and China's Independence, 1899–1900
The First Open Door Note, 1899

The Government of Her Britannic Majesty has declared that its policy and its very traditions precluded it from using any privileges which might be granted it in China as a weapon for excluding commercial rivals, and that freedom of trade for Great Britain in that Empire meant freedom of trade for all the world alike. While conceding by formal agreements, first with Germany and then with Russia, the possession of "spheres of influence or interest" in China in which they are to enjoy special rights and privileges, more especially in respect of railroads and mining enterprises, Her Britannic Majesty's Government has therefore sought to maintain at the same time what is called the "open-door" policy, to insure to the commerce of the world in China equality of treatment within said "spheres" for commerce and navigation. This latter policy is alike urgently demanded by the British mercantile communities and by those of the United States, as it is justly held by them to be the only one which will improve existing conditions, enable them to maintain their positions in the markets of China, and extend their

This document can be found in U.S. Department of State, *Papers Relating to the Foreign Relations of the United States, 1899* (Washington, D.C.: Government Printing Office, 1901), pp. 131–133.

operations in the future. While the Government of the United States will in no way commit itself to a recognition of exclusive rights of any power within or control over any portion of the Chinese Empire under such agreements as have within the last year been made, it can not conceal its apprehension that under existing conditions there is a possibility, even a probability, of complications arising between the treaty powers which may imperil the rights insured to the United States under our treaties with China.

This Government is animated by a sincere desire that the interests of our citizens may not be prejudiced through exclusive treatment by any of the controlling powers within their so-called "spheres of interest" in China, and hopes also to retain there an open market for the commerce of the world, remove dangerous sources of international irritation, and hasten thereby united or concerted action of the powers at Pekin[g] in favor of the administrative reforms so urgently needed for strengthening the Imperial Government and maintaining the integrity of China in which the whole western world is alike concerned. It believes that such a result may be greatly assisted by a declaration by the various powers claiming "spheres of interest" in China of their intentions as regards treatment of foreign trade therein. The present moment seems a particularly opportune one for informing Her Britannic Majesty's Government of the desire of the United States to see it make a formal declaration and to lend its support in obtaining similar declarations from the various powers claiming "spheres of influence" in China, to the effect that each in its respective spheres of interest or influence—

First. Will in no wise interfere with any treaty port or any vested interest within any so-called "sphere of interest" or leased territory it may have in China.

Second. That the Chinese treaty tariff of the time being shall apply to all merchandise landed or shipped to all such ports as are within said "sphere of interest" (unless they be "free ports"), no matter to what nationality it may belong, and that duties so leviable shall be collected by the Chinese Government.

Third. That it will levy no higher harbor dues on vessels of another nationality frequenting any port in such "sphere" than shall be levied on vessels of its own nationality, and no higher railroad charges over lines built, controlled, or operated within its "sphere" on merchandise belonging to citizens or subjects of other nationalities transported through such "sphere" than shall be levied on similar merchandise belonging to its own nationals transported over equal distances.

The recent ukase of His Majesty the Emperor of Russia, declaring the port of Ta-lien-wan open to the merchant ships of all nations during the whole of the lease under which it is to be held by Russia, removing as it does all uncertainty as to the liberal and conciliatory policy of that power, together with the assurance given this Government by Russia, justifies the expectation that His Majesty will cooperate in such an understanding as is here proposed, and our ambassador at the court of St. Petersburg has been instructed accordingly to submit the propositions above detailed to His Imperial Majesty, and ask their early consideration. . . .

The action of Germany in declaring the port of Kiaochao a "free port," and the aid the Imperial Government has given China in the establishment there of a Chinese custom-house, coupled with the oral assurance conveyed the United States by Germany that our interest within its "sphere" would in no wise be affected by its occupation of this portion of the province of Shang-tung, tend to show that little opposition may be anticipated from that power to the desired declaration.

The interests of Japan, the next most interested power in the trade of China, will be so clearly served by the proposed arrangement, and the declaration of its statesmen within the last year are so entirely in line with the views here expressed, that its hearty cooperation is confidently counted on.

The Second Open Door Note, 1900

In this critical posture of affairs in China it is deemed appropriate to define the attitude of the United States as far as present circumstances permit this to be done. We adhere to the policy initiated by us in 1857, of peace with the Chinese nation, of furtherance of lawful commerce, and of protection of lives and property of our citizens by all means guaranteed under extraterritorial treaty rights and by the law of nations. If wrong be done to our citizens we propose to hold the responsible authors to the uttermost accountability. We regard the condition at Pekin[g] as one of virtual anarchy, whereby power and responsibility are practically devolved upon the local provincial authorities. So long as they are not in overt collusion with rebellion and use their power to protect foreign life and property we regard them as representing the Chinese people, with whom we seek to remain in peace and friendship. The purpose of the President is, as it has been heretofore, to act concurrently with the other powers, first, in opening up communication with Pekin[g] and rescuing the American officials, missionaries, and other Americans who are in danger; secondly, in affording all possible protection everywhere in China to American life and property; thirdly, in guarding and protecting all legitimate American interests; and fourthly, in aiding to prevent a spread of the disorders to the other provinces of the Empire and a recurrence of such disasters. It is, of course, too early to forecast the means of attaining this last result; but the policy of the Government of the United States is to seek a solution which may bring about permanent safety and peace to China, preserve Chinese territorial and administrative entity, protect all rights guaranteed to friendly powers by treaty and international law, and safeguard for the world the principle of equal and impartial trade with all parts of the Chinese Empire.

✪ D O C U M E N T   5

The Boxers Lash Out at Christian Missionaries and Converts, 1900

Attention: all people in markets and villages of all provinces in China—now, owing to the fact that Catholics and Protestants have vilified our gods and sages, have deceived our emperors and ministers above, and oppressed the Chinese people below, both our gods and our people are angry at them, yet we have to keep silent. This forces us to practise the I-ho magic boxing so as to protect our country, expel the foreign bandits and kill Christian converts, in order to save our people from miserable suffering. After this notice is issued to instruct you villagers, no matter

The Second Open Door Note, 1900 can be found in U.S. Department of State, *Papers Relating to the Foreign Relations of the United States, 1901* (Washington, D.C.: Government Printing Office, 1902), Appendix, p. 12.

Document 5 can be found in Ssu-yu Teng and John K. Fairbank, *China's Response to the West* (Cambridge, Mass.: Harvard University Press, 1954), p. 190.

which village you are living in, if there are Christian converts, you ought to get rid of them quickly. The churches which belong to them should be unreservedly burned down. Everyone who intends to spare someone, or to disobey our order by conceal- ing Christian converts, will be punished according to the regulation when we come to his place, and he will be burned to death to prevent his impeding our program. We especially do not want to punish anyone by death without warning him first. We can- not bear to see you suffer innocently. Don't disobey this special notice!

DOCUMENT 6

Corporal Daniel J. Evans Describes the "Water Cure," 1902

Q. The committee would like to hear from you in regard to the conduct of the war, and whether you were the witness of any cruelties inflicted upon the natives in the Philippine Islands; and if so, under what circumstances.

A. The case I had reference to was where they gave the water cure to a native in the Ilieano Province at Ilocos Norte.

Q. That is in the extreme northern part of Luzon?

A. Yes, sir. There were two native scouts that were with the American forces. They went out and brought in a couple of insurgents. They were known to be insurgents by their own confession, and, besides that, they had the mark that most insurgents in that part of the country carry; it is a little brand on the left breast, generally inflicted with a nail or head of a cartridge, heated. They tried to find out from this native—

Q. What kind of a brand did you say it was?

A. A small brand put on with a nail head or cartridge.

Sen. [Albert J.] Beveridge: A scar on the flesh?

The Witness: Yes, sir.

They tried to get him to tell where the rest of the insurgents were at that time. We knew about where they were, but we did not know how to get at them. They were in the hills, and it happened that there was only one path that could get to them, and we did not get to them that time. They refused to tell this one path and they com- menced this so-called "water cure." The first thing one of the Americans—I mean one of the scouts for the Americans—grabbed one of the men by the head and jerked his head back, and then they took a tomato can and poured water down his throat un- til he could hold no more, and during this time one of the natives had a rattan whip, about as large as my finger, and he struck him on the face and on the bare back, and every time they would strike him it would raise a large welt, and some blood would come. And when this native could hold no more water, then they forced a gag into his mouth; they stood him up and tied his hands behind him; they stood him up against a post and fastened him so he could not move. Then one man, an American

This document can be found in Daniel Evans, testimony, "Affairs in the Philippine Islands." Senate Com- mittee on the Philippines, 57th Congress, 1st Session, April 1902. It can also be found in Henry F. Graff, ed., *American Imperialism and the Philippine Insurrection: Testimony Taken from Hearings on Affairs in the Philippine Islands Before the Senate Committee on the Philippines. 1902* (Boston: Little, Brown, 1969), pp. 80–89.

soldier, who was over six feet tall, and who was very strong, too, struck this native in the pit of the stomach as hard as he could strike him, just as rapidly as he could. It seemed as if he didn't get tired of striking him.

Sen. [William B.] Allison: With his hand?

A. With his clenched fist. He struck him right in the pit of the stomach and it made the native very sick. They kept that operation up for quite a time, and finally I thought the fellow was about to die, but I don't believe he was as bad as that, because finally he told them he would tell them, and from that on he was taken away, and I saw no more of him.

Q. Did he tell?

A. I believe he did, because I didn't hear of any more water cure inflicted on him. . . .

Q. How many American soldiers altogether were there present?

A. I can safely say there were fifty.

DOCUMENT 7

Major Cornelius Gardner Recalls
the Horrors of War, 1902

Of late by reason of the conduct of the troops such as the extensive burning of the barrios in trying to lay waste the country so that the insurgents cannot occupy it, the torturing of natives by so-called water-cure and other methods to obtain information, the harsh treatment of natives generally, and the failure of inexperienced, lately-appointed lieutenants commanding posts to distinguish between those who are friendly and those unfriendly and to treat every native as if he were, whether or no, an *insurrecto* at heart, . . . and a deep hatred toward us engendered. If these things need be done, they had best be done by native troops, so that the people of the United States will not be credited therewith.

Almost without exception, soldiers and also many officers refer to natives in their presence as "Niggers," and natives are beginning to understand what the word "Nigger" means. The course now being pursued in this province and in the provinces of Batangas, Laguna, and Samar is in my opinion sowing the seeds for a perpetual revolution against us hereafter whenever a good opportunity offers. Under present conditions the political situation in this province is slowly retrograding, the American sentiment is decreasing, and we are daily making permanent enemies. In the course above referred to, troops make no distinction often between the property of those natives who are insurgent or insurgent sympathizers, and the property of those who heretofore have risked their lives by being loyal to the United States and giving us information against their countrymen in arms. Often every house in a barrio is burned. In my opinion the small number of irreconcilable insurgents still in arms, although admittedly difficult to catch, does not justify the means employed, and especially when taking into consideration the suffering that must be undergone by the innocent and its effects upon the relations with these people hereafter.

This document can be found in B. D. Flower, "Some Dead Sea Fruit of Our War Subjugation," *The Arena*, Vol. 27 (1902), pp. 648–649.

🌐 *D O C U M E N T   8*

Governor-General William Howard Taft Envisions Partial Democracy for the Philippines, 1902

Sen. Culberson: . . . [U]nder your instructions, was not the [Taft] Commission under the control of the Secretary of War and were not all your acts subject to the approval of the Secretary of War?

Gov. Taft: Yes, sir; under the Secretary of War, who is a civilian. I am speaking now of the authorities resident in the islands.

I have studied, of course, the instructions issued by President McKinley with a great deal of care, and have watched their operation in the development of the government of those islands. . . . I think they constitute one of the greatest state papers ever issued in operating as they were intended to operate and in bringing about a state of affairs that they intended to bring about; and their operation was this: There was insurrection in the country. How far that insurrection attracted the sympathy of all the people is of course a mere matter of opinion, upon which there will always be a substantial difference. That there were two parties, however—those who favored the exclusion of American sovereignty altogether, and a substantial party who favored the government which we are now establishing—is undoubtedly true, and that there was a large body of ignorant people who were entirely indifferent, provided peace could be established and they could be protected from oppression and violence and assault, and who had very few political ideas at all, is also true.

Sen. Beveridge: This third division is the great[est] body of all?

Gov. Taft: Yes; ignorant people.

Now, the problem there was on the one hand to suppress the insurrection, and that had to be done with the Army. On the other hand, it was to teach the people that our purpose was not to continue a military government, but by object lessons to show them what civil government was by legislation and by putting it into force.

Now, here was a dual government. There was the military arm on the one hand and there was the civil arm on the other, and the effect of those instructions—you can see it operate every day—was to bring the Filipino—and I do not except anybody in that statement; I do not even except the insurrectos—to bring the people into more friendly relations with the civil government than with the military government.

The conduct of a dual form of government of that sort was of course difficult. The instructions were framed so that they have worked. But the coming into the minds of the people [of] a consciousness of the existence of power in the civil government and its effect on them, and the gradually [*sic*] placing [of] more and more power in the civil government, which the instructions contemplated, have had a marvelous effect in showing the people what our purpose was. . . .

This document can be found in William Howard Taft, testimony, "Affairs in the Pacific Islands," *Senate Committee on the Philippines*, 57th Congress, 1st Session, 31 January 1902, 3–46. It can also be found in Henry F. Graff, American Imperialism and the Philippine Insurrection: Testimony Taken from Hearings on Affairs in the Philippine Islands Before the Senate Committee on the Philippines (Boston: Little Brown, 1969), pp. 123–125.

[T]he theory of the Commission in its formation of civil government has been this: First, that the indispensable aid to the ultimate success of a popular government there, with qualified suffrage, is the extension of education through the islands; but that of course cannot have great effect short of a generation or two generations, because the people affected by education are those who are now children, though there are some ten thousand adults studying English in the night schools. But the main effect of education must be on those who are coming into manhood or will not come into manhood possibly for ten or fifteen years.

In the meantime the reliance of the Commission is on the small educated portion of the community. With this as a nucleus and with the aid of American control we think a stable government can be erected. A majority of the provincial board in each case is American, and I say without hesitation—of course it is an expression of opinion—that lacking the American initiative, lacking the American knowledge of how to carry on a government, any government there must be a complete failure until by actual observation and practice, under the guidance of a people who know how to carry on a government, who understand the institutions of civil liberty, there may be trained a Filipino element who may then be able to carry on the government without so much guidance and so much initiative as now are absolutely necessary to the carrying on of a decent government at all. . . .

The Federal party was projected in November. Its organization continued into December and January, and it spread, I may say, like wildfire.

Sen. Allison: January of last year?

Gov. Taft: Yes, sir. Now, it [has been] suggested . . . that the reason why the party spread with such rapidity was because of a plank in its platform which was for statehood. I have been trying to find that platform. Possibly some gentleman present may have it. I cannot find it among my papers. . . .

My recollection of the platform is that it is divided into two parts. The first part concerned what was at hand—the present purpose of the party—and the second part contained what may not be characterized as aspirations of the party, but something equivalent to that. In the first part they ask for amnesty to all political offenders, for the organization of a partially popular government, and some other things that do not now occur to me. In the second part is the statement of their hope that they may be made part of the States when fitted for self-government, and some other things.

Possibly in the first part, too, is the plank that they shall have two or three delegates representing them before the executive and legislative departments in Washington.

Now, the real reason for the spread of the Federal party was the urgent desire for peace on the part of substantially all classes except those people who were in the mountains. I make that statement without the slightest qualification. . . .

The only party of any organization at all throughout the islands is the Federal party. In the appointment of natives the fact that a man was a member of the Federal party was always a good recommendation for him for appointment, for the reason that we regarded the Federal party as one of the great elements in bringing about pacification, and if a man was in the Federal party it was fairly good evidence that he was interested in the government which we were establishing, and would do as well as he could.

🌐 *E S S A Y S*

In the first essay, Michael H. Hunt of the University of North Carolina at Chapel Hill explains the role of American businesses, missionaries, and diplomats—the three components of the "open door constituency"—in shaping the McKinley administration's efforts to defend U.S. interests in China against challenges from both the Chinese and the imperial powers. Given Washington's reluctance to join in partitioning China, Secretary of State John Hay's notes seemed a logical, if ineffective, means of disciplining the great powers and protecting U.S. interests.

In the second essay, Paul A. Kramer of The Johns Hopkins University anaylzes the U.S.-Philippine War through the prism of race. U.S. government officials, according to Kramer, dismissed Filipino demands for self-government on the grounds that the Philippine population was "tribal" rather than national. U.S. soldiers on the scene also racialized the colonial project, not simply by associating Filipinos with American racial minority groups such as African Americans and Indians but also by inventing new racial epithets—including the widely used term "gu-gu"—to identify the indigenous population. The stereotypes helped U.S. authorities dismiss the insurgents' resort to guerrilla war as "savage" and legitimized the extremely harsh tactics employed by the U.S. military, including the establishment of relocation camps, the torture of prisoners, and the erosion of distinctions between combatants and noncombatants.

The Open Door Constituency's Pressure for U.S. Activism in China

MICHAEL H. HUNT

In the latter part of the nineteenth century the open door constituency reached the apogee of its influence. It exercised that influence not in China, for a handful of Americans, however exaggerated their sense of self-importance, could have only an imperceptible impact on the lives of a people numbering some 400 million. It was rather in moving Washington toward a more active China policy that they made their mark. In effecting this policy transformation Americans in China were inadvertently assisted by Chinese hostile to the mission movement and by plotting foreign imperialists. The threat they posed led businessmen, missionaries, and diplomats—each in their own way—to employ a rhetoric that idealized their concrete self-serving goals. Because the activities of each group contributed (so they argued) to China's regeneration and to the realization of an American Pacific destiny, each could legitimately make a claim on Washington's support. A flurry of economic activity in the 1890s, viewed hopefully as the harbinger of more to come, strengthened the voice of commercial interests. But at the same time the articulate representatives of the expanding mission enterprise and a chain of vocal ministers in the Peking legation demanded that policy makers attend to their aspirations as well and thus by degrees diverted policy away from its earlier, essentially commercial orientation.

The Open Door Constituency's Pressure for U.S. Activism, pp. 143–144, 148–149, 150–154, 156–157, 158, 162–163, 168–169, 171–172, 174–175, 177–178, 179–180, 181–183, 186–187, 196–198. From *The Making of a Special Relationship: The United States and China to 1914,* by Michael H. Hunt, Copyright © 1983 Columbia University Press. Reprinted with the permission of the publisher.

For roughly two decades—from the 1860s through the 1880s—American economic enterprise in China stagnated, eroding the merchants' dominant position in the open door constituency. United States exports to China fell from a high of $9 million in 1864 to a low of $1 million in the mid-1870s, while the number of American firms operating in China declined from 42 to 31 between 1872 and 1880, a time when the enterprises operated by other nationalities actually grew in number. The most serious casualties were the great merchant houses that had dominated American economic activity before the 1860s. Augustine Heard and Company failed in 1875, Olyphant three years later. . . .

At last in the 1890s previously dim prospects gave way to China market fever. The trade statistics, already beginning to point upward in the 1880s, climbed at a rapid rate through the nineties. American exports, overwhelmingly cotton goods and kerosene, began the decade at $3 million and ended it at $14 million.

Cotton goods, sent to China as far back as the 1830s, had now become a major export as American mills gained a clear edge over the long dominant British in the markets of North China and Manchuria. While the British industry with its skilled work force and accumulated experience continued to excel in finer grades of cloth, Americans took over in the cheap coarse goods, thanks essentially to lower wages (particularly in the southern United States) and more advanced machinery. . . .

Kerosene, the other major component in the American export drive, had begun to enter the China market as early as 1867 chiefly for use by foreign residents. Not until the late 1870s did its sales begin to boom. The 5.4 million gallons (valued at $690,000) imported in 1879 were in turn to increase to 40.4 million ($2,436,000) by 1894. China's share of American kerosene exports climbed between those years from 1.6 percent to 5.5 percent. Supplying oil for the lamps of China was becoming big business. The chief beneficiary was Standard Oil of New York, the export arm of the Rockefeller petroleum trust. . . .

These commercial advances were accompanied by another burst of interest in investment; only this time Americans would in the end have something to show for their effort. Investments valued at $6 million in 1875 were to grow to $20 million by 1900, thus preserving for Americans approximately the same share in China relative to other nationals. American money began to go into direct investments early in the 1890s. At mid-decade the Treaty of Shimonoseki (ending the Sino-Japanese War) encouraged the investment of still more American capital by giving foreigners the undisputed right to establish industry and especially textile mills in China. Finally, Americans even moved into mining seriously for the first time. . . .

Speculators at last scored a triumph when the American China Development Company obtained the concession for a railway to be built between Hankow and Canton. The company, organized in 1895 in anticipation of expanded postwar investment opportunities, was headed by Calvin Brice, a former Ohio senator and railway lawyer who moved in New York financial circles. It included among its shareholders the railway magnate E. H. Harriman; Jacob Schiff of the investment house of Kuhn, Loeb and Company; the presidents of the National City Bank and the Chase National Bank; the former Vice President of the United States, Levi Morton; an associate of J. P. Morgan and Company; and the Carnegie Steel Corporation. . . .

A growing trade and a prize railway concession inspired the belief among Americans that they would enjoy a prominent part in the broad economic development that China was sure to undergo in the decades ahead. But roseate hopes for railway building, mining, and trade expansion contended against mounting fears that the advancing European powers and Japan might snatch away the China market just as it was at last about to realize its potential. The pattern of imperial penetration ending in formal territorial control, already worked out in Africa and parts of Asia, had begun to repeat itself in China. The powers were using political loans and their diplomatic and military muscle to stake out spheres of influence. The German seizure of Kiaochow in Shantung in November 1897 prompted the Russians in turn to take Port Arthur in Manchuria. France grabbed new concessions in the southern provinces of Yünnan and Kwangsi bordering on French Indochina. Japan laid claim to a sphere of influence in Fukien. Even Britain joined in, taking a naval base of her own on the Shantung peninsula and new lands adjoining Hong Kong, and strengthening her position in the Yangtze Valley. China's manifest weakness, growing great power rivalry, and Britain's wavering support for the principle of free trade and China's integrity suddenly made the carving up of the empire an imminent possibility.

With the future of American trade and the American role in the pending drama of Chinese economic development hanging in the balance, the commercial interests within the open door constituency appealed to Washington for support. A look at the sponsors of that appeal reveals the changing nature of American involvement in the China market. Once dominated for all practical purposes by a few merchant houses exclusively concerned with China, the business element in the open door constituency had become both broader and more diffuse. . . . It now embraced import-export firms; export industries such as cotton textiles, petroleum, and railroad equipment; and a class of speculative investors and promoters including some of the leading figures on Wall Street. This diverse group used an array of commercial pressure groups, including the National Association of Manufacturers (organized in 1895), regional chambers of commerce, and industry and trade associations, all as instruments for political action. . . .

The McKinley administration was slow to respond. The aged Secretary of State John Sherman was unsympathetic, and the administration as a whole was distracted by the prospect, then the complications, and finally the immediate consequences of the war with Spain. The tangible evidence—the hard facts and figures—that business could use to prove to policy makers the immediate importance of the China market simply was not there. Indeed, the available statistics showed that China was not crucial to American prosperity and that American enterprise was far from a formidable presence in the Chinese economy. The China trade, only 2 percent of total U.S. foreign trade at the turn of the century, was growing no faster than U.S. foreign trade generally. The same held true of China investments, then only 3 percent of all U.S. foreign investments. In China itself Americans could claim only 9 percent of total foreign trade and 2.5 percent of all foreign investments.

In 1899, with the China crisis none improved and business pressure unabated, the McKinley administration decided to act. Except for the rebellion in the Philippines, the crisis of the war had passed, leaving the United States in an unprecedentedly strong territorial position in the Pacific. McKinley had taken Hawaii and Guam as well as the Philippines, envisioned as commercial and naval stepping stones to China. John Hay, appointed the previous autumn to succeed Sherman, had had time to settle in at the State Department. His response to the China problem, drawn so insistently to his attention, was measured. In February he sent, for the "serious attention" of the Peking legation, a petition from the textile manufacturers and traders complaining of the Russian threat to their market in northern China. But it was not until seven months later that Hay took the next step. In August [State Department official W. W.] Rockhill, and through him Alfred Hippisley, a senior English employee of the Chinese Maritime Customs Service then visiting in the United States, urged Hay to take a public stand on behalf of the commercial open door. Hay accepted their advice and in September began addressing each of the major powers in turn, asking for guarantees against specific forms of trade discrimination—in regard to the treaty ports, customs duties, and railway and harbor rates. Their qualified and evasive responses he translated publicly the following March into a "final and definitive" acceptance, and the thing was done.

These first open door notes were a token nod to the future possibilities of the China market and a tribute to the influence and persistence of the China trade pressure groups. But not much more. They did not extend a mantle of protection to investments. Indeed, Hay nowhere mentioned investments in his correspondence on this occasion except to concede that wherever in China the powers had funneled their capital they had created special interests. Further, he would not free the Peking legation from the old restrictions, much criticized by promoters, strictly limiting its ability to intervene with the Chinese government on behalf of American business proposals. And McKinley in his address to Congress in December 1898 stressed that his administration's concern was limited to the protection of commerce from discrimination by the powers. It was not even clear how far the administration would go even in behalf of trade, the chief concern of Hay's notes. Neither in public nor in private did it envision forceful action against powers who might seal off their spheres of influence against American trade. It gave no thought to the persistent and no less serious obstructions thrown by Chinese economic nationalists in the way of exporters . . . and investors. . . . Nor did it follow up the notes with a program of trade promotion. When it cautiously proposed to Congress twice in 1898 and again the next year that at least a survey be made of ways to increase China trade, Congress withheld appropriations. The open door notes had not dramatically altered China policy or transformed conditions in China, but Hay had managed by his dramatic public gesture to inspire business confidence that Washington was more committed than ever before to preserving American economic opportunity.

Despite past disappointments, American missionaries soldiered on after 1860, adding new personnel and extending their efforts beyond the safety of the treaty ports into the interior. This policy of expansion gave rise to a shrill and often violent Chinese nativism prompting missionaries in turn to call for naval and diplomatic protection. The resulting interaction among determined missionaries, aroused nativists, and uncertain diplomats was to define the history of the mission movement through the balance of the century.

The mission crisis had its origins in an extension of missionary activities that was steadier and far more aggressive than the performance of economic enterprise and that was in global terms to make China the chief focus of American Protestant activity abroad. By 1899 the once "feeble band" of missionaries numbered nearly 500 (roughly one-third to two-fifths of the Protestant force). American missionaries had by then gathered about them some 1,400 Chinese "helpers," over 1,300 converts, 9,000 students, and close to $5 million worth of physical plant (equal at least one-quarter of business investments). Mission boards, both the long established and the newcomers, allocated ever higher levels of funding to extend their activities, first into many of the newly opened ports (some 32 by 1900) and then into the interior, with the treaty ports initially serving as a base of operations. To sustain the expansion new nondenominational mission organizations such as the Student Volunteer Movement for Foreign Missions sprang up in the late 1880s and after. . . .

Minister Anson Burlingame once predicted after watching the initial mission advance into the interior that it would "plant the shining cross on every hill and in every valley." The reality as the movement unfolded during the nineteenth century was, however, closer to the sardonic observation of one old China hand less given to enthusiasm: "poor Burlingame's 'cross' shines on the hills of China, only when the population burn it." The threat of mob violence, sometimes condoned or even abetted by local officials, hung almost constantly over the missionaries and their converts scattered over the interior.

Violence sprang from multiple sources of opposition, combining in a variety of ways to produce an "incident." To the difficulties of cultural incomprehension between missionary and Chinese that had plagued work early in the century was added the problem of deracination as a result of the growing incidence of successful conversions. By turning their back on some of the norms and obligations of the local community, converts destroyed its unity and harmony and became in a measure traitors to Chinese ways. No less objectionable to their Chinese antagonists was the missionaries' direct challenge to the local social and political order and the prerogatives of its elite defenders. The missionary appeared on the scene in a role coveted by the elite, that of teacher—and to make matters worse one whose irrational doctrine was sharply at odds with the prevailing Confucian ideology. . . .

Confronted by threats to converts and mission property as well as to his own life and those of his dependents, the missionary had no difficulty choosing between a fatalistic acceptance of providential adversity (even in extremity the martyr's crown) and invoking the state's protection. Missionaries, Americans notably included, were the source of ever more persistent appeals for intervention against Chinese persecution. They began by lodging at the door of consulates and the legation the problems of securing compensation for losses, release of imprisoned converts, punishment of offenders, and widespread publicity for the rights of missionary and converts. As the Chinese opposition became more violent, the problems became less tractable and increasingly commanded the attention of the State Department. . . .

The 1890s brought a major and lasting shift in policy favorable to the mission movement. By the end of the decade Washington had dramatically broadened its definition of missionary rights and demonstrated its willingness to defend the exercise of those rights, even in the face of undiminished Chinese opposition. Missionaries, though not fully satisfied, could no longer complain that they were treated as the stepchildren of the open door constituency. China policy had come to guarantee opportunity for missions as much as for commerce. . . .

In the United States missionaries undertook a lobbying and propaganda effort, comparable to the one China market enthusiasts were to launch only a few years later, to win the support of policy makers. At the core of the missionary argument was the contention that Chinese character and culture required mission uplift. To retreat in the face of violence—so contended spokesmen for the major boards, petitions from China, missionary journals, missionaries on home leave touring from congregation to congregation, and the writings of prominent missionaries whose long residence in China qualified them as experts—would be to betray decades of missionary sacrifice and forsake the obligations of a civilized nation to turn back barbarism. . . .

The anti-Christian movement in China from the mid-1880s through the mid-1890s, though it had resulted in the loss of not a single American life and in only one wounded, nonetheless had succeeded in altering missionary policy by undermining the essential assumption that restraint and reason might guide the encounter between missionary and Chinese in the interior. The legation and Washington had come to accept instead a new but no less ill-founded assumption and erected a more interventionist policy on it. The new assumption was that the Chinese government had the power to put a stop to violent opposition and could be induced to do so. Peking might be moved to act by appeals to self-interest, or in Denby's words to fear of loss of "character, credit, and standing before the world." Failing that, intimidation would have to do, and to prepare for such a case Washington increased its naval patrol on the Yangtze from the single gunboat available in 1895. . . .

The foreign service, the last element of the open door constituency to take root in China, came into its own after 1860. It gained a permanent legation in Peking, and by 1899 it had extended its consular system to a total of ten points along the coast and in the interior. It also began to consolidate its autonomy by increasingly excluding businessmen and missionaries from its ranks. Both American and Chinese officials recognized that to allow a regular merchant to serve as consul was to give him access to confidential trade information that put other American traders at a disadvantage and clothed him with a degree of immunity in carrying out illegal business activities. Missionaries fell from favor because they faced an even more acute conflict of interest with the rise of the explosive missionary question. S. Wells Williams and Chester Holcombe served as chargé on seven occasions between 1860 and 1882, but thereafter Washington appears to have acted on the view that it was "injurious" to have a missionary in the legation. (The Chinese were also opposed to having as head of mission such missionaries as Holcombe, denounced by [Chinese leader] Li Hung-chang as a cunning scoundrel with a bad reputation.) The slowing of the ministerial merry-go-round, the bane of the legation before 1860, and the emergence of a new breed of China specialists such as William Pethick, W. W. Rockhill, and Charles Denby, Jr., further enhanced the independence of the foreign service, especially by breaking the missionaries' near monopoly of expertise. . . .

From their bully pulpits in the legation and consulates Americans maintained an unflagging enthusiasm for the contribution American economic enterprise—the building of railroads and telegraphs, the opening of mines, an expanding volume of trade—would make to China's awakening as well as to increased American influence. Missionary work and education would serve the same end though they generally inspired less enthusiasm. Finally, the foreign service would make its own special contribution to progress by drawing China into the family of nations. Its advocacy of a responsible foreign office, an end to Chinese pretensions of superiority (as in its claim to suzerainty over tribute states and its insistence on the kowtow as an inseparable part of an imperial audience with foreign diplomats), the extension of Chinese legations abroad, and the removal of artificial barriers to trade (such as the internal transit tax known as likin) were all steps in this direction. . . .

Charles Denby, Sr., whose fourteen years (1885–1898) in the legation under no fewer than seven Secretaries of State made him its longest tenured occupant, was a transitional figure in the evolving tactics of reform. He began by essentially espousing the more temperate position—vis à vis China—of Burlingame and [John Russell] Young [American minister to China, 1882–1885]. Like them he believed it was possible to work with China's leaders. He also followed their methods when in late 1894 and early 1895 he tried to mediate an end to the war with Japan in order to minimize the damage done to China and the temptation by the powers to exploit her.

However, by 1895 the complete incapacity of China's government to deal effectively with the problems festering at the heart of Sino-foreign relations at last drew Denby into the coercive mold favored by [J. Ross.] Browne [American minister to China, 1868–1869]. Concerned particularly with the threat that the antimissionary agitation posed to "a handful of Americans surrounded by four hundred million Asiatics," he concluded that "the fear of interfering with international rights or offending China should not for a moment be allowed to stand in the way of ordering immediate, and armed protection to . . . all foreigners in China." Without the backing of force, he reminded Washington in 1891, "both mission work and commerce would languish."

The inability of Peking after 1895 to check the growing aggressiveness of the powers completed Denby's conversion to a coercive policy. His mediation effort in 1894 had shown the Chinese as children blundering in foreign affairs from crisis to crisis, unable to recognize their true interests or true friends. The government seemed to Denby a hopeless patchwork of ignorance, reaction, corruption, drift, and incompetence, and in 1897 even Li Hung-chang fell from grace when revealed as the architect of the alliance between Peking and St. Petersburg. The powers themselves failed to meet Denby's hopes that they would come to some accord on how best to promote China's development. In April 1895 Japan, earlier regarded by Denby as a "champion of civilization," made territorial demands which convinced him that she had under false pretenses "pursued her own aggrandizement" at the expense of the Western powers. Two years later Russia—whose railway plans Denby had expected would be a force for progress in Manchuria—also showed her true colors, refusing to cooperate with American railway interests, deserting her Chinese ally in the face of German demands in Shantung province, and responding with demands of her own for new concessions in Manchuria.

In the face of the powers' unchecked "colonial ambitions" and "plans of national aggrandizement," Denby at last felt constrained to recommend that the United States imitate them. Though he was to back away from advocating steps as radical as making alliances or joining in China's partition, he became convinced that the United States would have to pursue a more aggressive financial diplomacy. Denby had long believed the legation should have wide latitude "to push American material interests . . . and thereby to extend American influence and trade." The arrival at mid-decade of European concessionaries who enjoyed strong official backing intensified Denby's demand for greater freedom of action to advance the cause of American concession hunters in "this limitless field of financial and industrial operations." Visits to the foreign office became for Denby, a self-styled "old lawyer," occasions for arm twisting as he reiterated the American claim to a favored role in China's economic development. . . .

The reiterated invocation of the open door ideology by commercial groups, missionaries, and diplomats had by the end of the 1890s transformed a once passive, narrowly commercial China policy. This shift in thinking on China policy is evident in the message of a group of publicists and popularizers who stepped forward at this crucial juncture. Figures as diverse as Richard Olney, Henry Cabot Lodge, W. W. Rockhill, Charles Denby, John Barrett, Josiah Strong, D. Z. Sheffield, Charles Conant, Brooks Adams, and Alfred Thayer Mahan now made an important contribution to the apotheosis of the open door ideology by carrying the message of the open door constituency to a wider audience. Their China was the scene of two related struggles—between the regenerating forces of the West (best represented by the United States) and a stagnant China and between selfish and exclusive imperialism and American aspirations for long-term, benevolent involvement in Chinese affairs. Only a China reformed could stand off imperialism unaided. Only an immediate assertion of American interests, especially against Russia in North China and Manchuria, would preserve the national dream of China's eventual reformation and of access to this "gigantic" market with its "almost boundless possibilities." In global terms they saw China as the main or even, in Adams' estimate, the decisive scene in the struggle for control of world civilization. The open door ideology, embodying long-established ideas of westward expansion and moral and material uplift and pointing to a solution for the problem of excess production raised by the depression of the 1890s, made it easy for these popularizers to hold out in common the dramatic possibilities of China—ancient, vast, potentially rich—as a stage for national action. . . .

Washington was . . . reluctant to play the game of alliances and spheres of influence that the [Peking] legation moved steadily toward after 1895. In March 1898, for example, Washington turned aside overtures from London intended to get the United States to join in opposing any commercial restrictions that the other powers might institute in their spheres of influence and concessions in China. McKinley, then on the brink of war over Cuba, replied to the inquiring British ambassador that he saw no threat yet sufficiently serious to justify his breaking with the traditional policy of nonentanglement. John Hay accepted the wisdom of that position even after the war with Spain was out of the way. In his view Anglophobia at work in domestic politics ruled out alliance, though he personally thought there was much to be said for a common Anglo-American approach to China and had earlier as ambassador in London helped stir up the British overtures.

The remaining alternative was to strike out an independent course, strengthening the American position in East Asia the better to withstand the coming scramble for territory. McKinley had already anticipated such a line of action by taking the Philippines. Control of territory adjacent to China improved the American claim to a voice in China's ultimate disposition, while a Philippines naval base put Washington in a better position to back that claim. McKinley's predecessors had put in his hands a developing navy, successfully tested in the war with Spain, to turn those bases to good account.

The next logical step in an independent policy might have been to stake out a slice of Chinese territory. But McKinley publicly proclaimed in December 1898 that that was a step the United States did not have to take. Though coastal China might fall under foreign control, he confidently predicted that somehow

the "vast commerce" and "large interests" of the United States would be preserved without departing from traditional policy and without the United States
becoming "an actor in the scene." That disclaimer did not, however, prevent Hay
and McKinley from returning the following year repeatedly, though with characteristic caution and discretion, to the question of a land grab. In March Hay,
while conceding that the public would frown on the United States joining "the
great game of spoilation now going on," nonetheless added that the government,
"with great commercial interests" to safeguard, did "not consider [its] hands tied
for future eventualities." Again, after the Japanese in March 1899 demanded a
concession at the port of Amoy, Hay watched developments with interest—and
with the expectation that, whatever grants China made to Japan, she would be
prepared to make similar ones to the United States. Even the preparation of the
open door notes in September of that year did not remove the temptation. When
Hay wondered aloud whether the United States could in truth deny in the notes
any interest in Chinese territory, McKinley responded, "I don't know about that.
May we not want a slice, if it is to be divided?" In November rumors stirred up
by the dispatch of the notes brought the Chinese minister calling. Under examination, Hay freely admitted that the United States reserved its right to claim
"conveniences or accommodations on the coast of China," though for the moment such a demand was not in the cards.

The McKinley administration's ultimate recourse to note writing after toying
with the possibility of a more aggressive policy was for the moment an adequate
response to the China problem. Hay's qualified statement of anti-imperialism cost
little. It satisfied the domestic demand for action without stirring up controversy. It
was offensive to no one abroad. Rather than singling out Russia and Germany, the
most egregious offenders against the open door to date, Hay had blandly asked assent from all the powers. Yet Hay's stand with its implied promise of support served
as a gentle prod to the other commercial powers. Whether it would prove sufficient
to preserve China and—more to the point—the broad interests that the open door
constituency claimed to represent remained to be seen. . . .

The Boxer attack on Pao-ting, Tientsin, T'ai-yüan, and a score of smaller places
[in 1900] were sideshows to a world looking on aghast at the main drama going on
in Peking. A state of siege had descended on the legation quarter in mid-June, trapping within a motley, status-riven, and anxious community. Foreigners, both regular
troops and young, single, able-bodied volunteers, manned the outer defenses and
suffered heavily in dead and wounded. Missionaries, with the Americans in the lead,
threw themselves into directing work on the fortifications and organizing the life
of the besieged. The dignitaries and their wives sat leisurely on the sidelines in the
safety and comfort of the British legation where were the inner defenses. Two thousand Chinese (more than twice the number of foreigners) also waited. Some were
Christians brought by the missionaries to safety, others laborers and servants who
had fallen by chance into the trap and could not escape. All were regarded with suspicion and all, except for those who worked under missionary supervision or who
had a foreign patron, were kept on short rations. Though the troops shot birds and
carrion dogs for them, distended bellies were everywhere to be seen in the carefully
segregated Chinese section. Within the first month Chinese children were already
dying of starvation.

That first month of the siege was the hardest. By mid-July the court began to waver uncertainly as foreign forces gathered off the coast, overcame stout resistance at Tientsin, and began a forced inland march against disorganized Boxer and imperial units. Government troops took over the lines about the legation quarter from the Boxers, and rather than unlimbering their modern artillery, instead fraternized with the enemy in a truce that was to last down to the eve of relief. Finally on August 14 the international army fought its way into the capital. . . .

Following the capture of Peking in late August, McKinley—true to his word— at once began cutting back on the ten-thousand-man force assigned to China. Units en route were recalled, and two-thirds of the 6,300 already in China returned to suppressing Filipino "rebels." For a time McKinley had even leaned toward Secretary of War Elihu Root's call for an immediate and complete withdrawal (in response to the Russian evacuation of all their units back to Manchuria) before reluctantly acceding to the arguments of Hay, Rockhill, [and other state department officials] that a token military presence was needed to keep the pressure on the Chinese and to guarantee an American voice among the powers. Still concerned over excessive use of force, McKinley forbade the American troops wintering over in North China to engage in the punitive expeditions conducted by the other powers, brought an early end to aggressive patrolling immediately outside the city, and at last in the spring called back the remaining troops. . . . The result was, as McKinley wished, an exemplary record for the American occupation force that none but the Japanese could match and that Chinese officials singled out for praise.

While McKinley kept the American military response to the Boxers in check, Hay brought note-writing, exercised so successfully in 1899, back into play to restrain the powers. To forestall a new round of great power competition that might end with China's dismemberment, Hay sent out on July 3, 1900 his second major statement on the open door, calling this time for China's preservation, both administrative and territorial. This proposal invoked [Chinese official] Chang's fiction that the powers warred against neither the Chinese people nor the imperial government and hence could have only limited objectives. To avoid contradiction or evasion, Hay did not ask for a response from the powers since, he calculated, a unilateral assertion of the integrity principle was as likely to build an international consensus as a prolonged and involved diplomatic exchange. In early August Hay at last retired from the scene for two months, exhausted by his labors in the Washington heat and tormented by imagined "scenes of tragic horror" to which, as well he knew, his own delays in the spring may have contributed.

The Boxer crisis had sharpened for both Americans and Chinese leaders the specter of partition. But that it was averted was due less to the efforts of either than to the growing recognition in European capitals of the difficulties—the high cost, perhaps even the physical impossibility—of directly controlling China. . . .

Moreover, the Boxer summer enhanced the role of coercion in the tactical armory of the open door. American policy makers had confirmed a belief of growing importance since the late 1880s—that the Chinese respected only force. Accordingly, Washington retained occupation forces in Peking until a settlement was near conclusion, kept at the legation a guard of 150 men (increased to 300 in 1905), earmarked for emergency service in China an army force of 2,000 (that could be expanded to 5,000) in the Philippines, and in 1911, in the wake of the revolution, would post an infantry battalion to Tientsin (augmented with a second battalion in 1914) to guard the communications route to Peking. The Asiatic Squadron underwent a parallel buildup. By 1902 it would number some forty-eight ships, including gunboats to patrol Chinese waters as well as one battleship and two armored cruisers that might be quickly deployed to the China coast. Together this force stood ready to protect "the interests of civilization and trade" and deal out "severe and lasting punishment" to any Chinese who threatened Americans.

America's Race War in the Philippines

PAUL A. KRAMER

The task of rationalizing the war in its ends and means before the American public led to the active production of a novel, imperial-racial formation by the war's defenders. This formation had a dual character, simultaneously and reciprocally racializing Americans and Filipinos in new ways. Its first half racialized the U.S. population as "Anglo-Saxons" whose overseas conquests were legitimated by racial-historical ties to the British Empire. . . . Specifically, the war's advocates subsumed U.S. history within longer, racial trajectories of Anglo-Saxon history that folded together U.S. and British imperial histories. The Philippine-American war was a natural extension of Western conquest, and both taken together were the organic expression of the desires, capacities, and destinies of Anglo-Saxon peoples. "Blood," in the phrase widely used in this context, "was thicker than water," specifically the Atlantic that separated American and British "cousins." Americans, as Anglo-Saxons, shared Britons' racial genius for empire-building, a genius that they must exercise for the greater glory of the "race" and to advance civilization in general. . . .

If the advocates of war attempted to racialize the U.S. population as "Anglo-Saxon" in defense of empire, they simultaneously racialized the Philippine population in ways that would legitimate U.S. conquest of the islands before domestic and international skeptics. . . . [T]he Americans would develop their own imperial indigenism aimed at denying Filipinos political power on the basis of attributed socio-cultural and racial features. Specifically, the Philippine Republic would be derecognized as nothing more than the will to power of what was called a "single tribe" of Tagalogs. Conventional evolutionary theory held that societies, in evolving from savagery to civilization, moved in political terms from "tribal" fragmentation to "national" unity and toward the elusive goal of "ethnological homogeneity." To successfully recognize tribes—marked by language, religion, political allegiance, or other features—was to disprove a nation's existence. Enumerate a society's fragments, and what might otherwise have looked like a nation became merely the tyranny of one tribe over others; what might have appeared to be a state became instead a problem of imperial "assimilation."

The "tribalization" of the republic would rhetorically eradicate the Philippine Republic as a legitimate state whose rights the United States might have to recognize

---

From *The Blood of Government: Race, Empire and the Philippines, The United States and the Philippines* by Paul A. Kramer. Copyright © 2006 by the University of North Carolina Press. Used by permission of the publisher. www.uncpress.unc.edu

under international law. This argument was forcefully advanced by the Philippine Commission's report [(undertaken by a government advisory commission led by Cornell University President Jacob Gould Schurman)], whose first installment was issued in January 1900, and which represented the most influential effort to reduce the Philippine Republic to what came to be called the "single tribe" of the Tagalogs. . . .

"The most striking and perhaps the most significant fact in the entire situation," began the section of the commission's report entitled "Capacity for Self-Government," "is the multiplicity of tribes inhabiting the archipelago, the diversity of their languages (which are mutually unintelligible), and the multifarious phases of civilization—ranging all the way from the highest to the lowest—exhibited by the natives of the several provinces and islands.". . .

U.S. soldiers [also] racialized the "insurrection" with striking speed and intensity. . . . "A lively hatred of our newly declared enemy was the one enthusiasm of the camp," wrote a corporal in the Montana regulars in July 1899. The race-making process is vividly illustrated by terminological shifts in the diaries and letters home of U.S. volunteers in the early months of the war. . . .

Andrew Wadsworth, for example, a twenty-eight-year-old sergeant in the First Nebraska Volunteers, had observed shortly after arrival in Manila that "the natives are bright and intelligent as the average run of people" and admired their art, musicianship, and industriousness. Three months later, as tensions sharpened between U.S. and Filipino troops, Wadsworth's assessment darkened. "I didn't even like a negro, but they are pretty good people after seeing the natives that live here near the sunset," he wrote. Writing home from "the Field" two weeks after the beginning of the war, he wrote that "it was a hot time going over some of the ground. . . . [It] swarmed with the indians but we didn't do a thing to them." Within another two weeks, his racism was more matter-of-fact. "[H]ave forgotten whether I have written any of you folks since we commenced to chase niggers," he wrote offhandedly, "have no doubt read in the papers what we are doing." Despite rising tensions, Earl Pearsall of the same unit had recorded in his diary on January 5, with some regret, that "the insurgents have not been as friendly lately as they have been for they have not visited our camp for three or four days." The day war broke out, he imagined that "the dusky fellows don't care for any more of this warfare with the Americano." Less than three weeks later, however, he thrilled that U.S. artillery had "put the black rascals over the hills." Early in March, he reported being "attacked by the 'Gugos'" on the Mariquina road.

For the first two weeks of the war, Oregon volunteer William Henry Barrett referred to the enemy exclusively as "natives" or "Philippinos," as when "[n]atives [were] driven from their trenches and forced back all along the line." Just over two weeks later, he recorded that other companies had "chased out the niggers [and] run them across the swamps into Malabon." South Dakota volunteer Louis Hubbard, a leader in his unit's regimental band, had accepted the gift of a sword from "one of [insurgent leader Emilio] Aguinaldo's sergeants" in December 1898 and recruited a Filipino musician, "the finest clarinetist I ever heard in my life." Two weeks into the combat, angered by reports of Filipino atrocities against U.S. troops, he wrote that "[t]hey are just like any savage." In mid-March he recorded the hope for a speedy charge on Malolos, "for the quicker we get there and get these 'gugos' of[f] the face of the earth the quicker we will be ready to start for home.". . .

This "lively hatred" was not, however, a projection or an export, but a new racial formation developing on the ground. Its novelty was evidenced by the consistency with which reporters—imperialist and anti-imperialist—felt compelled to explain it to their domestic readers, as above. The new formation was strikingly illustrated by the appearance of a new term, "gu-gu," or "goo-goo," in U.S. soldiers' discourse, almost certainly the linguistic ancestor of "gook." Veteran Charles A. Freeman, writing in the 1930s, noted that "[o]f recent years the world [*sic*] has been shortened to gook, but gu-gu persists in Philippine fiction and fact written by Americans, and applies to the lower class Filipino." If the term had a sinister future, its origins remain speculative. One of two plausible explanations—far from incompatible with each other—roots the term in local dynamics: the term came from the Tagalog term for a slippery coconut-oil shampoo, pronounced *gu-gu,* which may have been used to convey a sense of the enemy's elusiveness. A second account suggests the term was born at the intersection of immediate sexual tensions and racialized U.S. popular culture. According to Freeman, among the songs sung by U.S. troops on the long voyage from San Francisco had been a minstrel tune with the chorus " 'Just because she made dem goo-goo eyes.' " When American soldiers first "gazed into the dark orbs of a Filipino *dalaga* [young woman]" on arrival, they had commented to each other, " 'Gee, but that girl can make *goo-goo* eyes.' " Filipino men had taken the term as an insult; when American soldiers learned this, "it stuck, and became a veritable taunt."

Whatever its specific origins, "gu-gu" formed part of a distinctive Philippine-American colonial vocabulary that focused hatreds around a novel enemy and lent American troops a sense of manly, insider camaraderie. . . .

The other common term assigned to the enemy by U.S. troops was "nigger." "Our troops in the Philippines . . . look upon all Filipinos as of one race and condition," wrote Henry Loomis Nelson, "and being dark men, they are therefore 'niggers,' and entitled to all the contempt and harsh treatment administered by white overlords to the most inferior races.". . .

On the surface, the application of the term "nigger" to Filipinos suggests the export of domestic U.S. racial formations. But in other ways it appears that the term itself was being transformed in the colonial setting. As with "gu-gu," soldiers felt compelled to explain its colonial meaning to family members, as when Corporal William Eggenberger observed in March 1899, of Filipino clothing, that "it is nothing to see a niger (we call them nigers) woman pretty near naked." In some cases, U.S. soldiers ridiculed their comrades who used it, as when John Jordan poked fun at white Southern soldiers. "It must have been very embarrassing to men almost entirely from Georgia, Ala., Miss. and Florida to be whipped and captured by 'niggers,' " he wrote of one recently defeated unit. "The Capt. is from Miss. and I have no doubt it will be an unpleasant recollection to him especially when he returns to Natchez.". . .

Black troops fighting in the islands had much to say about the race war emerging around them. "You have no idea the way these people are treated by the Americans here," wrote Sgt. Patrick Mason, excluding himself from this category. "The first thing in the morning is the 'Nigger' and the last thing at night is the 'Nigger.' " Some like Sgt. Maj. John W. Galloway accused whites of "establish[ing] their diabolical race hatred in all its home rancor in Manila . . . to be sure of the foundation of their supremacy" under civil rule. Unlike white soldiers, Galloway noted, black soldiers did not "push [Filipinos] off the streets, spit at them, call them damned 'niggers,' abuse them in all manner of ways, and connect race hatred with duty.". . .

If one way to rationalize a war of aggression was to declare the enemy state a "tribe," one way to end it was simply to declare it over by fiat. November 1899 saw the war's first end by U.S. proclamation. General [Arthur] MacArthur reported the U.S. mission accomplished, saying that there was "no organized insurgent force left to strike at," and declared that all future resistance be characterized as "banditry," and the killing of U.S. soldiers, murder. General [Elwell S.] Otis cabled Washington stating that the revolutionaries had been dispersed and that the "claim to government by insurgents can be made no longer under any fiction." In fact, Filipinos had undertaken a strategy of guerrilla war. Disbanding the regular army in the wake of defeats, Aguinaldo divided the country into military zones, each under a guerrilla commander, preparing for a regionally dispersed set of smaller campaigns through locally raised *sandatahan* (guerrilla) units. It was hoped that in these scattered settings, tropical disease, impassable roads, and unfamiliar conditions would weaken the American advance, while geographic knowledge and village-level support would sustain guerrilla ambushes and surprise attacks against isolated American patrols. . . .

U.S. commanders [thus] felt at greater liberty to widen the boundaries of violence, which General MacArthur achieved through a mass-circulated proclamation dated December 20. In content, it was a highly expedient interpretation of General Orders No. 100, the Civil War–era regulations on the conduct of combat; MacArthur selected those provisions he felt "most essential for consideration under present conditions." The proclamation was meant to "instruct all classes" and was circulated widely: the army distributed 10,000 copies to the Department of Southern Luzon alone, and copies of it were printed in Tagalog, Spanish, and English in the *Manila Times,* the first English-language daily in the islands. . . . Accordingly, he "reject[ed] every consideration of belligerency of those opposing the Government" and directed the document both at combatants and "noncombatants, native or alien, residing within occupied places." In those locations, the U.S. Army owed protection only to those Filipinos who demonstrated "strict obedience" to U.S. commanders. Noncombatants who in any way aided Filipino combatants, through "secret communities," collecting supplies, recruiting men, or sharing military information, would from then on be seen by the U.S. military as indistinguishable from combatants.

In broadening the enemy in this way, MacArthur invoked a category from the General Orders: "war rebels, or war traitors." Any such person residing in an occupied area and engaging in acts that were "inimical to the interests of the occupying army" would be punished "at the discretion of the tribunals of the occupying army.". . . MacArthur's proclamation defined these terms in ways that embraced the entire population in areas of combat as potential targets of punishment. It did not recognize intimidation by insurgents as a legitimate cause for cooperation: compliance with the rebels without reportage to the U.S. military "creates the presumption that the act is voluntary and malicious.". . .

Race was at the core of the U.S. Army's effort to rethink and redefine the enemy in a context of guerrilla war. . . .

By these lights, those who waged guerrilla war were, by definition, savage: Filipino warfare, therefore, did not take this form out of ignorance or strategy but because of race. Conventional wisdom to this effect issued from the top of the U.S.

military hierarchy in the Philippines. "War in its earlier from was an act of violence which, from the very nature of primitive humanity and of the forces employed, knew no bounds," General MacArthur had declared in the December 1900 proclamation. "Mankind, from the beginning of civilization, however, has tried to mitigate, and to escape, as far as possible, from the consequences of this barbarous conception of warlike accion." The Filipinos, in refusing these boundaries, had shown themselves to be less than civilized. "The war on the part of the Filipinos," wrote Secretary of War Elihu Root, "has been conducted with the barbarous cruelty common among uncivilized races.". . .

Racial exterminist impulses were also in evidence in U. S. soldiers' descriptions of violence against prisoners and civilians. The American torture of prisoners—some fraction of which appeared in soldiers' letters, newspaper accounts, and court-martial proceedings—was often, if not always, justified as a means of intelligence-gathering. The most notorious form of torture by the American side, if far from the only one, was the "water cure," in which a captured Filipino was interrogated while drowned with buckets of filthy water poured into his mouth. The scale of its practice and the frequency of death remain difficult if not impossible to establish. Later blamed almost exclusively on the United States' Macabebe Scous [(U.S.-trained Filipino forces)], it was in fact the tactical expression of the military policy of attraction, undertaken in many cases by U.S. and Filipino forces working together both secretly and with the tacit approval of U.S. officers. In the context of guerrilla war, the water cure would simultaneously cure Filipinos of their unknowability and Americans of their ignorance.

Despite later claims that distanced U.S. soldiers from torture, U.S. soldiers not only carried out the water cure but apparently did so in a jocular manner. In 1902, Albert Gardner, in Troop B of the First U.S. Cavalry, composed comic works that made light of torture in a way that suggested familiarity and ease. The first, playing with the torture's name, was a mock-testimonial patent-medicine advertisement addressed to "My Dear Doctor Uncle Sam," by a certain "Mariano Gugu." The author complained of a recent bout of "loss of memory, loss of speach [*sic*] and other symptoms" of a disease called "insurectos"; among other things, he "had forgotten where I placed my Bolo and my rifle." He had been miraculously cured with "only one treatment of your wonderful water cure." "No hombre's shack is complete without a barrel of it," he concluded in a postscript. . . .

Along with torturing them, U.S. soldiers also killed Filipino prisoners. Rumors of "no-prisoners" orders were common. Arthur C. Johnson of the Colorado Volunteers, for example, reported as early as February 1899 that Manila's prisons were already overflowing, and "the fiat is said to have gone forth that no more prisoners are to be taken"; he anticipated that "the Filipino death list promises to correspondingly increase." "They say our boys raised the cry of no quarter," Willis Platts wrote on the second day of the war, "([I] am glad of it) and disregarded the numerous white flags because of many treacherous deeds." Nearly two months into the war, George Telfer recorded his one line of thought while "jumping trenches—seeing mangled bodies, writhing figures, and hearing groans everywhere": " 'Guide right.' 'preserve touch.' 'Advance' 'Lay Down' 'Forward'—'Kill' 'Kill'—'Take no prisoners.' " . . .

Ultimately, the strategy that would crush the remaining resistance involved implementing MacArthur's December 1900 instructions most harshly by waging war against the entire rural population in hostile areas, a strategy represented best by the policy of reconcentration undertaken from 1901 to 1902 in numerous locations. The policy aimed at the isolation and starvation of guerrillas through the deliberate annihilation of the rural economy: peasants in resistant areas were ordered to relocate to garrisoned towns by a given date, leaving behind all but the most basic provisions. Outside of the policed, fenced-in perimeters of these "reconcentration camps," troops would then undertake a scorched-earth policy, burning residences and rice stores, destroying or capturing livestock, and killing every person they encountered. Americans had first become aware of this tactic during the final Cuban war of independence, when its use by the Spanish general Weyler had inflamed righteous American outrage and tilted the United States toward intervention against Spain. "This cruel policy of concentration," President McKinley himself had observed in his first message to Congress, while rationalized "as a necessary measure of war and as a means of cutting off supplies from the insurgents," was immoral, requiring the U.S. government to issue a "firm and earnest protest." "It was not civilized warfare," he stated. "It was extermination." . . .

Little if anything of the cruelties of the war became known to the U.S. public prior to early 1902, in part due to rigorous censorship of foreign correspondents by the U.S. Army. By mid-1902, however, the American press—particularly Democratic and independent papers—became more emboldened, particularly as editors learned of General [James Franklin] Bell's "reconcentration" program in [the province of] Batangas [(located just south of Manila)]. Some critical press attention was due to the energetic efforts of anti-imperialists like Herbert Welsh, who resourcefully culled for republication references to the water cure and other atrocities in hometown newspapers and sent agents to interview returning soldiers firsthand. These efforts would culminate in the publication of the pamphlet *"Marked Severities" in Philippine Warfare,* a compilation by Moorfield Storey and Julian Codman of descriptions of U.S. atrocities attributed to U.S. soldier-witnesses, with attempts to connect atrocity to administration policy.

These propaganda efforts coincided with a Senate investigation between January and June 1902, initiated by Senator George Hoar, Republican of Massachusetts, to "examine and report into the conduct of the war in the Philippine Islands, the administration of the government there, and the condition and character of the inhabitants." The Senate hearings would force open small windows onto U.S. Army conduct, although their potential challenge was blunted by [Republican] Senator [Henry Cabot] Lodge's able maneuvering of the hearings into his own, prowar Committee on Insular Affairs, which was closed to press and public, and where sympathetic witnesses and lengthy War Department reports would predominate. The anti-imperialist publicity campaign that would reach its height in April–May 1902 would be met by a determined administration counteroffensive, as Lodge, army officers, and ultimately President [Theodore] Roosevelt would answer charges of military misconduct. . . .

Theodore Roosevelt's 1902 Memorial Day speech at Arlington National Cemetery was both one of the final interventions in the administration's mid-1902 propaganda campaign and, as the first such address in the cemetery's history, a sign of the way that empire would become a foundation for national institutions. According to the *Boston Morning Journal,* an estimated 30,000 people attended, hearing a set of "harmonious" speeches in which the war in the Philippines was "most prominent."

Roosevelt had "never delivered a speech that more impressed his hearers." Turning to the Philippines after Civil War invocations, "[t]here was indignation in every word and every gesture." U.S. soldiers in the Philippines—"your younger brothers, your sons"—were bringing to completion "a small but peculiarly trying and difficult war" on which turned "not only the honor of the flag but the triumph of civilization over forces which stand for the black chaos of savagery and barbarism." Roosevelt formally acknowledged and regretted U.S. atrocities but claimed that "a very cruel and very treacherous enemy" had committed, for every American atrocity, "a hundred acts of far greater atrocity." Furthermore, while such means had been the Filipinos' "only method of carrying on the war," they had been "wholly exceptional on our part."

Roosevelt condemned the army's critics—those who "walk delicately and live in the soft places of the earth"—for dishonoring the "strong men who with blood and sweat" had suffered and laid down their lives "in remote tropic jungles to bring the light of civilization into the world's dark places." These were men, unlike their armchair counterparts, engaged in the heavy work of race and history. "The warfare that has extended the boundaries of civilization at the expense of barbarism and savagery has been for centuries one of the most potent factors in the progress of humanity," Roosevelt said. While "from its very nature it has always and everywhere been liable to dark abuses," to avoid such wars would show Americans to be "cravens and weaklings, unworthy of the sires from whose loins we sprang." Victory over the "Aguinaldan oligarchy" had been the only "effective means of putting a stop to cruelty in the Philippines." Now a regime of benevolence and uplift could begin.

FURTHER READING

Teodoro Agoncillo, *A Short History of the Philippines* (1975)
David R. Akush and Leo L. Lee, *Land Without Ghosts: Chinese Impressions of America from the Mid Nineteenth Century to the Present* (1989)
Warwick Anderson, *Colonial Pathologies* (2006) (on disease in the Philippines)
A. J. Bacevich, *Diplomat in Khaki* (1989) (on the Philippines)
David Howard Bain, *Sitting in Darkness* (1984)
Robert L. Beisner, *Twelve Against Empire* (1968)
H. W. Brands, *Bound to Empire: The United States and the Philippines* (1992)
Thomas A. Breslin, *China, American Catholicism, and the Missionary* (1980)
Gordon H. Chang, "Whose 'Barbarian'? Whose 'Treachery'? Race and Civilization in the Unknown United States-Korea War of 1871," *Journal of American History,* 89 (March 2003), 1331–1365
Carol C. Chin, "Beneficent Imperialists: American Women Missionaries in China at the Turn of the Century," *Diplomatic History,* 27 (June 2003), 327–352
Kenton J. Clymer, *John Hay* (1975)
_____, *Protestant Missionaries in the Philippines* (1986)
Warren I. Cohen, *America's Response to China* (2000)
Renato Constantino, *The Philippines* (1975)
Ken DeBevoise, *Agents of Apocalypse: Epidemic and Disease in Colonial Philippines* (1995)
Wayne Flint and Gerald W. Buckley, *Taking Christianity to China* (1997)
Julian Go, *American Empire and the Politics of Meaning* (2008)
Frank Golay, *Face of Empire* (1997) (on the Philippines)
Gael Graham, *Gender, Culture, and Christianity* (on China) (1996)
Patricia R. Hill, *The World and the Household* (1985) (on missionaries)

Kristin L. Hoganson, *Fighting for American Manhood* (1998)
Jane Hunter, *Gospel of Gentility* (1984) (on missionaries)
Abe Ignacio et al., eds., *The Forbidden Book* (2004) (on political cartoons and Philippines)
Akira Iriye, "Imperialism in East Asia," in James B. Crowley, ed., *Modern East Asia* (1970)
Arnold Xiangze Jiang, *The United States and China* (1988)
Stanley Karnow, *In Our Image* (1989) (on the Philippines)
Brian Linn, *The Philippine War* (2000)
Glenn A. May, *Battle for Batangas: A Philippine Province at War* (1991)
Thomas J. McCormick, *China Market* (1967)
Alfred W. McCoy, *An Anarchy of Families* (1998) (on the Philippines)
Stuart C. Miller, *"Benevolent Assimilation"* (1982) (on the Philippines)
Vicente L. Rafael, *White Love* (2000) (on the Philippines)
Michael Schaller, *The United States and China in the Twentieth Century* (1990)
Eileen P. Scully, *Bargaining with the State from Afar* (2001)
Richard Slotkin, "Buffalo Bill's 'Wild West' and the Mythologinization of the American
    Empire," Amy Kaplan and Donald Pease, eds., *Cultures of United States Imperialism*
    (1993), 164–181
Paul A. Varg, *The Making of a Myth* (1968) (on China market)
Richard Welch, *Response to Imperialism* (1979) (on the Philippines)
Laura Wexler, *Tender Violence* (2000)
Walter L. Williams, "United States Indian Policy and the Debate Over Philippine Annexa-
    tion: Implications for the Origins of American Imperialism," *Journal of American
    History,* 66 (1980), 810–831
William Appleman Williams, *The Tragedy of American Diplomacy* (1962)

CHAPTER
14

Theodore Roosevelt, the Big Stick, and U.S. Hegemony in the Caribbean

Theodore Roosevelt dominated the American diplomatic landscape in the early twentieth century. The bespectacled, mustachioed president (1901–1909) always spoke frankly and pursued political power with enviable energy. A formidable diplomat, he exercised American influence worldwide. A staunch nationalist, he championed American supremacy in a legendary, jingoistic rhetoric. In keeping with the upper-class culture into which he had been born, he preached that it was America's "manly" duty to spread the benefits of Anglo-Saxon civilization to the world's "inferior" peoples. An indefatigable expansionist, he exploited new opportunities to extend the U.S. empire in the Western Hemisphere. After the Spanish-American-Cuban-Filipino War, the United States, under Roosevelt's leadership, became a "police power" in the Caribbean, lecturing Europeans and Latin Americans alike on the virtues of the U.S. model for development. By means of the Platt Amendment and military occupation, he exerted American control over reluctant Cubans. He began the process of bringing Puerto Rico into the U.S. system. Through naval demonstrations and blunt warnings, he intimidated nations in the region. He imposed financial supervision on the Dominican Republic. In one of his most celebrated actions, he helped sever Panama from Colombia to gain U.S. rights to a canal across the isthmus. And his "corollary" to the Monroe Doctrine proclaimed U.S. hegemony in the Western Hemisphere. For both contemporaries and historians, Roosevelt was the "Rough Rider" who wielded the "Big Stick."

Some historians have admired Roosevelt's displays of toughness and assertions of national greatness in a world dominated by competing powers. They have applauded his recognition that the United States had become a major force in international affairs. But other scholars have found his behavior imperial and haughty, and hence shortsighted and dangerous, because its bullying quality proved insensitive to the sovereignty and nationalism of other peoples and fostered anti-Yankee resentments that later exploded, often violently, against the United States. Conversely, some historians have interpreted Roosevelt not as an aggressive promoter of power and empire but as a cautious, principled diplomat who cared about the well-being of other peoples and preferred negotiation over war. (Roosevelt won the Nobel Peace Prize for successfully mediating the end of the Russo-Japanese War in 1905.)

Most observers agree that Theodore Roosevelt was an expansionist, especially in the Caribbean region. Still, scholars have offered a variety of explanations for his actions and policies. Some have highlighted his role as a conservative reformer and his quest for orderly modernization and stability both at home and abroad. Others have accented his love of power and his drive to capitalize on economic and military opportunities. Still others have emphasized his racial arrogance and his belief in the manliness of America's mission to civilize others. The selections that follow illustrate the controversial nature of Roosevelt's diplomacy and raise fundamental questions about the impact of U.S. policies on the peoples of the Caribbean. Did Roosevelt's expansionism promote modernization, or deepen economic dependency? Did his policies establish political order, or nurture dictatorship, instability, and revolution? To answer such questions is to reach for an understanding of twentieth-century American intervention abroad.

D O C U M E N T S

Document 1, an excerpt from "The Strenuous Life," a speech given on April 10, 1899, by then governor of New York Theodore Roosevelt, outlines the future president's philosophy of vigorous, manly nationalism and overseas expansion. The United States, he lectured, should embrace new responsibilities in the Pacific and Caribbean, build an isthmian canal, and strengthen its military to enhance its power and contribute to world progress. As president, Roosevelt later put these ideas into action. Document 2, an excerpt from an official letter written on December 29, 1902, by Argentina's foreign minister, Dr. Luis M. Drago, to the Argentine minister to the United States, condemns creditor nations' use of force to collect debts. Written in response to Anglo-German threats against Venezuela, the "Drago Doctrine" also challenged the principle of intervention that Roosevelt later espoused in his corollary to the Monroe Doctrine. The Second Hague Conference of 1907 discussed Drago's proposal and adopted a convention in which the signatories pledged not to resort to military might for the collection of debts.

Document 3, the treaty of November 18, 1903, with Panama, came after the United States encouraged and assisted Panamanian independence from Colombia. The pact granted the United States canal rights and a zone of occupation. Document 4, Colombian president Rafael Reyes's answer of January 6, 1904, to a U.S. message of December 30, 1903, angrily protests the Panama affair and lists Bogotá's official grievances against the United States. On December 6, 1904, President Roosevelt issued his famous corollary to the Monroe Doctrine as part of his annual message to Congress. The declaration, Document 5, reserved for the United States the right to exercise police power over the Western Hemisphere. In 1905, Nicaragua's acclaimed poet Rubén Darío composed "To Roosevelt," a powerful expression of Latin American nationalism and cultural pride. Reprinted as Document 6, the poem reflects widespread Latin American indignation against U.S. interventionism in the early twentieth century.

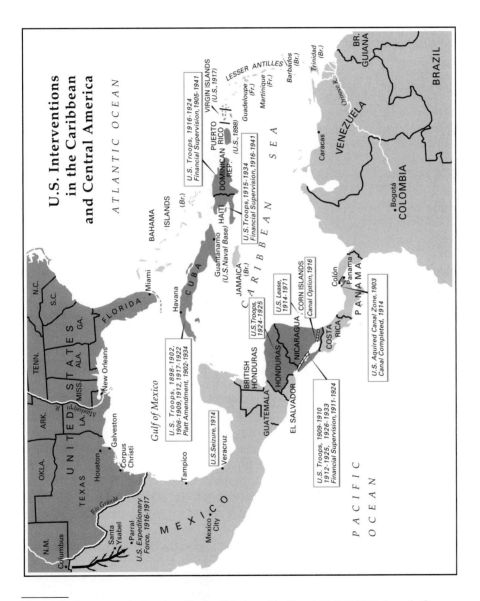

U.S. Interventions in the Caribbean and Central America

ATLANTIC OCEAN

U.S. Troops, 1916-1924
Financial Supervision, 1905-1941

VIRGIN ISLANDS
(U.S.,1917)

PUERTO RICO
(U.S.,1898)

LESSER ANTILLES

Guadeloupe
(Fr.)

Martinique
(Fr.)

Barbados
(Br.)

Trinidad
(Br.)

BR.
GUIANA

BRAZIL

DOMINICAN REP.

U.S.Troops, 1915-1934
Financial Supervision,1916-1941

HAITI

Orinoco R.

VENEZUELA

Caracas

CARIBBEAN SEA

BAHAMA
ISLANDS
(Br.)

Bogotá
COLOMBIA

Guantánamo
(U.S.Naval Base)

CUBA

JAMAICA
(Br.)

U.S. Lease,
1914-1971
CORN ISLANDS

Colón
Panama
PANAMA

Miami

S.C.

N.C.

FLORIDA

GA.

ALA.

TENN.

MISS.

Havana

U.S.Troops,
1924-1925

NICARAGUA

COSTA RICA

Canal Option,1916

U.S. Aquired Canal Zone,1903
Canal Completed, 1914

UNITED STATES

New Orleans

ARK.

LA.

Mississippi R.

OKLA.

TEXAS

Houston
Corpus Christi

Galveston

Gulf of Mexico

U.S. Troops, 1898-1902,
1906-1909,1912, 1917-1922
Platt Amendment, 1902-1934

Tampico

U.S.Seizure,1914
Veracruz

BRITISH
HONDURAS

GUATEMALA

HONDURAS

EL SALVADOR

U.S. Troops, 1909-1910
1912-1925, 1926-1933
Financial Supervision,1911-1924

PACIFIC
OCEAN

N.M.

Columbus

Santa Ysabel
Parral

U.S. Expeditionary
Force, 1916-1917

Rio Grande

MEXICO

Mexico
City

Thomas G. Paterson et al., *American Foreign Relations*, 6/e. Copyright © 2005 Wadsworth, Cengage Learning. Used with permission.

🌎 D O C U M E N T   1

New York Governor Theodore Roosevelt Champions the Manly Virtues of Overseas Expansion, 1899

I wish to preach, not the doctrine of ignoble ease, but the doctrine of the strenuous life, the life of toil and effort, of labor and strife; to preach that highest form of success which comes, not to the man who desires mere easy peace, but to the man who does not shrink from danger, from hardship, or from bitter toil, and who out of these wins the splendid ultimate triumph.

A life of slothful ease, a life of that peace which springs merely from lack either of desire or of power to strive after great things, is as little worthy of a nation as of an individual. I ask only that what every self-respecting American demands from himself and from his sons shall be demanded of the American nation as a whole. . . . We do not admire the man of timid peace. We admire the man who embodies victorious effort; the man who never wrongs his neighbor, who is prompt to help a friend, but who has those virile qualities necessary to win in the stern strife of actual life. It is hard to fail, but it is worse never to have tried to succeed. In this life we get nothing save by effort. . . .

We of this generation do not have to face a task such as that our fathers faced, but we have our tasks, and woe to us if we fail to perform them! We cannot, if we would, play the part of China, and be content to rot by inches in ignoble ease within our borders, taking no interest in what goes on beyond them, sunk in a scrambling commercialism; heedless of the higher life, the life of aspiration, of toil and risk, busying ourselves only with the wants of our bodies for the day, until suddenly we should find, beyond a shadow of question, what China has already found, that in this world the nation that has trained itself to a career of unwarlike and isolated ease is bound, in the end, to go down before other nations which have not lost the manly and adventurous qualities. If we are to be a really great people, we must strive in good faith to play a great part in the world. We cannot avoid meeting great issues. All that we can determine for ourselves is whether we shall meet them well or ill. In 1898 we could not help being brought face to face with the problem of war with Spain. All we could decide was whether we should shrink like cowards from the contest, or enter into it as beseemed a brave and high-spirited people; and, once in, whether failure or success should crown our banners. So it is now. We cannot avoid the responsibilities that confront us in Hawaii, Cuba, Porto Rico, and the Philippines. . . . To refuse to deal with them at all merely amounts to dealing with them badly. We have a given problem to solve. If we undertake the solution, there is, of course, always danger that we may not solve it aright; but to refuse to undertake the solution simply renders it certain that we cannot possibly solve it aright. The timid man, the lazy man, the man who distrusts his country, the over-civilized man, who has lost the great fighting, masterful virtues, the ignorant man, and the man of dull mind, whose soul is incapable of feeling the mighty lift that thrills "stern men with empires in their brains"—all these, of course, shrink from seeing the nation undertake its new duties; shrink from seeing us build a navy and an army adequate to our needs; shrink from seeing us do our share of the world's work, by bringing order out of chaos in the

This document can be found in Theodore Roosevelt, *The Strenuous Life: Essays and Addresses* (New York: The Century Company, 1900), pp. 4–5, 6–8, 9–10.

great, fair tropic islands from which the valor of our soldiers and sailors has driven the Spanish flag. These are the men who fear the strenuous life, who fear the only national life which is really worth leading. They believe in that cloistered life which saps the hardy virtues in a nation, as it saps them in the individual; or else they are wedded to that base spirit of gain and greed which recognizes in commercialism the be-all and end-all of national life, instead of realizing that, though an indispensable element, it is, after all, but one of the many elements that go to make up true national greatness. . . .

We cannot sit huddled within our own borders and avow ourselves merely an assemblage of well-to-do hucksters who care nothing for what happens beyond. Such a policy would defeat even its own end; for as the nations grow to have ever wider and wider interests, and are brought into closer and closer contact, if we are to hold our own in the struggle for naval and commercial supremacy, we must build up our power without our own borders. We must build the isthmian canal, and we must grasp the points of vantage which will enable us to have our say in deciding the destiny of the oceans of the East and the West.

So much for the commercial side. From the standpoint of international honor the argument is even stronger. The guns that thundered off Manila and Santiago left us echoes of glory, but they also left us a legacy of duty. If we drove out a medieval tyranny only to make room for savage anarchy, we had better not have begun the task at all. It is worse than idle to say that we have no duty to perform, and can leave to their fates the islands we have conquered. Such a course would be the course of infamy. It would be followed at once by utter chaos in the wretched islands themselves. Some stronger, manlier power would have to step in and do the work, and we would have shown ourselves weaklings, unable to carry to successful completion the labors that great and high-spirited nations are eager to undertake. . . .

Our army has never been built up as it should be built up. I shall not discuss . . . the puerile suggestion that a nation of seventy millions of freemen is in danger of losing its liberties from the existence of an army of one hundred thousand men, three fourths of whom will be employed in certain foreign islands, in certain coast fortresses, and on Indian reservations. No man of good sense and stout heart can take such a proposition seriously. If we are such weaklings as the proposition implies, then we are unworthy of freedom in any event. To no body of men in the United States is the country so much indebted as to the splendid officers and enlisted men of the regular army and navy. There is no body from which the country has less to fear, and none of which it should be prouder, none which it should be more anxious to upbuild. . . .

I have scant patience with those who fear to undertake the tasks of governing the Philippines, and who openly avow that they do fear to undertake it, or that they shrink from it because of the expense and trouble; but I have even scanter patience with those who make a pretense of humanitarianism to hide and cover their timidity, and who cant about "liberty" and the "consent of the governed," in order to excuse themselves for their unwillingness to play the part of men. Their doctrines, if carried out, would make it incumbent upon us to leave the Apaches of Arizona to work out their own salvation, and to decline to interfere in a single Indian reservation. Their doctrines condemn your forefathers and mine for ever having settled in these United States. . . .

I preach to you, then, my countrymen, that our country calls not for the life of ease but for the life of strenuous endeavor. The twentieth century looms before us big with the fate of many nations. If we stand idly by, if we seek merely swollen, slothful ease and ignoble peace, if we shrink from the hard contests where men must win at hazard of their lives and at the risk of all they hold dear, then the bolder and stronger peoples will pass us by, and will win for themselves the domination of the world. Let us therefore boldly face the life of strife, resolute to do our duty well and manfully; resolute to uphold righteousness by deed and by word; resolute to be both honest and brave, to serve high ideals, yet to use practical methods. Above all, let us shrink from no strife, moral or physical, within or without the nation, provided we are certain that the strife is justified, for it is only through strife, through hard and dangerous endeavor, that we shall ultimately win the goal of true national greatness.

🌐 D O C U M E N T   2

Argentina's Foreign Minister Luis Drago Condemns the Collection of Debts by Force, 1902

Among the fundamental principles of public international law which humanity has consecrated, one of the most precious is that which decrees that all states, whatever be the force at their disposal, are entities in law, perfectly equal one to another, and mutually entitled by virtue thereof to the same consideration and respect.

The acknowledgment of the debt, the payment of it in its entirety, can and must be made by the nation without diminution of its inherent rights as a sovereign entity, but the summary and immediate collection at a given moment, by means of force, would occasion nothing less than the ruin of the weakest nations, and the absorption of their governments, together with all the functions inherent in them, by the mighty of the earth. The principles proclaimed on this continent of America are otherwise. "Contracts between a nation and private individuals are obligatory according to the conscience of the sovereign, and may not be the object of compelling force," said the illustrious [Alexander] Hamilton. "They confer no right of action contrary to the sovereign will."

The United States has gone very far in this direction. The eleventh amendment to its Constitution provided in effect, with the unanimous assent of the people, that the judicial power of the nation should not be extended to any suit in law or equity prosecuted against one of the United States by citizens of another State, or by citizens or subjects of any foreign State. The Argentine Government has made its provinces indictable, and has even adopted the principle that the nation itself may be brought to trial before the supreme court on contracts which it enters into with individuals.

What has not been established, what could in no wise be admitted, is that, once the amount for which it may be indebted has been determined by legal judgment, it should be deprived of the right to choose the manner and the time of payment, in which it has as much interest as the creditor himself, or more, since its credit and its national honor are involved therein.

This is no wise a defense for bad faith, disorder, and deliberate and voluntary insolvency. It is intended merely to preserve the dignity of the public international entity which may not thus be dragged into war with detriment to those high ends which determine the existence and liberty of nations.

This document can be found in U.S. Department of State, *Papers Relating to the Foreign Relations of the United States, 1903* (Washington, D.C.: Government Printing Office, 1904), pp. 1–5.

The fact that collection can not be accomplished by means of violence does not, on the other hand, render valueless the acknowledgment of the public debt, the definite obligation of paying it. . . .

As these are the sentiments of justice, loyalty, and honor which animate the Argentine people and have always inspired its policy, your excellency will understand that it has felt alarmed at the knowledge that the failure of Venezuela to meet the payments of its public debt is given as one of the determining causes of the capture of its fleet, the bombardment of one of its ports, and the establishment of a rigorous blockade along its shores. If such proceedings were to be definitely adopted they would establish a precedent dangerous to the security and the peace of the nations of this part of America.

The collection of loans by military means implies territorial occupation to make them effective, and territorial occupation signifies the suppression or subordination of the governments of the countries on which it is imposed.

Such a situation seems obviously at variance with the principles many times proclaimed by the nations of America, and particularly with the Monroe doctrine, sustained and defended with so much zeal on all occasions by the United States, a doctrine to which the Argentine Republic has heretofore solemnly adhered.

Among the principles which the memorable message of December 2, 1823, enunciates, there are two great declarations which particularly refer to these republics, viz, "The American continents are henceforth not to be considered as subjects for colonization by any European powers," and ". . . with the governments . . . whose independence we have . . . acknowledged, we could not view any interposition for the purpose of oppressing them or controlling in any other manner their destiny by any European power in any other light than as the manifestation of an unfriendly disposition toward the United States."

The right to forbid new colonial dominions within the limits of this continent has been many times admitted by the public men of England. To her sympathy is due, it may be said, the great success which the Monroe doctrine achieved immediately on its publication. But in very recent times there has been observed a marked tendency among the publicists and in the various expressions of European opinion to call attention to these countries as a suitable field for future territorial expansion. Thinkers of the highest order have pointed out the desirability of turning in this direction the great efforts which the principal powers of Europe have exerted for the conquest of sterile regions with trying climates and in remote regions of the earth. . . .

And it will not be denied that the simplest way to the setting aside and easy ejectment of the rightful authorities by European governments is just this way of financial interventions—as might be shown by many examples. We in no wise pretend that the South American nations are, from any point of view, exempt from the responsibilities of all sorts which violations of international law impose on civilized peoples. We do not nor can we pretend that these countries occupy an exceptional position in their relations with European powers, which have the indubitable right to protect their subjects as completely as in any other part of the world against the persecutions and injustices of which they may be the victims. The only principle which the Argentine Republic maintains and which it would, with great satisfaction, see adopted, in view of the events in Venezuela, by a nation that enjoys such great authority and prestige as does the United States, is the principle, already accepted, that there can be no territorial expansion in America on the part of Europe, nor any oppression of the peoples of this continent, because an unfortunate financial situation may compel some one of them to postpone the fulfillment of its promises. In a word, the principle which she would like to see recognized is: that the public debt can not occasion armed intervention nor even the actual occupation of the territory of American nations by a European power.

DOCUMENT 3

The Panama Canal Treaty Grants the United States a Zone of Occupation, 1903

Article I.   The United States guarantees and will maintain the independence of the Republic of Panama.

Article II.   The Republic of Panama grants to the United States in perpetuity the use, occupation and control of a zone of land and land under water for the construction, maintenance, operation, sanitation and protection of said Canal of the width of ten miles extending to the distance of five miles on each side of the center line of the route of the Canal to be constructed. . . .

Article III.   The Republic of Panama grants to the United States all the rights, power and authority within the zone mentioned and described in Article II of this agreement and within the limits of all auxiliary lands and waters mentioned and described in said Article II which the United States would possess and exercise if it were the sovereign of the territory within which said lands and waters are located to the entire exclusion of the exercise by the Republic of Panama of any such sovereign rights, power or authority. . . .

Article XIV.   As the price or compensation for the rights, powers and privileges granted in this convention by the Republic of Panama to the United States, the Government of the United States agrees to pay to the Republic of Panama the sum of ten million dollars ($10,000,000) in gold coin of the United States on the exchange of the ratification of this convention and also an annual payment during the life of this convention of two hundred and fifty thousand dollars ($250,000) in like gold coin, beginning nine years after the date aforesaid. . . .

Article XVIII.   The Canal, when constructed, and the entrances thereto shall be neutral in perpetuity, and shall be opened upon the terms provided for by Section I of Article three of, and in conformity with all the stipulations of, the treaty entered into by the Governments of the United States and Great Britain on November 18, 1901. . . .

This document can be found in U.S. Department of State, *Papers Relating to the Foreign Relations of the United States, 1904* (Washington, D.C.: Government Printing Office, 1905), pp. 543–550.

Article XXIII.   If it should become necessary at any time to employ armed forces for the safety or protection of the Canal, or of the ships that make use of the same, or the railways and auxiliary works, the United States shall have the right, at all times and in its discretion, to use its police and its land and naval forces or to establish fortifications for these purposes. . . .

Article XXV.   For the better performance of the engagements of this convention and to the end of the efficient protection of the Canal and the preservation of its neutrality, the Government of the Republic of Panama will sell or lease to the United States lands adequate and necessary for naval or coaling stations on the Pacific coast and on the western Caribbean coast of the Republic at certain points to be agreed upon with the President of the United States.

🌎 *D O C U M E N T   4*

President Rafael Reyes Enumerates Colombia's Grievances Against the United States, 1904

First. That the said note of the 30th of December from your excellency is regarded by my Government as an intimation that the Colombian forces will be attacked by those of the United States on their entering the territory of Panama for the purpose of subduing the rebellion, and that for that reason, and owing to its inability to cope with the powerful American squadron that watches over the coasts of the Isthmus of Panama, it holds the Government of the United States responsible for all damages caused to it by the loss of that national territory.

Second. That since the 3d of November last the revolution of Panama would have yielded, or would not have taken place, if the American sailors and the agents of the Panama Canal had not prevented the Colombian forces from proceeding on their march toward Panama, and that I [Rafael Reyes], as commander in chief of the army of Colombia, would have succeeded in suppressing the revolution of Panama as early as the 20th of the same month if Admiral Coghlan had not notified me in an official note that he had orders from his Government to prevent the landing of Colombian forces throughout the territory of the Isthmus.

Third. That the charges officially made against the Government and Senate of Colombia that it was opposed to the work of the Panama Canal, and that its purpose was to obtain a greater amount of money from the American Government and to recover the concession of the French company are unfair and groundless, and the proof of this assertion is that the Colombian Senate refused to ratify the Hay-Herrán treaty, not because a greater sum of money was demanded, but because the treaty was contrary to the constitution of the country, which prohibits the cession of sovereignty over national territory; but the necessity of the canal is so well recognized in Colombia that it was proposed, in the discussion of the Senate, to amend the constitution in

This document can be found in *Diplomatic History of the Panama Canal, Senate Documents,* Doc. No. 474 (Washington, D.C.: Government Printing Office, 1914), p. 504.

order to remove the constitutional difficulty, and the minister of foreign relations, after the sessions of Congress were closed, directed the chargé d'affaires, Doctor [Tomás] Herrán, to advise the Government of your excellency that that of Colombia was ready to enter into renewed negotiations for a canal convention, and that it purposed to remove the existing constitutional difficulties. The charge made against the Government of Colombia that it purposed to cancel the concession of the French company vanishes as soon as it be known that under the latest extension granted to it by Colombia the said concession would not lapse until the year 1910. . . .

Fifth. That while the treaty of 1846 gives to the Government of the United States the right to maintain and protect the free transit of the Isthmus at the request of Colombia and when the latter is unable to do so, it places it under the obligation of enforcing the respect of Colombia's sovereignty over the territory of the Isthmus, and that the American Government has now not only failed to discharge that duty, but has prevented the Colombian forces from recovering the national sovereignty on the Isthmus, and thus the said treaty of 1846 being in full force, Colombia holds that the Government of the United States has no other reason than that of its own strength and of Colombia's weakness for interpreting and applying it in the manner it has; that is to say, for availing itself of the advantages and rights conferred by the treaty, and refusing to fulfill the obligations imposed thereby.

Sixth. That it is known, from sworn statements, that the garrisons of Panama and Colón were bought with gold brought from the United States, toward the end of October, by the Panama revolutionists.

Seventh. That if these revolutionists had not relied, and did not now rely, on the armed protection of the United States, whose powerful squadrons on both the Pacific and Atlantic oceans have prevented, and are preventing, since the 3d of November, the Colombian army from landing its forces, the Panama revolution would have been foiled by Colombia in a few hours. . . .

Ninth. That on the grounds above stated, the Government of Colombia believes that it has been despoiled by that of the United States of its rights and sovereignty on the Isthmus of Panama, and not being possessed of the material strength sufficient to prevent this by the means of arms (although it does not forego this method, which it will use to the best of its ability), solemnly declares to the Government of the United States:

1. That the Government of the United States is responsible to that of Colombia for the dismemberment that has been made of its territory by the separation of Panama, by reason of the attitude that the said Government assumed there as soon as the revolution of the 3d of November broke out.
2. That the contract made between the United States and the French canal company is null, since it lacks the consent of Colombia, and the latter has already brought suit against the said canal company before the French courts in the defense of its interests.
3. That the Government of Colombia does not nor will it ever relinquish the rights it possesses over the territory of the Isthmus, . . . and that for that reason the title over the territory of the Isthmus that may be acquired by the United States for the opening of the canal is void. . . .
4. That if the work of the Panama Canal is undertaken and carried to completion in disregard and trespass of the rights of Colombia, the latter puts it on record that

she was denied justice by the United States; that she was forcibly despoiled of the territory of the Isthmus in clear violation of the treaty of 1846. . . .

5. That Colombia, earnestly wishing that the work of the canal be carried into effect, not only because it suits her interests but also those of the commerce of the world, is disposed to enter into arrangements that would secure for the United States the execution and ownership of the said work and be based on respect for her honor and rights.

6. That the United States has never protected Colombia on the Isthmus of Panama against foreign invasion, and that when it has intervened to prevent the interruption of the traffic it has been in help, or be it at the suggestion of the Government of Colombia. In this one instance it did so on its own initiative, with the obvious purpose of protecting the secession of the Isthmus. The guarantee of neutrality, if it were privileged, would estop the sovereign of the land from maintaining order, which is contrary to the fundamental principles of every government; and

7. That the course followed by the American Government at Panama at the time when Colombia enjoyed peace, after overcoming a revolution of three years' duration, which left her exhausted, is in favor of any rebellion, but not of the maintenance of order, which is contrary to the principles and antecedents of the policy of this great nation as established in the war of secession.

DOCUMENT 5

The Roosevelt Corollary Asserts U.S. Police Power over the Western Hemisphere, 1904

It is not true that the United States feels any land hunger or entertains any projects as regards the other nations of the Western Hemisphere save such as are for their welfare. All that this country desires is to see the neighboring countries stable, orderly, and prosperous. Any country whose people conduct themselves well can count upon our hearty friendship. If a nation shows that it knows how to act with reasonable efficiency and decency in social and political matters, if it keeps order and pays its obligations, it need fear no interference from the United States. Chronic wrongdoing, or an impotence which results in a general loosening of the ties of civilized society, may in America, as elsewhere, ultimately require intervention by some civilized nation, and in the Western Hemisphere the adherence of the United States to the Monroe Doctrine may force the United States, however reluctantly, in flagrant cases of such wrongdoing or impotence, to the exercise of an international police power. If every country washed by the Caribbean Sea would show the progress in stable and just civilization which with the aid of the Platt amendment Cuba has shown since our troops left the island, and which so many of the republics in both Americas are constantly and brilliantly showing, all question of interference by this Nation with their affairs would be at an end. Our interests and those of our southern neighbors are in reality identical. They have great natural riches, and if within their borders the reign of law and justice obtains, prosperity is sure to come to them. While they thus obey the primary laws of civilized society they may rest assured that they will be

This document can be found in the *Congressional Record,* XXXIX (December 6, 1904), Part I, 19.

treated by us in a spirit of cordial and helpful sympathy. We would interfere with them only in the last resort, and then only if it became evident that their inability or unwillingness to do justice at home and abroad had violated the rights of the United States or had invited foreign aggression to the detriment of the entire body of American nations. It is a mere truism to say that every nation, whether in America or anywhere else, which desires to maintain its freedom, its independence, must ultimately realize that the right of such independence can not be separated from the responsibility of making good use of it.

🌐 D O C U M E N T   6

A Latin American Poet Fires Back: Ruben Dario's "To Roosevelt," 1905

The voice that would reach you, Hunter, must speak
in Biblical tones, or in the poetry of Walt Whitman.
You are primitive and modern, simple and complex;
you are one part George Washington and one part Nimrod.
    You are the United States,
future invader of our naive America
with its Indian blood, an America
that still prays to Christ and still speaks Spanish.

You are a strong, proud model of your race;
you are cultured and able; you oppose Tolstoy.
You are an Alexander-Nebuchadnezzar,
breaking horses and murdering tigers.
(You are a Professor of Energy,
as the current lunatics say).

You think that life is a fire,
that progress is an irruption,
that the future is wherever
your bullet strikes.

                                                No.

The United States is grand and powerful.
Whenever it trembles, a profound shudder
runs down the enormous backbone of the Andes.
If it shouts, the sound is like the roar of a lion.
And Hugo said to Grant: "The stars are yours."
(The dawning sun of the Argentine barely shines;
the star of Chile is rising . . .) A wealthy country,
joining the cult of Mammon to the cult of Hercules;
while Liberty, lighting the path
to easy conquest, raises her torch in New York.

But our own America, which has had poets
since the ancient times of Nezahualcóyotl;
which preserved the footprints of great Bacchus,
and learned the Panic alphabet once,
and consulted the stars; which also knew Atlantis
(whose name comes ringing down to us in Plato)
and has lived, since the earliest moments of its life,
in light, in fire, in fragrance, and in love—
the America of Moctezuma and Atahualpa,
the aromatic America of Columbus,
Catholic America, Spanish America,
the America where noble Cuauhtémoc said:
"I am not on a bed of roses"—our America,
trembling with hurricanes, trembling with Love:
O men with Saxon eyes and barbarous souls,
our America lives. And dreams. And loves.
And it is the daughter of the Sun. Be careful.
Long live Spanish America!
A thousand cubs of the Spanish lion are roaming free.
Roosevelt, you must become, by God's own will,
the deadly Rifleman and the dreadful Hunter
before you can clutch us in your iron claws.

And though you have everything, you are lacking one thing:
    God!

☉ *E S S A Y S*

Mark T. Gilderhus of Texas Christian University paints a negative portrait of Theodore Roosevelt's Caribbean policies in the first essay. Acknowledging that Roosevelt most likely viewed the exercise of U.S. military and economic power as defense, Gilderhus nonetheless concludes that TR's vigorous diplomatic and military intervention in the region sprang from a drive to create a U.S. sphere of influence. According to Gilderhus, the president's blustering stirred incessant controversy among Latin Americans, who viewed U.S. activism as imperialism and domination.

In the second selection, Emily S. Rosenberg of the University of California, Irvine combines economic and cultural analysis to explain Roosevelt's expansionism. Rosenberg argues that TR drew on cultural discourses on gender and race that equated "manliness" with civilization and authority to justify "dollar diplomacy" in the Caribbean. Dollar diplomacy, first practiced in the Dominican Republic in 1905, relied on partnerships among banks, government officials, and professional financial managers to establish U.S. protectorate status over acquiescing foreign governments—without necessitating outright colonial possession.

Richard H. Collin of the University of New Orleans differs fundamentally with Gilderhus and Rosenberg. In the last essay, Collin posits that Roosevelt was a man of vision who labored to enlarge America's role in the world, to engineer a global balance of power, and to foster modernization in Latin America. Control rather than expansion ranked as TR's foremost objective in the Caribbean, and he pursued that goal through the measured use of force and diplomacy. Collin faults reactionary Latin American nationalists, such as President José Manuel Marroquín of Colombia, and clumsy foreign intruders such as Germany, for creating chaos in the region and inviting U.S. police actions. The three essays demonstrate the vast differences in viewpoints and approaches among scholars who seek to understand and interpret U.S. hegemony in the Caribbean during the Roosevelt era.

Bravado and Bluster:
TR's Sphere of Influence in the Caribbean

MARK T. GILDERHUS

On 6 September 1901 an assassin twice shot William McKinley at a reception in Buffalo, New York. McKinley lingered for eight days before dying, and then Theodore Roosevelt became the president. Conservative reformer, nationalist, and exponent of the vigorous life, the former vice president assumed the conduct of foreign relations at a critical time, the aftermath of the war with Spain. As president, he reveled in the responsibilities of his office and brought the New Diplomacy to a kind of fulfillment. Above all, he wanted his country to function as "a force for stability in the world" and saw "no escape from the exercise of American influence." Among his fundamental aims, Roosevelt sought a balance of power in Europe, an Open Door policy in Asia, and U.S. hegemony in the Western Hemisphere. His outspoken views and bellicose rhetoric always produced high levels of controversy. Critics sometimes characterized him as an imperialist and a militarist. As a young man, according to historian Richard Hofstadter, "it had always been his instinct to fight, to shoot things out with someone or something—imaginary lovers of his fiancée, Western Indians, Mexicans, the British navy, Spanish soldiers, American workers, Populists." By the time he became president, however, Roosevelt had acquired self-control and discharged "his penchant for violence . . . on a purely verbal level." The recent scholarship plays down his propensity for war. Though typically ready to use force if necessary, according to Lewis L. Gould, he "sent no troops into action, and no Americans died in armed combat while he was in office" except in the Philippines, where the fighting had started before he assumed the presidency.

Roosevelt scholar Richard H. Collin insists that historians have too often misrepresented and misunderstood the president by failing to take into account the appropriate "contexts." Collin particularly dislikes present-minded, neo-Marxist accounts because they are more concerned with "the Cold War or America's role as a superpower than with Kaiser Wilhelm II's Germany." This misplaced emphasis has obscured the principal point that "Roosevelt's main purpose" in the New World was "not the subjugation of Latin America" but "the exclusion of Europe" from the Western Hemisphere. Europe was "central" for Roosevelt. Moreover, his concern about German intrusions was legitimate, "not because Germany could conquer substantial parts of Latin America" but "because the introduction of European national rivalries into the New World, combined with the growing instability of Central America—Latin America's Balkans—would destabilize the entire region."

"Bravado and Bluster: TR's Sphere of Influence in the Caribbean," from excerpts from Gilderhus, Mark T., "Expansion, Empire, and Intervention," in *The Second Century: U.S.-Latin American Relations Since 1889* (Wilmington, Del.: Scholarly Resources, 2000), pp. 23–33. Copyright © 2000 by Scholarly Resources, 2000. Reprinted with permission of Mark T. Gilderhus.

Roosevelt valued order. He also encouraged capitalist enterprise, not so much for purposes of moneygrubbing as for tactical reasons: He hoped thereby to promote material progress, peace, and stability.

Roosevelt earned much of his reputation for bravado and bluster in Latin America, where his spheres-of-influence policies in the Caribbean region stirred pincessant controversy. Though probably geared in his own thinking to the defense of strategic purposes and the Monroe Doctrine, his actions served U.S. economic interests as well. Secretary of State Elihu Root acknowledged as much in 1906, when he remarked upon the importance of Latin American markets for the United States. He also looked upon the region as an outlet for "a surplus of capital beyond the requirements of internal development." During this time the total overseas investments of the United States grew impressively from $0.7 billion in 1897 to $2.5 billion in 1908 to $3.5 billion in 1914. About half went into Latin America.

Roosevelt's actions during the Venezuela crisis in 1902–03 illustrated his strategic concerns. Germany, already a source of mistrust, posed the problem. The difficulty developed when Cipriano Castro, the Venezuelan president and strongman, defaulted on European loans and disregarded an ultimatum demanding payment from Germany, Italy, and Great Britain. Germany then instituted a naval blockade, sank some Venezuelan ships, landed troops, and shelled the forts along the coastline. Though initially acquiescent, Roosevelt later became alarmed. He would not allow the collection of international debts to serve as a pretext for the establishment of a European base in the Western Hemisphere. Among other things, his plans for a trans-Isthmian canal ruled out European obstructions.

In this instance, Roosevelt's own historical account has generated a controversy. Thirteen years later, when the United States was struggling to maintain neutrality in the First World War, the former chief executive suggested in an interview that he knew better than President Woodrow Wilson how to deal with the Germans. Indeed, Roosevelt claimed that during the Venezuela crisis he had obtained good effects behind the scenes by employing coercion with threats of force, warning of war unless the Germans accepted arbitration as the means of settlement. In this way, by his own account, Roosevelt applied the adage "speak softly and carry a big stick." For historians the difficulty resides in assessing the credibility of the claim. Since no corroborating evidence exists in the archives of the United States, Great Britain, or Germany, some scholars regard Roosevelt's version as an exaggeration or a fabrication, perhaps the product of fading memory or mounting personal disgust with Woodrow Wilson's efforts to stay out of the war. Other historians credit Roosevelt with truthfulness, citing earlier renditions of the story in his correspondence and even the possibility of a cover-up, that is, the removal of documents from governmental archives to avoid political embarrassment. Whatever the case, German leaders in the end terminated the crisis by consenting to arbitration, thus presumably giving way when faced with Roosevelt's resolve.

Roosevelt's efforts to build a canal in Panama also displayed a robust readiness to act. This complicated and contentious affair raised difficult questions about the propriety of his means in promoting Panamanian independence to secure the route. Panama, a province of the South American country of Colombia, had possessed strategic significance since colonial times as "a crossroads of global trade" and "the keystone of the Great Spanish Empire." For U.S. entrepreneurs the region became particularly important as a consequence of "their quest for continental and commercial empire." As early as 1825, New York interests had laid plans for the construction of a canal to link the Atlantic and Pacific Oceans. The British had similar aims. To head off competition the United States and Great Britain negotiated the Clayton-Bulwer Treaty of 1850, in which they promised to make any such project a joint venture. The construction of a railroad by New York financiers in 1855 established U.S. influence as dominant.

The French posed a challenge in 1878, when Ferdinand de Lesseps, the builder of the Suez Canal in Egypt, announced plans for the construction of a sea-level waterway across Panama. This project went forward for a decade, despite U.S. opposition, and then failed because of insuperable obstacles, including varieties of poisonous snakes, mud and rock slides, and tropical diseases such as malaria and yellow fever. Unimpressed by the French collapse, U.S. leaders during the economic depression of the 1890s retained a strong interest in reviving the project. Indeed, as McKinley noted in his annual message to the Congress in December 1898, "The prospective expansion of our influence and commerce in the Pacific" provided a strong incentive for building a canal. This commercial justification ran parallel with and reenforced the recommendations of another vocal pressure group, the advocates of sea power in the U.S. Navy and elsewhere, for whom Captain Alfred Thayer Mahan of the U.S. Naval War College in Newport, Rhode Island, functioned as a leading publicist and theorist. Mahan argued from the British example that battle fleets always had sustained national power, commerce, and greatness. According to him, the construction of a canal formed an essential part of a grandiose design to advance U.S. interests around the world. For such champions the voyage of the USS *Oregon* during the war with Spain illustrated the obvious point: The 14,000-mile voyage from San Francisco around the southern tip of South America to Cuba took sixty-eight days. A canal would make it much shorter.

One problem was whether to construct the passageway in Nicaragua or Panama. In 1901 the Walker Commission, a group of engineers named by McKinley to study the issue, recommended Nicaragua, mainly because of difficulties with the French-owned New Panama Canal Company over the purchase of equipment and assets. The asking price ran to $109 million, an excess valuation of $69 million, according to the Walker Commission. Panama in other respects displayed advantages, chief among them cheaper construction and maintenance costs and a shorter distance from sea to sea. Roosevelt knew of these benefits, but before choosing Panama he had to deal with other complications.

Lobbyists pressed hard on Panama's behalf. As advocates of the New Panama Canal Company, William Nelson Cromwell, the head of a prestigious New York City law firm, and Philippe Bunau-Varilla, a French engineer formerly employed by de Lesseps, sought to rig a deal by which the United States would designate Panama as the choice and pay for the privilege. Cromwell cultivated support among Republican leaders with arguments and campaign contributions and also reduced the purchase price to $40 million. The Walker Commission responded by issuing a new report in favor of Panama. Meanwhile, Bunau-Varilla pushed for acceptance of a proposal suggested by Republican Senator John C. Spooner of Wisconsin. Once adopted into law, the Spooner amendment authorized President Roosevelt to buy the assets of the New Panama Canal Company for $40 million and to employ Panama as the site—provided, of course, that he could obtain the treaty rights.

The diplomatic solution consisted of two parts. First, U.S. leaders wanted to break free from the Clayton-Bulwer Treaty of 1850 in order to exercise exclusive control and fortification rights. Discussions between Secretary of State John Hay and British Minister Julian Pauncefote produced an agreement in November 1901. Second, the United States devised a treaty with Colombia to obtain a long-term lease on a swatch of land six miles wide across Panama. In return, the United States would pay Colombia $10 million and an annual rental fee of $250,000. The stockholders of the New Panama Canal Company also would benefit from the sale of assets to the United States.

John Hay's treaty, worked out with the Colombian diplomat Tomás Herrán, obtained ratification in the United States but was rejected by the Colombian Senate in August 1903. Colombians wanted more money for sacrificing sovereignty in Panama. Only recently their country had emerged from a disastrous civil war. By stalling until 1904, when the charter of the New Panama Canal Company ran out, Colombian leaders conceivably could rake in a $40-million profit, additional resources for their devastated nation. Moreover, President José Marroquín, a provincial and reactionary ideologue, would not support the work of his own government's more cosmopolitan diplomats by endorsing the treaty with the United States. His unyielding stance based on conservative Catholic views "confounded" Roosevelt by ruling out the transfer of land in Panama to a Yankee, Protestant nation. Viewed from another angle, Marroquín possessed "as little understanding of the commercial aspects of Panama canal diplomacy as Theodore Roosevelt had for Colombia's religious politics."

Furious, Roosevelt denounced the Colombians for bad faith. He told the secretary of state, "I do not think the Bogotá lot of jack rabbits should be allowed permanently to bar one of the future highways of civilization." Conscious of the consequences "not merely decades, but centuries hence," Roosevelt wanted to take "the right step." A convergence of purposes with Panamanian separatists seeking independence from Colombia provided the solution. Remote and isolated by mountains and jungle, Panama had produced fierce nationalism and a series of revolts in the nineteenth century. New efforts got under way in the fall of 1903, when Philippe Bunau-Varilla assumed the role of intermediary between Panamanian dissidents and U.S. officials. The latter included President Roosevelt, who conveyed a clear impression that he would not permit the failure of a new bid for independence. Coordinating plans with Dr. Manuel Amador Guerrero, the head of a revolutionary junta, Bunau-Varilla brought about an uprising on 3 November. The Panamanian rebels swiftly seized control of strategic points, and the arrival of the USS *Nashville* on the following day prevented Colombia from striking back. The revolution cost hardly any bloodshed.

Seeking to salvage something, the Colombian government attempted to revive the previously rejected treaty, this time at a lower price. Not much interested, the Roosevelt administration concentrated its attention on negotiations with the dexterous and omnipresent Bunau-Varilla, who now represented the interests of both newly independent Panama and the New Panama Canal Company. Because of the administration's political concerns, Roosevelt needed favorable terms to assure Senate ratification and got them in the Hay-Bunau-Varilla Treaty of 18 November 1903. This document provided for a perpetual grant of land ten miles wide within which the United States possessed "all rights, power, and authority" as "if it were the sovereign of the territory." In return, the United States agreed to protect

Panama's independence, pay $10 million down and after nine years remit an annual fee of $250,000. For the sale of its assets the New Panama Canal Company received $40 million. The prime loser, Colombia, received nothing until 1921, when, under the terms of the Thomson-Urrutia Treaty, the government accepted the loss of Panama and also an indemnity of $25 million from the United States.

Negotiated hastily without benefit of Panamanian representation, the Hay-Bunau-Varilla Treaty distressed officials in the new country's government. They protested "the manifest renunciation of sovereignty" over the Canal Zone, a central issue during the ensuing years, but could not change the provisions. A rejection at this point could have precipitated even worse outcomes. The United States might have seized a canal route without payment or moved the site to Nicaragua, leaving Panama without protection against Colombia. The Panamanians really had no choice. Although the U.S. Senate ratified the treaty by a large margin on 23 February 1904, the acquisition of Panama as a second protectorate in the Caribbean region left a legacy of bitterness and ill will. Colombian leaders objected to the U.S. role in bringing about the loss of the rebellious province. Panamanian nationalists disliked the loss of sovereignty. In each instance, the issue created difficulties for the future.

In the annual message to Congress in December 1904, Roosevelt enunciated his most comprehensive statement of policy toward Latin America. As an expression of preferred assumptions and favorite techniques, his corollary to the Monroe Doctrine uncompromisingly affirmed U.S. responsibility to stand against European intervention in the Western Hemisphere and also to take corrective action when Latin Americans reneged on international debts. Roosevelt advised preventive intervention by which the United States would step in and set things right. Such measures inverted the original intent of the Monroe Doctrine. Initially a prohibition on European intrusion into the New World, it now became a sanction for U.S. intervention when, in T.R.'s words, "chronic wrongdoing" or "impotence" caused a breakdown of "the ties of civilized society" and forced intercession "by some civilized nation." In the Western Hemisphere the United States, "however reluctantly, in flagrant cases" should assume the responsibility by carrying out "the exercise of an international police power." As Roosevelt explained to Secretary of State Elihu Root, a decision "to say 'Hands off' to the powers of Europe" meant that "sooner or later we must keep order ourselves."

A test occurred soon afterward: An international debt exceeding $32 million threatened the Dominican Republic with bankruptcy and the possibility of European intervention. When Dominican leaders asked the United States for help, Roosevelt first hesitated and then, after his reelection in 1904, accepted a commitment. An agreement in January 1905 engaged the United States to manage the foreign debt in such a way as to "restore the credit, preserve the order, increase the efficiency of the civil administration and advance [the] material progress and welfare of the Republic." Senate opponents, mainly Democrats, delayed ratification until February 1907, but Roosevelt characteristically worked around the problem by obtaining authority through an executive agreement. It enabled U.S. officials to take over the collection of Dominican customs receipts, the principal source of revenue, and also to arrange for a new schedule of payments.

Roosevelt employed strong measures in Cuba as well. Following a presidential election denounced by critics as coercive, corrupt, and fraudulent, Liberal party opponents of President Tomás Estrada Palma rebelled in 1906, hoping thereby to provoke U.S. intervention on their behalf. As required by the Platt amendment, Roosevelt responded to the breakdown of public order by sending in occupation troops. This time they stayed until 1909, retiring finally after U.S. authorities supervised another election resulting in a Liberal party victory. As [the historian] Louis Pérez notes, "That the United States intervened . . . to displace a government held in disfavor by the opposition . . . suggested that there was more than one way to redress grievances and obtain political ascendancy" in Cuba. The United States became a mediator of local disputes, in this instance "with almost unlimited entrée into Cuban internal affairs."

Such affirmations of power and prerogative established the principal attributes of U.S. hegemony in the Western Hemisphere. Though Roosevelt annexed no new territory and, indeed, denied any interest in doing so, he upheld his definition of U.S. interest by vigorous means. Through the exercise of a self-proclaimed international police authority, supposedly sanctioned by the Monroe Doctrine, Roosevelt created not colonies but protectorates, using intervention as a major instrument of control. For him, such methods probably suggested paternalism rather than outright imperialism. Yet for many Latin Americans the prospect of domination—political, commercial, and cultural—seemed threateningly real. Among intellectuals especially, suspicion of the United States ran deep and appeared in expressions of Yankeephobia. In 1900, for example, José Enrique Rodó, a Uruguayan, published *Ariel,* a book in which he defended Latin American spirituality against North American materialism, for him a prime distinction between the two cultures. In 1904, similarly, Rubén Darío, a Nicaraguan, incorporated anti-imperial themes into his poem "To Roosevelt," which represented the president as a symbol of arrogant condescension toward Latin America.

Although historians generally have depicted negative reactions to Roosevelt among Latin Americans, Frederick W. Marks III has argued to the contrary that "American prestige south of the border was exceptionally high under Roosevelt." If correct, this assessment probably pertains to ruling elites who appreciated the U.S. president's techniques as a defense against forcible European debt collections. But Latin American resentment of U.S. intervention appeared at a succession of Pan American conferences: at Mexico City in 1901, Rio de Janeiro in 1906, and Buenos Aires in 1910. Even though these were mainly ceremonial occasions to celebrate appearances of hemispheric unity, the rituals could not disguise the differences. The Argentines especially pressed for formal endorsements of the Calvo and Drago doctrines, both favorite projects. Carlos Calvo, an Argentine expert on international law, upheld the inviolability of national sovereignty, opposed the Roosevelt corollary, and insisted on the principle of nonintervention on grounds that no state should intervene in the affairs of another for any reason. Luis María Drago, an Argentine diplomat, similarly argued against the use of force in collecting international debts. . . .

[During the early twentieth century] the United States created protectorates, practiced intervention in the Caribbean region, and established, if not an empire, something very much like one. Within this sphere of influence, successive administrations affirmed a need for stability and invoked the authority of a self-proclaimed international police power. This practice, a form of hegemony, required the subordination of Latin American sensibilities to U.S. preferences, sometimes justified on grounds of serving lesser peoples. U.S. policies aimed at peace, order, and predictability but could not sustain such conditions. During the second decade of the twentieth century the violent disorder of revolution and war assailed U.S. interests all around the world.

TR's Civilizing Mission: Race, Gender, and Dollar Diplomacy

EMILY S. ROSENBERG

President Roosevelt was a dedicated internationalist, advocated a large navy, and believed in the civilizing mission of the United States. Even most anti-imperialists agreed that national interest and international benevolence required exerting some kind of influence overseas. Secretary of State Elihu Root warned that differences in race and culture made outright acquisition of colonies undesirable, but that the United States still had a responsibility to spread its commercial and moral influence. He took seriously the country's obligations to lead the hemisphere and was the first Secretary of State to take a good-will tour of South America. During the first five years of the twentieth century, the Roosevelt administration thus developed clear and expansive policies that sanctioned the creation of dependencies but not colonies. The justifications of spreading civilization and securing a favorable economic and geopolitical position would provide the rationales for dollar diplomacy—a means of establishing some control while avoiding outright colonial possession.

Whether advocating formal imperialism or rejecting it, the leading policymakers in the Roosevelt administration shaped their views of the civilizing mission within the professional-managerial outlook that envisioned progress as the spread of markets and monetary exchange through scientific application of economic laws. These themes also intermingled with presumably scientific thinking about gender and race. Notions of gender and racial hierarchy would reinforce the civilizationist justifications for dollar diplomacy.

The changes sweeping through American life at the turn of the century seemed to provoke widespread concern with manhood. The term "manhood" should be understood as connoting neither a transhistorical, biological essence nor a unified collection of specific traits. It describes, rather, a dynamic *cultural process* through which men asserted a claim to certain authority as though it had a status immutably rooted in nature. In the formulation that was widespread among middle-class white men in the Victorian era, manliness emphasized strength of character, especially defined as self-control and self-mastery. According to the social evolutionary doctrine of the day, humans advanced by establishing mastery over themselves and the larger environment. The lack of self-discipline and ability to plan for the future marked a lower status. Thus, a worthy man had a duty to protect those who were weaker, self-indulgent, and less rational: women, children, and nonwhite races. Manly restraint, both in monetary and sexual matters, would bring capital accumulation and

Emily S. Rosenberg, "The Roosevelt Corollary and the Dominican Model of 1905 . . . [excerpts only]," in *Financial Missionaries to the World: The Politics and Culture of Dollar Diplomacy, 1900–1930*, pp. 32–34, 36, 39–46, 56, 59–60. Copyright 2003, Duke University Press. All rights reserved. Used by permission of the publisher.

family (thus social) stability. In this view, civilization advanced as men became more cognizant of manly duties and as gender roles diverged to become almost mirror opposites. . . .

Gender distinctions had symbolic links to the emerging political economy that was to be organized by dollar diplomacy. Just as manhood implied restraint, self-mastery, and supervision over dependents, uncivilized peoples were marked by feminine attributes, especially lack of planning and weak self-discipline. Against the moral and financial effeminacy of unbacked, inflating paper money could be set the manly, civilizing force of a gold standard, careful regulation by a national banking system, and supervised revenue collection and expenditure. Civilized men conserved value by restraining and regulating use; whether the currency of potential value was semen or money, civilized men kept control of the quantities produced. Manly orientations toward sexual relations and money (there was a quantity theory of both) shared discursive similarities. . . .

Like many others of his day, Roosevelt co-mingled the meanings of manhood, whiteness, and nationhood. His *Strenuous Life* (1899) was about manhood and the *nation's* duty to be manly. One of his most famous speeches, "National Duties," was about "the essential manliness of the American character." Roosevelt explained that "exactly as each man, while doing first his duty to his wife and the children within his home, must yet, if he hopes to amount to much, strive mightily in the world outside his home, so our nation, while first of all seeing to its own domestic well-being, must not shrink from playing its part among the great nations without." By using such domestic metaphors, Roosevelt made international involvements seem more familiar and natural. He wrote, "man must be glad to do a man's work, to dare and endure and to labor; to keep himself, and to keep those dependent upon him. . . . As it is with the individual, so it is with the nation." Nations, like men, had duties to perform.

Although many middle-class men, or aspirants to that status, performed and perpetuated this particular discourse of manhood well past the Victorian age, some significant reformulations emerged during the late nineteenth century. The new immigration, the New Woman, the growth of professions and office work, and a perception of decline in economic predictability and in professional wages all challenged middle-class male identity and authority. Claims that manhood was in decline became pervasive as doctors developed heightened concerns about male homosexuality, worried about male effeminacy, and warned about growing neurasthenia (nervous strain) in men. These concerns gave rise to a relatively new word—masculinity—which gained sudden popularity and had slightly different connotations than manliness.

Neurasthenia was an illness that George M. Beard, in his *American Nervousness* (1881), had defined as "nervelessness—a lack of nerve force." Beard traced the condition to the stresses of overcivilization—men were becoming weak and sickly by depleting their nerve force. Nerve force could be depleted by masturbation, a moral problem that Beard believed sapped masculine energy, but the disease also could stem from the *cultural* problem of modern civilization, as it was common among *white men* who did "brain work." The neurasthenic man, exhausted by the demands of ambition, achievement, and work, was retreating into passivity and invalidism—in effect, into the feminine realm. . . .

Roosevelt brilliantly molded all of [the] associations of manliness, whiteness, adulthood, and nationhood into a powerful projection of the civilizing mission.

In his person he embodied the two (somewhat contradictory) models of manhood: civilized manliness (representing duty and self-mastery) and primitive masculinity (representing primitive urge toward assertiveness, spontaneity, and battle). As a young president at the start of a new century, he persuasively claimed these attributes not just for himself but for the white American race in its relationship to the world. The Roosevelt Corollary reflected this mix of manly duty, masculine threat of force, and the white race's destiny to organize and uplift child-like races.

The Roosevelt administration marshaled these images to shape a new vision of the U.S. presidency. Political leaders were to pursue high-minded goals, especially in foreign affairs, without paying too much attention to possibly ill-informed public clamor. Although popular opinion might set certain boundaries for policy, it should never guide it. As Roosevelt's brash action in Panama suggested, his presidency elevated the power of the executive branch, while new civil service requirements, organizational specialization, and a stronger navy made it operate more effectively. A proponent of expertise and the cult of efficiency, Roosevelt also advanced the professional-managerial faith in the civilizing power of monetary exchange and envisioned a strong working relationship between government and large, efficient businesses to transform backward groups, whether at home or abroad. The modern presidency, he believed, should be an activist office, mobilizing public and the private sectors to operate on behalf of an expansive view of the public good. . . .

The Venezuelan crisis of 1902 helped define Roosevelt's approach and prompted the formulation of his Roosevelt Corollary. In Venezuela, European intervention over defaulted debts provoked difficulties. The global economic depression of the mid-1890s, which had been preceded by a tremendous volume of Latin American borrowing in European markets, had brought widespread defaults throughout the area and made financial irresponsibility a major diplomatic concern. As Roosevelt saw it, European gunboats sent against Venezuela diminished the prestige of the Monroe Doctrine. Moreover, the Hague Court decision that helped resolve Venezuela's dispute with England and Germany implied preferential treatment in debt settlement to states that used armed force, a precedent that, Roosevelt feared, might encourage more European military interventions against defaulted states in the Western hemisphere.

In his Corollary to the Monroe Doctrine (1904), Roosevelt stated that when nations of the Western hemisphere conducted their economic affairs irresponsibly enough to raise the possibility of European intervention, the United States would assume the role of an "international police power." Roosevelt wrote privately to his son that the United States "should assume an attitude of protection and regulation in regard to all these little states in the neighborhood of the Caribbean." The doctrine blended discourses about manhood, race, adulthood, managerial expertise, and national interest into a program for spreading civilization.

It was initially unclear how Roosevelt planned to implement the Corollary. Widespread anti-imperial sentiments prevented acquisition of new colonies. Cuba and Panama provided models of protectorates—that is, nations bound by treaty obligations to be "protected" by the United States from external threats or internal disorder—but Congress and the public were reluctant to acquire more protectorates. In 1904 the Dominican Republic became, in effect, a laboratory for working out the question of how other forms of dependency might be devised. . . .

Deeply in debt to European bondholders and threatened by European warships, the Dominican Republic in 1904, with its harbor at Samaná Bay and its proximity to the Panama Canal, seemed of strategic importance to President Roosevelt. The credibility of the Roosevelt Corollary also appeared to rest on how the United States would handle the Dominican case. Although Roosevelt would later claim to Congress that he had to act because European intervention was imminent, Europeans were probably less eager to intervene themselves than to force action by the United States on their behalf. If European governments were to live with the Caribbean as a U.S. sphere of influence, then they wanted assurance that the United States would uphold what they perceived as their legitimate interests in the area. As Roosevelt told the Senate in 1905, U.S. handling of the Dominican crisis afforded "a practical test of the efficiency of the United States Government in maintaining the Monroe Doctrine." . . .

Between 1904 and 1907, U.S. emissaries incrementally pieced together a plan for rehabilitating the Dominican Republic. In the spring of 1904, the new U.S. minister, Thomas C. Dawson, a veteran of the diplomatic service in Brazil and author of a two-volume history of South America, reported that fiscal insolvency was the basis of the endemic political disorder. He recommended "a radical change in the system of collecting revenue and a great reduction in current expenditure." The Dominican government requested readjustment of the country's current outstanding debt so that bankruptcy and intervention could be avoided. Dawson worked out a protocol that reflected both of these goals: the U.S. government would take over collection of Dominican customs, applying up to 55% of the receipts to debt service; it would also review the internal and external debt claims and work out private bank refinancing. [Financial expert] Jacob Hollander was hired to put the plan together. To help convince the Dominican government to allow the United States to "establish an orderly and businesslike administration" through the protocol, the Secretary of State ordered a visit by naval commander Albert C. Dillingham. In the meantime, the Dominican government officially established a gold standard, based on the U.S. gold dollar, to facilitate the proposed reforms.

When Roosevelt took Dawson's protocol to the Senate for ratification, he hit a roadblock. The president appealed to senators to uphold the credibility of the Monroe Doctrine, do a service to humanity, and increase "the sphere in which peaceful measures for the settlement of international difficulties gradually displace those of a warlike character." But many senators questioned the idea that the U.S. government could bind itself to refund private debts. Sufficient support for the protocol seemed so unlikely that the measure was not brought up for vote.

The president who had bragged about taking the canal while congresses debated remained undeterred. Feminizing his opponents as prattling pacifists, proponents of inefficiency, and reactionaries, Roosevelt simply took over Dominican customs collection without the consent of Congress. He encouraged the Dominican president, who was increasingly desperate about his [nation's revolutionary political climate], to issue by decree a *modus vivendi* under which the U.S. government was invited to assume control of the customs houses. A retired army colonel and veteran of the colonial customs service in the Philippines took over as General Receiver of customs. Roosevelt claimed that these measures were only temporary stopgaps until Congress formally consented to the protocol. "The Constitution," Roosevelt explained, "did not explicitly give me the power to bring about the necessary agreement with Santo Domingo. But the Constitution did not forbid me." . . .

Because a U.S. government obligation for Dominican debt had been the stumbling block to the protocol's ratification, Hollander turned to bankers to work out refunding. If the plan proved successful, the U.S. government would then only need to oversee revenue collection, not assume responsibility for debt. Hollander was asking investment bankers to use a process similar to that employed with bankrupt domestic companies: provide new money to pay off creditors and to reorganize fiscal affairs in return for assurances of some control over future management (in this case the Dominican government) so that the problems that had produced the crisis in the first place would not recur. The creation of a receivership, a common practice in the domestic business sector during the late nineteenth century, provided a ready technique for dealing with foreign bankrupt governments. With Secretary of State Root's personal encouragement, Hollander finally obtained Kuhn, Loeb, and Company's cooperation and worked out an adjustment of past debts with the Protective Committee of Bondholders in Antwerp and others. . . .

The Dominican model provided a compromise between the ideal of limited government and the need for structures that would secure and "civilize" the sphere of interest proclaimed in the Roosevelt Corollary to the Monroe Doctrine. The basic formula of dollar diplomacy involved three groups. First were the investment bankers, seeking new bond issues with higher rates of interest and willing to sponsor a loan that both paid off old bonds and added new money for domestic improvements. On the government side were officials who wanted the United States to dominate the area; they promised to establish a receivership that would oversee the fiscal affairs of a bankrupt government and remit regular repayments on the loan. Finally, professionals who had already gained financial experience in U.S. colonies oversaw the financial rehabilitation, including debt renegotiation, more effective revenue collection, and gold-standard currency reform. Of course, cooperation or acquiescence by the foreign government was also required. A foreign government escaped the strategic and economic uncertainties of bankruptcy and expected to solidify its own governing power by uniting with a powerful and capital-rich protector. For all, managerial capitalism provided a framework for action. . . .

If the Panama Canal symbolized [the] dream of a growing empire of commerce and well-ordered amity, the Dominican model seemed a practical step to the dream's fulfillment. With U.S. experts controlling the customs houses, [the architects of the Dominican model] claimed, Dominican revolutionaries could no longer seize a port and use customs revenue to finance a revolt against the central government. Internal disorder initially subsided, as the U.S.-backed government successfully crushed its opponents. Moreover, trade rose steadily and receipts from the Dominican customs houses shot up dramatically. A nation burdened by bankruptcy and default seemed to acquire, through U.S. supervision, the steady habits of thrift and regular payment of bills. U.S. direct investment in the Dominican Republic also soared. . . .

Although dollar diplomacy would not acquire its name until the [William Howard] Taft administration, the process took shape under Theodore Roosevelt as a way of negotiating two seemingly incompatible trends: a distaste for colonialism along with a commitment to stabilize and provide manly uplift to the darker-skinned peoples of nations touching the Caribbean. In the Dominican Republic between 1905 and 1907 the United States instituted financial controls without, at first, incurring the burdens or backlash associated with formal colonialism. The Dominican Republic's receivership, fiscal protectorate, or controlled loan (any of these terms were and may be used) represented an attempt by policymakers to find an alternative to colonialism that would still institute the supervision they deemed necessary for fiscal and social reform.

TR's Measured Response to
Political Instability and European Encroachment

RICHARD H. COLLIN

When Theodore Roosevelt assumed the presidency on September 14, 1901, the United States was already a major world power. The United States had won a small world war with Spain in 1898—a war decided by naval victories continents apart at Manila Bay and Santiago, Cuba. As an articulate American expansionist, President William McKinley's assistant secretary of the Navy, and hero of the Rough Riders, Roosevelt played a vital role in the Spanish-American War. Roosevelt prepared the Navy for war and helped win the Asiatic command for Commodore George Dewey. His legendary charge at San Juan Hill made him and Dewey America's first modern war heroes. Roosevelt was a unique world leader, a writer-intellectual who became a successful soldier, an aristocrat who led a democratic people, a global visionary who deprovincialized his nation, and an international nationalist who championed world civilization and patriotic nationalism at the same time. Theodore Roosevelt was one of the most effective charismatic phrase-makers to ever capture the world's imagination.

Roosevelt's colorful use of language proved to be both an asset and a liability. He made the "big stick" into a household phrase, winning public support for an expanded navy, a more efficient military bureaucracy, and an activist foreign policy. But the same big stick that impressed Kaiser Wilhelm II frightened Latin Americans. American historiography has consistently stressed Latin American rather than European reaction to the big stick policy. Although Latin America was the battleground in the turn-of-the-century struggle between the United States and Europe, Latin America was never Roosevelt's target. Control, not expansion, was Roosevelt's primary object. His union of power and responsibility, his intellectual commitment to the idea of civilization, and his personal indifference to the economic side of capitalism tempered the big stick.

U.S. willingness to accept responsibility in Roosevelt's Corollary to the Monroe Doctrine of 1905 made Roosevelt's policy acceptable to Europe. What pleased Europe displeased Latin America. But Latin American intellectuals were frustrated by Latin American cultural and economic dependency on Europe and their awareness of Latin American vulnerability to the emerging modernism of the twentieth-century world of which the United States was the chief symbol. Latin American

"The Big Stick of Weltpolitik: Europe and Latin America in Theodore Roosevelt's Foreign Policy," by Richard H. Collin in Natalie A. Naylor et al., eds., *Theodore Roosevelt: Many Sided American,* Interlaken: Heart of the Lakes Publishing, 1992, pp. 295–316.

concern was justified. Roosevelt's success in removing Europe eliminated the effective Latin American diplomatic tactic of using divisions among competing European interests to win whatever diplomatic victories were possible to weak, pre-industrial nations. Dealing with the colossus to the north was far more difficult than playing British, Germans, or French off against one another, and, when that failed, invoking the Monroe Doctrine to prevent European military intervention.

Latin American political dependency preceded Roosevelt's time. In the 1820s Simón Bolívar despaired of finding a political solution to authoritarian Iberian traditions. Latin America may well have been a victim of Roosevelt's success, but it was already a victim of Spanish colonialism and European cultural dependency. The Americans who wanted Europe out did not want themselves in. Roosevelt's graphic disclaimer, "I have about the same desire to annex it [Santo Domingo] as a gorged boa constrictor might have to swallow a porcupine wrong-end to," is an accurate statement of American feelings. Germany (mainly) and Great Britain were the main focus of American fears and policies. Only after the United States established control in the Caribbean—in Roosevelt's method through the measured use of power and diplomacy—could U.S. policy attempt to deal with its Latin American relationships. Roosevelt won his battle with Europe but in so doing became the historical demon blamed for losing Latin America.

Great Britain had gradually begun to come to terms with the American demand for hegemony in Central America. When Roosevelt signed the Hay-Pauncefote II Treaty on December 21, 1901—his first treaty as president—Britain finally gave in to American ambitions to be rid of the Clayton-Bulwer Treaty of 1850 which prohibited either nation from building a canal unilaterally. When the Senate rewrote Secretary of State John Hay's first version of the treaty, it insisted that an isthmian canal be American in word as well as deed, though the British fleet remained the sovereign of the seas. Resisting any conciliatory gesture to the British, including a linkage of the Alaskan boundary dispute or Canadian fishing rights, Hay-Pauncefote II was a measured public expression of American nationalism. Roosevelt fully supported the diction of the treaty even while reassuring his English friends that he conceded the British navy's control of an isthmian canal in time of war. Roosevelt's concession, which was true in 1901, was no longer true in 1905 when the U.S. naval building program and Britain's more pressing interests gave the Americans actual control of the Caribbean.

American concern over Germany's threat also began well before Roosevelt's presidency. When Kaiser Wilhelm II supplanted Chancellor Otto von Bismarck as chief architect of German foreign policy in 1890, Germany abandoned Bismarck's continental strategy and determined to become a world power. German attempts to match Britain's naval power were disastrous to world stability. No matter how brilliant or determined the German plans, Germany could not transcend its geographical limitations nor catch up with Britain's colonial and trade empire nor with its superior industrial capacity. German timing was bad. Both Japan and the United States emerged as new world powers; eventually, Germany's challenge to Britain moved both of the new powers to align with Britain and widen the German gap. German friction with the United States intensified in disputes over food tariffs and American ability to export agricultural products cheaply; likewise in naval skirmishes at Samoa in 1889 and Rio de Janiero in 1893, the German seizure of Kiaochow, China in 1897, and the constant presence of German naval forces in conflict with U.S. interests at Manila Bay and the Caribbean Sea. . . .

Although American fear of Germany, the beginnings of the immense U.S. naval mobilization, a strategic naval board, an isthmian canal commission, and colonial responsibilities in Asia and the Caribbean all began under William McKinley's presidency, it was Theodore Roosevelt who dramatized America's new role as a world power. McKinley was a reluctant statesman; Roosevelt was an exuberant world leader who welcomed the new role for the United States and the new technologies of modernism. As president, TR flew in an early airplane, dived in an early submarine, and embraced the new dreadnought-class big gun battleship. Roosevelt abandoned the fortress-America mentality, fully supported Mahan's concept of offensive sea power, and welcomed the chance to make the United States not just an equal world power but an influential one. Roosevelt possessed geographical advantages the kaiser lacked. He understood that, by exploiting American isolation from European rivalries, the United States could become the center of a new balance of power, neutralizing Germany and tempering British supremacy. He played a decisive role in the Asian struggle between Russia and Japan and the European dispute over Morocco in 1905. Roosevelt's intense nationalism was tempered by his equally important belief in responsibility and a commitment to the concept of civilization. By linking civilization, responsibility, and power, Roosevelt transformed his provincial nation into one with global consciousness, able to influence events not only in the Caribbean but also in Asia and Europe. McKinley was an adept American national leader. Roosevelt became the preeminent world leader of his time and America's most successful globalist, willing and able to prevent wars from becoming world wars by intervening in gesture and word before military force was necessary.

The German threat the Americans feared materialized in 1902, Roosevelt's first full year as president. The Anglo-German intervention of December 1902 [in Venezuela] demonstrated how even friendly European powers little appreciated the symbolism of the Monroe Doctrine, how vulnerable the Americans were to a concert of Europe, and how foolish the Europeans were to even consider such a harebrained scheme. British judgment was skewed by the deaths of Lord Julian Pauncefote, the longtime British ambassador to Washington, and Queen Victoria, followed by King Edward's unexpected illness, the end of the Boer War, Lord Lansdowne's replacement of Lord Salisbury as foreign minister, and the complications of the growing naval race with Germany.

Germany's diplomatic clumsiness matched its opportunistic naval policies. The kaiser hated the Monroe Doctrine and German diplomats referred to America as the United States of North America. To deflect U.S. disapproval of his Venezuelan intervention, the kaiser relied on a silly goodwill visit by his brother Prince Heinrich to Washington in April 1902. Heinrich's visit was a fiasco; the Americans remained wary, and Germany hoped to shift blame for the intervention to Britain. Both European powers proceeded as if the Americans could be easily sidetracked. Lansdowne . . . and the kaiser . . . [both] ignored known American sensitivity to European interventions. Italy joined the intervention through a trade off for concessions in the African colony of Somaliland. Even though Germany did not have enough vessels to effectively blockade Venezuela, let alone seriously challenge the United States, German recklessness—its willingness to proceed even with obvious naval deficiencies—validated American fear of German opportunism. . . .

The American naval maneuvers scheduled in June 1902 at Culebra island, five miles north of Puerto Rico, served a triple purpose. Culebra, the only deep harbor port outside of Guantánamo (still in the process of negotiation with Cuba) which could serve as an effective Caribbean naval base, had to be used, developed, and protected. The U.S. Navy shifted its emphasis from coastal defense and its mainly ceremonial role in scattered outposts throughout the world into a fighting fleet using Alfred Mahan's theories of sea power. Culebra was ideally situated for possible Venezuelan operations. Roosevelt, a master of the symbolic use of naval power and a naval intellectual of long standing, publicized the Culebra maneuvers and put Admiral Dewey, a well-known Germanophobe in charge. But the Germans and British blithely ignored the presence of a U.S. fleet that easily outnumbered the Europeans in the same way they ignored the Monroe Doctrine.

U.S. naval intelligence predicted both the Venezuelan resistance and the European overreaction. Roosevelt with a large navy in strategic and logistical control—and with sufficient supplies of nearby coal—could suddenly switch the U.S. posture from passive onlooker to decisive diplomatic force. The Anglo-Germans were in an untenable position. Venezuela could resist any attempted invasion with impunity. Once the United States aligned with Venezuela against European intervention, the Anglo-German undertaking was doomed. Roosevelt, however, made the most of the opportunity, capitalizing on public reaction to the European show of force to establish the Monroe Doctrine, for the first time, in both principle and practice. Five days after Secretary of State John Hay demanded the end of intervention and the settlement of the dispute by international arbitration—a demand consistent with President Grover Cleveland's Venezuelan policy in 1895—Britain and Germany agreed on December 17, 1902. Prime Minister Arthur Balfour publicly conceded support of the Monroe Doctrine in a speech to Parliament on December 15. The kaiser replaced his American ambassador Theodor von Holleben, with Herman (Speck) von Sternburg, Roosevelt's closest German diplomatic friend. The continuance of the blockade through February and the legal victory of the blockading powers in the Hague Court of Arbitration ruling in 1904 do not diminish the magnitude of Roosevelt's diplomatic victory. He raised European consciousness of American resistance to New World adventurism and made Europe aware that the United States was now an effective world power.

Roosevelt knew exactly what had happened. He used the "speak softly and carry a big stick" phrase in Chicago on April 2, 1903, to describe his foreign policy of defending the Monroe Doctrine and to win more support for a larger navy. Unlike Grover Cleveland, who blustered (effectively), Roosevelt allowed the Europeans to escape gracefully by agreeing to keep the ultimatums off the record and by rebuking Admirals Henry Clay Taylor and Dewey for their anti-German remarks, though he privately sympathized with them.

Although most accounts of the Panama Canal controversies focus on U.S. mistreatment of Colombia, Colombian domestic politics and the changing role of Europe in Central America better explain the breakdown in U.S.-Colombian relations. Carlos Martínez Silva, the first Colombian diplomat to negotiate with the United States about a Panama canal, fully understood Colombia's lost advantage when the Hay-Pauncefote II Treaty eliminated Britain and the leverage Europe provided Latin American nations in their dealings with the United States. Roosevelt, Hay, and Mark

Hanna, the Senate's main Panama route advocate, all realized the importance of removing the French interests before the U.S.-Colombian negotiations began. The diplomatic complications between the United States and Colombia were caused by Colombian domestic conflicts between Liberals and Conservatives, culminating in the War of the Thousand Days (1899–1902), which the United States helped settle at Colombia's request on board the battleship *Wisconsin* on November 21, 1902.

When Colombian President José Marroquín stymied American negotiations for a Panama canal, an opposition rooted in his own resistance to Liberal modern capitalism, Roosevelt made a two-stage change in U.S. policy. Under the terms of the Bidlack-Mallarino Treaty of 1846 between Colombia (then New Granada) and the United States, the U.S. recognized Colombia's sovereignty over Panama in return for an ambiguous "right of transit" across the isthmus. The United States from 1846 to 1902 acted as Colombia's ally, keeping order in Panama and preventing its independence. In its 1902 naval intervention, the United States limited its obligation to keeping the Panama railroad open, even barring Colombian troops from using it—a new policy of neutrality rather than alliance.

The Colombian Senate's 24–0 rejection of the Hay-Herrán Treaty in August 1903 was a challenge to U.S. prestige and ability, reflected in the increasing demands by American newspapers for a strong U.S. response including annexation of Panama. Colombia's demands for part of the $40 million the United States agreed to pay the French Compagnie Nouvelle (for the completed work on the canal and its physical property) underscored the European complications Roosevelt struggled to eliminate. U.S. abhorrence at European involvement in Panama began with Presidents [Rutherford B.] Hayes and [Ulysses S.] Grant and help explain the deep American attachment to an inferior Nicaraguan canal route uncorrupted by French involvement. When Panamanians became convinced in 1903 that the United States would no longer automatically support Colombian hegemony if Panama seceded and Colombia remained intransigent, the Panamanians revolted and Roosevelt shifted U.S. support to Panama.

Colombia responded to Panama's independence by asking Germany to establish a European protectorate against the United States. Germany quickly declined the Colombia intervention, even though just a year before it sought desperately to find a way of controlling the Panama canal. Although U.S. historians focus on Roosevelt's naval intervention in Panama in November 1903 as a questionable extension of U.S. power, Roosevelt's response was measured and effective. Colombia's brinkmanship diplomacy with her only ally was irresponsible and foolhardy. Colombia's only claim to sovereignty over Panama rested in the Bidlack-Mallarino Treaty of 1846. By tradition, geography, and preference, Panama was never an integral part of Colombia. The U.S. Navy provided Panama's main police force, intervening twelve times between 1856 and 1903. But Colombia in 1903 was as indifferent to U.S. wishes as Britain and Germany in 1902—with the same result. The humiliating 24–0 rejection of a treaty it had negotiated, and the constant demands for renegotiation of French and American concessions the Americans considered settled, were caused by the pressures of Colombia's chaotic domestic politics.

By openly challenging the United States when Roosevelt was trying to discourage European involvement in the Caribbean, Colombia made U.S. support of Panamanian independence an attractive option. Nicaragua was not a feasible alternative.

Had Roosevelt taken the Nicaraguan alternative there would be two competing canals in Central America. A partly finished Panama canal and Colombia's unsettled politics might well have transformed the isthmus into a Central American Balkans. The Americans would have been stuck with the inferior canal route, the canal question would have remained unsettled, and Europe would have remained at the center of New World diplomacy. Roosevelt's haste in settling an isthmian canal was essential to the U.S. policy of excluding Europe and eliminating potential trouble spots. Nor could Roosevelt have backed down when Colombia defied the Americans. Backing down for no real purpose (except to appease a confused Colombian leadership that used diplomacy as part of its ongoing domestic revolutions, and remained indifferent to canals, development, or Panama) would have created a fatal inconsistency in Roosevelt's policy to convince Europe that the United States was strong. Historians, who insist that TR could or should have waited patiently, miss the point of U.S. policy. Europe, not Colombia or Latin America, was the reason to resolve the Panama canal issue quickly. Roosevelt originally planned to ask the Senate to approve a unilateral seizure of the canal zone under the American interpretation of the Bidlack-Mallarino Treaty and subsequently let an international arbitration court assess the cost and the question of sovereignty. When he learned from his own intelligence sources that a Panamanian revolution was imminent, Roosevelt supported Philippe Bunau-Varilla's alliance with the Panamanian revolutionaries, a political error which muddied the waters and made Colombia's victimization and later Latin American displeasure the main historical question of TR's Panama policies.

The rape of Panama has remained a popular theme in U.S. and Colombian historiography, but it is time that sentimentality over Colombia's martyrdom be put to rest. Colombia had no real right in Panama from the start. Colombia's subjection of Panama was always based on its obligation to encourage development of a Panama canal in alliance with the United States, the treaty protector of the Colombian-Panama relationship since 1846. When Colombia, distracted by its domestic politics, played foolish games with both the United States and Panama, Roosevelt acted to protect U.S. interests and punish Colombia. His policy was supported by Europeans and Latin Americans, who wanted a canal and welcomed the American ability and willingness to build it. Colombia's argument was with other Colombians. American historians, who make Roosevelt responsible, ignore the real cause of the conflict: the catastrophic disordering of Colombian society in the War of the Thousand Days.

European diplomats were deeply concerned at the breakdown of law and decency in what had been one of Latin America's most civilized nations. French Vice-Consul Pierre Bonhenry, present at the Colombian siege of Colón, credited the United States with preventing a blood bath in Panama, not fomenting a revolution. The Europeans understood the two complementary parts of Roosevelt's Panama policy: support of Panama's independence and U.S. willingness to undertake the building of a Panama Canal, a monumental engineering challenge which eventually cost $340 million, took ten years to complete, and transformed the Latin American economy.

U.S. historiography has overemphasized Latin American disaffection. Latin American problems were rooted in the traditions of Spanish and Catholic authoritarianism, compounded by nineteenth-century experiments with European positivism, caudillo localism, and constant struggles between positivist liberals and conservative Catholics. By Theodore Roosevelt's time, Latin America had failed to become politically, culturally, or economically self-sufficient. . . .

In 1903 Latin America was peripheral to U.S. policy. The United States needed to keep Germany from exploiting Latin American weakness as a springboard to regional domination and as a threat to Balkanize the Caribbean. Colombia, the Dominican Republic, Venezuela, and Cuba, were all adept at playing the European card—one power or creditor against the other with the United States as the ultimate wild card to play when the Europeans tired of the game and threatened intervention. When Roosevelt took Europe out of Latin America, he did in fact disarm it by removing the only weapon that weak Latin American governments had been able to use effectively. But Roosevelt did not make Latin America dependent. Colombia, after the loss of Panama and even before the discovery of oil, was stronger than it was before, economically and politically. What made Latin America weak was not the colossus to the North but its traditions of Spanish authoritarianism, its romance with French intellectual elitism in the nineteenth century, its ill-defined political borders and heterogeneous populations, and the same problems in coping with modernist thought and technology that bedevilled the industrial powers. . . .

It is time to put the devil theories to rest. Roosevelt was successful in ending European activism in Latin America. He never used or intended to use the "big stick" against Latin America. He did not need to. Latin America was too weak to require a big stick. Until the discovery of oil changed its status, there was not enough of economic consequence to tempt Europe to fight the United States for it. Nor did Roosevelt lose Latin America; it was never Roosevelt's to lose. The inequities of the disparity between North American wealth and political unity and Latin American poverty and political disunity continue to frustrate Latin [American] intellectuals who have blamed Spain, Bolívar, Europe, and the United States for Latin America's problems. Latin American governments have proven more adept at manipulating whatever power was dominant than American historians or Latin American writers have given them credit for. TR makes a convenient Protestant devil, useful for a culture with a genius for magical realism. American historians should stop making this useful fiction into inaccurate history.

F U R T H E R   R E A D I N G

Stuart Anderson, *Race and Rapprochement: Anglo-Saxonism and Anglo-American Relations, 1895–1904* (1981)

Louis Auchinloss, *Theodore Roosevelt* (2001)

Gail Bederman, *Manliness and Civilization* (1995)

Mark T. Berger, *Under Northern Eyes* (1995)

H. W. Brands, *TR: The Last Romantic* (1997)

Bruce Calder, *The Impact of Intervention: The Dominican Republic During the U.S. Occupation, 1916–1924* (1984)

Raymond Carr, *Puerto Rico* (1984)

Arturo M. Carrión, *Puerto Rico* (1983)

Richard H. Collin, "Symbiosis versus Hegemony: New Directions in the Foreign Relations Historiography of Theodore Roosevelt and William Howard Taft," *Diplomatic History,* 19 (Summer 1995), 473–498

——, *Theodore Roosevelt, Culture, Diplomacy, and Expansionism* (1985)

Pedro Cabán, *Constructing a Colonial People* (1999) (on Puerto Rico)
———, *Theodore Roosevelt's Caribbean: The Panama Canal, the Monroe Doctrine, and the Latin American Context* (1990)
Michael L. Conniff, *Panama and the United States* (1992)
John M. Cooper Jr., *The Warrior and the Priest: Woodrow Wilson and Theodore Roosevelt* (1983)
Marcos Cueto, *Missionaries of Science: The Rockefeller Foundation in Latin America* (1994)
Kathleen Dalton, *Theodore Roosevelt* (2002)
Aida Donald, *Lion in the White House* (2007) (on TR)
Paul J. Dosal, *Doing Business with Dictators: A Political History of United Fruit Company in Guatemala, 1899–1944* (1993)
Paul W. Drake, *Money Doctors, Foreign Debts, and Economic Reforms in Latin America* (1994)
Thomas G. Dyer, *Theodore Roosevelt and the Idea of Race* (1980)
Raymond A. Esthus, *Theodore Roosevelt and the International Rivalries* (1970)
———, *Double Eagle and the Rising Sun* (1988)
Joseph A. Fry, "In Search of an Orderly World," in John M. Carroll and George C. Herring, eds., *Modern American Diplomacy* (1986), pp. 1–20
Piero Gleijeses, *Shattered Hope* (1991) (on Guatemala)
Lewis L. Gould, *The Presidency of Theodore Roosevelt* (1991)
Julie Greene, *The Canal Builders* (2009) (on labor in Panama)
John Mason Hart, *Empire and Revolution* (2002) (on Mexico)
David Healy, *Drive to Hegemony: The United States in the Caribbean, 1898–1917* (1988)
James R. Holmes, *Theodore Roosevelt and World Order* (2006)
Gerald Horne, *Black and Brown* (2005) (on race and U.S.-Mexican relations)
Michael H. Hunt, *Ideology and U.S. Foreign Policy* (1987)
Richard L. Lael, *Arrogant Diplomacy: U.S. Policy Toward Colombia, 1903–1922* (1987)
Walter LaFeber, *The American Search for Opportunity* (1993)
———, *Inevitable Revolutions: The United States in Central America* (1993)
———, *The Panama Canal* (1989)
Lester D. Langley, *The Banana Wars* (1983)
———, *The United States and the Caribbean in the Twentieth Century* (1985)
Lester Langley and Thomas Schoonover, *The Banana Men* (1995) (on Central America)
Kyle Longley, *The Sparrow and the Hawk* (1997) (on the United States and Costa Rica)
John Major, *Prize Possession: The U.S. and the Panama Canal, 1903–1979* (1993)
David McCullough, *The Path Between the Seas: The Creation of the Panama Canal, 1870–1914* (1977)
Frederick Marks, *Velvet on Iron: The Diplomacy of Theodore Roosevelt* (1979)
Nancy Mitchell, *The Danger of Dreams* (1999) (on Germany and the United States)
Edmund Morris, *Theodore Rex* (2001)
Thomas O'Brien, *The Revolutionary Mission: American Business in Latin America, 1900–1945* (1996)
Louis A. Pérez Jr., *Cuba Between Reform and Revolution* (1988)
———, *Cuba in the American Imagination* (2008)
———, *Cuba Under the Platt Amendment* (1990)
Brenda Gail Plummer, *Haiti and the Great Powers* (1988)
———, *Haiti and the United States* (1992)
Stephen J. Randall, *Colombia and the United States* (1992)
Mary Renda, *Taking Haiti* (2001)
Ramón Ruíz, *The Making of a Revolution* (1968) (on Mexico)
Gregory Russell, *The Statecraft of Theodore Roosevelt* (2009)
Thomas D. Schoonover, *The United States in Central America, 1860–1911* (1991)
David Spurr, *The Rhetoric of Empire* (1993)
Cyrus Veeser, "Inventing Dollar Diplomacy: The Gilded Age Origins of the Roosevelt Corollary to the Monroe Doctrine," *Diplomatic History,* 27 (June 2003), 301–326
Sarah Watts, *Rough Rider in the White House* (2003)

Woodrow Wilson, the First World War, and the League Fight

In August 1914, Europe descended into war. Then an imperial power and an active trader on the high seas, the United States became ensnared in a deadly conflict. Until April 1917, however, President Woodrow Wilson struggled to define policies that would protect U.S. interests and principles, end the carnage, and permit him to influence the peace settlement. The president protested violations of U.S. neutral rights that interrupted trade and took human life (dramatized by the sinking of the Lusitania *by a German submarine in May 1915) and offered to mediate a "peace without victory." Britain's naval blockade of the continent meanwhile directed the bulk of U.S. cargo to British ports, provoking Germany to denounce the trade as not neutral. When his peace advocacy faltered and Germany launched unrestricted submarine warfare, Wilson asked a divided but ultimately supportive Congress for a declaration of war.*

Once the United States became a belligerent, Wilson strove not only to win the war but also to shape the peace. He called for a nonvindictive peace treaty and urged the creation of an association of nations, the League of Nations, to deter war. The president's Fourteen Points outlined his plans for shelving balance-of-power politics in favor of disarmament, the self-determination of nations, and open diplomacy. Having tipped the balance in favor of the Allies, the United States helped to force Germany to surrender on November 11, 1918. In January of the following year, Wilson journeyed to Versailles Palace near Paris to negotiate a peace treaty and a covenant for the League of Nations that he believed would sustain a world order.

At home, however, many Americans questioned Wilson's handling of foreign policy, especially after they learned that he had compromised many of his principles at the conference to win approval for his League. Republican leaders, who had defeated Democrats in the 1918 congressional elections, calculated that the Democrat Wilson had become politically vulnerable. Supreme nationalists feared that an international organization would undermine American sovereignty and violate George Washington's venerable advice to avoid permanent alliances. Anti-imperialists noted that the Treaty of Versailles had not included provisions for the dismantling of European empires. Wilson battled back, denouncing the naysayers as narrow-minded, backward-looking people who did not understand humanity's demand for a new world order. He refused to abandon the collective security provision of Article 10 of the League Covenant. Unwilling to bargain with senators who demanded "reservations" (amendments), opposed to "irreconcilables" who rejected the League outright, and laid low by a debilitating stroke suffered in the summer of 1919, Wilson lost the fight. The Senate rejected the treaty and U.S. membership in the League of Nations.

America's participation in the First World War further elevated the nation to great-power status and enshrined many of Wilson's ideals as the cornerstone of U.S. foreign policy. Thus, it is not surprising that scholars have disagreed strongly in assessing "Wilsonianism." Some have praised Wilson for his breadth of vision, his willingness to make America assume a leadership role in world affairs, and his noble crusade against power politics. Others have labeled Wilson an impractical idealist, whose moralism led him to adopt an inconsistent neutrality in the early stages of the war, to underestimate the great-power nationalism of the Allies at war's end, and to render people of color residing in colonial areas incapable of governing themselves. Still others have analyzed the impact of partisan politics, the adversarial relationship between the executive and legislative branches of the U.S. governments, and Wilson's deteriorating health to explain the ultimate failure of Wilsonian diplomacy. Should Wilson be credited with designing a multilateral system that, once adopted after World War II, preserved the peace for over half a century? Or was Wilson's principal legacy the flawed Versailles treaty, which unwisely punished Germany, left the United States absent from the League of Nations, set the stage for the Second World War, and dodged the all-important issue of decolonization? To grapple with Wilsonianism and its legacy is to reach for an understanding of America's place in twentieth-century world affairs.

🌐 D O C U M E N T S

When a German U-boat sank the British liner *Lusitania* on May 7, 1915, killing 1,198, including 128 Americans, President Woodrow Wilson sent a strong note to Berlin. The May 13 warning, Document 1, demands that Germany disavow submarine warfare and respect the right of Americans to sail on the high seas. In January 1917, Germany declared unrestricted submarine warfare, and Wilson broke diplomatic relations with Berlin. On April 2, after the sinking of several American vessels, the president asked Congress for a declaration of war. His war message, Document 2, outlines U.S. grievances against Germany. One of the few dissenters in the Senate—the war measure passed, 82 to 6—was Robert M. La Follette of Wisconsin. In his speech of April 4, Document 3, the great reform politician reveals his fear of an American "war machine."

President Wilson issued his Fourteen Points in a speech on January 8, 1918, reprinted here as Document 4. Articles 10 through 16 of the Covenant of the League of Nations hammered out at the Paris Peace Conference in 1919 are included as Document 5. Wilson explained during his busy western U.S. speaking tour in September 1919 that these provisions would prevent wars. Excerpts from his speeches are featured in Document 6. Led by Senator Henry Cabot Lodge of Massachusetts, critics worked to add "reservations" to the covenant through a Lodge resolution dated November 19, 1919, Document 7. But neither an amended peace treaty (which contained the covenant) nor an unamended treaty passed the Senate.

Wilsonianism inflamed passions far beyond U.S. borders. Advocates of self-determination in colonial areas took umbrage when the great powers refused to consider decolonization at Versailles in 1919. In Document 8, an excerpt from his *The Youth Movement in China* (1927), the Chinese educator and nationalist Tsi C. Wang recalls the historic May Fourth protest against the transfer of Germany's concessions at Jiaozhou (Kiaochow) and Qingdao (Tsing-tao) on the Shandong (Shantung) peninsula in northern China to arch-rival Japan. The student-led uprising pressured the divided Chinese government to reject the Treaty of Versailles in June of that year and marked the radicalization of modern Chinese nationalism.

D O C U M E N T   1

The First *Lusitania* Note Demands That Germany Halt Submarine Warfare, 1915

The Government of the United States has been apprised that the Imperial German Government considered themselves to be obliged by the extraordinary circumstances of the present war and the measures adopted by their adversaries in seeking to cut Germany off from all commerce, to adopt methods of retaliation which go much beyond the ordinary methods of warfare at sea, in the proclamation of a war zone from which they have warned neutral ships to keep away. This Government has already taken occasion to inform the Imperial German Government that it cannot admit the adoption of such measures or such a warning of danger to operate as in any degree an abbreviation of the rights of American shipmasters or of American citizens bound on lawful errands as passengers on merchant ships of belligerent nationality: and that it must hold the Imperial German Government to a strict accountability for any infringement of those rights, intentional or incidental. It does not understand the Imperial German Government to question those rights. It assumes, on the contrary, that the Imperial Government accept, as of course, the rule that the lives of noncombatants, whether they be of neutral citizenship or citizens of one of the nations at war, can not lawfully or rightfully be put in jeopardy by the capture or destruction of an unarmed merchantman, and recognize also, as all other nations do, the obligation to take the usual precaution of visit and search to ascertain whether a suspected merchantman is in fact of belligerent nationality or is in fact carrying contraband of war under a neutral flag.

The Government of the United States, therefore, desires to call the attention of the Imperial German Government with the utmost earnestness to the fact that the objection to their present method of attack against the trade of their enemies lies in the practical impossibility of employing submarines in the destruction of commerce without disregarding those rules of fairness, reason, justice. and humanity, which all modern opinion regards as imperative. It is practically impossible for the officers of a submarine to visit a merchantman at sea and examine her papers and cargo. It is practically impossible for them to make a prize of her; and, if they can not put a prize crew on board of her, they can not sink her without leaving her crew and all on board of her to the mercy of the sea in her small boats. These facts it is understood the Imperial

This document can he found in U.S. Department of State, *Papers Relating to the Foreign Relations of the United States, 1915. Supplement* (Washington, D.C.: Government Printing Office, 1928), 393–396.

German Government frankly admit. We are informed that, in the instances of which we have spoken, time enough for even that poor measure of safety was not given, and in at least two of the cases cited, not so much as a warning was received. Manifestly submarines can not be used against merchantmen, as the last few weeks have shown, without an inevitable violation of many sacred principles of justice and humanity.

American citizens act within their indisputable rights in taking their ships and in traveling wherever their legitimate business calls them upon the high seas, and exercise those rights in what should be the well-justified confidence that their lives will not be endangered by acts done in clear violation of universally acknowledged international obligations, and certainly in the confidence that their own Government will sustain them in the exercise of their rights.

🌐 D O C U M E N T   2

President Woodrow Wilson Asks Congress to Declare War Against Germany, 1917

On the third of February last I officially laid before you the extraordinary announcement of the Imperial German Government that on and after the first day of February it was its purpose to put aside all restraints of law of humanity and use its submarines to sink every vessel that sought to approach either the ports of Great Britain and Ireland or the western coasts of Europe or any of the ports controlled by the enemies of Germany within the Mediterranean. That had seemed to be the object of the German submarine warfare earlier in the war, but since April of last year the Imperial Government had somewhat restrained the commanders of its undersea craft in confomity with its promise then given to us that passenger boats should not be sunk and that due warning would be given to all other vessels which its submarines might seek to destroy, when no resistance was offered or escape attempted, and care taken that their crews were given at least a fair chance to save their lives in their open boats. The precautions taken were meagre and haphazard enough, as was proved in distressing instance after instance in the progress of the cruel and unmanly business, but a certain degree of restraint was observed. The new policy has swept every restriction aside. Vessels of every kind, whatever their flag, their character, their cargo, their destination, their errand, have been ruthlessly sent to the bottom without warning and without thought of help or mercy for those on board, the vessels of friendly neutrals along with those of belligerents. Even hospital ships and ships carrying relief to the sorely bereaved and stricken people of Belgium, though the latter were provided with safe conduct through the proscribed areas by the German Government itself and were distinguished by unmistakable marks of identity, have been sunk with the same reckless lack of compassion or of principle.

I was for a little while unable to believe that such things would in fact be done by any government that had hitherto subscribed to the humane practices of civilized nations. International law had its origin in the attempt to set up some law which would be respected and observed upon the seas, where no nation had right of dominion

---

This document can he found in *Congressional Record,* LV (April 2, 1917), Part 1, 102–104.

where lay the free highways of the world. By painful stage after stage has that law been built up, with meagre enough results, indeed, after all was accomplished that could be accomplished, but always with a clear view, at least of what the heart and conscience of mankind demanded. This minimum of right the German Government has swept aside under the plea of retaliation and necessity and because it had no weapons which it could use at sea except these which it is impossible to employ as it is employing them without throwing to the winds all scruples of humanity or of respect for the understandings that were supposed to underlie the intercourse of the world. I am not now thinking, of the loss of property involved, immense and serious as that is, but only of the wanton and wholesale destruction of the lives of noncombatants, men, women, and children, engaged in pursuits which have always, even in the darkest periods of modern history, been deemed innocent and legitimate. Property can be paid for; the lives of peaceful and innocent people cannot be. The present German submarine warfare against commerce is a warfare against mankind.

It is a war against all nations. American ships have been sunk, American lives taken, in ways which it has stirred us very deeply to learn of, but the ships and people of other neutral and friendly nations have been sunk and overwhelmed in the waters in the same way. There has been no discrimination. The challenge is to all mankind. Each nation must decide for itself how it will meet it. The choice we make for ourselves must be made with a moderation of counsel and a temperateness of judgment befitting our character and our motives as a nation. We must put excited feeling away. Our motive will not be revenge or the victorious assertion of the physical might of the nation, but only the vindication of right, of human right, of which we are only a single champion. . . .

With a profound sense of the solemn and even tragical character of the step I am taking and of the grave responsibilities which it involves, but in unhesitating obedience to what I deem my constitutional duty, I advise that the Congress declare the recent course of the Imperial German Government to be in fact nothing less than war against the government and people of the United States; that it formally accept the status of belligerent which has thus been thrust upon it; and that it take immediate steps not only to put the country in a more thorough state of defense but also to exert all its power and employ all its resources to bring the Government of the German Empire to terms and end the war. . . .

Does not every American feel that assurance has been added to our hope for the future peace of the world by the wonderful and heartening things that have been happening within the last few weeks in Russia? Russia was known by those who knew it best to have been always in fact democratic at heart, in all the vital habits of her thought, in all the intimate relationships of her people that spoke their natural instinct, their habitual attitude towards life. The autocracy that crowned the summit of her political structure, long as it had stood and terrible as was the reality of its power, was not in fact Russian in origin, character, or purpose; and now it has been shaken off and the great, generous Russian people have been added in all their naive majesty and might to the forces that are fighting for freedom in the world, for justice, and for peace. Here is a fit partner for a League of Honour.

One of the things that has served to convince us that the Prussian autocracy was not and could never be our friends is that from the very outset of the present war it has filled our unsuspecting communities and even our offices of government with spies and set criminal intrigues everywhere afoot against our national unity of counsel, our peace within and without, our industries and our commerce. . . . That it means to stir up enemies against us at our very doors the intercepted note to the German Minister at Mexico City [the Zimmerman telegram] is eloquent evidence.

We are accepting this challenge of hostile purpose because we know that in such a government, following such methods, we can never have a friend; and that in the presence of its organized power, always lying in wait to accomplish we know not what purpose, there can be no assured security for the democratic governments of the world. We are now about to accept gauge of battle with its natural foe to liberty and shall, if necessary, spend the whole force of the nation to check and nullify its pretensions and its power. We are glad, now that we see the facts with no veil of false pretence about them, to fight thus for the ultimate peace of the world and for the liberation of its peoples, the German peoples included: for the rights of nations great and small and the privilege of men everywhere to choose their way of life and of obedience. The world must be made safe for democracy. . . .

It is a distressing and oppressive duty, Gentlemen of the Congress, which I have performed in thus addressing you. There are, it may be, many months of fiery trial and sacrifice ahead of us. It is a fearful thing to lead this great peaceful people into war, into the most terrible and disastrous of all wars, civilization itself seeming to be in the balance. But the right is more precious than peace, and we shall fight for the things which we have always carried nearest our hearts—for democracy, for the right of those who submit to authority to have a voice in their own governments, for the rights and liberties of small nations, for a universal dominion of right by such a concert of free peoples as shall bring peace and safety to all nations and make the world itself at last free. To such a task we can dedicate our lives and our fortunes, everything that we are and everything that we have, with the pride of those who know that the day has come when America is privileged to spend her blood and her might for the principles that gave her birth and happiness and the peace which she has treasured. God helping her, she can do no other.

DOCUMENT 3

Senator Robert M. La Follette
Voices His Dissent, 1917

The poor, sir, who are the ones called upon to rot in the trenches, have no organized power, have no press to voice their will upon this question of peace or war; but, oh, Mr. President, at some time they will be heard. I hope and I believe they will be heard in an orderly and a peaceful way. I think they may be heard from before long. I think, sir, if we take this step, when the people to-day who are staggering under the burden of supporting families at the present prices of the necessaries of the life find those prices multiplied, when they are raised a hundred percent, or 200 percent, as they will be quickly, aye, sir, when beyond that those who pay taxes come to have their taxes doubled and again doubled to pay the interest on the nontaxable bonds held by Morgan and his combinations, which have been issued to meet this war,

This document can he found in *Congressional Record*, LV (April 4, 1917), Part I, 226, 228.

there will come an awakening; they will have their day and they will be heard. It will be as certain and as inevitable as the return of the tides, and as resistless, too. . . .

Just a word of comment more upon one of the points in the President's address. He says that this is a war "for the things which we have always carried nearest to our hearts—for democracy, for the right of those who submit to authority to have a voice in their own government." In many places throughout the address is this exalted sentiment given expression. . . .

But the President proposes alliance with Great Britain, which, however liberty-loving its people, is a hereditary monarchy, with a hereditary ruler, with a hereditary House of Lords, with a hereditary landed system, with a limited and restricted suffrage for one class and a multiplied suffrage power for another, and with grinding industrial conditions for all the wageworkers. The President has not suggested that we make our support of Great Britain conditional to her granting home rule to Ireland, or Egypt, or India. We rejoice in the establishment of a democracy in Russia, but it will hardly be contended that if Russia was still an autocratic Government, we would not be asked to enter this alliance with her just the same. Italy and the lesser powers of Europe, Japan in the Orient; in fact all of the countries with whom we are to enter into alliance, except France and newly revolutionized Russia, are still of the old order—and it will be generally conceded that no one of them has done as much for its people in the solution of municipal problems and in securing social and industrial reforms as Germany. . . .

Who has registered the knowledge or approval of the American people of the course this Congress is called upon in declaring war upon Germany? Submit the question to the people, you who support it. You who support it dare not do it, for you know that by a vote of more than ten to one the American people as a body would register their declaration against it.

In the sense that this war is being forced upon our people without their knowing why and without their approval, and that wars are usually forced upon all peoples in the same way, there is some truth in the statement; but I venture to say that the response which the German people have made to the demands of this war shows that it has a degree of popular support which the war upon which we are entering has not and never will have among our people. The espionage bills, the conscription bills, and other forcible military measures which we understand are being ground out of the war machine in this country is the complete proof that those responsible for this war fear that it has no popular support and that armies sufficient to satisfy the demand of the entente allies can not be recruited by voluntary enlistments.

DOCUMENT 4

Wilson Proclaims U.S. War Aims: The Fourteen Points, 1918

I. Open covenants of peace, openly arrived at, after which there shall be no private international understandings of any kind but diplomacy shall proceed always frankly and in the public view.

This document can be found in *Congressional Record,* LVI (January 8, 1918), Part 1, 680–682.

II. Absolute freedom of navigation upon the seas, outside territorial waters, alike in peace and in war, except as the seas may be closed in whole or in part by international action for the enforcement of international covenants.

III. The removal, so far as possible, of all economic barriers and the establishment of an equality of trade conditions among all the nations consenting to the peace and associating themselves for its maintenance.

IV. Adequate guarantees given and taken that national armaments will be reduced to the lowest point consistent with domestic safety.

V. A free, open-minded, and absolutely impartial adjustment of all colonial claims, based upon a strict observance of the principle that in determining all such questions of sovereignty the interests of the populations concerned must have equal weight with the equitable claims of the government whose title is to be determined.

VI. The evacuation of all Russian territory and such a settlement of all questions affecting Russia as will secure the best and freest cooperation of the other nations of the world in obtaining for her an unhampered and unembarrassed opportunity for the independent determination of her own political development and national policy and assure her of a sincere welcome into the society of free nations under institutions of her own choosing; and, more than a welcome, assistance also of every kind that she may need and may herself desire. The treatment accorded Russia by her sister nations in the months to come will be the acid test of their good will, of their comprehension of her needs as distinguished from their own interests, and of their intelligent and unselfish sympathy.

VII. Belgium, the whole world will agree, must be evacuated and restored, without any attempt to limit the sovereignty which she enjoys in common with all other free nations. No other single act will serve as this will serve to restore confidence among the nations in the laws which they have themselves set and determined for the government of their relations with one another. Without this healing act the whole structure and validity of international law is forever impaired.

VIII. All French territory should be freed and the invaded portions restored, and the wrong done to France by Prussia in 1871 in the matter of Alsace-Lorraine, which has unsettled the peace of the world for nearly fifty years, should be righted, in order that peace may once more be made secure in the interest of all.

IX. A readjustment of the frontiers of Italy should be effected along clearly recognizable lines of nationality.

X. The peoples of Austria-Hungary, whose place among the nations we wish to see safeguarded and assured, should be accorded the freest opportunity of autonomous development.

XI. Rumania, Serbia, and Montenegro should be evacuated; occupied territories restored; Serbia accorded free and secure access to the sea; and the relations of the several Balkan states to one another determined by friendly consul along historically established lines of allegiance and nationality; and international guarantees of the political and economic independence and territorial integrity of the several Balkan states should be entered into.

XII. The Turkish portions of the present Ottoman Empire should be assured a secure sovereignty, but the other nationalities which are now under Turkish rule should be assured an undoubted security of life and an absolutely unmolested opportunity of autonomous development, and the Dardanelles should be permanently opened as a free passage to the ships and commerce of all nations under international guarantees.

XIII. An independent Polish state should be erected which should include the territories inhabited by indisputably Polish populations, which should be assured a free and secure access to the sea, and whose political and economic independence and territorial integrity should be guaranteed by international covenant.

XIV. A general association of nations must be formed under specific covenants for the purpose of affording mutual guarantees of political independence and territorial integrity to great and small states alike.

DOCUMENT 5

Articles 10 Through 16 of the
League of Nations Covenant, 1919

Article 10. The Members of the League undertake to respect and preserve as against external aggression the territorial integrity and existing political independence of all Members of the League. In case of any such aggression or in case of any threat or danger of such aggression the Council shall advise upon the means by which this obligation shall be fulfilled.

Article 11. Any war or threat of war, whether immediately affecting any of the Members of the League or not, is hereby declared a matter of concern to the whole League, and the League shall take any action that may be deemed wise and effectual to safeguard the peace of nations. . . .

It is also declared to be the friendly right of each Member of the League to bring to the attention of the Assembly or of the Council any circumstance whatever affecting international relations which threatens to disturb international peace or the good understanding between nations upon which peace depends.

Article 12. The Members of the League agree that if there should arise between them any dispute likely to lead to a rupture, they will submit the matter either to arbitration or to inquiry by the Council, and they agree in no case to resort to war until three months after the award by the arbitrators or the report by the Council.

In any case under this Article the award of the arbitrators shall be made within a reasonable time, and the report of the Council shall be made within six months after the submission of the dispute.

Article 13. The Members of the League agree that whenever any dispute shall arise between them which they recognise to be suitable for submission to arbitration and which cannot be satisfactorily settled by diplomacy, they will submit the whole subject-matter to arbitration. . . .

This document can be found in U.S. Department of State, *Papers Relating to the Foreign Relations of the United States, 1919* (Washington, D.C.: Government Printing Office, 1942–1947), XIII, 83–89.

Article 14.   The Council shall formulate and submit to the Members of the League for adoption plans for the establishment of a Permanent Court of International Justice. The Court shall be competent to hear and determine any dispute of an international character which the parties thereto submit to it. The Court may also give an advisory opinion upon any dispute or question referred to it by the Council or by the Assembly.

Article 15.   If there should arise between Members of the League any dispute likely to lead to a rupture, which is not submitted to arbitration in accordance with Article 13, the Members of the League agree that they will submit the matter to the Council. . . .

Article 16.   Should any Member of the League resort to war in disregard of its covenants under Articles 12, 13 or 15, it shall *ipso facto* be deemed to have committed an act of war against all other Members of the League, which hereby undertake immediately to subject it to the severance of all trade or financial relations, the prohibition of all intercourse between their nationals and the nationals of the covenant-breaking State, and the prevention of all financial, commercial or personal intercourse between the nationals of the covenant-breaking State and the nationals of any other State, whether a Member of the League or not.

It shall be the duty of the Council in such case to recommend to the several Governments concerned what effective military, naval or air force the Members of the League shall severally contribute to the armed forces to be used to protect the covenants of the League.

🌐 D O C U M E N T   6

Wilson Defends the Peace Treaty and League, 1919
Indianapolis, Indiana, September 4

You have heard a great deal about article 10 of the covenant of the league of nations. Article 10 speaks the conscience of the world. Article 10 is the article which goes to the heart of this whole bad business, for that article says that the members of this league, that is intended to be all the great nations of the world, engage to respect and to preserve against all external aggression the territorial integrity and political independence of the nations concerned. That promise is necessary in order to prevent this sort of war from recurring, and we are absolutely discredited if we fought this war and then neglect the essential safeguard against it. You have heard it said, my fellow citizens, that we are robbed of some degree of our sovereign independent choice by articles of that sort. Every man who makes a choice to respect the rights of his neighbors deprives himself of absolute sovereignty, but he does it by promising never to do wrong, and I can not for one see anything that robs me of any inherent right that I ought to retain when I promise that I will do right, when I promise that I will respect the thing which, being disregarded

This document can he found in *Congressional Record,* LVIII (September 1919): Part 5, 5001–5002, 5005; Part 6, 5593, 6244–6245, 6249, 6254; Part 7, 6417, 6422.

and violated, brought on a war in which millions of men lost their lives, in which the civilization of mankind was in the balance, in which there was the most outrageous exhibition ever witnessed in the history of mankind of the rapacity and disregard for right of a great armed people. We engage in the first sentence of article 10 to respect and preserve from external aggression the territorial integrity and the existing political independence not only of the other member States, but of all States, and if any member of the league of nations disregards that promise, then what happens? The council of the league advises what should be done to enforce the respect for that covenant on the part of the nation attempting to violate it, and there is no compulsion upon us to take that advice except the compulsion of our good conscience and judgment. So that it is perfectly evident that if in the judgment of the people of the United States the council adjudged wrong and that this was not a case of the use of force, there would be no necessity on the part of the Congress of the United States to vote the use of force. But there could be no advice of the council on any such subject without a unanimous vote, and the unanimous vote includes our own, and if we accepted the advice we would be accepting our own advice, for I need not tell you that the representatives of the Government of the United States would not vote without instructions from their Government at home, and that what we united in advising we could be certain that the American people would desire to do. There is in that covenant not only not a surrender of the independent judgment of the Government of the United States, but an expression of it, because that independent judgment would have to join with the judgment of the rest.

But when is that judgment going to be expressed, my fellow citizens? Only after it is evident that every other resource has failed, and I want to call your attention to the central machinery of the league of nations. If any member of that league or any nation not a member refuses to submit the question at issue either to arbitration or to discussion by the council, there ensues automatically, by the engagements of this covenant, an absolute economic boycott. There will be no trade with that nation by any member of the league. There will be no interchange of communication by post or telegraph. There will be no travel to or from that nation. Its borders will be closed. No citizen of any other State will be allowed to enter it and no one of its citizens will be allowed to leave it. It will be hermetically sealed by the united action of the most powerful nations in the world. And if this economic boycott bears with unequal weight, the members of the league agree to support one another and to relieve one another in any exceptional disadvantages that may arise out of it. . . .

I want to call your attention, if you will turn it up when you go home, to article 11, following article 10 of the covenant of the league of nations. That article, let me say, is the favorite article in the treaty, so far as I am concerned. It says that every matter which is likely to affect the peace of the world is everybody's business; that it shall be the friendly right of any nation to call attention in the league to anything that is likely to affect the peace of the world or the good understanding between nations, upon which the peace of the world depends, whether that matter immediately concerns the nation drawing attention to it or not.

St. Louis, Missouri, September 5

There can hereafter be no secret treaties. There were nations represented around that board—I mean the hoard at which the commission on the league of nations sat, where 14 nations were represented—there were nations represented around that board who had entered into many a secret treaty and understanding, and they made not the least objection to promising that hereafter no secret treaty should have any validity whatever. The provision of the covenant is that every treaty or international understanding shall be registered, I believe the word is, with the general secretary of the league, that the general secretary shall publish it in full just so soon as it is possible for him to publish it, and that no treaty shall be valid which is not thus registered. It is like our arrangements with regard to mortgages on real estate, that until they are registered nobody else need pay any attention to them. And so with the treaties; until they are registered in this office of the league nobody, not even the parties themselves, can insist upon their execution. You have cleared the deck thereby of the most dangerous thing and the most embarrassing thing that has hitherto existed in international politics.

Sioux Falls, South Dakota, September 8

I can not understand the psychology of men who are resisting it [the treaty]. I can not understand what they are afraid of, unless it is that they know physical force and do not understand moral force. Moral force is a great deal more powerful than physical. Govern the sentiments of mankind and you govern mankind. Govern their fears, govern their hopes, determine their fortunes, get them together in concerted masses, and the whole thing sways like a team. Once get them suspecting one another, once get them antagonizing one another, and society itself goes to pieces. We are trying to make a society instead of a set of barbarians out of the governments of the world. I sometimes think, when I wake in the night, of all the wakeful nights that anxious fathers and mothers and friends have spent during those weary years of this awful war, and I seem to hear the cry, the inarticulate cry of mothers all over the world, millions of them on the other side of the sea and thousands of them on this side of the sea, "In God's name, give us the sensible and hopeful and peaceful processes of right and of justice."

America can stay out, but I want to call you to witness that the peace of the world can not be established without America. America is necessary to the peace of the world. And reverse the proposition: The peace and good will of the world are necessary to America. Disappoint the world, center its suspicion upon you, make it feel that you are hot and jealous rivals of the other nations, and do you think you are going to do as much business with them as you would otherwise do? I do not like to put the thing on that plane, my fellow countrymen, but if you want to talk business, I can talk business. If you want to put it on the low plane of how much money you can make, you can make more money out of friendly traders than out of hostile traders. You can make more money out of men who trust you than out of men who fear you.

San Francisco, California, September 17

The Monroe doctrine means that if any outside power, any power outside this hemisphere, tries to impose its will upon any portion of the Western Hemisphere the United States is at liberty to act independently and alone in repelling the aggression; that it does not have to wait for the action of the league of nations; that it does not have to wait for anything but the action of its own administration and its own Congress. This is the first time in the history of international diplomacy that any great government has acknowledged the validity of the Monroe doctrine. Now for the first time all the great fighting powers of the world except Germany, which for the time being has ceased to be a great fighting power, acknowledge the validity of the Monroe doctrine and acknowledge it as part of the international practice of the world.

They [critics] are nervous about domestic questions. They say, "It is intolerable to think that the league of nations should interfere with domestic questions," and whenever they begin to specify they speak of the question of immigration, of the question of naturalization, of the question of the tariff. My fellow citizens, no competent or authoritative student of international law would dream of maintaining that these were anything but exclusively domestic questions, and the covenant of the league expressly provides that the league can take no action whatever about matters which are in the practice of international law regarded as domestic questions.

San Francisco, California, September 18

In order that we may not forget, I brought with me the figures as to what this war [First World War] meant to the world. This is a body of business men and you will understand these figures. They are too big for the imagination of men who do not handle big things. Here is the cost of the war in money, exclusive of what we loaned one another: Great Britain and her dominions, $38,000,000,000; France, $26,000,000,000; the United States, $22,000,000,000 (this is the direct cost of our operations); Russia, $18,000,000,000; Italy, $13,000,000,000; and the total, including Belgium, Japan, and other countries, $123,000,000,000. This is what it cost the Central Powers: Germany, $39,000,000,000, the biggest single item; Austria-Hungary, $21,000,000,000; Turkey and Bulgaria, $3,000,000,000; a total of $63,000,000,000, and a grand total of direct war costs of $186,000,000,000—almost the capital of the world. The expenditures of the United States were at the rate of $1,000,000 an hour for two years, including nighttime with daytime. The battle deaths during the war were as follows: Russia lost in dead 1,700,000 men, poor Russia that got nothing but terror and despair out of it all; Germany, 1,600,000; France, 1,385,000; Great Britain, 900,000; Austria, 800,000; Italy, 364,000; the United States, 50,300 dead. The total for all the belligerents, 7,450,200 men—just about seven and a half million killed because we could not have arbitration and discussion, because the world had never had the courage to propose the conciliatory methods which some of us are now doubting whether we ought to accept or not.

San Diego, California, September 19

It is feared that our delegates will be outvoted, because I am constantly hearing it said that the British Empire has six votes and we have one. I am perfectly content to have only one when the one counts six, and that is exactly the arrangement under the league. Let us examine that matter a little more particularly. Besides the vote of Great Britain herself, the other five votes are the votes of Canada, of South Africa, of Australia, of New Zealand, and of India. We ourselves were champions and advocates of giving a vote to Panama, of giving a vote to Cuba—both of them under the direction and protectorate of the United States—and if a vote was given to Panama and to Cuba, could it reasonably be denied to the great Dominion of Canada? Could it be denied to that stout Republic in South Africa, that is now living under a nation which did, indeed, overcome it at one time, but which did not dare retain its government in its hands, but turned it over to the very men whom it had fought? Could we deny it to Australia, that independent little republic in the Pacific, which has led the world in so many liberal reforms? Could it be denied

New Zealand? Could we deny it to the hundreds of millions who live in India? But, having given these six votes, what are the facts? For you have been misled with regard to them. The league can take no active steps without the unanimous vote of all the nations represented on the council, added to a vote of the majority in the assembly itself. These six votes are in the assembly, not in the council. The assembly is not a voting body, except upon a limited number of questions, and whenever those questions are questions of action, the affirmative vote of every nation represented on the council is indispensable, and the United States is represented on the council.

Salt Lake City, Utah, September 23

I am not going to stop, my fellow citizens, to discuss the Shantung provision [which shifted control of the area from Germany to Japan] in all its aspects, but what I want to call your attention to is that just so soon as this covenant is ratified every nation in the world will have the right to speak out for China. And I want to say very frankly, and I ought to add that the representatives of those great nations themselves admit, that Great Britain and France and the other powers which have insisted upon similar concessions in China will be put in a position where they will have to reconsider them. This is the only way to serve and redeem China, unless, indeed, you want to start a war for the purpose. At the beginning of the war and during the war Great Britain and France engaged by solemn treaty with Japan that if she would come into the war and continue in the war, she could have, provided she in the meantime took it by force of arms, what Germany had in China. Those are treaties already in force. They are not waiting for ratification. France and England can not withdraw from those obligations, and it will serve China not one iota if we should dissent from the Shantung arrangement; but by being parties to that arrangement we can insist upon the promise of Japan—the promise which the other Governments have not matched—that she will return to China immediately all sovereign rights within the Province of Shantung. We have got that for her now, and under the operations of article 11 and of article 10 it will be impossible for any nation to make any further inroads either upon the territorial integrity or upon the political independence of China.

Denver, Colorado, September 25

The adoption of the treaty means disarmament. Think of the economic burden and the restraint of liberty in the development of professional and mechanical life that resulted from the maintenance of great armies, not only in Germany but in France and in Italy and, to some extent, in Great Britain. If the United States should stand off from this thing we would have to have the biggest army in the world. There would be nobody else that cared for our fortunes. We would have to look out for ourselves, and when I hear gentlemen say, "Yes; that is what we want to do; we want to be independent and look out for ourselves" I say, "Well, then, consult your fellow citizens. There will have to be universal conscription. There will have to be taxes such as even yet we have not seen. There will have to be concentration of authority in the Government capable of using this terrible instrument. You can not conduct a war or command an army by a debating society. You can not determine in community centers what the command of the Commander in Chief is going to be;

you will have to have a staff like the German staff, and you will have to center in the Commander in Chief of the Army and Navy the right to take instant action for the protection of the Nation." America will never consent to any such thing.

DOCUMENT 7

Senator Henry Cabot Lodge Proposes Reservations to the League Covenant, 1919

1. . . . In case of notice of withdrawal from the league of nations, as provided in said article [Article 1], the United States shall be the sole judge as to whether all its international obligations . . . have been fulfilled, and notice of withdrawal . . . may be given by a concurrent resolution of the Congress of the United States.

2. The United States assumes no obligation to preserve the territorial integrity or political independence of any other country . . . under the provisions of article 10, or to employ the military or naval forces of the United States under any article of the treaty for any purpose, unless in any particular case the Congress, which . . . has the sole power to declare war . . . shall . . . so provide.

3. No mandate shall be accepted by the United States under article 22 . . . except by action of the Congress of the United States.

4. The United States reserves to itself exclusively the right to decide what questions are within its domestic jurisdiction. . . .

5. The United States will not submit to arbitration or to inquiry by the assembly or by the council of the league of nations . . . any questions which in the judgment of the United States depend upon or relate to . . . the Monroe doctrine; said doctrine is to be interpreted by the United States alone and is . . . wholly outside the jurisdiction of said league of nations. . . .

6. The United States withholds its assent to articles 156, 157, and 158 [Shantung clauses]. . . .

7. The Congress of the United States will provide by law for the appointment of the representatives of the United States in the assembly and the council of the league of nations, and may in its discretion provide for the participation of the United States in any commission. . . . No person shall represent the United States under either said league of nations or the treaty of peace . . . except with the approval of the Senate of the United States. . . .

9. The United States shall not be obligated to contribute to any expenses of the league of nations . . . unless and until an appropriation of funds . . . shall have been made by the Congress of the United States.

10. If the United States shall at any time adopt any plan for the limitation of armaments proposed by the council of the league . . . it reserves the right to increase such armaments without the consent of the council whenever the United States is threatened with invasion or engaged in war. . . .

14. The United States assumes no obligation to be bound by any election, decision, report, or finding of the council or assembly in which any member of the league

---

This document can be found in *Congressional Record,* LVIII (November 19, 1919), Part 9, 877–878.

and its self-governing dominions, colonies, or parts of empire, in the aggregate have cast more than one vote.

The Chinese Reformer Tsi C. Wang Recalls the Shandong Question and China's May Fourth Movement, 1927

Japan took possession of Kiaochow [Jiaozhou] and Tsing-tao [Qing-dao] in Shantung [Shandong] Province in 1914, and in 1915 she sent the so-called Twenty-one Demands to China which China was forced to accept. The intellectuals with high hope believed that the principles of Woodrow Wilson would prevail at the Peace Conference, and that Japan would be forced to withdraw. When on April 30, 1919, the Peace Conference decided the Shantung issue in favor of Japan, the alert in China were deeply stirred. . . .

The famous parade of the Peking students on May 4th, was the outcome of this unrest. The following description is written by one of the students who took part in the strike:

"At 1 P.M., May 3rd, 1919, a notice was posted calling for a mass meeting. More than 1,000 students were present at the meeting. Mr. Lo, one of the student-leaders in the Literary Revolution Movement was among those in charge of the meeting.

"We first discussed the problem of our national crisis and we all agreed that the Shantung Problem was caused by corruption and injustice, and that we as students must fight to show the world that 'Might should never be right!' Four methods of procedure were then discussed. They were as follows: 1. To get the people of the country to fight together; 2. To send telegrams to the Chinese delegates in Paris and ask them not to sign the treaty; 3. To send telegrams to all Provinces in the country asking them to parade on May 7th, the National Humiliation Day; 4. To decide on the coming Sunday (May 4th) to meet the students of all of the schools in Peking at 'Tieng-Ang Mien' [Tiananmen Gate] and to show our discontent by a great mass parade.

"During the meeting, a student of the Law School, Mr. Tshia, deliberately broke his finger and wrote on the wall in blood 'Return Our Tsing-tao.' The students were all quiet.

"Next morning at 10 o'clock, a meeting of the school representatives of about eighteen leading schools in Peking was held at the Peking Law College to plan the procedure of the afternoon mass parade. After dinner all of us marched out toward Tieng-Ang Mien. A representative of the Board of Education came to our school and advised us not to go, but we refused to listen. When we arrived at Tieng-Ang Mien, a few thousand students of other schools had already gathered there. All of them met in the big yard in front of the gate. They stood in order, group after group, according to their schools. All of them had in their hands white flags made of paper or cloth, bearing the inscriptions, 'Self-determination'; 'International Justice'; 'Abolish the Twenty-one Demands'; 'Return Our Tsing-tao'; 'Down with the Traitors' [(a reference to three

From Tsi C. Wang, *The Youth Movement in China* (New York: New Republic, 1927), pp. 160–161, 163–167, 170, 175–176, 180–181.

Chinese government officials who signed secret treaties that ceded Shandong to Japan)];
and the like. About thirty schools were present with more than 10,000 students! . . .

"It was about 2 o'clock in the afternoon, more than 10,000 strong, we paraded
the streets, and the people in Peking were greatly aroused. Three thousand of us
paraded to the Legation Quarter to ask the Allied Ministers to aid us in securing justice, but the police of the special extraterritorial district refused to let us enter. Four
representatives, including Mr. Lo, were then appointed to see the American Minister. The Minister was absent; it was Sunday.

"After waiting in vain for a time, we marched on through Chang-Ang Street,
and passed by the residence of one of the so-called 'traitors,' Tsao Ju-lin, then Minister of Communication. The students tried to see him, but his home was guarded by
soldiers and policemen. All of us called loudly, 'The Traitor! The Traitor!' We threw
all our small white flags through the windows, and there were so many that we could
see the array of white colored flags from a long distance. Finally a conflict took
place, for suddenly the door of the building was opened and the students marched in.
They saw one of the 'traitors' conversing with a group of Japanese. . . . They went
forward to question him, but they were stopped by the Japanese. . . . The students
dispersed because a fire suddenly broke out from the building and the soldiers fired
at them. Thirty-two were arrested.". . .

Not only were students of other schools sympathetic with the movement, but
merchants, newspaper organizations, scholars, and others sent telegrams to Peking,
directed both to the Government and to the students in Peking. . . .

Although the thirty-two students were released, the Government continued to
make many arrests. . . . At the same time the Government used mandates to suppress
the activities of students in different places. . . .

The indifference of the Government led to a general strike of all Peking students.
Propaganda spread. Student unions organized throughout the whole country. Strikes
in other cities occurred as follows: Peking, May 19th; Tientsin, May 23rd; Tsinan,
May 24th; Shanghai, May 26th; Nanking, May 27th; Paotingfu, May 28th; Anking,
May 30th; Hankow, Wushang, and Kaifeng, May 31st. In Foochow, Canton, Amoy,
Hangchow, and practically all over the country there were also student strikes. . . .

Places of detention for students were getting full. The fact that Shanghai merchants had struck and Peking merchants had threatened to take similar steps at last
brought the government to its senses. On June 6th guards were taken away from the
prisons. Doors were thrown open, but the students proposing to be released on their
own terms, embarrassed the government by remaining in "jail" all night and the day
following, sending four demands to the government. 1. That three officials in the
government should be dismissed; 2. That the students should be allowed freedom
of speech; 3. That they should be allowed to parade through the streets of Peking on
being released from prison; 4. That the government make them a public apology.

It is significant that the government of its own accord, through fear of its own
security and understanding of the grave situation, and out of admiration for the spirit
demonstrated, sent an apology to the students by a pacification delegate, a condemnation as it were of its wrong moves. The police apologized and sent automobiles to
the prison doors.

The day that the students marched triumphantly from prison was a gala one for
Peking. Everywhere bands played, schoolmates applauded. The masses cheered and

shouted: "Long live the Republic of China! Long live the Students!" and "Long live the National University of Peking!" Even the janitor of the University congratulated the freed students with a thousand pieces of "red flower."

More than that, the resignations of the three so-called "traitors" were accepted, the cabinet was altered, and the Chinese delegates at the Paris Peace Conference refused to sign the treaty.

E S S A Y S

In the first essay, Thomas J. Knock of Southern Methodist University delivers a sympathetic but not uncritical assessment of Wilson. Knock argues that Wilson drew on both progressive and conservative internationalists in pursuing neutrality toward Europe's war but rallied a left-of-center coalition to win reelection in 1916, advance his liberal domestic agenda, and mediate a "peace without victory." Once America entered the war, however, the president failed to win support for his controversial peace treaty, including the League of Nations, primarily because the backing of the progressives he needed for victory eroded in the face of wartime reaction at home and abroad.

In the second essay, Robert W. Tucker of The Johns Hopkins University delivers a biting assessment of Wilson's efforts to stay out of the war. Tucker maintains that the president's response to the Great War was grounded in his visionary espousal of neutral rights, rather than a coherent national security strategy. Wilson's neutrality did not take into account modern U.S. power and fed a mistaken American notion that Europe awaited a blueprint for "peace without victory." As his dream of a U.S. mediated peace collided with the reality of German submarine warfare, Wilson convinced himself that the war he had once viewed as a sordid blood feud represented a noble battle between democracy and autocracy.

In the last essay, Erez Manela of Harvard University analyzes the impact of Wilsonianism on the colonial world and finds the U.S. president less supportive of self-determination than his rhetoric indicated. Initially inspired by the president's crusade for international justice, nationalists in colonial societies experienced deep disillusionment when Wilson turned down their pleas for national self-determination at Versailles. Manela attributes the double standard that championed nation state status for Europeans but not for Afro-Asians to Wilson's conviction that non-European peoples lacked the capacity for self-government and would be best off under a League of Nations trusteeship imposed by more civilized powers. The disappointment that accompanied the "Wilsonian moment" led anticolonial patriots in China, Egypt, India, Indochina, and Korea to embrace revolutionary ideologies in their struggles for sovereignty, thus transforming international history.

From Peace to War: Progressive Internationalists Confront the Forces of Reaction

THOMAS J. KNOCK

As the historian Frederick Jackson Turner once remarked, the age of reform in the United States was "also the age of socialistic inquiry." Indeed, by 1912, the Socialist Party of America and its quadrennial standard-bearer, Eugene Debs, had attained

---

This is an original essay written for this volume based on *To End All Wars: Woodrow Wilson and the Quest for a New World Order* (New York: Oxford University Press, 1992).

respectability and legitimacy. The party's membership exceeded 115,000, and some 1,200 socialists held public office in 340 municipalities and twenty-four states. As many as three million Americans read socialist newspapers on a regular basis. Julius Wayland's *Appeal to Reason,* with 760,000 weekly subscribers, ranked among the most widely read publications in the world.

The general cast of the four-way presidential campaign of 1912 also lent credence to Turner's observation. Notwithstanding the conservatism of the incumbent, William Howard Taft, the impact of progressivism on the two main parties, in tandem with the success of the Socialist party, caused a certain blurring of traditional political lines. To millions of citizens, a vote for either Woodrow Wilson, the progressive Democrat, Theodore Roosevelt, the insurgent "Bull Moose" who bolted the Republicans to form the Progressive party, or Debs, the Socialist, amounted to a protest against the status quo of industrial America. And that protest, from top to bottom, sanctioned an unfolding communion between liberals and socialists practically unique in American history.

In this new age of progressive reform and socialistic inquiry, it would be Woodrow Wilson's opportunity and challenge to reconcile and shape domestic and foreign concerns in ways that no previous chief executive had ever contemplated. . . .

Feminists, liberals, pacifists, socialists, and reformers of varying kinds filled the ranks of the progressive internationalists. Their leaders included many of the era's authentic heroes and heroines: Jane Addams of Hull House, the poet-journalist John Reed, Max Eastman of the *Masses,* the civil-rights crusader Oswald Garrison Villard, and Lillian Wald of New York's Henry Street Settlement, to name a few. For them the search for a peaceful world order provided a logical common ground. Peace was indispensable to change itself—to the survival of the labor movement, to their campaigns on behalf of women's rights and the abolition of child labor, and to social justice legislation in general. If the war in Europe were permitted to rage on indefinitely, progressive internationalists believed, then the United States could not help but get sucked into it; not only their great causes, but also the very moral fiber of the nation would be destroyed should its resources be diverted from reform to warfare. Thus, their first goal (and one in keeping with Wilson's policy of neutrality) was to bring about a negotiated settlement of the war.

The Woman's Peace party, founded in January 1915, in Washington, D.C., and led by Jane Addams, played a pivotal role in the progressive internationalist movement. Guided by the principle of "the sacredness of human life," the platform of the Woman's Peace party constituted the earliest manifesto on internationalism advanced by any American organization throughout the war. The party's "program for constructive peace" called for an immediate armistice, international agreements to limit armaments and nationalize their manufacture, a reduction of trade barriers, self-determination, machinery for arbitration, and a "Concert of Nations" to supersede the balance-of-power system. The platform also pressed for American mediation of the war. Its authors made sure that the president received all of their recommendations. . . .

Many progressive internationalists regarded the reactionary opponents of domestic reform and the advocates of militarism and imperialism as twins born of the same womb; they watched with alarm as the champions of "preparedness" mounted what they viewed as an insidious offensive to thwart social and economic progress at home, as well as disarmament and the repudiation of war as an instrument of foreign policy. In response to the preparedness movement, liberal reformers and leading socialists joined forces to establish the American Union Against Militarism (AUAM). Within months, the AUAM had branches in every major city in the country. When, in the wake of the *Lusitania* disaster, Wilson introduced legislation to increase substantially the size of the army and navy, it appeared that he had surrendered to the enemy. Then, too, a competing, conservative vision of internationalism was vying for national attention.

The program of the conservative internationalists was different in both subtle and conclusive ways. It was developed by the organizers of the League to Enforce Peace (LEP), founded in June 1915, and led by former president William Howard Taft and other Republicans prominent in the field of international law. Within two years, they had established four thousand branches in forty-seven states. The LEP's platform, "Warrant from History," called for American participation in a world parliament, which would assemble periodically to make appropriate changes to international law and employ arbitration and conciliation procedures to settle certain kinds of disputes. While more or less endorsing the general principle of collective security, most conservative internationalists also believed that the United States should build up its military complex and reserve the right to undertake independent coercive action whenever the "national interest" was threatened. Unlike progressive internationalists, the LEP did not concern itself with self-determination or advocate disarmament or even a military standoff in Europe. These internationalists were openly pro-Allied; in fact, the slogan, "The LEP does *not* seek to end the present war," appeared on their letterhead in the autumn of 1916.

Throughout that year, Wilson met and corresponded with representatives of both wings of the new internationalist movement. In May 1916, for example, he delivered an important address before a gathering of the LEP, the occasion for his first public affirmation on behalf of American membership in some kind of postwar peacekeeping organization. Yet Wilson's sympathies lay decidedly with the progressive internationalists. Two weeks earlier, for the first time, he had articulated to persons other than his absolute confidants his ideas for a "family of nations," during a lengthy White House colloquy with leaders of the AUAM.

The AUAM stood neither for "peace at any price" nor against "sane and reasonable" military preparedness, Lillian Wald explained to the president; but they were anxious about those agents of militarism who were "frankly hostile to our institutions of democracy." Wilson contended that his preparedness program conformed to his interlocutors' criteria—that it would provide adequate security "without changing the spirit of the country" and that one of his motives for it was to achieve a league of nations. "[I]f the world undertakes, as we all hope it will undertake, a joint effort to keep the peace, it will expect us to play our proportional part," he said. "Surely that is not a militaristic ideal. That is a very practical, possible ideal." . . .

Wilson could not have made a truly plausible case for a new diplomacy and a league—nor would he have been continued in office—if, at the same time, he had not been willing and able to move plainly to the left of center in American politics. Indeed, the array of social justice legislation he pushed through Congress on the eve of his reelection campaign gave legitimacy to his aspirations in foreign affairs like nothing else could have. Wilson could boast of a number of accomplishments for his first two years in office: the Underwood Tariff, the Clayton Antitrust Act, the Federal Reserve System, and the Federal Trade Commission. Then, as his polestar moved comparatively leftward with the approach of the 1916 campaign, he put two "radicals" (Louis D. Brandeis and John Hessin Clarke) on the Supreme Court. Over the protests of conservatives in and out of Congress, he secured passage of the Adamson Act, which established the eight-hour day for railroad workers, and the Keating-Owen bill, which imposed restrictions on child labor. Finally, he had defused the conservatives' appeal to jingoism with his "moderate" preparedness program, which, in conjunction with the Revenue Act of 1916, yielded the first real tax on wealth in American history. . . .

But this was only the half of it. As the complement to his advanced progressivism, Wilson also made American membership in a league of nations one of the cardinal themes of his campaign, a theme that complemented the Democratic chant, "He Kept Us Out Of War!" His utterances on the league exerted a significant impact on the outcome. [The leftist journalist] Max Eastman predicted that Wilson would win reelection because "he has attacked the problem of eliminating war, and he has not succumbed to the epidemic of militarism." Indeed, his speeches on the league constituted "the most important step that any President of the United States has taken towards civilizing the world since Lincoln." Herbert Croly, the influential editor of the *New Republic,* threw his support to Wilson not only on the grounds of the president's domestic record but also because he had "committed himself and his party to a revolutionary doctrine": American participation in a postwar league of nations. . . .

In any event, the election returns suggested that Wilson and the progressive internationalists had not merely checked the reactionaries; they had presided over the creation of a left-of-center coalition that seemed to hold the balance of political power in the United States. Precisely what all of this portended for future domestic struggles could hardly be predicted. As for foreign policy, the deeper meaning of their victory was unmistakable. "[T]he President we reelected has raised a flag that no other president has thought or perhaps dared to raise," [the left-liberal journalist] Amos Pinchot submitted. "It is the flag of internationalism."

American neutrality was a fragile thing. Wilson had always shared the conviction of fellow peace seekers that the best way to keep the country out of the war was to try to bring about a negotiated settlement. Twice, to that end, in 1915 and 1916, he had sent his personal emissary, Colonel Edward M. House, to Europe for direct parlays with the heads of all the belligerent governments. These appeals had proved futile. Now, fortified by reconfirmation at the polls, he decided on a bold stroke. In a climactic attempt to end the war, he went before the Senate on January 22, 1917, and called for "peace without victory." In this address, Wilson drew together the strands of progressive internationalist thought and launched a penetrating critique of European imperialism, militarism, and balance-of-power politics—the root causes of the war, he said. In their stead, he held out the promise of a "community of nations"—a new world order sustained by procedures for the arbitration of disputes between nations, a dramatic reduction of armaments, self-determination, and collective security. The chief instrumentality of this sweeping program was to be a league of nations. Thus, Wilson began his ascent to a position of central importance in the history of international relations in the twentieth century.

Responses to the address varied. The governments of both warring coalitions, still praying for decisive victory in the field, either ignored it or received it with contempt. Many pro-Allied Republicans, such as Senator Henry Cabot Lodge of Massachusetts, heaped scorn upon the very notion of "peace without victory" and wondered exactly what membership in a league might entail. Nonetheless, Wilson's manifesto met with an unprecedented outpouring of praise from progressive groups at home and abroad. . . .

One week later, Germany announced the resumption of unrestricted submarine warfare against all flags. After three American ships were sunk without warning, public opinion shifted markedly. On March 20, the cabinet unanimously recommended full-fledged belligerency. Wilson, too, had concluded that after some thirty months of neutrality, war had "thus been thrust upon" the United States. "But," the secretary of interior recorded in his diary, "he goes unwillingly."

In his address to Congress on April 2, 1917, the president explained why neutrality no longer seemed tenable and outlined the measures necessary for getting the country on a war footing. He then turned to more transcendent matters. His goals were the same as when he had addressed the Senate in January; he said. "The world must be made safe for democracy. Its peace must he planted upon the tested foundations of political liberty. We have no selfish ends to serve. We desire no conquest, no dominion. We seek no indemnities for ourselves, no material compensation for the sacrifices we shall freely make." He implied that Americans would be fighting to establish some degree of "peace without victory," or, as he put it, "for a universal dominion of right by such a concert of free nations as shall bring peace and safety to all nations and the world itself at last free"—a program now attainable apparently only through the crucible of war. . . .

Then, just as the United States entered the war, Russia, staggering under the relentless blows of the German army, was seized by revolutionary upheaval. By the end of 1917, the Bolshevik leaders, V. I. Lenin and Leon Trotsky, pulled their ravaged nation out of the war. They thereupon issued proclamations on behalf of a democratic peace based on self-determination and summoned the peoples of Europe to demand that their governments—the Allies and the Central Powers alike—repudiate plans for conquest.

In the circumstances, Wilson really had no choice but to respond to the Bolshevik challenge. In his Fourteen Points Address, of January 8, 1918, the most celebrated speech of his presidency, he reiterated much of the anti-imperialist "peace without victory" formula and once again made the League of Nations the capstone. In answer to Lenin's entreaty to stop the war, he argued that German autocracy and militarism must be crushed so that humanity could set about the task of creating a new and better world. Wilson's endeavor to remove the suspicions hanging over the Allied cause and rally doubters to see the war through to the bitter end succeeded magnificently. The popular approbation that greeted the Fourteen Points in both Europe and America approached phenomenal proportions. (Even Lenin hailed the address as "a great step ahead towards the peace of the world.") But as before, the Allied governments declined to endorse or comment on Wilson's progressive war aims.

At home, Wilson's own immediate priorities inexorably shifted toward the exigencies of war mobilization. And, in part owing to stinging Republican criticism of "peace without victory" and, later, the Fourteen Points as the basis for the postwar settlement, he refused to discuss his plans for the League in any concrete detail throughout the period of American belligerency. He also neglected to lay essential political groundwork for it at home. By the autumn of 1918, important segments among both conservative and progressive internationalists had grown disenchanted with Wilson, albeit for entirely different reasons.

This development would prove to be as unfortunate as the partisan opposition led by the president's arch-nemeses, Theodore Roosevelt and Henry Cabot Lodge. For example, Wilson grievously offended Taft by frustrating the wartime efforts of the LEP and other conservative internationalists, who wanted to make formal plans for the League of Nations in cooperation with the British government. (There were, of course, serious ideological differences between his and Taft's conception of the League, but Wilson might have found a way to use the Republican-dominated LEP to defuse some of the incipient senatorial criticism.)

Perhaps just as consequential, Wilson failed to nurture the left-of-center coalition of 1916, a dynamic political force that, had it remained intact, might have made it possible for him to secure and validate American leadership in a peacekeeping organization intended to serve progressive purposes. But he began to lose his grip on his former base of support as a tidal wave of anti-German hysteria and superpatriotism swept over the country in 1917–1918. Like a giant wrecking machine, "One Hundred Percent Americanism," as it was known, had the potential to batter the progressive wing of the American internationalist movement to ruins. In every part of the United States, acts of political repression and violence (sanctioned by federal legislation) were committed against German-Americans as well as pacifists and radicals. Only at risk of life or limb did antiwar dissenters express their views in public. For example, for speaking out against American participation in the war, Eugene Debs was sentenced to ten years in prison. The postmaster general denied second-class mailing privileges to such publications as the *Milwaukee Leader,* the *Appeal to Reason,* and the *Masses,* virtually shutting them down. The majority of progressive internationalists steadfastly supported the war effort, but they could not abide these kinds of violations of basic First Amendment rights, for which, ultimately, they held Wilson responsible. And so, because he acquiesced in the suppression of civil liberties, Wilson himself contributed to a gradual unraveling of his coalition.

The circumstances in which the war ended compounded the larger problem. By September 1918, the combined might of the Allied and American armies had pushed the enemy back toward Belgium. On October 6, German Chancellor Max von Baden appealed to Wilson to take steps for the restoration of peace based on the Fourteen Points. The armistice was signed on November 11. Meanwhile, a midterm congressional election more important than most presidential elections in American history had taken place. Against the Wilsonian peace plan, the Republicans launched a fiercely partisan, ultraconservative campaign. This time around, endorsements on behalf of the administration by leading progressives outside the Democratic party hardly matched those of the 1916 contest. Even so, the centralization of the wartime economy and the core of Wilson's foreign policy placed him far enough to the left to make all Democrats vulnerable to Republican charges that they were "un-American." Most historians maintain that Wilson committed the worst blunder of his presidency in countering the attacks: He asked the public for a vote of confidence— an ostensibly partisan appeal to sustain the Democrats' control of Congress. When the Republicans won majorities of forty-five in the House and two in the Senate, they could claim that the president, who planned to attend the Paris Peace Conference personally, had been repudiated. The Republicans also thereby gained control over congressional committees, including the Senate Foreign Relations Committee, which would be chaired by Lodge.

Yet despite these political setbacks, the Fourteen Points had acquired the status of sacred text among the war-weary peoples of Europe, and "Wilson" was becoming something more than the name of a president. Italian soldiers placed his picture in their barracks. An old woman said she heard that in America "there was a great saint who is going to make peace for us." Romain Rolland, the French Nobel laureate, pronounced him the greatest "moral authority" in the world. The whole world seemed to come to a halt to honor Wilson when he arrived in Europe. Into the streets and piazzas of Paris, London, Rome, and Milan, millions of people turned out to hail "the Moses from Across the Atlantic." . . .

Whereas he could not have prevailed without the massive outpouring of public support, Wilson still had to pay a heavy price for the League. If he was adored by the "common people," the statesmen of Europe—David Lloyd George, Georges Clemenceau, and Vittorio Orlando—held grave reservations about a Wilsonian peace. They were also keen students of American politics. Fully aware of the arithmetic of the Senate, they used their acceptance of the covenant as a lever to gain concessions on other vital and contentious issues.

For instance, Wilson was compelled to swallow a less-than-satisfactory compromise on the disposition of captured enemy colonies, which the Allies (in particular, Australia and South Africa) coveted for themselves. Clemenceau, on threat of withdrawal of his certification of the League, demanded for France military occupation of the Rhineland; Orlando claimed for Italy the Yugoslav port city of Fiume; and the Japanese insisted on retaining exploitative economic privileges in China's Shantung province. On several occasions, Wilson was able to moderate the more extreme Allied demands and uphold at least the spirit of the Fourteen Points. But, then, on verge of physical collapse, he permitted the Allies to impose upon Germany a huge reparations burden and, on top of everything else, a "war-guilt" clause—saddling it with the moral responsibility for allegedly having started the war. Wilson tried to take comfort in the hope that, once the "war psychosis" had receded, the League would be in position to arbitrate and rectify the injustices contained in the peace treaty itself. After six long months of often acrimonious deliberations, however, the signing of that document in the Hall of Mirrors at Versailles, on June 28, 1919, was at best a fleeting triumph for the exhausted president.

By the time Wilson returned to the United States in the summer of 1919, thirty-two state legislatures and thirty-three governors had endorsed the covenant. According to a *Literary Digest* poll, the vast majority of nearly 1,400 newspaper editors, including a majority of Republican editors, advocated American membership in some kind of league. Had a national referendum been held at just that moment, the country almost certainly would have joined. The reasons for its failure to do so are still debated by historians. To begin, Wilson had already lost the active support of most left-wing progressives, not to mention that of the socialists. Many liberals, too, shook their heads in dismay upon reading the Versailles settlement. They believed that, regardless of his motives, he had forsaken the Fourteen Points; that he had conceded too much to the Allies in the territorial compromises: and that vindictiveness, not righteousness, had ruled at the Paris conclave. In short, they feared that the League of Nations would be bound to uphold an unjust peace.

The great debate also coincided with the opening phase of the Red Scare, an even more hysterical and pervasive manifestation of "One Hundred Percent Americanism" whose focus had shifted from the German menace to the threat of bolshevism. Deterioration of civil liberties continued to discourage many progressive internationalists from giving Wilson's crusade their full devotion. . . .

In the Senate on the one hand sheer partisanship motivated much of the opposition. Until the autumn of 1918, Wilson had been the most uniformly successful (if controversial) president since Lincoln. What would become of the Republican party, a friend asked Senator Lodge, if Wilson got his League and the Democrats could boast of "the greatest constructive reform in history"? On the other hand, many of the senatorial objections were grounded in ideological principles. Most Republicans acknowledged that the United States should cooperate with the Allies and play its part in upholding the peace settlement; but they also believed that Wilson had consigned too many vital national interests to the will of an international authority. (At one point, Wilson had frankly admitted, "Some of our sovereignty would be surrendered.") The Republicans found Article X of the covenant particularly troubling. It obliged contracting nations to "preserve as against external aggression the territorial integrity and political independence of all Members of the League." Thus, at least on paper, the United States might be required to take part in some far-flung military intervention in which it had no compelling interest; at the same time, the United States apparently would be prevented from using its military power unilaterally whenever it wanted to. Although during the peace conference he had responded to early criticisms and amended the covenant—to provide for withdrawal from the League and nominally to exempt the Monroe Doctrine and domestic matters (such as immigration) from its jurisdiction—Wilson had not done enough to assuage the anxieties of the majority of Republicans.

Then, too, a small but sturdy knot of senators known as the "irreconcilables" flat-out opposed the League in any form. Not all of the fifteen or so irreconcilables were partisans or reactionaries (though most, like Albert Fall, were); several of them, including Robert La Follette and George Norris, were bona-fide progressives who based their opposition on convictions similar to those of many liberals and socialists. Irreconcilable or no, only a few of Wilson's opponents were strict isolationists. No one had cut through to the crux of the debate with more discernment than Gilbert M. Hitchcock of Nebraska, the Democratic leader in the Senate, when he observed, "Internationalism has come, and we must choose what form the internationalism is to take." The *Appeal to Reason,* though disillusioned with the president and highly dubious of his labors, was harsher: Republicans feared Wilson's League because it placed restrictions on "America's armed forces . . . [and] the commercial and territorial greed of American capitalists." The Lodge crowd hardly advocated isolationism, but rather "the internationalism of unrestrained plunder and competition."

By summer's end, the Senate Foreign Relations Committee, dominated by Republicans and irreconcilables and with Lodge at the helm, had formulated forty-six amendments as the conditions for ratification; by autumn, these had evolved into formal reservations—curiously, fourteen in number. The most controversial one pertained to Article X of the covenant: "The United States assumes no obligation to preserve the territorial integrity or political independence of any country . . . unless in any particular case the Congress . . . by act or joint resolution [shall] so provide." . . .

Meanwhile, Wilson held a series of White House meetings with groups of Republicans known as "mild reservationists" and tried to persuade them to ratify the treaty as it was written. In fact, there was very little difference between their views and those of the senators called "strong reservationists." Hence, none of these conferences changed anyone's mind. Then, against the advice of his personal physician and the pleading of the First Lady, Wilson determined that he must take his case directly to the American people and let them know what was at stake. For three weeks in September 1919, he traveled ten thousand miles by train throughout the Middle and Far West, making some forty speeches to hundreds of thousands of people.

Wilson appealed to his audiences on both the intellectual and the emotional level. Despite the importance of Article X, he told them, military sanctions probably would not have to come into play very often—in part because of the deterrent manifest within the threat of collective force, in part because of the cooling-off provisions in the arbitration features of the League, and in part because disarmament, which he heavily emphasized, would help to eliminate most potential problems from the start. He also addressed the question of sovereignty, as it related to the Senate's concern over arbitration and the hindrance to unilateral action that League membership implied: "The only way in which you can have impartial determinations in this world is by consenting to something you do not want to do." And the obvious corollary was to agree to refrain from doing something that you *want* to do, for there might be times "when we lose in court [and] we will take our medicine."

But there could be no truly effective League without America's participation. Should Americans turn their backs, he said, they would have to live forever with a gun in their hands. And they could not go in grudgingly or on a conditional basis. The "Lodge Reservations" would utterly "change the entire meaning of the Treaty." If the League were thus crippled, he would feel obliged to stand "in mortification and shame" before the boys who went across the seas to fight and say to them. " 'You are betrayed. You fought for something that you did not get.' " . . .

As the crowds grew larger and the cheers louder, Wilson looked more haggard and worn out at the end of each day. His facial muscles twitched. Headaches so excruciating that he could hardly see recurred. To keep from coughing all night, he slept propped up in a chair. At last, his doctor called a halt to the tour and rushed him hack to Washington. Two days later, on October 2, he suffered a stroke that nearly killed him and permanently paralyzed the left side of his body. From that point onward, Wilson was but a fragile husk of his former self, a tragic recluse in the White House, shielded by his wife and doctor.

The Senate roll was called three times, in November 1919 and March 1920. But whether on a motion to ratify the treaty unconditionally or with the fourteen Lodge reservations attached to it, the vote always fell short of a two-thirds majority. In November 1920, Warren G. Harding, the Republican presidential candidate, won a landslide victory over the Democrat, James M. Cox. The Republicans were only too happy to interpret the returns as the "great and solemn referendum" that Wilson had earlier said he had wanted for his covenant. "So far as the United States is concerned," Lodge now declared, "that League is dead."

In surveying the ruins, many historians have cited the president's stroke as the primary factor behind the outcome. A healthy Wilson, they argue, surely would have grasped the situation and strived to find a middle ground on the question of reservations. Other historians have maintained that his refusal to compromise was consistent with his personality throughout his life, that he would never have yielded to the Republicans (especially to Lodge), regardless of the state of his health. Although there is merit in both of these interpretations—the stroke and Wilson's personality are of obvious relevance—neither provides a complete explanation. They do not take adequate account of the evolution of the League idea, the ideological gulf that had always separated progressive and conservative internationalism, or the domestic political conditions that had taken shape long before the treaty was in the Senate.

In a very real sense, Wilsonian, or progressive, internationalism had begun at home, as part of the reform impulse in the "age of socialistic inquiry." By the touchstone of Wilson's advanced reform legislation and his synthesis of the tenets of the New Diplomacy, progressive internationalists had been able to define the terms of the debate and claim title to the League until 1917–1918—that is, until "One Hundred Percent Americanism" released uncontrollable forces that overwhelmed them. Wilson contributed to this turn of events by losing sight of the relationship between politics and foreign policy—by refusing to acknowledge his administration's culpability in the wartime reaction and by declining to take any action to combat it. . . .

Whatever the central cause of his historic failure, Wilson's conservative and partisan adversaries earnestly believed that his was a dangerously radical vision, a new world order alien to their own understanding of how the world worked. His severest critics among progressive internationalists believed he had not done enough to rally the people to his side and resist the forces of reaction—either in America or at the Paris Peace Conference. Wilson's response to them was a cry of anguish. "What more could I have done?" he asked historian William E. Dodd shortly before leaving the presidency. "I had to negotiate with my back to the wall. Men thought I had all power. Would to God I had had such power." His voice choking with emotion, he added, "The 'great' people at home wrote and wired every day that they were against me."

On all counts, and no doubt for all concerned, it had been, as Dodd himself concluded, "one long wilderness of despair and betrayal, even by good men."

A Passionate Visionary Stumbles into War

ROBERT W. TUCKER

Woodrow Wilson was heir to a tradition of neutrality. That tradition was not without ambiguity. Neutrality was the corollary of isolation; it was the policy of isolation in periods of war between the great European powers. Although closely linked, isolation and neutrality were nevertheless different. . . . If isolation meant maintaining a separateness from Europe's politics and wars, neutrality meant remaining apart

Tucker, Robert W., *Woodrow Wilson and the Great War: Reconsidering America's Neutrality, 1914–1917.* © 2007 by Rector and Visitors of the the University of Virginia. Reproduced with permission of the University of Virginia Press.

from Europe's wars, while insisting upon a broad right to trade with the belligerents. From the outset, the American tradition of neutrality laid emphasis on rights and invested those rights with a status that did not readily permit of compromise. This was, at any rate, the Jeffersonian side of the tradition, and it may be seen as the prevailing one. The vindication of neutral rights was equated with the nation's honor and prestige and even its independence, values that could not be compromised, let alone sacrificed, however great the price of defending them. The War of 1812, with Great Britain, was the price Jefferson's successor, James Madison, had finally paid.

A century later, in another great European conflict over the balance of power, neutral rights were again equated with interests that did not readily admit of compromise. "The rights of neutrals in time of war," Woodrow Wilson insisted, in terms strikingly similar to Jefferson's, "are based upon principle not upon expediency, and the principles are immutable.". . . And as it had been for Jefferson and Madison before him, the price of doing so was war. . . .

The difficulty of Wilson's position began with the recognition that the European war was not just another conflict but one that would determine the future order of the world. The normal indifference of neutrals toward the outcome of the wars of the nineteenth century, an indifference that rested on the assumption of the limited consequences of war, no longer held. In the case of the smaller neutral states of Europe, this consideration might be acknowledged, yet, in view of their weakness, considered irrelevant. In the case of a great power, even one separated from Europe by an ocean and long committed to a policy of isolation from Europe's politics, the response had to prove more difficult. The fate of a civilization of which America was a part could not simply be viewed with indifference, particularly given the role that Wilson had assigned to the nation. The responsibility imposed upon America by a world in crisis was one that inescapably followed from her power and ideals. America could not be indifferent to the war and its consequences, content merely to observe it from afar and relieved not to be involved. . . .

Although foreshadowed by statements made very early in the war, it was not until almost eight months following the outbreak of war that Wilson fully set forth his thoughts on neutrality and on America's vocation as a neutral. The basis of neutrality, the president explained, "is not indifference; it is not self-interest. The basis of neutrality is sympathy for mankind. It is fairness, it is good will at bottom. It is impartiality of spirit and of judgment." The commitment to neutrality did not stem from "the petty desire to stay out of trouble" but from the conviction that "there is something so much greater to do than fight: there is a distinction waiting for this nation that no nation has ever yet got. That is the distinction of absolute self-control and self-mastery." For America, in stark contrast to the nations of Europe, which had abandoned their respective fates to the arbitrament of armed force, the president coveted "this splendid courage of reserve moral force." America's vocation was to be the mediating nation of the world, if only by virtue of being a nation "compounded of the nations of the world. We mediate their blood . . . their traditions . . . their sentiments, their tastes, their passions; we are ourselves compounded of those things. We are, therefore, able to understand all nations; we are able to understand them in the compound, not separately as partisans, but unitedly, as knowing and comprehending and embodying them all." It was in this sense, Wilson explained, that America was a mediating nation, a nation without a past that impelled it in a fixed direction, a nation that had no "hampering ambitions" to take what did not belong to it. . . .

Wilson equated America's neutrality with a noble vision. Yet it was manifestly a vision that also expressed what Wilson believed to be the nation's interests. The president saw no conflict between the two. The advantages neutrality conferred upon the nation were ultimately advantages to the world as well. America's "reserve moral force" might, it was hoped would, one day help to bring peace with justice to a wartorn world. That task could only be undertaken by a great power that preserved an "absolute self-control and self-mastery." The financial benefits that accrued to America by virtue of the war would facilitate this high undertaking. In . . . April 1915 . . . Wilson noted: "Our resources are untouched; we are more and more becoming, by the force of circumstances, the mediating nation of the world in respect to its finance." This was the Wilsonian version of Jefferson's earlier view of a general European war that enabled the United States "to become the carriers for all parties" at sea, thus enabling the new world "to fatten on the follies of the old." What to Jefferson was benefiting from Europe's infatuation with war and conquest was to Wilson the prospect of inheriting the position of world leadership by staying out of the war. To [his fiancée] Edith Bolling Galt he wrote in August 1915: "Yes, I think the [newspaper] clipping about America now standing as likely heir to the influence and power hitherto possessed by England and her continental neighbors and rivals does contain a thought . . . and is it not a pretty safe prediction, always supposing we succeed in keeping out of the deadly maelstrom ourselves?" The expectation of an exhausted Europe incapable of resisting a neutral America's growing influence and power persisted to the end of the period of neutrality. In mid-February 1917, during the final days of Wilson's crumbling determination to remain out of the war, the president reportedly said that "he is not in sympathy with any great preparedness— that Europe would be man and money poor by the end of the war." It was by then a familiar calculation. . . .

Wilson was not blind to the prospective threat of a triumphant Germany to the nation's security interests. He appreciated that a German victory, even if it were not immediately to give rise to a challenge to the Monroe Doctrine, might eventually impose a burden of military preparedness, which the country had been able to escape in the past. He realized that a German triumph might carry with it a threat to many of the values that defined American and, indeed, Western civilization. These considerations, however, were not sufficiently compelling to overturn long-held views about the nature and basis of American security. Despite a later concern over the possible consequences a German victory held out for American security, Wilson could never bring himself to view those consequences with the seriousness needed to prompt the abandonment of neutrality. Whatever fears he may have entertained of a German victory, he nevertheless continued to see America's security as essentially unconditioned by events in Europe. And to the limited extent that he did draw a connection between the two, what weighed heavily in his calculations was not the threat to the nation's security that *might* arise in a distant future when a victorious Germany had recovered from the devastating effects of war but the threat to America's institutions and well-being that, he was utterly persuaded, *would* arise were it to become a party to the war. Between what he saw as a distant and hypothetical threat and what he considered an immediate and real danger, he had little difficulty in choosing.

Wilson's determined hold on neutrality, then, had the simplest of explanations: he wanted to stay out of the war. He wanted to stay out of the war because, as he said on numerous occasions, the people relied on him to keep the nation out of the war and because he himself believed to the very end that participation in the war held out the greatest threat to the nation's democratic values and institutions. Yet though Wilson's neutrality was ultimately rooted in his profound fear of war's effects, he was nevertheless unable to candidly avow the compelling reason for his determination to remain out of the war. Instead, that reason had to be disavowed as one unworthy of a great nation committed to the ideals Wilson had set out.

In this his task was greatly facilitated by a view of the war that found right and justice on neither side. Against a growing chorus of criticism at home and abroad that his neutrality was self-serving when it was not simply driven by fear, Wilson replied that the war offered little, if any, grounds for moral choice. The theme of the belligerents' moral equivalence, of the war as being simply a struggle for power, was Wilson's last line of defense on behalf of his neutrality. The view that the war was devoid of moral significance was one the president had come to only some months after the outbreak of hostilities. In the beginning he had appeared to think otherwise and even to privately endorse Allied claims respecting the causes and objects of the war. But it soon became apparent that whatever his initial reaction, his studied position was one of skepticism toward the moral claims of the belligerents. . . .

This refusal to see any moral significance in the conflict found repeated expression in Wilson's campaign speeches during the fall of 1916. "The singularity of the present war," he stated in Omaha on October 5, 1916, "is that its origin and objects have never been disclosed. They have obscure European roots which we do not know how to trace." Three weeks later, in Cincinnati, he asked: "Have you ever heard what started the present war? If you have, I wish you would publish it, because nobody else has." These were expressions of a president seeking reelection. Yet they bear a close resemblance to his most considered utterances as a statesman. Once the campaign was over, Wilson turned to his last and greatest effort to bring the war to an end. The December peace note to the belligerents [asking each to state their war aims] was preceded by the November prolegomenon to a peace note; Wilson's private memorandum to himself on the meaning of the war. In that memo, which reflected the quintessential Wilson, the president averred that the war had no meaning save its immense suffering and utter futility, that neither side's claims could be endorsed, that German militarism and British navalism had been equally important as causes of the war, and that a lasting peace could not he obtained by accepting either side's position. . . .

Considered in isolation, Wilson's belief that the war was no more than a struggle for power might well have proved a sufficient justification for his continued neutrality, whatever the outcome of the war. But, of course, it could not be considered in isolation. The neutrality to which the president had long been committed . . . was pushing him inexorably toward war. Wilson's awareness of his deepening predicament was reflected in two themes that emerged in this period: the intolerableness of neutrality in modern war and the need for a cause in defense of which Americans would be willing to undertake the sacrifices of war. In a campaign speech in late October 1916 he elaborated on the first theme: "[This] is the last war of the kind, or of any kind that involves the world, that the United States can keep out of. I say that because I believe that the business of neutrality is over. Not because I want it to be over, but I mean this—that war has now such a scale that the position of neutrals sooner or later becomes intolerable." . . .

[I]f neutrality had become intolerable, this did not mean that war had become tolerable, let alone desirable. It might be both if only a worthy cause for fighting could be found. "It has been said," he observed in an address at Shadow Lawn mansion, in Monmouth, New Jersey, on October 14, 1916, "that the people of the United States do not want to fight about anything. That is profoundly false. But the people of the United States want to be sure what they are fighting about, and they want to be sure that they are fighting for the things that will bring to the world justice and peace. Define the elements. Let us know that we are not fighting for the prevalence of this nation over that, for the ambitions of this group of nations as compared with the ambitions of that group of nations. Let us once be convinced that we are called into a great combination to fight for the rights of mankind, and America will unite her force and spill her blood for the great things she has always believed in and followed." What Europe must realize, the president went on to declare, was that "we are saving ourselves for something greater that is to come. We are saving ourselves in order that we may unite in that final league of nations in which it shall be understood that there is no neutrality where any nation is doing wrong, in that final league of nations which must, in the providence of God, come into the world, where nation shall be leagued with nation in order to show all mankind that no man may lead any nation into acts of aggression without having all the other nations of the world leagued against it."

The statement was representative of Wilson's public utterances in the fall of 1916. What did it mean? Clearly the most reasonable interpretation was one that supported the Allied view that the president was indifferent to, even condemnatory of, the objects and purposes of the war. The "rights of mankind," the cause "in which it was a glory to shed human blood," as Wilson said on another occasion, were never expressly defined. But one definition did emerge by implication. It was the right of the peoples of all states to be free of armed aggression. Wilson had proclaimed this right in his address of May 27, 1916, to the League to Enforce Peace, saying that "the world has a right to be free from every disturbance of its peace that has its origin in aggression and disregard of the rights of peoples and nations," and had declared America's willingness "to become a partner in any feasible association of nations formed in order to realize" the right of peoples to be free of aggression. However, if this was the meaning of his statement, it referred to the future, not the present. America would shed her blood in a cause to which a future league of nations was to be dedicated, not in a cause, the war, intent on establishing the dominance of one group of nations over another. In that future league neutrality would have no place; for the present, neutrality, though intolerable, would be held to as long as honor permitted. . . .

In the end, these disparities between reality and vision would lead Wilson to the renunciation of neutrality. In his war address [in April 1917] the president declared: "Neutrality is no longer feasible or desirable where the peace of the world is involved and the freedom of its peoples, and the menace to that peace and freedom lies in the existence of autocratic governments backed by organized force which is controlled wholly by their will, not by the will of the people. We have seen the last of neutrality in such circumstances." In the new order, the war address proclaimed, there would be no place for an institution that was based upon the refusal to distinguish between the just and unjust resort to armed force. Wilson would later say, in defending the League of Nations, that "international law has been the principle of minding your own business, particularly when something outrageous was up." But the covenant of the League made "matters of that sort everybody's business." In the new system there was to be no place for neutrality.

Until the winter of 1917, however, Wilson was still in the old system. Neutrality had become intolerable for him, but not so intolerable as to lead him to accept the alternative. There is sheer pathos in his repeated call in the fall of 1916 for "some cause which will elevate your spirit, not depress it, some cause in which it seems a glory to shed human blood, if it be necessary." What Wilson desperately searched for, he must have known he could not find. There was no cause that, once recognized, would free him from the dilemma that was in no small measure of his own making. Only the German decision to pursue unrestricted submarine warfare could do that. . . .

In late February, Wilson changed his initial position on armed neutrality. Having initially opposed the government's arming of American merchantmen, on February 26 he wrote to the Congress requesting authority to place naval guns and gun crews on board merchant ships. In doing so, he emphasized that he was not "contemplating war or any step that need lead to it." He continued to hold to the "ideal of peace." Even so, a significant change had occurred in what Wilson now deemed it necessary to do in responding to the German challenge. When Congress failed to give him the authorization sought, by virtue of a Senate filibuster that ended the session, he declared his intention to arm American ships under authority he claimed already to possess.

By the end of February, Wilson had already begun to abandon old positions. While not yet ready to accept the dread alternative, he was steadily moving toward doing so. The news of the Zimmermann telegram undoubtedly helped. On February 24 the president learned through the British government of the proposal made by German Foreign Minister Zimmermann to the Mexican government of an alliance in the event of war with the United States. The German offer, made on January 19, 1917, read in part: "make war together, make peace together, generous financial support, and an understanding on our part that Mexico is to reconquer the lost territory in Texas, New Mexico, and Arizona."

Wilson was shocked and indignant on receiving the news of the German offer. Mexico was a very sensitive issue for him, given the considerable difficulties still attending Mexican-American relations in the winter of 1917. An American military force had only recently been withdrawn from Mexico, and Wilson was confronted with the issue of whether to recognize the Mexican government of Venustiano Carranza despite objectionable features in the new constitution. . . .

Wilson's embrace of armed neutrality proved to be very brief. In his second inaugural address, on March 5, he declared that "we stand firm in armed neutrality." In the days immediately following, days in which Wilson was confined to his private quarters with a bad cold, measures were initiated by the government to implement the new status. On March 18, two days after the president returned to his office, Washington learned that German submarines had attacked and sunk three American vessels, one with considerable loss of life. This was the event that Wilson had earlier said would alone be sufficient to persuade him that the Germans intended to carry out their declaration against American vessels.

The presidential conversion to war came, to all outward appearances, very suddenly. On March 20, . . . Wilson held a meeting of his cabinet devoted to the issue of war with Germany. The questions the president put to his cabinet were whether he should summon Congress to meet in special session at an earlier date than he had already called for (April 16) and once Congress was assembled, what he should lay before it. The cabinet was unanimous in the view that war was inevitable and that Congress should be called in extraordinary session as soon as possible. . . .

The day following the cabinet meeting of March 20, the president called Congress to meet in special session on April 2. His reason for doing so was to "advise" the Congress that a state of war existed between Germany and the United States.

Wilson's war address brought to an end the long and increasingly difficult period of American neutrality. It afforded to a divided nation release from an uncertainty and tension that had become almost unendurable. It marked for the first time since the period of independence the country's participation in a European war, thereby breaking a long tradition of isolation from the old continent's politics. Both supporters and opponents of intervention agreed that once America had entered the war, the nation's destiny would be radically altered. In his popular history *Our Times* Mark Sullivan wrote of the night of April 2, 1917: "To every person present, from members of the cabinet in the front row, to observers in the remote seats in the gallery, that evening was the most-to-be-remembered of their lives." . . .

The war address held out a new understanding of the meaning and significance of the great conflict. What had been a struggle for power now became a conflict between democracy and autocracy. . . .

Wilson's explanation of the origins of the war had a familiar ring. It had been given before by Thomas Paine and Thomas Jefferson. "Why are not republics plunged into war," Paine had asked, "but because the nature of their government does not admit of an interest distinct from that of the nation?" Paine's answer was given again by Wilson: "Self-governed nations do not fill their neighbor states with spies or set the course of intrigue to bring about some critical posture of affairs which will give them an opportunity to strike and make conquest." Only when the decision for war rested on the will of the community rather than on the will of an unrepresentative government, Paine and Jefferson had insisted, would this ever-present specter of Europe's old diplomacy recede and a great step toward permanent peace be taken. Wilson's war message embraced this view: "A steadfast concert for peace can never be maintained except by a partnership of democratic nations. No autocratic government could be trusted to keep faith within it or observe its covenants."

The war address did not expressly abandon the vision of a peace without victory. Not only did it emphasize that toward the German people, as distinct from the German government, America had only a feeling of "sympathy and friendship" but it pledged that in conducting the war America would fight "without rancor and without selfish object, seeking nothing for ourselves but what we shall wish to share with all free peoples." Once liberated from their government, these words plainly implied, the Germans too would be reckoned among free peoples. At that moment, Wilson's peace without victory, "a peace the very principle of which is equality and a common participation in a common benefit," would presumably apply.

These were the words of a visionary who still stood outside the great conflict. When Wilson uttered them, the effects of war were but foreseen, not experienced. Only the experience could test the resolve to "fight without rancor" and to "conduct . . . operations as belligerents without passion." Involvement was bound to alter Wilson's pledge. It had always done so before in the lesser political battles he had waged, battles he had never conducted without passion or rancor. Wilson had not been insincere in his earlier commitment to a peace without victory, but he had made the commitment as an outsider, when he had seen the war as a mere struggle for power, not as a struggle for justice. Once the war was seen as a struggle for justice, peace without victory would recede into a forgotten past.

Wilsonianism and Anticolonial Nationalism: A Dream Deferred

EREZ MANELA

In June 1919, Nguyen Tat Thanh, a twenty-eight-year-old kitchen assistant from French Indochina, set out to present a petition to the world leaders then assembled in Paris for the peace conference. The document, entitled "The Claims of the People of Annam," echoed the rhetoric of the president of the United States, Woodrow Wilson, who had recently emerged in the international arena as a champion of the right of all peoples to self-determination. In the tumultuous months following the end of the First World War, Wilson was hailed around the world as the prophet of a new era in world affairs, one in which justice, rather than power, would be the central principle of international relations. The young man from Indochina, who signed the petition as Nguyen Ai Quoc, or "Nguyen the Patriot," sought a personal audience with the American president to plead his people's case before Wilson. According to some accounts, he even rented a formal morning suit in preparation for the occasion. The meeting, however, did not materialize. Wilson probably never even saw Nguyen's petition, and he certainly did not respond to it. Within less than a year the man, who would later become known to the world as Ho Chi Minh, adopted Bolshevism as his new creed, and Lenin replaced Wilson as his inspiration on the road to self-determination for his people. . . .

The major leaders who convened for the peace conference in Paris in January 1919 were concerned mainly with fashioning a settlement in Europe. But Europeans were not the only ones who had high hopes for the conference. For colonized, marginalized, and stateless peoples from all over the world—Chinese and Koreans, Arabs and Jews, Armenians and Kurds, and many others—the conference appeared to present unprecedented opportunities to pursue the goal of self-determination. They could now take the struggle against imperialism to the international arena, and their representatives set out for Paris, invited or otherwise, to stake their claims in the new world order. A largely unintended but eager audience for Wilson's wartime rhetoric, they often imagined the president as both an icon of their aspirations and a potential champion of their cause, a dominant figure in the world arena committed, he had himself declared, to the principle of self-determination for all peoples.

Erez Manela, "Wilsonianism and Anti-Colonial Nationalism: A Dream Deferred" from *The Wilsonian Moment: Self-Determination and the International Origins of Anti-Colonial Nationalism* (New York: Oxford University Press, 2007), pp. 3–5, 216–222, 224–225. By permission of Oxford University Press, Inc.

Based on these perceptions, groups aspiring to self-determination formed delegations, selected representatives, formulated demands, launched campaigns, and mobilized publics behind them. They composed and circulated a flood of declarations, petitions, and memoranda directed at the world leaders assembled in Paris and directed at public opinion across the world. Many of the petitioners adopted Wilson's rhetoric of self-determination and the equality of nations to formulate their demands and justify their aspirations, both because they found his language appealing and, more importantly, because they believed it would be effective in advancing their cause. They quoted at length from the president's Fourteen Points address and his other wartime speeches, praised his plan for a League of Nations, and aimed to attract his support for their struggles to attain self-determination.

Hundreds of such documents, many addressed to President Wilson himself, made their way to the Paris headquarters of the American Commission to Negotiate Peace at the Hôtel Crillon, but most got no further than the president's private secretary, Gilbert Close. The president read only a small fraction of them, and he acted on fewer still. The complex and contentious issues of the European settlement were foremost on his mind during his months in Paris, and relations with the major imperial powers—Britain, France, Japan—loomed larger in the scheme of U.S. interests as Wilson saw them than did the aspirations of colonized groups or weak states. Though the dispensation of territories that belonged to the defunct empires—German colonies in Africa and the Pacific, Ottoman possessions in the Arab Middle East—was an important topic in the peace negotiations, the leading peacemakers had no intention of entertaining the claims for self-determination of dependent peoples elsewhere, least of all those that ran against their own interests. To himself and to others, Wilson explained this lapse by asserting that the peace conference already had enough on its plate and that the League of Nations would take up such claims in due time.

Many in the colonial world who had followed Wilson's increasingly dramatic proclamations in the final months of the war, however, came to expect a more immediate and radical transformation of their status in international society. As the outlines of the peace treaty began to emerge in the spring of 1919, it became clear that such expectations would be disappointed and that outside Europe the old imperial logic of international relations, which abridged or entirely obliterated the sovereignty of most non-European peoples, would remain largely in place. The disillusionment that followed the collapse of this "Wilsonian moment" fueled a series of popular protest movements across the Middle East and Asia, heralding the emergence of anticolonial nationalism as a major force in world affairs. . . .

The Chinese in 1919 . . . [, for example] had envisioned the coming of a new era of self-determination and equality in international relations, and though their faith in Wilson crumbled when he failed to apply his principles to China, the experience left its mark. Sun Yat-sen, the icon of Chinese nationalism, suggested a few years later the far-reaching implications of this process, which he . . . viewed within a broad global context:

> Wilson's proposals, once set forth, could not be recalled; each one of the weaker, smaller nations . . . stirred with a great, new consciousness; they saw how completely they had been deceived by the Great Powers' advocacy of self-determination and began independently and separately to carry out the principle of the "self-determination of peoples."

China had failed to win its case in Paris, but the failure was only temporary. The Japanese had won Wilson's agreement to their claims in Shandong [(formerly a German sphere of influence in Northern China, transferred to Japan by secret treaty during the war)] only by promising to return the territory shortly to China, and in fact they did so, under U.S. pressure, on the margins of the Washington Naval Conference of 1921–1922. By then, however, it was too late to reverse the broader consequences of the Paris decision, and in any case, Chinese nationalists now wanted nothing less than a complete abrogation of the unequal treaties [first imposed on China in the 1840s and 1850s following the Opium Wars]. That goal, too, was largely achieved by 1928, as China, newly reunited under the Guomindang leader Chiang Kai-shek [(Jiang Jieshi)], renegotiated its treaties with foreign powers, achieving tariff autonomy and doing away with legal extraterritoriality. But this successful self-assertion was quickly overshadowed by the Japanese encroachments of the 1930s, which began with the conquest of Manchuria in 1931 and culminated in the outbreak of all-out war between China and Japan in 1937. When Mao Zedong, now head of the victorious Chinese Communist Party, announced in 1949 that the Chinese people had "stood up," he declared the attainment of the goal that Chinese nationalists had pursued for the better part of a century.

Even as Mao, in 1919 still a twenty-five-year-old activist in a remote Chinese province, analyzed the international events from Changsha [the capital city of Hunan Province], the urbane, Cambridge-educated twenty-nine-year-old [Indian patriot] Jawaharlal Nehru made similar observations in Allahabad. Penning a review of the philosopher Bertrand Russell's 1918 book, *Roads to Freedom*, Nehru suggested the turn away from the Wilsonian millennium with the quote from Karl Marx with which he chose to preface his review: "A spectre is haunting Europe, the spectre of communism." "Much was expected of the war," Nehru lamented. "It was to have revolutionised the fabric of human affairs, but it has ended without bringing any solace or hope of permanent peace or betterment. President Wilson's brave words have remained but words, and the 'fourteen points,' where are they?" . . .

The Wilsonian moment had encouraged Indian and other nationalists to formulate their claims for self-government in language that resonated with a wider, international discourse of legitimacy. Veteran nationalists like [Bal Gangadhar] Tilak and [Lala] Lajpat Rai left the confines of the British Empire, physically and conceptually, to take their case before world opinion. The principle of self-determination supported both Indian demands for home rule and their claim for representation in the international arena, and though India's colonial masters denied those demands, they could not deny their legitimacy. The new radicalism of the Indian National Congress [(INC)] under [Mohandas K.] Gandhi was reflected in its continued rejection of [Britain's] postwar reforms [which granted only limited political rights instead of independence] as insufficient, as it boycotted the elections for new provincial councils in 1921 and the visit of the Simon Commission, sent to propose further reforms, in 1928. Indian nationalists were no longer willing to accept the measured, piecemeal process that London wanted. In 1929, at the annual gathering of the INC in Lahore, Nehru, now presiding over the session, officially announced the Indian goal as *purna swaraj*, or complete independence. . . .

In Egypt, too, Wilson's rhetoric led nationalists to expect immediate independence after the war and helped to shape their demands and the ways they pursued them as they prepared for the postwar world. Like . . . Indians, Egyptian nationalists believed that with Wilsonian principles on the ascendant, the formation of the League of Nations would allow demands for self-determination to come before a tribunal of the world community, shifting the balance of power in colonial relationships away from the colonial powers. Egyptian nationalists saw the numerous representatives of subject nations who rushed to Paris to present their demands and could see little reason that they should be excluded from that opportunity. The violent clashes that erupted [in Cairo and Alexandria in the spring of 1919] in response to British intransigence escalated Egyptian resistance to their rule, broadened the social base of the movement, and hardened Egyptians' commitment to nationalist goals. . . .

The ad hoc alliance that [the Egyptian Nationalist Sa'd] Zaghlul had created to bring Egyptian claims to the peace conference became a political party [(the Wafd, or delegation party)] that dominated Egyptian politics for nearly three decades. Zaghlul himself, who returned from his European sojourn in 1920, remained the most popular political figure in Egypt. He served as prime minister for ten months in 1924 following a landslide election victory for the Wafd, and when he died in August 1927 he was widely hailed in Egypt as the "Father of the Nation." The British, attempting to accommodate nationalist sentiment while preserving their interests, ended the protectorate and granted Egypt limited independence in 1922, but the nationalists found it inadequate and continued to demand full sovereignty. They won a greater measure of independence in 1936, but the struggle against British influence in Egypt continued until 1956, when the last of the British forces evacuated Egyptian territory in the wake of the Suez crisis [sparked by Egypt's nationalization of the British and French-operated Suez Canal]. By then, however, Egyptians no longer imagined the United States as a benevolent and well-intentioned force in international affairs as they had in 1919. In 1958, when tensions between the United States and a newly assertive Egypt were at a peak, Egyptian president Gamal Abdel Nasser—who was born on January 15, 1918, exactly one week after Wilson's Fourteen Points address—accused the United States of forgetting "the principles invoked by Wilson." . . .

The millenarian, quasi-religious renderings of Woodrow Wilson—[the Indian scholar V. S. Srinivasa] Sastri's description of Wilson as "Christ, or Buddha," [the philosopher S. Subramanya] Aiyar's rendering of him as an agent of "salvation," or [the Chinese reformer] Kang Youwei's hope that the president could be the purveyor of [the Confucian Concept of] *datong* [(or Great Harmony)] utopia—reflected a powerful if fleeting sense in the immediate wake the war that a historical moment had arrived in which humanity could transcend the logic of Darwinian competition and long-established power relationships and found an international community in which all nations would enjoy recognition and dignity. . . .

Such views of Wilson, of course, hardly reflected the man himself. A supporter of the U.S. conquest of the Philippines, Wilson thought that non-European peoples needed the trusteeship of more "civilized" powers in order to develop the capabilities for self-determination. Though his wartime rhetoric did not explicitly exclude non-Europeans from self-determination, he never specified how that principle would apply to them beyond a vague promise, perfectly compatible with the reigning theory of colonial trusteeship, to take into account the "interests of the populations concerned." Moreover, Wilson's background and approach was well known to some colonial leaders, who noted and criticized the injustices of American society and foreign policy. Lala Lajpat Rai had carefully studied and documented the state of American race relations, and Chinese intellectuals had long deplored and protested the ill treatment and exclusion in the United States of Chinese migrants. During the height of the Wilsonian moment, however, the deficiencies of the United States and its president as champions of freedom seemed to be overshadowed by Wilson's image as a vigorous advocate of international justice. . . .

In the campaigns that they launched to claim the right to self-determination for their own peoples, anticolonial nationalists appropriated Wilsonian language to articulate their goals and mobilize support for them both at home and abroad. Western-educated nationalists like [Korea's] Syngman Rhee and [China's] Wellington Koo and expatriate communities more generally played central roles in speaking for their nations in international society, reflecting their geographic, intellectual, and cultural proximity to the arenas of power and influence in international society. But diverse groups back home—religious communities, local councils, professional organizations, and women's groups—also mobilized to ask the peace conference for self-determination. In thousands of petitions, pamphlets, declarations, and memoranda, they adopted Wilson's language, refracted it through the lenses of local conditions and sensibilities, and harnessed it to claim their rights in international society.

The simultaneous eruption of anticolonial upheavals in the spring of 1919 occurred in this context. In [Japanese-occupied] Korea and Egypt, the protests initially broke out as part of the campaigns to bring demands for self-determination to international attention. In China and India, the upheavals reflected the collapse of the expectations for change, as the peace conference rejected Chinese claims and the promulgation of the Rowlatt acts [(British legislation passed in 1919 that severely restricted legal rights in India)] signaled that Britain had little intention of loosening its grip on the empire's crown jewel. By the spring of 1919, as the contours of the peace settlement began to emerge, it became clear that the leading powers, including the United States, had little intention of applying the principle of self-determination significantly beyond Europe. The faith in Wilson's commitment to a more just international order, or in his ability to fashion one, began to ebb, and disenchantment with the Wilsonian promise spread.

Still, the experiences of the Wilsonian moment cemented ideological and political commitments to anticolonial agendas, and the movements launched then did not disappear with its demise. The colonial authorities moved to stem the anticolonial wave, and the popular momentum of the spring of 1919, driven by international events, could not last indefinitely. In its wake, however, political programs and organizations committed to self-determination became more powerful and more pervasive than before. Moreover, the upheavals of the spring of 1919 themselves created narratives of colonial violence and popular resistance that quickly became etched into collective memories and that came to symbolize each nation's striving for liberation. These movements—the 1919 Revolution [in Egypt], the May Fourth movement [in China], [Gandhi-led, nonviolent] the Rowlatt Satyagraha and Amritsar [(where British forces killed some 400 peaceful, civilian protestors)], and the March First movement [in Korea]—became focal points in the construction of national identity and inspired continued commitment to nationalist agendas. The language of self-determination as a central norm of legitimacy in international relations remained central in the rhetoric of anticolonial movements, useful in mobilizing public opinion and action both at home and abroad and in rejecting any accommodation with empire.

Wilson himself did acknowledge that the peace conference failed to deal with colonial claims, especially those related to the possessions of the Allied powers, in accordance with his much-advertised principles. In Paris, he said shortly after his return to the United States, there were numerous delegations clamoring to be heard, and though the conference, limited to issues that arose directly from the war, could not take up their demands, it did lay the institutional groundwork for dealing with them. Now that the League of Nations was established, oppressed peoples would receive justice in the court of world opinion. Soon after, however, the president suffered the stroke that ended his career, and on March 19, 1920, the U.S. Senate finally rejected the Treaty of Versailles and with it the League of Nations covenant. The United States never joined the League of Nations, and even if it had, it is hard to imagine that the league, controlled as it was by the major imperial powers, would have been sympathetic to colonial demands for self-determination. In the end, the Wilsonian moment did alter the relationship between colonizer and colonized, but it did not do so in the consensual, evolutionary manner that Wilson had envisioned.

Framing the Wilsonian moment in the colonial world as an international and transnational event is not merely an analytical device or an expression of a particular historical method. Rather, it reflects the perceptions and actions of historical actors at the time, and much of what they saw and did at the time is rendered incomprehensible, even invisible outside that framework. The moment was inherently international in that it played out in an arena defined by the interactions between sovereign nation-states and in which such states were the primary actors. It was also transnational, meaning that the perceptions and actions of the actors regularly transcended and crossed existing political boundaries; indeed, in many cases such crossings—for example, in order to travel to Paris or to Washington—were among the primary purposes of their activities at the time. . . .

The nationalist leaders of 1919 pursued an anticolonial agenda and sought to challenge an international order in which the groups they represented were subordinated, but, as their perceptions of Wilson suggest, their aims and sentiments were not anti-Western as such. Most of the leaders of the anticolonial campaigns of 1919—men like Sa'd Zaghlul, Lala Lajpat Rai, Wellington Koo, and Syngman Rhee, many of them with a Western education—were reformers who proclaimed their ambitions to remake their societies along the lines of liberal democratic models. The campaigns they led in 1919 did not set out to tear down the existing international order but rather to join it as members of equal status. When the quest to achieve self-determination through the peace conference failed, however, many anticolonial activists, disillusioned with the results of Wilson's liberal internationalism, began to seek alternative ideological models and sources of practical support in their struggles for self-determination. The "revolt against the West," to use [the historian] Geoffrey Barraclough's term, that was launched after 1919 emerged not from the experiences of the war; rather, it came from the failure of the peace to break the power of imperialism and allow colonial peoples a voice as full-fledged members in international society.

The history of the Paris Peace Conference is often read as a tragic failure to fashion a European settlement that would bring lasting peace. But the story of the

Wilsonian moment in the colonial world illuminates another, no less important facet of that central turning point in twentieth-century international history. From the perspective of the periphery, rather than the center, of international society, the conference appears as a tragedy of a different sort, as the leading peacemakers, Wilson foremost among them, failed to offer the populations of the non-European world the place in international society that Wilson's wartime speeches had implied that they deserved. At the Wilsonian moment, Egyptians, Indians, Chinese, Koreans, and others glimpsed the promised land of self-determination, but enter into it they could not. That experience, inasmuch as it shaped the formative stages of major national movements in the colonial world, helped to displace the liberal, reformist anticolonialism that failed in 1919 in favor of the more radical, revisionist nationalism that became an important force in the subsequent history of the twentieth century.

🌐 F U R T H E R   R E A D I N G

David A. Adelman, *A Shattered Peace* (2007) (on Versailles)

Lloyd Ambrosius, "Woodrow Wilson and George W. Bush: Historical Comparisons of Means and Ends in their Foreign Policies," *Diplomatic History* (June 2006): 509–543

_____, *Woodrow Wilson and His Legacy in American Foreign Relations* (2002)

H. W. Brands, *Woodrow Wilson* (2003)

Kendrick A. Clements, *The Presidency of Woodrow Wilson* (1992)

G. R. Conyne, *Woodrow Wilson: British Perspectives* (1992)

John W. Coogan, "Wilsonian Diplomacy in War and Peace," in *American Foreign Relations Reconsidered, 1890–1993,* ed. Gordon Martel (1994)

John Milton Cooper Jr., *Breaking the Heart of the World* (2001)

_____, *Woodrow Wilson* (2009)

David E. Davis and Eugene P. Trani, *The First Cold War* (2000)

Richard R. Doerries, *Imperial Challenge: Ambassador Count von Bernstorff and German–American Relations, 1908–1917* (1989)

David M. Esposito, *The Legacy of Woodrow Wilson* (1996)

Byron Farrell, *Over There* (1999)

Robert H. Ferrell, *Woodrow Wilson and World War I* (1985)

David S. Foglesong, *America's Secret War Against Bolshevism* (1995)

Lloyd C. Gardner, *Safe for Democracy* (1984)

Godfrey Hodgson, *Woodrow Wilson's Right Hand* (2006) (on Colonel Edward House)

Michael Kazin, *A Godly Hero* (2006) (on William Jennings Bryan)

Ross A. Kennedy, "Woodrow Wilson, World War I, and American National Security," *Diplomatic History* 25 (Winter 2001): 1–31

William R. Keylor, *The Legacy of the Great War* (1998)

Antony Lentin, *Lloyd George, Woodrow Wilson, and the Guilt of Germany* (1985)

Arthur S. Link, *Wilson,* 5 vols. (1947–1965)

_____, *Woodrow Wilson: Revolution, War, and Peace* (1979)

David W. McFadden, *Alternative Paths: Soviets and Americans, 1917–1920* (1993)

Margaret, MacMillan, *Paris, 1919* (2003)

Herbert F. Margulies, *The Mild Reservationists and the League of Nations Controversy in the Senate* (1989)

John H. Mauer, *The Outbreak of the First World War* (1995)

Elizabeth McKillen, *Chicago Labor and the Quest for a Democratic Diplomacy* (1995)

_____, "Ethnicity, Class, and Wilsonian Internationalism Reconsidered: The Mexican and Irish-American Immigrant Left and U.S. Foreign Relations, 1914–1922," *Diplomatic History* 25 (Fall 2001): 553–87

Bert E. Park, *Ailing, Aging, Addicted: Studies of Compromised Leadership* (1993)
David S. Patterson, *The Search for Negotiated Peace* (2007) (on women's activism)
Ann R. Pierce, *Woodrow Wilson and Harry Truman* (2003)
Jim Powell, *Wilson's War* (2005)
Diane Preston, *"Lusitania": An Epic Tragedy* (2001)
Daniela Rossini, *Woodrow Wilson and the American Myth in Italy* (2008)
Norman E. Saul, *War and Revolution* (2001)
Jan W. Schulte-Nordholt, *Woodrow Wilson: A Life for Peace* (1991)
Klaus Schwabe, *Woodrow Wilson, Revolutionary Germany, and Peacemaking, 1918–1919* (1985)
Richard Slotkin, *Lost Batallions* (2005)
Tony Smith, *America's Mission* (1995)
David Steigerwald, "The Reclamation of Woodrow Wilson," *Diplomatic History* 23
    (Winter 1999): 79–99
John A. Thompson, *Woodrow Wilson* (2001)
Marc Trachtenburg, *Reparations in World Politics* (1980)
Barbara Tuchman, *The Zimmermann Telegram* (1958)
Edwin A. Weinstein, *Woodrow Wilson: A Medical and Psychological Biography* (1981)
William C. Widenor, *Henry Cabot Lodge and the Search for an American Foreign Policy* (1980)
Robert H. Zeiger, *America's Great War* (2001)